Pharmaceutical Antitrust

An Analysis of US and EU Law

Editors

Mélanie THILL-TAYARA
George GORDON

Managing Editors

Laurence BARY
Rani HABASH

106 West 32nd Street, Suite 144, New York, NY 10001, USA
www.concurrences.com
books@concurrences.com

First Printing, November 2023
978-1-954750-10-4 (Hardcover)
Library of Congress Control Number: 2023951192

Cover: Yves Buliard, www.yvesbuliard.fr
Book design and layout implementation: Nord Compo

Concurrences Books

Tributes

Eleanor M. Fox – Antitrust Ambassador to the World, *2021*

Herbert Hovenkamp – The Dean of American Antitrust Law, *2021*

Frédéric Jenny – Standing Up for Convergence and Relevance in Antitrust, (Vol. I & II), *2019 & 2021*

Albert Foer – A Consumer Voice in the Antitrust Arena, *2020*

Richard Whish – Taking Competition Law Outside the Box, *2020*

Douglas H. Ginsburg – An Antitrust Professor on the Bench (Vol. I & II), *2018 & 2020*

Wang Xiaoye – The Pioneer of Competition Law in China, *A. Emch, W. Ng (eds.), 2019*

Ian S. Forrester – A Scot without Borders (Vol. I & II), *A. Komninos (eds.), 2015*

William E. Kovacic – An Antitrust Tribute (Vol. I & II), *2013 & 2014*

Practical Books

Global Dictionary of Competition Law, *D. Healey, W. Kovacic, P. Trevisan, R. Whish, 2023*

Innovation Paradox in Merger Control, *G. Gurkaynak, 2023*

State Aid & the Energy Transition, *D. Buschle, L. Hancher, M.-T. Richter-Kuhnert (eds.), 2023 (in collaboration with the Energy Community)*

State Aid & National Enforcement, *J. Derenne, D. Jouve, C. Lemaire, F. Martucci (eds.), 2023*

Antitrust and the Digital Economy, *Y. Katsoulacos (ed.), 2023 (in collaboration with CRESSE)*

Judicial Review of Competition Cases, *D. Ginsburg, T. Eicke (eds.), 2023*

Competition Law Treatment of Joint Ventures, *B. Bleicher, N. Campbell, A. Hamilton, N. Hukkinen, A. Khan, A. Mordaunt (eds.), 2022 (in collaboration with the IBA)*

Information Exchange & Related Risks, *Z. Marosi, M. Soares (eds.), 2022 (in collaboration with the IBA)*

Rulemaking Authority of the US Federal Trade Commission, *D. Crane (ed.), 2022*

The International Competition Network at Twenty, *D. Anderson & P. Lugard (eds.), 2022*

Competition Case Law Digest – 5th Edition, *F. Jenny, N. Charbit (eds.), 2022*

Competition Inspections in 21 Jurisdictions – A Practitioner's Guide, *N. Jalabert-Doury (ed.), 2022*

Perspectives on Antitrust Compliance, *A. Riley, A. Stephan, A. Tubbs (eds.), 2022 (in collaboration with the ICC)*

Turkish Competition Law, *G. Gürkaynak, 2021*

Competition Law – Climate Change & Environmental Sustainability, *S. Holmes, D. Middelschulte, M. Snoep (eds.), 2021*

Merger Control in Latin America – A Jurisdictional Guide, *P. Burnier da Silveira, P. Sittenfeld (eds.), 2020*

Competition Inspections under EU Law – A Practitioner's Guide, *N. Jalabert-Doury, 2020*

Gun Jumping in Merger Control – A Jurisdictional Guide, *C. Hatton, Y. Comtois, A. Hamilton (eds.), 2019 (in collaboration with the IBA)*

Choice – A New Standard for Competition Analysis? *P. Nihoul (ed.), 2016*

PhD Theses

Abuse of Platform Power, *F. Bostoen, 2023*

Reform of Chinese State-Owned Enterprises, *X. Bai, 2023*

Competition & Regulation in Network Industries – Essays in Industrial Organization, *J-M. Zogheib, 2021*

The Role of Media Pluralism in the Enforcement of EU Competition Law, *K. Bania, 2019*

Buyer Power, *I. Herrera Anchustegui, 2017*

General Interest

Great Antitrust Enforcers, *W. E. Kovacic, 2023*

Competition – How to Speak Like an Expert, *E. Combe , 2023*

Women and Antitrust – Voices from the Field (Vol I & II), *E. Kurgonaite & K. Nordlander, 2020*

Conference Proceedings

Antitrust in Emerging and Developing Countries – (Vol I & II), *E. Fox, H. First, 2015 & 2016*

Global Antitrust Law – Current Issues in Antitrust Law and Economics, *D. Ginsburg, J. Wright, (eds.) 2015*

Competition Law on the Global Stage – David Gerber's Global Competition Law in Perspective, *D. Gerber, 2014*

OVERVIEW

FOREWORD

ALDEN ABBOTT
George Mason University

The life sciences industries (covering such fields as pharmaceuticals, biotechnology, medical devices, biomedical technologies, research and manufacturing support, and health care provision)[1] continue to grow in global importance. The rapid launch of successful vaccines and therapeutics to combat the COVID-19 pandemic,[2] and the development of simple blood tests that will diagnose many cancers prior to the emergence of symptoms,[3] are just two among many prominent examples of the enormous impact this sector is having on human health around the world.

The life sciences sector is also of great importance to the economies of many countries, the United States[4] and European nations[5] in particular. Not surprisingly, therefore, life sciences firms receive a great deal of government oversight in the United States and Europe, not just from health and safety regulators, but from antitrust enforcers as well.

Life sciences company leaders must be especially attentive to plans by US and EU officials[6] to "reinvigorate" already aggressive antitrust enforcement in health care.[7] As such, there is a vital need for clear up-to-date guidance on the application of US and European Union competition laws to the life sciences sector.

---

1 *See* generally, *What is the Life Sciences Industry*? PROCLINICAL (2023), *available at* https://www.proclinical.com/life-sciences#:~:text=The%20life%20sciences%20industry%20consists,improve%20the%20lives%20of%20organisms.

2 *See, e.g.,* Helen Branswell, *Why Covid-19 Vaccines Are a Freaking Miracle*, STAT (Feb. 14, 2022), *available at* https://www.statnews.com/2022/02/14/why-covid-19-vaccines-are-a-freaking-miracle/; Philip C. Robinson et al., *COVID-19 Therapeutics: Challenges and Directions for the Future*, PNAS (Apr. 6, 2022), *available at* https://www.pnas.org/doi/10.1073/pnas.2119893119.

3 *See, e.g.,* Ian Sample, *Blood Test Spots Multiple Cancers Without Clear Symptoms, Study Finds*, THE GUARDIAN (Sept. 11, 2022), *available at* https://www.theguardian.com/science/2022/sep/11/galleri-blood-test-multiple-cancers-before-clear-symptoms-study.

4 *See* generally, *e.g.,* Alex Keown, *BIO Report Outlines Economic Impact of Booming Life Sciences Industry*, BIOSPACE (Jan. 21, 2022), *available at* https://www.biospace.com/article/bio-report-outlines-economic-impact-of-booming-life-sciences-industry/.

5 *See* generally, *e.g.,* European Commission, Biotechnology (Biotechnology and life sciences contribute to the modernization of European industry), (2023), *available at* https://single-market-economy.ec.europa.eu/sectors/biotechnology_en.

6 *See, e.g.,* Margrethe Vestager Speech, at the Fordham's 49th Annual Conference on International Antitrust Law and Policy, *Antitrust for the Digital Age*, (Sept. 14, 2022), *available at* https://ec.europa.eu/commission/presscorner/detail/en/SPEECH_22_5590.

7 *See, e.g.,* Andrew Forman Keynote Remarks, Deputy Assistant Attorney General, US Department of Justice, Before the American Bar Association Antitrust in Health Care Conference, *The Importance of Vigorous Antitrust Enforcement in Health Care*, (June 3, 2022), *available at* https://www.justice.gov/opa/speech/deputy-assistant-attorney-general-andrew-forman-delivers-keynote-abas-antitrust; Salomé Cisnal de Ugarte et al., *European Union: Commission Still at the Forefront, While Pay-for-Delay Cases Set New Precedents*, GLOBAL COMPETITION REVIEW (Oct. 21, 2022), *available at* https://globalcompetitionreview.com/guide/guide-life-sciences/first-edition/article/european-union-commission-still-the-forefront-while-pay-delay-cases-set-new-precedents.

Concurrences admirably fulfills this need with a one-volume book, *Pharmaceutical Antitrust: An Analysis of US and EU Law*, edited by Mélanie Thill-Tayara and George Gordon of the Dechert LLP (experts in EU and US antitrust law, respectively). Throughout the volume, each specific legal topic presents clear back-to back comparisons of European Union and United States legal requirements.

The book's first chapter (Patent and Regulatory Framework) provides an excellent comparative overview of the EU and US regulatory frameworks applicable to health care products (medicinal products and medical devices). Specifically, it focuses on patent law and the many laws governing marketing authorization and exclusivity in the two jurisdictions. The chapter closes with a special section on the pricing and distribution complexities governing EU market access.

The rest of the book addresses the full gamut of antitrust issues that may confront health care market participants in the United States and Europe. The second chapter (Applicable Procedural and Legal Antitrust Framework) explores the institutional antitrust framework, including international cooperation among antitrust authorities, public and private enforcement, and analysis of product markets and market power in life sciences. The third chapter (Mergers and Acquisitions) deals with the procedural and substantive aspects of mergers. The fourth chapter (Concerted Conduct) explores horizontal and vertical non-merger agreements among firms. The fifth chapter (Unilateral Conduct) assesses unilateral conduct by a firm that may affect competition. The sixth and final chapter (Private Enforcement) provides a detailed exposition of private antitrust enforcement (a longstanding feature of US antitrust that is becoming increasingly significant in Europe).

The book is user friendly in all respects. Its detailed table of contents allows the reader to hone in quickly on a narrow topic of particular interest, or explore a broader topic in depth. Patent-antitrust issues, that are rapidly gaining significance in innovative life sciences markets (especially in pharmaceuticals and biologics), are concisely yet thoroughly evaluated. The comprehensive coverage of antitrust procedural questions (such as standing, jurisdiction, and discovery) is particularly well-suited to readers who want an initial sense of the scope of legal risks they may face in different jurisdictions.

In sum, *Pharmaceutical Antitrust: An Analysis of US and EU law* is a gem. It should be on the bookshelves of both in-house counsel to life-science companies and private practitioners who may represent those firms. University law libraries should stock up on this valuable information-packed book also.

FOREWORD

Ian S. Forrester KC

General Court of the European Union (Former Judge)

European competition law, like European law itself, was in its infancy when I arrived in Brussels. There were not many Court cases, and the judgements were short; there were not many Commission decisions, each one usually a flagship disposition of a new point of principle. Lunchtime roundtable discussions parsed each new decision or judgement. Indeed, enthusiasts could claim to read (more likely skim) each judgement of the ECJ. Each decision about competition or free movement of goods or intellectual property would be given especially close scrutiny.

The Court was making its way towards a mature set of legal principles to make sense of an economic constitutional document. The Court evidently found difficulty in resolving conflicts between IP rights and competition principles. Early challenges focused on whether the use of IP rights could be anticompetitive and in what circumstances marked the 1970s and 1980s. Competition law aspired to be continental in its reach; trademarks and patents were national. Which was to prevail?

The law was shaped or precipitated by the entrepreneurial activities of a Dutch pharmaceutical wholesaler called Centrafarm. It turned previous principles of trademark and patent law upside down or at least somewhat askew. The patentee in one Member State could no longer object to the importation and resale in its territory of genuine goods placed on the market in another Member State by the patentee or one of its affiliates. I should not exaggerate, as the national rules on "grey imports" of genuine goods gave support to the Commission's thesis.

The principle of the free movement of goods prevailed over the technical infringement of the patentee's rights. Public authorities should welcome such trade, said the Court, not harass it. In order to justify this conclusion, the court created a distinction between core rights and ancillary rights: between "essential subject matter" and "exercise". This early tussle between classical IP Law and the almost sacred goal of the border-free internal market established that despite the Treaty of Rome's provisions on property, the Court was willing to give primacy to other goals and policies.

The authors give a clear account of the principles on both sides of the Atlantic governing classic competition problems: mergers, unilateral conduct, concerted practices, price-fixing and the rest, while noting the necessary adaptations to make them relevant to the healthcare. We know that European competition law sharply differs from US law in that the latter is uninterested in the creation of a common market. So, there is no real equivalent in US law to these early European dramas, though the end result may not be so significantly different.

But there were implications to Europe from the United States. The application of competition law to the economics of the pharmaceutical industry created its own set of challenges.

The classic reason for favoring the prohibition of contractual obstacles to the making of exports to countries where the price is lower is consumer benefit. Since pharmaceutical prices are set by the state for most prescription drugs (not all and not all states, however) one part of the industry argued that parallel trade did not confer consumer advantage. Parallel trade in pharmaceuticals does not bring about an approximation of retail prices to patients who pay for drugs in the pharmacy; but on the other hand it offers a rich opportunity for wholesalers whose activities are also valuable. And in some countries it conferred actual consumer benefit. The company cannot prohibit its customers in low price countries to export, but are there any limits to how much it must deliver to those who export? Such were the controversies of the European scene from say 1990 to 2005.

Once a patent has expired, to what extent may the patentee seek to maintain its former exclusivity? Some have suggested that process patents may be regarded as an unfair or, rather, undesirable means of prolonging exclusivity, although that is really an issue for patent law and policy not competition law, and access by generic producers to the regulatory data of the former patentee is a frequent source of controversy. In the field of patent litigation, enforcement of European patent rights is pursued before national courts on a national basis. If a settlement of one patent litigation emerges, what commitments should be given by the "infringer" regarding the validity of the patent and exports to countries where parallel litigation is progressing? (The so-called "pay for delay" cases). Parallel controversies have arisen in the United States, where efforts have focused on eliminating alleged efforts by patent holders to improperly induce alleged infringers to end meritorious patent challenges.

The book gives a useful account of the fundamentals of US antitrust law, and of EU competition law not skewed either "for" or "against" any particular viewpoint: indeed, these chapters contain a useful resumé of the classic authorities, relevant to any antitrust practitioner in any industry.

This excellent book describes very clearly the highly regulated world of health care. Pharmaceuticals go through a prolonged series of tests, in the laboratory, on healthy adult volunteers, and then on patients. The decisions, positive or negative, on whether a medicine is safe and efficacious are subject to judicial review, at the instance of different stakeholders. How much discretion should the court leave to the expert agency? At what point may or should the judge intervene in a highly technical regulatory matter?

I am delighted to have had the opportunity of reading the proofs of this book before publication and can confirm that it seems thoroughly to describe the regulatory framework within which competition law principles are with some adaptions applied in the health care sector. I am pleased to commend it to practitioners, officials (and judges' réferendaires).

LIST OF ABBREVIATIONS

Abbreviation	Meaning
AAC	Average Avoidable Cost
ACM	Dutch Authority for Consumers & Markets
AFSSAPS	*Agence Française de Sécurité Sanitaire des Produits de Santé* (French Agency for Medicines and Health Products Safety)
AG	Authorized Generic under the Hatch-Waxman Act
AGCM	*Autorità Garante della Concorrenza e del Mercato* (Italian Competition Authority)
AIFA	*Agenzia Italiana del Farmaco* (Italian Medicines Agency)
ALJ	US Administrative Law Judge
ANDA	Abbreviated New Drug Application
ANSM	*Agence Nationale de Sécurité du Médicament et des Produits de Santé* (French Agency for Medicines and Health Products Safety – formerly AFSSAPS)
API	Active Pharmaceutical Ingredient
Article 22 Guidelines	European Commission Communication, Guidance on the application of the referral mechanism set out in Article 22 of the Merger Regulation to certain categories of cases
ATC	Anatomical Therapeutic Chemical Classification
BfArM	*Bundesinstitut für Arzneimittel und Medizinprodukte* (German Health Agency)
BGH	*Bundesgerichtshof* (German Supreme Court)
Bioequivalence	Absence of a significant difference in the rate and extent to which the active ingredient or active moiety in pharmaceutical equivalents or pharmaceutical alternatives becomes available at the site of drug action when administered at the same molar dose under similar conditions in an appropriately designed study
Biologics	Large-molecule pharmaceutical products whose active pharmaceutical ingredient is made by or derived from living organisms
Biosimilars drugs	Biological medicinal products highly similar to another authorized biologic product (i.e., the innovator or reference medicinal product) in terms of structure, biological activity and efficacy, safety, and immunogenicity profile

BPCIA	Biologics Price Competition and Innovation Act
Branded pharmaceutical products	Originator drugs, typically protected by patents for a certain duration
CAFA	Class Action Fairness Act
Captive use restrictions	Obligation on the licensee to limit its production of the licensed product to the quantities required for the production of its own products and for the maintenance and repair of its own products
CAT	UK Competition Appeal Tribunal
CBER	Center for Biologics Evaluation and Research within the US Food and Drug Administration
CCPC	Irish Competition and Consumer Protection Commission
CDER	Center for Drug Evaluation and Research within the US Food and Drug Administration
CDMO	Contract Development and Manufacturing Organization
Centralized Procedure	EU procedure to obtain a single EU-wide marketing authorization, delivered by the European Commission, which is valid throughout the EU
CFR	Code of Federal Regulations
CHC	US Consumer Health Classification
CHMP	Committee for Medicinal Products for Human Use within the European Medicines Agency
CID	US Civil Investigative Demand
Clinical Trial Regulation	Regulation 536/2014 of the European Parliament and of the Council of April 16, 2014 on clinical trials on medicinal products for human use repealing Directive 2001/20
CMA	UK Competition and Markets Authority
CMO	Contract Manufacturing Organization
CNMC	*Comisión Nacional de los Mercados y la Competencia* (Spanish Competition Authority)
Collaboration Guidelines	US Antitrust Guidelines for Collaborations Among Competitors
Co-marketing agreements	Commercialization of a specific medical product by multiple parties under separate trademarks
Commercialization agreements	Agreements which cover the commercialization of a final medical product through co-operation between pharmaceutical companies for the sale, distribution and/or promotion of their products

Commission Communication on Guidelines for national courts	European Commission Communication on Guidelines for national courts on how to estimate the share of overcharge which was passed on to the indirect purchaser
Consolidated Jurisdictional Notice	European Commission Communication, Consolidated Jurisdictional Notice under Council Regulation 139/2004 on the control of concentrations between undertakings
Co-promotion agreements	The joint commercialization of a specific medical product under one single trademark under the Pharmaceutical Sector Inquiry – Final Report
CPUs	Central Processing Units
CREATES Act	Creating and Restoring Equal Access to Equivalent Samples Act
DAMITT	Dechert Antitrust Merger Investigation Timing Tracker
De Minimis Notice	European Commission Communication, Notice on agreements of minor importance which do not appreciably restrict competition under Article 101(1) of the Treaty on the Functioning of the European Union, 2014 (C 291) 1
DG COMP	Directorate-General for Competition within the European Commission
DOJ	US Department of Justice
DOJ & FTC Antitrust Guidelines	DOJ & FTC Antitrust Guidelines for the Licensing of Intellectual Property
EC Treaty	Treaty Establishing the European Community
EC Pharmaceutical Enforcement Report	Report on Competition Enforcement in the Pharmaceutical Sector 2009–2017
ECN	European Competition Network
EEA	European Economic Area
EEC	European Economic Community
ECJ	Court of Justice of the European Union
EMA	European Medicines Agency
EMEA	Europe, Middle East and Africa
EPC	Convention on the Grant of European Patents of October 5, 1973
EphMRA	European Pharmaceutical Market Research Association
EPI	Exocrine Pancreatic Insufficiency
EPO	European Patent Office
EU	European Union
EU Antitrust Implementing Regulation	European Commission Regulation 802/2004 implementing Council Regulation 139/2004 on the control of concentrations between undertakings

EU Damages Directive	Directive 2014/104 of the European Parliament and of the Council of November 26, 2014 on certain rules governing actions for damages under national law for infringements of the competition law provisions of the Member States and of the European Union
EU Guidelines on Technology Transfer Agreements	Communication from the European Commission and Guidelines on the application of Article 101 of the Treaty on the Functioning of the European Union to technology transfer agreements
EU Horizontal Merger Guidelines	European Commission, Guidelines on the assessment of horizontal mergers under the Council Regulation on the control of concentrations between undertakings
EU Merger Regulation	European Council Regulation 139/2004 on the control of concentrations between undertakings
EU Notice on Market Definition	European Commission Notice on the definition of relevant market for the purposes of Community competition law
European Commission	European Commission of the European Union
FCA	*Autorité de la concurrence* (French Competition Authority)
FDA	US Food and Drug Administration
FDCA	Food, Drug, and Cosmetic Act
FTC	US Federal Trade Commission
GAIN	Generating Antibiotic Incentives Now (part of the US Food and Drug Administration Safety and Innovation Act)
General Court	General Court of the European Union
GDP	Pharmaceutical Good Distribution Practices
Green Paper on Damages Actions	European Commission Green Paper on Damages actions for breach of the EC antitrust rules
Hatch-Waxman Act	Drug Price Competition and Patent Term Restoration Act of 1984
HHI	Herfindahl-Hirschman Index
Horizontal Guidelines	European Commission, Guidelines on the applicability of Article 101 of the Treaty on the Functioning of the European Union to horizontal cooperation agreements
Hospital-only	Drugs prescribed and/or delivered at the hospital and that can be subject to restricted prescription, e.g., by specialist doctors
HSR Act	Hart-Scott-Rodino Antitrust Improvements Act of 1976, as amended, a US federal law requiring pre-notification of certain transactions

Hybrid drugs	Drugs similar to generics that either do not meet the strict definition of generics because their bioequivalence cannot be demonstrated through bioavailability studies, or they have different active substances, therapeutic indications, strengths, pharmaceutical forms, or routes of administration than the innovator drug
ICN	International Competition Network
IP	Intellectual Property
LRAIC	Long-run Average Incremental Cost
Magnuson-Moss Act	Magnuson-Moss Warranty Act of 1975
MDL	US Multidistrict Litigation
MDL Panel	US Judicial Panel on Multidistrict Litigation
Medicaid	US federal health insurance for adults and children with limited income and resources
Medicare	US federal health insurance program for seniors 65 or older, certain younger people with disabilities, and people with permanent kidney failure requiring dialysis or a transplant
Medicare Part D	Medicare coverage for prescription drugs in the US for Medicare-eligible persons
Mutual Recognition Procedure	EU procedure for the recognition of a local marketing authorization granted by one Member State in the other Member States
NAICS	North American Industry Classification System
National Procedure	Procedure to obtain a local marketing authorization in the EU Member State where the application is filed
NCA	National Competition Authority within the European Union
NCE	New Chemical Entities
NCRPA	US National Cooperative Research and Production Act
NDA	US New Drug Application
NFC	US New Form Code
No-AG	No-Authorized Generic Agreements (US)
Non-horizontal Merger Guidelines	European Commission Communication, Guidelines on the assessment of non-horizontal mergers under the Council Regulation on the control of concentrations between undertakings
Notice on Case Referral	European Commission Communication, Notice on Case Referral in respect of concentrations
Notice on Effect on Trade	European Commission Notice, Guidelines on the effect on trade concept contained in Articles 81 and 82 of the Treaty

Notice on Leniency	European Commission Notice on Immunity from fines and reduction of fines in cartel cases
Notice on Market Definition	European Commission Notice on the definition of relevant market for the purposes of Community competition law
Notice on Remedies	European Commission Communication, Notice on Remedies acceptable under Council Regulation 139/2004 and under Commission Regulation 802/2004
Notice on Settlement	European Commission Notice on the conduct of settlement procedures in view of the adoption of Decisions pursuant to Article 7 and Article 23 of Council Regulation 1/2003 in cartel cases
Notice on Simplified Procedure	European Commission Notice on a simplified treatment of certain concentrations under Council Regulation 139/2004 on the control of concentrations between undertakings
OECD	Organization for Economic Co-operation and Development
OEM	Original Equipment Manufacturer
Off-label	Medication prescribed outside of the terms of their marketing authorization
OFT	UK Office of Fair Trading
Orange Book	US list of Approved Drug Products with Therapeutic Equivalence Determinations
Originator drugs	*See* Branded pharmaceutical products
OTC	Over-the-Counter medicines that can be purchased without a prescription
Part D Sponsors	Private insurance companies approved by the US federal government within the Medicare program
PCT	Patent Cooperation Treaty
Pharmaceutical Sector Inquiry – Final Report	European Commission, Staff Working Document, Pharmaceutical Sector Inquiry – Final Report, July 8, 2009
PHSA	Public Health Service Act
PNO	Federal Trade Commission Premerger Notification Office
Practical Guide	European Commission Staff Working Document Practical Guide on Quantifying Harm in Actions for Damages Based on Breaches of Article 101 or 102 TFEU
PTE	Patent Term Extension
PTO	US Patent and Trademark Office
QIDP	Qualified Infectious Disease Product
R&D	Research and Development

R&D Block Exemption Regulation	European Commission Regulation 2023/1066 of June 1, 2023 on the application of Article 101(3) of the Treaty on the Functioning of the European Union to certain categories of research and development agreements
REMS	Risk Evaluation Mitigation Strategy (safety program required by the US Food and Drug Administration for certain prescription medications)
RLD	Reference Listed Drug (US Food and Drug Administration)
RMS	Reference Member State: EEA Member State that leads the review of an application in a mutual recognition procedure or decentralized procedure
RP Act	Robinson-Patman Act of 1936
RPM	Resale Price Maintenance
Second Request	Under the US HSR Act, second initial waiting period to address competitive issues that remain unresolved and potentially avoid a more in-depth investigation
SESCAM	Regional Health Service of Castilla-La Mancha
Sherman Act	Sherman Anti-trust Act of 1890
SIEC	Significant Impediment to Effective Competition
Simons Phillips Wilson AbbVie Statement	Federal Trade Commission, Statement of Chairman Joseph J. Simons, Commissioner Noah J. Phillips & Commissioner Christine S. Wilson Concerning the Proposed Acquisition of Allergan plc by AbbVie Inc., 191-0169, 2020, 1, (May 5, 2020)
SME	Small and Medium-Sized Business
SmPC	EU Summary of Product Characteristics
SO	Statement of Objections sent by the European Commission or a National Competition Agency
Soft product hop	When an innovation is introduced, the old product is left on the market to compete with the new product
SPC	Supplementary Protection Certificate
Specialization Block Exemption Regulation	European Regulation 2023/1067 of June 1, 2023 on the application of Article 101(3) of the Treaty on the Functioning of the European Union to certain categories of specialization agreements
SSNIP	Small but Significant and Non-Transitory Increase in Price
SSR	Single Shared System REMS (US)
Statement of Antitrust Enforcement	Antitrust Guidelines for Collaborations; US DOJ & FTC, Statement of Antitrust Enforcement Policy in Health Care (August 1996)

Study report on the relevant market	Support study accompanying the Commission Notice on the evaluation of the definition of relevant market for the purposes of Community competition law, June 2021
TEU	Treaty of the European Union
TFEU	Treaty on the Functioning of the European Union
Package insert or PI	FDA-approved product labeling in the US
EU Transparency Directive	Directive 89/105 relating to the transparency of measures regulating the prices of medicinal products for human use and their inclusion in the scope of the national health insurance systems
TRIPS Agreement	Agreement on Trade-Related Aspects of Intellectual Property Rights
TTBER	European Commission Regulation 316/2014 on the application of Article 101(3) of the Treaty on the Functioning of the European Union to categories of technology transfer agreements
U.S.C.	United States Code
UK	United Kingdom
US	United States
US Antitrust Agencies	FTC and DOJ
US Horizontal Merger Guidelines	US DOJ & FTC, Horizontal Merger Guidelines
VBER	European Commission Regulation 2022/720 on the application of Article 101(3) of the Treaty on the Functioning of the European Union to categories of vertical agreements and concerted practices
Vertical Guidelines	European Commission Communication, Guidelines on Vertical Restraints
White Paper on Damages Actions	European Commission White Paper on Damages actions for breach of the EC antitrust rules

INTRODUCTION*

Why This Book and Why Now?

For one, the life sciences industry presents unique challenges for antitrust law practitioners. It is a sector characterized by an overlapping thicket of specialized market dynamics, intellectual property issues, and regulatory oversight, all intended to foster the innovation necessary to develop new medicines while also managing the increasing costs of those medicines and insuring patient access and safety. It is no wonder that the industry gives rise to such complex and interesting competition law issues.

In addition, enforcement agencies and private antitrust plaintiffs continue to show an unrelenting interest in the industry. For better or for worse, it remains in the antitrust enforcement spotlight and looks likely to stay there for the foreseeable future. As a result, antitrust practitioners face a proliferation of new competition law theories being pursued before the agencies and courts. Life sciences are often used by enforcers as an area where they can test innovative approaches before they are translated into other industries. Counseling in this environment thus requires an in-depth knowledge of how competition law principles apply in the specific and unique context of the life sciences industry.

Finally, an increasing number of life sciences companies are facing scrutiny from enforcers, including government agencies and private plaintiffs, in both the United States and Europe, and, although there has been remarkable progress in harmonizing approaches across different jurisdictions, important differences remain both with respect to process and substantive competition law theory. Practitioners in the United States and Europe must be knowledgeable regarding the areas of harmony and of tension.

For all of these reasons, we thought practitioners might benefit from a work providing a comprehensive but accessible treatment of the competition law issues facing the life sciences industry in the United States and Europe. We thought it important to start from the ground up. The book therefore begins with chapters covering the relevant intellectual property, regulatory, antitrust enforcement context (Chapters I–II). The chapters that follow dive into competition law issues arising from mergers (Chapter III), concerted conduct (Chapter IV) and unilateral conduct (Chapter V). We have concluded with a chapter on private antitrust enforcement (Chapter VI), which accounts for the majority of antitrust enforcement litigation in the United States and is playing a growing role in Europe as well.

---

* The editors would like to thank David Costigan and Elvire Jolimoy for his very valuable help and contribution to this work.

We have written this work for non-antitrust specialists in the life sciences sector seeking to understand the competition law issues facing the industry and also for antitrust specialists representing life sciences clients on such issues. We hope it is helpful for both groups, and of assistance in navigating companies through this dynamic and complex area of the law.

Melanie Thill-Tayara
George G. Gordon
Laurence Bary
Rani Habash

CHAPTER I

Patent and Regulatory Framework

Katherine Helm and Sophie Pele*

* The authors would like to thank Dr. Ivan J. Burnside and Gilbert T. Voy at Eli Lilly, as well as Brian Goldberg, Margaux Lasseigne, and Seth Ray at Dechert LLP for their very valuable help and contribution to this chapter.

1. The pharmaceutical sector is complex and highly regulated. In particular, no drug can be placed on the market without a marketing authorization which, as regards originator drugs, is usually granted following years of costly research and development (R&D), with only very few (10% on average) research programs actually reaching the finish line. Because it takes time to develop a new drug, pharmaceutical companies engaging in R&D activity enjoy a certain level of protection against competition, through the grant of intellectual property (IP) rights conferring upon them a legal monopoly for a certain amount of time. However, as any other economic sector, the pharmaceutical sector does not escape the application of competition law rules, which serve as a powerful tool to meet wider policy objectives on both sides of the Atlantic: ensure patients access to both innovative and affordable healthcare products and services.
2. This specific environment often gives rise to conflicting interests, which health economists have illustrated as an "iron triangle"[1]:

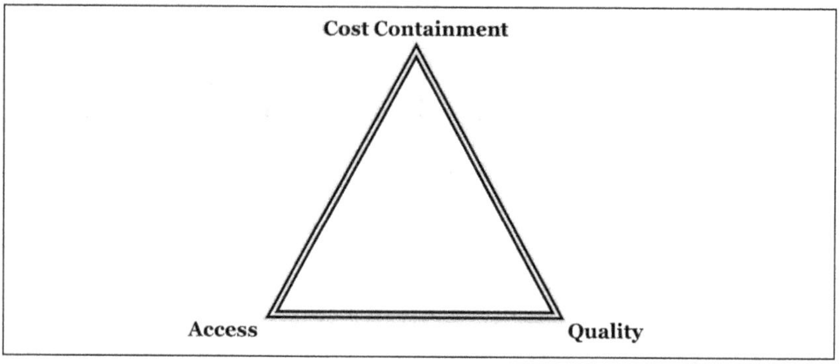

3. From an economic perspective, the equilateral triangle with points representing cost containment, access, and quality reflects the reality that progress toward one of the points often comes at the expense of another. The tension in attempting to increase access, lower costs, and improve the quality of healthcare is reflected in the patent protection and regulatory policies at play in the life sciences and pharmaceutical industries. On the one hand, it is important to promote innovation in the pharmaceutical and life sciences industry and facilitate the expensive and time-consuming R&D necessary to bring new therapies to the market. On the other hand, it is important to provide a pathway for less-expensive generic or biosimilar alternatives to come to the market either once the innovator company is deemed to have derived sufficient profit from its legal monopoly to fund research into next generation medicines or after a certain period of time.
4. The patent, regulatory, and competition law frameworks governing the healthcare industry in the European Union (EU) and United States (US) thus play an important role in balancing these competing interests. This Chapter provides a brief overview of the patent framework for pharmaceutical products in the EU and US

---

[1] William L. Kissick, MEDICINE'S DILEMMAS: INFINITE NEEDS VERSUS FINITE RESOURCES (Yale Univ. Press 1994).

and examines the unique regulatory framework that applies in the healthcare industry, each of which impose some constraints on pharmaceutical companies that are of particular importance for the application of competition law rules to the pharmaceutical sector.

I. Patent Framework in the US and EU

1. Patents and Patentability

5. A patent grants the patent holder, for the duration of the life of the patent, the right to exclude others from making, using, selling, offering for sale, or importing patented articles, or from performing a patented method. The purpose of this temporary legal monopoly is to protect and encourage those who take risks and make substantial investments to innovate and bring new treatments to the market, ultimately to the benefit of patients. In return for this grant of exclusivity, the public obtains public disclosure of enhancements to the state of the art. When a patent expires (or is declared invalid), the invention enters the public domain, meaning that anyone can make or use the patented invention free of patent infringement and of royalties payable to the patentee.

6. The requirements for patentability are similar in the EU and US. The two most important are novelty and non-obviousness (meaning that there must be an inventive step). Therefore, in broad terms, to be patentable, an invention must generally be an entirely new idea or a non-obvious improvement to an existing idea.[2]

7. Patents generally last for 20 years in both the US and EU. Furthermore, in both the EU and the US, specific provisions allow patentees to prolong their exclusivity for additional periods of time, provided they meet certain conditions. For example, in the EU, patentees can sometimes obtain a supplementary protection certificate (SPC) to effectively extend the protection of a patent for a period of up to a maximum of 5 years after expiry of the patent or 15 years from the date of the first marketing authorization in the Europe, Middle East and Africa (EMEA), whichever is earlier.[3] In certain circumstances, they can also obtain a further six-month extension. SPCs are a *sui generis* right, not a patent term extension (PTE). As such, SPCs do not extend the entire scope of the patent, but instead extend exclusivity over the marketed product only. As patents are national property rights, SPCs are only awarded on a national basis. If an applicant desires SPC protection, it must submit individual SPC applications to each national patent office in the countries within the EU where it desires such protection.

---

2 Convention on the Grant of European Patents, Oct. 5, 1973, 13 I.L.M. 270 (1974) (the EPC), art. 52.1; *see also* Agreement on Trade-Related Aspects of Intellectual Property Rights, art. 35, Apr. 15, 1994, Marrakesh Agreement Establishing the World Trade Organization, Annex 1C, 1869 U.N.T.S. 299, 33 I.L.M. 1197 (1994) (the TRIPS Agreement), art. 27. Note that the use of old medicines for the treatment of new indications (*e.g.*, second medical uses (2MUs)) can be patented. 35 U.S.C. §§ 101, 102, 103, 112.

3 Article 3 of the SPC Regulation sets forth the requirements for obtaining an SPC. They are not available for medical devices. Only one SPC may be granted per product per company group.

8. In the US, the term of a patent can be lengthened through PTE.[4] PTE extends patent life to compensate patent holders for marketing time lost while developing the product and awaiting government approval. A maximum of 5 years can be restored to the patent, and the total patent life after PTE cannot exceed 14 years from the product's approval date. In addition, only the first approval of a new active ingredient qualifies for a PTE, and only one patent may be extended per new active ingredient.

2. Patent Approval Process

9. **In the US**, the patent approval process is called patent prosecution and is overseen by the US Patent and Trademark Office (PTO). An inventor can apply for a national patent from the PTO or an international patent under the Patent Cooperation Treaty (PCT). International applications have the same effect as national patents[5] but undergo two stages: an "international stage" and a "national stage." The international stage involves an international patentability search and international patentability opinion, and the national stage involves regular review by the PTO.[6]

10. **In the EU**, an applicant has three different options for seeking patent protection. First, an inventor, successor in title, or assignee can apply for a national patent directly at the patent office of a particular Member State; if granted, the protection would be limited to the territory of said Member State. Second, the inventor can apply for a European patent before the European Patent Office (EPO) designating the European countries where it is seeking patent protection.[7] If granted, the holder of a European patent must validate the patent in each Member State it designated within three months of the grant of the patent. Third, the inventor can apply for an international patent under the PCT.[8] The PCT procedure consists of two main phases: it begins with the filing of an international application and, if the outcome of this first phase is positive, it is followed by the grant of national patents by the national offices of the countries where protection is sought (so-called "national phase") or by the grant of a European patent if the applicant chooses to go before the EPO (so-called "regional phase"). In this second case, the EPO procedure applies and the patent granted by the EPO will thus subsequently have to be validated in the designated Member States.

---

4 *See* 35 U.S.C. § 156. Patent-term extension allows the extension of the term of a patent claiming a product that requires regulatory approval prior to being sold, or a method of using or manufacturing the product. The FDA is involved in determining which patent applications are granted PTE.

5 *See* 35 U.S.C. § 363 ("An international application designating the United States shall have the effect, from its international filing date under article 11 of the treaty, of a national application for patent regularly filed in the Patent and Trademark Office.").

6 *See id.* § 364 (describing procedure in international stage); *id.* §§ 371–372 (describing procedure in national stage).

7 While European patents are granted by the EPO following a single application, a European patent is in fact a bundle of identical national patents.

8 An applicant who has filed a PCT application and seeks a patent in any Member State of the EPC: (i) may apply to enter the national phase and designate a particular country, or (ii) may apply to enter into the regional phase before the EPO and later validate the patent in the particular country once granted.

3. Challenging Patents

11. Patents are not absolute and can be challenged.

12. **In the US**, patent validity may be challenged in federal court. Because patents are presumed valid upon issuance, absent a showing of fraud on the PTO or inequitable conduct,[9] the patent challenger bears a high burden of proof (clear and convincing evidence) in order to obtain invalidation of the patent.[10]

13. Patent validity may also be challenged in PTO proceedings. Patent challenges in the PTO include *Inter Partes* Review (IPR), Post-Grant Review (PGR), and *Ex-Parte* Reexamination. In contrast to federal court challenges, patents subject to a PTO challenge are not presumed valid.

14. Like federal court patent challenges, IPR and PGR are adversarial proceedings in which the party that files the petition challenging the patent participates in the proceeding and bears the burden of proving unpatentability, albeit by the lower "preponderance of the evidence" standard.[11] For IPR, patentability challenges are limited to § 102 (anticipation) and § 103 (obviousness), and only on the basis of prior art consisting of patents or printed publications.[12] PGR challenges can be based on any statutory unpatentability basis, including, § 101 (eligibility, utility, double patenting), § 112 (written description, enablement, definiteness), and all §§ 102 and 103 bases, but not non-statutory obviousness-type double patenting.[13]

15. A PGR petition can only be filed against a patent having an effective filing date on or after March 16, 2013, and it must be filed within nine-months of the challenged patent's issue date.[14] An IPR petition may be filed against any patent, and a party can file an IPR petition provided it is not "filed more than one year after the date on which the petitioner, real party in interest, or privy of the petitioner is served with a complaint [in federal court] alleging infringement of the patent."[15]

16. A third party requesting an *Ex-Parte* Reexamination does not participate in the challenge beyond submitting the initial request, but an *Ex-Parte* Reexamination request can raise any statutory unpatentability basis as well as non-statutory obviousness-type double patenting.[16] There are no time limits on when an *Ex-Parte* Reexamination request can be filed.[17]

17. **In the EU**, if a patent is granted by the EPO, a challenger has nine months to file an opposition before the EPO. If the patent is successfully challenged before the EPO, this will invalidate the patent in all designated countries, even if a national

---

9 *See* Section II.C.a.(4), Chapter V, for a discussion of fraud and inequitable conduct before the PTO.

10 35 U.S.C. § 282.

11 *See id.* §§ 316, 326.

12 *Id.* § 311(b).

13 *Id.* § 321(b).

14 *Id.* § 321(c).

15 *Id.* § 315(b).

16 *See id.* §§ 301, 302; USPTO, Manual of Patent Examining Procedure (MPEP) ¶2258 (Feb. 2023).

17 37 C.F.R. § 1.510(a).

court has upheld the patent. Alternatively, at any time during the life of the patent, a challenger can file a revocation action in the national courts of the Member States or, in some cases, the national patent office to challenge the patent's validity.

II. Pharmaceutical Regulatory Process

18. By way of principle, while there exist simplified procedures for generics and biosimilars, any medicinal product must be approved by the relevant regulatory authority before it can be marketed. The marketing authorization aims to safeguard public health and is issued by competent authorities only after the safety and efficacy of the medicinal product has been assessed and the authorities have concluded that the risk-benefit ratio of the drug candidate merits approval. The marketing authorization of a medicinal product defines the approved indication(s) for which the product may be marketed, the target population of patients, the instructions for use, and any special warnings and precautions for use of the product. This information can be found in the summary of product characteristics (SmPC) in the EU, which is part of the marketing authorization, and in the FDA-approved product labeling (the Package insert or PI) in the US, which is available to the public.[18]

19. This section provides an overview of the relevant authorities in charge of the regulatory process in the EU and the US as well as of the rules which govern the marketing authorization of each type of medicinal product (originator drugs, generics, biosimilars). Once authorized, marketing authorization holders are also subject to post-approval obligations.

1. Regulatory authorities

20. **In the US**, the US Food and Drug Administration (FDA)[19] is responsible for ensuring the safety and efficacy of pharmaceutical products before they can be placed on the market. It reviews all new drug applications (NDAs) and Abbreviated New Drug Applications (ANDAs), 505(b)(2) applications submitted under the Federal Food, Drug, and Cosmetic Act (FDCA),[20] all biologic license applications under the Public Health Service Act (PHSA).[21] Certain branches of FDA oversee specialized products:
    - The FDA's Center for Drug Evaluation and Research (CDER) is responsible for oversight of small molecule drugs. Most NDAs and 505(b)(2) applications are reviewed by divisions within the Office of New Drugs (OND). CDER's Office of Therapeutic Biologics & Biosimilars reviews certain BLAs and biosimilar applications. ANDAs are reviewed by CDER's Office of Generic Drugs (OGD).
    - The FDA's Center for Biologics Evaluation and Research (CBER) is responsible for oversight of biologic drugs. CBER's Office of Therapeutic Products reviews BLAs for certain therapeutic biologics.

---

18 Health professionals can also sometimes prescribe medication "off-label," which means that they are prescribed outside of the terms of their marketing authorization.

19 The FDA was created in 1938 by the FDCA.

20 21 U.S.C. § 355.

21 42 U.S.C. § 262.

21. The FDA has extensive authority to regulate drug products after approval, including monitoring for adverse events; testing and sampling products; and conducting investigations, inspections, and audits.

22. **In the EU**, the medicines regulatory system comprises a network of around 50 regulatory authorities which are responsible for assuring the quality, safety, and efficacy of pharmaceutical products. Amongst them:

    - The European Medicines Agency (EMA) is a decentralized agency of the EU,[22] whose role is to provide scientific advice to the institutions of the EU[23] as well as to the Member States. It enables these stakeholders to exercise their competencies – authorizing medicinal products (for both human and veterinary use) and monitoring their post-approval use on the market – in accordance with EU legislation. Within the EMA, the Committee for Medicinal Products for Human Use (CHMP) scientifically evaluates the quality, safety, and efficacy of drugs for which a centralized marketing authorization application has been submitted. The CHMP is also responsible for assessing variations (e.g., modifications or extensions) to existing centralized marketing authorizations (such as including new special warnings and precautions for use in the SmPC following new pharmacovigilance data) and, when applicable, for recommending to the European Commission of the European Union (the European Commission), which is responsible for granting a marketing authorization upon positive opinion of the EMA, changes to, suspensions, or withdrawals of centralized marketing authorizations on the basis of pharmacovigilance and safety concerns. In addition, the EMA may under certain circumstances arbitrate disputes concerning the safety or risk-benefit balance of medicinal products. Finally, the EMA promotes the development and innovation of new medicinal products through scientific guidelines, scientific advice program and specific incentives.[24] It also coordinates the Member States' actions and enables the sharing of information at the EU level through different databases.
    - EU Member State national authorities[25] are responsible for implementing and ensuring compliance with the EU and local applicable directives and regulations in their territories.[26] The national authorities assess and grant national marketing authorizations to medicinal products that have not received centralized authorization or are not eligible for the centralized procedure.

---

22 The EMA was created by Council Regulation 726/2004 of the European Parliament and of the Council of Mar. 31, 2004, laying down Community procedures for the authorization and supervision of medicinal products for human and veterinary use and establishing a European Medicines Agency (Council Regulation 726/2004).

23 Notably to the European Commission, in charge of granting the marketing authorizations at the EU level.

24 Incentives notably apply to drugs intended for the treatment of children and rare diseases.

25 For example, in France, the National Agency for Medicines and Health Products Safety (*Agence Nationale de Sécurité du Médicament et des Produits de Santé* (ANSM)), in Germany, the German Health Agency (*Bundesinstitut für Arzneimittel und Medizinprodukte* (BfArM)), and, in Italy, the Italian Medicines Agency (*Agenzia Italiana del Farmaco* (AIFA)).

26 The manufacturing, marketing, and distribution of medicinal products are regulated at the EU level by above-mentioned Council Regulation 726/2004 and the Directive 2001/83 of the European Parliament and of the Council of Nov. 6, 2001 on the Community code relating to medicinal products for human use whose provisions have been implemented by each Member State.

National authorities are responsible for surveilling the market and monitoring the safety of health products. To this end, they enjoy wide powers. They can conduct audits or investigations of pharmaceutical companies. They can also, at any time, test and sample products to ensure that they comply with the applicable regulations and are safe and effective enough to continue to be marketed. Finally, where necessary, they can impose penalties, including the suspension of withdrawal from the market of a given product, or close any site or entity which is not compliant with the applicable regulations.

2. Marketing Authorization Process

23. The marketing authorization process differs for originator drugs and for generics and biosimilars, for which simplified procedures are available.

A. *Marketing Authorization Process for Originator Drugs*

24. Except in exceptional circumstances where early access can be granted subject to certain conditions, obtaining a marketing authorization is mandatory before any drug can be placed on the market. Separate from patent protection, Originator companies then benefit, for a certain period of time, from regulatory exclusivity protecting them from the competition of generics and biosimilars as a reward for the time and efforts spent in the approval process.

a. *Regular procedure*

25. **In the US**, the regulatory approval process for innovator drugs depends on the type of drug. Originators seeking approval for a new small molecule drug must submit an NDA under the FDCA.[27] Those seeking approval for new biological products must submit a Biologic License Application ("BLA") under the PHSA.[28]

26. The US drug approval process takes place within a structured framework that includes an analysis of the target condition and available treatments; an assessment of benefits and risks from the pre-clinical and clinical data, including data regarding the product's efficacy, safety, and quality, such as the results of pre-clinical (toxicological and pharmacological) tests and clinical trials; strategies for managing risks demonstrated by the data (e.g., warnings in drug labeling; Risk Evaluation and Mitigation Strategies or REMS;[29] and an FDA inspection of the facility where the drug will be manufactured. Application also includes information about any patents that cover the drug.[30] If FDA scientists conclude that the drug's benefits outweigh its known risks, the NDA may be approved (a BLA is "licensed") and the drug can be marketed in the US. Such approval can also be conditioned on the performance of certain post-approval clinical studies to provide further data on the product that the FDA concludes require additional analysis but should not hold up approval.

---

27 21 U.S.C. § 355(b)(1).

28 42 U.S.C. § 262(a).

29 A Risk Evaluation and Mitigation Strategy (REMS) is a drug safety program that FDA can require for certain drugs/biologics with serious safety concerns to help ensure the benefits of the drug/biologic outweigh its risks. *See* 21 U.S.C. § 355-1.

30 *Id.* § 355(a), (b).

27. The FDA has implemented an accelerated approval program which allows for earlier approval, through an expeditious procedure, of drugs that treat serious or life-threatening conditions and provide therapeutic benefit over available therapies based on a surrogate endpoint.[31] In practice, this leads to earlier availability of promising therapies for patients and is often used in oncology. If subsequently mandatory confirmatory trials show that the drug actually provides a clinical benefit, the FDA grants traditional approval for the drug. But if they in fact show that the drug is not effective and/or not safe, the FDA has expedited procedures in place that can ultimately lead to the removal of the drug from the market. Additionally, FDA employs several approaches to encourage the development and/or speed the review of drugs that may represent the first available treatment for a serious illness, or drugs that have a significant benefit over existing drug treatments (e.g., Fast Track and Breakthrough Therapy designations, Priority Review).

28. **In the EU**, in order to obtain a marketing authorization for an originator drug, the applicant must be established within the EU[32] and submit sufficient information to demonstrate the product's efficacy, safety, and quality, such as the results of pre-clinical (toxicological and pharmacological) tests and clinical trials.[33] When a medicinal product has been granted an initial marketing authorization, any additional dosage, pharmaceutical form, administration route, presentation, or variation and extensions must receive a separate marketing authorization or be incorporated into the initial marketing authorization.[34]

29. There are four different routes to obtain a marketing authorization: (1) the centralized procedure, (2) the national procedure (the National Procedure), (3) the decentralized procedure, and the (4) mutual-recognition procedure (the Mutual Recognition Procedure). Each route has a unique sequence of steps and associated timeframe:

    - The Centralized Procedure allows an inventor to obtain a single EU-wide marketing authorization, delivered by the European Commission, which is valid throughout the EU. The use of this procedure is mandatory for orphan drugs, biotechnology products, and new active substances in certain therapeutic areas and is optional for other new active substances and innovative medicines. Most innovating products can follow the centralized procedure through an accelerated (so called fast track) process.
    - By contrast, the National Procedure only allows to obtain a local marketing authorization in the EU Member State where the application is filed. The marketing authorization will be limited to the territory of the Member State concerned.

---

31 A surrogate endpoint is a marker, such as a laboratory measurement, radiographic image, physical sign or other measure that is reasonably likely to predict clinical benefit, but is not itself a measure of clinical benefit.

32 Council Directive 2001/83, art. 8.2.

33 *Id.* art. 8.3(i). The conduct of clinical trials is regulated by Council Regulation 536/2014 of the European Parliament and of the Council of Apr. 16, 2014 on clinical trials on medicinal products for human use repealing Directive 2001/20 (Clinical Trial Regulation), that entered into force on Jan. 31, 2022.

34 *Id.* art. 6.1.

- The Decentralized Procedure can be used when the applicant seeks to obtain simultaneous local marketing authorizations for its medicine in more than one EU Member State, provided that the product concerned has not yet been authorized in any EU country and does not fall within the scope of the centralized procedure.[35] The first Member State to review the application is the Reference Member State (RMS), and subsequent states are called Concerned Member States (CMS).
- Finally, the Mutual Recognition Procedure allows for the recognition of a local marketing authorization granted by one Member State, the RMS, in the other Member States, the CMS. The decision of the RMS is forwarded to the CMSs. If there is a dispute over granting the authorization, the EMA will arbitrate the dispute.

b. *Early access programs*

30. Under certain conditions, in the interest of public health, both the EU and US allow drugs to be marketed and used before having formally obtained a market authorization.

31. **In the US**, FDA's Expanded Access Program (sometimes referred to as "compassionate use") offers a potential route for patients to gain access to investigational drugs and biologics for "treatment use" outside of a clinical trial, provided that the following criteria are met: (1) The patient has a serious or immediately life-threatening disease or condition, (2) There is no comparable or satisfactory alternative therapy to diagnose, monitor, or treat the patient's disease or condition, (3) Patient enrollment in a clinical trial is not possible or feasible, (4) The potential patient benefit justifies the potential risks of treatment use, and those potential risks are not unreasonable in the context of the disease or condition to be treated; and (5) Providing the investigational drug product will not interfere with clinical investigations that could support a product's development or marketing approval for the expanded access use. FDA's Expanded Access regulations also include provisions for Individual Patient treatment use (including for emergency use), Intermediate-size patient populations, and for widespread treatment use under a "Treatment IND or Treatment Protocol."

32. **In the EU**, conditional marketing authorizations[36] may be granted by the European Commission for medicines that address unmet medical needs, without full clinical data supporting the safety and efficacy of a product, provided that the benefit of their immediate availability outweighs the risk inherent in the fact that additional data are still required and must be supplied at a later stage. Medicinal products for human use intended for the treatment, prevention, or medical diagnosis of seriously debilitating or life-threatening diseases are eligible for conditional marketing authorizations. Unauthorized medicinal products can also be made available

---

35 *Id.*

36 For more details, refer to Council Regulation 726/2004, art. 14-a, and to the European Commission Regulation 507/2006 of Mar. 29,2006 on the conditional marketing authorization for medicinal products for human use falling within the scope of Council Regulation 726/2004 of the European Parliament and of the Council, 2006 OJ (L 92) 6.

on a compassionate basis under strict conditions[37] to groups of patients with chronically or seriously debilitating diseases or whose diseases are considered to be life-threatening and whose diseases cannot be treated satisfactorily by an authorized medicinal product.[38]

c. *Market exclusivities*

33. To foster innovation in the pharmaceutical industry, both the EU and US protect innovator drugs by regulating when generics or biosimilars can enter the market, aside from the protection inherent from patents rights. This is achieved by preventing generics and biosimilars manufacturers to apply for a marketing authorization using the data of the original marketing authorization for a certain period of time (so-called regulatory data protection) and to launch the product for an additional period of time (so-called market exclusivity).

34. **In the US**, the length of market exclusivity depends on whether the product is a small molecule drug or a biologic. Small molecule drugs generally have 5 years of market exclusivity and 4 years of data exclusivity,[39] for new chemical entities (NCE), and 3 years of market exclusivity for sponsors who conduct new clinical investigations of approved drugs leading to changes in the marketed products. Biologics have 12 years of market exclusivity and 4 years of data exclusivity.

35. **In the EU**, aside from the protections granted by IP rights, an innovator drug may receive up to 11 years in total of data and market exclusivity, during which it can market its product without risk of competition. This regime is comprised of 8 years of data exclusivity, 2 years of market exclusivity, and, in very rare circumstances, a one-year extension.[40]

36. Certain drugs are eligible for even longer exclusivity periods. For example, both the EU and US incentivize developing drugs for children by granting slightly longer exclusivity periods for pediatric drugs. Similarly, so-called "orphan drugs" that treat rare diseases or conditions are eligible for longer exclusivities periods. The below chart – which is meant to be illustrative rather than exhaustive – summarizes some exclusivity periods in the US and EU:

---

37 In particular, to be provided on a compassionate basis, a product must either be subject to an application for a marketing authorization or undergoing clinical trials.

38 Council Regulation 726/2004, art. 83.

39 During the 5 years of NCE exclusivity, FDA cannot approve or accept a competitor's 505(b)(2) or ANDA for a product based on the same active ingredient, regardless of indication, with one exception. If the 505(b)(2) or ANDA filer challenges the patent (file a Paragraph IV certification), FDA can accept the application one year before the expiration of the five-year exclusivity. Thus, the NDA holder enjoys 4 years of data exclusivity during which another applicant cannot rely on clinical data obtained by the NDA holder, but no approval can occur until the five-year expiration date.

40 The eight-year period of data exclusivity prevents companies seeking to submit generic applications for marketing approval that seek to rely on the pre-clinical and clinical data of the initial innovator marketing authorization holder in order to establish the safety and efficacy of its product. After the eight-year data exclusivity period ends, generic applicants are permitted to file an application relying on the innovator's data in place of investing in generating their own data. During the two-year period of marketing exclusivity, however, EU authorities may not approve a marketing authorization for the generic product. The additional one year can for example be granted if during the first 8 years, the marketing authorization holder obtains an authorization for one or more new therapeutic indications based on a new clinical investigation which establishes a significant clinical benefit in comparison with existing therapies.

	US		EU
Exclusivity Type	**Small Molecule**	**Biologic**	**Innovator Drug**
Data Exclusivity	4 years (if patents listed)	4 years	8 years
Market Exclusivity	5 years (new chemical entity)	12 years	2 years
Pediatric Exclusivity	6 months (additive with others)	6 months (additive with others)	2 years if orphan drug[41]
Orphan Drug Exclusivity	7 years	7 years	10 years (reduced to 6 years if conditions not met at end of 5th year)
Generating Antibiotic Incentives Now (GAIN) Exclusivity	5 years (additive with others)	N/A	
New Clinical Investigation Exclusivity	3 years	N/A	
Qualified Infectious Disease Product (QIDP) Exclusivity	5 years (additive with others)	N/A	
ANDA First-Filer Exclusivity	180 days (for first filers of certain ANDAs, see below)	N/A	
New Formulation/ Composition Exclusivity	3 years	N/A	
New Indication Exclusivity	3 years	N/A	

41 Although not linked to regulatory exclusivities, SPCs are also extended by six months for pediatric drugs.

B. *Generic Drugs*

37. Generally speaking, "generic" drugs are copies of previously authorized small molecule drugs. At a high level, both the EU and US allow for an abbreviated application process for generic drugs that allows applicants to forgo the full approval process, including full safety and efficacy studies.[42] This is because the generic applicant is allowed to rely on certain data from the innovator's original authorization.

38. **In the US**, there are two types of abbreviated application pathways for generic drugs: (1) an ANDA or (2) a 505(b)(2) application. In an ANDA, a generic company generally satisfies FDA's safety and efficacy requirements if (with some exceptions) the active ingredient, route of administration, dosage form, and strength of the generic drug is the same as the branded drug and the generic company demonstrates that its generic product is bioequivalent[43] to the branded reference listed drug (RLD). In 505(b)(2) applications, applicants can rely on data not generated by the applicant (such as publicly available scientific literature) to establish safety and efficacy of the drug necessary for approval. The approval process for *ANDAs* and 505(b)(2) applications under the Hatch-Waxman Act[44] share many similarities.

39. When the FDA approves an NDA for a drug, patents that cover the drug's substance (i.e., active ingredient), drug product, or a method of using the drug are required to be listed in the *Approved Drug Products with Therapeutic Equivalence Determinations*, colloquially referred to as the "Orange Book."[45] A generic drug company submitting an ANDA or 505(b)(2) application for a generic drug must make one of the following certifications for each patent listed for an RLD in the Orange Book:[46]

    - Paragraph I certification that no relevant patent is listed in the Orange Book.
    - Paragraph II certification that the listed patent has expired.
    - Paragraph III certification that the listed patent, plus any other exclusivity, will expire before the requested approval.
    - Paragraph IV certification that the listed patent is invalid or will not be infringed by the commercialization of the generic drug.

40. A generic company submitting a Paragraph IV certification must provide notice to the NDA holder and patentee within 20 days after FDA accepts the ANDA for

---

42 The EU also has a "hybrid" drug concept. Hybrid drugs are similar to generics but either do not meet the strict definition of generics because their bioequivalence cannot be demonstrated through bioavailability studies, or they have different active substances, therapeutic indications, strengths, pharmaceutical forms, or routes of administration than the innovator drug. *See* Council Directive 2001/83, art. 10.3.

43 Bioequivalence is defined in 21 C.F.R. § 314.3, in part, as "the absence of a significant difference in the rate and extent to which the active ingredient or active moiety in pharmaceutical equivalents or pharmaceutical alternatives becomes available at the site of drug action when administered at the same molar dose under similar conditions in an appropriately designed study."

44 Drug Price Competition and Patent Term Restoration (Hatch-Waxman) Act, Pub. L. No. 98-417, 98 Stat. 1585 (1984).
No. 98-417, 98 Stat. 1585 (1984).

45 21 U.S.C. § 355(b)(1)(G).

46 *See id.* § 355(b)(2)(A)(i)-(iv); *id.* § 355(j)(2)(A)(vii)(I)–(IV).

filing. The act of filing an ANDA constitutes an "artificial act of infringement" providing the basis for an NDA holder to file suit under 35 United States Code (U.S.C.) § 271(e)(2) even though actual infringement under 35 U.S.C. § 271(a)–(c) may not have occurred yet.[47] At this point, if the NDA holder files suit within 45 days, the FDA may not grant final approval of the ANDA for 30 months. This 30-month stay can be terminated early if the court issues a final order determining that the patent is invalid, unenforceable, or not infringed.[48] Should a generic drug obtain FDA approval upon expiration of the 30-month stay (or if no 30-month stay is applicable), but before a court has had an opportunity to resolve patent disputes, the generic has the option to market its product. This is commonly referred to as an "at-risk" launch because the generic company is still subject to potential liability for patent infringement and, therefore, assumes the risk that a court could find those sales to be infringing, with the generic liable for the patentee's potentially significant lost-profit damages. Should the NDA holder not sue a generic within 45 days, the generic company can bring a declaratory judgment action against the NDA holder for a declaration that the Orange Book-listed patents are not infringed or invalid.[49] The ability of a generic company to bring a declaratory judgment action can be important for the purposes of triggering the 180 days of exclusivity granted for a first filer ANDA (described below). An important exception to this rule exists – it does not apply to the brand manufacturer, and they are free to market an Authorized Generic (AG) version of the product that competes with the first-to-file generic.[50]

41. To facilitate ANDA development, Congress created a "safe harbor" for generic companies seeking to prepare an ANDA. Under the safe harbor provision of 35 U.S.C. § 271(e)(1):

> It shall not be an act of infringement to make, use, offer to sell, or sell within the United States or import into the United States a patented invention… solely for uses reasonably related to the development and submission of information under a Federal law which regulated the manufacture, use or sale, of drugs or veterinary biological products.

42. In addition, and to create an incentive for generic companies to challenge Orange Book listed patents, the first generic company to successfully challenge an innovator's patents can receive 180 days of exclusivity where FDA will not approve another ANDA.[51] A generic can forfeit its 180 days of exclusivity in certain circumstances such as when the generic fails to market its product or fails to obtain

---

47 *See Eli Lilly and Co. v. Medtronic, Inc.*, 496 U.S. 661, 676 (1990).

48 21 U.S.C. § 355(c)(3)(C); *id.* § 355(j)(5)(B)(iii).

49 *Id.* § 355(j)(5)(C).

50 An authorized generic is a generic drug that is sold pursuant to the brand manufacturer's NDA, as opposed to a generic manufacturer's ANDA. *Mylan Inc. v. SmithKline Beecham Corp.*, 723 F.3d 413, 416 n. 4 (3d Cir. 2013) (citing 21 U.S.C. § 355(t)(3)).

51 *See id.* § 355(j)(5)(B)(iv). Section 505(b)(2) applications, as a form of NDA, are not eligible for 180-days of exclusivity. However, FDA will similarly not subject a 505(b)(2) application to a 180-day exclusivity period granted to an ANDA. Therefore, a 505(b)(2) application could launch during an ANDA's exclusivity period.

tentative approval within certain timeframes.[52] These forfeiture provisions can be particularly important for subsequent ANDA filers whose applications FDA will not approve due to a first generic filer's 180 day exclusivity.

43. **In the EU**, the applicant is not required to provide the results of pre-clinical tests and clinical trials if it can demonstrate that its product is a generic of an innovator which has been authorized for at least 8 years in the Member State or in the EU. Save for exceptional circumstances, the bioequivalence between the generic and its innovator must be demonstrated through bioavailability studies. The generic status generally allows for certain sorts of substitution by the pharmacist. At the national level, Member States have also adopted specific rules and put in place various incentives to encourage the use of generic products.

C. *Biosimilar Drugs*

44. Biological medical products[53] differ from traditional pharmaceuticals, which typically are small-molecule compounds manufactured through chemical synthesis. Examples include immunological products and medicines derived from human blood and plasma.

45. As with traditional pharmaceuticals created through chemical synthesis, biologics typically begin with a branded originator product. Once any patent protections expire, so-called "biosimilars" then aim to mimic the original patented biologic therapy with an identical therapeutic mechanism and clinical attributes and can be described as "generic" versions of originator biologics. Unlike traditional generic pharmaceuticals, however, biosimilars are not as close copies of the originator biologics. Making an exact copy is impossible as biologics are based on either mammalian or microbial cell cultures and the Active Pharmaceutical Ingredient (API) is never exactly the same as the biological originator product. One medical journal summarizes these differences as follows:

> Biologic production uses specialized processes that do not always resemble facilities, machinery, or equipment used to produce chemical drugs. Construction and validation of new facilities is disproportionately expensive and also time consuming. This helps explain the global shortage of biomanufacturing capacity and the cost differential between biologic and chemical drugs.[54]

---

52 *See* FDA, U.S. Department of Health and Human Services, CDER, *Draft Guidance for Industry, 180-Day Exclusivity: Questions and Answers*, (Jan. 2017), *available at* https://www.fda.gov/media/102650/download.

53 Council Directive 2001/83, annex I, ¶3.2.1.1 ("A biological medicinal product is a product, the active substance of which is a biological substance. A biological substance is a substance that is produced by or extracted from a biological source and that needs for its characterisation and the determination of its quality a combination of physico-chemical-biological testing, together with the production process and its control. The following shall be considered as biological medicinal products: immunological medicinal products and medicinal products derived from human blood and human plasma as defined, respectively in paragraphs (4) and (10) of Article 1; medicinal products falling within the scope of Part A of the Annex to Regulation (EEC) No. 2309/93; advanced therapy medicinal products as defined in Part IV of this Annex.").

54 Thomas Morrow & Linda Hull Felcone, *Defining the Difference: What Makes Biologics Unique*, 1 Biotechnology Healthcare 24, 24–29 (Sept. 2004), *available at* https://www.ncbi.nlm.nih.gov/pmc/articles/PMC3564302/. *See also* Lea Chrisl, *From Bench to Bedside, Biologics Require Excellence at Every*

46. Biosimilars are therefore biological medicinal products highly similar to the innovator or reference medicinal product in terms of structure, biological activity and efficacy, safety, and immunogenicity profile.[55]

47. Biologics and biosimilars are relatively recent innovations. The first biosimilar was approved in the EU in 2006, and the first biosimilar was approved in 2015 in the US.[56]

48. **In the US**, regulatory approval for biosimilars is governed by the Biologics Price Competition and Innovation Act (BPCIA). Biosimilars are licensed by submitting an abbreviated biologic license application (aBLA) to FDA. Under the BPCIA, biological products may be licensed as "Biosimilar" (highly similar to the reference product notwithstanding minor differences in clinically inactive components) or "Interchangeable" (the product is biosimilar and can be expected to produce the same clinical result as the reference product).

49. Also under the BPCIA, innovator biologics are afforded two types of regulatory exclusivities that are often referred to as: (1) data exclusivity and (2) marketing exclusivity. Under the data exclusivity, no application for an abbreviated aBLA can be filed until 4 years after the date the reference product was first licensed. Under the marketing exclusivity, FDA cannot approve an aBLA until 12 years after the date the reference product was first licensed.[57]

50. The first aBLA to obtain FDA approval as Interchangeable to the reference product is eligible for up to one year of regulatory exclusivity.[58] During this one-year period, FDA cannot approve any additional applications for an Interchangeable product but can approve additional applications as biosimilar. As with the 180-day exclusivity period for generics under the Hatch-Waxman Act, the one-year exclusivity period of interchangeable products can be shortened or forfeited.[59]

51. A key difference between the Hatch-Waxman Act and the BPCIA is that the BPCIA's analog of the Orange Book – commonly referred to as the Purple Book – does not *require* the reference product sponsor to list patents that it believes cover the reference product or a method of using the reference product.[60] Accordingly, there is less clarity for an aBLA sponsor as to what patents it will have to overcome in order to market its

---

Stage, STAT (Feb. 13, 2020) ("Biologic medicines are more complex and require mastery of manufacturing processes involving living cells that are inherently more variable than components involved in chemical synthesis."), *available at* https://www.statnews.com/2020/02/13/biologics-require-manufacturing-excellence-at-every-stage/.

55 EMA, *Guideline on Immunogenicity Assessment of Therapeutic Proteins* (May 18, 2017), *available at* https://www.ema.europa.eu/en/documents/scientific-guideline/guideline-immunogenicity-assessment-therapeutic-proteins-revision-1_en.pdf.

56 Unlike the US, the EU's system for approval of drugs and biologics is centralized and not divided between the EU and the Member States. Biotechnology-derived products are approved at the European level, which lead in the early 2000s to a much-simplified adoption process for biosimilars. *See* Krista Hessler Carver et al., *An Unofficial Legislative History of the Biologics Price Competition and Innovation Act of 2009*, 65 Food & Drug L.J. 671, 688 (2010).

57 42 U.S.C. § 262(k)(7)(A).

58 *Id.* § 262(k)(6).

59 *Id.*

60 In addition, method of manufacture (or process) patents are a prevalent and important aspect of protecting innovations in the field of biologic pharmaceuticals. Biologics are complex molecules that are produced by living cells through multistep manufacturing processes that must be monitored and reproduced to ensure correct product identity. In this way, a biologic is defined by its process. By contrast, small molecule pharmaceuticals are simpler chemical compounds that can be manufactured by chemical synthesis. Accordingly, method of

product. The BPCIA attempts to navigate this via a two-phase process that has been termed the "patent dance". As part of the first phase, the aBLA applicant submits a copy of its aBLA to the reference product sponsor. Then, the reference product sponsor responds with a list of patents it could reasonably assert against the applicant. The applicant responds with its own counter-list and explains why its biosimilar does not infringe any of the patents identified by the reference product sponsor. The parties then negotiate over the lists to try to narrow the list of patents that will be the subject of any patent infringement lawsuit by the reference product sponsor.

52. Unlike the Hatch-Waxman Act, filing suit under the BPCIA triggers no automatic 30-month stay. Rather, the Section 262(k) applicant must provide notice at least 180 days before first commercial marketing of its biosimilar product, which can trigger the second phase of litigation under the BPCIA.[61] In the second phase, the reference product sponsor may then seek a preliminary injunction not only with respect to the patents-in-suit, but with respect to *any* patent identified under paragraph (3)(A), (3)(B), (4), or (5)(B) that had not already been resolved in the first phase of litigation.[62]

53. **In the EU**, a specific framework has been put in place to authorize the marketing and sale of biosimilars.[63] Biosimilar medicinal products must be registered under the centralized procedure;[64] therefore, the EMA is solely responsible for evaluating application for biosimilar drugs. Unlike generics which can rely on bioavailability studies, a biosimilar applicant must submit evidence showing comparable safety and efficacy of the biosimilar product as compared to the reference product in accordance with the requirements of Directive 2001/83. In particular, comparability studies need to demonstrate the similar nature of a biosimilar with its innovator biological medicinal product in terms of quality characteristics, biological activity, safety, and efficacy based on a comprehensive comparability exercise.[65] As with generics, several mechanisms have been put in place at the Member States level to facilitate the entry and encourage the penetration of biosimilars in the market.

3. Post-Approval Obligations

54. Both the EU and US impose post-approval obligations on manufacturers of medical products.

55. **In the US**, once FDA approves a drug application, FDA will monitor its via post-approval adverse experience monitoring and reporting requirements imposed on the drug applicant.[66] In addition, companies that hold approved drug applications are required to (a) file annual reports with FDA that summarize new information

---

manufacture patents generally play a lesser role in small molecule drug patents and are not listable in the Orange Book. *See generally*, Jeffrey Wu & Claire W. Cheng, *Into the Woods: A Biologic Patent Thicket Analysis*, 19 CHI.-KENT J. INTELL. PROP. 93, 100, 159–160, 162, nn. 22, 265, 272, fig. 22 (2020).

61 42 U.S.C. § 262(l)(8)(A).

62 *Id.* § 262(l)(8)(B).

63 *See* Council Directive 2001/83, as amended, where the European Commission created new authorization procedures for biosimilar products.

64 Council Regulation 726/2004, art. 3.1 and annex I.

65 EMA, *Guideline on Similar Biological Medicinal Products* (Oct. 23, 2014), *available at* https://www.ema.europa.eu/en/documents/scientific-guideline/guideline-similar-biological-medicinal-products-rev1_en.pdf.

66 *See, e.g.*, 21 C.F.R. 314.84.

that might affect the safety, effectiveness, or labeling of the drug product, and other data; (b) submit copies of labeling and advertising used for promotion of the drug product; conduct post-approval studies and clinical trials, and provide status reports to FDA on their progress; notify FDA of drug shortages; among other requirements. Furthermore, companies are required to cooperate with FDA during periodic inspections, audits, and investigations.

56. **In the EU**, competent authorities and marketing authorization holders[67] interact periodically throughout the life cycle of a product. Marketing authorization holders have a regulatory obligation to vigilantly monitor their own products. Therefore, companies marketing medicinal products are subject to post-marketing vigilance obligations (known as pharmacovigilance). These obligations include the collection, assessment, investigation, and interpretation of real-world data to identify any adverse reactions to marketed products. Marketing authorization holders must provide the EMA and the local health agencies with periodic reports and any information they have collected that demonstrates or tends to demonstrate that their products may cause adverse reactions and must continuously reassess the risk-benefit tradeoff of their products. Post-marketing authorization vigilance might result in the discontinuation of medicinal products.

57. Discontinuation of certain treatments may be detrimental to public health if there are no other therapeutic alternatives available, and certain national legislations allow competent authorities to order companies to continue selling certain products on a temporary basis (e.g., until the identification of an adequate alternative solution).[68]

III. Marketing and Sales

1. Pricing

58. **In the US**, the government does not directly regulate or negotiate the price of drugs. Instead, US drug companies set their own list prices, which may then be discounted through negotiations with payors. For Americans covered by Medicare (those age 65 or older and those receiving social security disability), the Medicare Part D program helps cover the cost of prescription drugs. Medicare Part D is optional and only provided through private insurance companies approved by the federal government (Part D Sponsors) (costs and coverage varies from plan to plan). Part D Sponsors negotiate prices with drug manufacturers and contract with pharmacies to dispense drugs to Medicare Part D beneficiaries. For the first time, pursuant to the Inflation Reduction Act of 2022 (IRA),[69] the Secretary of Health and Human Services (HHS) was authorized to negotiate prices with drug companies for certain drugs covered under Medicare Part D. Drugs qualify for price negotiation for 2026 if they are covered under Medicare Part D, are single-source brand name drugs or biological products (i.e., without therapeutically

---

[67] For the purposes of this sub-section, marketing authorization holders are pharmaceutical companies marketing medicinal products and companies marketing medical devices.

[68] In France, for instance, pharmaceutical companies marketing medicinal products of major therapeutic interest must inform the ANSM of their intention to discontinue a product at least one year in advance.

[69] Inflation Reduction Act of 2022, Pub. L. No. 117-169, 136 Stat. 1818 (2022).

equivalent generic or biosimilars), and are a specified number of years past their FDA approval or licensure date. In addition, Medicaid is a joint Federal–State program that provides coverage for outpatient prescription drugs to individuals and families with low incomes and relatively few assets.

59. **In the EU**, pricing and reimbursement of medicinal products is not regulated at the EU level. To the contrary, price setting of medicines is, within the EU, determined by individual Member States. Therefore, the same product might be sold at significantly divergent prices in various Member States.[70]

2. Status of drugs (prescription, OTC, hospital-only)

60. When granting a marketing authorization, the competent authority in the EU and the US classifies a medicinal product[71] as either "prescription"[72] or "over-the-counter" (OTC), meaning that the product can be delivered in pharmacies without a prescription. The initiative to qualify as an OTC is made by marketing authorization holders. Certain products are both available with a prescription or OTC but, if bought without a prescription, they cannot be reimbursed.

61. In the EU, certain drugs – qualified as "hospital-only" – can only be prescribed and/or delivered at the hospital and can be subject to restricted prescription, e.g., by specialist doctors. In the US, drugs are not qualified as "hospital-only," however, under FDA's REMS authority, drug approvals may have "Elements to Assure Safe Use," including restrictions limiting dispensing to patients only in certain health care settings, such as hospitals.

3. Distribution channels

62. **In the US**, wholesale distributors purchase drug products from manufacturers and distribute them to a variety of customers, including pharmacies (retail and mail-order), hospitals, and long-term care and other medical facilities. Some wholesalers sell to a broad range of potential customers while others specialize in sales of particular products (e.g., biologic products) or sales to particular types of customers (e.g., nursing homes).

63. The Drug Quality and Security Act (DQSA) was enacted in the US in 2013, in order to better regulate the drug supply chain. The DQSA outlines steps to achieve electronic tracing of drug products at the package level to identify and trace certain prescription drugs as they are distributed in the US. These requirements are intended to enhance FDA's ability to detect and remove drugs that are

---

70 Despite the lack of harmonization at the EU level regarding medicinal products pricing and reimbursement, Member States' medicinal product pricing practices must comply with the provisions of Council Directive 89/105 of Dec. 21, 1988 relating to the transparency of measures regulating the prices of medicinal products for human use and their inclusion in the scope of the national health insurance systems (the EU Transparency Directive). The EU Transparency Directive provides for procedural obligations to ensure fair, objective and equal treatment in the pricing decision making process, along appropriate deadlines and procedural rights.

71 Council Directive 2001/83, arts. 70, 71.

72 Subject to specific criteria defined at EU-level, Member States may provide for sub-categories of medicinal products, including medicinal products on medical prescription for renewable or non-renewable delivery, medicinal products subject to special medical prescription, and medicinal products on restricted medical prescription reserved for use in certain specialized areas.

counterfeit, stolen, contaminated, or otherwise harmful. In addition, the DQSA directed FDA to establish national licensure standards for wholesale distributors and third-party logistics providers and requires these entities to report licensure and other information to FDA annually.

64. **In the EU**, the wholesale distribution of medicinal products comprises all activities consisting of procuring, holding, supplying, or exporting medicinal products, apart from supplying medicinal products to the public. These activities are carried out by manufacturers or their depositories, importers, other wholesale distributors, or with pharmacists and persons authorized or entitled to supply medicinal products to the public in the concerned Member State.[73]

65. Distribution to hospitals is generally taken care of directly by the marketing authorization holder, through tender procedures or negotiated contracts. For the sale of drugs to public hospitals, specific procedures set out in Directive 2014/24 of 16 February 2014 on public procurement apply.

66. To the contrary, community pharmacies rarely purchase drugs directly from the marketing authorization holder. Rather, they go through specialized wholesalers. Within their territory of distribution, wholesalers are bound by Pharmaceutical Good Distribution Practices (GDP)[74] and have public service obligations to timely deliver products, the breadth of which may vary across Member States. Manufacturers, importers, and distributors also have the obligation to ensure that medicinal products are authorized before carrying out regulated activities.

67. Parallel trade is the cross-border sale of medicinal products within the EU outside of a manufacturer's distribution system. As developed in Section III.1. above, because prices are not harmonized within the EU and can therefore vary significantly from one Member State to the other, the goal of parallel trade is to purchase medicinal products at a low price in a given Member State to resell them in another Member State where the price is higher. Certain wholesalers (sometimes called shortliners) have made a business out of this activity. While parallel trade of medicinal products is in principle compatible with the free movement of goods enshrined in the Treaty on the Functioning of the European Union (TFEU), Member States may restrict parallel trade, as long as the measures are justified, reasonable, and proportionate to ensure a legitimate public interest, for instance to ensure an adequate and continuous supply of medicinal products to the public within the Member State. Restrictions on parallel trade are under the close watch of European and national competition authorities (NCAs) as they are not only considered harmful to competition but also hinder the free movement of goods between the Member States of the EU. The European Commission has however acknowledged that parallel trade may be contributing to shortages of medicinal products and thus affect the availability of medicines for the patients.[75]

---

[73] Council Directive 2001/83, art. 1.17.

[74] European Commission, Guidelines of Nov. 5, 2013 on Good Distribution Practice of Medicinal Products for Human Use, 2013 OJ (C 343) 1.

[75] European Commission, Press Release, *Infringement: Parallel trade of medicines: Commission closes infringement proceedings and complaints against Poland, Romania and Slovakia* (May 17, 2018).

CHAPTER II

Applicable Procedural and Legal Antitrust Framework

James Fishkin and Clemens York*

* The authors would like to thank Isabella Egetenmeir, Dennis Schmelzer, and Delphine Strohl for their very valuable help and contribution to this chapter.

I. General Aspects of the Legal Antitrust Framework

68. Competition law, both in the US and in the EU, is subject to parallel enforcement by both (a) public enforcement agencies with significant investigative powers and (b) private parties. Although the enforcement systems differ significantly on each side of the Atlantic, the legal and institutional frameworks are designed to insure effective application of the antitrust rules.

1. US

A. *Federal Antitrust Law and Public Enforcement Agencies*

69. The principal federal antitrust statutes in the US are the Sherman Act,[1] the Clayton Act,[2] the Hart-Scott-Rodino Antitrust Improvements Act of 1976 (HSR Act),[3] the Federal Trade Commission Act (FTC Act),[4] and the Robinson-Patman Act (RP Act).[5] The Federal Trade Commission (FTC) and the Department of Justice (DOJ) are charged with the primary responsibility for enforcing these laws (together the US Antitrust Agencies).

70. Section 1 of the Sherman Act prohibits unreasonable coordinated restraints of trade, including agreements that are illegal per se such as price-fixing and market allocation, as well as other forms of agreements that are evaluated under what is called the antitrust rule of reason (*see* Chapter IV). The rule of reason requires an analysis and weighing of the anticompetitive effects of the restraint and its potential procompetitive benefits, and whether those procompetitive benefits could have been achieved through less restrictive alternative means.[6]

71. Section 2 of the Sherman Act prohibits certain unilateral conduct, including using predatory or exclusionary means to obtain or maintain a monopoly, attempt to obtain a monopoly, or conspire to obtain a monopoly (*see* Chapter V).[7]

72. Section 7 of the Clayton Act, along with the provisions of the HSR Act, regulate mergers and acquisitions. In particular, Section 7 of the Clayton Act prohibits mergers and acquisitions "where the effect... may be substantially to lessen competition," or to "tend to create a monopoly' in "any line of commerce" in "any section of the country."[8] The HSR Act in turn requires companies to notify both the US Antitrust Agencies in advance of any planned mergers or acquisitions (or certain joint ventures) exceeding specific size thresholds and to observe a waiting period.[9] Of note, acquisitions of exclusive pharmaceutical licenses can be reportable under the HSR Act.[10]

---

1 15 U.S.C. §§ 1–2.
2 *Id.* §§ 12–27.
3 *Id.* § 18a.
4 *Id.* §§ 41–58.
5 *Id.* § 13.
6 *Id.* § 1.
7 *Id.* § 2.
8 *Id.* § 18.
9 *Id.* § 18a.
10 16 C.F.R. § 801.2(g)(3). The reportability of exclusive pharmaceutical licenses is established by the implementing regulations for the HSR Act rather than the text of the HSR Act itself, but the D.C. Circuit Court of Appeals has upheld the validity of these implementing regulations. *Pharm. Research Mfrs. Am. v. FTC*, 790 F.3d 198 (D.C. Cir. 2015).

73. The FTC Act authorizes the FTC to bring enforcement actions against "unfair methods of competition" and "unfair or deceptive acts or practices," and generally prohibits the same types of conduct that would violate the Sherman Act.[11]

74. Finally, the RP Act prohibits certain forms of price discrimination in the sale of commodities, including pharmaceuticals, to resellers or distributors.[12]

75. At the national level, public enforcement of US antitrust laws falls to the Bureau of Competition at the FTC and the Antitrust Division of the DOJ, which share concurrent jurisdiction over the enforcement of federal antitrust laws. Attorneys General for each US state also may pursue either separate or joint enforcement actions under both the federal antitrust laws above and other individual state antitrust laws in either federal or state courts. Each state Attorney General is generally bound by its own state laws that govern its own investigative powers and jurisdiction.

a. *FTC*

76. The FTC was created by the FTC Act in 1914 as an independent agency reporting to Congress empowered to prevent unfair methods of competition and unfair or deceptive acts or practices in or affecting commerce.[13] The FTC is led by five Commissioners nominated by the President and subject to Senate confirmation to serve staggered terms of 7 years. No more than three Commissioners can be part of the same political party. The US President designates the Chairman of the FTC from among the Commissioners.

77. **Overall Authority.** The FTC's Premerger Notification Office (PNO) has primary responsibility for administering pre-merger notifications filed by parties under the HSR Act, but the US Antitrust Agencies otherwise share concurrent jurisdiction for the review of mergers and acquisitions and other civil enforcement of the federal antitrust laws. While there is no formal allocation of authority, the US Antitrust Agencies typically utilize an informal process based on each agency's expertise to allocate responsibility for any given matter. The FTC does not have authority to prosecute criminal matters, but rather refers such matters to the DOJ when necessary.

78. The FTC's Bureau of Competition traditionally has taken the lead on civil antitrust enforcement in the pharmaceutical industry. This includes reviewing pharmaceutical mergers and acquisitions to determine whether they may be unlawful under Section 7 of the Clayton Act.[14] Its Mergers I division typically reviews pharmaceutical mergers, whereas the Health Care division traditionally has taken a leading role investigating other alleged anticompetitive practices, such as certain reverse payment or "pay-for-delay" agreements between pharmaceutical companies, alleged sham litigation, improper Orange Book patent listings and the like.

---

11 15 U.S.C. §§ 41–58; FTC, *Policy Statement Regarding the Scope of Unfair Methods of Competition Under Section 5 of the Federal Trade Commission Act* (Nov. 10, 2022), *available at* https://www.ftc.gov/system/files/ftc_gov/pdf/P221202Section5PolicyStatement.pdf.

12 15 U.S.C. § 13.

13 *Id.* §§ 41–58.

14 *Id.* § 18a. Mergers may also be challenged under the Sherman Act, which prohibits agreements that unreasonably restrain trade as well as monopolization, attempted monopolization, and conspiracy to monopolize, or the FTC Act, which focuses on unfair methods of competition and unfair or deceptive acts or practices. The HSR Act, which governs the premerger notification process in the USA, is incorporated into the Clayton Act.

79. Beyond the review of mergers and acquisitions, the FTC has broad authority to investigate other conduct that may violate the Sherman Act or other federal antitrust laws. Section 5 of the FTC Act, for example, prohibits "unfair or deceptive acts or practices in or affecting commerce."[15] Although not without controversy, Section 5 has been described as embodying "the Commission's congressionally mandated duty to use its expertise to identify and combat unfair methods of competition even if they do not violate a separate antitrust statute."[16]

80. The FTC similarly has authority under the Magnuson-Moss Warranty Act of 1975 (Magnuson-Moss Act)[17] to prescribe "rules which define with specificity acts or practices which are unfair or deceptive acts or practices in or affecting commerce."[18] Under Section 19 of the FTC Act, the FTC can pursue civil penalty and equitable relief for violations of properly promulgated rules.

81. **Investigative Powers.** The FTC has considerable investigative powers to pursue potential violations of the antitrust laws. At a high level, the Commission is authorized to "prosecute any inquiry necessary to its duties in any part of the United States,"[19] and, with some limited exceptions, "to gather and compile information concerning, and to investigate from time to time the organization, business, conduct, practices, and management of any person, partnership, or corporation engaged in or whose business affects commerce."[20] To conduct pre-complaint inquiries, the FTC has the following investigatory powers.

- *Subpoenas.* Section 9 of the FTC Act permits the FTC to issue subpoenas requiring "the attendance and testimony of witnesses and the production of all such documentary evidence relating to any matter under investigation."[21] If a party fails to comply, the FTC may seek to enforce compliance in "[a] y of the district courts of the United States within the jurisdiction of which such inquiry is carried on."[22]
- *Civil Investigative Demands (CIDs).* Pursuant to Section 20 of the FTC Act, the FTC may issue a CID to obtain existing documents, oral testimony, or "written reports or answers to questions."[23] Of note, a CID may be issued to require the production of other "tangible things" or to provide service on entities outside of the jurisdiction of US federal courts.[24]

82. Where its investigation provides "reason to believe" that a violation of law has occurred, the FTC may issue a complaint with formal charges under Section 5(b) of

---

15 15 U.S.C. § 45(a)(1).

16 FTC, *Statement of Chair Lina M. Khan Joined by Commissioner Rohit Chopra and Commissioner Rebecca Kelly Slaughter on the Withdrawal of the Statement of Enforcement Principles Regarding "Unfair Methods of Competition" Under Section 5 of the FTC Act* (July 1, 2021), *available at* https://www.ftc.gov/system/files/documents/public_statements/1591498/final_statement_of_chair_khan_joined_by_rc_and_rks_on_section_5_0.pdf.

17 Magnusn-Moss Warranty Act, Pub. L. No. 93-637, 88 Stat. 2183 (1975).

18 15 U.S.C. § 46(b).

19 *Id.* § 43.

20 *Id.* § 46(a).

21 *Id.* § 49.

22 *Id.*

23 *Id.* § 57(c).

24 *Id.*

the FTC Act.[25] If the FTC and the relevant parties agree to settle those charges, the FTC may resolve its complaint through the entry of a consent decree. If the relevant parties contest the charges, however, the complaint will proceed to adjudication before an administrative law judge (ALJ). Through this process, the FTC ultimately has the authority to seek injunctions, restitution, and civil penalties.[26] Where necessary, the FTC may also rely upon Section 13(b) of the FTC Act to file an action in a US District Court seeking both preliminary and, in some cases, permanent injunctions to remedy "any provision of law enforced by the Federal Trade Commission."[27] Of note, however, Section 13(b) requires that the FTC show a defendant "is violating, or is about to violate" the law,[28] and the courts have found that this provision limits the ability of the FTC to pursue injunctive relief for past anticompetitive conduct without alleging current or imminent conduct that violates the laws.[29]

83. At any point in the investigative process or after litigation is filed, a party may settle with the FTC. In particular, a party can negotiate a consent agreement with FTC staff, which must be accepted by the FTC.[30]

84. Finally, separate from its other investigative powers, the FTC has authority under Section 6(b) of the FTC Act to require companies to file "annual or special… reports or answers in writing to specific questions" to provide information about their "organization, business, conduct, practices, management, and relation to other corporations, partnerships, and individuals."[31] Section 6(b) accordingly enables the FTC to effectively conduct studies apart from any alleged violations of existing antitrust laws.

b. *DOJ – Antitrust Division*

85. The DOJ Antitrust Division is led by an Assistant Attorney General who reports to the US Attorney General. The US President nominates the Assistant Attorney General for the Antitrust Division, and the nominee is subject to Senate confirmation. In general, the DOJ is empowered to investigate and pursue enforcement of federal antitrust laws, including both the Sherman Act and the Clayton Act.[32] Like the FTC, the DOJ may exercise this authority through the review of pharmaceutical mergers and acquisitions to determine whether they may be unlawful under Section 7 of the Clayton Act and civil conduct investigations for potential violations of the Sherman Act.

86. The DOJ also has the authority to issue CIDs to investigate non-merger violations of the antitrust laws.[33] As a practical matter, although the FTC typically has taken

---

25 *Id.* § 45(a).

26 *See generally* 15 U.S.C. § 45.

27 *Id.*§ 53(b).

28 *Id.* § 53(b)(1).

29 *See FTC v. Shire ViroPharma, Inc.*, 917 F.3d 147, 150, 161 (3d Cir. 2017) ("Under Section 13(b) of the FTC Act, the FTC must plead that Shire 'is' violating or 'is about to' violate the law. But Shire indisputably is not currently violating the law, nor is it alleged to be poised to do so anytime in the foreseeable future. The FTC thus fails to state a claim upon which relief can be granted.").

30 *See* 16 C.F.R. §§ 2.31–2.41.

31 15 U.S.C. § 46(b).

32 *See generally* 15 U.S.C. §§ 1–2, 18a.

33 15 U.S.C. § 1312.

the lead for civil investigations in the pharmaceutical industry, the DOJ maintains exclusive jurisdiction to issue subpoenas and pursue investigations and enforcement for potential criminal violations.[34] Criminal violations of the Sherman Act are generally punishable by fines of up to US$100 million for a corporation and US$1 million for an individual, although those fines may be increased to twice the amount gained by the conspirators or double the amount lost by the victims. Individuals also may be sentenced to imprisonment for up to 10 years.

87. To aid its criminal enforcement authority, the DOJ has established a leniency program that allows corporations and individuals involved with antitrust violations to self-report criminal conspiracies and therefore avoid criminal convictions and the resulting fines and/or incarceration.[35] The DOJ can also enter into plea agreements or deferred prosecution agreements with defendants.[36]

c. *State Attorneys General*

88. Attorneys General for each US state also are independently authorized to pursue investigations and enforcement actions against mergers or other anticompetitive conduct alleged to violate federal and/or state antitrust laws. State Attorneys General may elect to pursue such actions independently or as part of a multi-state action. State Attorneys General also may join US Antitrust Agencies investigations and enforcement actions.

89. In pursuing enforcement, a state Attorney General may file actions in an enforcement capacity, in its own capacity to recover monetary damages on behalf of state agencies, and/or in a *parens patriae* capacity to recover monetary damages on behalf of its citizens.[37] In pursuing actions on its own behalf or in a *parens patriae* capacity in particular, state Attorneys General may choose to join with other private parties, including private plaintiffs in class action cases.

90. As with the FTC or DOJ, parties can always attempt to settle claims asserted by state Attorneys General. Such settlements will typically be memorialized in the form of a stipulated court order. Parties entering into settlements with Attorneys General should research the law of the particular state regarding the Attorneys General's authority to resolve claims by state agencies, counties, municipalities, and other subdivisions,

B. *Private Litigation*[38]

91. Private parties in the US can also file claims in federal and state courts for alleged violations of federal and/or state antitrust laws. The Clayton Act in particular permits private parties to seek both injunctive and monetary relief. Monetary relief

---

[34] Where criminal prosecution may be warranted on a matter initially handled by FTC staff, the FTC may refer cases to the DOJ for enforcement.

[35] *See* DOJ, *Leniency Program*, (2022), *available at* https://www.justice.gov/atr/leniency-program.

[36] *See* DOJ, *Model Annotated Corporate Plea Agreement*, (2022), *available at* https://www.justice.gov/atr/page/file/1490321/download (providing a model plea agreement between the Antitrust Division and a corporate defendant and citing prior antitrust plea agreements and deferred prosecution agreements).

[37] In *parens patriae* actions, the state Attorney General acts like a putative class representative for its citizens, but, notably, there is no class certification requirement.

[38] *See* Chapter VI for a detailed discussion of antitrust private litigation.

in civil cases can be significant, as the Clayton Act provides for treble damages[39] and the recovery of attorneys' fees and costs for successful plaintiffs.

92. Other federal and state antitrust laws may provide additional grounds for relief. The 2019 Creating and Restoring Equal Access to Equivalent Samples Act (CREATES Act),[40] for example, provides a private right of action for generic drug manufacturers against branded drug manufacturers for failing to provide product samples for the creation of generic drugs if certain criteria are met. (*See* Section II.2.A., Chapter IV, for more details.)

93. Companies and individuals can pursue their claims as either individuals or groups of plaintiffs. Individuals and companies can also file class action claims on behalf of similarly situated individuals and/or entities provided that they can satisfy the elements of Rule 23 of the Federal Rules of Civil Procedure. Depending on the specific claims, potential plaintiffs may include customers, suppliers, or competitors of the parties alleged to have violated the antitrust laws.

94. Of note, the US Supreme Court has established that only direct purchasers of goods or services can recover damages for violations under federal antitrust laws.[41] At the same time, indirect purchasers impacted further down the chain of distribution may have viable claims under individual state antitrust laws where they can establish that increased costs were passed down to customers through the supply chain. Even where they do not have claims for damages under federal antitrust laws, indirect purchasers may bring claims for injunctive relief under Section 16 of the Clayton Act and include state law claims for damages, where available. For example, California and North Carolina have enacted broader state antitrust acts that have a more expansive reach compared to the federal antitrust laws. Under the California Cartwright Act, indirect purchasers plaintiffs have antitrust standing and can bring claims for damages that are prohibited under the Clayton Act.[42] Another example is the North Carolina Unfair and Deceptive Trade Practices Act, which allows indirect purchasers plaintiffs to sue for damages for antitrust violations, and automatically provides for treble damages.[43] Nevertheless, not all states permit the recovery of damages by indirect purchaser plaintiffs.[44]

---

39 Under the Clayton Act, a party injured by a violation of the antitrust laws may recover treble damages, or three times the actual damages incurred. *See* 15 U.S.C. § 15(a) ("[A]ny person who shall be injured in his business or property by reason of anything forbidden in the antitrust laws may sue therefor in any district court of the United States in the district in which the defendant resides or is found or has an agent, without respect to the amount in controversy, and shall recover threefold the damages by him sustained, and the cost of suit, including a reasonable attorney's fee.").

40 Further Consolidated Appropriation Act, 2020, Pub. L No. 116-94, 133 Stat. 2534 (2019) ¶610 (CREATES Act incorporated into appropriations bill).

41 *See generally Illinois Brick Co. v. Illinois*, 431 U.S. 720 (1977).

42 Cal. Bus. & Prof. Code § 16720; *see also Knevelbaard Dairies v. Kraft Foods, Inc.*, 232 F.3d 979, 987–89 (9th Cir. 2000) ("California law affords standing more liberally than does federal law.").

43 N.C. Gen. Stat. § 75-16 (2011); *see also Hyde v. Abbott Labs., Inc.*, 473 S.E.2d 680, 683–84, 686 (1996) (finding that "[s]ince we are not required to construe our antitrust statute in harmony with the federal antitrust laws," indirect purchaser plaintiffs have standing to sue under North Carolina law).

44 States that permit recovery by indirect purchasers under "*Illinois Brick* repealer" statutes include Alabama, Alaska, Arizona, Arkansas, California, Colorado, Florida, Hawaii, Idaho, Illinois, Iowa, Kansas, Maine, Maryland, Massachusetts, Michigan, Minnesota, Mississippi, Nebraska, Nevada, New Hampshire, New Mexico,

95. Where many federal cases are filed based on the same underlying conduct, procedures exist for private litigation to be transferred and consolidated for purposes of pre-trial discovery in a single federal court as part of a Multidistrict Litigation (MDL) proceeding.[45] This process is supervised by the US Judicial Panel on Multidistrict Litigation (MDL Panel).

C. *Standard of Review*

96. Anticompetitive conducts (and in particular anticompetitive agreements) can be subject to different standards of review depending on the potential harm to competition.

97. As the Supreme Court has explained, "there are certain agreements or practices which because of their pernicious effect on competition and lack of any redeeming virtue are conclusively... unreasonable and therefore illegal without elaborate inquiry as to the precise harm they have caused or the business excuse for their use."[46] As such, there is a presumptive harm to competition from these types of agreements.[47] The "per se rule is appropriate... only if courts can predict with confidence that [the challenged conduct] would be invalidated in all or almost all instances under the rule of reason..."[48] With limited exceptions, only horizontal agreements are analyzed under the per se rule, while vertical restrains are generally analyzed under the rule of reason.[49] Restraints which are analyzed under the per se rule include: (1) price fixing, (2) market division, (3) bid rigging, (4) concerted refusals to deal, and (5) potentially, no poach agreements.

98. The rule-of-reason analysis applies presumptively to all other types of agreements (except when the hybrid "quick look" analysis applies, *see* below).[50] When applying the rule of reason, the inquiry is whether the restraint "is one that promotes competition or one that suppresses competition."[51] Courts apply the rule of reason through a burden shifting test:

> [(1)] [T]he plaintiff has the initial burden to prove that the challenged restraint has a substantial anticompetitive effect that harms consumers in the relevant market. [(2)] If the plaintiff carries its burden, then the burden shifts to the defendant to show a procompetitive rationale for the restraint. [(3)] If the defendant makes this showing, then the burden shifts back to

---

New York, North Carolina, North Dakota, Oregon, Rhode Island, South Dakota, Tennessee, Utah, Vermont, Washington, and Wisconsin. The District of Columbia also permits indirect purchaser recovery.

45 28 U.S.C. §§ 1407, 2112.

46 *Northern Pac. Ry. Co. v. United States*, 356 U.S. 1, 5 (1958).

47 *See, e.g., Socony-Vacuum Oil Co.*, 310 U.S. 150, 224 n. 59.

48 *Leegin Creative Leather Prod., Inc. v. PSKS, Inc.*, 551 U.S. 877, 886–87 (2007) (holding vertical price restraints must be analyzed under the rule of reason).

49 All vertical restraints are subject to the rule of reason analysis, with one exception: tying agreements. Tying agreements are those in which a party conditions the sale of one product on a buyer taking another product. While the tying test is still known as a per se test, it is effectively a structured rule of reason test. *Illinois Tool Works Inc. v. Independent Ink, Inc.*, 547 U.S. 28, 36–38 (2006).

50 *Texaco Inc. v. Dagher*, 547 U.S. 1, 5 (2006).

51 *National Soc'y of Prof. Engineers v. United States*, 435 U.S. 679, 691 (1978).

the plaintiff to demonstrate that the procompetitive efficiencies could be reasonably achieved through less anticompetitive means.[52]

99. The types of agreements that are analyzed under the rule of reason include vertical agreements, joint ventures, competitor collaborations, and information sharing agreements.

100. The final standard of review courts apply is the quick look standard or a truncated rule-of-reason standard. The quick look standard applies to "business activities that are so plainly anticompetitive that courts need undertake only a cursory examination before imposing antitrust liability."[53] This standard has been applied in cases in which "an observer with even a rudimentary understanding of economics could conclude that the arrangements in question would have an anticompetitive effect on customers and markets."[54] In applying the quick look test, "no elaborate industry analysis… to demonstrate anticompetitive character" is required.[55] Therefore, while the restraints are not automatically illegal like per se restraints, they "require[…] some competitive justification even in the absence of a detailed market analysis."[56]

101. Cases in which the quick look standard has been used will be further discussed in Chapter IV below.

2. EU

102. The EU is a supra-national organization established in 1957 by the Treaty of Rome,[57] and currently governed by the Treaty on European Union (TEU) and the TFEU.[58] Under the Treaties, the Member States confer "competences" to the EU so that it can fulfil its objectives, one of which is to establish a highly competitive social market economy.[59] As such, the EU is competent to carry out public enforcement actions in order to protect competition in the internal market,[60] even as private enforcement still takes place at the Member State level, with some EU coordination.

---

52 *Ohio v. American Express Co.*, 138 S. Ct. 2274, 2284 (2018).

53 547 U.S. 1, 7 n. 3 (2006) (rejecting application of quick look analysis).

54 *California Dental Ass'n v. FTC*, 526 U.S. 756, 770 (1999); *see also 1-800 Contacts, Inc. v. FTC*, 1 F.4th 102, 115 (2d Cir. 2021) (explaining that the FTC "calls the standard it applies in these situations the 'inherently suspect' framework"); *In re Polygram Holding, Inc.*, 416 F.3d 29, 36–37 (2d Cir. 2005) ("Although the Commission uses the term 'inherently suspect' to describe those restraints that judicial experience and economic learning have shown to be likely to harm consumers, … we note that, under the Commission's own framework, the rebuttable presumption of illegality arises not necessarily from anything 'inherent' in a business practice but from the close family resemblance between the suspect practice and another practice that already stands convicted in the court of consumer welfare.").

55 *National Soc'y of Prof. Engineers*, 435 U.S. 692.

56 *NCAA v. Bd. of Regents of the Univ. of Oklahoma*, 468 U.S. 85, 110 (1984).

57 Treaty establishing the European Economic Community (EEC), signed on Mar. 25, 1957 (the EC Treaty).

58 The EU currently includes Austria, Belgium, Bulgaria, Croatia, Republic of Cyprus, Czech Republic, Denmark, Estonia, Finland, France, Germany, Greece, Hungary, Ireland, Italy, Latvia, Lithuania, Luxembourg, Malta, Netherlands, Poland, Portugal, Romania, Slovakia, Slovenia, Spain and Sweden. The United Kingdom (the UK) was a member of the EU until Jan. 31, 2020. Since Feb. 1, 2020, the UK is no longer part of the EU as a consequence of Brexit.

59 Article 3 TEU.

60 The internal market of the EU encompasses the territory of the 27 Member States and constitutes a single market in which the free movement of goods, services, capital and persons is assured, and in which citizens are free to live, work, study and do business.

A. *Public Enforcement Agencies*

103. At the level of the EU, competition law enforcement powers are vested in the European Commission, which in turn operates under the supervision of the General Court of the European Union (General Court) and the Court of Justice of the European Union (ECJ). At the level of the Member States, NCAs can also apply EU competition rules, with powers similar to those of the European Commission in terms of investigations and fines, under the control of the national courts.[61]

a. *European Commission*

104. The European Commission is the executive branch of the EU and acts as the Guardian of the Treaties. Its task is to promote the general interest of the EU and to ensure and oversee the application of the Treaties.[62] From a competition law standpoint, the European Commission reviews mergers and investigates anti-competitive behavior. It can issue binding decisions, which are subject to review by the European courts. The European Commission is composed of 33 departments, the Directorates General. Each is headed by a Director General under the responsibility of a Commissioner[63] and deals with a specific policy area.

105. The Directorate-General for Competition (DG COMP) is responsible for establishing and implementing competition policy for the EU, covering in particular (i) the application of Articles 101 and 102 TFEU, and (ii) the application of European Council Regulation 139/2004 on the control of concentrations between undertakings (the EU Merger Regulation).[64] DG COMP is structured into various units depending on the sector and types of cases handled. Life sciences cases are primarily handled by Unit E, which is dedicated to basic industries, manufacturing, and agriculture. Unit E has a sub-unit dedicated to conduct cases relating to pharmaceuticals and health services (E.1), and another one for mergers (E.4). DG COMP also include a separate unit dedicated to cartel enforcement (G).

(1) Application of Articles 101 and 102 TFEU

106. **Anticompetitive Agreements.** The European Commission is tasked with investigating anticompetitive behavior prohibited under Articles 101 and 102 TFEU.

107. Article 101(1) TFEU prohibits all agreements between undertakings, decisions by associations of undertakings and concerted practices having as their object or effect the prevention, restriction or distortion of competition in the internal market. This

---

61 Even when NCAs apply EU competition rules, the review of their decisions is governed by national procedural rules under the principle of the procedural autonomy of the Member States and may therefore differ from one country to the other.

62 TEU, art. 17(1).

63 The College of Commissioners includes 27 Commissioners from the 27 EU Member States. Together, the 27 Members of the College are the European Commission's political leadership during a five-year term. They are assigned responsibility for specific policy areas by the President.

64 Council Regulation 139/2004 of Jan. 20, 2004 on the control of concentrations between undertakings (the EU Merger Regulation), 2004 OJ (L 24) 1.

can apply to agreements both between competitors (horizontal agreements) and between companies active at different levels of the supply chain (vertical agreements).[65] Article 101(1) TFEU is interpreted broadly by the European Commission and covers actual agreements, gentlemen's agreements, general understandings, and exchanges of information.

108. Generally speaking, the most frequent types of Article 101(1) infringements relate to price fixing, sharing of markets and customers, restrictions on output, innovation or investment, or impositions of unfair trading conditions on trading partners. However, many of these infringements are relatively rare in the pharmaceutical sector; in particular, given that the price of drugs is regulated in many Member States, price fixing cartels are infrequent in this sector. On the other hand, since IP disputes are common in the pharmaceutical sector, it is worth noting that Article 101(1) is also applicable to anticompetitive conduct related to IP rights.[66] For example, such conduct might include "pay-for-delay" agreements involving a patent holder agreeing to compensate a potential or alleged infringer for refraining from competing with the patent holder for a certain period of time (*see* Chapter IV for more details).

109. Article 101(3) TFEU provides a safe harbor for agreements that would otherwise be prohibited by Article 101(1) if the agreements: (i) contribute to improving the production or distribution of goods, or promote technical or economic progress, (ii) allow consumers a fair share of the resulting benefit, (iii) only impose restrictions indispensable to achieving those objectives, and (iv) do not eliminate competition.[67]

110. Undertakings must self-assess their compliance with Article 101 TFEU and any possible exemptions.[68] In order to assist companies in such self-assessment, the European Commission adopted various implementing regulations and guidance that outline its enforcement approach to various types of conducts.[69] In the pharmaceutical sector, regulations relating to technology transfer agreements,[70] R&D agreements,[71] and specialization agreements[72] are key sources of information for companies.

---

65 *See* David Bailey, *Competition Law and Policy in the EU*, *in* BELLAMY & CHILD: EUROPEAN UNION LAW OF COMPETITION 4 (David Bailey and Laura Elizabeth John eds., 2018).

66 *See id.*

67 Commission Regulation 316/2014 of Mar. 21, 2014 on the application of Article 101(3) of the Treaty on the Functioning of the European Union to categories of technology transfer agreements, 2014 OJ (L 93) 14.

68 Council Regulation 1/2003 of Dec. 16, 2002 on the implementation of the rules on competition laid down in Articles 81 and 82 of the Treaty, 2003 OJ (L 1) 1–25, art. 1.

69 Commission Communication, Guidelines on Vertical Restraints (the Vertical Guidelines), 2022 OJ (C 248) 1; Guidelines on the applicability of Article 101 TFEU to horizontal cooperation agreements, 2023 OJ (C 259) 1; Guidelines on the application of Article 81(3) of the Treaty, 2004 OJ (C 101) 97; Commission Communication, Notice on agreements of minor importance which do not appreciably restrict competition under Article 101(1) TFEU (the De Minimis Notice), 2014 OJ (C 291) 1–4.

70 Commission Regulation 316/2014 of Mar. 21, 2014, on the application of Article 101(3) TFEU to categories of technology transfer agreements (the TTBER).

71 Commission Regulation 2023/1066 of June 1, 2023 on the application of Article 101(3) TFEU to certain categories of research and development agreements (the R&D Block Exemption Regulation).

72 Commission Regulation 2023/1067 of June 1, 2023 on the application of Article 101(3) TFEU to certain categories of specialization agreements (the Specialization Block Exemption Regulation).

111. It is important for companies to be able to accurately evaluate any agreements they enter because any agreement infringing Article 101(1) TFEU is automatically null and void[73] and unenforceable in the national courts of the Member States (doctrine of direct effect).[74] However, the ECJ has stated that this applies only to the anticompetitive provisions, not the entire agreement, assuming it can still be implemented absent the problematic provisions.[75] Infringements of Article 101 TFEU can also result in fines of up to 10% of the infringer's entire group worldwide turnover.[76] Infringements of Article 101 TFEU can also trigger follow-on cartel damage claims (*see* Section I.B.2 of this chapter and Chapter VI).[77]

112. To facilitate cartel detection, the European Commission's leniency program offers companies the possibility of reducing fines for infringements of Article 101 TFEU if they provide the European Commission with sufficient information about a cartel.[78] A leniency application can result in complete immunity from fines for the applicant in certain cases.

113. The current notice on leniency,[79] which was published by the European Commission in 2006, sets out the framework for the regulator to apply leniency to undertakings that are or have been part of a secret cartel and that are cooperating with the European Commission investigations. The European Commission's policy is to allow total immunity to the first undertaking in a cartel to "blow the whistle,"[80] and to impose lower fines (up to a 50% reduction) on undertakings that provide further substantial evidence that enables it to proceed more effectively with the investigation of a case.

114. It is important to note that immunity will not be granted if the European Commission already has sufficient evidence to proceed either to an inspection or to a final decision.[81] The undertaking may nonetheless be qualified for a reduced fine where it provides evidence to the European Commission, "which represents significant added value."[82]

115. Additionally, undertakings can enter into a settlement with the European Commission, acknowledging their participation in a cartel in exchange for a fine

---

73 TFEU, art. 101(2).

74 Case 26/62, *NV Algemene Transport- en Expeditie Onderneming van Gend & Loos v. Netherlands Inland Revenue Administration*, ECLI:EU:C:1963:1, (Feb. 5, 1963).

75 Case 56/65, *Société Technique Minière v. Maschinenbau Ulm,* ECLI:EU:C:1966:38, ¶250 (June 30, 1966); Case 319/82, *Société de Vente de Ciments et Bétons v. Kerpen & Kerpen*, ECLI:EU:C:1983:374, ¶¶4184–4185 (Dec. 14, 1983).

76 Council Regulation 1/2003, *supra* n. 68, Chapter II, art. 23(2).

77 *See* Alison Jones et al., *The Consequences of Infringement*, *in* EU COMPETITION LAW 140 (Alison Jones et al., eds., 2019).

78 European Commission, Notice on Immunity from fines and reduction of fines in cartel cases (the Notice on Leniency), 2006 OJ (C 298) 17–22.

79 *Id.*

80 *See generally* Wouter PJ Wils, *Leniency in antitrust Enforcement: Theory and Practice*, 30 WORLD COMPETITION: LAW AND ECONOMICS REVIEW (2007).

81 Notice on Leniency, ¶¶10–11; on the evidence required to qualify for immunity *see* Case T-521/09, *Alstom Grid SAS v. Commission*, ECLI:EU:T:2014:1000, ¶¶44–89 (2014).

82 Notice on Leniency, *supra* n. 78, Chapter II, ¶¶24–25.

reduction.[83] While the leniency program is an instrument to gather evidence, a settlement is an instrument to increase procedural efficiency. Applying for leniency is not a prerequisite for a settlement application, but an undertaking that has filed a leniency application can also enter into a settlement.

116. The settlement system allows for cases to be resolved quicker and lowers the risk of appeals. Parties opting for the settlement procedure must make a formal request in the form of settlement submission at any point in time, but no later than the date on which the European Commission issues a Statement of Objections (SO) against the parties concerned.[84] Paragraph 5 of the European Commission's settlement notice clearly states that the European Commission retains a broad discretion to determine which cases may be suitable for settlement. In most settlement decisions, the European Commission will settle with all cartel participants and tries to avoid so-called "hybrid settlements," when one or more of the parties decline to settle while the rest move forward with the procedure.[85]

117. The settlement system cannot be applied to non-cartel cases under Article 101 TFEU nor to abuse cases under Article 102 TFEU; however, the European Commission may still reduce a fine to reflect the cooperative approach taken by an undertaking under investigation.[86]

118. **By-Object vs By-Effect Infringements**. EU competition law distinguishes between two types of infringements: infringements by object and infringements by effect.

119. The distinction originates from the wording of Article 101 TFEU which prohibits agreements "which have as their *object* or *effect* the prevention, restriction or distortion of competition" (emphasis added). The ECJ established the distinction between the two types of agreements early on, clarifying: (i) their alternative nature, and (ii) the different standard of proof applying to each type of infringement:

> The fact that these are not cumulative but alternative requirements, indicated by the conjunction "or", leads first to the need to consider the precise purpose of the agreement, in the economic context in which it is to be applied. This interference with competition referred to in Article [101 TFEU] must result from all or some of the clauses of the agreement itself. Where, however, an analysis of the said clauses does not reveal the effect on competition to be sufficiently deleterious, the consequences of the agreement should then be considered and for it to be caught by the prohibition it is then necessary to find that those factors are present which show that competition has in fact been prevented or restricted or distorted to an appreciable extent.[87]

---

83 European Commission, Notice on the conduct of settlement procedures in view of the adoption of Decisions pursuant to Article 7 and Article 23 of Council Regulation 1/2003 in cartel cases (the Notice on Settlement), 2008 OJ (C 167) 1–6.

84 *Id.* ¶20.

85 *See e.g.*, Case COMP/38866, *Animal Feed Phosphates* (2010); Case COMP/39914, *Euro Interest Rate Derivatives (Euribor)* (2016); Case COMP/39861, *Yen Interest Rate Derivatives* (2013).

86 *See* European Commission, Guidelines on the method of setting fines imposed pursuant to Article 23(2)(a) of Regulation 1/2003 2006 OJ (C 210) 2, ¶37.

87 *See* Case 56/65, *Société Technique Minière v. Maschinenbau Ulm*, ECLI:EU:C:1966:38, (June 30, 1966).

120. The ECJ clarified that when an agreement aims to prevent, restrict, or distort competition, there is no need to take account of the concrete effects of such agreement.[88] As such, the burden of proof is significantly lower on the European Commission in the case of infringements by object, as the European Commission does not have to demonstrate the anticompetitive effects of the agreement. However, the alternative nature of the object/effect dichotomy does not preclude the European Commission from concluding that a practice has at the same time both the object and the effect of restricting competition.[89]

121. In light of the significant consequences of classifying an agreement as a by-object infringement, the question of what constitutes an infringement by object is crucial. This has led to extensive debates and case law controversies. Although the two notions are distinct, infringements by object tend to correlate with practices that are treated as hard-core restrictions in the European Commission block exemptions regulations, guidance and notices, such as price fixing, output limitation, allocation of markets and customers, fixed and minimum resale price maintenance (RPM), and restrictions providing absolute territorial protection, including restrictions on passive sales.[90]

122. The European Commission and the EU courts have been criticized for interpreting the by-object category too broadly for quite some time,[91] but this trend seems to have reversed since the *Cartes bancaires* case in 2014.[92] The ECJ reiterated that by definition, the notion of infringement by object covers coordination between undertakings that can be regarded, by their very nature, as being harmful to the proper functioning of normal competition.[93] As such, only agreement or conduct which, based on experience, is likely to produce negative effects on the market and

---

88 *See* Joined Cases 56/64 and 58/64, *Établissements Consten S.à.R.L. and Grundig-Verkaufs-GmbH v. Commission*, ECLI:EU:C:1966:41, (July 13, 1966).

89 *See* Case C-228/18, *Gazdasági Versenyhivatal v. Budapest Bank Nyrt. And Others*, ECLI:EU:C:2019:678, ¶44 (Sept. 5, 2019).

90 European Commission Notice, Guidelines on the application of Article 81(3) of the Treaty, 2004 OJ (C 101) 97–118.

91 In particular following Case C-209/07, *Competition Authority v. Beef Industry Development Society Ltd and Barry Brothers (Carrigmore) Meats Ltd*, ECLI:EU:C:2008:643, (Nov. 20, 2008), where the ECJ first stated that the "types of agreements covered by Article [101(1)(a) to (e) TFEU] do not constitute an exhaustive list of prohibited collusion.", and Case C-8/08, *T-Mobile Netherlands BV v. Raad van bestuur van de Nederlandse Mededingingsautoriteit*, ECLI:EU:C:2009:343, (June 4, 2009), when the ECJ took an extensive view of the notion of by-object infringements with regards to information exchanges "an exchange of information which is capable of removing uncertainties between participants as regards the timing, extent and details of the modifications to be adopted by the undertaking concerned must be regarded as pursuing an anticompetitive object" (¶41).

92 Case C-67/13 P, *CB v. Commission*, ECLI:EU:C:2014:2204, (Sept. 11, 2014).

93 *Id.*; *see also* European Commission Notice, Guidelines on the application of Article 81(3) of the Treaty, 2004 OJ (C 101) 97–118, ¶21: "Restrictions of competition by object are those that by their very nature have the potential of restricting competition. These are restrictions which in light of the objectives pursued by the Community competition rules have such a high potential of negative effects on competition that it is unnecessary for the purposes of applying Article [101(1) TFEU] to demonstrate any actual effects on the market. This presumption is based on the serious nature of the restriction and on experience showing that restrictions of competition by object are likely to produce negative effects on the market and to jeopardize the objectives pursued by the Community competition rules. Restrictions by object such as price fixing and market sharing reduce output and raise prices, leading to a misallocation of resources, because goods and services demanded by customers are not produced. They also lead to a reduction in consumer welfare, because consumers have to pay higher prices for the goods and services in question."

to jeopardize the objectives pursued by the EU competition rules can be defined as an infringement by object. The ECJ also stressed that although there is no exhaustive list of infringements by object, this notion should be interpreted restrictively.[94]

123. The ECJ has consistently held that in order to determine whether an agreement involves a restriction of competition "by object", regard must be had to the content of its provisions, its objectives, and the economic and legal context of which it forms a part.[95] The ECJ Advocate General Bobek recently provided a more detailed framework for establishing that an agreement constitutes an infringement by object in its opinion relating to the *Budapest Bank* case:[96]

- *Preliminary Step*. The European Commission should clearly identify the conduct alleged to constitute a restriction of competition by object, and explain its key elements, such as the parties responsible, the markets affected, the nature of the conduct in question, and the relevant time frame.[97]
- *Step 1–- Is the agreement of a harmful type?* The European Commission should focus on the content of the agreement and its specific provisions, "to ascertain whether the agreement in question falls within a category of agreements whose harmful nature is, in the light of experience, commonly accepted and easily identifiable."[98] In practice, this means that the European Commission needs to establish whether the agreement is of a type that has previously been assessed and has systematically been viewed as leading to negative effects. This follows the view taken by Advocate General Whal in *Cartes bancaires,* where he stated that "it is only when experience based on economic analysis shows that a restriction is constantly prohibited that it seems reasonable to penalize it directly for the sake of procedural economy."[99] For instance, horizontal price-fixing in the context of cartels would fit this definition as experience shows that such behavior leads to decreases in production and price increases, resulting in poor allocation of resources to the detriment, in particular, of consumers.[100] Similarly, with regards to exchange of information, the ECJ has consistently held that "[a]n exchange of information which is capable of removing uncertainty between participants as regards the timing, extent and details of the modifications to be adopted by the undertakings concerned in their conduct on the market must be regarded as pursuing an anticompetitive object."[101]

---

94 *Id.*; Case C-228/18, *Budapest Bank Nyrt. and Others*, ECLI:EU:C:2019:678, ¶54 (Sept. 5, 2019).

95 *See* Case C-32/11, *Allianz Hungária Biztosító Zrt. and Others v. Gazdasági Versenyhivatal*, ECLI:EU:C:2013:160, (Mar. 14, 2013); *see also* Case C-439/09, *Pierre Fabre Dermo-Cosmétique SAS v. Président de l'Autorité de la Concurrence, Ministre de l'Économie, de l'Industrie et de l'Emploi*, ECLI:EU:C:2011:649, (Oct. 13, 2011).

96 Case C-228/18, *Budapest Bank Nyrt. and Others*, ECLI:EU:C:2019:678, (Sept. 5, 2019), Opinion of Advocate General Bobek delivered on Sept. 5, 2019.

97 *Id.* ¶54.

98 *Id.* ¶42.

99 Case C-67/13 P, *CB*, ECLI:EU:C:2014:2204, (Sept. 11, 2014), Opinion of Advocate General Wahl delivered on Mar. 27, 2014, ¶55.

100 *See* Case C-345/14, *SIA, "Maxima Latvija" v. Konkurences padome*, ECLI:EU:C:2015:784, ¶19 (Nov. 26, 2015); Case C-67/13 P, *CB*, ECLI:EU:C:2014:2204, ¶51 (Sept. 11, 2014).

101 *See e.g.*, Case T-799/17, *Scania AB and Others v. Commission*, ECLI:EU:T:2022:48, ¶318 (Feb. 2, 2022) and the case law cited.

- *Step 2 – Robustness Test.* The European Commission should ensure that the legal and economic context in which the agreement takes place does not question the presumed anticompetitive nature of the agreement.[102] For this analysis, the European Commission should in particular take account of the nature of the products/services at issue, as well as the real conditions of the functioning and structure of the markets.[103] The European Commission is, however, not required to take into account the parties' intention, but it can still be a relevant factor.[104] The ECJ has, for instance, stated that when an agreement serves no purpose other than the restriction of competition, it can be characterized as an infringement by object;[105] but the mere fact that an agreement pursues a legitimate interest does not prevent it from being viewed as a by-object restriction.[106] Furthermore, for types of agreements that have been consistently viewed as constituting serious breaches of the competition rules, analysis of the economic and legal context may be limited to what is strictly necessary in order to establish the existence of a restriction of competition by object.[107]

124. It must be noted that although a by-object infringement is presumed to be harmful, it does not in theory deprive the agreement of the benefit of the exemption provided by Article 101(3) TFEU if it meets the relevant conditions;[108] it is however very rare for an infringement by object to meet the high threshold required by Article 101(3) TFEU.

125. In all other cases, i.e., when the agreement cannot be viewed as infringing competition by object, actual or potential effects of the agreement should then be considered and the agreement will only be deemed to infringe Article 101(1) TFEU if concrete facts show that competition has in fact been prevented, restricted or distorted to an appreciable extent.[109] In order to carry out such analysis, the European Commission should rely on a counterfactual scenario, i.e., how competition would have taken place absent the agreement.[110] Finally, the effects of the agreement can be either real or potential but should in any case be appreciable.[111]

126. **Abuse of Dominance.** Article 102 TFEU deals with the conduct of undertakings holding significant market power. While holding a dominant position is not

---

[102] Case C-228/18, *Budapest Bank Nyrt. and Others*, ECLI:EU:C:2019:678, (Sept. 5, 2019), Opinion of Advocate General Bobek delivered on Sept. 5, 2019, ¶43.

[103] *See* Case C-67/13 P, *CB*, ECLI:EU:C:2014:2204, ¶78 (Sept. 11, 2014); Case C-228/18, *Budapest Bank Nyrt. and Others*, ECLI:EU:C:2019:678, ¶67 (Sept. 5, 2019).

[104] *See* Case C-67/13 P, *CB*, ECLI:EU:C:2014:2204, ¶78 (Sept. 11, 2014); Case C-228/18, *Budapest Bank Nyrt. and Others*, ECLI:EU:C:2019:678, ¶53 (Sept. 5, 2019).

[105] *See* Case C-307/18, *Generics (UK) Ltd and Others v. Competition and Markets Authority*, ECLI:EU:C:2020:52, ¶87 (Jan. 30, 2020).

[106] *See* Case C-67/13 P, *CB*, ECLI:EU:C:2014:2204, ¶70 (Sept. 11, 2014).

[107] *See* Case C-373/14 P, *Toshiba Corporation v. Commission*, ECLI:EU:C:2016:26, ¶29 (Jan. 20, 2016).

[108] European Commission Notice, Guidelines on the application of Article 81(3) of the Treaty, 2004 OJ (C 101) 8.

[109] *See e.g.*, Case C-345/14, *SIA, "Maxima Latvija"*, ECLI:EU:C:2015:784, ¶17 (Nov. 26, 2015); Case C-32/11, *Allianz Hungária Biztosító Zrt. and Others*, ECLI:EU:C:2 013:160, ¶34 (Mar. 14, 2013).

[110] Case C-306/20, *SIA "Visma Enterprise" v. Konkurences padome*, ECLI:EU:C:2021:935, ¶74 (Nov. 18, 2021); Case C-307/18, *Generics (UK) Ltd and Others*, ECLI:EU:C:2020:52, ¶117 (Jan. 30, 2020).

[111] Case C-307/18, *Generics (UK) Ltd and Others*, ECLI:EU:C:2020:52, ¶117 (Jan. 30, 2020).

prohibited, dominant undertakings have a special responsibility regarding their behavior in a market.[112] Article 102 TFEU prohibits the abuse by one or more undertakings of a dominant position within the internal market or a substantial part thereof. The definition of what constitutes an abuse depends on various factors (*see* for more detail Chapter V), but the European Commission outlined its enforcement priorities in a guidance paper in 2009 that provides useful advice.[113]

127. The majority of abuse of dominance cases stem from complaints by competitors submitted to the European Commission and NCAs.[114] However, the European Commission's pharmaceutical sector enquiry in 2009 also led to the intervention of competition authorities due to breaches of Article 102 TFEU.[115]

128. As will be developed in Chapter V below, in the pharmaceutical sector, the misuse of IP rights has attracted significant enforcement scrutiny, when IP rights are used as a tool to hinder market entry or push competitors out of the market. NCAs have also been particularly active, especially with regard to issues related to excessive pricing and disparagement.[116]

129. With regard to Article 102 TFEU cases, although the wording of the provision does not provide the same dichotomy between by-object and by-effect restrictions as Article 101 TFEU does, the ECJ has clearly stated that Articles 101 and 102 TFEU seek the same aim, and that a restriction of competition which is prohibited under Article 101 TFEU cannot become permissible by the fact that such behavior succeeds under the influence of a dominant undertaking.[117] There was some controversy based on the fact that Article 102 TFEU requires the abuse to have an effect on competition. However, the approach taken by the ECJ confirms that the reasoning is similar to the one applied in relation to anti-competitive agreements. The General Court clearly stated that "if it is shown that the object pursued by the conduct of an undertaking in a dominant position is to limit competition, that conduct will also be liable to have such an effect."[118]

130. The ECJ clarified early on that the presumed anticompetitive effects of an infringement by object can however be rebutted if the dominant undertaking

---

112 Case 322/81, *NV Nederlandsche Banden Industrie Michelin v. Commission*, ECLI:EU:C:1983:313, ¶57 (Nov. 9, 1983); Case C-413/14 P, *Intel v. Commission*, ECLI:EU:C:2017:632, ¶135 (Sept. 6, 2017).

113 European Commission Communication, Guidance on the Commission's enforcement priorities in applying Article 82 of the EC Treaty to abusive exclusionary conduct by dominant undertakings, 2009 OJ (C 45), ¶2.24.

114 *See* Alison Jones et al., *The Enforcement of Article 102 TFEU*, *in* EU Competition Law 281 (Alison Jones et al., eds., 2019).

115 *See* European Commission SWD, Pharmaceutical Sector Inquiry – Final Report (the Pharmaceutical Sector Inquiry – Final Report) (July 8, 2009), *available at* https://ec.europa.eu/competition/sectors/pharmaceuticals/inquiry/staff_working_paper_part1.pdf.

116 *See e.g.*, in the Netherlands, Case No. ACM/20/041239, *Leadiant*; in Italy, Decision No. A524, *Leadiant Biosciences/Farmaco per la cura della Xantomasi erebrotendinea* (May 31, 2022), *available at* https://www.agcm.it/dotcmsCustom/getDominoAttach?urlStr=192.168.14.10:8080/41256297003874BD/0/5F6041FF7929D-043C125849B0046F058/$File/p27940.pdf; in the UK, CMA, Case No. CE/9742-13, *Unfair pricing in respect of the supply of phenytoin sodium capsules in the UK* (2016), *available at* https://assets.publishing.service.gov.uk/media/594240cfe5274a5e4e00024e/phenytoin-full-non-confidential-decision.pdf.

117 Case 6/72, *Europemballage Corporation and Continental Can Company Inc. v. Commission*, ECLI:EU:C:1973:22, ¶25 (Feb. 21, 1973).

118 Case T-203/01, *Manufacture française des pneumatiques Michelin v. Commission*, ECLI:EU:T:2003:250, ¶241 (Sept. 30, 2003).

is able to demonstrate that its conduct is not capable of restricting competition in the specific economic and legal context at stake.[119] The ECJ even stated that the European Commission has a duty to examine evidence submitted by the dominant undertaking to that effect.[120] It should however be noted that while the fact that a conduct did not generate any exclusionary effects in practice can constitute an element showing that the conduct was not capable of hindering competition, it is in no way sufficient alone to rebut the presumption.[121]

(2) Application of the EU Merger Regulation

131. The EU Merger Regulation provides for an EU level merger control, requiring mergers involving companies meeting specific revenue thresholds[122] to be notified to and approved by the European Commission before completion.[123]

132. According to the one-stop-shop principle, when a merger meets the EU thresholds, the European Commission has exclusive jurisdiction to review the transaction.[124]

133. The EU Merger Regulation also provides for various referral mechanisms to catch below-thresholds deals that may nevertheless lead to anticompetitive effects: Articles 4(4) and (5)[125] and Article 22 of the EU Merger Regulation. The latter allows one or more Member States to request the European Commission to examine any concentration that does not meet the turnover thresholds but affects trade between Member States and threatens to significantly affect competition within the territory of the Member State or States making the request.

134. Although originally introduced to allow Member States without national merger control to refer significant transactions to the European Commission, it was slowly set aside as Member States introduced national regimes.[126] However, the importance of Article 22 of the EU Merger Regulation was recently revived. On March 26, 2021, the European Commission published revised guidance (Article 22 Guidance)[127] to use this tool to address so-called "killer acquisitions,"

---

119 *See* Case C-413/14 P, *Intel*, ECLI:EU:C:2017:632, (Sept. 6, 2017); Case T-286/09 RENV, *Intel Corporation Inc. v Commission*, ECLI:EU:T:2022:19, (Jan. 26, 2022).

120 *See* Case C-413/14 P, *Intel*, ECLI:EU:C:2017:632, (Sept. 6, 2017); Case T-286/09 RENV, *Intel Corporation Inc.*, ECLI:EU:T:2022:19, (Jan. 26, 2022): "where an undertaking in a dominant position 'submits, during the administrative procedure, on the basis of supporting evidence, that its conduct was not capable of restricting competition and, in particular, of producing the… foreclosure effects [alleged against it]', the European Commission must analyse the foreclosure capability of the scheme."

121 Case C-377/20, *Servizio Elettrico Nazionale SpA and Others v. Autorità Garante della Concorrenza e del Mercato and Others*, ECLI:EU:C:2022:379, ¶58 (May 12, 2022).

122 The turnover thresholds relate only to the economic size of the parties taking into account: (i) worldwide, (ii) EU-wide, and (iii) Member-State-wide turnovers, regardless of any effects of the transaction within the EU.

123 Council Regulation 139/2004 (EU Merger Regulation), *supra* n. 64, Chapter II, art. 1(2)–(3).

124 *Id.* art. 9 however allows the European Commission to refer a deal to a Member State if justified by the specificities of the deal.

125 *Id.* Art. 4(4) and (5) allow the European Commission to review a merger: (i) upon request of the parties, or (ii) upon referral by at least three Member States.

126 Today, all EU Member States have a national merger control regime, with the exception of Luxemburg. However, Luxemburg launched a consultation in Dec. 2022 about the possible introduction of a merger control regime.

127 *See* European Commission Communication, Guidance on the application of the referral mechanism set out in Article 22 of the Merger Regulation to certain categories of cases (the Article 22 Guidelines), COM (2021) 1959 final (Mar. 26, 2021).

i.e., acquisitions by a company with a strong market position of a small, nascent company in the early stage of operations (i.e., a company with low or no turnover but high actual or future competitive potential). The General Court confirmed the legality of the new guidance on July 13, 2022.[128] The newly revised guidance lists illustrative examples of cases which may fall under Article 22 of the EU Merger Regulation (e.g., where the target carries out important research or has access to key IP rights).[129] Another key factor taken into account by the European Commission is the premium paid for the target.[130]

135. Article 22 Guidance singles out the pharmaceuticals sector as of particular interest.[131] In this sector, transactions likely involve companies carrying out R&D with significant competitive potential that have not yet launched their products or have not yet realized the long-term value of their products. Indeed, the first case where the European Commission applied the revised approach to the Article 22 referral process involved two pharmaceutical companies, Illumina and Grail.[132] At the time, Grail was a start-up active in cancer testing.[133]

(3) The European Commission investigative powers

136. **Subsidiarity Principle.** The European Commission and NCAs have concurrent powers for the enforcement of competition law. The allocation of cases between the EU and the national level is regulated by the subsidiarity principle.[134] According to this principle, in areas that do not fall within the EU's exclusive competence, the EU shall act only if and insofar as the objectives of the proposed action cannot be sufficiently achieved by the Member States, either at the central level or at the regional and local level.[135]

137. The subsidiarity principle is reflected in EU competition law in the sense that a merger or certain market behavior must affect trade between Member States for the European Commission to have jurisdiction. European Commission jurisdiction does not extend to cases where the effect is limited to one Member State.[136]

---

128 *See* Case T-277/21, *Illumina, Inc. v. Commission*, ECLI:EU:T:2022:447, (July 13, 2022).

129 *See id.* ¶¶19–20.

130 *See id.* ¶19.

131 *See id.* ¶¶9–10.

132 The Article 22 referral often involves cooperation between competition authorities in the EU and their counterparts outside the EU: In case COMP/M.10188, *Illumina/Grail* (2022), the FTC alerted the European Commission to the anticompetitive aspects of the proposed acquisition.

133 Illumina acquired Grail for approx. US$7 billion. The transaction did not meet the relevant EU merger control thresholds as US-based Grail did not have any EU-wide sales. It was also not notifiable under any national merger control regime in the EU. Illumina and Grail have implemented the transaction while the European Commission's investigation was still ongoing. On Sept. 6, 2022, the European Commission issued a prohibition decision against the deal (*see* case COMP/M.10188, *Illumina/Grail* (2022)). On July 12, 2023, the European Commission fined Illumina €432 million for implementing the merger before receiving EU merger clearance (*see* case COMP/M.10483, *Illumina/Grail* (2023)). On Oct. 12, 2023, the European Commission ordered Illumina to divest Grail in the next 12 months (*see* case COMP/M.10939, *Illumina/Grail* (2023)).

134 TEU art. 5, ¶3 and Protocol (No. 2) on the application of the principles of subsidiarity and proportionality.

135 *See* Consolidated version of the Treaty on the TFEU – Protocols – Protocol (No. 2) on the application of the principles of subsidiarity and proportionality, 2008 OJ (C 115) 206–209.

136 *See* Case 22/78, *Hugin v. Commission*, ECLI:EU:C:1979:138, (May 31, 1979).

138. The definition of what affects trade between Member States depends on the specific case in question, but the ECJ and the European Commission Notice on the concept of effect on trade between Member States provides helpful guidance.[137] As established by European case law, trade between Member States is interpreted broadly and does not only cover exchanges of goods and services in a traditional sense.[138] In line with the EU's aim to foster free movement of goods, services and capital, the notion of trade follows a broad interpretation and includes all economic activity across borders. Additionally, an impact on the flow of goods and services between at least two Member States is a prerequisite.

139. In order for an agreement or a conduct to affect trade between Member States, there needs to be a sufficient probability that it will exert a direct or indirect, actual or potential influence on the pattern of trade between Member States.[139] This means that there is no requirement that the agreement or conduct have an actual effect on trade; the mere fact that it is capable of affecting intra-EU trade is sufficient.[140] According to settled case law, an agreement covering the entire territory of a single Member State is capable of affecting trade between Member States.[141] The effect must, however, be appreciable and the European Commission considers that agreements will not meet this threshold if the parties' combined market shares are below 5% on all relevant markets affected by the agreement and their individual (or combined in case of horizontal agreements) EU turnover is below EUR 40 million.[142]

140. In a merger control context, the effect on trade, or so-called "Community dimension" is established if the parties meet the EU Merger Regulation turnover thresholds.[143] However, under the European Commission's new Article 22 Guidance, mergers that do not meet the thresholds can also be seen as affecting trade between Member States in specific circumstances. According to the European Commission, the following factors could be relevant for this assessment: location of (potential) customers, the availability and offering of the products or services at stake, the collection of data in several Member States, or the development and implementation of R&D projects whose results, including IP rights, if successful, may be commercialized in more than one Member State.

141. **Investigative Powers of the European Commission.** The European Commission's investigative powers to enforce Articles 101 and 102 TFEU are detailed in Chapter V of Council Regulation 1/2003 of Dec. 16, 2002 on the implementation of the rules on competition laid down in Articles 81 and 82 of the Treaty [now Articles 101 and 102 TFEU] (Regulation 1/2003).

---

137 *See* Guidelines on the effect on trade concept contained in Articles 81 and 82 of the Treaty (the Notice on Effect on Trade), 2004 OJ (C 101) 81.

138 *See* Case C-41/90, *Höfner and Elser v. Macrotron*, ECLI:EU:C:1991:161, (Apr. 23, 1991); Case 172/80, *Züchner v. Bayerische Vereinsbank AG*, ECLI:EU:C:1981:178, (July 14, 1981).

139 Notice on Effect on Trade, *supra* n. 137, Chapter II, ¶24.

140 *Id.* ¶26.

141 *Id.* ¶77.

142 *Id.* ¶52.

143 Council Regulation 139/2004 (EU Merger Regulation), *supra* n. 64, Chapter II, art. 1(2).

142. The main powers granted to the European Commission may be summarized as follows:

- *Requests for Information (Article 18).* Under Article 18(1) of Regulation 1/2003, the European Commission has wide powers to obtain all necessary information from the governments and competent authorities of the Member States, as well as from undertakings and associations of undertakings. Article 18(2) deals with simple requests, for which there is no obligation for the undertaking to comply. On the other hand, undertakings must respond to a European Commission Decision requiring information pursuant to Article 18(3). Under these provisions, the European Commission is not entitled to request information for a purpose other than the enforcement of the competition rules and must comply with the principle of proportionality.[144] At the request of the European Commission, the governments and competition authorities of the Member States shall provide all necessary information required by the European Commission; in some cases, such assistance may however require a judicial authorization under national rules.
- *Power to Take Statements (Article 19).* The European Commission can interview natural or legal persons, with their consent, for the purpose of collecting information relating to the subject-matter of an investigation. Any interview must be recorded to preserve the rights of the defendants.[145]
- *Commission's Powers of Inspection (Articles 20–21).* Article 20(1) enables the European Commission to conduct "all necessary inspections." Under Article 20(3), undertakings may submit to an inspection voluntarily upon production of a written authorization specifying the subject matter and purpose of the inspection and the penalties incurred in case of misleading information is provided. Under Article 20(4), undertakings must submit to an inspection ordered by a European Commission decision; such inspections, also called "dawn raids", may be conducted without prior announcement or judicial authorization.[146] Additionally, Article 21 confers the power on the European Commission to inspect "other premises", which can include private homes; in that case, Article 21(3) requires prior authorization by a national court, though.

143. The European Commission, in exercising its powers of investigation, is however limited by: (1) general EU law principles and (2) the duty to respect the rights of the defense:[147]

- *Privilege against Self-incrimination.* Privilege against self-incrimination[148] entitles undertakings to refuse to answer questions that would require them

[144] *See* for example Case C-247/14 P, *HeidelbergCement AG v. Commission*, ECLI:EU:C:2016:149, (Mar. 10, 2016); Case C-466/19, *Qualcomm, Inc and Qualcomm Europe, Inc v. Commission*, ECLI:EU:C:2021:76, (Jan. 28, 2021); Cases T-451/20 R and T-452/20 R, *Facebook Ireland Ltd v. Commission*, ECLI:EU:T:2020:515 and ECLI:EU:T:2020:516, (Oct. 29, 2020).

[145] *See* Case C-413/14 P, *Intel*, ECLI:EU:C:2017:632, ¶¶ 90–91 (Sept. 6, 2017); Case C-466/19, *Qualcomm, Inc and Qualcomm Europe, Inc.*, ECLI:EU:C:2021:76, (Jan. 28, 2021).

[146] Joined Cases 97/87, 98/87 and 99/87, *Dow Chemical Ibérica, SA, and others v. Commission*, ECLI:EU:C:1989:380, (Oct. 17, 1989); *see also* C-583/13 P, *Deutsche Bahn and Others v. Commission*, ECLI:EU:C:2015:404, (June 18, 2015).

[147] Cristina Teleki, *Limits on the European Commission's Powers of Investigation*, *in* 18 DUE PROCESS AND FAIR TRIAL IN EU COMPETITION LAW: THE IMPACT OF ARTICLE 6 OF THE EUROPEAN CONVENTION ON HUMAN RIGHTS 248 (2021).

[148] *See* Case C-374/87, *Orkem v. Commission*, ECLI:EU:C:1989:387, ¶35 (Oct. 18, 1989).

to admit to the very infringement the European Commission is seeking to establish.[149] However, privilege against self-incrimination applies only where the European Commission requires answers to questions addressed to undertakings under investigation or their employees.[150]

- *Attorney-client Privilege.*[151] Correspondence between a client and an independent lawyer based in the European Economic Area (EEA) is privileged provided that it was conducted for the purposes and in the interest of the client's rights of defense under competition law.[152] Dealings with an in-house lawyer or with a lawyer in a third country are not covered by the legal professional privilege.[153]
- *Confidentiality.* Any commercially sensitive information obtained under Regulation 1/2003 must be protected by confidentiality and may not be disclosed by the European Commission.[154]

144. Although the NCAs generally have similar powers of investigation as the European Commission to apply Articles 101 and 102 TFEU, their exact powers are governed by national law under the principle of procedural autonomy of the Member States. Key elements such as the possibility for the NCAs to carry out inspections without the prior authorization of a national court or the extent of attorney-client privilege may therefore vary from one Member State to the other.

145. **Pharmaceutical Sector Inquiry.** Under Article 17 of the Regulation 1/2003, the European Commission may also initiate general inquiries into markets where it believes competition might be restricted or distorted.[155] The aim of this provision is to enable the European Commission to learn about business models, markets, strategies and practices in a given sector or part of the economy in order to identify possible infringements of competition rules. The European Commission has extensive powers in this context.[156]

146. In 2008, the European Commission opened an 18-month sector inquiry into the pharmaceutical sector. The sector inquiry was prompted by the European Commission's concerns about the competitive relationship between originator and

---

149 Council Directive 2019/1 of the European Parliament and of the Council of Dec. 11, 2018 to empower the competition authorities of the Member States to be more effective enforcers and to ensure the proper functioning of the internal market, art. 8.

150 Case C-301/04 P, *Commission v. SGL Carbon AG*, ECLI:EU:C:2006:432, (June 29, 2006); *see also* Case C-466/19, *Qualcomm, Inc and Qualcomm Europe, Inc.*, ECLI:EU:C:2021:76, (Jan. 28, 2021), where the General Court stated that there is no absolute right to silence on the part of a recipient of a request for information under art. 18(3).

151 *See generally* Case 155/79, *AM & S Europe Ltd. v Commission*, ECLI:EU:C:1982:157, (May 18, 1982); *see also* C-550/07 P, *Akzo Nobel Chemicals Ltd and Akcros Chemicals Ltd v. Commission*, ECLI:EU:C:2010:512, (Sept. 14, 2010) where the ECJ reaffirmed its judgement in *AM & S.*

152 Joint Cases T-125/03 and T-253/03, *Akzo Nobel Chemicals Ltd v. Commission*, ECLI:EU:T:2007:287, (Sept. 17, 2007).

153 *See generally* Richard Whish & David Bailey, *Articles 101 and 102: public enforcement by the European Commission and national competition authorities under Regulation 1/2003*, *in* COMPETITION LAW 281–288 (Richard Whish & David Bailey eds., 10th ed., 2021).

154 Commission Regulation 773/2004 of Apr. 7, 2004 relating to the conduct of proceedings by the European Commission pursuant to Articles 81 and 82 of the EC Treaty, art.16(1).

155 Council Regulation 1/2003, *supra* n. 68, Chapter II, art. 17.

156 *Id.* art. 17 ¶1, art. 20 ¶1.

generic companies and between originator companies. The European Commission's inquiry focused in detail on the reasons for the delayed market entry of generic medicines and the decline in market entry of new medicines in Europe, including the use by originator companies of various patent and regulatory strategies.[157] It confirmed that the behavior of originator companies contributed to the delay of generic entry. The European Commission found that delaying strategies against generic entry included, for example filing a large number of patents for a single drug (creating so-called "patent clusters"), initiating expensive and lengthy patent litigation against generic companies, and/or entering into patent settlement agreements with generic companies that limit generic entry and involve a transfer of value from the original manufacturer to the generic company.

147. In 2019, the European Commission issued a new report following up on its initial sector inquiry and focusing on competition enforcement in the pharmaceutical sector for the period 2009 to 2017.[158] It found that over this period, European competition authorities investigated more than 100 cases, with 20 possible antitrust infringements still being examined as of 2019. The European Commission also reviewed more than 80 transactions; competition concerns were detected in 19 merger cases, and the European Commission cleared these mergers only after the companies offered to address concerns and modify the transaction. The European Commission concluded: "The past enforcement record provides a solid basis for competition authorities to continue and to focus their enforcement efforts. Effective enforcement of EU competition rules in the pharmaceutical sector remains a matter of high priority and the competition authorities will continue to monitor and be pro-active in investigating potential anticompetitive situations."[159]

148. In parallel, also as a follow-up to its sector inquiry of 2009, the European Commission started monitoring all patent settlements between originator and generic companies and publishing annual reports on this specific issue. Eight reports were released, covering years 2009 to 2016.[160] During that period, the European Commission investigated several originator and generic companies and imposed sanctions under Article 101 TFEU for entering into patent settlements with reverse payments that involved a significant transfer of value and were in fact intended to restrict market entry of generics, as discussed in more details in Chapter IV.[161] In its report for 2016, published on 9 March 2018, the European Commission found that patent settlements continue to be widely used

---

157 Pharmaceutical Sector Inquiry – Final Report, *supra* n. 115, Chapter II, ¶1554, 520.

158 Report from the European Commission to the Council and the European Parliament, Competition enforcement in the pharmaceutical sector (2009–2017), (Jan. 28, 2019), *available at* https://ec.europa.eu/competition/sectors/pharmaceuticals/report2019/report_en.pdf.

159 *Id.* 4.

160 *See* European Commission Reports on the Monitoring of Patent Settlements (2009–2016), *available at* https://competition-policy.ec.europa.eu/sectors/pharmaceuticals-health-services/pharmaceutical-sector-inquiry_en.

161 *See* Cases C-591/16 P, *Lundbeck v. Commission*, ECLI:EU:C:2021:243, (Mar. 25, 2021) and T-472/13, *Lundbeck v. Commission*, ECLI:EU:T:2016:449, (Sept. 8, 2016); Case COMP/AT.39612, *Perindopril (Servier)* (2014); Case COMP/AT.39686, *Cephalon* (2020).

in the European pharmaceutical sector, as demonstrated by the number of patent settlements concluded in 2016, i.e., 107 patent settlement agreements in the EU.[162] However, it also noted that most of these settlements (89%) do not raise *prima facie* competition concerns.[163] As a result, the European Commission therefore decided to stop the publication of the annual reports, although patent settlements remain an enforcement priority.

b. *The EU courts*

149. The EU courts are located in Luxembourg and consist primarily of the ECJ and the General Court.[164] Their task is to ensure respect for the law in the interpretation and application of the Treaties. Each Member State can appoint one judge to the ECJ. Eleven Advocates General assist the ECJ by delivering independent and impartial opinions on cases. For the General Court, each Member State appoints two judges.

150. In the context of competition law, the EU courts are involved in two types of cases.

151. First, any act of the European institutions is subject to judicial review before the EU courts.[165] The General Court is the first instance court for any appeal against a decision by the European Commission, including competition decisions. The General Court hears on a relatively regular basis appeals concerning infringement decisions, decisions rejecting complaints, and procedural decisions taken during investigations. The General Court has unlimited jurisdiction when reviewing these cases. The ECJ then acts as court of appeal but will only review the legality of the judgment, not any alleged factual inaccuracy.

152. Second, in order to ensure a coherent application of EU law throughout the EU, any Member State court can – or must, in some cases – refer to the ECJ any question on the interpretation of EU law. The ECJ has exclusive jurisdiction over such cases. As such, it will have to review questions referred by national courts as provided for by Article 267 TFEU, which arise in the course of the application of Articles 101 and 102 TFEU. This can be the case when legal questions arise in connection with these two provisions in private law disputes or in judicial review of NCA decisions. National courts can obtain a preliminary ruling on the interpretation of EU law from the ECJ, which allows them to form an opinion in the relevant case and come to a judgment.

B. *Private Litigation*[166]

153. In addition to public enforcement, private damages claims can be brought in the EU for violations of Articles 101 and 102 TFEU. These must be pursued before the national courts of the Member States.

---

162 *See* European Commission, Eighth Report on the Monitoring of Patent Settlements (Jan.–Dec. 2016) (Mar. 9, 2018), *available at* https://ec.europa.eu/competition/sectors/pharmaceuticals/inquiry/patent_settlements_report8_en.pdf.

163 *Id.*

164 TEU, art. 19(1).

165 *Id.* art. 263.

166 *See* Chapter VI for a more detailed discussion of private litigation.

154. Private enforcement is becoming increasingly important and companies that have been found by the European Commission or NCAs to have infringed Article 101 TFEU regularly face follow-on claims for damages. In addition, the adoption of the EU Damages Directive on November 26, 2014 (the EU Damages Directive), has led to an increase in private enforcement cases.[167] The EU Damages Directive aims to ensure that claimants can rely on a minimum set of substantive and procedural rules, regardless of the Member State in which they bring their claim. By way of example, the EU Damages Directive stipulates that anyone who has suffered harm as a result of an infringement of competition law can claim the right to full compensation for that harm.[168] Indirect purchasers who have had to pay more because of the passing-on of cartel-induced overpricing by direct purchasers can also claim damages.[169] A plaintiff can also demand the disclosure of evidence needed to pursue his claim.[170]

155. The EU Damages Directive lays down minimum standards, and Member States are free to adopt higher standards, leading to differences between the jurisdictions of the individual Member States. To avoid harmful divergences, the ECJ plays a harmonization role and guides Member States on the application and interpretation of individual provisions of the EU Damages Directive. Since the EU Damages Directive only applies to violations committed after its entry into force, and considering the length of competition law investigations, the most important provisions of the EU Damages Directive will not apply for several years.[171]

156. The question of collective redress is not addressed in the EU Damages Directive and as such there are considerable differences between Member States in that respect. (*See* Chapter VI.)

3. International Cooperation

A. *European Competition Network*

157. The European Competition Network (ECN) is a cooperation network set up between NCAs and the European Commission. Within this framework, authorities mutually exchange information on cases and decisions, provide mutual assistance in investigations, and share evidence or other information.

158. The leading forum of the ECN is the Meeting of Directors General, which defines the work program for the entire network. The ECN is structured around working groups, including sectoral ones, such as for the pharmaceutical sector. The NCAs worked together through the ECN on the Pharmaceuticals Sector Inquiry and the Report on Competition Enforcement in the Pharmaceutical Sector 2009–2017

167 Council Directive 2014/104 of the European Parliament and of the Council of Nov. 26, 2014 on certain rules governing actions for damages under national law for infringements of the competition law provisions of the Member States and of the EU (the EU Damages Directive), 2014 OJ (L 349) 1–19.

168 *Id.* art. 3.

169 *Id.* Chapter IV.

170 *Id.* Recitals 14–29, Chapter II.

171 *Id.* art. 22.

(EC Pharmaceutical Enforcement Report).[172] The ECN also allows for enforcement cooperation, as was the case in the Aspen investigation where the Irish Competition Authority (Competition and Consumer Protection Commission (CCPC)) provided investigatory assistance to the Italian Competition Authority (*Autorità Garante della Concorrenza e del Mercato* (AGCM)). Following the AGCM's request for investigatory assistance, the CCPC conducted inspections at the premises of the company's undertakings located in Ireland and shared seized documents with the AGCM.[173]

B. *International Competition Network*

159. European competition authorities also cooperate with their counterparts beyond the borders of Europe. The International Competition Network (ICN) includes 140 member authorities from 129 jurisdictions. The ICN offers competition authorities worldwide an informal, project-oriented network to intensify their cooperation in matters of antitrust law application.

160. The ICN working groups deal with issues from all areas of antitrust law (merger control, antitrust, abuse of dominance) as well as a number of cross-jurisdiction issues. An example is the Multilateral Task Force on pharmaceutical mergers, which was launched in May 2021 and consists of staff from the FTC, the European Commission's Directorate-General for Competition, the Canadian Competition Bureau and the UK Competition and Markets Authority (CMA). This task force is re-evaluating how to analyze the effects of mergers in the pharmaceutical industry.[174]

II. Market Definition

161. The definition of the relevant market, both from a product and geographic standpoint, is often a starting point for the analysis of antitrust and competition law issues in both merger and non-merger cases in the US and the EU.[175] In practice, it is often necessary to identify the boundaries of competition between firms, through an assessment of the competitive constraints that those firms face, in order to then move on to consider the extent to which any firms may either exercise

---

172 European Commission Report to the Council and European Parliament on Competition Enforcement in the Pharmaceutical Sector (2009–2017), *available at* https://ec.europa.eu/competition/publications/reports/kd0718081enn.pdf.

173 AGCM, Case A480, Decision No. 26185, *Incremento Prezzo Farmaci Aspen* (Sept. 29, 2016) published on the AGCM Bulletin No. 36/2016. A non-official English translation of the decision is *available at* https://en.agcm.it/dotcmsdoc/pressrelease/a480_eng.pdf. *See* ¶5 of the decision about the cooperation with the CCPC.

174 *See* FTC, *Multilateral Pharmaceutical Merger Task Force Seeks Public Input* (May 11, 2021), *available at* https://www.ftc.gov/news-events/news/press-releases/2021/05/multilateral-pharmaceutical-merger-task-force-seeks-public-input.

175 *See, e.g.*, *Walker Process Equip., Inc. v. Food Mach. & Chem. Corp.*, 382 U.S. 172, 177 (1965) ("Without a definition of th[e] market there is no way to measure [a defendant's] ability to lessen or destroy competition."); Case 6/72, *Europemballage Corporation and Continental Can Company Inc.*, ECLI:EU:C:1973:22, ¶32 (Feb. 21, 1973) (noting the "fundamental significance" of market definition for both abuse of dominance and merger control).

or acquire market power. In fact, the relevant market definition is frequently outcome determinative.[176]

1. General Principles

162. The antitrust and competition laws generally require that markets be defined by: (A) a specific line of commerce (the relevant product market); and (B) a specific section of the world, region, country or other area (the relevant geographic market).

A. *Relevant Product Market*

163. In both the US and the EU, product market definition is generally guided by the concepts of substitutability and cross-elasticities of demand. In the US, this approach was established in long-standing US Supreme Court precedent holding that "[t]he outer boundaries of a product market are determined by the reasonable interchangeability of use or the cross-elasticity of demand between the product itself and substitutes for it."[177] In the EU, the ECJ has similarly emphasized that "the possibilities of competition must be judged in the context of the market comprising the totality of the products which, with respect to their characteristics, are particularly suitable for satisfying constant needs and are only to a limited extent interchangeable with other products."[178] While the US and EU may at times reach different conclusions when applying this approach in practice, both jurisdictions share a common commitment to defining the relevant product market by identifying the actual universe of products or services that serve as real competitive constraints to the specific product or service in question.

---

176 *See, e.g.*, *FTC v. RAG-Stiftung*, 436 F. Supp. 3d 278, 288 (D.D.C. 2020) ("[T]the FTC pleaded and argued for a single market for all 'non-electronics' hydrogen peroxide. And because evaluating a merger's competitive effects on a market requires the FTC to properly define a market in terms of both product and geography, that oversimplification all but precludes the Court from siding with it."); *FTC v. Staples, Inc.*, 970 F. Supp. 1066, 1073 (D.D.C. 1997) ("As with many antitrust cases, the definition of the relevant product market in this case is crucial. In fact, to a great extent, this case hinges on the proper definition of the relevant product market."); Commission Notice on the definition of relevant market for the purposes of Community competition law (the Notice on Market Definition), 1997 OJ (C 372) 5–13, ¶4 ("The definition of the relevant market in both its product and its geographic dimensions often has a decisive influence on the assessment of a competition case.").

177 *Brown Shoe Co. v. United States*, 370 U.S. 294, 325 (1962); *see also United States v. E.I. du Pont de Nemours & Co.*, 351 U.S. 377, 404 (1956) ("The 'market' which one must study to determine when a producer has monopoly power will vary with the part of commerce under consideration. The tests are constant. That market is composed of products that have reasonable interchangeability for the purposes for which they are produced – price, use and qualities considered.").

178 Case 31/80, *NV L'Oréal and SA L'Oréal v PVBA "De Nieuwe AMCK"*, ECLI:EU:C:1980:289, ¶25 (Dec. 11, 1980). *See also* Notice on Market Definition, *supra* n. 176, Chapter II, ¶7 ("A relevant product market comprises all those products and/or services which are regarded as interchangeable or substitutable by the consumer, by reason of the products' characteristics, their prices and their intended use.") (citations omitted); Form CO, annex to Consolidated version of the Commission Regulation 802/2004 of Apr. 21, 2004 implementing Council Regulation 139/2004 on the control of concentrations between undertakings, 2004 OJ (L 24) 1 (the EC Merger Regulation), as amended by Commission Regulation 1033/2008 2008 OJ (L 279) 3–12 and by Commission EU Antitrust Implementing Regulation 1269/2013 of Dec. 5, 2013 OJ (L 336) 1–36, ¶6.1 ("A relevant product market comprises all those products and/or services which are regarded as interchangeable or substitutable by the consumer, by reason of the products' characteristics, their prices and their intended use. A relevant product market may in some cases be composed of a number of individual products and/or services which present largely identical physical or technical characteristics and are interchangeable.").

164. Defining a relevant product market often requires a fact-intensive inquiry into the potential substitutes to market participants and the ability and willingness of market participants to switch between available products or services in the event of an increase in price.

165. In practice, the US Antitrust Agencies and the European Commission have primarily looked to *demand* substitutability (i.e., which products or services customers view as adequate substitutes).[179] For mergers in particular, it is common for enforcers in both jurisdictions to probe how customers would react to a hypothetical small but significant and non-transitory increase in price (SSNIP) on at least one product in the market.[180] Despite some differences in how this test is articulated in each jurisdiction,[181] the test essentially evaluates whether substitution would be enough to make the hypothetical price increase unprofitable because of the resulting loss of sales. In the US, the Antitrust Agencies typically use a SSNIP of 5% when applying this test, but this benchmark varies depending on the nature of the market and the merging parties' positions in it.[182] Similarly, the European Commission typically applies a benchmark SSNIP in the range of 5 to 10%.[183]

166. In limited circumstances, however, both the US Antitrust Agencies and the European Commission may also look at *supply-side* substitutability (i.e., the ability of suppliers to switch production between different products) for products that are not otherwise demand substitutes.[184] In the US, a market may be defined by supply-side substitution if supply-side substitution is: (1) "nearly universal among the firms selling one or more of a group of products," (2) "easy," and (3) "profitable."[185] Firms that meet the criteria for supply-side substitution are called "rapid entrants" because they "are not current producers in a relevant market" defined by product substitution, but "would very likely provide rapid supply responses with direct competitive impact in the event of a SSNIP, without incurring significant sunk costs[.]"[186] Similarly,

---

179 *See, e.g.*, US Antitrust Agencies, Horizontal Merger Guidelines, § 4 (2010) (the US Horizontal Merger Guidelines) ("Market definition focuses solely on demand substitution factors, *i.e.*, on customers' ability and willingness to substitute away from one product to another in response to a price increase or a corresponding non-price change such as a reduction in product quality or service."); Notice on Market Definition, *supra* n. 176, Chapter II, ¶13 ("From an economic point of view, for the definition of the relevant market, demand substitution constitutes the most immediate and effective disciplinary force on the suppliers of a given product, in particular in relation to their pricing decisions.").

180 *Compare* US Horizontal Merger Guidelines, *supra* n. 179, Chapter II, § 4.1.1 *with* Notice on Market Definition, *supra* n. 176, Chapter II, ¶¶15–19.

181 In the US, this tool has historically been tied to the application of the so-called "Hypothetical Monopolist Test," which asks whether "a hypothetical profit-maximizing firm, not subject to price regulation, that was the only present and future seller of those products ('hypothetical monopolist') likely would impose a [SNIPP] on at least one product in the market, including at least one product sold by one of the merging firms." US Horizontal Merger Guidelines, *supra* n. 179, Chapter II, § 4.1.1. In the EU, the European Commission asks "whether the parties' customers would switch to readily available substitutes or to suppliers located elsewhere in response to a hypothetical small (in the range 5% to 10%) but permanent relative price increase in the products and areas being considered."

182 US Horizontal Merger Guidelines, *supra* n. 179, Chapter II, § 4.1.2.

183 Notice on Market Definition, *supra* n. 176, Chapter II, ¶¶17–18.

184 *See, e.g.*, US Horizontal Merger Guidelines, *supra* n. 179, Chapter II, § 5.1 & n.8; *id.* ¶¶20–23.

185 *FTC v. RAG-Stiftung*, 436 F. Supp. 3d 278, 293 (D.D.C. 2020) (quoting US Horizontal Merger Guidelines, *supra* n. 179, Chapter II, § 5.1 & n. 8).

186 *Id.* § 5.1.

supply-side substitution is mainly relevant in the EU only where "most of the suppliers are able to offer and sell the various qualities immediately and without the significant increases in costs[.]"[187] As the European Commission has explained: "When supply-side substitutability would entail the need to adjust significantly existing tangible and intangible assets, additional investments, strategic decisions or time delays, it will not be considered at the stage of market definition."[188]

167. Beyond supply-side substitution, both the US Antitrust Agencies and the European Commission often exclude the likelihood of new entry from other potential competitors when defining a product market.[189] In the US, an exception is made for "[f]irms not currently earning revenues in the relevant market, but that have committed to entering the market in the near future," which are considered market participants.[190] Similarly, the European Commission often includes pipeline products when there is a sufficient degree of certainty that they will enter the market in the short term.[191] Otherwise, while entry may not play a role in defining relevant markets, entry can play a role in any subsequent assessment of competitive effects once the relevant market is defined.[192]

168. When defining a relevant product market, it is important to keep in mind that the approach described above does not necessarily lead to only one relevant product market. Instead, especially when evaluating mergers, the US Antitrust Agencies and the European Commission often consider multiple potential product markets and may assess competitive effects in each.[193] For example, because demand substitutability is the guiding principle, separate product markets may be defined in both the US and the EU based around targeted subsets of customers.[194] In practice, "[b]ecause the relative competitive significance of more distant substitutes is apt to be overstated by their share of sales," the US Antitrust Agencies tend to rely on market shares and concentration in the smallest allowable relevant

---

187 Notice on Market Definition, *supra* n. 176, Chapter II, ¶¶17–18.

188 *Id.* ¶23.

189 *See, e.g.*, Notice on Market Definition, *supra* n. 176, Chapter II, ¶24 ("The third source of competitive constraint, potential competition, is not taken into account when defining markets, since the conditions under which potential competition will actually represent an effective competitive constraint depend on the analysis of specific factors and circumstances related to the conditions of entry.").

190 US Horizontal Merger Guidelines, *supra* n. 179, Chapter II, § 5.1.

191 *See, e.g.*, Case COMP/M.7559, *Pfizer/Hospira* ¶269 (2015) (pipeline products taken into consideration when they are planned to enter the market within 2 years).

192 *See, e.g.*, US Horizontal Merger Guidelines, *supra* n. 179, Chapter II, § 9; Notice on Market Definition, *supra* n. 176, Chapter II, ¶24; *FTC v. Sanford Health*, 926 F.3d 959 (8th Cir. 2019) (explaining timely, likely, and sufficient entry "can offset anticompetitive effects").

193 *See, e.g.*, US Horizontal Merger Guidelines, *supra* n. 179, Chapter II, § 4.1.1 ("The Agencies may evaluate a merger in any relevant market satisfying the [hypothetical monopolist test]."); Notice on Market Definition, *supra* n. 176, Chapter II, ¶26 ("In general, and for all practical purposes when handling individual cases, the question will usually be to decide on a few alternative possible relevant markets."); Case COMP/M.5865, *Teva/Ratiopharm* (2010).

194 *See, e.g.*, US Horizontal Merger Guidelines, *supra* n. 179, Chapter II, § 4.1.4 ("If a hypothetical monopolist could profitably target a subset of customers for price increases, the Agencies may identify relevant markets defined around those targeted customers, to whom a hypothetical monopolist would profitably and separately impose at least a SSNIP."); Notice on Market Definition, *supra* n. 176, Chapter II, ¶43 ("A distinct group of customers for the relevant product may constitute a narrower, distinct market when such ha group could be subject to price discrimination.").

market based on the view that narrow markets "are more likely to capture the relative competitive significance of these products, and often more accurately reflect competition between close substitutes."[195]

B. *Relevant Geographic Market*

169. **In the US**, "[t]he criteria to be used in determining the appropriate geographic market are essentially similar to those used to determine the relevant product market."[196] When evaluating the area of effective competition, the geographic market selected must "correspond to the commercial realities of the industry and be economically significant."[197] In practice, this can lead to wide variation. As the US Supreme Court has explained: "Although the geographic market in some instances may encompass the entire Nation, under other circumstances it may be as small as a single metropolitan area."[198] In some cases, the US Antitrust Agencies have even defined geographic markets on a supranational or worldwide basis.[199]

170. In practice, the US Antitrust Agencies have explained that "[t]he scope of geographic markets often depends on transportation costs."[200] In addition, "[o]ther factors such as language, regulation, tariff and non-tariff trade barriers, custom and familiarity, reputation, and service availability may impede long-distance or international transactions."[201] In most cases, the US Antitrust Agencies define geographic markets based around the location of each supplier.[202] For markets where suppliers can discriminate on price based on customer location (such as when suppliers deliver products or services to customer locations), geographic markets may be defined based on the location of the target customers, even if some suppliers that sell into that territory may be located outside of the boundaries of the relevant geographic market.[203]

171. As a practical matter, in most antitrust cases involving pharmaceutical products, the geographic market will likely be the US. Given the regulatory restrictions, pharmaceutical product markets are usually limited by national boundaries.

---

195 US Horizontal Merger Guidelines, *supra* n. 179, Chapter II, § 4.1.1.

196 *Brown Shoe Co. v. United States*, 370 US 294, 336–337 (1962).

197 *Id.* (internal citations omitted).

198 *Id.* a relevant geographic market in "highly urban areas" can also be as small as "no broader than a half-mile radius around a given store."; *see* Complaint, *In the Matter of Dollar Tree, Inc.*, FTC File No. 141-0207, § 8 (July 2, 2015).

199 Complaint, *In the Matter of American Securities Partners/Ferro,* FTC File No. 211-0121, §§ 10–11 (Apr. 21, 2022) (defining a separate North America market for porcelain enamel frit and worldwide market for glass enamel and forehearth colorants); Complaint, *United States v. Inco Ltd.*, Case No. 1:06-cv-01151, §§ 25–26 (June 23, 2006) ("All of the High-Purity Nickel sold in the world in mined, processed, and refined outside of the United States. Both Inco and Falconbridge sell High-Purity Nickel throughout the world. Both companies import High-Purity Nickel into the United States and sell that nickel to customers located throughout the United States. Accordingly, the world is the relevant geographic market within the meaning of Section 7 of the Clayton Act.").

200 US Horizontal Merger Guidelines, *supra* n. 179, Chapter II, § 4.2.

201 *Id.*

202 *Id.* § 4.2.1.

203 *Id.* § 4.2.2.

172. **In the EU,** a similar approach to geographic market definition is followed, also grounded in commercial realities. In brief, the European Commission has explained that the relevant geographic market "comprises the area in which the undertakings concerned are involved in the supply and demand of products or services, in which the conditions of competition are sufficiently homogeneous, and which can be distinguished from neighboring areas because the conditions of competition are appreciably different in those area."[204]

173. In assessing the geographic scope of a market, the European Commission will generally first look at the distribution of market shares of various competitors as well as price differences between Member States.[205] The European Commission will also take into account any specificities of demand, such as the importance of national or local preferences, current patterns of purchases of customers, or product differentiation/brands across countries.[206] It will consider barriers that may separate one geographic area from another, including both regulatory barriers (e.g., price regulations, quotas and tariffs limiting trade or production, technical standards, monopolies, freedom of establishment, requirements for administrative authorizations) and financial barriers (such as costs associated with setting up a distribution network).[207] Finally, the European Commission will look at actual trade flows to confirm its preliminary assessment.[208]

C. *Official Guidance*

174. **In the US**, the general principles governing market definition under the antitrust laws have been established by the courts through a vast body of case law over the last century. Practitioners can also look to voluminous complaints and other documents filed by the US Antitrust Agencies in enforcement actions to understand how they may address similar markets in the future.

175. Because these decisions have evolved on a case-by-case basis and can be cumbersome to interpret, the US Antitrust Agencies historically have developed and been guided by separate "Horizontal" and "Vertical" (or "Non-Horizontal") Merger Guidelines. The US Horizontal Merger Guidelines assist the US Antitrust

---

204 Notice on Market Definition, *supra* n. 176, Chapter II, ¶8. Council Regulation 139/2004 (EU Merger Regulation), *supra* n. 64, Chapter II, art. 9(7), 1–22 ("The geographical reference market shall consist of the area in which the undertakings concerned are involved in the supply and demand of products or services, in which the conditions of competition are sufficiently homogeneous and which can be distinguished from neighboring areas because, in particular, conditions of competition are appreciably different in those areas. This assessment should take account in particular of the nature and characteristics of the products or services concerned, of the existence of entry barriers or of consumer preferences, of appreciable differences of the undertakings' market shares between the area concerned and neighboring areas or of substantial price differences."); Form CO, ¶6.2 ("The relevant geographic market comprises the area in which the undertakings concerned are involved in the supply and demand of relevant products or services, in which the conditions of competition are sufficiently homogeneous and which can be distinguished from neighboring geographic areas because, in particular, conditions of competition are appreciably different in those areas.").

205 Notice on Market Definition, *supra* n. 176, Chapter II, ¶28.

206 *Id.* ¶29.

207 *Id.* ¶30.

208 *Id.* ¶31.

Agencies in evaluating mergers between companies at the same level of the market (e.g., two manufacturers of a drug to treat the same condition).[209] By contrast, Vertical Merger Guidelines help the Antitrust Agencies review mergers between companies at different levels of the supply chain (e.g., between the manufacturer of an API and therapies relying on that ingredient).[210] In principle, the merger guidelines are primarily intended to "assist the business community and antitrust practitioners by increasing the transparency of the analytical process underlying the Agencies' enforcement decisions," but the US Antitrust Agencies also anticipate that the merger guidelines may "assist the courts in developing an appropriate framework for interpreting and applying the antitrust laws" related to mergers.[211]

176. It is important to remember, however, that the merger guidelines are always subject to revision by the US Antitrust Agencies and do not have the same weight as judicial precedent. As suggested by their name, they also are intended primarily for the assessment of mergers. That said, because market definition principles do not change across the various US antitrust statutes, courts often look to the merger guidelines as persuasive authority on market definition – even for non-merger matters.[212] As such, the merger guidelines are a valuable source when evaluating market definition principles under the antitrust laws.

177. **In the EU**, there are several decades of precedents from the EU courts that establish market definition principles. The established decisional practice of the European Commission can also be invaluable for understanding market definition across a wide range of industries. That said, the intricate link between market definition and the economic competitive dynamics of a market also means that market definitions evolve over time. Although European Commission precedents can be a useful tool to anticipate how a market would be assessed in a specific case, these precedents do not prevent the European Commission from departing from previous market definitions to account for evolving market conditions.

---

209 The 2010 US Horizontal Merger Guidelines are currently in effect, but the US Antitrust Agencies announced in Jan. 2022 that a joint inquiry aimed at updating the existing guidelines. FTC, *Federal Trade Commission and Justice Department Seek to Strengthen Enforcement Against Illegal Mergers* (Jan. 18, 2022), *available at* https://www.ftc.gov/news-events/news/press-releases/2022/01/federal-trade-commission-justice-department-seek-strengthen-enforcement-against-illegal-mergers.

210 The most recent Vertical Merger Guidelines were issued by the US Antitrust Agencies in June 2020, but those guidelines were subsequently withdrawn by the FTC in Sept. 2021. FTC, *Federal Trade Commission Withdraws Vertical Merger Guidelines and Commentary* (Sept. 15, 2021), *available at* https://www.ftc.gov/news-events/news/press-releases/2021/09/federal-trade-commission-withdraws-vertical-merger-guidelines-commentary. The 2020 Vertical Guidelines remain in force with the DOJ, but the DOJ is collaborating with the FTC on a review intended to update those guidelines. DOJ, *Justice Department Issues Statement on the Vertical Merger Guidelines* (Sept. 15, 2021), https://www.ftc.gov/news-events/news/press-releases/2021/05/multilateral-pharmaceutical-merger-task-force-seeks-public-input.

211 *See* US Horizontal Merger Guidelines, *supra* n. 179, Chapter II, § 1; US Antitrust Agencies, Vertical Merger Guidelines § 1 (June 30, 2020), *available at* https://www.ftc.gov/system/files/documents/reports/us-department-justice-federal-trade-commission-vertical-merger-guidelines/vertical_merger_guidelines_6-30-20.pdf.

212 *E.g., FTC v. Lundbeck, Inc.*, 650 F.3d 1236, 1240 (8th Cir. 2011); *Rebel Oil Co., Inc. v. Atlantic Richfield Co.*, 51 F.3d 1421, 1440–41 (9th Cir. 1995); *United States v. Syufy Enterprises*, 903 F.2d 659, 664 (9th Cir. 1990); *United States v. Visa U.S.A., Inc.*, 163 F. Supp. 2d 322, 335–36 (S.D.N.Y. 2001); *Anti-Monopoly Inc. v. Hasbro, Inc.*, 958 F. Supp. 895, 902 (S.D.N.Y. 1997).

178. The framework for market definition was historically provided in regulations providing for notification forms of both agreements between undertakings and mergers; this aimed to assist practitioners with navigating complex precedents. Then, in 1997, the European Commission adopted the Notice on Market Definition[213] to provide better transparency on its proceedings and help undertakings in their assessment of their behavior. Like the merger guidelines in the US, however, the Notice on Market Definition is always subject to change.[214]

179. In both the US and the EU, the market definition methodology and principles remain relatively consistent across both merger and non-merger cases, but it is important to note that the resulting market may differ in some cases depending on the type of assessment carried out. This is due in part to the fact that the time horizon can differ, especially between the assessment of mergers, which requires a prospective analysis, and the assessment of anticompetitive behavior, which is by nature backward looking and can more closely study the past competitive dynamics and structure of the market.[215] Some caution accordingly may be warranted when extrapolating market definition from different types of cases even within the same industry.

D. *Issues Regarding Market Definitions in Life Sciences*

180. While basic market definition principles in the US and the EU do not vary by industry, applying those principles to the life sciences can present some relatively unique challenges.

181. First, assessing demand substitutability in the life sciences sector is less straightforward than in many other industries. Indeed, the peculiarities of this industry and in particular the multiplicity of actors involved in the choice of a product complicate the assessment. For instance, depending on the country, the type of life sciences, and the applicable regulations, the ultimate decision to purchase a product can depend on determinations made by a variety of actors other than the final patient or consumer (such as national authorities, health insurance providers, and healthcare professionals). The specificities of some patients (e.g., for pediatric or geriatric drugs) may also complicate the analysis. Because of these factors, customers may be less sensitive to price and may focus on more qualitative criteria. Price competition in pharmaceutical markets also may manifest in other ways, including through rebates and formulary negotiations that are not transparent to the ultimate consumer.

182. In the EU, the General Court recently addressed this situation with its judgment in *Servier SAS e.a. v. Commission*,[216] which highlighted the specificities of the pharmaceutical sector and emphasized that non-price elements, such as therapeutic

---

213 Notice on Market Definition, *supra* n. 176, Chapter II, 5–13.

214 Most recently, the European Commission carried out a public consultation on the Notice on Market Definition in 2020 and commissioned a study report of the same that was published in June 2021. Support study accompanying the European Commission Notice on the evaluation of the definition of relevant market for the purposes of Community competition law (study report on the relevant market), June 2021, *available at* https://competition-policy.ec.europa.eu/system/files/2021-06/kd0221712enn_market_definition_notice_2021_1.pdf.

215 Notice on Market Definition, *supra* n. 176, Chapter II, ¶12.

216 Case T-691/14, *Servier SAS e.a. v. Commission*, ECLI:EU:T:2018:922, (Dec. 12, 2018).

indication, should be taken into account when defining the relevant market.[217] The General Court also flagged that the lower price competition in the pharmaceutical sector, due to the focus of healthcare providers on therapeutic indication and the specific regulatory framework, is a key element of market definition that can justify defining narrower markets.[218] This does not mean that price indicators are not relevant when defining a market in the life sciences industry. To the contrary, the General Court has separately confirmed that "the specific features which characterize competitive mechanisms in the pharmaceutical sector do not negate the relevance of price-related factors in the assessment of competitive constraints, although those factors must be assessed in their specific context."[219] Where prices are regulated or set by public authorities, the General Court suggested, the price granted to a product may relate to a large extent to the public authorities' perception of the products relative therapeutic added value relative to other existing products.[220]

183. The interplay between different decision-makers results in some relatively unique market dynamics.[221] For example, while considering competition between two originator companies to market patented medicine targeting the same therapeutic area, the decision-making process often focuses primarily on the medicine's relative efficacy and its perceived lack – or lower frequency of occurrence – of adverse effects rather than price. At the same time, competition also takes place through marketing and promotional activities. These competitive dynamics can play a significant role when considering market definition issues. The same is true of the overall regulatory framework regulating the sales of such products. As the General Court has explained: "In the pharmaceutical sector, competitive relationships respond to mechanisms which differ from those determining competitive interactions normally present in markets which are not so heavily regulated."[222]

184. Finally, life sciences also are often characterized by fierce competition for the development of new products, which in turn may create new markets (i.e., introducing a patented product on the market to meet a currently unmet need). In order to bring such a product to market, competitors initially compete through innovation, with the goal of obtaining a patent. Patents will reward innovation as they allow the originator to benefit from a legal monopoly on sales for the patented innovation throughout the exclusivity period. This has two main consequences. First, for products already on the market, IP rights can create barriers to entry influencing market definitions.[223] Second, when assessing substitutability between pipeline products that have not yet received regulatory approval, this dynamic requires an assessment of whether and when each of the future products are sufficiently likely to enter the market.

---

217 *Id.* ¶1385.

218 *Id.* ¶1390.

219 Case T-321/05, *AstraZeneca AB and AstraZeneca plc v. Commission*, ECLI:EU:T:2010:266, ¶183 (July 1, 2010).

220 *Id.* ¶¶162–165.

221 *See generally* Pharmaceutical Sector Inquiry – Final Report, *supra* n. 115, Chapter II.

222 Case T-321/05, *AstraZeneca AB and AstraZeneca plc*, ECLI:EU:T:2010:266, ¶183 (July 1, 2010).

223 *See, e.g.*, Case COMP/M.6944, *Thermo Fisher Scientific/ Life Technologies* (2013).

2. Life Sciences Product Markets

A. *Pharmaceuticals*

185. While the US and the EU use a very similar substitutability framework for market definition, the initial approach to defining pharmaceutical markets does have some notable differences. It is also worth noting that, in both the US and the EU, market definition for pharmaceutical products has at times been heavily litigated given its complexity and the unique challenges for market definition in the life sciences.

186. **In the US**, while existing precedents can be a helpful guide, the market definition is typically adduced from the available evidence on a case-by-case basis. The US Antitrust Agencies thus tend to define pharmaceutical markets by reference to one or more of the following criteria:

- the disease or condition the product is approved to treat;[224]
- the chemical composition, compound, molecule, or mechanism by which the product works;[225]
- the manner through which the product is administered (galenic form in particular);[226]
- the strength of dosage;[227]
- the frequency of the dosage;[228]
- whether the product is branded or generic;[229]

---

224 *See, e.g.*, Complaint, *In the Matter of C.H. Boehringer Sohn AG & Co. KG*, FTC File No. 161-0077 § 12 (Dec. 27, 2016) (defining a market for rabies vaccines); Complaint, *In the Matter of Prestige Brand Holdings, Inc. and Insight Pharmaceuticals Corp.*, FTC File No. 141-0159, § 7 (Aug. 28, 2014) (defining a market for sickness medication); Complaint, *In the Matter of Pfizer and Pharmacia*, FTC File No. 021-0192, § 20 (May 30, 2003) (defining separate markets for the R&D, and the manufacture and sale, of prescription drugs for the treatment of conditions like erectile dysfunction and canine arthritis).

225 *See, e.g.*, Complaint, *In the Matter of Novartis AG*, FTC File No. 141-0141, § 5 (Apr. 8, 2015) (defining separate relevant markets for BRAF and MEK inhibitors, which are cancer treatment drugs that inhibit specific molecules associated with the development of cancer).

226 *See, e.g.*, Complaint, *In the Matter of Mylan N.V.*, FTC File No. 161-0102, ¶8 (July 27, 2016) (defining a market certain tablets); Complaint, *In the Matter of Lupin Ltd.*, FTC File No. 151-0202, ¶9 (Feb. 19, 2016) (defining a relevant market for certain capsules); *In the Matter of Pfizer Inc. / Hospira, Inc.*, FTC File No. 151-0074, ¶5 (Aug. 24, 2015) (defining separate relevant markets for an inhalation solution and several injection products).

227 *See, e.g.*, Complaint, *In the Matter of Mylan N.V.*, FTC File No. 161-0102, ¶8 (July 27, 2016) (defining a market for 400 mg and 600 mg generic felbamate tablets); Complaint, *In the Matter of Hikma Pharmaceuticals PLC*, FTC File No. 151-0198, ¶4 (Feb. 26, 2016) (defining a market for 5 mg, 10 mg, and 20 mg generic prednisone tablets).

228 *See, e.g.*, Complaint, *In the Matter of Lupin Ltd.*, FTC File No. 151-0202, ¶9 (Feb. 19, 2016) (defining a relevant market for certain extended-release capsules); Complaint, *In the Matter of Watson Pharmaceuticals / Actavis Inc.*, FTC File No. 121-0132, ¶¶7–8, 12–17, 20, 24–26 (Oct. 15, 2012) (defining separate markets for various extended-release pharmaceutical products).

229 *See, e.g.*, *Geneva Pharmaceuticals Technology Corp. v. Barr Labs. Inc.*, 386 F. 3d 485, 496–99 (2d Cir. 2004) (defining a separate market for generics alone); Complaint, *In the Matter of Amneal Holdings, LLC*, FTC File No. 181-0017, ¶¶7–16 (Apr. 27, 2018) (defining separate markets for various generic pharmaceutical products); Complaint, *In the Matter of Hikma Pharmaceuticals PLC*, FTC File No. 151-0198, ¶ 4 (Feb. 26, 2016) (same); Complaint, *In the Matter of Lupin Ltd.*, FTC File No. 151-0202, ¶¶8–9 (Feb. 19, 2016) (defining separate relevant markets for generic doxycycline monohydrate capsules and generic mesalamine ER capsules); Complaint, *In the Matter of Prestige Brand Holdings, Inc. and Insight Pharmaceuticals Corp.*, FTC File No. 141-0159, ¶7 (Aug. 28, 2014) (defining a market for branded OTC motion sickness medication).

- whether the product requires a prescription or is sold over the counter;[230]
- whether the product is currently marketed or at various stages of the development pipeline;[231]
- the branded product and generic substitutes (in conduct cases).[232]

187. In each case, the focus is on the perceived substitutability of the product for market participants, typically without significant deference to formal medical classifications. Substitutability in this context may have multiple dimensions, including therapeutic substitutability from the perspective of a physician and economic substitutability on price from the perspective of a payer or consumer. Market definition is often heavily contested, and US courts do not always accept the definition alleged by the US Antitrust Agencies, even as US courts do generally engage in the same overall substitutability analysis.[233]

188. **In the EU**, the European Commission typically relies in the first instance on the Anatomical Classification of Pharmaceutical Products (also called Anatomical Therapeutic Classification or ATC), which is a five-level classification system developed and maintained by the European Pharmaceutical Market Research Association (EphMRA).[234] The starting point for market definition of pharmaceutical products is to group drugs according to their therapeutic functionality (i.e., by reference to the third level of the EphMRA classification referenced as ATC3).[235]

189. At the same time, where it finds that the ATC3 level is not appropriate, the European Commission may instead adopt a narrower market definition based on factors like product characteristics (e.g., efficacy, safety profile, mode of administration, or galenic form),[236] a more detailed ATC level (e.g., ATC4),[237] the API[238] (whether as a group or as a single molecule), or other therapeutic criteria. For instance, in oncology, the European Commission defines markets based on (i) the form of therapies (surgery, radiation therapy, chemotherapy, targeted therapies and immunotherapies) and (ii) the type of cancer.[239] For orphan drugs, markets are usually defined based on the rare disease they are intended to treat, rather than the ATC3 level.[240]

---

230 *See, e.g.*, Complaint, *In the Matter of Prestige Brand Holdings, Inc. and Insight Pharmaceuticals Corp.*, FTC File No. 141-0159, ¶7 (Aug. 28, 2014) (defining a market for branded OTC motion sickness medication).

231 *See*, e.g., Complaint, *In the Matter of Watson Pharmaceuticals / Actavis Inc.*, FTC File No. 121-0132, ¶¶22–27 (Oct. 15, 2012) (defining markets for certain pipeline products not yet marketed where the parties were "among a limited number of likely potential suppliers").

232 *See, e.g., FTC v. Actavis, Inc.*, 570 U.S. 136, 146 (2013).

233 *See, e.g., FTC v. Lundbeck, Inc.*, 650 F.3d 1236, 1240–42 (8th Cir. 2011) (upholding district court ruling rejecting FTC proposed market definition).

234 *See, e.g.*, Case COMP/M.6613, *Watson/Actavis* (2012).

235 Case COMP/M.1397, *Sanofi/Synthelabo* (1999).

236 *See e.g.*, Case COMP/M.5865, *Teva/Ratiopharm* ¶¶16–21 and 39–41 (2010); Case COMP/M.737, *Ciba-Geigy/ Sandoz* ¶21 (1996); Case COMP/M.1846, *Glaxo Wellcome/Smithkline Beecham* ¶38 (2000); COMP/M.5999, *Sanofi Aventis/ Genzyme* ¶42 (2011).

237 *See e.g.*, Case COMP/M.6613, *Watson/Actavis* ¶7 (2012).

238 *See e.g.*, Case COMP/M.6113, *DSM/Sinochem/JV* ¶¶20–23 (2011).

239 *See, e.g.*, Case COMP/M.7275, *Novartis/GlaxoSmithKline Oncology Business* (2015).

240 *See, e.g.*, Case COMP/M.9461, *AbbVie/Allergan* ¶9 (2010). In that case, the European Commission pointed out that, in autoimmune diseases, has typically identified relevant product markets by reference to indications.

190. Over time, a trend can be observed towards narrow markets and away from the traditional ATC3 level, in particular for the application of Article 102 TFEU. The General Court has confirmed, for example, that the European Commission can rely on differentiated therapeutic uses to distinguish between medicines indicated for the same pathologies even if those medicines are technically at the same ATC level.[241]

191. The European Commission also takes into account the dosage, pharmaceutical form, and the route of administration of a drug (i.e., its galenic form) when defining the market for prescription drugs.[242] To assess the galenic form, the European Commission usually refers to the first letter of the New Form Code (NFC) of the EphMRA, which typically differentiates between forms for systemic and topical effect, site of application, and also between long-acting and ordinary forms.[243] The European Commission considers that different galenic forms cater to the needs of different patients group and are not substitutable from a supply-side standpoint.[244] Finally, it should be noted that in the merger context, depending on the circumstances, the European Commission can take into account discontinued products as part of the relevant market when the exit decision can be viewed as reversible and may be assessed as related to the merger.[245]

192. While the European Commission may begin with a more formulaic approach to market definition for pharmaceutical products, courts in the EU ultimately require that market definition takes into account the wide variety of factors healthcare providers consider when choosing a product for their patients, including the therapeutic indication of the product, the adequacy of the product for a given patient's needs, known adverse effects, brand recognition, and healthcare provider familiarity and knowledge of each treatment.[246] This approach strongly resembles the approach applied by courts in the US. The ECJ even acknowledges that a pharmaceutical product used off-label in a different indication than that for which it was approved may still belong to the relevant market, provided that this use complies with the rules governing the off-label prescription of a medicinal product and its repackaging for such use.[247]

193. With this framework in mind, it is worth considering how product markets have been defined for the following groups of pharmaceutical products and services on both sides of the Atlantic: (a) branded pharmaceuticals; (b) generic pharmaceuticals; (c) biologics and biosimilars; (d) OTC drugs; (e) products in the developmental pipeline (pipeline products); (f) APIs and excipients; and (g) contract manufacturing services.

---

241 Case T-691/14, *Servier SAS e.a.*, ECLI:EU:T:2018:922, § 1388 (Dec. 12, 2018).

242 Case COMP/M.5865, *Teva/Ratiopharm* (2010).

243 *See, e.g.*, Case COMP/M.6613, *Watson/Actavis* (2012).

244 Case COMP/M.5865, *Teva/Ratiopharm* (2010).

245 *Id.*

246 Case T-691/14, *Servier SAS e.a.*, ECLI:EU:T:2018:922, § 1396–97 (Dec. 12, 2018).

247 Case C-179/16, *F. Hoffmann-La Roche Ltd and Others v. Autorità Garante della Concorrenza e del Mercato*, ECLI:EU:C:2018:25, (Jan. 23, 2018).

a. *Branded Pharmaceuticals*

194. Branded pharmaceutical products are also referred to as originator drugs, and they are typically protected by patents for a certain duration.

195. A patent, by definition, is exclusive. Nearly all legal systems contain a process for granting patents that provide innovators with the right to practice their invention on an exclusive basis and exclude others from doing so.[248] Antitrust and competition laws recognize that, while patents allow exclusivity for a limited period, they serve important, procompetitive public policy interests, including incentivizing innovation and providing for the disclosure of innovations to the public.[249]

196. In the US, the Patent Act specifically gives patent holders the explicit "right to exclude others from making, using, offering for sale, or selling the invention throughout the United States" during the term of the patent.[250] Similarly, courts in the EU have consistently held that the ability to use a protected technology or work to the exclusion of others is the very heart of an IP right.[251]

197. Any patent protections for branded pharmaceuticals are important constraints that are considered when defining a relevant product market, but the boundaries of any underlying exclusivity under the patent laws do not on their own define the contours of the relevant product market for branded pharmaceutical products under the antitrust and competition laws.[252]

---

248 All 164 members of the World Trade Organization, for example, are parties to the TRIPS Agreement. Section 5 of the TRIPS Agreement specifies that patents shall be available for certain inventions (Article 27), confer exclusive rights (Article 28), and extend for a period of at least 20 years (Article 33).

249 *See, e.g.*, FTC, *To Promote Innovation: The Proper Balance of Competition and Patent Law and Policy*, 2 (Oct. 2003), *available at* https://www.ftc.gov/sites/default/files/documents/reports/promote-innovation-proper-balance-competition-and-patent-law-and-policy/innovationrpt.pdf ("A patent confers a right to exclude others from making, using, or selling in the United States the invention claimed by the patent for twenty years from the date of filing the patent application. This property right can enable firms to increase their expected profits from investments in R&D, thus fostering innovation that would not occur but for the prospect of a patent. Because the patent system requires public disclosure, it can promote a dissemination of scientific and technical information that would not occur but for the prospect of a patent."). *See also Bonito Boats, Inc. v. Thunder Craft Boats, Inc.*, 489 U.S. 141, 150–51 (1989) ("The federal patent system thus embodies a carefully crafted bargain for encouraging the creation and disclosure of new, useful, and nonobvious advances in technology and design in return for the exclusive right to practice the invention for a period of years.").

250 35 U.S.C. § 154(a)(1); *see also* U.S. C. art. 1, § 8, cl. 8 (granting Congress the power "To promote the progress of science and useful arts, by securing for limited times to authors and inventors the exclusive right to their respective writings and discoveries."); *FTC v. Actavis, Inc.*, 570 U.S. 136, 147 (2013) ("[A] valid patent excludes all except its owner from the use of the protected process or product." (quoting *United States v. Line Material Co.*, 333 U.S. 287, 308 (1948)).

251 Case 238/87 *Volvo v. Veng*, ECLI:EU:C:1988:477, ¶8 (Oct. 5, 1988). This position was reconfirmed by the ECJ in Joined Cases C-241/91 P and C-242/91 P, *Radio Telefis Eireann (RTE) and Independent Television Publications Ltd (ITP) v. Commission*, ECLI:EU:C:1995:98, ¶34 (Apr. 6, 1995) ("Further, the exclusive right of reproduction forms part of the author's rights, so that refusal to grant a licence, even if it is the act of an undertaking holding a dominant position, cannot in itself constitute abuse of a dominant position.").

252 *See, e.g.*, *Illinois Tool Works Inc. v. Independent Ink, Inc.*, 547 U.S. 28, 31 (2006) ("The question presented to us today is whether the presumption of market power in a patented product should survive as a matter of antitrust law despite its demise in patent law. We conclude that the mere fact that a tying product is patented does not support such a presumption."); US Antitrust Agencies, *Antitrust Guidelines for the Licensing of Intellectual Property* § 2.2 (2017) (DOJ & FTC Antitrust IP Guidelines) ("Although the intellectual property

198. Instead, in both the US and the EU, the relevant product market for branded pharmaceutical products typically includes other comparable branded products viewed as substitutes for the same therapeutic uses.[253] While the European Commission relies on the ATC3 level as a starting point for this analysis, it tends to then further narrow the product market based on different qualities like therapeutic effectiveness, especially when applying Article 102 TFEU.[254] On the other hand, in performing this substitutability analysis, the relevant product market may not be limited to products that are specifically authorized for the indications at issue; instead, a relevant product market may also take into account products that have received a marketing authorization for one indication, but are used for the treatment of other indications in practice.[255] Similarly, the European Commission has left open the possibility of aggregating products across ATC3 classes where those products "are considered interchangeable so as to exercise competitive pressure on each other."[256]

199. The analysis above assumes that generic pharmaceuticals are not available, but, as discussed below, the availability of generic pharmaceuticals and biosimilars may further complicate the definition of a relevant product market.

b. *Generic Pharmaceuticals*

200. Generics are in general less expensive versions of branded originator pharmaceuticals. In regulatory approval procedures, a generic drug manufacturer is required to demonstrate that its generic version of the originator drug is bioequivalent to the originator drug.

201. Here, it is worth noting that the US and the EU tend to approach the relevant product market for generic pharmaceuticals from a different perspective.

202. **In the US**, when generic pharmaceuticals are available, the relevant product market is commonly limited to just the generic versions of the branded product.[257] Particularly where multiple generic products are available for a given branded product, these generic drugs, by virtue of their bioequivalence to the originator

---

right confers the power to exclude with respect to the specific product, process, or work in question, there will often be sufficient actual or potential close substitutes for such product, process, or work to prevent the exercise of market power."), *available at* https://www.justice.gov/atr/IPguidelines/download.

253 *See, e.g.*, Complaint, *In the Matter of AbbieVie Inc. and Allergan PLC*, FTC File No. 191-0169, ¶5(a), 7 (May 5, 2020) (defining a market for prescription drugs used to treat exocrine pancreatic insufficiency (EPI) consisting of four separate branded pharmaceutical products); European Commission, Case COMP/AT.37507, *Generics/AstraZeneca* (2005) (defining a market for branded Proton-Pump Inhibitors, including several different branded pharmaceuticals).

254 *See, e.g.*, Case COMP/AT.37507, *Generics/AstraZeneca* ¶37, 504 (2005), (concluding that Proton-Pump Inhibitors did not face significant competitive constraints from other products at the same ATC level such that Proton-Pump Inhibitors constated a separate product market that "corresponds to the fourth ATC level").

255 *See, e.g.*, Case C-179/16, *F. Hoffmann-La Roche Ltd and Others*, ECLI:EU:C:2018:25, ¶67 (Jan. 23, 2018). ("Article 101 TFEU must be interpreted as meaning that, for the purposes of the application of that article, a national competition authority may include in the relevant market, in addition to the medicinal products authorized for the treatment of the diseases concerned, another medicinal product whose [marketing authorization] does not cover that treatment but which is used for that purpose and is thus actually substitutable with the former.").

256 Case COMP/M.8974, *Procter & Gamble/Merck Consumer Health Business* ¶¶11, 38 (2018).

257 *See, e.g.*, Complaint, *In the Matter of Teva Pharmaceutical Industries and Barr Pharmaceuticals*, FTC File No. 081-0224, ¶8 (Feb. 10, 2009).

product, are viewed as the closest substitutes for each other. At the same time, while these generics are also bioequivalent to the branded originator drug, the branded pharmaceutical product is typically excluded from the relevant product market because of the expected significant differences in demand and pricing between branded drugs and generics. Nevertheless, the FTC has stated that, where a branded drug manufacturer chooses to lower its price and compete against generics, the branded drug "is a participant in the generic drug market."[258] Similarly, in conduct cases alleging efforts to prevent or delay generic entry, the FTC and private plaintiffs typically allege that branded and generic products are part of the same relevant market,[259] while there is some recognition of differences in the demand for originator or generic drugs, the European Commission considers that these differences are not sufficient to conclude that generic and branded pharmaceuticals are in separate markets.[260]

203. Although, **in the EU**, the starting point when defining a market for generic pharmaceutical products in the EU is theoretically the same as for branded pharmaceuticals, the European Commission has increasingly considered a narrower market based on the molecule or active ingredient used in the pharmaceutical product.[261] It has acknowledged that the ATC3 level in particular is not likely to be appropriate in the generics market because "generic pharmaceutical companies typically produce copies of originator drugs which therefore can normally be viewed as the closest substitute to those drugs."[262] As a consequence, even in this narrower market for generics, the European Commission – unlike the US Antitrust Agencies – defines the relevant product market to include both the originator and its generic pharmaceutical alternatives.

c. *Biologics and Biosimilars*

204. Biologics (or "macromolecular" therapies) are large-molecule pharmaceutical products whose API is made by or derived from living organisms. As described in Chapter I, because of their more complex structures due to their larger size, most biologics cannot be copied identically. Biosimilars are biological medicinal products highly similar to the originator biologics in terms of structure, biological activity and efficacy, safety and immunogenicity profile (*see* Chapter I, Section II.2.C.). While biologics and biosimilars have distinct characteristics, in practice they are likely to receive similar treatment as branded pharmaceuticals and their generic counterparts in both the US and the EU when it comes to defining the overall contours of the relevant product market. The European Commission, for example, has already defined a relevant product market as limited to an originator

---

258 FTC, Analysis of Agreement Containing Consent Orders to Aid Public Comment, *In the Matter of Mylan Inc, Agila Specialties Global Pte Limited*, FTC File No. 131-0112, 2 (Dec. 18, 2013).

259 *See, e.g.*, Complaint, *In the Matter of Endo Pharmaceuticals Inc./Amneal Pharmaceuticals, Inc.*, FTC File No. 191-0104, ¶110 (Jan. 25, 2021) (alleging a relevant market "no broader than extended-release oxymorphone tablets approved by the FDA for sale in the United States" covering both branded and generic products).

260 Case COMP/M.5865, *Teva/Ratiopharm* (2010).

261 *See, e.g.*, Case COMP/M.6613, *Watson/Actavis* (2012); Case COMP/M.5865, *Teva/Ratiopharm* (2010); Case COMP/M.5253, *Sanofi-Aventis/Zentiva* (2009).

262 Case COMP/M.5865, *Teva/Ratiopharm* ¶12 (2010).

biologic and its related biosimilars, to the exclusion of other products belonging in the same ATC3 category.[263] As for chemical drugs, markets are especially likely to be defined narrowly when applying Article 102 TFEU and its national equivalent.[264]

205. At the same time, the European Commission has recognized in other cases that the level of substitutability between an originator biologic and its biosimilars can be more limited than between originator and generics, as the clinical risks from switching between an originator and a biosimilar could be significant. Although like generic products, biosimilars are new versions of an originator products, biologics are not as close copies of the originator and require more extensive and costly R&D efforts, as well as more complex regulatory approvals.[265] Due to these differences in terms of product differentiation, interchangeability, the regulatory framework, the cost structure, and barriers to entry, the European Commission has explained that the assessment of competitive effects will be different for generics and biosimilars, even if they are grouped together in the same relevant product market.[266] Similar issues are likely to arise in the US. Although the FTC views biosimilars as important drivers of competition, not all biosimilars are designated by the FDA as "interchangeable" with the reference product, which may make substitutability more difficult than with traditional generic drugs.[267]

d. *OTC Drugs*

206. OTC drugs are pharmaceutical products that can be purchased without a health-care professional prescription, in either a pharmacy or other retail establishment.

207. In both the US and the EU, separate product markets are traditionally defined for OTC medicines and prescription pharmaceuticals.[268] This separation takes into account the fact that the medical indications (including possible side-effects), legal framework, marketing, and distribution of OTC medicines all tend to differ from prescription pharmaceuticals, even when their active ingredients are otherwise identical.[269] Of particular note, OTC medicines are normally not prescribed by a physician and involve pharmacists taking a more significant role, and patients usually bear the full cost of the medicine.[270] As such, while the marketing of prescription drugs targets prescribers, marketing of OTC products tends to reach more directly to pharmacists and consumers.

---

263 *See, e.g.*, Case COMP/M.7559, *Pfizer/Hospira* ¶25 (2015) (defining a relevant product market for infliximab pharmaceuticals, including both the originator and its biosimilars).

264 *See, e.g.*, CMA, Case No. 50236, *Remicade: alleged abusive discount scheme* (2015).

265 Case COMP/M.5479, *Lonza / Teva / JV* ¶12 (2009).

266 Case COMP/M.7559, *Pfizer/Hospira* ¶¶18, 32–38 (2015).

267 Summary Report on the FDA/FTC Workshop on a Competitive Marketplace for Biosimilars (Mar. 9, 2020), *available at* https://www.fda.gov/media/165710/download.

268 *See, e.g.*, Complaint, *In the Matter of Prestige Brand Holdings, Inc. and Insight Pharmaceuticals Corp.*, FTC File No. 141-0159, ¶7 (Aug. 28, 2014) (defining a separate market for branded OTC motion sickness medication); Case COMP/M.6613, *Watson/Actavis* (2012).

269 Case COMP/M.5253, *Sanofi-Aventis/Zentiva* (2009).

270 Case COMP/M.5865, *Teva/Ratiopharm* (2010).

208. Although the general rule is to define separate markets for OTC drugs and prescription pharmaceuticals, the European Commission has noted that in some cases, it may not be excluded that these products compete with each other, especially in cases where the status of the drug is not clearly limited to either OTC or prescription.[271] This is in particular the case when the same drug can be delivered either with a prescription – and therefore reimbursed by health insurance – or without a prescription at the patient's own expense. In cases where an OTC drug can also be prescribed by a medical practitioner, the price of the OTC drug may be a key factor in the patient's decision to obtain a prescription before purchasing the product, which may impact the market definition.[272]

209. When defining the market for an OTC drug, the European Commission usually relies on the US Consumer Health Classification (CHC) standard developed and managed by IQVIA. Just as the European Commission starts at the ATC3 level for prescription pharmaceuticals, the European Commission uses the third CHC level (CHC3) as a starting point but has also considered narrower definitions for a relevant product market.[273] In addition, with regard to OTC drugs, the European Commission acknowledged that there could be more substitutability between galenic forms.[274]

210. The FTC has viewed branded OTC drugs that treat the same condition (e.g., motion sickness medications, nighttime sleep aids) as within the same product market.[275] Despite generating substantial sales, the FTC has viewed private label OTC products as part of a separate market because OTC products allegedly "have only a limited competitive impact in the market because they are usually priced at a fixed discount to branded OTC… products, and are not promoted or marketed."[276]

e. *Pipeline Products*

211. The notion of potential competition and entry in the pharmaceutical sector is relatively unique given the extended process required for product development and regulatory approval, which has key public milestones that are known to all market players. The process begins with the discovery and development of the potential new product and related preclinical trials. Once preclinical research is complete, researchers move on to several phase of clinical drug development through the following three stages of clinical trials before a pharmaceutical product can be submitted for regulatory approval.[277]

---

271 Case COMP/M.5778, *Novartis/Alcon* ¶14 (2010); Case COMP/M.8889, *Teva/PGT OTC Assets* ¶25 (2018).

272 Case COMP/M.5865, *Teva/Ratiopharm* (2010).

273 Case COMP/M.10247, *CVC / Cooper* (2021).

274 Case COMP/M.5865, *Teva/Ratiopharm* (2010).

275 Complaint, *In the Matter of Johnson & Johnson and Pfizer Inc.*, FTC Docket No. C-4180, §§ 8–17 (Dec. 12, 2006); Complaint, *In the Matter of Prestige Brands Holdings, Inc. and Insight Pharmaceuticals Corp.*, FTC Docket No. C-4487m §§ 5–7 (Aug. 28, 2014).

276 Complaint, *In the Matter of Prestige Brands Holdings, Inc. and Insight Pharmaceuticals Corp.*, FTC Docket No. C-4487, ¶7 (Aug. 28, 2014).

277 Although covered by different regulations, these phases are relatively consistent in the US and the EU. *Compare* FDA, Step 3: Clinical Research (Jan. 4, 2018), *available at* https://www.fda.gov/patients/drug-development-process/step-3-clinical-research, *with* European Federation of Pharmaceutical Industries and Associations, Clinical Trials, *available at* https://www.efpia.eu/about-medicines/development-of-medicines/regulations-safety-supply/clinical-trials/.

Phase	Description
I	An initial trial of the product on around 20–80 healthy volunteers to determine if the product leads to any severe side effects.
II	An initial trial with several hundred participants who have the condition the medication is intended to treat to evaluate the effect the product has on the underlying condition and to evaluate any potential side effects that develop in patients with the condition.
III	A secondary trial with thousands of participants who have the condition the medication is intended to treat to evaluate the efficacy and safety of the product in comparison to other treatments for the same condition.

212. While well-defined, this process can be cumbersome, time-consuming, and expensive. On average, it takes at least 10 years for a new product to complete this process, with more than half of that period spent in the three clinical trial phases outlined above. The overwhelming majority of pipeline products never make it through the full process.

213. In the US and, to a lesser extent, the EU, the uncertainty surrounding approval typically means that early-stage pipeline products are not viewed as competitive constraints on current market participants. As the FTC has summarized in the merger context:

> New entry would require significant investment of time and money for product research and development, regulatory approval by the FDA, developing clinical history supporting the long-term efficacy of the product, and establishing a US sales and service infrastructure. Such development efforts are difficult, time-consuming, and expensive, and often fail to result in a competitive product reaching the market.[278]

214. As a result of this uncertainty, in the context of assessing possible competitors to merging entities, the FTC commonly alleges that market entry by third parties would not be timely, likely, or sufficient.[279]

215. At the same time, since merger analysis is future-looking, the US Antitrust Agencies and the European Commission typically do look closely at the merging

---

[278] FTC, Analysis of Agreement Containing Consent Orders to Aid Public Comment, *In the Matter of AbbVie Inc. and Allergan plc*, FTC File No. 191-0169, 3 (May 5, 2020), *available at* https://www.ftc.gov/system/files/documents/cases/191_0169_abbvie_and_allergan_-_aapc.pdf (the Analysis of Agreement in the Matter of AbbVie Inc./ Allergan plc).

[279] *See, e.g.*, Complaint, *In the Matter of Stryker and Wright Medical*, FTC Docket No. C-4728, ¶10 (Nov. 3, 2020); Complaint, *In the Matter of Pfizer Inc., Upjohn, Inc., Viatris, Inc, Mylan Inc., and Utah Acquisition Sub Inc.*, FTC Docket No. C-4727, ¶20 (Oct. 13, 2020); Complaint, *In the Matter of Össur Hf, Össur American Holdings, Inc., and College Park Industries, Inc.*, FTC Docket No. C-4712, ¶11 (Apr. 6, 2020); Complaint, *In the Matter of Danaher Corp. and General Electric Co.*, FTC Docket No. C-4710, ¶16–17 (Mar. 10, 2020); Complaint, *In the Matter of Bristol-Myers Squibb Co. and Celgene Corp.*, FTC Docket No. 4690, ¶8 (Nov. 15, 2019); Complaint, *In the Matter of Grifols S.A. and Grifols Shared Services North America Inc.*, FTC Docket No C-4654, ¶14 (July 31, 2018); Complaint, *In the Matter of Abbott Laboratories and Alere, Inc.*, FTC Docket No. C-4625, ¶10 (Sept. 28, 2017); Complaint, *In the Matter of Integra Lifesciences Holdings Corp. and Johnson & Johnson*, FTC Docket No. C-4624, ¶13 (Sept. 26, 2017).

parties' pipeline products to ensure that the merger does not eliminate future competition. When performing this analysis, the US Antitrust Agencies and the European Commission often define markets for pipeline products more broadly than existing pharmaceuticals. The European Commission, for example, typically assesses pipeline products by therapeutic indication, mode of administration, and line of treatment when relevant.[280] At the same time, the European Commission has explained that, when "research and development activities are assessed in terms of importance for future markets, the product market definition can be less clearly defined than for marketed products, reflecting the intrinsic uncertainty in analyzing products that do not exist yet."[281]

216. Traditionally, pipeline products in Phases II and III clinical trials – those that are most likely to come on the market in the next 3–5 years – have received the most attention from the US Antitrust Agencies and the European Commission.[282] Nevertheless, both the US Antitrust Agencies and the European Commission have shown a willingness to reach even further back to Phase I trials and broader innovation markets.

217. To some extent, the relevant product market defined by the US Antitrust Agencies and the European Commission when evaluating pipeline products may depend upon the specific nature of the overlap. For example, one circumstance that frequently arises in merger analysis is the so-called "pipeline-to-product" situation, where one party has a pipeline product that competes with an approved pharmaceutical product of the other party.[283] In such cases, the US Antitrust Agencies and the European Commission may be more likely to limit its inquiry to potentially competitive pipeline products that are in Phase III clinical trials or even pending regulatory approval where regulatory approval is expected in the near future.[284]

218. A key exception for pipeline-to-product cases arises for biosimilars, which, because of the different nature of biologics, are required to go through clinical trials. In these cases, the European Commission has explained that the key step in the development of a biosimilar product is establishing similarity, which occurs prior to clinical trials, which is the point at which the European Commission considers the eventual launch "sufficiently certain for the pipeline to be considered a potential competitive constraint."[285]

219. There is also the so-called "pipeline-to-pipeline" situation, where both parties have pipeline products that may be likely to compete in the future. In this situation, the US Antitrust Agencies and the European Commission may be more likely to also consider products in Phase I and Phase II of clinical trials. In particular, in

---

280 *See, e.g.*, Case COMP/M.1397, *Sanofi/Synthelabo* (1999).

281 Case COMP/M.9461, *AbbVie/Allergan* ¶11 (2020); *see also* Case COMP/M.7275, *Novartis/GlaxoSmithKline Oncology Business* ¶26 (2015).

282 *See, e.g.*, Case COMP/M.1397, *Sanofi/Synthelabo* (1999).

283 *See, e.g.*, Case COMP/M.7559, *Pfizer/Hospira* (2015); Case COMP/M.7275, *Novartis/GlaxoSmithKline Oncology Business* (2015).

284 *See, id.*; Analysis of Agreement Containing Consent Orders to Aid Public Comment, *In the Matter of Baxter International Inc., Claris Lifesciences Limited, and Arjun Handa*, FTC Docket No. C-4620, 2 (July 20, 2017); Analysis to Aid Public Comment, *In the Matter of Bristol-Myers Squibb/Celgene*, FTC File No. 191-0061 2–3 (Nov. 15, 2019).

285 Case COMP/M.5865, *Teva/Ratiopharm* ¶¶426–27 (2010).

oncology, the European Commission has considered the impact on competition of transactions involving the combination of Phase I and Phase II products.[286]

220. It is an open question whether the US Antitrust Agencies or the European Commission might define a broader relevant product market based on preclinical innovation or R&D efforts in the pharmaceutical sector. In the US, for example, the FTC has in the past investigated broader theories of harm to preclinical innovation markets potentially impacted by pharmaceutical mergers but stopped short of adopting a broader market for pharmaceutical innovation.[287]

221. Similarly, the European Commission has gone further in some non-pharmaceutical cases, focusing on so-called "innovation spaces." In the *Dow/Dupont* case, for example, the European Commission assessed competition at the innovation level by reference to areas where the parties both had overlapping lines of research and early pipeline products, or where such lines of research and early pipeline products overlapped with existing or upcoming products.[288] In this respect, the European Commission defined lines of research as "set[s] of scientists, patents, assets, equipment and chemical class(es) which are dedicated to a given discovery target whose final output are successive pipeline [active ingredients] targeting a given innovation space."[289] The European Commission also reviewed the overlap between the parties' R&D activities, defined as "resources, personnel, facilities, and other tangible and intangible assets dedicated to research, development and registration of new active ingredients (including lines of research, field testing facilities, registration capabilities)."[290]

---

286 *See, e.g.*, Case COMP/M.7275, *Novartis/GlaxoSmithKline Oncology Business* ¶¶85–94 (2015) (defining a relevant product market for competing clinical research programs "by reference to the mechanism of action of the pipeline products concerned, the cancer type for which the pipeline products are being trialed in clinical studies and the Phase of these clinical trials"); Case COMP/M.8401, *J&J/Actelion* (2017).

287 *See, e.g.*, FTC, *Statement of Chairman Joseph J. Simons, Commissioner Noah Joshua Phillips, and Commissioner Christine S. Wilson Concerning the Proposed Acquisition of Allergan plc by AbbVie Inc.*, File No. 191-0169, 9–10 (May 5, 2020), *available at* https://www.ftc.gov/system/files/documents/public_statements/1574619/abbvie-allergan_majority_statement_5-5-20.pdf, (the Simons, Phillips, Wilson AbbVie Statement) ("Consistent with the Horizontal Merger Guidelines, staff investigated whether the 'merger will diminish innovation competition by combining two of a very small number of firms with the strongest capabilities to successfully innovate in a specific direction.'"); Statement of Commissioner Christine Wilson *In the Matter of Bristol-Myers Squibb Company/Celgene Corporation*, FTC File No. 191-0061, 1 n. 2 (Nov. 15, 2019) ("The investigation identified a likely harm to innovation involving oral products to treat moderate-to-severe psoriasis; the identified overlap includes a product that is still in development by BMS. In addition, staff investigated whether the proposed transaction would decrease innovation competition; instead, the investigation found that reduced innovation competition was unlikely."); Statement of the FTC Concerning *Pfizer/Wyeth*, FTC File No. 091-0053, 2, 3 (Oct. 14, 2009) ("Beyond the[] specific overlaps, the staff thoroughly investigated whether the transaction could have an impact on competition in human pharmaceutical markets more broadly, whether on innovation, the intellectual property landscape, clinical development, or marketing."); Statement of Chairman Timothy J. Muris *In the Matter of Genzyme Corporation/Novazyme Pharmaceuticals, Inc.*, FTC File No. 021-0026, 12, 17 (Jan. 13, 2004) ("[T]he competition between Genzyme and Novazyme would not have had a substantial effect on the amount or timing of Genzyme's or Novazyme's R&D spending on Pompe, or on when the first Pompe therapy would reach the market... There is no evidence that the merger reduced R&D spending on either the Genzyme or the Novazyme program or slowed progress along either of the R&D paths.").

288 Case COMP/M.7932, *Dow/Dupont* ¶1957 (2017); *see also* Case COMP/M.8084, *Bayer/Monsanto* (2018).

289 Case COMP/M.7932, *Dow/Dupont* ¶1958 (2017).

290 *Id.* ¶1957.

222. It is possible that the European Commission would follow a similar approach in the life sciences industry. Along similar lines, the study report on the relevant market issued by the European Commission in 2021 has suggested defining relevant product markets for pipeline products based on existing products when R&D efforts are "directed towards specific products, their link to existing products is clear, and substitutability between innovative and existing products is likely high" and emphasized that R&D processes may be more predictable in regulated industries such as the pharmaceutical sector.[291] This recommendation hints at looking further down the development pipeline to earlier stage pharmaceutical products.

f. *APIs and Excipients*

223. Beyond finished pharmaceutical products, both the US Antitrust Agencies and the European Commission have considered separate upstream markets for the development, production, supply, and marketing of APIs and inactive pharmaceutical ingredients (excipients).[292] At a high level, the European Commission has suggested that each API would constitute a separate market on its own, but that in some cases APIs might be more appropriately grouped by application.[293]

224. As far as other excipients, the European Commission has considered that separate product markets should be defined for each excipients based on the substance from which each excipient was made (e.g., lactose, starch, cellulose), and that these substance-based markets could be further divided into relevant sub-markets (i.e., lactose can be sub-segmented into wet granulation lactose and direct compression lactose).[294] The European Commission also previously considered whether separate markets should be defined for binders and coatings but ultimately left the market definition open.[295]

g. *Contract Manufacturing Services*

225. Contract Manufacturing Organization (CMO) and Contract Development and Manufacturing Organization (CDMO) providers manufacture finished dose pharmaceutical products or APIs on behalf of third-party pharmaceutical companies. These CMO/CDMO services are likely to be considered in a separate market from the finished pharmaceutical products made available for sale by pharmaceutical companies under their own label.

226. The European Commission has previously considered the market for CMO/CDMO services and whether it could be segmented into four separate markets for (i) solid dose and powder pharmaceuticals, (ii) liquids and semi-solid pharmaceuticals,

---

291 Study Report on the Relevant Market, Box 13; *available at* https://competition-policy.ec.europa.eu/system/files/2021-06/kd0221712enn_market_definition_notice_2021_1.pdf.

292 *See, e.g.*, Complaint, *In the Matter of Teva Pharmaceutical Industries Ltd./Allergan PLC*, FTC File No. 151-0196, ¶¶5, 8 (July 27, 2016), (defining separate relevant product markets for various APIs); Case COMP/M.5865, *Teva/Ratiopharm* (2010); Case COMP/M.3394, *Johnson & Johnson/Johnson & Johnson MSD Europe* (2010).

293 Case COMP/M.10247, *CVC/Cooper* (2021); Case COMP/M. 7746, *Teva/Allergan Generics* (2016).

294 Case COMP/M.10247, *CVC/Cooper* (2021); Case COMP/M.5046, *Friesland Foods/Campina* (2008).

295 Case COMP/M.6313, *Ashland/International Specialty Products* (2011).

(iii) sterile liquid pharmaceuticals, and (iv) medicated confectionary pharmaceuticals.[296] Separately, the European Commission has also considered that the markets of the provision of CMO/CDMO for finished pharmaceutical products and APIs should be viewed as separate product markets.[297]

B. *Pharmaceutical Distribution*

227. Beyond product markets for finished pharmaceutical products and upstream inputs like APIs and excipients or contract manufacturing services, separate product markets may be defined for supplying pharmaceuticals at various levels of the supply chain, including: (a) wholesale or supply services; and (b) pharmacies and retail distribution.

a. *Wholesalers and Supply Services*

228. Separate product markets have also been defined in both the US and the EU for the wholesale sale of finished pharmaceutical products.

229. **In the US**, at least one court has defined the relevant product market for wholesalers as a single market for the wholesale distribution of prescription drugs.[298] It is however worth noting that this case involved the largest national wholesalers, which had argued that the relevant product market should be defined more broadly to include the entire prescription drug industry, including direct manufacturer, mail order, and retail self-warehousing sales.[299] It is possible that narrower markets would be defined for more specific services provided by smaller or more specialized suppliers.

230. **In the EU**, the European Commission has more explicitly considered that the wholesale supply of pharmaceutical products does not constitute a single market but should be further subdivided on the basis of the following elements:[300]

- *Categories of Wholesalers.* Wholesalers can be distinguished between full-line wholesalers (i.e., wholesalers offering a full range of products, including prescription drugs and OTC products) and short-line wholesalers (i.e., wholesalers offering a smaller range of products, typically specific pharmaceuticals sold in large quantities). The European Commission considered in various cases, notably with regards to Germany and Belgium, that the two types of wholesalers will belong to separate markets in light of differences in product ranges, prices, and frequency of delivery.[301]
- *Categories of Customers.* Differences in purchasing and delivery patterns could also justify defining separate product markets depending on customer type. In the past, the European Commission has considered distinguishing

296 *See also* Case COMP/M.10238, *Nordic Capital/Leo Foundation/Leo Pharma* (2021); Case COMP/M.9962, *Mylan/Aspen's EU Thrombosis Business* (2020); Case M.5253, *Sanofi-Aventis/Zentiva* (2009); Case COMP/M.5953, *Reckitt Benckiser/SSL* (2010).

297 *See, e.g.*, Case COMP/M.10247, *CVC/Cooper* (2021); Case COMP/M.9315, *CHR. Hansen/Lonza/JV* (2019).

298 *FTC v. Cardinal Health*, 12 F. Supp. 2d 34, 45–46 (D.D.C. 1998).

299 *Id.*

300 *See, e.g.*, Case COMP/M.7818, *Mckesson/Udg Healthcare (Pharmaceutical Wholesale and Associated Businesses)* (2016).

301 *See, e.g.*, Case COMP/M.4301, *Alliance Boots/Cardinal Health* (2006); Case COMP/M.9711, *Alliance Healthcare Deutschland/Gehe Pharma Handel* (2020); Case COMP/M.7935, *Mckesson Deutschland/Belmedis/Cophana/Espafarmed/Alphar Partners/Sofiadis* (2016).

between wholesalers selling to: (i) retail pharmacies; (ii) dispensing doctors (i.e., healthcare professional licensed to dispense pharmaceuticals to patients who live in areas with few or no retail pharmacies); and (iii) hospitals.[302] However, the European Commission tends to leave the market definition open on this point, and it has even rejected such segmentation in other cases.[303]

- *Categories of Products.* Wholesalers can also be distinguished depending on product types, including: (i) prescription drugs; (ii) OTC products; (iii) originator, generic or parallel import pharmaceuticals; and (iv) whether the medicine may only be sold in retail pharmacies under the supervision of a pharmacist or is also in other outlets such as supermarkets.[304]

231. In each case, the analysis will consider the national Member State specificities and regulatory framework, and the relevant product market might not be defined in the same way in each Member State.

b. *Pharmacies and Other Retail Distribution*

232. In both the US and the EU, defining a relevant product market for pharmacies and other retail distributors can be complicated and may vary depending upon the specific products being sold and the different categories of customers for those products.

233. **In the US**, the FTC has separated "the provision of prescription medications by a licensed pharmacist who is able to provide usage advice and other relevant information as may be required by law" from the sale of OTC drugs. It has further defined separate product markets for pharmacy sales to patients who pay a price negotiated by or paid through a third party (such as an insurance plan or a pharmacy benefits manager) versus so-called "cash customers" who generally pay the price set by a pharmacy or the list price for a prescription drug or some discounted amount of a posted or list price.[305] The FTC also has defined separate relevant product markets for more specialized pharmacy services, including long term care pharmacies and nuclear pharmacies that sell radiopharmaceutical products.[306]

234. **In the EU,** the European Commission tends to consider that the market may be segmented based on the channel of distribution for the product, in particular

---

302 Case COMP/M.7818, *Mckesson/Udg Healthcare (Pharmaceutical Wholesale and Associated Businesses)* (2016); Case COMP/M.9711, *Alliance Healthcare Deutschland/Gehe Pharma Handel* (2020).

303 Case COMP/M.4301, *Alliance Boots/Cardinal Health* (2006).

304 Case COMP/M.7818, *Mckesson/Udg Healthcare (Pharmaceutical Wholesale and Associated Businesses)* (2016); Case COMP/M.9711, *Alliance Healthcare Deutschland/Gehe Pharma Handel* (2020).

305 *See, e.g.*, Complaint, *In the Matter of Rite Aid Corporation and The Jean Coutu Group (PJC), Inc.*, FTC File No. 061-0257, 2–3 (June 4, 2007).

306 *See, e.g.*, Complaint, *In the Matter of Omnicare, Inc.*, FTC File No. 111-0239, 6 (Jan. 27, 2012) (defining a relevant product market for long term care pharmacy products and services provided to Medicare Part D Sponsors for their skilled nursing home residents); Complaint, *In the Matter of Cardinal Health, Inc.*, FTC File No. 091-0136, 4 (July 21, 2011) (defining a relevant product market for the sale and distribution of low energy radio pharmaceuticals).

between prescription pharmaceuticals and OTC medicines.[307] Yet the situation is further complicated within the EU because of significant differences in the regulatory framework for the retail sale of pharmaceuticals across different Member States. As a result, the European Commission tends to rely on the decisional practice of NCAs as a guide to the national specificities of the countries where the relevant parties are active. A few examples are described below:

- *Ireland.* While not reaching definitive conclusions, the European Commission has considered segmentation by categories of products, especially between prescription and OTC medicines, as well as a specific market segment for the pharmacy services to hospitals, which present distinct features from community retail pharmacies.[308]
- *The Netherlands.* The European Commission has previously considered, based on precedents from the Authority for Consumers & Markets (ACM), that the market could be subdivided between: (i) regular pharmacies (the pharmacy "around the corner"); (ii) polyclinic pharmacies (associated with a hospital); and (iii) self-dispensing general practitioners.[309]
- *UK.* When the UK was still part of the EU, the European Commission considered possible subdivisions between: (i) "ethical" (prescription only medicines); (ii) "P medicines" (pharmacy only medicines that do not require a prescription but can only be dispensed by a pharmacist); and (iii) "GLS medicines" (medicines which do not need to be sold in pharmacies and can therefore be found in supermarkets).[310] At the time, the European Commission also considered that the provision of pharmacy services to hospitals could be a separate market.[311]

3. Geographic Markets in the Life Sciences

A. *Pharmaceuticals*

235. Due in part to strong national regulatory barriers, geographic markets for finished pharmaceutical products tend to be defined as at most national in scope.

236. **In the US**, the relevant geographic market for pharmaceuticals is typically defined broadly as covering the country as a whole, because the US has a single national regulatory scheme for drug approvals and sales.[312] Exceptions are possible but,

---

307 *See, e.g.*, Case COMP/M.7494, *Brocacef/Mediq Netherlands* (2015).

308 Case COMP/M.7818, *Mckesson/UDG Healthcare (Pharmaceutical Wholesale and Associated Businesses)* (2016).

309 Case COMP/M.7494, *Brocacef/Mediq Netherlands* (2015).

310 Case COMP/M.7721, *Celesio/Sainsbury's UK pharmacy business* (2015).

311 *Id.*

312 *See, e.g.*, Complaint, *In the Matter of Amneal Holdings, LLC*, FTC File No. 181-0017, ¶6 (Apr. 27, 2018); Complaint, *In the Matter of Mylan N.V.*, FTC File No. 161-0102, ¶7 (July 27, 2016); Complaint, *In the Matter of C.H. Boehringer Sohn AG & Co. KG*, FTC File No. 161-0077, ¶9 (Dec. 27, 2016); Complaint, *In the Matter of Lupin Ltd.*, FTC File No. 151-0202, ¶7 (Feb. 19, 2016); Complaint, *In the Matter of Watson Pharmaceuticals / Actavis Inc.*, FTC File No. 121-0132, ¶6 (Oct. 15, 2012). Parties typically do not contest the national scope of the market in pharmaceutical matters. *See, e.g.*, *Mylan Pharmaceuticals v. Warner/Chilcott*, 838 F.3d 421, 435 n. 57 (3d Cir. 2016) ("Defendants do not contest Mylan's expert's conclusion that the relevant geographic market is the United States. We therefore focus solely on the product component.").

in practice, geographic markets for the manufacture and sale of pharmaceuticals are typically viewed as limited to the US.

237. **In the EU**, despite the existence of a centralized approval procedure for pharmaceutical products (*see* Chapter I), each Member State also has its own national regulatory scheme for drug approvals, pricing and sales. On that basis, the European Commission has typically defined the markets for the sales of finished pharmaceutical products (whether branded, generic, biosimilar, or OTC) as limited to the national, or EU Member State, level.[313]

238. Exceptions to this practice are certainly possible, especially for products or services that are less regulated or upstream from the production of a finished pharmaceutical product. The European Commission, for instance, has defined broader geographic markets for:

- pipeline pharmaceutical products, as (i) the assessment relates to R&D, which usually takes place on a global scale, and (ii) national regulations have a lower importance;[314]
- APIs and excipients (considered at least EEA-wide, if not worldwide in scope);[315] and
- CMO/CDMO services (considered at least EEA-wide, if not worldwide in scope).[316]

B. *Pharmaceutical Distribution*

239. In both the US and the EU, the relevant geographic market for the distribution of pharmaceutical products may be either national or more local depending on the level of the supply chain and the nature of competition with other distributors at that level.

a. *Wholesalers and Supply Services*

240. **In the US**, the relevant geographic market for wholesale sales may occur at both: (a) the national level (for customers that purchase nationally, including retailer chains, hospital chains, hospital group purchasing organizations, and some independent pharmacy buying groups); and (b) a more limited regional level (for smaller customers in smaller areas of the US).[317] Where wholesale markets are defined as narrower than the US as a whole, the specific contours of any regional geographic markets will depend upon the evidence presented to show that competition in this region is distinct from competition at the national level.

241. **In the EU**, the European Commission has similarly described how the geographic scope of wholesale markets can vary. Along those lines, the European Commission

---

313 *See, e.g.*, Case COMP/M.9995, *Permira/Neuraxpharm* ¶11 (2020); Case COMP/M.9962, *Mylan/Aspen's EU Thrombosis Business* ¶11 (2020); Case COMP/M.5865, *Teva/Ratiopharm* (2010).

314 Case COMP/M.9461, *AbbVie/Allergan* ¶13 (2020); Case COMP/M.7275, *Novartis/GlaxoSmithKline Oncology Business* ¶32 (2015); Case COMP/M.737, *Ciba-Geigy/Sandoz* ¶51 (1996).

315 Case COMP/M.1397, *Sanofi/Synthelabo* (1999); Case COMP/M.10247, *CVC/Cooper* (2021).

316 Case COMP/M.9962, *Mylan/Aspen´s EU Thrombosis Business* (2020); Case COMP/M.5953, *Reckitt Benckiser/SSL* (2010).

317 *See FTC v. Cardinal Health*, 12 F. Supp. 2d 34, 49–52 (D.D.C. 1998).

has noted in particular that most retail pharmacies will receive various deliveries each day from their wholesale supplier; as such, depending on the size of the Member State and its transport infrastructure, a wholesaler may or may not be able to serve the entire national territory. As a result, the European Commission has consistently considered that "wholesaling is either national or regional (sub-national) in scope."[318] As an example of a regional market, the European Commission has previously defined a regional wholesaling market by reference to a catchment area of 2 hours 14 minutes driving time (2 hours 30 minutes, minus 8 to 10 stops) around each depot.[319]

b. *Pharmacies and Other Retail Distribution*

242. Geographic markets for pharmacies and other retail distribution points are defined somewhat differently in the US and the EU.

243. **In the US**, pharmacy services – like other retail healthcare services – may be defined narrowly around local markets defined by demand substitutability.[320] However, where reimbursement for pharmacy services is negotiated at the national level, the FTC may allege a national market.[321]

244. **In the EU**, the European Commission will also evaluate competition from a demand substitutability standpoint, where the market has traditionally been viewed as fundamentally local in nature since patients will not cross the entire country to purchase needed medicines.[322] At the same time, the European Commission considers that in most countries there are national chains of retail pharmacies which implement national advertising and promotion campaigns and for which pricing decisions are usually taken on a national basis. For that reason, the European Commission also will assess competition from a supply side standpoint, where it typically considers that the geographic market is national in scope.[323]

---

318 Case COMP/M.7818, *Mckesson/Udg Healthcare (Pharmaceutical Wholesale and Associated Businesses)* ¶24 (2016). *See also* Case COMP/M.4301, *Alliance Boots/Cardinal Health* (2006); Case COMP/M.9711, *Alliance Healthcare Deutschland/Gehe Pharma Handel* (2020); Case COMP/M.7935, *Mckesson Deutschland/Belmedis/Cophana/Espafarmed/Alphar Partners/Sofiadis* (2016).

319 Case COMP/M.9711, *Alliance Healthcare Deutschland/Gehe Pharma Handel* (2020).

320 *See, e.g.*, Complaint, *In the Matter of Rite Aid Corp. / The Jean Coutu Group (PJC), Inc.*, FTC File No. 61-0257, ¶9 (June 4, 2007) (defining geographic markets for 24 small cities and towns, such as Berlin, NH, Lyndonville, VT, and Franklin, VA). *FTC v. Hackensack Meridian Health, Inc.*, No. 21-2603, 20 (3d Cir. Mar. 22, 2022) (affirming district court treatment of "Bergen County, including all hospitals that serve its residents," as a relevant geographic market for inpatient general acute care hospital services); Complaint, *In the Matter of Inova Health System Foundation / Price William Health System, Inc.*, FTC File No. 061-0166, ¶21 (May 9, 2008) (defining a geographic market for inpatient hospital services "in an area no larger than Northern Virginia or the Commonwealth of Virginia's Health Planning Region II ('HPR II') and Fauquier County").

321 *See, e.g.*, Complaint, *In the Matter of Omnicare, Inc.*, FTC File No. 111-0239, 6–7 (Jan. 27, 2012) (defining a national geographic market for long term care pharmacy products and services provided to Medicare Part D Sponsors for their skilled nursing facility residents).

322 The European Commission has previously considered a definition based on a specific radius around each pharmacy but ultimately left the definition open. *See, e.g.*, Case COMP/M.7494, *Brocacef/Mediq Netherlands* (2015); Case COMP/M.4301, *Alliance Boots/Cardinal Health* (2006).

323 *See, e.g.*, Case COMP/M.7494, *Brocacef/ Mediq Netherlands* (2015); Case COMP/M.4301, *Alliance Boots/ Cardinal Health* (2006).

III. Establishing Market Power

245. Competition law, on both sides of the Atlantic, aims at preserving free and fair competition in the market. To that end, an assessment of market power is often critical. In practice, however, there is no single one-size-fits-all approach to market power. Different perspectives emerge, for instance, from the distinct temporal assessment carried out in merger and non-merger cases. Merger cases by nature are forward-looking and more preventive, aiming to avoid strengthening of market power through combinations and acquisitions instead of organic growth. Non-merger cases, by contrast, examine current market dynamics, but even there the relevant measure of market power can depend upon the specific law applied in both the US and the EU. Different measures of market power can be appropriate in each of these circumstances, as described below.

1. Merger Cases

246. In both the US and the EU, the goal of merger control laws is to preserve fair competition by preventing undue concentrations of market power. The precise language for this objective varies across jurisdictions. In the US, the relevant standard is set forth in Section 7 of the Clayton Act, which prohibits mergers and acquisitions the effect of which "may be substantially to lessen competition, or to tend to create a monopoly."[324] In the EU, by contrast, the relevant standard is set forth in the EU Merger Regulation, which prohibits concentrations "which would significantly impede effective competition, in the common market or in a substantial part of it, in particular as a result of the creation or strengthening of a dominant position[.]"[325]

247. In practice, however, the US Antitrust Agencies and the European Commission take a similar approach in evaluating when transactions are likely to have adverse competitive effects. They take into account a wide array of factors, such as barriers to entry and any countervailing buyer power. This analysis is described at greater length in Chapter III below. At the same time, as a starting point, the US Antitrust Agencies and the European Commission look primarily at two areas to assess whether a proposed transaction may raise competitive concerns: (A) market shares; and (B) market concentration.

A. *Market Shares*

248. Both the US Antitrust Agencies and the European Commission typically look at market shares for an initial assessment of the potential for competitive harm.

249. **In the US**, this approach is informed by Supreme Court precedent explaining that "[t]he market share which companies may control by merging is one of the most important factors to be considered when determining the probable effects of the combination on effective competition in the relevant market."[326] While

---

324 15 U.S.C. § 18a. Mergers may also be challenged under the Sherman Act, 15 U.S.C. §§ 1–2, which prohibits agreements that unreasonably restrain trade as well as monopolization, attempted monopolization and conspiracy to monopolize, or the FTC Act, which focuses on unfair methods of competition and unfair or deceptive acts or practices.

325 Council Regulation 139/2004 (EU Merger Regulation), *supra* n. 64, Chapter II, art. 2(3).

326 *Brown Shoe Co. v. United States*, 370 U.S. 294, 343 (1962).

referencing market shares as "the primary index of market power," however, the Supreme Court added that "only a further examination of the particular market – its structure, history and probable future – can provide the appropriate setting for judging the probable anticompetitive effect of the merger."[327] Of note, the Supreme Court has never set a bottom market share threshold below which a merger is presumptively lawful.[328] By contrast, the Supreme Court has previously held that a combined market share of at least 30% was presumptively unlawful.[329] Based on this case law, parties with combined market shares of 30% or higher should be aware that their transactions may receive scrutiny.[330]

250. **In the EU,** the European Commission, relying on well-established case law, European Commission has explained that "very large market shares – 50% or more – may in themselves be evidence of the existence of a dominant market position."[331] At the same time, market shares above 50% are not dispositive; instead, the European Commission has emphasized that "smaller competitors may act as a sufficient constraining influence if, for example, they have the ability and incentive to increase their supplies."[332] Market shares below 50% are similarly not dispositive; to the contrary, the European Commission has explained that even parties whose combined market shares remain below 50% may "raise competition concerns in view of other factors such as the strength and number of competitors, the presence of capacity constraints or the extent to which the products of the merging parties are close substitutes."[333] Taking into account these factors, the European Commission has "in several cases considered mergers resulting in firms holding market shares between 40% and 50%, and in some cases below 40%, to lead to the creation or the strengthening of a dominant position."[334] There is however a presumption in the EU that combined market shares below 20–25% will not have adverse competitive effects.[335] Similarly, a vertical merger where

---

327 *Id.* 322.

328 *Cf. id.* 343–44 (finding a 5% share sufficient to determine probably anticompetitive effects); *United States v. Von's Grocery Co.*, 384 U.S. 270, 272–75 (1966) (finding a 7.5% share sufficient to show a substantial lessening of competition). While these cases involved low combined market shares, it is worth noting that those shares were calculated based on markets that were defined very broadly by modern standards.

329 *United States v. Philadelphia Nat'l Bank*, 374 U.S. 321, 364–65 (1963).

330 This market share analysis primarily applies to horizontal mergers (*i.e.*, between competitors at the same level of the supply chain), but vertical mergers (*i.e.*, between companies at different levels of the same supply chain) are generally also only likely receive scrutiny if at least one of the merging parties has already elevated market shares in its own relevant market).

331 European Commission, Guidelines on the assessment of horizontal mergers under the Council Regulation on the control of concentrations between undertakings (the EU Horizontal Merger Guidelines), 2004 OJ (C 31) 5, ¶17 (citing Case T-221/95, *Endemol v. Commission*, ECLI:EU:T:1999:85, ¶134 (Apr. 28, 1999) and Case T-102/96, *Gencor v. Commission*, ECLI:EU:T:1999:65, ¶205 (Mar. 25, 1999)).

332 *Id.*

333 *Id.*

334 *Id.* (citing Case COMP/M.2337, *Nestlé/Ralston Purina* ¶¶44–50 (2001) and Case COMP/IV/M.1221, *Rewe/Meinl* ¶¶98–114 (1999)).

335 EU Horizontal Merger Guidelines indicate that below 25% combined market share a merger is unlikely to restrict competition (¶18); the European Commission Notice on a simplified procedure for treatment of certain concentrations under Council Regulation 139/2004 2013 OJ (C 366) 5 however sets the bar a little lower, allowing horizontal mergers where parties have a combined market share below 20% to be reviewed under the simplified procedure.

neither party's share exceeds 30% will be seen as unlikely to adversely affect competition.[336]

251. Here it is worth noting that, when calculating market shares, past market shares may not always be an appropriate basis for a forward-looking analysis.

252. **In the US**, for example, the Supreme Court has previously found that evidence of past market shares was not an appropriate indicator of market power where evidence existed indicating that resource constraints would limit a company's ability to compete in the future.[337]

253. **In the EU**, the General Court has agreed with the European Commission that in highly dynamic market environments (like consumer and enterprise communications services), even exorbitantly high market shares may turn out to be ephemeral, such that other means of establishing market power may need to be relied upon.[338] To the contrary, small market shares may underestimate the market position of a party which could be a significant competitive force due to e.g., pipeline products.[339]

B. *Market Concentration*

254. Beyond the merging parties' market shares, the US Antitrust Agencies and the European Commission also look to measures of market concentration to get a better sense of the competitive significance of the merging parties within their market.

255. At the most basic level, market concentration can be measured by the number of competitors in the market.[340] At a higher level, the US Antitrust Agencies and the European Commission also have traditionally looked to the Herfindahl–Hirschman Index (HHI) as a guide.[341]

256. The HHI is a simple metric that is calculated by summing the squares of the individual firms' market shares, for a maximum combined HHI score of 10,000 (for a market consisting of only one monopolist or dominant firm). This methodology is perceived as valuable because it gives proportionately greater weight to larger market shares. In practice, the US Antitrust Agencies and the European Commission look to both the value of the post-merger HHI and the increase in the post-merger HHI over the pre-merger HHI to evaluate the merger's effect on market concentration. At the same time, the US Antitrust Agencies and the European Commission have historically used different HHI thresholds to evaluate whether a merger requires additional scrutiny.

257. **In the US**, in their 2010 US Horizontal Merger Guidelines, the US Antitrust Agencies divided markets into the following categories by HHI level.

---

336 European Commission Notice on a simplified procedure for treatment of certain concentrations under Council Regulation 139/2004 2013 OJ (C 366) 5, ¶5.

337 *United States v. General Dynamics Corp.*, 415 U.S. 486, 501–02 (1974).

338 Case COMP/M.6281, *Microsoft/Skype* ¶¶78, 99 (2011); Case T-79/12, *Cisco Systems & Messagenet v. Commission* ECLI:EU:T:2013:635, ¶69 (Dec. 11, 2013).

339 EU Horizontal Merger Guidelines, *supra* n. 331, Chapter II, ¶38. *See also* Article 22 Guidance.

340 US Horizontal Merger Guidelines, *supra* n. 179, Chapter II, ¶5.3; EU Horizontal Merger Guidelines, *supra* n. 331, Chapter II, ¶17.

341 US Horizontal Merger Guidelines, *supra* n. 179, Chapter II, ¶5.3; EU Horizontal Merger Guidelines, *supra* n. 331, Chapter II, ¶¶19–21.

HHI	Category	Characterization
Under 1500	Unconcentrated	Unlikely to have adverse competitive effects and ordinarily require no further analysis
1500 to 2500	Moderately Concentrated	Potentially raise significant competitive concerns and often warrant scrutiny when HHI increases by more than 100 points
Above 2500	Highly Concentrated	Potentially raise significant competitive concerns and often warrant scrutiny when HHI increases by 100 to 200 points and presumed to enhance market power when HHI increases by more than 200 points

258. In the EU, the European Commission, has historically defined the following categories for its analysis.

HHI	Characterization
Under 1000	Unlikely to identify horizontal competition concerns or to require extensive analysis
1000 to 2000	Unlikely to identify horizontal competition concerns when HHI increases by less than 250 points
Above 2000	Unlikely to identify horizontal competition concerns when HHI increases by less than 150 points, except in special circumstances[342]

259. In the EU, there is no HHI level that gives rise to a presumption of the existence of competitive concerns.

2. Non-Merger Cases

260. An assessment of market power is also often necessary for non-merger cases in the US and the EU. Indeed, establishing market power is a basic requirement for many non-merger cases. Of course, this is not always the case; for some claims, especially in the context of anticompetitive agreements considered per se illegal, the mere fact of entering into the agreement can be sufficient to establish a violation without establishing market power. Nevertheless, even where it is not a requirement, establishing market power can be important when considering anticompetitive effects.

261. As in merger cases, an assessment of market power in non-merger cases takes into account a wide range of competitive factors, including market structure, barriers to entry, countervailing buyer power, and any vertical integration at different levels of the supply chain. As a starting point, however, both the US Antitrust Agencies

342 *See* EU Horizontal Merger Guidelines, *supra* n. 331, Chapter II, ¶10 (defining special circumstances as those involving: (a) a potential entrant or a recent entrant with a small market share; (b) important innovators in ways not reflected in market shares; (c) significant cross-shareholdings among the market participants; (d) a maverick firm with a high likelihood of disrupting coordinated conduct; (e) indications of past or ongoing coordination, or facilitating practices; or (f) a merging party with a pre-merger market share at or above 50%).

and the European Commission tend to look at market shares as an initial indicator and proxy for market power, as described below.

A. *Monopoly Power and Single-Firm Dominance*

262. **In the US**, the standard for market power in non-merger cases focuses on "monopoly power," which has been defined by the US Supreme Court as "the power to control prices or exclude competition."[343] In practice, barring more direct evidence of control over pricing or the power to exclude rivals, US courts rely on market shares as a proxy for market power.[344] The Supreme Court has established that market shares above 66% would be sufficient to establish monopoly power,[345] but the Supreme Court has never set a lower limit. That said, lower courts generally required market shares of at least 50% to establish monopoly power.[346]

263. **In the EU**, the standard for market power in non-merger cases focuses on whether an entity has a "dominant position," which is defined as "a position of economic strength enjoyed by an undertaking which enables it to prevent effective competition being maintained on the relevant market by giving it the power to behave to an appreciable extent independently of its competitors, customers and ultimately of its consumers."[347] In practice, EU courts consider that a market share exceeding 50% constitutes a very large market share and triggers a presumption of dominance.[348] By contrast, the European Commission stated that a company with a market share below 40% is unlikely to be dominant,[349] although a significant discrepancy between the market shares of the market leader and those of its closest competitor (e.g., where the market leader has twice the market shares of the second player) may still indicate dominance.

264. In both the US and the EU, the concept of market power can be applied across a variety of separate relevant markets. While discussion often focuses on the primary products or services sold by a company, for example, market power also may be determined separately for aftermarket or add-on parts or services that are ancillary to the company's main activities.[350] Similarly, while discussions about monopoly power and dominance often focus on sellers, a firm also can be a

---

343 *Eastman Kodak Co. v. Image Technical Services, Inc.*, 504 U.S. 451, 481 (1992) (quoting *United States v. E.I. du Pont de Nemours & Co.*, 351 U.S. 377, 391 (1956)); *United States v. Grinnell Corp.*, 384 U.S. 563, 571 (1966) (same).

344 *Jefferson Parish Hospital District No. 2 v. Hyde*, 466 U.S. 2, 17 (1984); *Eastman Kodak Co*, 504 U.S. 469 n. 15; *Grinnell Corp.*, 384 U.S. at 571 (1966); *United States v. Microsoft*, 253 F.3d 34, 51 (D.C. Cir. 2001) (*en banc*).

345 *Eastman Kodak Co*, 504 U.S. 481; *Grinnell Corp.*, 384 U.S. 571.

346 Brian A. Facey & Dany H. Assaf, *Monopolization and Abuse of Dominance in Canada, the United States, and the European Union: A Survey*, 70 ANTITRUST L.J. 513, 537, n. 100 (2002).

347 Case 27/7, *United Brands Company and United Brands Continentaal BV v. Commission*, ECLI:EU:C:1978:22, ¶65 (Feb. 14, 1978); Case 322/81, *NV Nederlandsche Banden Industrie Michelin*, ECLI:EU:C:1983:313, ¶57 (Nov. 9, 1983).

348 Case C-62/86, *AKZO Chemie BV v. Commission*, ECLI:EU:C:1991:286, ¶60 (July 3, 1991); Case T-30/89, *H ilti v. Commission*, ECLI:EU:T:1991:70, ¶89 (1991); Case T-83/91, *Tetra Pak v. Commission*, ECLI:EU:T:19 94:246, ¶109 (Oct. 6, 1994).

349 *See*, https://competition-policy.ec.europa.eu/antitrust/procedures/article-102-investigations_fr.

350 *See, e.g., Eastman Kodak Co*, 504 U.S. at 477–78 (upholding allegations of market power in a market for aftermarket parts and service); Case 226/84, *British Leyland Public Limited Company v. Commission*, ECLI:EU:C:1986:421, (Nov. 11, 1986).

"buyer's monopoly" (monopsonist) or a dominant purchaser.[351] In both the US and the EU, the same legal standards apply to a monopsonist or dominant purchaser as to a monopolist or dominant seller.[352]

B. *Collective Dominance*

265. Beyond single-firm dominance, the EU has adopted a notion of collective dominance to address certain rare cases where a group of firms with certain characteristics holds significant market power. Collective dominance is rooted in the wording of Article 102 TFEU, which refers to a dominant position held by "one or more" undertakings. According to the EU case law, collective dominance can be established in two types of situations.

266. First, collective dominance can be established for so-called "linked undertakings" when two or more independent firms are "united by such economic links that, by virtue of that fact, together they hold a dominant position *vis-à-vis* the other operators on the same market."[353] For the purpose of establishing collective dominance, economic links can be demonstrated through agreements or licenses between the parties.[354]

267. Second, collective dominance can be established based on the structure of the market absent any agreement or legal link.[355] Though a high bar, collective dominance can be shown based on market structure when each of the following three criteria are met: (a) the relevant market is oligopolistic and transparent; (b) market participants are capable of retaliation; and (c) other competitive constraints do not restrain the market participants.[356] For the first criteria in particular, the General Court has found that "the market structures which encourage oligopolistic conduct most are those in which two, three or four suppliers each hold approximately the same market share, for example two suppliers each holding 40% of the market, three suppliers each holding between 25% and 30% of the market, or four suppliers each holding approximately 25% of the market."[357] Conversely, the European Commission found that a collective dominant position can be excluded in markets that are characterized by asymmetric market positions.[358]

---

351 *Weyerhaeuser Co. v. Ross-Simmons Hardwood Lumber Co. Inc.*, 549 U.S. 312, 320 (2007).

352 *See, e.g., id.* 322 ("The kinship between monopoly and monopsony suggests that similar legal standards should apply to claims of monopolization and to claims of monopolization."); Case T-219/99, *British Airways v. Commission* ECLI:EU:T:2003:343, ¶101 (Dec. 17, 2003) ("[T]he fact that BA is to be regarded as an undertaking in a dominant position in its capacity as a purchaser of services, rather than as a provider of services, is irrelevant.").

353 *See* Joined Cases T-68/89, T-77/89 and T-78/89, *Società Italiana Vetro SpA, Fabbrica Pisana SpA and PPG Vernante Pennitalia SpA v. Commission*, ECLI:EU:T:1992:38, ¶358 (Mar. 10, 1992).

354 *See id.*; *See also* judgment of the Court in C-179/16, *F. Hoffmann-La Roche Ltd and Others*, ¶¶38, 48 (Jan. 23, 2018), cited above.

355 *See* Joined Cases C-395/96 P and C-396/96 P, *Compagnie maritime belge transports SA/Compagnie maritime belge SA and Dafra-Lines A/S v. Commission*, ECLI:EU:C:2000:132, ¶45 (Mar. 16, 2000).

356 *See generally* Case T-342/99, *Airtours plc v. Commission*, ECLI:EU:T:2004:192, (June 28, 2004); Case T-193/02, *Laurent Piau v. Commission*, ECLI:EU:T:2005:22, (Jan. 26, 2005).

357 *See* T-102/96, *Gencor*, ECLI:EU:T:1999:65, ¶134 (Mar. 25, 1999).

358 *See* Case COMP/IV/M.358, *Pilkington-Techint/SIV* (1993); Case COMP/IV/M.523, *Akzo Nobel/Monsanto* (1995); Case COMP/IV/M.1440, *Lucent Technologies/Ascend Communications* (1999); Case COMP/M.1943, *Telefónica/Endemol* (2000); Case COMP/M.6106, *Caterpillar/MWM* (2011).

C. *Note on Intellectual Property Rights and Market Power*

268. While patents and other IP rights may provide their holders with the right to exclude, such rights do not necessarily confer market power. The reason is simple: most products covered by IP rights still face actual or potential competition from other close substitutes.[359] Nevertheless, where products covered by IP rights are deemed not to have other close substitutes, those products may be deemed to have market power. This situation frequently arises in the pharmaceutical sector when branded originator drugs are nearing the end of their patent protection and face potential competition from generic or biosimilar products.[360]

359 *See, e.g.*, DOJ & FTC Antitrust IP Guidelines, *supra* n. 252, Chapter II, § 2.2 ("Although the intellectual property right confers the power to exclude with respect to the specific product, process, or work in question, there will often be sufficient actual or potential close substitutes for such product, process, or work to prevent the exercise of market power.").

360 *See, e.g.*, Case C-307/18, *Generics (UK) Ltd and Others*, ECLI:EU:C:2020:52, ¶7, 124–25, 141–72 (Jan. 30, 2020), (finding that GSK held a dominant position for sales of paroxetine, an originator drug marketed under the brand name Seroxat, because other similar serotonin re-uptake inhibitors "exercised little pressure on the prices of Seroxat set by GSK" and holding that potential settlements intended to delay the entry of potential settlers could constitute "an abuse of a dominant position" under certain conditions).

CHAPTER III

Mergers and Acquisitions

Alec Burnside and Rani Habash*

* The authors would like to thank Marjolein de Backer, Isabella Egetenmeir, Jonathan Greengarden, Konstantin Medvedovsky, and Thirith von Doeren for their very valuable help and contribution to this chapter.

269. The pharmaceutical industry is characterized by two features that impact merger control review. First, R&D is part and parcel of the industry, with a broad spectrum of companies involved in different stages from research to the marketing of products. Second, as discussed in Chapter I, the sector is subject to a comprehensive legislative and regulatory framework. These factors impact the dynamics of competition and therefore play an important role in the review of pharmaceutical mergers both in the EU and the US.[1]

270. As identified in its EC Pharmaceutical Enforcement Report, the European Commission considers three main risks to competition: (1) price increases for some medicines, (2) depriving patients and the national healthcare systems of some medicinal products, and (3) diminishing innovation in relation to certain treatments.[2] In the US, where the FTC typically is in charge of merger reviews, enforcement has similarly been concerned about the impact of mergers on prices, consumer choice, and innovation.[3]

271. Parties merging companies may see more harmonized and aggressive enforcement between the US and EU authorities following a March 2021 initiative to establish a cross-Atlantic working group that aims to "bring enhanced scrutiny and more detailed analysis" to pharmaceutical mergers.[4] As one FTC Commissioner explained: "Working hand in hand with international and domestic enforcement partners, we intend to take an aggressive approach to tackling anticompetitive pharmaceutical mergers."[5] The European Commission's press release added that "the number of mergers in the pharmaceutical sector has grown in recent years, and there is the need to scrutinize closely to detect those that could lead to higher drug prices, lower innovation or anticompetitive conduct."[6] The cross-Atlantic working group has solicited public input from all stakeholders about relevant theories of harm, the effects of pharmaceutical mergers on innovation, the relevance of regulatory processes, market definition, relevant evidence, and effective remedies.[7] In June 2022, the FTC and DOJ also organized a two-day public workshop. The

---

1 Given many commonalities in the EU and US approaches to assessing pharmaceutical mergers, Chapter III compares and contrasts the analyses in both jurisdictions together where similarities exist.

2 Report from the European Commission to the Council and the European Parliament, Competition enforcement in the pharmaceutical sector (EC Pharmaceutical Enforcement Report) (2009–2017), ¶11 (Jan. 28, 2019), *available at* https://ec.europa.eu/competition/sectors/pharmaceuticals/report2019/report_en.pdf.

3 FTC, Overview of FTC Actions in Pharmaceutical Products and Distribution, 26–75 (June 2019), *available at* https://www.ftc.gov/system/files/attachments/competition-policy-guidance/overview_of_ftc_actions_in_pharmaceutical_products_and_distribution.pdf.

4 European Commission, Press Release IP/21/1203, *Competition: The European Commission forms a Multilateral Working Group with leading competition authorities to exchange best practices on pharmaceutical mergers* (Mar. 16, 2021), *available at* https://ec.europa.eu/commission/presscorner/detail/en/ip_21_1203.

5 FTC, Press Release, *FTC Announces Multilateral Working Group to Build a New Approach to Pharmaceutical Mergers* (Mar. 16, 2021), *available at* https://www.ftc.gov/news-events/news/press-releases/2021/03/ftc-announces-multilateral-working-group-build-new-approach-pharmaceutical-mergers.

6 European Commission, Press Release IP/21/1203, *supra* n. 4, Chapter III.

7 FTC, Press Release, *Multilateral Pharmaceutical Merger Task Force Seeks Public Input* (May 11, 2021), *available at* https://www.ftc.gov/news-events/news/press-releases/2021/05/multilateral-pharmaceutical-merger-task-force-seeks-public-input.

discussions were held to provide additional insights for adjusting the competition analysis of mergers in the pharmaceutical industry.[8]

272. This increased focus on innovation and preserving R&D in the broadest sense is already showing both in the EU and US. The *Illumina/Grail* transaction[9] is a prime recent example. The deal was blocked by the European Commission and was challenged by the FTC.[10] The transaction involves the acquisition by Illumina – a global leader in DNA testing – of Grail, which produces a cancer blood test not yet widely available. The case demonstrates that enforcement agencies[11] are not limiting their analysis to the effects of a merger in the specific markets related to actual or pipeline products, even at early stages. More than that, agencies are increasingly focusing on innovation even before candidate products reach the pipeline, a point at which there is often substantial uncertainty about whether the products will ever be launched. In this case there is not only uncertainty about the ability of Grail to launch its cancer detection product, but more fundamentally about the prospects for any market for these nascent future products. The European Commission's press release explained: "The merger would have stifled innovation, and reduced choice in the emerging market for blood-based early cancer detection tests."[12]

273. Concerns about "killer acquisitions," where larger companies buy up smaller firms before they have the chance to develop into more important players, are also becoming more prevalent. Agencies are concerned that incumbents will acquire mavericks at an early stage so that these challengers cannot make markets more competitive. This is an area, critics have complained, that the agencies have not focused on sufficiently, allegedly leading to under-enforcement. An example is AbbVie's acquisition of Pharmacyclics in 2015. The transaction did not meet the European merger filing thresholds, and the FTC decided not to launch an in-depth investigation of the increased significance of AbbVie in the specific oncology markets.[13]

274. Agencies have responded to the under-enforcement concerns in the pharmaceutical industry as demonstrated by the *Illumina/Grail* transaction. That case would not normally have come within the remit of EU (or national) merger control because

---

8 FTC, Press Release, *FTC and Justice Department to Hold Two-Day Virtual Public Workshop Examining Antitrust Enforcement in the Pharmaceutical Industry* (May 31, 2022), *available at* https://www.ftc.gov/news-events/news/press-releases/2022/05/ftc-justice-department-hold-two-day-virtual-public-workshop-examining-antitrust-enforcement.

9 Case COMP/M.10188, *Illumina/Grail* (2021); *In the Matter of Illumina, Inc., and GRAIL, Inc.*, FTC File No. 201-0144 (2021).

10 *See* Complaint Counsel's Appeal of the Initial Decision, *In the Matter of Illumina, Inc. and Grail, Inc.*, FTC Docket No. 9401 (Oct. 4, 2022), *available at* https://www.ftc.gov/system/files/ftc_gov/pdf/D09401%20-%20COMPLAINT%20COUNSEL_S%20APPEAL%20OF%20THE%20INITIAL%20DECISION%20-%20PUBLIC%20%281%29.pdf.

11 This chapter refers to "agencies" including the European Commission and US Antitrust Agencies.

12 European Commission, Press Release IP/22/5364, *Mergers: Commission prohibits acquisition of GRAIL by Illumina* (Sept. 6, 2022), *available at* https://ec.europa.eu/commission/presscorner/detail/en/ip_22_5364. The decision was not yet published at September 2023.

13 *See* Sebastian Muller & Arthur Stril, *European Merger Control and Innovation Competition: Moving the Goalpost*, 2 Comp. L. & Policy Debate 52, 61–62 (2016) (citing the *AbbVie/Pharmacyclics* merger as an example of a "jurisdictional gap" in antitrust enforcement).

Grail had no products or sales in Europe. However, the European Commission has encouraged European Member States to make new use of an old mechanism under Article 22 of the EU Merger Regulation,[14] which the European Commission has re-purposed in the Article 22 Guidelines to allow national agencies to request that the European Commission review transactions which are likely problematic but which do not trigger existing EU or national merger control regimes.[15] In the case of *Illumina/Grail*, the European Commission sent an invitation to all Member States suggesting they use the Article 22 mechanism to refer the transaction to the EC, which the FCA and others then did.

275. Several EU Member States also have or are about to introduce mechanisms allowing them to capture "killer acquisitions." Germany and Austria have chosen to introduce transaction value-based thresholds, €400 million and €200 million, respectively. In other Member States, such as Sweden, Slovenia, Latvia, and Lithuania, the competition authorities have or will obtain the power to review below-threshold transactions if they meet certain criteria, in particular, if a transaction bears potential risks to competition. Italy and Ireland have already established this power.

I. Procedural Aspects of Merger Reviews

1. Jurisdictional thresholds

276. The US and EU rules defining when a transaction must be notified have fundamentally different implications in each jurisdiction. In the US a transaction that does not require a pre-merger notification filing under the HSR Act[16] may nevertheless be investigated by the agencies, either before or after consummation. By contrast, the substantive test under the EU Merger Regulation only applies to transactions meeting the relevant turnover thresholds, or those specifically referred to the European Commission from the Member State level. Unlike in the US, therefore, a transaction not subject to review under the EU Merger Regulation is not exposed to examination under the substantive EU test.

277. Beyond this basic conceptual difference, the two regimes also employ different methodologies in identifying the transactions that must be reported. The information required when filing is also different. A European filing includes detailed descriptions of products, markets, and market dynamics. The US HSR form is more limited in this respect. However, both forms require companies to attach key internal transaction and synergies documents to the initial filing. Additionally, in the EU, there is no filing fee, whereas the US charges fees that vary in size depending on the value of the transaction.

---

14 Council Regulation 139/2004 of Jan. 20, 2004 on the control of concentrations between undertakings (the EU Merger Regulation), 2004 OJ (L 24) 1; European Commission Communication, Guidance on the application of the referral mechanism set out in Article 22 of the Merger Regulation to certain categories of cases (the Article 22 Guidelines), COM (2021) 1959 final (Mar. 26, 2021), 1–6.

15 The legality of this use of Article 22 EU Merger Regulation is under challenge before the ECJ in the *Illumina/Grail* case at the time of writing.

16 15 U.S.C. § 18a.

278. The sections below discuss the filing thresholds in the US (Section A) and EU (section B), as well as the information parties must provide at the outset.

A. *US Filings*

279. Under the Hart-Scott-Rodino Antitrust Improvements (HSR) Act,[17] the FTC's Premerger Notification Office (PNO)[18] applies three checks to determine whether a pre-merger notification filing is required:[19]

- *Commerce Test.* The first prong of the test is whether either party is engaged in commerce or any activity affecting commerce. In practice, nearly every pharmaceutical merger would pass this test.
- *Size of Transaction Test.* Transactions are bucketed into one of three categories, based on the transaction value. The thresholds for these buckets are indexed to changes in the US's Gross National Product. The statutory and adjusted levels as of 2023 are:
  - $50 million or less (adjusted to $111.4 million as of 2023). No filing is necessary.
  - Between $50 million and $200 million (adjusted to between $111.4 million and $445.5 million as of 2023). A filing may be necessary if the size of person test below is met.
  - Over $200 million (adjusted to $445.5 million as of 2023). A filing is required unless another exemption applies.
- *Size of Person Test.* The parties to the transaction must meet certain size requirements. Although these requirements can be complicated, generally the basic "size of person" test requires a filing for transactions valued between $50 million and $200 million (as adjusted) where at least one person has at least $100 million (as adjusted, to $222.7 million as of 2023) in assets or annual sales, and the other has at least $10 million (as adjusted, to $22.3 million as of 2023) in assets or annual sales. In calculating the size of person, it is important to properly identify the relevant "Ultimate Parent Entity," which is an entity not controlled by any other entity. Under the HSR rules, a "person" includes all entities having the same Ultimate Parent Entity.

280. There are a few additional considerations relevant to pharmaceutical transactions:

- *Jurisdictional Thresholds Generally.* The acquisition price, which includes all forms of cash or non-cash consideration, is used to determine whether the "size of transaction" test is met in most transactions, including the formation of joint ventures where the contributors will acquire equity interests in a newly formed entity. Furthermore, the "size of transaction" includes the value of any voting securities or non-corporate interests held by the acquiring person in the acquired person prior to the acquisition, if any. For asset acquisitions, "size of transaction" purposes should also include the value

---

17 *Id.*

18 The PNO first receives the HSR filing on behalf of both the US Antitrust Agencies.

19 FTC Premerger Notification Program, *Steps for Determining Whether an HSR Filing Is Required*, *available at* https://www.ftc.gov/enforcement/premerger-notification-program/hsr-resources/steps-determining-whether-hsr-filing.

of assets acquired – or assets for which a letter of intent or agreement in principle has been signed to acquire – from the same acquired person within the 180 days preceding the execution of the letter of intent or agreement in principle in the present transaction, unless an HSR filing was made and the waiting period observed for the earlier acquisition.

One overarching issue in pharmaceutical transactions is that typically a significant portion of the consideration may be contingent upon future events, in the form of earnouts, royalties, milestone payments, or other payouts, the likelihood of which may be uncertain at the time of closing. In such cases, the size-of-transaction is assessed based on "fair market value." Under the HSR rules, fair market value (whether it is an asset deal or a stock deal) is to be determined in good faith by the board of the acquirer's Ultimate Parent Entity (i.e., an entity which is not controlled by any other entity) or such board's designee. The valuation must be made as of any date that is within 60 days prior to closing.

While there is no specific HSR mandate as to the valuation methodology to be used, the fair market value determination is made on a commercially reasonable basis. The idea is for the fair market value to approximate the amount a reasonable third party would pay, up front and in cash, for the relevant interests/assets in an arm's length transaction.

- *Exemptions Relevant to the Pharmaceutical Industry.* Transfers of pharmaceutical patent rights or exclusive licenses to such rights are considered asset acquisitions under the HSR statute. Accordingly, rights that are only effective outside the US (e.g., a license to commercialize exclusively in Europe) are treated as foreign assets and are typically exempt under the HSR statute because there are no US sales associated with such rights.
- *R&D Agreements.* Research and collaboration arrangements, whereby two parties may collaborate on R&D activities, are potentially reportable. In these transactions, typically one party will receive an option to acquire the exclusive license after the development targets have been identified or certain development milestones have been achieved. Until recently, the PNO's guidance in these cases allowed parties to treat an entire collaboration as a single, upfront acquisition of exclusive rights. Therefore, parties could make an HSR filing prior to embarking on a proposed collaboration, which would also cover any future option exercises. The PNO's most recent informal interpretation, however, is that any such option exercises made more than one year after the expiration or termination of the HSR waiting period would not be covered by such filing.[20]
- *Licensing Agreements.* Licensing agreements may also be reportable under HSR rules. For a license to be reportable, it must be exclusive – that is, the license must prevent the licensor from: (1) practicing the patent themselves

[20] *See* the fact pattern set forth in FTC Premerger Notification Program, *1709004 Informal Interpretations* (Sept. 12, 2017), *available at* https://www.ftc.gov/legal-library/browse/hsr-informal-interpretations/1709004, which was subsequently superseded by FTC Premerger Notification Program, *1907007 Informal Interpretations* (July 19, 2019), *available at* https://www.ftc.gov/legal-library/browse/hsr-informal-interpretations/1907007.

or (2) licensing a party other than the licensee to practice the patent.[21] Specific rules apply to pharmaceutical patents to determine exclusivity. Under the HSR Act, a reportable asset acquisition occurs "if all commercially significant rights to a patent … for any therapeutic area (or specific indication within a therapeutic area) are transferred to another entity."[22] Thus, if a pharmaceutical patent holder grants an exclusive license for a specific indication but retains the right to use the patent for other indications, the transaction may still be reportable.[23] Notably, however, the transaction must still meet the HSR Act's "size-of-person" or "size-of-transaction" tests for the reporting requirement to apply. By enacting these rules, the FTC addressed concerns that pharmaceutical companies could transfer all patent rights for a drug to a competitor and potentially eliminate competition in the market for that product.

- *Commercially Significant Rights.* In addition to pharmaceutical mergers, the HSR Act may also apply to other types of transfers and collaboration arrangements. In 2013, the FTC adopted specific rules applicable to pharmaceutical licensing agreements. Generally, while HSR filings may be required for transfers of *exclusive* licenses or patents if they meet the jurisdictional thresholds above, *non-exclusive* licenses are not treated as a potentially reportable asset acquisition. Under the updated rules, the FTC explained that in the pharmaceutical sector, any licenses that transfer "all commercially significant rights" could trigger a filing even where the licensor retains limited manufacturing or other co-rights (such as the right to co-develop, co-promote, co-market and co-commercialize alongside the licensee). Such limited manufacturing rights and co-rights are no longer deemed sufficient to render a license "non-exclusive" for purposes of the HSR Act.

  These changes were driven by concerns that pharmaceutical companies could transfer exclusive rights to commercially use a patent (or part thereof) to a competitor, while retaining certain limited rights (such as the right to manufacture the product) and thus lessen competition. The new FTC rules came into effect shortly after the transfer of US patent rights relating to the drug Synacthen from Novartis (which retained some manufacturing rights) to Questcor in June 2013. The FTC later sued Questcor with respect to conduct related to this acquisition.[24]

281. HSR filings require the parties to submit information including, among other things, the companies' corporate information and structure, a description of the transaction and its value, a copy of the transaction agreement, documents prepared by or for officers or directors "for the purpose of evaluating or analyzing the acquisition with respect to market shares, competition, competitors, markets,

---

21 16 C.F.R. § 801.2(g)(3).

22 *Id.*

23 *See id.*

24 FTC, Press Release, *Mallinckrodt Will Pay $100 Million to Settle FTC, State Charges It Illegally Maintained its Monopoly of Specialty Drug Used to Treat Infants* (Jan. 18, 2017), *available at* https://www.ftc.gov/news-events/news/press-releases/2017/01/mallinckrodt-will-pay-100-million-settle-ftc-state-charges-it-illegally-maintained-its-monopoly.

potential for sales growth or expansion into product or geographic markets," deal synergies documents, and a list of North American Industry Classification System (NAICS) codes in which the companies operate.[25]

B. *EU Filings*

282. EU merger control rules[26] cover "concentrations"[27] that have a "Union dimension."[28] Under the arrangements which govern the European Economic Area (EEA), where a merger has a Union dimension, the jurisdiction of the European Commission will extend to the whole of the EEA, which includes also Iceland, Liechtenstein and Norway.[29]

283. *Concentrations.* A concentration is defined as a merger of two or more previously independent "undertakings," parts of undertakings, or the acquisition of direct or indirect sole or joint control of the whole or parts of another undertaking. In practice, the ultimate issue is whether a transaction results in a lasting change of control over one or more previously independent undertakings or parts thereof.

284. The object of a transaction is considered an "undertaking" when it is a business with a market presence to which turnover can be clearly attributed[30] in the present or the foreseeable future. The European Commission construes the concept of "undertaking" very broadly. For example, the transfer of intangible assets such as brands or patents can under certain circumstances constitute a concentration. In the pharmaceutical sector, transactions may involve companies with products still in development or undergoing authorization, referred to commonly as pipeline products. The European Commission has found that the acquisition of rights to develop, manufacture, and commercialize a pipeline product currently undergoing Phase III clinical trials is a concentration because the transaction is expected to enable the acquirer to successfully launch a product and generate turnover within a reasonable time frame. In the *Novartis/GSK* case,[31] Novartis acquired sole

---

[25] FTC Premerger Notification Program, *The Form and Instructions* (2017), *available at* https://www.ftc.gov/enforcement/premerger-notification-program/form-instructions.

[26] European Commission, Guidelines on the applicability of Article 101 TFEU to horizontal co-operation agreements (the EU Horizontal Guidelines), 2023 OJ (C 259) 5–18; European Commission Communication, Consolidated Jurisdictional Notice under Council Regulation 139/2004 on the control of concentrations between undertakings (the Consolidated Jurisdictional Notice), 2008 OJ (C 95) 1–48; European Commission Communication, Guidelines on the assessment of non-horizontal mergers under the Council Regulation on the control of concentrations between undertakings (Non-Horizontal Merger Guidelines), 2008 OJ (C 265) 6–25; European Commission Communication, Notice on Case Referral in respect of concentrations (the Notice on Case Referral), 2005 OJ (C 56) 2–23; European Commission Communication, Notice on Restrictions directly related and necessary to concentrations (the Notice on Ancillary Restraints), 2005 OJ (C 56) 24–31; European Commission Communication, Notice on Remedies acceptable under Council Regulation 139/2004 and under Commission Regulation 802/2004 (the Notice on Remedies), 2008 OJ (C 267) 1–27; Commission Explanatory Note, *Best Practice Guidelines: the European Commission's Model Texts for Divestiture Commitments and the Trustee Mandate under the EC Merger Regulation*, (Dec. 5, 2013), *available at* https://ec.europa.eu/competition/mergers/legislation/best_practice_commitments_trustee_en.pdf

[27] Council Regulation 139/2004 (EU Merger Regulation), *supra* n. 14, Chapter III, art. 3.

[28] *Id.* art. 2.

[29] Following the UK's exit from the EU with effect from Dec. 31, 2020 concentrations meeting the requirements under UK competition law will also be subject to a review by the CMA.

[30] Consolidated Jurisdictional Notice, *supra* n. 26, Chapter III, ¶24.

[31] Case COMP/M.7872, *Novartis /GSK (Ofatumumab autoimmune indications)* (2015).

control over GSK's portfolio of oncology pharmaceutical products, including two pipeline products. The acquired business comprised the transfer of rights, licenses, marketing authorizations and employees necessary for the commercialization and R&D in respect of the oncology pharmaceuticals concerned.

285. In a concentration, the concept of control includes the acquisition of sole or joint, legal or de facto, control over a previously independent undertaking. Control is defined as the possibility to exercise decisive influence over an undertaking's commercial strategy and may be based on rights, agreements, or other means. Minority shareholdings often fall outside of the EU Merger Regulation, but, under certain circumstances, they can also result in control if they enable an investor, in combination with other rights or due to specific factual circumstances (such as historical patterns of attendance at annual general meetings) to exercise decisive influence over the target's strategic commercial behavior and go beyond the usual protection rights granted to a minority shareholder. This is especially the case if such rights are granted with respect to the target's business plan, operating budget, or the appointment of senior management.

286. "Joint" control is a situation where an undertaking has more than one shareholder, but none with sole control. This is most often the case where two shareholders each hold 50% of voting rights and are each equally represented in the controlled undertaking's decision-making bodies. Joint control can also occur where a minority shareholder is vested with (veto) rights over the strategic matters described above.

287. The EU Merger Regulation also covers "full function" joint ventures. The full functionality of a joint venture generally requires that it will operate on the market as an autonomous economic entity, on a lasting basis, and cannot be considered as a part of its parent company. The assessment whether a joint venture is "fully functional" within the meaning of the EU Merger Regulation is often difficult. The European Commission will consider a joint venture to be fully functional if it has sufficient resources (such as financial, personnel, and assets) to operate independently on a lasting basis like any other undertaking operating in the same market. Other relevant issues include whether the joint venture has its own management, whether its operations are limited to specific activities (e.g., complementing those of the parents), or any dependence of the joint venture on its parents as customer or supplier.

288. *Union Dimension*. The EU merger control rules seek to ensure that large scale concentrations that have a Union dimension are reviewed exclusively by the European Commission rather than by any national authority of the Member States. Union dimension is defined by two alternative sets of thresholds:[32]

- *Primary Thresholds*: combined aggregate worldwide turnover of all the undertakings concerned exceeds €5 billion; and the aggregate EU-wide turnover of each of at least two of the undertakings concerned exceeds €250 million, unless each of the undertakings concerned achieves more than two-thirds of its aggregate EU-wide turnover within one and the same Member State.

---

32 Council Regulation 139/2004 (EU Merger Regulation), *supra* n. 14, Chapter III, art. 1.3 and art. 2.

- *Secondary Thresholds*: the combined aggregate worldwide turnover of all the undertakings concerned is more than €2.5 billion; and in each of at least three Member States the combined aggregate turnover of all the undertakings concerned is more than €100 million; and in each of at least the same three Member States included for the purposes of the previous criterion, the aggregate turnover of each of at least two of the undertakings concerned is more than €25 million; and the aggregate EU-wide turnover of at least two of the undertakings concerned is more than €100 million; unless each of the undertakings concerned achieves more than two-thirds of its aggregate EU-wide turnover within one and the same Member State.

289. Both sets of thresholds are designed to capture transactions in which at least two involved undertakings meet certain turnover criteria. Which undertakings are concerned, and whose turnover needs to be taken into account, will depend on the type of concentration. These issues become particularly relevant where two large undertakings acquire joint control over a third business. If the parent companies acquire joint control over a newly created joint venture which does not yet have any turnover, it is only the turnover of the parents that is taken into account. That is also the case where a business originally solely controlled by one parent will become a joint venture with a newly investing parent (or parents). In contrast, where a pre-existing separate business will come under the joint control of newly investing parents, both the parents and the future joint venture are treated as separate relevant undertakings.

290. Where the seller disposes of only part of its activities, only the turnover of that part is taken into account, but not the turnover of the seller's retained businesses.

291. The assessment as to whether the turnover thresholds under the EU Merger Regulation are met requires the correct geographical allocation of turnover of the undertakings concerned.[33]

292. Concentrations satisfying the EU turnover tests are by the exclusive domain of the EC, to the exclusion of the jurisdiction of Member State authorities. Conversely, concentrations that do not meet the EU thresholds may fall within the jurisdiction of the NCAs if they meet the relevant national thresholds. But the national authorities can also refer transactions to the European Commission for review under the EU Merger Regulation. The EU Merger Regulation provides for two referral mechanisms from EU Member States level to the European Commission.[34] One operates at the initiative of the parties, and the other at the initiative of the Member State(s).

293. Under the first referral mechanism, the parties to a transaction which does not have Union dimension, but is notifiable in at least three Member States, can request that the European Commission examine the transaction instead of the NCAs. If

---

33 For both the sale of goods and the provision of services, the general rule is that turnover should be attributed to the place where the customer is located. The underlying principle is that turnover should be allocated to the location where competition with alternative suppliers takes place. This location is normally also the place where the characteristic action under the contract in question is to be performed, *i.e.*, where the service is actually provided and the product is actually delivered.

34 Council Regulation 139/2004 (EU Merger Regulation), *supra* n. 14, Chapter III, art. 4.5 and art. 22.

none of the Member States expresses any disagreement the transaction is deemed to have a Union dimension and must be notified to the European Commission.

294. Under the second referral mechanism, one or several Member States can request the European Commission to examine a transaction not meeting the EU thresholds but affecting trade between EU Member States and threatening to significantly affect competition within the territory of the requesting Member State. In March 2021, the European Commission announced a significant change in its approach as regards the use of this Article 22 referral mechanism.[35] The European Commission declared that it would review mergers falling short of the EU turnover thresholds and invite the NCAs to use the referral mechanism even in cases where those authorities do not themselves have jurisdiction to review a transaction. This change of approach was implemented in response to the perception of an enforcement gap in relation to so-called "killer acquisitions" mentioned in the introduction to this chapter. It applies to all sectors, but the pharmaceutical and the digital sectors were specifically highlighted in the Article 22 Guidelines as sectors where innovation is a key parameter of competition.[36]

295. As noted above, the European Commission encouraged Member States to use the Article 22 referral mechanism in the *Illumina/Grail* transaction, which would otherwise have fallen outside of the national and EU merger control regimes because Grail did not generate any revenues in Europe. Both parties challenged the referrals on several grounds but the General Court confirmed that Article 22 can be applied by Member States that have a merger control regime but whose thresholds do not capture a particular transaction.[37] The Court held that Article 22 can be interpreted broadly, allowing the European Commission to review transactions that do not meet EU or national merger control thresholds but could nevertheless significantly impede effective competition.[38] One reason for the decision was that thresholds are not at all times appropriate to cover all transactions that require scrutiny because of the risk of distortion of competition. Therefore, as the reasoning goes, thresholds should not be supplemented with rules on the referrals which must "constitute effective corrective mechanisms."[39] The case has been appealed to the ECJ.[40] If upheld, the European Commission would have the ability to review any transaction it deems to be of competitive relevance, regardless of turnover or market share. Pharmaceutical companies would therefore need to thoroughly assess whether a transaction could become subject to a review by the European Commission via the "referral route" even if the transaction does not meet the relevant EU or national turnover thresholds.

296. A referral can also go in the other direction, i.e., from the European Commission level to the Member State(s). The European Commission can refer a transaction with a Union dimension in whole or in part to a Member State if a Member State

---

35 Article 22 Guidelines, *supra* n. 14, Chapter III.

36 *Id.* § 9.

37 Case T-277/21, *Illumina, Inc. v. Commission*, ECLI:EU:T:2022:447, (2022).

38 *Id.* §§ 94, 116, 139, 148.

39 *Id.* §§ 123, 141–148.

40 Case C-611/22 P, *Illumina, Inc. v. Commission*, ECLI:EU:C:2023:205, (Mar. 10, 2023).

so requests.[41] This kind of referral can occur when the transaction: (i) threatens to significantly affect competition within that Member State, which presents all the characteristics of a distinct market, or (ii) affects competition in a market within that Member State, which presents all the characteristics of a distinct market and does not constitute a substantial part of the common market.[42] Parties to a transaction can also request a referral to the national level, in similar circumstances, under Article 4.4 of the EU Merger Regulation.[43]

297. If an EU Merger Regulation notification is required, the parties must complete a "Form CO" pursuant to the EU Antitrust Implementing Regulation.[44] The form provides a long series of questions, including a description of the transaction and relevant revenues of the undertakings concerned. Further, the Form CO asks parties to provide information about the markets in which they meet certain market-share tests on the basis of which it is assumed that these markets are affected by the transaction and may raise concerns. The information includes market size, market shares of the parties and competitors, capacities, structure of supply and demand, product differentiation and closeness of competition, market entry and exit, R&D, and cooperative agreements.

298. The Form CO also lists supporting documents that must be submitted. Supporting documentation includes all documents bringing about the concentration (e.g., agreements between the parties or the offer document in case of a public bid), annual reports, and accounts and copies of analyses, reports, studies, and surveys assessing or analyzing the concentration with respect to market shares, competitive conditions, competitors (actual and potential), the rationale for the concentration, potential for sales growth, or expansion into other markets, and/or general market conditions prepared by or for or received by any member of the board of management (or directors), the supervisory board or other persons with similar functions, or the shareholders' meeting. Over and above this documentary production specified in the Form CO, the European Commission now routinely requires extensive production of relevant internal documents.

299. Finally, the Form CO also asks about efficiencies created by the transaction.

300. Transactions which obviously do not raise serious doubts can benefit from a "simplified procedure" for which a less extensive form, the Short Form CO, can be completed. The European Commission has recently expanded the use of this simplified procedure to mergers where the combined market share of all the parties

---

[41] Case COMP/M.10404, *McKesson /Phoenix (wholesale of pharmaceutical goods)* (2022). The European Commission cleared the transaction outside of France but, at the request of the FCA, referred the transaction in as far as it concerned France to the French authority.

[42] Council Regulation 139/2004 (EU Merger Regulation), *supra* n. 14, Chapter III, art. 9.

[43] Prior to the notification of a concentration, the notifying parties may inform the European Commission, by means of a reasoned submission, that the concentration may significantly affect competition in a market within a Member State which presents all the characteristics of a distinct market and should therefore be examined, in whole or in part, by that Member State. The European Commission then has 25 working days to accept or refuse the referral request.

[44] EU Antitrust Implementing Regulation 1269/2013 of Dec. 5, 2013 amending Regulation 802/2004 implementing Council Regulation 139/2004 on the control of concentrations between undertakings (EU Antitrust Implementing Regulation), 2013 OJ (L 336) 1–39.

to the concentration that are engaged in a horizontal overlap remains below 25% or, in the case of vertical mergers, to cases where they are lower than 35% in both the upstream and downstream markets.[45]

2. Timing for reviews

301. The European Commission and US review periods differ in both their procedural aspects and duration. For example, the European Commission process has strict deadlines for proposing remedies and, in general, the European Commission process may be more frontloaded than the US process. Extensive pre-filing discussions are a standard practice in the EU even in transactions that are expected to receive clearance without an in-depth review, whereas pre-filing discussions in the US are not as common and, in any case, do not last as long. Additionally, the European Commission has the power to block transactions prior to consummation, with any court appeal coming only later. In the US, agencies typically must go to federal court and win an injunction to halt a transaction prior to consummation.[46]

302. The sections below discuss in more detail the procedural steps of a review both in the EU and the US: initial review (Section A), in-depth investigation (Section B), and court proceedings (Section C).

A. *Initial Reviews*

a. *EU Phase I*

303. The European Commission has 25 working days to conduct its Phase I review.[47] This review period begins on the working day after the receipt of a "complete" notification, meaning that the European Commission considers that the parties have provided all the necessary information allowing it to start an investigation. If the simplified procedure is applied during Phase I review, the European Commission often clears a transaction before the full review period has expired.

304. The European Commission can suspend the 25-working day period in certain circumstances. These include where one of the undertakings involved is responsible for not providing requested information about the transaction to the European Commission in time, and the European Commission must request the information through a formal decision or even launch an inspection. Such suspension is often referred to as a "stop-the-clock." The Phase I review period is extended to 35 working days if the parties propose remedies to alleviate possible competition concerns, or if the European Commission receives requests for referrals from any EU Member State. If the European Commission still has serious competitive

---

45 *See* the Commission Notice on a simplified treatment for certain concentrations under Council Regulation 139/2004 on the control of concentrations between undertakings (the Notice on Simplified Procedure), 2023 OJ (C 160) 1–10.

46 Although the FTC does have its own administrative authority to block an anticompetitive transaction, the agency typically will first seek a preliminary injunction in federal court to prevent the parties from closing pending completion of a full administrative hearing.

47 Council Regulation 139/2004 (EU Merger Regulation), *supra* n. 14, Chapter III, art. 10.1.

concerns, the European Commission must open a Phase II investigation; it cannot prohibit a transaction after a Phase I review.[48]

305. Although the European Commission has only 25 working days for Phase I following receipt of a complete notification, the actual duration for a European Commission Phase I clearance process, with or without remedies, is typically much longer. In line with explicit encouragement from the EC, notifying parties invariably engage in pre-notification discussions with the European Commission prior to formally notifying a transaction. Parties usually submit a draft of the Form CO and/or briefing papers explaining the background and the context of the intended transaction. The European Commission may then invite the parties to meetings and even start a market inquiry. Pre-notification discussions can last several weeks to several months and are particularly long in the case of transactions likely to be subject to remedies or a Phase II review. According to the Dechert Antitrust Merger Investigation Timing Tracker (DAMITT), pre-notification discussions for first phase remedy cases in 2022 lasted an average of 8.3 months from deal announcement to the notification with the European Commission.[49]

b. *US HSR preliminary investigation*

306. In the US, the initial waiting period during which the transaction may not close is 30 calendar days (15 days for cash tender offers and certain bankruptcy transactions) from completion of a valid filing. If this initial waiting period expires without either the FTC or the DOJ taking action, the transaction may be consummated. Transactions that do not involve current or potential competitive overlaps typically receive clearance within 30 calendar days after filing unless early termination is requested and granted.

307. If there are competitive overlaps, however, either US agency may open a preliminary investigation of the proposed transaction during the initial waiting period to decide if a more in-depth investigation is required. During a preliminary investigation, the US agencies typically ask merging parties to voluntarily produce basic competitive information, such as a list of competitive overlaps, market shares within these overlapping areas, the companies' strategic business plans, and competitive research (e.g., surveys, industry reports, internal competitive landscape documents) or data (e.g., win/loss reports). The US agencies also typically ask for a list of each company's top customers, whom they often will contact during the waiting period to understand the customers' views of the expected impact of the transaction.

308. If competitive concerns cannot be resolved within the initial waiting period, the HSR rules give merging parties the option to withdraw their filing and refile within two business days without paying a second filing fee. This "pull-and refile" option provides the agencies' staff and the parties with a second initial waiting period to address competitive issues that remain unresolved and potentially avoid

---

48 *Id.* art. 6.

49 Dechert LLP, *DAMITT: How Long Does It Take to Conduct Significant Antitrust Merger Investigations, available at* https://www.dechert.com/knowledge/hot-topic/damitt--how-long-does-it-take-to-conduct-significant-u-s--antitr.html.

a more in-depth, "Second Request" investigation. Alternatively, rather than limit the agencies' time during these waiting periods to the statutory waiting periods, parties may engage in pre-filing discussions with the US Antitrust Agencies to work "off the clock" to address any concerns before the HSR filing triggers the statutory waiting period.

309. Prior to the expiration of the waiting period, if the FTC or DOJ chooses to formally request additional documents and information as part of a Second Request, the waiting period is suspended until 30 days after the parties certify substantial compliance. More information on the Second Request process is provided below.

B. *In-depth investigations*

a. *EU Phase II*

310. If the European Commission concludes that a transaction raises serious competitive concerns, it initiates proceedings for an in-depth Phase II review. The European Commission has 90 working days from the date of initiation of Phase II to reach a decision; this will be extended to 105 working days if the parties offer remedies 55 working days or more after the initiation of a Phase II. There is also a possibility to extend the Phase II by 20 working days, giving a total of 125 working days, at the request of the parties.[50] In practice, however, the duration of Phase II proceedings is often longer and increasingly includes "stop-the-clock" periods.[51] Including pre-notification contacts, according to DAMITT, EU merger cases that proceeded to Phase II averaged 18.4 months in 2022.[52]

311. If the European Commission intends to prohibit a transaction, it must issue a Statement of Objections (SO) to inform the parties about the competitive concerns raised with respect to the intended transaction. When this occurs, the parties gain access to the European Commission's file and usually have about two weeks to express their written views on the objections raised by the European Commission. The parties may also request an oral hearing.

b. *US Second Request*

312. If a US agency issues a Second Request, that begins a more in-depth investigation that could last many months. Second Requests require the merging parties to produce large volumes of documents and data from company employees and corporate databases.[53] The agencies will request transaction-specific documents

---

50 According to the findings of DAMITT these voluntary extensions have become fairly standard as such extensions were implemented in 88% of the Phase II cases in the period between 2011 and 2020, and even in 100% of the Phase II cases in 2021: *id.* The reality is often that the European Commission prompts the parties to request the extra time.

51 Pre-notification discussions are particularly long for cases proceeding to a Phase II review. According to DAMITT these pre-notification discussions had an average duration of 7.3 months in 2022. This is due to the fact that such transactions are often more complex and often pose competitive issues which the undertakings involved try to address/remove already at the pre-notification stage: *id.*

52 *Id.*

53 *See* DOJ Model Second Request, *Request for Additional Information and Documentary Material Issued to [Weebyewe Corporation], available at* https://www.justice.gov/atr/file/706636/download.

as well as contemporaneous business records (e.g., emails, presentations, spreadsheets, reports, voicemails, text messages) on a variety of topics, including sales, marketing, customers, and competition. Second Requests also contain several interrogatories, which require the parties to provide written answers to specific questions about the company's business, the transaction, or the industry. The agencies typically will negotiate modifications to their requests for documents or data if certain information demands are overly burdensome.

313. Once each party has complied with its Second Request, the waiting period resumes and extends by statute for an additional 30 calendar days. As a practical matter, however, the US Antitrust Agencies typically seek to require parties to enter "timing agreements" that may add 30 to 120 days to the review process after the statutory waiting period expires.

314. According to DAMITT, "significant" merger investigations resolved during 2022 lasted an average of 11.8 months from deal announcement to completion of the review.[54] Significant US merger investigations include HSR-reportable transactions for which the result of the investigation by the FTC or DOJ is a consent order, a complaint challenging the transaction, an official closing statement by the reviewing antitrust agency, or the abandonment of the transaction with the antitrust agency issuing a press release regarding its review of the deal.

315. If the FTC or DOJ still has competitive concerns at the conclusion of a Second Request investigation and a settlement cannot be reached, the agency may seek to block the transaction in court. The agency cannot block the transaction on its own without the entry of an order from a court or, in the case of the FTC, an order by the administrative law judge (ALJ) or the FTC Commissioners on the merits.

C. *Potential court proceedings*

a. *EU Appeals*

316. European Commission merger decisions can be appealed to the General Court within two months of the European Commission's decision. This includes prohibition and clearance decisions, as well as certain other decisions that the European Commission can adopt (e.g., referral decisions). A further appeal against judgments of the General Court can be brought before the ECJ (on points of law only).

317. Technically speaking the appeal is an "application to annul" under the TFEU.[55] It is not a *de novo* assessment of the case or its facts, but rather a marginal review in which some deference is given to the European Commission's appraisal of the facts. Where an appeal succeeds, the court does not substitute its own decision

54 DAMITT, *supra* n. 49, Chapter III.

55 Appeals against decisions of the European Commission are based on French administrative rules, whereby the judge rules on the legality or illegality of the decision made by the administration based on the procedural and substantial grounds put forward by the appellants. Since the appeal tribunal does not have the same investigative powers as the administration, though, it cannot substitute its own decision to that of the administration. Instead, it is for the administration to make a new decision based on the court's legal guidance.

– instead, the parties have to file again before the European Commission to get a new decision, provided that their interest to do so remains.

318. The parties to a transaction, EU Member States, and third parties (such as customers or competitors) who can demonstrate a sufficient interest can bring appeals.

b. *US Litigation Process*

319. If a US agency determines that a transaction is anticompetitive, it may sue to block the transaction. The process differs depending on whether the DOJ or FTC seeks enforcement. Generally, the US Antitrust Agencies assign merger reviews based on industry expertise, with the FTC traditionally taking responsibility for life sciences industry mergers.

320. If the DOJ is the reviewing agency, it may file in federal district court a complaint seeking a permanent injunction to block the transaction in violation of Section 7 of the Clayton Act. The DOJ must show with a "reasonable probability" that the merger may substantially lessen competition. In addition to seeking to block mergers prior to consummation, the DOJ also has the power to seek judicial action to unwind a merger that has already been consummated.[56]

321. Unlike the DOJ, the FTC may only seek a preliminary injunction in federal district court to place transactions on hold pending an FTC administrative trial. To obtain a preliminary injunction, the FTC must make "a proper showing that, weighing the equities and considering the European Commission's likelihood of ultimate success, such action would be in the public interest."[57] Practically, these preliminary injunction hearings are similar in size and scope to the DOJ actions seeking permanent injunctions.

322. In parallel to the preliminary injunction proceedings, the FTC typically commences a proceeding in its own administrative court before an FTC-employed ALJ. These trials involve extensive discovery as well as witness testimony as in federal courts. The ALJ's decision or recommendations at the end of a trial may be appealed to the full Commission which originally voted to block the transaction. If the federal court decides to enjoin a transaction, the FTC will typically continue with the administrative trial unless the parties decide to abandon the transaction. But if the federal court denies the FTC a preliminary injunction, the FTC traditionally has decided to dismiss the administrative trial, though it is not required to do so. Following an administrative trial, the FTC could enter an order prohibiting a merger or, if already consummated, requiring divestiture of the acquired assets.

323. DAMITT shows that US Antitrust Agencies litigations seeking to enjoin proposed mergers last just under 10 months from the filing of the complaint to the federal judge's decision, adding substantial time to a lengthy review process.[58]

---

56 DOJ, Merger Remedies Manual (Sept. 2020), 19, *available at* https://www.justice.gov/atr/page/file/1312416/download.

57 15 U.S.C. § 53(b)(2).

58 DAMITT, *supra* n. 49, Chapter III.

II. Substantive Assessments of Mergers

324. The European Commission and US agencies technically apply different substantive tests for purposes of merger analysis. The European Commission analyzes whether notified mergers – concentrations under the EU Merger Regulation – are compatible with the internal market,[59] more specifically whether a transaction will cause a "significant impediment to effective competition" (the so-called SIEC test). In particular the European Commission assesses whether the deal will result in the creation or strengthening of a dominant position, although the test is wider, too[60]. The EU Horizontal and Non-Horizontal Merger Guidelines provide guidance on the European Commission's assessment.[61] The US agencies consider whether "the effect of an acquisition may be substantially to lessen competition, or to tend to create a monopoly."[62] The US Antitrust Agencies have periodically published merger guidelines explaining how the agencies evaluate the particular facts of a merger in making this determination.[63]

325. The EU and US agencies' examinations start from the definition of the different markets on which the parties are active to identify the competitive overlaps and thus the markets where concerns may arise. In the pharmaceutical industry, the approach can differ depending on the condition being treated.

326. The Sections below discuss two different types of effects mergers may have on competition: (1) horizontal effects, and (2) non-horizontal effects, including vertical and conglomerate effects.

1. Horizontal Effects

327. Horizontal mergers may raise competitive concerns when the transaction leads to meaningful overlaps between the parties and risks a reduction in competition.

328. The FTC has a long-established framework applied across many horizontal pharmaceutical industry mergers, focusing on actual competition (i.e., direct overlaps between the merging parties' products), potential competition (e.g., competition where one party's pipeline product is not yet approved but may directly compete with the other party's product in the future), and innovation markets (e.g., where neither firm has an approved product for sale on the market but the merging companies are among the firms with a chance to enter the market).

329. In its decisional practice, the European Commission has identified a specific competitive assessment framework for pharmaceutical cases which corresponds to the overlaps between the parties:[64]

---

59 Council Regulation 139/2004 (EU Merger Regulation), *supra* n. 14, Chapter III, art. 2.1.

60 *Id.* art. 2.2.

61 EU Horizontal and Non-Horizontal Merger Guidelines, *supra* n. 26, Chapter III.

62 Clayton Act § 7, 15 U.S.C. § 18.

63 *See, e.g.*, US Horizontal Merger Guidelines, *available at* https://www.justice.gov/sites/default/files/atr/legacy/2010/08/19/hmg-2010.pdf; US Antitrust Agencies, Vertical Merger Guidelines (June 30, 2020), *available at* https://www.ftc.gov/system/files/documents/reports/us-department-justice-federal-trade-commission-vertical-merger-guidelines/vertical_merger_guidelines_6-30-20.pdf.

64 Case COMP/M.9461, *AbbVie/Allergan* ¶19 (2020); Case COMP/M.9294, *BMS/Celgene* ¶22 (2019).

- actual (product and price) competition, assessing the overlaps between the parties' existing (marketed) products;
- potential (product and price) competition, assessing the overlaps between marketed products and/or pipeline products at advanced stages of development;
- innovation competition in relation to the parties' ongoing pipeline products; and
- innovation competition in relation to the capability to innovate in certain "innovation spaces."

330. The European Commission and FTC will examine whether a proposed transaction eliminates important competitive constraints on the merging parties. Such effects can arise not only in existing markets but also in new product markets. Section A below discusses horizontal overlaps in existing markets. Section B below discusses horizontal overlaps in new product markets which could lead to restrictions in innovation regarding pipeline products but also innovation spaces. Section C below addresses overlaps that are portfolio based rather than product based. Each of these sections discusses case examples, most of which address overlaps between both existing marketed products and new innovative products.

A. *Market overlaps*

331. The EU and US agencies will typically evaluate mergers between pharmaceutical companies on an individual therapy or drug-level, or on a narrower basis such as molecules, to determine whether any overlaps exist between the companies' existing drug portfolios. If any market overlaps exist that harm competition, the agencies may require the merging firms to divest the overlapping assets of one of the two firms depending on the circumstances of the market at issue. It is not uncommon for a single merger to result in multiple asset divestitures in the event of multiple overlapping marketed product lines.[65]

332. Because pharmaceutical mergers often feature a vast number of overlapping marketed products, the European Commission has adopted a system of filters aimed at reducing the number of overlapping markets to be examined, so as to focus the investigation on the group of existing product markets where concerns are most likely.[66] For marketed products, the groups are defined on the basis of the parties' combined market shares and the increment caused by the transaction, occasionally with a further segmentation into sub-groups. The three main groups are: (1) parties' combined market share exceeds 35% and the increment exceeds 1%, (2) parties' combined market share exceeds 35% but the increment is below 1%, and (3) parties' combined market share is between 20%–35%.[67]

333. For all overlapping markets, the European Commission will analyze how a transaction affects actual price or quality competition between marketed products.[68] The EU Horizontal Merger Guidelines identify a number of factors that can be taken

---

65 *See, e.g.*, Case COMP/M.9517, *Mylan/Upjohn* (2022).

66 *See, e.g.*, Case COMP/M.7746, *Teva/Allergan Generics* ¶58 (2016).

67 *See, e.g.*, Case COMP/M.9274, *GlaxoSmithKline/Pfizer Consumer Healthcare Business* ¶34 (2019).

68 For the third group, the European Commission does generally not assess each overlap market individually but examines the competitive situation on these markets by considering the nature and the number of existing competitors. *Id.*; Case COMP/M.8889, *Teva/PGT OTC Assets* ¶36 (2018).

into account: large market shares of the merging parties, the fact that the parties are close competitors, limited possibilities for customers to switch suppliers, or the fact that the merger would eliminate an important competitor.[69] This is not an exhaustive list, nor do all elements need to be present for the European Commission to consider that a merger will negatively affect competition for marketed products. In recent years, the European Commission has intervened in several pharmaceutical mergers that allegedly may have resulted in higher prices, in particular in mergers involving generic and biosimilar products which themselves are price challengers to originator products. This activity is unsurprising given that the EC Pharmaceutical Enforcement Report identified price as a key concern, stating that "a key objective of merger control in the pharmaceutical sector is to ensure that the changes in the market structure due to a merger do not result in higher prices."[70]

334. Although the US Antitrust Agencies do consider market shares to be an important factor in merger reviews, they do not use fixed share thresholds to reduce the overlapping markets to be examined. However, the agencies do in addition to market shares consider market concentration using Herfindahl–Hirschman Index (HHIs), the number of competing drugs, the closeness of competition between two overlapping products in terms of method of administration (e.g., oral versus injectable), efficacy, safety, and side effects, potential effects on future innovation, and the likelihood of timely and sufficient entry, among other factors.

335. Where concerns relate to innovation rather than marketed overlaps in pharmaceutical mergers, the European Commission and US agencies may seek to block the merger outright rather than seek divestitures of overlapping products.[71] This happens rarely in Europe, although the European Commission did recently block the *Illumina/Grail* transaction.

336. The *AbbVie/Allergan* and *Teva/Allergan* mergers provide illustrative examples of conditional clearance decisions:

- *AbbVie Inc./Allergan plc (2020).*[72] Both the FTC and European Commission concluded this transaction would harm competition. The FTC alleged that AbbVie's $63 billion acquisition of Allergan would reduce competition in the market for the treatment of EPI, a condition that results in the inability to digest food properly. According to the FTC, the combined firm would control 95% of the US market for EPI treatments.[73] As part of a negotiated

---

69 European Commission, Guidelines on the assessment of horizontal mergers under the Council Regulation on the control of concentrations between undertakings (the EU Horizontal Merger Guidelines), 2004 OJ (C 31) 5, ¶27.

70 EC Pharmaceutical Enforcement Report, *supra* n. 2, Chapter III, 35.

71 FTC, *Statement of Commissioner Rohit Chopra Joined by Commissioner Rebecca Slaughter, In the Matter of Pfizer Inc./Mylan N.V.*, FTC File No. 191-0182 (Oct. 30, 2020), *available at* https://www.ftc.gov/system/files/documents/public_statements/1582382/191_0182_pfizer-mylan_-_dissenting_statement_of_commrs_chopra_and_slaughter_1.pdf.

72 FTC, Press Release, *FTC Imposes Conditions on AbbVie Inc.'s Acquisition of Allergan plc* (May 5, 2020), *available at* https://www.ftc.gov/news-events/news/press-releases/2020/05/ftc-imposes-conditions-abbvie-incs-acquisition-allergan-plc.

73 FTC, *Analysis of Agreement Containing Consent Orders to Aid Public Comment, In the Matter of AbbVie Inc. and Allergan plc,* FTC File No. 191-0169, 3 (May 5, 2020), *available at* https://www.ftc.gov/system/files/documents/cases/191_0169_abbvie_and_allergan_-_aapc.pdf.

consent, the FTC required the merged firm to divest the assets and rights to two EPI drugs (Zenpep and Viokace) to preserve the status quo in EPI treatment competition. The FTC also alleged that the acquisition would eliminate future competition between AbbVie and Allergan in interleukin-23 (IL-23) inhibitor drugs for the treatment of moderate-to-severe Crohn's disease and moderate-to-severe ulcerative colitis. While neither firm had IL-23 inhibitor drugs on the market at the time, both firms had IL-23 inhibitors in late-stage development at the time of the merger. Accordingly, the FTC required the divestiture of Allergan's rights and assets related to its not-yet-approved IL-23 product.

The EC[74] similarly concluded that the transaction would negatively affect competition for biologic treatments for ulcerative colitis and Crohn's disease, collectively termed inflammatory bowel diseases (IBD). AbbVie's product portfolio included several biologic drugs for IBD: Risankizumab, an IL-23 pipeline drug and Humira, a marketed Tumor Necrosis Factor (TNF) drug. Allergan was also developing an IL-23 inhibitor (Brazikumab). The European Commission found that Brazikumab was likely to compete closely with AbbVie's Risankizumab as both are IL-23 inhibitors. Based on its market investigation the European Commission concluded that the transaction would have led to a loss of innovation for IBD treatments, as AbbVie would not continue to develop Allergan's IL-23 inhibitor while IL-23 inhibitors were found to be a promising class of biologics for which only two other competing pipeline products (in addition to those of the merging parties) were being developed. To address the European Commission's concerns AbbVie offered to divest Allergan's pipeline product, including development, manufacturing and marketing rights at worldwide level to a purchaser that would continue the drug's development.

Such "pipeline" product divestitures are common, and likewise part of the established European Commission and FTC framework for analyzing horizontal pharmaceutical mergers. Additional information on how the agencies evaluate issues of nascent competition is provided below.

- *Teva/Allergan (2016).*[75] The FTC alleged that Teva's acquisition of Allergan's generic pharmaceutical business would reduce competition in 79 separate product markets. The product markets included anesthetics, antibiotics, weight loss drugs, oral contraceptives, and treatments for a wide variety of diseases and conditions, including attention deficit hyperactivity disorder (ADHD), allergies, arthritis, cancers, diabetes, high blood pressure, high cholesterol, mental illnesses, opioid dependence, pain, Parkinson's disease, and respiratory, skin, and sleep disorders.

  In 25 of the 79 markets at least one of the merging parties did not yet have a competing product, including some cases where neither firm had yet entered the market. However the FTC alleged a loss of future competition in these

[74] Case COMP/M.9461, *AbbVie/Allergan* (2020).

[75] FTC, *In the Matter of Teva and Allergan*, FTC File No. 151-0196 (Sept. 15, 2016), *available at* https://www.ftc.gov/legal-library/browse/cases-proceedings/151-0196-teva-allergan-matter.

markets because one or both of the parties were developing competing products and were part of a limited number of firms capable of entry. The FTC required the parties to divest rights and assets to all 79 pharmaceutical products.

Additionally, the FTC identified 15 products where Teva supplied the APIs to current or future Allergan competitors. In these cases, Teva was required to offer these customers long-term API supply contracts.

Because of the unusual breadth of the divestitures, the FTC also issued a statement explaining that they evaluated the effect of the merger on generic pharmaceutical competition generally, beyond the 79 divested drugs.[76] Specifically, the FTC considered but rejected a theory that the merger would lead to anticompetitive effects from the bundling of generic products to foreclose smaller competitors. The FTC likewise rejected theories that the merger would dampen incentives to develop new generic products, or to challenge brand exclusivity.

The scale of the *Teva/Allergan* merger, combining two of the top four generics players globally, raised many novel issues for the European Commission.[77] The European Commission not only examined hundreds of product-by-product overlaps at the molecule level but also at the level of the overall sale of generics in certain EEA countries, including the UK (which was at the time still a member of the EU), Ireland, and Iceland. The European Commission concluded that price competition would have been adversely affected in several national markets. In the UK, the European Commission focused on the unique pricing pressure between the two parties, finding that they were the only two generics companies able to sell their drugs to pharmacies. All other generics companies allegedly lacked the commercial scale to do so and could only sell their medicines to wholesalers. This led to the divestment of the majority of Allergan's generics business in the UK and Ireland in addition to the divestiture of 159 marketed and 20 pipeline molecules in 26 additional EEA countries. The complexity of the remedies, and the portfolio and vertical analysis, are discussed in the Sections below.

B. Restriction of innovation

337. Given that innovation is a key part of the pharmaceutical sector, both the European Commission and the FTC scrutinize how mergers in the industry might compromise R&D efforts. This Section first addresses the assessment of restrictions on innovations generally before focusing on the following specific topics: (a) product overlaps involving at least one pipeline product, (b) pipeline-pipeline mergers, and (c) innovation spaces.

---

76 FTC, *Statement of the Federal Trade Commission, In the Matter of Teva Pharmaceuticals Industries Ltd. And Allergan plc*, FTC File No. 151-0196 (July 27, 2016), *available at* https://www.ftc.gov/system/files/documents/public_statements/973673/160727tevaallergan-statement.pdf.

77 Case COMP/M.7746, *Teva/Allergan Generics* (2016); European Commission, Press Release IP/16/727, *Mergers: Commission approves acquisition of Allergan Generics by Teva, subject to conditions* (Mar. 10, 2016), *available at* https://ec.europa.eu/commission/presscorner/detail/en/IP_16_727.

338. The European Commission identified harm to innovation as a key concern in its EC Pharmaceutical Enforcement Report:

> Reducing competition on innovation means that patients and healthcare systems would forego future benefits from innovative and affordable medicines. Harmful effects may include a loss of potentially better treatments, reduced future variety of medicines on the market, delayed access to medicines needed for the treatment of their conditions and higher prices.[78]

339. The EU Horizontal Merger Guidelines expressly mention innovation as one of the benefits of effective competition and specify that mergers involving pipeline products can affect competition in relation to innovation.[79] Typically this would involve overlapping pipeline products that are relatively developed, within sight of commercialization, and known to target specific product markets.[80] An example is *Novartis/GSK Oncology*[81] where the European Commission considered inter alia that the transaction would reduce innovation, with the likely abandonment of Novartis' broad clinical trial programs for two skin cancer inhibitors (LGX818 and MEK16) which were being trialed for a number of other cancers (ovarian, colorectal, or lung cancer).[82] In *J&J/Actelion*,[83] the European Commission raised issues in relation to overlap of Phase II pipeline products. The European Commission's concerns focused on the development of the parties' overlapping development programs for insomnia drugs and found that the parties would have the incentive to reduce, discontinue, or delay the development programs. An example in the medical devices sector is *Medtronic/Covidien*,[84] where the European Commission considered that there was reasonable certainty that a pipeline product in Phase III, the last stage of clinical trials, would reach the market upon completion of the regulatory approval process and thus in the near future. But "innovation" is not limited to pipeline products and may also cover earlier-stage innovation projects which may not yet identify concrete products and remain uncertain.[85] In all innovation cases, similar to potential competition cases, one of the main concerns the European Commission identifies is the discontinuation, delay, or re-orientation of pipeline or innovation efforts of one of the merging parties. The pharmaceutical sector is highly R&D intensive and therefore is a sector where the European Commission regularly identifies competition concerns related to the overlaps in the parties' pipeline products, including those at relatively early stages.[86]

---

78 EC Pharmaceutical Enforcement Report, *supra* n. 2, Chapter III, 42.

79 EU Horizontal Merger Guidelines, *supra* n. 69, Chapter III, ¶¶37–38, 81.

80 OECD Background Note, *Start-ups, Killer Acquisitions and Merger Control*, ¶¶30–31 (2020), *available at* https://www.oecd.org/daf/competition/start-ups-killer-acquisitions-and-merger-control-2020.pdf.

81 Case COMP/M.7276, *Novartis/GlaxoSmithKline Oncology Business* (2015).

82 European Commission, Press Release IP/15/3842, *Competition: Commission approves acquisition of GSK's oncology business by Novartis, subject to conditions* (Jan. 28, 2015), *available at* https://ec.europa.eu/commission/presscorner/detail/en/IP_15_3842.

83 Case COMP/M.8401, *J&J/Actelion* (2017).

84 Case COMP/M.7326, *Medtronic/Covidien* (2014).

85 Note by the OECD Background Note, *supra* n. 80 Chapter III, ¶32.

86 *Id.* ¶¶33–35.

340. In the US, the US Horizontal Merger Guidelines state that "[c]ompetition often spurs firms to innovate."[87] Pharmaceutical companies may compete with one another through innovation to develop new or improved drugs. When companies that compete in innovation merge, the US Antitrust Agencies may be concerned that the combined entity will cause a "curtailment of innovation" through a "reduced incentive to continue with an existing product-development effort or reduced incentive to initiate development of new products."[88] Agencies believe that fewer potential entrants could lead to less experimentation for new discoveries, causing concentrated R&D efforts with a focus on a narrower selection of products, and industry innovation as a whole to suffer.

341. In recent years, the FTC has taken enforcement actions to specifically address these potential harms to innovation. As stated in the US agencies' 2010 guidelines, "Agencies may consider whether a merger is likely to diminish innovation competition by encouraging the merged firm to curtail its innovative efforts below the level that would prevail in the absence of the merger."[89] Many recent FTC enforcement actions across different areas within the pharmaceutical industry address theories of harm related to a reduction in innovation and the remedies used to resolve such concerns.

342. For example, the FTC's May 2020 complaint challenging AbbVie's proposed acquisition of Allergan highlighted the FTC's approach to analyzing a restriction to innovation theory of harm.[90] AbbVie focused on the research, development, manufacturing, and sale of pharmaceutical and biologic products in the immunology, oncology, and virology areas.[91] Allergan focused on some of the same pharmaceutical areas.[92] These areas included EPI drugs and inhibitors used to treat moderate-to-severe Crohn's disease and ulcerative colitis.[93] In the three relevant markets in which the FTC alleged the transaction would pose anticompetitive concerns, AbbVie and Allergan were two of only a limited number of firms with products that were either currently on the market or in development.[94]

343. The FTC investigated whether the "merger will diminish innovation competition by combining two of a very small number of firms with the strongest capabilities to successfully innovate in a specific direction."[95] In the course of its investigation, the FTC determined entry into the relevant markets would require significant investment and not be "timely, likely, or sufficient in magnitude" to deter the anticompetitive nature of the transaction, and future competition between

---

87 US Horizontal Merger Guidelines, *supra* n. 63, Chapter III, ¶6.4.

88 *Id.*

89 *Id.*

90 *See* Analysis of Agreement in the Matter of AbbVie Inc./ Allergan plc, *supra* n. 73, Chapter III.

91 *See* FTC, *Statement of Chairman Joseph J. Simons, Commissioner Noah Joshua Phillips, and Commissioner Christine S. Wilson Concerning the Proposed Acquisition of Allergan plc by AbbVie Inc.*, File No. 191-0169, 9–10 (May 5, 2020), *available at* https://www.ftc.gov/system/files/documents/public_statements/1574619/abbvie-allergan_majority_statement_5-5-20.pdf.

92 *Id.*

93 *See* Analysis of Agreement in the Matter of AbbVie Inc./ Allergan plc, *supra* n. 73, Chapter III.

94 *Id.* 3.

95 *See* Simons, Phillips, Wilson AbbVie Statement, *supra* n. 91 Chapter III, 9.

the two companies would be eliminated.[96] The FTC specifically considered the "transaction's effect on the parties' R&D programs and investments, as well as on innovation competition."[97] While the agency ultimately allowed the merger to go through, it did so on the condition that Allergan divest three drugs that overlapped with drugs in AbbVie's portfolio. Two of these drugs at the time were competing on the market with one of AbbVie's drugs used to treat EPI, and the third was in the development stage that also overlapped with a developing drug AbbVie supplied to treat ulcerative colitis and Crohn's disease.[98] The parties were required to divest not only Allergan's businesses related to these drugs (including the regulatory approvals, IP, contracts, and inventory), but also to transfer all business information, R&D information, regulatory, formulation, and manufacturing reports related to the divested products, and provide access to knowledgeable employees to assist in the transfer.[99]

344. In other FTC investigations in the pharmaceutical industry, the FTC's innovation-related theories of harm differ based on where the parties are in product development. For example, the analysis may change based on whether one or both parties have an existing product on the market, are still in the R&D stage, or have overlapping product portfolios that combine top-selling drugs across multiple therapeutic areas.

345. When a drug sponsor develops a new compound and seeks approval for sale in the EU or US, the sponsor must take the drug through various tests to generate data on the safety and efficacy of the compound. In the US, the sponsor may first test the drug on animals to gather basic information about the safety and efficacy of the compound being researched.[100] The sponsor will then submit this data to the FDA in a formal request, also known as the Investigational New Drug (IND) Application, that includes a plan for clinical testing of the drug.[101] In the EU, medicine developers who wish to conduct clinical trials need to submit applications to the national competent authorities of the countries where they want to conduct the trials. The EMA does not have a role in the authorization of clinical trials which is instead the responsibility of the competent national authorities.[102]

346. Once approval is received, the sponsor can proceed to the three phases of clinical trials: Phase I (reviewing the most frequent side effects of the drug), Phase II (reviewing the efficacy of the drug and whether it works in people

---

96 Complaint, *In the Matter of AbbVie Inc., and Allergan plc*, FTC File No. 191-0169, 3 (May 5, 2020), *available at* https://www.ftc.gov/system/files/documents/cases/191_0169_abbvie_and_allergan_-_complaint_0.pdf.

97 *See* FTC, *Dissenting Statement of Commissioner Rebecca Kelly Slaughter, In the Matter of AbbVie /Allergan*, FTC File No. 191-0169, 2 (May 5, 2020), *available at* https://www.ftc.gov/system/files/documents/public_statements/1574577/191_0169_dissenting_statement_of_commissioner_rebecca_kelly_slaughter_in_the_matter_of_abbvie_and_0.pdf.

98 *See* Analysis of Agreement in the Matter of AbbVie Inc./ Allergan plc, *supra* n. 73, Chapter III, 2.

99 *Id.* 3.

100 *See* FDA, *Drug Approval Process*, *available at* https://www.fda.gov/drugs/development-approval-process-drugs.

101 *Id.*

102 EMA, *From Laboratory to Patient: The Journey of a Medicine Assessed by EMA* (2019), *available at* https://www.ema.europa.eu/en/documents/other/laboratory-patient-journey-centrally-authorised-medicine_en.pdf.

with certain diseases or conditions), and Phase III (gathering additional information about safety, effectiveness, and adverse reactions to the drug).[103] A study tracking FDA approval rates for drugs indicated that among pipeline products moving through the three FDA trial phases, about 70% of Phase I drugs moved to the next phase, about 33% of Phase II drugs advanced to Phase III, and about 25–30% of drugs made it past Phase III. Due to the rigorous FDA drug approval process, only about 10% of brand drugs that begin Phase I clinical trials are actually approved by the FDA.[104] Historically, the FTC has most seriously reviewed Phase III pipeline products for potential competition concerns because they are most likely to make it to market, but the agency does not have rigid rules and may also review products in earlier phases for potential competition concerns.

347. In the EU, it was well-established that harm to innovation was only possible if concerns arose in relation to late-stage pipeline products, for example, Phase III of clinical trials when market entry was supposed to occur in a short time frame, of 2 to 3 years. However, since 2014 the European Commission has been expanding its approach to harm to innovation and pipeline products. In general, the European Commission examines the potential for pipeline products to enter into competition with other marketed or pipeline products by reference to their characteristics and intended therapeutic use.[105] In the same way as for overlaps between marketed products, the European Commission applies a system of filters to focus on the product overlaps that are most likely to raise concerns. Based on established practice, the European Commission generally identifies the following categories:

- pipeline in affected markets: one party is planning to launch a pipeline product in a market where both parties already hold a combined market share in excess of 35%;
- pipeline-to-marketed affected markets: one party is planning to launch a pipeline in a market where the other party is the originator or holds a market share in excess of 35%;
- pipeline-to-pipeline affected markets: both parties are planning to launch a pipeline in a market where there are only one or two competitors (including the originator); this is the case for example in relation to molecules close to patent expiry; and
- originator-to-generic pipeline overlaps: one party is planning to launch a generic version of a product for which the other party is the originator.

348. The sections below discuss specific areas of focus for the agencies, namely product overlaps involving at least one pipeline product, pipeline-pipeline mergers, and innovation spaces.

---

103 FDA, *Step 3: Clinical Research* (Jan. 4, 2018), *available at* https://www.fda.gov/patients/drug-development-process/step-3-clinical-research#Clinical_Research_Phase_Studies; Dave DiProspero, *The Basics and the Process of Drug Approval* (CRB Group), *available at* https://www.crbgroup.com/insights/pharmaceuticals/drug-approval-process.

104 *Id.*

105 Case COMP/M.7275, *Novartis/GlaxoSmithKline Oncology Business* (2015).

a. *Mergers Where the Product Overlap Involves At Least One Pipeline Product*

349. In analyzing the potential diminution in innovation as a result of a merger or acquisition, the FTC and the European Commission have expressed concerns over transactions involving competing firms with identifiable products on the market, and in development.[106] This category includes "product-to-pipeline" overlaps in which one merging firm has an existing product and the other is developing a product that could capture substantial revenues from the existing product on the market.[107] An identifiable feature of some of these mergers is that the pipeline product will typically be associated easily and directly with the existing product, such as the "next generation" of an existing product.[108] EU and US agencies may be concerned that the merged entity may discontinue or prevent the entry of the new and innovative product developed by the acquired firm in order to maintain its market power for the existing product. Furthermore, agencies may theorize that the merged firm may devote fewer resources to certain pipeline projects or reduce the number of pipeline projects that are funded, thereby harming innovation.[109]

350. In these types of transactions, particularly involving complex pharmaceutical products that are difficult to manufacture, the FTC prefers a divestiture of the on-market product rather than the pipeline product, so as to place the greater risk of manufacturing difficulties on the merging parties.[110] But where a pipeline product is divested, the FTC explained: "The goal of a divestiture is to put the product development effort (including any pending regulatory filings) in the hands of a new firm with the same ability and incentive to bring the pipeline product to market."[111] In the EC, divestitures generally relate to the overlapping pipeline product, rather than the marketed product.

351. A few notable investigations in this area demonstrate how the FTC and European Commission review these types of transactions, as well as the types of remedies used to resolve product-to-pipeline issues.

352. In November 2019, the FTC filed a complaint challenging Bristol-Myers Squibb's (BMS) proposed $74 billion acquisition of Celgene Corporation[112]

---

106 US Horizontal Merger Guidelines, *supra* n. 63, Chapter III, 23–24; EU Horizontal Merger Guidelines, *supra* n. 69, Chapter III, 5–18.

107 Giulio Federico et al., *Antitrust and Innovation: Welcoming and Protecting Disruption*, 20 INNOVATION POLICY AND THE ECONOMY 125, 137 (Univ. Chicago Press, 2020), *available at* https://www.journals.uchicago.edu/doi/pdf/10.1086/705642.

108 *Id.* 139.

109 *Id.* 140.

110 *See* FTC, Analysis of Agreement, *In the Matter of Amneal Holdings and Impax Laboratories*, FTC File No. 181-0017, 4 (Apr. 27, 2018), *available at* https://www.ftc.gov/system/files/documents/cases/1810017_amneal_impax_analysis_4-27-18.pdf (the Analysis of Agreement in the Matter of Amneal Holdings and Impax Laboratories).

111 *Id.* 4–5.

112 FTC, Press Release, *FTC Requires Bristol-Myers Squibb Company and Celgene Corporation to Divest Psoriasis Drug Otezla as a Condition of Acquisition* (Nov. 15, 2019), *available at* https://www.ftc.gov/news-events/news/press-releases/2019/11/ftc-requires-bristol-myers-squibb-company-celgene-corporation-divest-psoriasis-drug-otezla-condition; FTC, Press Release, *FTC Approves Final Order Requiring Bristol-*

even though the transaction was unconditionally cleared in the EU.[113] BMS and Celgene are both researchers, developers, and sellers of prescription pharmaceutical and biologic products, and BMS had a pipeline oral product in development at Phase III to treat moderate-to-severe psoriasis.[114] Celgene already had the most popular oral product on the market in the US that was approved to treat moderate-to-severe psoriasis, marketed under the brand name Otezla.[115] BMS' pipeline product was currently the most advanced oral treatment for moderate-to-severe psoriasis in production and the most likely rival to Otezla.[116]

353. The FTC was concerned that this transaction would result in "substantial competitive harm to consumers" because Celgene was the market leader and BMS would likely be the next entrant.[117] The FTC's investigation identified a likely harm to innovation involving oral products to treat moderate-to-severe psoriasis due to the elimination of future competition between BMS and Celgene.[118] Additionally, given the lengthy FDA approval process, new entry was not expected to be timely, likely, or sufficient in magnitude to counteract the anticompetitive effects of the transaction.[119] However in the distinct field of oncology, the FTC's investigation also found that "reduced innovation competition" as a result of this transaction was unlikely, in part, because "no fewer than 711 companies [were] conducting late-stage R&D in oncology, the therapeutic category in which BMS and Celgene conduct[ed] research."[120]

354. The FTC ultimately allowed the merger to go through on the condition that the merged entity divest Celgene's existing product, Otezla. The divestment raised $13.4 billion in what has been considered the largest divestiture that

---

Myers Squibb Company and Celgene Corporation to Divest Psoriasis Drug Otezla as a Condition of Acquisition (Jan. 13, 2020), *available at* https://www.ftc.gov/news-events/news/press-releases/2020/01/ftc-approves-final-order-requiring-bristol-myers-squibb-company-celgene-corporation-divest-psoriasis.

113 The European Commission concluded that "the proposed transaction would raise no competition concerns given the number of actual and potential competitors, and its limited impact in the EEA.", European Commission, Press Release MEX/19/4849, *Mergers: Commission clears acquisition of Celgene by BMS*, (July 30, 2019), *available at* https://ec.europa.eu/commission/presscorner/detail/en/MEX_19_4849.

114 *See* FTC, Analysis of Agreement, *In the Matter of Bristol-Myers Squibb Company and Celgene Corporation*, FTC File No. 191-0061, 1 (Nov. 15, 2019), *available at* https://www.ftc.gov/system/files/documents/cases/bms-celgene_aac.pdf (the Analysis of Agreement in the Matter of Bristol-Myers Squibb Company and Celgene Corporation).

115 *Id.* 2.

116 FTC, Press Release, *FTC Requires Bristol-Myers Squibb Company and Celgene Corporation to Divest Psoriasis Drug Otezla as a Condition of Acquisition* (Nov. 15, 2019), *available at* https://www.ftc.gov/news-events/news/press-releases/2019/11/ftc-requires-bristol-myers-squibb-company-celgene-corporation-divest-psoriasis-drug-otezla-condition.

117 Analysis of Agreement in the Matter of Bristol-Myers Squibb Company and Celgene Corporation, *supra* n. 114, Chapter III, 2–3.

118 Complaint, *In the Matter of Bristol-Myers Squibb Company and Celgene*, FTC Docket No. C-4690, 3 (Nov. 15, 2019), *available at*https://www.ftc.gov/system/files/documents/cases/191_0061_c4690_bms_celgene_complaint_0.pdf; *see* FTC, *Statement of Comm'r Christine S. Wilson In the Matter of Bristol-Myers Squibb Company / Celgene Corporation*, FTC File No. 191-0061, 1 (Nov. 15, 2019), *available at* https://www.ftc.gov/system/files/documents/public_statements/1554278/bms-celgene_-_wilson_statement.pdf (the Statement of Comm'r Christine S. Wilson).

119 Analysis of Agreement in the Matter of Bristol-Myers Squibb Company and Celgene Corporation, *supra* n. 114, Chapter III, 3.

120 Statement of Comm'r Christine S. Wilson, *supra* n. 118, Chapter III, 1.

the FTC or DOJ has ever required in a merger enforcement matter.[121] As part of the divestiture, BMS was required to divest Otezla's regulatory approvals, IP, contracts, and inventory.[122] Additionally, BMS and Celgene were required to transfer all confidential business information, R&D information, formulation and manufacturing reports related to Otezla, and provide access to employees that possessed or were able to identify such information.[123] BMS and Celgene were also required to supply the divestiture buyer with Otezla for a limited time while the buyer established its own manufacturing capability.[124] In doing so, the FTC's Chair stated that the divestiture was needed "to preserve BMS's incentive to continue developing its own oral product for treating moderate-to-severe psoriasis."[125] This statement further emphasized that that "[t]he antitrust laws protect not only competition today, but competition in the future, especially when it comes to the development of new treatments for chronic conditions."[126]

355. In 2018, another FTC investigation resulted in a challenge of Amneal Pharmaceuticals LLC's proposed $1.45 billion acquisition through a series of transactions of equity interests of Impax Laboratories, LLC.[127] This transaction was not notifiable under the EU Merger Regulation because it did not meet the filing thresholds. Both Amneal and Impax were involved in the development, license, manufacture, marketing, distribution, and sale of generic pharmaceutical products. Of seven out of ten generic pharmaceutical products where the FTC alleged harm, either Amneal or Impax was a current competitor and the other was viewed as a likely entrant. For example, Amneal was the only existing generic competitor in the market for generic aspirin and dipyridamole extended-release capsules, but Impax had been approved to enter the same market. Similarly, Impax was one of only three generic competitors for azelastine nasal spray, but Amneal allegedly was one of a few suppliers capable of entering the market in the imminent future.[128] The FTC alleged that by eliminating future competition between Amneal and Impax in these seven markets, there would be an increased likelihood that the combined firm would "forego or delay the launch of each product" as well as "delay, eliminate, or otherwise reduce the substantial additional price competition that would have resulted from an additional supplier of each product."[129] To remedy this harm, the FTC required the parties to divest all of

---

121 FTC, Press Release, *FTC Approves Final Order Requiring Bristol-Myers Squibb Company and Celgene Corporation to Divest Psoriasis Drug Otezla as a Condition of Acquisition* (Jan. 13, 2020).

122 *Id.*

123 Analysis of Agreement in the Matter of Bristol-Myers Squibb Company and Celgene Corporation, *supra* n. 114, Chapter III, 3.

124 *Id.*

125 FTC, Press Release, *FTC Requires Bristol-Myers Squibb Company and Celgene Corporation to Divest Psoriasis Drug Otezla as a Condition of Acquisition* (Nov. 15, 2019), *available at* https://www.ftc.gov/news-events/news/press-releases/2019/11/ftc-requires-bristol-myers-squibb-company-celgene-corporation-divest-psoriasis-drug-otezla-condition.

126 *Id.*

127 Complaint, *In the Matter of Amneal et al. And Impax Laboratories, LLC.*, FTC Docket No. C-4650, 3 (Apr. 27, 2018), *available at* https://www.ftc.gov/system/files/documents/cases/1810017_amneal_impax_complaint_final.pdf.

128 Analysis of Agreement in the Matter of Amneal Holdings and Impax Laboratories, *supra* n. 110, Chapter III, 4.

129 Complaint in the Matter of Amneal et al and Impax Laboratories, LLC, *supra* n. 127, Chapter III, 5–6.

Impax's rights and assets related to the seven products in which either Amneal or Impax was a current market participant and the other a capable or imminent entrant, as well as two markets in which Amneal and Impax were two out of only four existing generic competitors.[130]

356. In *Medtronic/Covidien*,[131] the European Commission examined the proposed acquisition of Covidien, an Irish manufacturer of medical devices, by Medtronic, a US-based company active in medical technologies and therapies. Medtronic allegedly was the market leader and Covidien had a promising pipeline product called Stellarex for drug-coated balloons to treat vascular diseases. According to the EC, once launched Stellarex would compete with Medtronic's leading drug coated balloon device, In Pact. The European Commission raised concerns that the transaction would remove a credible future competitor to Medtronic and reduce innovation in this area, because there were only a few other competitors active in the market for drug-coated balloons, who could only exert limited competitive pressure on Medtronic. The European Commission found that Covidien would have constrained Medtronic in the near future based on Stellarex's promising first clinical trial results. To address these concerns Medtronic committed to sell Covidien's worldwide Stellarex business, including manufacturing equipment, related IP rights and scientific and regulatory material necessary for ensuring the completion of the Stellarex trials. Medtronic further committed to supply the purchaser, during a transitional period, with the balloons on which the drug is applied as well as to transfer staff, including some key personnel. This was considered necessary to provide the purchaser with all assets necessary to bring Stellarex to the market.

357. In 2017, the European Commission approved the acquisition of Hospira by Pfizer subject to divestment of Pfizer's biosimilar pipeline drug infliximab, which was used to treat certain autoimmune diseases.[132] The European Commission observed that because biological drugs are some of the most expensive therapies available, the entry of biosimilars would likely allow price decreases and increased access for patients to biological drugs. Infliximab was one of the top three best-selling pharmaceuticals globally, and is used to treat autoimmune diseases such as rheumatoid arthritis and Crohn's disease. One biosimilar had been approved in the EEA (developed by Celltrion but co-marketed by Hospira and Celltrion) and two companies had biosimilars in advanced stages of development (Samsung Bioepis and Pfizer). Based on its market investigation, the European Commission concluded that Pfizer's acquisition of Hospira could cause competition concerns in the market for infliximab drugs because Pfizer would be likely to ether delay or discontinue development of its biosimilar drug in order to focus on Hospira's marketed product. These scenarios allegedly would lead to either the net loss of future competition by one of only three

---

130 *Id.* 3.

131 Case COMP/M.7326, *Medtronic/Covidien* (2014).

132 Case COMP/M.7559, *Pfizer/Hospira* (2015); European Commission, Press Release IP 15/5470, *Mergers: Commission approves acquisition of Hospira by Pfizer, subject to conditions* (Aug. 4, 2015), *available at* https://ec.europa.eu/commission/presscorner/detail/en/IP_15_5470.

differential biosimilars already in advanced stages of development, or to the loss of current price competition between Hospira and Celltrion. Both outcomes – reduction of differentiated biosimilars from three to two or loss of price competition – would be detrimental to competition in the infliximab drug market. The parties had to divest Pfizer's biosimilar drug and its development, manufacturing, and marketing rights including appropriate IP, technology and know-how; however the marketing rights outside of the EEA remained with the merging entity.

b. *Pipeline/Pipeline Merger*

358. The FTC and European Commission have similarly expressed concerns specifically relating to a potential reduction in innovation in the pharmaceutical industry where both parties to a transaction have overlapping products in the pipeline. In this scenario, the drugs at issue are those that will compete with each other if and when they are introduced but are still in clinical testing Phases I, II, and III and not yet in the market.[133]

359. The European Commission first assessed merging parties' early-stage research projects (i.e., those not yet in Phase III final trials) in the 2015 *Novartis/GlaxoSmithKline Oncology Business* decision.[134] Both Novartis and GlaxoSmithKline had advanced pipeline products in Phase III for the treatment of skin and ovarian cancer. Both parties were also testing the same inhibitors and mechanisms of action for the treatment of other cancers; however, those tests were in early Phase I and II stages of development. Only one other competitor, Roche, had a late stage competing pipeline product for those other treatments. The parties offered a series of behavioral remedies to address the European Commission's concerns that Novartis would stop developing its pipeline products because the target had identical projects in the pipeline, and continuing similar clinical programs is lengthy and costly. For the first time, the European Commission looked at early-stage pipeline products where the timeframe for successful market entry was uncertain. And where before the European Commission's analysis was focused on specific products, the European Commission instead zoomed in on the merger's effect on the parties' "incentive to innovate," which highlights the European Commission's more recent focus on innovation spaces, i.e., the impact of mergers on competition in innovation as such without any link to specific products.

360. In August 2015 the FTC challenged Pfizer's acquisition of Hospira, alleging the transaction would reduce future competition in, among other areas, melphalan hydrochloride injection products, an alleged market in which both Pfizer and Hospira were developing their own generic versions and were the only well-positioned firms capable of entering the market in the near future.[135] The FTC

---

133 Federico et al., *Antitrust and Innovation: Welcoming and Protecting Disruption*, *supra* n. 107, Chapter III, 137–39.

134 Case COMP/M.7275, *Novartis/GlaxoSmithKline Oncology Business* (2015).

135 FTC, Analysis of Agreement Containing Consent Orders to Aid Public Comment, *In the Matter of Pfizer Inc. And Hospira, Inc.*, FTC File No. 151-0074 2 (Aug. 24, 2015), *available at* https://www.ftc.gov/system/files/documents/cases/150824pfizerhospiraanalysis.pdf.

raised concerns that the transaction would increase the likelihood that the combined entity would forego or delay the launch of Hospira's melphalan hydrochloride product.[136] While the FTC ultimately allowed the merger to go through, it required Hospira to divest, among other things, all of its rights and assets related to melphalan hydrochloride injection to another supplier, Alvogen.[137] The combined Pfizer/Hospira entity was also required to transfer the third-party development and contract manufacturing agreements for melphalan hydrochloride injection to Alvogen, along with all transitional service to assist Alvogen in establishing its manufacturing capabilities and securing all necessary FDA approvals.[138]

361. In October 2006 the FTC filed a complaint to block Barr Pharmaceutical's proposed acquisition of Pliva, alleging the transaction would have eliminated current or future competition between the two parties across multiple markets.[139] Both parties participated in the research, development, manufacture, and sale of generic pharmaceutical products.[140] While the transaction allegedly would have significantly increased the merged firm's market share across three separate markets in which the parties supply overlapping products – generic pharmaceuticals treating depression, high blood pressure, and organ preservation solutions – the FTC also alleged anticompetitive harm in a fourth market, generic nimodipine soft-gel capsules used to treat symptoms from a ruptured blood vessel in the brain, in which Barr and Pliva each had a generic product in its pipeline.[141] With the expiry of the patent on branded nimodipine, Barr and Pliva were the only companies seeking approval for generic nimodipine.[142] As a result, the FTC was concerned that the proposed transaction would eliminate potential competition in the generic market between Barr and Pliva, possibly leading to the delay or elimination of another innovative generic product. As part of the FTC's consent order, Barr was required to divest its generic antidepressant trazodone, its generic blood pressure medication triamterene/HCTZ, and Pliva's branded organ preservation solution Custodial. Additionally, the merged entity was required to divest either Barr's or Pliva's generic nimodipine. This outcome illustrates that the continuation of pipeline generic drugs, like pipeline branded drugs, may create competitive concerns even though generic entry is often considered easier than branded entry in the US.

362. In 2017 the European Commission conditionally approved the acquisition of Actelion Pharmaceuticals by Johnson & Johnson.[143] Both parties developed and

---

136 *Id.* 4.

137 *Id.* 3.

138 *Id.* 4.

139 Complaint, *In the Matter of Barr Pharma., Inc.*, FTC Docket No. C-4171, 2 (Oct. 19, 2006), *available at* https://www.ftc.gov/sites/default/files/documents/cases/2006/10/0610217barrcomplaint.pdf.

140 *Id.*

141 FTC, Analysis of Proposed Consent Order to Aid Public Comment, *In the Matter of Barr Pharmaceuticals, Inc. And Pliva d.d.*, FTC File No. 061-0217, 2 (Oct. 20, 2006), *available at* https://www.ftc.gov/sites/default/files/documents/cases/2006/10/0610217barranalysis.pdf.

142 *Id.*

143 Case COMP/M.8401, *J&J/Actelion* (2017.

sold innovative pharmaceutical products, and their activities were found to be largely complementary. Actelion marketed medicines in the EEA primarily for the treatment of pulmonary arterial hypertension, a market in which Johnson & Johnson was not active. However, the merging parties were each developing an innovative drug for insomnia. Both products were at an early stage – Phase II – of development. Both treatments under development were based on a novel mechanism of action, and no other treatments of this kind were being marketed in the EEA, and this new mechanism of action was only being developed for a limited number of medicines. The European Commission concluded that the merger would negatively affect competition because the merged parties would likely not be incentivized to continue both research projects post-transaction. The parties had proposed in their notification that Actelion's insomnia research program would be transferred before the merger to Idorsia, a newly created company in which Johnson & Johnson would have a minority shareholding of maximum 32%. The European Commission found that Idorsia would not be independent but instead controlled by Johnson & Johnson because allegedly it could influence Actelion's strategic decisions and Johnson & Johnson would be an important shareholder and finance provider to Idorsia. Johnson & Johnson's pipeline product was being co-developed with a third party, Minerva Neurosciences, which planned to commercialize the product in the EEA. Nevertheless, the European Commission found that Johnson & Johnson could still have influenced the research, in particular through the information it could have obtained through its minority shareholding in Idorsia. For these reasons, the European Commission required the parties to provide behavioral remedies. First, Johnson & Johnson had to reduce its shareholding in Idorsia to maximum 10%, or 16% if Johnson & Johnson would not be the largest shareholder and not have the right to nominate a board member. This was to ensure that Johnson & Johnson could not influence Idorsia's strategic decisions nor obtain any commercially sensitive information about Idorsia's insomnia medicine. Second, Johnson & Johnson had to grant Minerva Neurosciences new rights over the global development of its insomnia research program and waive Johnson & Johnson's royalty rights on Minerva's sales in the EEA. The European Commission considered that this requirement would remove Johnson & Johnson's incentives to negatively influence the development of its own insomnia research program.

c. *Innovation Spaces*

363. Another category of mergers that have raised innovation concerns both for the European Commission and FTC involves mergers between firms with competing R&D capabilities and longer-term innovation competition.[144] In contrast to pipeline-pipeline mergers, these transactions are more focused on the pre-clinical trial stage in which parties are still occupied with R&D. The merging parties typically have a broad set of assets targeted at similar innovation areas or trajectories including IP, access to technology, skilled scientists or engineers, R&D facilities, and an existing strong client base that can be upgraded to innovative products.[145]

---

144 Federico et al., *Antitrust and Innovation: Welcoming and Protecting Disruption*, *supra* n. 107, Chapter III, 137.

145 *Id.* 146.

The concern of the enforcement agencies is that the merger can lead to a "reduction in the incentives to initiate new R&D efforts in the overlapping areas," thereby depriving consumers of future competition in the relevant product market.[146]

364. One of the seminal FTC pharmaceutical cases in the innovation space involved the 1996 proposed merger agreement among Ciba-Geigy and Sandoz Ltd., providing that both companies would merge into a new entity, Novartis.[147] The resulting merged entity allegedly would have control over worldwide assets totaling approximately $80 billion.[148] Ciba and Sandoz were both engaged in the discovery, development, manufacture, and sale of proprietary and generic pharmaceutical products, largely gene therapy products.[149] One of the specific markets in which the FTC alleged harm was the market for "gene therapy technology and R&D of gene therapies."[150] This particular market allegedly was already highly concentrated with Ciba and Sandoz as two of only a few entities capable of commercially developing gene therapy products. Additionally, Ciba and Sandoz controlled the substantial proprietary rights that were necessary to commercialize gene therapy products and were the only firms that possessed the technological, manufacturing, clinical, regulatory expertise, and manufacturing capability to commercially develop gene therapy products.[151] Among other theories of harm, the FTC alleged that eliminating Ciba and Sandoz as substantial, independent competitors would result in the reduction in innovation competition among researchers and developers of gene therapy products, including reduction in, delay of, or redirection of R&D tracks.[152] The FTC was also concerned that the merger would lead to heightened barriers to entry in the market for gene therapy by allowing one entity to hold such an extensive portfolio of patents and patent applications, thereby requiring potential entrants to invent around or challenge a wide array of patents, and create a disincentive for the merged firm to license IP rights or collaborate with other companies.[153] As a result, the FTC concluded that the transaction would likely impede the ability of other gene therapy researchers and developers to continue developing their products.[154]

365. The FTC ultimately allowed the merger to go through with a consent agreement designed to ensure that the merger did not "slow research and development or raise prices for gene therapy products closest to marketability, or slow innovation toward future products."[155] Rather than requiring divestitures from the merging parties, as

---

146 *Id.* 147.

147 FTC, Analysis of Proposed Consent Order to Aid Public Comment, *In the Matter of Ciba-Geigy Limited, et al., and Novartis AG*, FTC File No. 961 0055, 1 (1997), *available at* https://www.ftc.gov/system/files/documents/cases/961217cibaanalysis.pdf.

148 *Id.*

149 Complaint, *In the Matter of Ciba-Geigy et al., and Novartis AG*, FTC File No. 961 0055, 1 (1997), *available at* https://www.ftc.gov/system/files/documents/cases/961217cibacmpt.pdf.

150 *Id.* 3.

151 *Id.* 5.

152 *Id.* 9.

153 *Id.*

154 Analysis of Proposed Consent Order to Aid Public Comment, *supra* n. 147, Chapter III, 6.

155 FTC, Press Release, *FTC Accord in Ciba-Geigy/Sandoz Merger to Prevent Slowdown in Gene Therapy Development & Preserve Competition in Corn Herbicides, Flea-Control Markets* (Dec. 17, 1996), *available at* https://www.ftc.gov/news-events/news/press-releases/1996/12/ftc-accord-ciba-geigysandoz-merger-prevent-slowdown-gene-therapy-development-preserve-competition.

the FTC has typically done for pharmaceutical mergers, the consent order provided for a set of patent licenses that would allow other companies to replace the competition that may be lost as a result of the transaction.[156] In wanting to maintain the ongoing innovation efforts in the impacted markets, the FTC was concerned that an asset divestiture would "create substantial disruption in the parties R&D efforts."[157] Therefore, among other things, the consent decree required the merged entity to provide another gene therapy R&D firm, Rhone-Poulenc Rorer, with non-exclusive licenses or sublicenses to certain essential proprietary and patented technologies for the competitive development and commercialization of gene therapy products in order to place it in a position to continue with R&D efforts and effectively compete against the combined firm.[158] In discussing the consent decree, the Director of the FTC's Bureau of Competition at the time, commented, "This case is about saving lives. Today there are two firms racing to develop new gene therapies to combat deadly diseases. This deal threatened to eliminate that competition. Our order ensures that this sprint to the finish line will continue."[159]

366. The European Commission introduced "innovation spaces" in EU merger control in the non-pharmaceutical case *Dow/Dupont*.[160] The European Commission defined innovation spaces as discovery targets that are located in early R&D pipelines,[161] referring to the EU Horizontal Merger Guidelines[162] that specify a concentration may not only affect competition in existing markets, but also competition in innovation and new product markets. Since the European Commission's decision from 2018 in *Bayer/Monsanto*, so-called innovation competition has also been referred to in later pharmaceutical mergers, including the 2020 merger *AbbVie/Allergan*, which related to treatments for autoimmune diseases. Referencing the *Bayer/Monsanto* decision, the European Commission explicitly stated in its *AbbVie/Allergan* decision that:

> Competition is understood to mean product and price competition (actual or potential), as well as innovation competition … The European Commission considers that a concentration may not only affect competition in existing markets, but also competition in innovation and new product markets. This may be the case when a concentration concerns entities currently developing new products or technologies which may one day replace existing ones or which are being developed for a new intended use and will therefore not replace existing products but create a completely new demand.
>
> In the pharmaceutical industry, the process of innovation is structured in such a way that it is typically possible to identify competing research programmes (or "pipeline" programmes) at an early stage of clinical trials. Competing pipeline programmes can be defined as R&D efforts aimed at

156 Analysis of Proposed Consent Order to Aid Public Comment, *supra* n. 147, Chapter III, 6.

157 *Id.* 7.

158 FTC Decision and Order, *In the Matter of Ciba-Geigy et al., and Novartis AG*, FTC Docket No. C-3725 (Mar. 24, 1997), *available at* https://www.ftc.gov/sites/default/files/documents/cases/1997/04/c3725.do.pdf.

159 FTC, Press Release, *supra* note 155, Chapter III.

160 Case COMP/M.7932, *Dow/Dupont* (2017).

161 *Id.* ¶¶2150–2168.

162 EU Horizontal Merger Guidelines, *supra* n. 69, Chapter III, ¶8.

developing substitutable products and having similar timing. The timing of a research programme should be assessed by reference to the stage of the on-going preclinical or clinical trials.[163]

367. The European Commission also concluded in *AbbVie/Allergan*, however, that the transaction did not raise innovation competition concerns because there were a very large number of R&D organizations competing globally in the field of autoimmune diseases, the area in which the parties' activities mostly overlapped. Examples of other innovators were not only pharmaceutical and biotechnology companies but also university research programs.[164]

368. Nevertheless the European Commission has moved away from focusing on single product overlaps (including pipeline products) and is considering broader R&D activity. In the pharmaceutical industry the European Commission will likely focus on all R&D in which the merging parties are involved, regardless of the stage of development of any particular project, to try to prevent early elimination of duplicative R&D pipelines and to preserve opportunities for innovation. This means that the European Commission will consider earlier R&D phases, including research for drug discovery, before later, clinical trials; and pre-clinical development where some testing takes place for the efficacy of a variety of compounds; and Phase I clinical trials after which, if successful, the Phase II and Phase III trials will continue.

369. The European Commission's *Illumina/Grail* merger prohibition also focuses on innovation as Illumina was found to have the ability and incentive to foreclose Grail's rivals on the emerging market for innovative cancer tests: "The European Commission is concerned that the proposed acquisition may reduce competition and innovation in the emerging market for the development and commercialization of cancer detection tests based on sequencing technologies." The European Commission – like the FTC, which also challenged the transaction – is particularly concerned that the transaction will foreclose competitors of Grail who are also developing next generation cancer detection tests in a nascent market: "The [EC] found that GRAIL and its rivals are currently engaged in an innovation race to develop and commercialize early cancer detection tests. While there is still uncertainty about the exact results of this innovation race and the future shape of the market for early cancer detection tests, protecting the current innovation competition is crucial to ensure that early cancer detection tests with different features and price points will come to the market." The vertical concerns raised in the European Commission's prohibition decision are addressed separately in Section II.2.A of this Chapter.

C. Single Product/Portfolio

370. The theories of harm mentioned in the above European Commission and FTC investigations largely focused on transactions in which the merging parties had overlapping products that were either in existence, in the pipeline, or still in the

---

163 Case COMP/M.9461, *AbbVie/Allergan* ¶¶17–18 (2020).

164 *Id.* ¶19, n. 27.

R&D phase. In addition, EU and US agencies have also expressed concerns over mergers between parties with overlapping drug portfolios across therapeutic areas. In the EU, this is the standard approach in generics since generics markets are defined by reference to the portfolio rather than individual drugs.

371. Transactions in which the parties have broad portfolios containing more than one type of drug typically raise additional theories of harm. According to the FTC, these include the tying or bundling of generic products requiring other firms to purchase a second product in order to get the first; withholding vital IP assets from other firms thereby foreclosing smaller competitors; decreasing the incentive for the merged firm or other firms to challenge the applicability or validity of patents, and a reduced incentive to bring new generic products to market, thereby reducing the introduction of new and innovative products.[165]

372. In the FTC's complaint challenging Teva's proposed acquisition of Allergan's generic pharmaceutical business,[166] the FTC alleged, among a number of theories of harm, "other potential theories of harm" related to the imminent combination of each party's robust product portfolios.[167] Specifically, the FTC warned that the merger would lead to anticompetitive effects from the bundling of generic products by the merged firm, a decreased incentive for the merged firm to bring Paragraph IV challenges, and a decreased incentive for the merged firm to bring new generic drugs to market.[168] However, after analyzing the issues, the FTC determined that none of these "other theories" were applicable.

373. Regarding the bundling theory, the FTC found that although both Teva and Allergan had broad generic drug portfolios, "the evidence did not show that the breadth of their portfolios significantly affects their ability to win business in individual drug product markets. Nor have they been able to use their portfolios to foreclose smaller competitors."[169] Despite its broad generic portfolio, the FTC determined that Teva's overall share of US generic prescriptions declined from 2010 to 2015, and the share of total prescriptions filled by the five largest generic suppliers similarly fell during that same period.[170]

374. Similarly, the FTC found no evidence to support the theory that the merger would lead to a decrease in Paragraph IV challenges by the merged firm or competing

---

165 FTC, Statement in the Matter of Teva Pharmaceuticals Industries Ltd. And Allergan plc, *supra* n. 76, Chapter III, 2–3; FTC, Dissenting Statement of Commissioner Rohit Chopra, *In the Matter of AbbVie, Inc. / Allergan plc Commission*, FTC File No. 191-0169 (May 5, 2020), *available at* https://www.ftc.gov/system/files/documents/public_statements/1574583/191-0169_dissenting_statement_of_commissioner_rohit_chopra_in_the_matter_of_abbvie-allergan_redacted.pdf.

166 Complaint, *In the Matter of Teva Pharma Industries LTD and Allergan PLC*, FTC Docket No. C-4589, 2 (July 26, 2016), *available at* https://www.ftc.gov/system/files/documents/cases/160727tevaallergancmpt.pdf.

167 FTC, Statement in the Matter of Teva Pharmaceuticals Industries Ltd. And Allergan plc, *supra* n. 76, Chapter III, 2.

168 *Id.* 2–3. A Paragraph IV challenge under the Hatch-Waxman Act is the process by which a generic drug manufacturer can challenge the validity of a branded drug company's patent or certify that its generic drug does not infringe the branded drug's patent. The first company to successfully file a Paragraph IV certification is entitled to market the generic drug exclusively for 180 days against other generic manufacturers also filing Paragraph IV certifications.

169 *Id.* 2.

170 *Id.* 3.

firms. The FTC found that Paragraph IV challenges were not concentrated among a small group of large firms and, in fact, many of the smaller firms were particularly active in bringing these challenges.[171] Furthermore, there was no evidence that the merged firm would be better positioned to win a Paragraph IV challenge than other, smaller, firms.[172] Additionally, there was no evidence that the merger would reduce the combined entity's incentive to continue pursuing Paragraph IV challenges.[173] Lastly, the FTC determined that the transaction would not "dampen incentives to develop new generic products."[174] To the extent that there were complex generic products for which both companies had already engaged in development efforts, the FTC did not have concerns that other smaller competitors would be foreclosed from partnering with either Teva or Allergan in order to bring a generic product to market.[175] The FTC explained that there were a number of other firms with similar technical capabilities to develop complex generics with whom smaller companies could partner, and there was no evidence to suggest these types of partnerships would disappear post-merger.[176]

375. The EC,[177] on the other hand, did raise concerns in relation to the parties' generics portfolios, in the *Teva/Allergan* merger. The European Commission found that in Iceland, Ireland and the UK, the remaining players would have been unable to compete effectively with the merged entity. In Iceland, Allergan was the incumbent and dominant generics supplier and its only challenger was Teva's wholesaler Lyfis. In Ireland, Teva and Allergan were recent entrants that quickly became market leaders because of their aggressive pricing, which challenged the existing generic companies. In the UK, Teva and Allergan allegedly were the only two generics manufacturers whose portfolio was large enough to be able to sell directly to pharmacies offering competitive discount schemes and a level of service valued by customers. The European Commission concluded that the merger would negatively affect competition for the sale of generics due to the risk of price increases and the loss of quality of service and supply. In order to address these concerns, the parties offered to divest Teva's portfolio of marketed and pipeline molecules in Iceland as well as a majority of Allergan's marketed generic activities and generics pipeline activities in Ireland and the UK. The Irish and UK divestment included all the main steps in the manufacture, supply, and distribution of these products, including Allergan's manufacturing plant in Barnstaple in the UK where most of the generics Allergan sells in Ireland and the UK were manufactured.

2. Non-horizontal effects

376. Beyond horizontal effects, the European Commission and FTC will also examine the potential non-horizontal effects caused by a transaction. We discuss below the most common vertical and conglomerate concerns.

---

171 *Id.*
172 *Id.*
173 *Id.*
174 *Id.*
175 *Id.* 3–4.
176 *Id.*
177 Case COMP/M.7746, *Teva/Allergan Generics* (2016).

A. *Vertical integration*

377. Pharmaceutical mergers may lead to instances where the merging firms will become vertically integrated in one or more areas, including the manufacture of APIs. APIs are central inputs in the manufacture of finished dose form pharmaceutical products (FDPs) such as tablets or solutions.

378. In the US, API supply sources must be designated in a drug's FDA marketing authorization. Switching to a non-designated API source requires a drug maker to supplement its NDA, a process that can take as long as two or more years.[178]

379. A pharmaceutical merger may also result in the merged firm becoming a significant API supplier to its competitors. The European Commission narrows its examination of these relationships to the areas where it believes concerns are most likely to arise, i.e., (1) downstream vertically affected markets where either party has a market share of more than 30% in the upstream API market and the other party has a market share that exceeds 5% in the downstream FDP market; and (2) upstream vertically affected markets where either party has a market share of more than 5% in the upstream API market and the other party has a market share that exceeds 30% in the downstream FDP market. To determine input foreclosure risks, the European Commission will consider the likelihood of entry, whether dual sourcing is significant, and whether there is spare capacity in the API industry, as well as the market share of the parties at the upstream level.

380. For example, prior to the merger in *Teva/Allergan* 2016, Teva was the primary API supplier for Allergan's competitors for 15 separate drugs. The FTC concluded that the acquisition would lessen current or future competition in these drugs by creating the incentive and ability for Teva to foreclose competitors in the sale of those drugs by withholding supply of the API. The European Commission identified 136 upstream and 33 downstream vertically affected markets, but it dismissed input foreclosure concerns. First, the market investigation did not identify any input foreclosure concerns. Second, the European Commission found that in the instances where Teva had a significant market share in the upstream API market, the API volumes needed by Allergan's competitors on the downstream market were very limited compared to the overall demand and could easily be sourced from the remaining upstream API suppliers. And some of Allergan's downstream competitors were also vertically integrated with respect to APIs and therefore not affected by any potential input foreclosure strategy.[179]

381. In these types of cases, the EU and US agencies may require the merging firm to offer the API customers long-term API supply contracts to address future competitive concerns.

382. The European Commission has identified another potential vertical theory of harm in pharmaceutical mergers: out-licensing, where one company licenses to another

---

178 FTC Federal Register 51892, 81 (Aug. 5, 2016), *available at* https://www.ftc.gov/system/files/documents/federal_register_notices/2016/08/teva_frn_080516.pdf.

179 Case COMP/M.7746, *Teva/Allergan Generics* ¶¶648–53 (2016).

company the rights to use a dossier to obtain marketing authorization for a product in one or more countries and to commercialize the licensed products in those countries to another company.[180] Such out-licensing agreements are generally accompanied by a supply agreement by which the out-licensor supplies the licensee with the FDP in question whether it is produced by the licensor or by a third party.[181] Out-licensing has been found to be a separate market which is upstream of the markets for the supply of FDPs, and the European Commission will examine the out-licensing relationship for each individual molecule (or API) as potentially constituting a relevant market.[182] According to the EC, outsourcing results in a vertically affected market where: (1) one party is active on a downstream FDP market, (2) the other party is active upstream as a licensor, and (3) the combined market share of the parties and their licensee(s) on the downstream market are in excess of 30%. From this starting point, the European Commission will identify and focus its analysis on filters aimed at determining the groups of vertically affected markets where concerns are most likely. These are markets where one party is active on a downstream FDP market, the other party is active upstream as a licensor, and the combined market share of the parties and their licensee(s) on the downstream market is more than 35% with an increment exceeding 1%. To assess potential input foreclosure whereby the merged entity would have the ability and incentive to raise the costs of downstream rivals (in the supply of FDPs) by restricting their access to out-licensing, the European Commission evaluates the merging parties' position in the out-licensing markets. But it also weighs whether it would be profitable for the merged entity to forego license fees from downstream competitors if it were to terminate the license agreements.

383. A good example is *Teva/Allergan*, where the European Commission identified input foreclosure risks for certain vertically affected markets where the merged entity allegedly would have the ability and incentive to decide not to out-license and supply a number of molecules to customers with which it was competing downstream. The European Commission found that the merged firm would have the ability to foreclose because the out-licensor can generally terminate its supply relationship with its out-licensee and the market investigation suggested that the technological transfer to a third-party supplier would not be an option for many out-licensees.[183] The European Commission also identified 103 out of a total 177 affected markets where the parties may have had the incentive to foreclose out-licensees. On these 103 affected markets, the European Commission concluded that there would be a risk of price increase downstream.[184] In order to address the European Commission's concerns in relation to molecules where there was no overlap between the parties, the companies committed to maintain the out-licensing relationship with equivalent terms for 39 molecules. For the other 71 molecules, Teva committed to either divest: (1) the out-licensing business,

---

180 *Id.* ¶594.
181 *Id.* ¶595.
182 *Id.* ¶596.
183 *Id.* ¶625.
184 *Id.* ¶637.

i.e., the upstream business, conducted by either of the two parties for the relevant product, or (2) the marketed generic pharmaceutical of either of the two parties in the relevant country, so the downstream business.[185]

384. The European Commission prohibited the completed *Illumina/Grail* merger because it allegedly interfered with the "innovation race" between Grail and its rivals to develop and commercialize early detection cancer tests. The merger leads to vertical integration of Illumina, an unrivalled supplier for next generation sequencing (NGS) systems for genetic and genomic analysis, with Grail, a customer of Illumina using NGS systems in its cancer detection tests The European Commission considered that there is a risk that the merged entity can engage in vertical input foreclosure strategies given its leading position in the NGS systems which are crucial inputs for the development and commercialization of NGS-based cancer detection tests. Based on its in-depth investigation, the European Commission concluded that the merged entity has both the ability and the incentive to foreclose its rivals. Grail has the ability to foreclose its rivals who equally rely on Illumina's NGS-systems to develop and run their early detection cancer tests. The European Commission's market investigation showed that there were no alternatives in the short to medium term to Illumina's reliable products and support network with little prospect of successful entry. Even if alternative NGS-system producers would enter the market, switching NGS providers allegedly would be a long and costly process for Grail's rivals without guarantee of success. Given the enormous market potential and the ongoing close innovation competition in the development of early cancer detection test, the European Commission considered that Illumina would have an incentive to foreclose Grail's rivals already today, despite benefiting from this action only at a later stage. The European Commission also considered that Illumina could adopt different strategies to foreclose Grail's rivals, e.g., stop supplying NGS systems, increase prices, or degrade quality and delay supplies. Such strategies allegedly would result in a significant detrimental effect on competition in developing and marketing NGS-based cancer detection tests in the EEA.[186]

385. Illumina offered remedies to remove the ability and incentive to foreclose Grail's rivals, but these were deemed insufficient by the European Commission. The proposed license for NGS suppliers to some of Illumina's NGS patents and a commitment to stop patent lawsuits in the US and EU to reduce IP related entry barriers was found insufficient to ensure the entry of a credible alternative to Illumina for Grail's rivals in the short to medium term. This is because the proposed license allegedly did not cover all relevant patents, other non-IP related barriers to entry exists, and even if the barriers to entry would be reduced, switching itself is a long and costly process without a guarantee of success. The proposed commitment to conclude agreements with Grail's rivals under conditions set out in a standard contract to ensure that Grail's rivals would enjoy continued access to Illumina's

---

185 *Id.*, ¶¶670–672.

186 European Commission, Press Release IP/22/7403, *Mergers: The Commission adopts a Statement of Objections outlining measures to unwind Illumina's blocked acquisition of GRAIL* (Dec. 5, 2022), available *at* https://ec.europa.eu/commission/presscorner/detail/en/ip_22_7403.

NGS systems were found to be ineffective in practice because they did not address all the possible foreclosure strategies Illumina could adopt. For example, it did not address that Illumina could degrade the technical support for NGS systems to rivals. In addition, the market test showed that Illumina could have circumvented the commitments, given Grail preferential treatment, and overall the commitments would have been too difficult to monitor.[187]

386. The European Commission therefore decided to block the transaction to protect "the current innovation competition" between Grail and its rivals and ensure that "early cancer detection tests with different features and price points will come to market." The prohibition is under appeal. The European Commission sent a SO to the parties on December 5, 2022 outlining the measures the European Commission considers Illumina must implement to unwind the transaction, and the transitional measures the parties must comply with until Illumina has dissolved the transaction.[188] On October 12, 2023, the European Commission issued an order for Illumina to divest rail within 12 months.[189] In addition, on July 19, 2022, the European Commission sent a SO to the parties because they had implemented the transaction while the European Commission's investigation was pending.[190] Following its investigation, on July 12, 2023, the European Commission fined Illumina €432 million for closing the transaction before receiving the EU merger clearance.[191]

387. The FTC similarly challenged the same transaction by filing an administrative complaint in March 2021. The complaint alleged that the merger "would substantially lessen competition in the market for the research, development, and commercialization of MCED tests" used to detect various types of cancers.[192] A key concern for the FTC was Illumina's ability to foreclose Grail's current and future competitors by withholding a "critical input" for all multi-cancer early detection (MCED) tests, for which Illumina was the "only provider."[193] Following an administrative trial in August and September of 2021, the ALJ dismissed the FTC's complaint. The ALJ determined the FTC failed to prove "that Illumina's post-Acquisition ability and incentive to advantage Grail to the disadvantage of Grail's alleged rivals is likely to result in a substantial lessening of competition in the relevant market for the research, development, and commercialization of MCED tests."[194] In support of this decision, the ALJ noted that the evidence presented by the FTC fell short of proving that "Grail's rivals are poised to imminently launch their products commercial in direct competition with Grail."[195]

---

187 *Id.*

188 *Id.*

189 Case COMP/M.10939, *Illumina/Grai* (2023).

190 European Commission, Press Release IP/22/4604, *Mergers: Commission alleges Illumina and GRAIL breached EU merger rules by early implementation of their acquisition* (July 19, 2022), *available at* https://ec.europa.eu/commission/presscorner/detail/en/IP_22_4604.

191 Case COMP/M.10483, *Illumina/Grai* (2023).

192 Complaint, *In the Matter of Illumina, Inc. and Grail, Inc.*, FTC Docket No. 9401, 12 (Mar. 30, 2021), *available at* https://www.ftc.gov/system/files/documents/cases/redacted_administrative_part_3_complaint_redacted.pdf.

193 *Id.* 25, 134.

194 Initial Decision, *In the Matter of Illumina, Inc. and Grail, Inc.*, FTC Docket No. 9401, 197 (Sept. 9, 2022), *available at* https://www.ftc.gov/system/files/ftc_gov/pdf/D09401InitialDecisionPublic.pdf.

195 *Id.* 143.

Rather, representatives from other companies creating MCED tests testified that they "hoped to," "aspired to," or "planned to" launch a test at some point in the future (anywhere from 3 to 10 years).[196] Furthermore, even if other companies launched MCED tests within five to 7 years, there was no evidence to indicate that such tests were "reasonably interchangeable" with Grail's tests.[197] The FTC Commissioners overturned the ALJ's decision on appeal. Illumina and Grail then appealed the FTC's decision in the federal court system and the decision could be reversed yet again in the future.

B. *Conglomerate effects*

388. Conglomerate theories of harm have historically not often been applied by the EC, but since 2016–2017, the European Commission has increasingly invoked conglomerate issues and their complexity generally triggers a more in-depth Phase 2 investigation. Based on publicly available information, the FTC has not sought to block any pharmaceutical mergers in cases where there were no horizontal product market overlaps or resulting vertical integration. But these theories of competitive harm in pharmaceutical mergers are an emerging area and may generate additional activity in the future.

389. The European Commission approved the *Dentsply/Sirona* merger subject to behavioral commitments.[198] Dentsply was active in the market for dental consumables. Sirona supplied dental technology and equipment and chairside computer-aided design (CAD) and computer-aided manufacturing systems (CAM) used to manufacture dental restorative materials such as crowns and bridges. The European Commission did not consider the existing horizontal overlaps as problematic because the merged entity's market shares were limited, there were several strong competitors, and the merger-specific increase in market share was not significant. But the European Commission did find that the merged entity allegedly would be able to produce both CAD/CAM systems and blocks. The European Commission was concerned that the merged entity would use Sirona's dominant position in CAD/CAM systems to favor its own CAD/CAM blocks and foreclose those of Dentsply's competitors that need access to Sirona's systems in order to compete effectively. The European Commission determined that such customer foreclosure would lead to reduced innovation and investment in R&D by competitors.

390. The FTC has not sought to block a merger outright on the basis of a conglomerate theory of harm. But in the 2020 *Upjohn/Mylan* merger, two FTC commissioners dissented from the FTC's conditional approval of the merger in part because of concerns that pharmaceutical manufacturers may "trade" favorable competitive terms in one market for favorable competitive terms in another.[199] The dissenting commissioners opposed merger clearance because

196 *Id.*

197 *Id.* 145.

198 Case COMP/M.7822, *Dentsply/Sirona* (2015), *available at* https://ec.europa.eu/competition/mergers/cases/decisions/m7822_494_3.pdf

199 FTC, *Statement of Commissioner Rohit Chopra Joined by Commissioner Rebecca Slaughter, In the Matter of Pfizer Inc./Mylan N.V., supra* n. 71, Chapter III.

they believed additional pharmaceutical consolidation, even absent product market overlaps, would make collusion more likely by reducing the number of pharmaceutical competitors generally.[200] The dissenting commissioners cited to the ongoing generic drug price fixing litigation, where private plaintiffs and state Attorneys General have alleged that Pfizer and Mylan engaged in such cross-market trading.[201]

391. The FTC has previously investigated mergers for conglomerate effects generally. In *Teva/Allergan* (2016), for example, the FTC issued a statement stating that they considered, but ultimately dismissed, the following theories:[202]

- *Bundling of Generic Products.* The FTC investigated whether the merger of Teva and Allergan (two large generic manufacturers) would lead to anti-competitive effects from the bundling of generic products. The FTC rejected such a theory because of a lack of evidence that either firm had been able to use their broad portfolios to foreclose smaller competitors previously. The FTC concluded purchasers of generic drugs would seek to diversify their supply base by sourcing from smaller suppliers.[203]
- *Patent Challenges.* The FTC investigated whether the merger would lead to a decreased incentive to challenge patents for branded drugs, specifically Paragraph IV challenges. The FTC concluded that the rewards associated with being the "first-to-file" a Paragraph IV challenge had led to robust competition for being the first to file such a challenge and that the merger was unlikely to increase the combined firm's incentive or ability to continue to pursue Paragraph IV challenges.[204]
- *New Product Development.* The FTC considered whether the merger would lead to a decreased incentive to develop new generic products. The FTC rejected this theory because the parties' in-house technical capabilities for new drug development were largely non-overlapping. The FTC also took note of the existence of specialized third-party CDMOs, which assist generic manufacturers with new product development. Thus, the FTC did not find evidence of a decreased incentive or ability to develop new drugs as result of the merger.[205]

3. Remedies

A. *General*

392. The European Commission and FTC both favor structural remedies, in particular divestitures of a viable business that can compete effectively with the merged entity.[206]

---

200 US Horizontal Merger Guidelines, *supra* n. 63, Chapter III, § 7.

201 Complaint, *In re Generic Pharms. Pricing Antitrust Litig.*, No. 17-3768 §§ 103–105 (E.D. Pa. Filed June 15, 2018); Complaint, *Connecticut v. Sandoz, Inc.*, No. 20-cv-802 ¶1299 (D. Conn. Filed June 10, 2020).

202 FTC, Statement in the Matter of Teva Pharmaceuticals Industries Ltd. And Allergan plc, *supra* n. 76, Chapter III.

203 *Id.* 2.

204 *Id.* 3.

205 *Id.* 3–4.

206 Notice on Remedies, *supra* n. 26, Chapter III, ¶¶22–31.

393. In the EU and the US, divestments therefore typically consist of all assets needed to help an up-front divestiture buyer maintain the status quo and fill the shoes of the divesting party. In the EU this has meant that divestitures include marketing authorizations, usually accompanied by licenses of IP rights, technology transfers as well as relevant assets, including plants or manufacturing and supply agreements with third parties. As mentioned above, the parties in *Teva/Allergan* offered to divest the great majority of Allergan's marketed generic activities and generics pipeline activities in Ireland and the UK. This included all the main steps in the manufacture, supply and distribution of these products, including Allergan's manufacturing plant in the UK where most of the generics Allergan sold in Ireland and the UK were manufactured. A divestment is not necessarily limited to a product but has also included a distribution business. In *Novartis/Alcon*, for example, the European Commission required that not only the product but also the distribution business was divested to facilitate entry and ongoing competitiveness. The distribution business included the existing product inventory, assignment of relevant rights under all contracts, leases, customer, credit and order records and commitments related to or necessary for the operation of the distribution business and relating to the divested products. Novartis would transfer all rights, title and interests as a distributor of the relevant products, including the termination of existing distribution agreements and the transfer of those rights.[207]

394. In the US, merger remedies require divestment of regulatory approvals, IP, contracts and inventory as well as all confidential business information, R&D information, and formulation and manufacturing reports for the divestiture drug. Merging parties may also be required to provide access to employees who were able to identify and provide such information.[208] In addition, the FTC looks favorably upon divestiture buyers with "expertise, US sales infrastructure, and resources to restore the competition that otherwise would have been lost due to the proposed Acquisition." And if a divestiture buyer does not have manufacturing capabilities for the divested products, the merging parties may be required to supply the buyer for a transition period while the buyer established its own manufacturing capabilities.[209]

395. When pipeline products raise concerns, remedies can include the divestment of the problematic pipeline product, including worldwide development, manufacturing and marketing rights, to suitable purchasers that will carry on the development. This occurred in *AbbVie/Allergan*, where AbbVie offered to divest Allergan's pipeline product including development, manufacturing and marketing rights worldwide to a purchaser who would continue the drug's development. Similarly, to obtain approval for the *Pfizer/Hospira* transaction, the parties had to divest Pfizer's biosimilar drug and its development, manufacturing, and marketing rights including

207 Case COMP/M.5778, *Novartis/Alcon* 291 (2010).

208 Analysis of Agreement in the Matter of Bristol-Myers Squibb Company and Celgene Corporation, *supra* n. 114, Chapter III, 3.

209 *Id.*3.

appropriate IP, technology, and know-how.[210] The marketing rights outside of the EEA remained with the merging entity.

396. In the case of vertical or conglomerate concerns, the European Commission has accepted behavioral remedies. For example, in *Teva/Allergan* the parties addressed the European Commission's concerns in relation to molecules where there was no overlap by maintaining the out-licensing relationship on equivalent terms. For conglomerate concerns, as noted by the European Commission in *Dentsply/Sirona*, "in the conglomerate case at stake, remedies other than divestiture remedies appear best suited to directly address the concerns raised." Dentsply committed to offer each existing licensed block manufacturer the right to continue to supply its CAD/CAM blocks under the existing agreements for ten more years.

B. *US Merger Remedies Retrospective Study Findings*

397. The FTC published an extensive retrospective study of merger remedies in January 2017.[211] Although the study found that the vast majority of remedies were successful, specific policy adjustments were needed to try to correct past failures, including ensuring transfer of manufacturing capabilities and ensuring a buyer does not have to establish a new production source. Preference for divestiture of on-market products also flowed from this study.

398. The study covered 89 Commission merger orders spanning over 400 markets across a variety of industries between 2006 and 2012. More than 90% of these orders required some form of structural relief. The study analyzed 24 pharmaceutical industry mergers resulting in 92 pharmaceutical product divestitures between 2006 and 2012, of which 60 were on-market products, and 32 involved products in development. The FTC found that remedies succeeded for 84% of these pharmaceutical products. Success rates were highest for oral solid generic pharmaceuticals where a transfer of manufacturing capabilities was not required. But the success rates were lower where the transfer of manufacturing capabilities for an on-market product was required and where the product's manufacturing process was more complex than that for an oral solid. The FTC also identified risk where the remedy required a divestiture buyer to establish a new production source.

399. As a result of this study, the FTC concluded that it would begin to require divestiture of "easier-to divest products where possible, particularly when the product was manufacturing under a third-party agreement that could transfer to a buyer." For overlaps between on-market and pipeline drugs, the FTC has signaled that to increase the success rate of its pharmaceutical merger remedies, it may require firms to divest the on-market drug to obtain antitrust clearance. For example, as part of the remedy granting clearance to BMS's acquisition of Celgene, the

---

210 Case COMP/M.7559, *Pfizer/Hospira*, (2015).

211 FTC, *The FTC's Merger Remedies 2006–2012* (Jan. 2017), *available at* https://www.ftc.gov/system/files/documents/reports/ftcs-merger-remedies-2006-2012-report-bureaus-competition-economics/p143100_ftc_merger_remedies_2006-2012.pdf.

FTC required divestiture of Celgene's on-market product valued at $13.4 billion rather than the rights to BMS's pipeline drug that had not yet been approved by the FDA.[212] Prior to this merger, the FTC had often given parties the option to choose between two overlapping products, with parties often opting to divest the pipeline drug.

C. *European Commission Purchaser, Timing and Transitional Requirements*

400. In order for a divestment business to compete effectively with the merged parties, the business must not only itself be viable as mentioned above, but must also be operated by a suitable purchaser. This means a purchaser which is independent of the parties, who has the financial resources, expertise, incentive, and ability to maintain and develop the divested business, and which will be in a position to acquire the business without regulatory problems.[213] These standard purchaser requirements may have to be supplemented on a case-by-case basis.[214] The following are some representative examples of additional criteria applied in pharmaceutical cases:

- The purchaser must have a complementary product portfolio in a specific area.[215]
- The purchaser already carries out similar activities to those that are part of the divestment business, e.g., the purchaser must be a generics company already active in the EEA,[216] or the purchaser must already have out-licensing activities in the EEA.[217]
- The purchaser has an existing and strong distribution and sales footprint in the relevant countries to guarantee a successful and prompt commercialization of the divested products.[218]

401. Sometimes, the suitable purchaser criteria are insufficient to address implementation risks, particularly if there are serious concerns whether such a suitable purchaser exist. In those circumstances, the European Commission has required the merging parties to identify a buyer post-clearance but before the transaction can be completed, i.e., an "upfront-buyer" remedy,[219] or to conclude a legally binding agreement with a suitable purchaser prior to the European Commission's conditional clearance decision, i.e., a fix-it-first remedy.[220]

---

212 FTC, Press Release, *FTC Requires Bristol-Myers Squibb Company and Celgene Corporation to Divest Psoriasis Drug Otezla as a Condition of Acquisition* (Nov. 15, 2019), *available at* https://www.ftc.gov/news-events/news/press-releases/2019/11/ftc-requires-bristol-myers-squibb-company-celgene-corporation-divest-psoriasis-drug-otezla-condition.

213 Notice on Remedies, *supra* n. 26, Chapter III, ¶48.

214 *Id.* ¶49.

215 *See, e.g.*, Case COMP/M.8955, *Takeda/Shire* ¶122 (2018).

216 *See, e.g.*, Case COMP/M.7746, *Teva/Allergan Generics* ¶706 (2016); Case COMP/M.7975, *Mylan/Meda* ¶627 (2016); and Case COMP/M.9517, *Mylan/Upjohn* ¶641 (2022).

217 *See, e.g.*, Case COMP/M.7746, *Teva/Allergan Generics* ¶¶648–53 (2016).

218 *See, e.g.*, Case COMP/M.7975, *Mylan/Meda* ¶628 (2016).

219 Notice on Remedies, *supra* note 26, Chapter III, ¶¶53–55.

220 *Id.* ¶¶56–57.

402. Upfront buyer remedies are not uncommon, in particular in cases where the market test has shown limited interest of potentially suitable purchasers for the proposed divestment(s), or other reasons for which there is uncertainty whether a suitable purchaser will be found, e.g., declining sales. A recent example of a conditional Phase 1 clearance in which the European Commission made the closing of the transaction subject to an upfront buyer remedy is *Mylan/Upjohn* where the market test had not only shown limited interest by purchasers and declining sales, but also mixed responses as to whether the viability and competitiveness of the divestment business would be negatively affected if the transfer of that divestment business would only occur after closing of the transaction. A significant number of respondents considered that the merged entity had a strategic advantage over potential purchaser(s) because the merged entity marketed "must-have" originator products and, unlike generic companies, therefore did not need to handle contract assignments, transfers and the uncertainty of robust supply.[221] The completion of the transaction was therefore made conditional upon identifying a suitable purchaser prior to the clearance decision.

403. The *AbbVie/Allergan* transaction could also not be completed until the European Commission gave its approval on the suitability of a purchaser for the divestment business, to mitigate what the European Commission considered an inherent risk relating to the development of pipeline products.[222] Other examples of upfront buyer cases are *Zimmer/Biomet* (addressing on-market and pipeline overlap concerns),[223] *Teva/Allergan Generics* (addressing on-market and pipeline overlap concerns),[224] *Mylan/Meda* (addressing on-market overlap concerns),[225] and *Takeda/Shire* (addressing on-market and pipeline overlap concerns).[226]

404. Fix-it-first remedies are rare in practice. The Notice on Remedies indicates that fix-it-first remedies are welcomed in particular where the identity of the purchaser is crucial for the effectiveness of the proposed remedy.[227] This is the case where the business in itself is not a viable business and its viability can only be ensured by specific assets of the purchaser or where the purchaser needs to have specific characteristics.[228] On this basis, the European Commission required a fix-it-first remedy in an animal health related case, *Boeringher Ingelheim/Sanofi Animal Health*.[229] The European Commission had identified competition concerns in a number of animal vaccine and pharmaceutical markets. The parties proposed a remedy involving the transfer of vaccine technology which is a highly complex process including risks. Ceva was identified as a suitable purchaser and was found to fulfill the strict criteria to takeover the divested vaccine business. In addition Ceva had a complementary vaccine to the divested vaccine in its portfolio

221 Case COMP/M.7975, *Mylan/Meda* ¶628 (2016).
222 Case COMP/M.9461, *AbbVie/Allergan* ¶¶127 (2020).
223 Case COMP/M.7265, *Zimmer/Biomet* (2015).
224 Case COMP/M.7746, *Teva/Allergan Generics* ¶725 (2016).
225 Case COMP/M.7975, *Mylan/Meda* ¶628 (2016).
226 Case COMP/M.8955, *Takeda/Shire* (2018).
227 Notice on Remedies, *supra* n. 26, Chapter III, ¶57.
228 *Id.*
229 Case COMP/M.7917, *Boehringer Ingelheim/Sanofi Animal Health* (2016).

which would allow for joint marketing making successful commercialization of the divested vaccine more likely.

405. In addition to the viable purchaser criteria and the timing of the divestments, the European Commission has required parties to introduce agreements ancillary to the divestments to ensure viability and a smooth transfer of the divestment business.

406. In *Johnson & Johnson/Pfizer Consumer Healthcare*, for example, the merging parties committed, at the option of the purchaser, to provide reasonable technical assistance to take over the production, sale and marketing of the divested formulation for a period of time at a cost-plus basis to be agreed with the purchaser.[230] More recently, in *Takeda/Shire*, the merging parties proposed a number of transitional supply arrangements for a certain period, including the supply of services (e.g., technical assistance); the supply of the active ingredient – SHP647; the continued sponsorship of the clinical trials; and the supply of products and services provided to Shire by third parties, through back-to-back arrangements, if the contracts in questions could not be transferred.[231] The commitment to provide the Contract Research Company with all the input required to ensure that development of the active ingredient (SHP647) continues uninterrupted during the transitional period, was added by the parties in the final commitments to address concerns raised in the market test about implementation risks.[232]

407. In *Teva/Allergan Generics*, the parties committed to a number of transition agreements to address various concerns raised with the original remedies package. First, for certain of the on-market divestment businesses, the option for the purchases was introduced to benefit from: (1) a supply arrangement for the relevant product for a certain period at full manufacturing costs for products that the merging parties manufactured in-house, (2) a supply arrangement for the relevant API for a certain period under commercially reasonable terms if the merging parties currently manufactured the API in-house, and (3) necessary technical assistance from Teva during the transitional supply arrangement for the purchaser to assume responsibility for the manufacture and the procurement of raw materials necessary for the manufacturing of the product, and the sale and marketing of the product, for such a period as required by the purchaser to establish it as a viable independent business.[233] For certain pipeline divestments, the merging parties committed not only to a contract manufacturing agreement for a transition period, if necessary for a timely launch of the pipeline product, until the purchaser secures a supply source, but also to complete the development of the pipeline product to the extent necessary for the purchaser to launch and market the product in the relevant countries. In addition, Teva would provide expeditiously and at its costs the necessary technical assistance to assume responsibility for the transfer of the manufacturing process.[234]

---

230 Case COMP/M.4314, *Johnson & Johnson/Pfizer* ¶¶139–140 (2006).

231 Case COMP/M.8955, *Takeda/Shire* ¶108 (2018).

232 *Id.* ¶¶106, 108, 117, and 122.

233 Case COMP/M.7746, *Teva/Allergan Generics* ¶¶685 (2016).

234 *Id.* ¶690.

III. Conclusion

408. While the US and EU differ procedurally in their merger control proceedings, there is much convergence in the substantive analysis and remedies imposed in pharmaceutical transactions. The outcome of investigations may still vary depending on the actual or potential overlaps that affect the US or EU market. Further convergence may occur following the establishment of the cross-Atlantic working group on pharmaceuticals. This group may develop broader theories of harm to innovation resulting from pharmaceutical mergers, which could lead to increased enforcement.

CHAPTER IV

Concerted Conduct

Laurence Bary and Shari Ross Lahlou*

* The authors would like to thank Marion Lécole, Forrest Lovett, and Thomas Miller for the very valuable help and contribution to this chapter.

409. This chapter addresses concerted conduct in the pharmaceutical sector, including agreements between competitors or potential competitors (horizontal agreements) and agreements between firms that are active at different levels of the distribution chain (vertical agreements).

410. Although there may be good reasons for competitors to enter into lawful agreements reflecting legitimate business arrangements, horizontal agreements between competitors may breach antitrust rules when they actually or potentially restrict competition. Certain horizontal agreements involving price fixing, customer allocations or production restraints are so obviously anticompetitive that they have been deemed *per se* unlawful. Other horizontal agreements require a more in-depth analysis and weighing of their competitive effects. In the life sciences sector, such agreements include those related to patent rights, R&D, or joint manufacturing or co-marketing. If the competitive benefits of such agreements outweigh and alleged anticompetitive effects, they may be justified under both US and EU antitrust laws.

411. Generally speaking, vertical agreements are considered less likely to harm competition on both sides of the Atlantic, although EU enforcement agencies (including NCAs and courts), in particular, have taken a hard stance on some type of vertical arrangements (*see* Chapter IV).

I. Concerted Conduct Under the antitrust and competition laws

1. US Framework for Evaluating Concerted Conduct

412. Under US antitrust law, the legality of most concerted conduct – i.e., agreements between both horizontally-situated and vertically-situated parties – is evaluated under Section 1 of the Sherman Act. Section 1 of the Sherman Act prohibits "[e]very contract, combination in the form of trust or otherwise, or conspiracy, in restraint of trade or commerce among the several States, or with [the] foreign nations."[1] As all commercial agreements restrain trade in some respect, the US Supreme Court has clarified that only agreements that *unreasonably* restrain trade violate Section 1.[2] To establish a violation of Section 1, there must be: (1) an agreement, (2) the agreement must be an unreasonable restraint of trade, and (3) there must be an effect on interstate commerce or foreign commerce. This subsection focuses on the first two elements because the commerce element is typically easily satisfied and rarely litigated.

---

1 15 U.S.C. § 1.

2 *See Standard Oil Co v. United States*, 221 U.S. 1, 58 (1911); *see also Standard Oil Co. v. Khan*, 522 U.S. 3, 10 (1997) ("[T]his Court has long recognized that Congress intended to outlaw only unreasonable restraints."); *American Needle, Inc. v. NFL*, 560 U.S. 183, 189 (2010) (explaining that "even though, read literally, § 1 would address the entire body of private contract, that is not what the statute means") (internal quotation marks and citation omitted).

A. *Issues Related to Existence of Agreement*

a. *Requirement of Multiple Actors*

413. Because Section 1 requires a "contract, combination… or conspiracy" – or, simply put, an agreement – that unreasonably restrains trade,[3] it does not proscribe unilateral activity but rather is concerned with concerted action between or among multiple parties.[4]

414. One critical issue is whether the relevant parties are considered as distinct entities capable of conspiring under Section 1. This issue "does not turn simply on whether the parties involved are legally distinct entities."[5] Instead, courts consider "how the parties involved in the alleged anticompetitive conduct actually operate."[6] The question of whether there are multiple actors may be a significant legal question when the alleged agreement involves different parts of a common enterprise or entities such as joint ventures or trade associations. In *Copperweld Corp. v. Independence Tube Corp.*, the Supreme Court considered this issue in the context of an alleged conspiracy between a parent and its subsidiary.[7] The Court held that, in this context, the test for determining whether parties are separate entities capable of conspiring together is whether the agreement is "amongst separate economic actors pursuing separate economic interests, such that the agreement deprives the marketplace of independent centers of decision-making, and therefore of diversity of entrepreneurial interests."[8]

415. Lower courts have extended *Copperweld* beyond the parent-subsidiary context. To evaluate the fact-specific question of whether a particular combination of entities constitutes a single entity under Section 1, lower courts have found the *Copperweld* rule extends to, for example, sister corporations,[9] corporations with common ownership,[10] and parent corporations and majority-owned subsidiaries.[11]

---

3 15 U.S.C. § 1; *see also* Phillip E. Areeda (late) & Herbert Hovenkamp, ANTITRUST LAW: AN ANALYSIS OF ANTITRUST PRINCIPLES AND THEIR APPLICATION ¶1400 (5th ed. 2020) (hereinafter ANTITRUST LAW), (noting "[t]he three quoted terms are generally understood as a single concept").

4 *See, e.g., Monsanto Co. v. Spray-Rite Serv. Corp.*, 465 U.S. 752, 761 (1984) (explaining independent action is not proscribed under Section 1).

5 *American Needle*, 560 U.S. 191.

6 *Id.*

7 467 U.S. 752 (1984).

8 *Id.* 195 (internal quotation marks and citations omitted).

9 *See, e.g., Eichorn v. AT&T Corp.*, 248 F.3d 131 (3d Cir. 2001) (finding two subsidiaries that where wholly owned by the same parent were not separate entities capable of conspiring under *Copperweld*); *Davidson Schaaf, Inc. v. Liberty Nat'l Fire Ins.*, 69 F.3d 868, 871 (8th Cir. 1995); *Century Oil Tool, Inc. v. Prod. Specialties, Inc.*, 737 F.2d 1316, 1317 (5th Cir. 1984); *Directory Sales Mgmt. Corp. v. Ohio Bell Tel. Co.*, 833 F.2d 606, 611 (6th Cir. 1987).

10 *See, e.g., Century Oil Tool*, 737 F.2d 1316 (finding no plurality of actors between two corporations each of which was owned by same three people who together manage all the affairs of the two companies); *Guzowski v. Hartman*, 969 F.2d 211, 214 (6th Cir. 1992) (finding no plurality of actors where the shareholders of the corporations are identical); *Cf. American Vision Ctrs v. Cohen*, 711 F. Supp. 721 (E.D.N.Y. 1989) (refusing to reject as a matter of law a charge of conspiracy between two firms and their shareholders as individuals where same individuals owned 100% of one corporation, but only 54% of competing firm).

11 *See, e.g., Siegel Transfer, Inc. v. Carrier Express*, 54 F.3d 1125, 1133 (3rd Cir. 1995) (finding no plurality of actors where parent owned 99.02% of the subsidiary); *Bell Atlantic Business Systems Services v. Hitachi Data Systems Corp.*, 849 F. Supp. 702, 706 (N.D. Cal. 1994) (finding no plurality of actors where parent owned 80% of the subsidiary).

In short, if an alleged anticompetitive agreement involves related corporate entities, there may be a question of whether there are separate actors as required to find liability under Section 1.

416. Joint ventures may also raise questions as to whether there are multiple actors present capable of reaching an agreement subject to Section 1. A "joint venture typically refers to a research, production, or marketing enterprise created by several persons other than ordinary investors."[12] For joint ventures, the key question is whether there is sufficient integration to count as a single entity. For example, in *Texaco, Inc. v. Dagher*,[13] the Supreme Court examined whether a fully integrated joint venture formed by Shell Oil and Texaco to refine and sell gas in the western US to retailers at the same price could violate Section 1. Rather than individually competing in the relevant market, Texaco and Shell Oil participated jointly in the market through their investment in the joint venture.[14] The Court held that "the pricing policy challenged here amounts to little more than price setting by a single entity – albeit within the context of a joint venture – and not a pricing agreement between competing entities with respect to their competing products."[15]

417. In the life sciences sector, questions about whether the actors involved in the challenged conduct are considered distinct for purposes of Section 1 may arise in different contexts. For example, pharmaceutical companies sometimes enter licensing arrangements or joint ventures related to the development or sale of a patented product. When a patent holder licenses patent rights to a separate entity, issues arise as to whether conduct involving the two parties can constitute "concerted action."[16] Generally, courts have held that where the alleged anti-competitive behavior "is purely derivative of the legal patent monopoly and legal exclusive distributorship," there can be no claim for an antitrust conspiracy.[17] Thus, there is no concerted action when "the alleged antitrust conduct involved the use of the patent by [a] licensee after the license had been granted."[18]

418. The mere existence of a patent-licensing arrangement, however, does not immunize parties from Section 1 claims. Parties to a patent license agreement may still be capable of conspiring when "the patentee/licensee relationship… is ancillary to

---

12 Phillip E. Areeda (late) & Herbert Hovenkamp, ANTITRUST LAW ¶1478 (2020) (internal quotations omitted).

13 547 U.S. 1 (2006).

14 *Id.* 6.

15 *Id.*

16 Parties to these licensing arrangements have argued that they constitute a single economic entity, and therefore cannot be held liable for Section 1 claims involving conduct arising out of the relationship. *See, e.g., In re Suboxone (Buprenorphine Hydrochloride & Naloxone) Antitrust Litig.*, No. 13-MD-2445, 2017 WL 4910673, at *8 (E.D. Pa. Oct. 30, 2017) ("In re Suboxone").

17 *Sheet Metal Duct, Inc. v. Lindab, Inc.*, No. 99-6299, 2000 WL 987865, at *6 (E.D. Pa. July 18, 2000); *Shionogi Pharma, Inc. v. Mylan, Inc.*, No. 10-1077, 2011 WL 2174499, at *5 (D. Del. May 26, 2011) (dismissing conspiracy claim because the complaint inadequately pled a plausible conspiracy and because of the relationship between the alleged conspirators as exclusive licensee and patent holder which gave them unified interests); *Levi Case Co., Inc. v. ATS Prods., Inc.*, 788 F. Supp. 428, 432 (N.D. Cal. 1992) (holding that where a patentee conveyed an exclusive licensee in three patents to a licensor who executed a sublicense with a sub-licensor, the patentee and sub-licensor "were not independent sources of economic power" and did not have "any independent decision making authority regarding the exploitation of the patent").

18 *In re Suboxone*, 2017 WL 4910673, *8.

the anticompetitive conduct at the heart of the alleged conspiracy."[19] For example, in *Subuxone*, two pharmaceutical defendants entered into a licensing and joint development agreement regarding a patented product.[20] The complaint alleged that the defendants conspired to delay the entry of generic drugs that would compete with the patented product through product hopping and sham Citizen Petitions to the FDA.[21] In response, the defendants claimed that the existence of the licensing arrangement brought them within the *Copperweld* doctrine.[22] The court rejected this argument and explained that "[t]he mere fact that this overall scheme included the existence of an exclusive license relationship" failed to "bring[] it within the realm of the *Copperweld* doctrine."[23]

419. Questions regarding whether or not an alleged conspiracy involves the required plurality of actors also arise in the context of trade associations or other professional organizations which impose rules on their members. "[A] trade association is not by its nature a walking conspiracy… ."[24] Rather, in assessing the conduct of a trade association, courts evaluate whether the conduct is that of the organization or of the individual members.[25] Mere membership in a trade association is not sufficient to find an agreement; instead, there must be some knowing participation by the members.[26]

b. *Requirement of Sufficient Evidence of Agreement*

420. In addition to involving a plurality of actors, an agreement also requires concerted action. To prove concerted action, there must be "a unity of purpose or a common design and understanding, or a meeting of minds in an unlawful [agreement]."[27] To prove concerted action, a formal agreement is not required.[28] Rather, the agreement may be tacit or informal, with one court explaining, "[a] knowing wink can mean more than words."[29]

---

19 *Id.* *9.

20 *Id.*

21 *Id.*

22 *Id.*

23 *Id.* The Supreme Court has also considered whether a plurality of actors exists when a professional sports league collectively licenses its member teams' IP. In *American Needle*, the Court found that although the NFL joint venture had a degree of integration, the member team participants are "still separate, profit-maximizing entities" which "have distinct, potentially competing interests." 560 U.S. 198. The Court, therefore, ruled that the NFL was not a single entity and, thus, the NFL's joint licensing was an agreement subject to Section 1. *Id.* 201–02.

24 *Consol. Metal Prods., Inc. v. Am. Petroleum Inst.*, 846 F.2d 284, 293–94 (5th Cir. 1988) (internal quotation marks omitted); *see also American Dental Assoc. v. Cigna Corp.*, 605 F.3d 1283, 1295 (11th Cir. 2010) ("[P]articipation in trade organizations provides no indication of conspiracy.").

25 *See, e.g., Alvord-Polk, Inc. v. F. Schumacher & Co.*, 37 F.3d 996, 1009 (3d Cir. 1994) (noting "an association's actions satisfy the concerted action requirement only when taken in a group capacity").

26 *See, e.g., Moore v. Boating Indus. Ass'ns*, 819 F.2d 693, 712 (7th Cir. 1987) (requiring "some evidence of actual knowledge of, and participation in, an illegal scheme in order to establish a violation of the antitrust laws by a particular association member").

27 *Am. Tobacco Co. v. United States*, 328 U.S. 781, 810 (1946) (finding a conspiracy based on a pattern of parallel conduct for which there was no economic justification).

28 *See, e.g., United States v. Gen. Motors Corp.*, 384 U.S. 127, 142–43 (1966) ("[I]t has long been settled that explicit agreement is not a necessary part of a Sherman Act conspiracy.").

29 *Esco Corp. v. United States*, 340 F.2d 1000, 1007 (9th Cir. 1965).

421. Whether there is enough evidence to prove an alleged conspiracy is often the central question litigated in US conspiracy cases. To establish concerted action, "there must be evidence that tends to exclude the possibility of independent action by the [alleged conspirators]. That is, there must be direct or circumstantial evidence that reasonably tends to prove that the [alleged conspirators] had a conscious commitment to a common scheme designed to achieve an unlawful object."[30]

422. Direct evidence of an agreement is evidence which does not require the fact finder to make any inferences.[31] For example, testimony from a senior executive of one of the parties admitting the existence of a conspiracy may constitute direct evidence, at least of the existence of a conspiracy. Similarly, a document reflecting the terms of an agreement – such as a signed settlement agreement – would constitute direct evidence of an agreement between the parties.

423. By contrast, circumstantial evidence requires the fact finder to infer an agreement. The range of inferences that may be drawn from circumstantial evidence is limited in Section 1 cases.[32] To prove an agreement based on circumstantial evidence, a plaintiff may allege parallel conduct by competitors, but parallel conduct alone is not enough.[33] When relying on evidence that alleged conspirators undertook similar kinds of conduct – sometimes referred to as "conscious parallelism"[34] – plaintiffs must also allege "plus factors," which suggest that conduct was not merely parallel.[35] Such plus factors must tend to exclude the possibility that parallel conduct was the result of unilateral action.[36]

424. There is no set list or hierarchy of such plus factors.[37] But courts have emphasized the following factors: "(1) evidence that the defendant had a motive to enter into a price fixing conspiracy; (2) evidence that the defendant acted contrary to its interests; and (3) evidence implying a traditional conspiracy."[38] While "the first two factors largely restate the phenomenon of interdependence," the last factor

---

30 *Monsanto Co. v. Spray-Rite Serv. Corp.*, 465 U.S. 752, 768 (1984).

31 *See, e.g., In re Insurance Brokerage Antitrust Litigation*, 618 F.3d 300, 324 (3d Cir. 2010) ("Allegations of direct evidence of an agreement, if sufficiently [p]led, are independently adequate.").

32 *Matsushita Elec. Indus. Co. v. Zenith Radio Corp.*, 475 U.S. 574, 588 (1986) (noting "conduct as consistent with permissible competition as with illegal conspiracy does not, standing alone, support an inference of antitrust conspiracy").

33 *See, e.g., Theatre Enter. v. Paramount Film Distrib. Corp.*, 346 U.S. 537, 541 (1954) (explaining "this Court has never held that proof of parallel business behavior conclusively establishes agreement").

34 *See, e.g., Brooke Grp. Ltd. v. Brown & Williamson Tobacco Corp.*, 509 U.S. 209, 227 (1993) ("[C]onscious parallelism describes the process, not in itself unlawful, by which firms in a concentrated market might in effect share monopoly power, setting their prices at a profit-maximizing, supracompetitive level by recognizing their shared economic interests and their interdependence with respect to price and output decisions." (citation omitted)).

35 *See, e.g., In re Flat Glass Antitrust Litig.*, 385 F.3d 350, 360 (3d Cir. 2004) ("Existence of these plus factors tends to ensure that courts punish 'concerted action' – an actual agreement – instead of the 'unilateral, independent conduct of competitors.'").

36 *Matsushita*, 475 U.S. 588 ("[T]o survive a motion for summary judgment or for a directed verdict, a plaintiff seeking damages for a violation of § 1 must present evidence 'that tends to exclude the possibility' that the alleged conspirators acted independently."); *Monsanto Co. v. Spray-Rite Serv. Corp.*, 465 U.S. 752, 753, (1984) (explaining that "that there must be evidence that tends to exclude the possibility" of independent conduct).

37 *In re Flat Glass*, 385 F.3d 360 (noting there is "no finite set of [plus factors to defeat summary judgment]; no exhaustive list exists").

38 *Id.* (internal quotations and citation omitted).

looks for "proof that the defendants got together and exchanged assurances of common action or otherwise adopted a common plan even though no meetings, conversations, or exchanged documents are shown."[39] Another example of a plus considered by courts is pretextual justifications for a course of conduct.[40] If a court finds that a plaintiff put forth sufficient circumstantial evidence, the defendant is given an opportunity to rebut the inference of concerted action by showing that no reasonable fact finder could find defendant entered into the conspiracy.[41]

425. In addition to proving the existence of a conspiracy, an antitrust plaintiff must also prove that each particular defendant knowingly committed to participating in the conspiracy.[42] To do, so, an antitrust plaintiff must establish that each defendant "knew 'the essential nature and general scope' of the joint plan and joined it."[43]

B. *Evaluating Whether the Challenged Agreement is Unreasonable*

a. *Background on Antitrust Standards of Review*

426. In addition to assessing whether an alleged agreement exists, courts must consider whether the restraint is unreasonable. As explained in Chapter II, in determining whether a restraint is unreasonable, courts traditionally apply one of two tests: the rule of reason or the per se rule.[44] The rule of reason is the presumptive test under Section 1.[45] However, certain types of agreements, like horizontal price-fixing, are automatically considered unreasonable because they are obviously anticompetitive and are thus condemned as per se illegal.[46] Finally, in some cases, courts may apply the hybrid "quick look" approach, which is essentially a truncated version of the rule-of-reason standard where it is immediately obvious that the conduct is anticompetitive, but the conduct does not fall into any of the per se categories.[47] These categories of standards of review (i.e., per se treatment, quick look rule of reason, and the "full" rule of reason) are not rigid, fixed categories and the Supreme Court has moved toward considering the standards on a continuum.[48]

---

39 *Id.* 361 (noting while the first two factors are important, "since these factors often restate interdependence (at least in the context of an alleged price-fixing conspiracy), they may not suffice – by [definition] – to defeat summary judgement on a claim of horizontal price-fixing among oligopolists").

40 *See, e.g., Dimidowich v. Bell & Howell*, 803 F.2d 1473, 1480 (9th Cir. 1986).

41 *See, e.g., Williamson Oil Co., Inc. v. Philip Morris USA*, 346 F.3d 1287, 1301 (11th Cir. 2003).

42 *See, e.g., MM Steel, L.P. v. JSW Steel (USA) Inc.*, 806 F.3d 835, 844 (5th Cir. 2015) (explaining that to affirm liability, a "reasonable jury must have been able to conclude that [defendants] knowingly joined the conspiracy.").

43 *Id.* 845 (quoting *H & B Equip. Co. v. Int'l Harvester Co.*, 577 F.2d 239, 245 (5th Cir. 1978)).

44 *California Dental Ass'n v. FTC*, 526 U.S. 756, 770 (1999).

45 *Dagher*, 547 U.S. 5 ("[T]his Court presumptively applies rule of reason analysis."); *Business Elecs. Corp. v. Sharp Elecs. Corp.*, 485 U.S. 717, 726 (1988) ("[T]here is a presumption in favor of [the] rule-of-reason standard.").

46 *United States v. Socony-Vacuum Oil Co.*, 310 U.S. 150, 230 (1940).

47 *California Dental Ass'n*, 526 U.S. 770.

48 *Id.* 779–780 ("There is always something of a sliding scale in appraising reasonableness, but the sliding scale formula deceptively suggests greater precision than we can hope for …" (internal quotation marks and citation omitted)).

427. Under Section 1, agreements can be classified as: (1) horizontal, involving agreements among competitors, (2) vertical, involving agreements between parties at different levels of a distribution chain,[49] or (3) a combination of both, a so-called hub-and-spoke agreement.[50] The classification of the agreement is important because it may determine whether the per se or rule-of-reason analysis applies.

b. *Per Se Illegal Agreements*

428. As explained in Chapter II, certain agreements and practices are so harmful to competition that they can be considered illegal per se. This includes: (1) horizontal price fixing, market allocation, and bid rigging, (2) certain concerted refusal to deal, and (3) potentially, no poach agreements.

429. Horizontal "price fixing" encompasses a range of different kinds of agreements. "Under the Sherman Act a combination formed for the purpose and with the effect of raising, depressing, fixing, pegging, or stabilizing the price of a commodity in interstate or foreign commerce is illegal per se."[51] The agreement need not establish a specific, particular price.[52] Furthermore, an agreement on terms of sale can constitute price fixing, as long as it relates to a component of price.[53] The courts have held price fixing agreements per se illegal in situations involving, for example, agreements to use a specific price quoting method,[54] agreements that restrict advertising,[55] and agreements which eliminate or reduce discounts.[56] One situation in which the court does not apply the per se rule to horizontal agreements on price is where the agreement on price is ancillary to a legitimate arrangement that promotes competition and is reasonably necessary to achieving the procompetitive effect.[57]

430. In recent years, horizontal price fixing lawsuits have been brought against both generic and brand pharmaceutical manufacturers. In 2016, US state attorneys general and private plaintiffs filed wide-ranging lawsuits against generic drug

---

49 *See, e.g.*, *Business Elecs. Corp. v. Sharp Elecs. Corp.*, 485 U.S. 717, 730 (1988) ("Restraints imposed by agreement between competitors have traditionally been denominated as horizontal restraints, and those imposed by agreement between firms at different levels of distribution as vertical restraints.").

50 A hub-and-spoke conspiracy may exist where a powerful player (the hub), either upstream or downstream, enters into a series of vertical agreements (the spokes), which facilitates a horizontal agreement among the spokes. *United States v. Apple, Inc.*, 791 F.3d 290, 314 n.15 (2d Cir. 2015) (finding Apple participated in a hub-and-spoke conspiracy with e-book publishers). "[T]he 'hub-and-spoke' metaphor is somewhat inaccurate – the plaintiff must also prove the existence of a 'rim' to the wheel in the form of an agreement among the horizontal competitors." *Id.* (citing *Dickson v. Microsoft Corp.*, 309 F.3d 193, 203–04 (4th Cir. 2002)); *see also Toys "R" Us, Inc. v. FTC*, 221 F.3d 928 (7th Cir. 2000) (finding Toys "R" Us participated in a hub-and-spoke conspiracy).

51 *Socony-Vacuum Oil*, 310 U.S. 223.

52 *See, e.g.*, *id.* (finding an agreement among gasoline companies to purchase surplus gasoline on the spot market to prevent deceases unlawful per se).

53 *See Catalano, Inc. v. Target Sales*, 446 U.S. 643 (1980) (finding an agreement among competing wholesalers to standardize credit terms offered to retailers per se illegal).

54 *See, e.g.*, *id.*

55 *See, e.g.*, *Blackburn v. Sweeney*, 53 F.3d 825, 827 (7th Cir. 1995) (finding agreement imposing advertising restrictions was per se illegal).

56 *See, e.g.*, *Catalano*, 446 U.S. 648 (noting "[a]n agreement to terminate the practice of giving credit is thus tantamount to an agreement to eliminate discounts, and thus falls squarely within the traditional per se rule against price fixing").

57 *See Broad. Music, Inc. v. Columbia Broad. Sys., Inc.*, 441 U.S. 1 (1979) (holding the rule of reason should apply).

manufacturers accusing them of conspiring to inflate the prices of various drugs. In addition to Section 1 claims related to individual drugs, plaintiffs have claimed that dozens of generic drug manufacturers engaged in an overarching conspiracy related to hundreds of different generic drugs.

431. Market division or allocation occur when competitors agree to divide territories or allocate customers. Horizontal market division, even when it is unaccompanied by an agreement on price, is per se illegal as it is viewed as having "no purpose except [the] stifling of competition."[58] Market division is per se illegal even where the competitors are only potential rivals.[59] For example, in *Palmer*,[60] the US Supreme Court held that an agreement among bar preparation course companies to effectively not compete in a state was "unlawful on its face."[61]

432. Bid rigging is an "agreement between competitors pursuant to which contract offers are to be submitted or withheld from a third party[.]"[62] Courts have applied the per se rule to bid rigging cases where, for example, competitors compared bids prior to submission,[63] competitors engaged in bid rotation,[64] competitors refrained from submitting bids,[65] or competitors submitted sham or fraudulent bids to create the illusion of competition.[66]

433. Concerted refusals to deal – sometimes called "group boycotts" – may also be per se illegal in some circumstances, but there is no precise test for determining which such agreements will receive such treatment.[67] Per se illegal concerted refusals to deal typically involve a horizontal combination of companies whose purpose is to exclude a direct competitor from the market. In *Northwest Wholesale Stationers*,[68] the US Supreme Court explained that a concerted refusal to deal may be per se illegal when it involves an agreement or joint conduct among competitors that have a dominant market position – which cuts off access to something a competitor needs to compete, and there is no justification for the refusal to deal.[69] While "a concerted refusal to deal need not necessarily possess all of these traits to merit per se treatment, not every cooperative activity involving a restraint or exclusion will share with the per se forbidden boycotts the likelihood of predominantly anticompetitive consequences."[70] The Supreme Court also

---

58 *United States v. Topco Assocs., Inc.*, 405 U.S. 596, 608–09 (1972) (noting "[o]ne of the classic examples of a per se violation of § 1 is an agreement between competitors at the same level of the market structure to allocate territories in order to minimize competition").

59 *Palmer v. BRG of Georgia, Inc.*, 498 U.S. 46 (1990).

60 *Id.*

61 *Id.* 49–50.

62 *United States v. Mobile Materials, Inc.*, 881 F.2d 866, 869 (10th Cir. 1989).

63 *See, e.g.*, *United States v. J.L. Hammett Co.*, No. 31655, 1964 U.S. Dist. LEXIS 8966 (E.D. Pa. Aug. 21, 1964).

64 *See, e.g.*, *United States v. Giraudo*, No. 14-cv-00534-CRB-1, 2018 WL 2197703, *4 (N.D. Cal. May 14, 2018) (explaining "an agreement to 'rotate' bids [as] I win this round, you win [the] next round").

65 *See, e.g.*, *United States v. MMR Corp. (LA)*, 907 F.2d 489, 496 (5th Cir. 1990).

66 *See, e.g.*, *United States v. Reicher*, 983 F.2d 168 (10th Cir. 1992).

67 *See Northwest Wholesale Stationers, Inc. v. Pacific Stationery & Printing Co.*, 472 U.S. 284, 294 (1985) ("[T]here is more confusion about the scope and operation of the per se rule against group boycotts than in reference to any other aspect of the per se doctrine." (internal quotation marks and citation omitted)).

68 *Id.*

69 *Id.* 294.

70 *Id.* (finding member's expulsion from a cooperative should be analyzed under the rule of reason).

addressed concerted refusals to deal in *FTC v. Superior Ct. Trial Law. Ass'n*,[71] which involved an agreement among lawyers who represented indigent criminal defendants to refuse to take any more cases until their fee was raised.[72] The Court explained that the lawyers' agreement consisted of "not only a boycott but also a horizontal price-fixing agreement – a type of conspiracy that has been consistently analyzed as a per se violation for many decades."[73]

434. Courts have sometimes applied the per se rule to no poach agreements, under which competitors agree not to solicit each other's employees. In 2016, the DOJ and the FTC issued joint guidance explaining that they view naked no-poach and wage-fixing agreements as per se illegal and subject to criminal penalties.[74] While courts have not ruled on whether no-poach agreements should be analyzed under the per se rule, the DOJ continues to file statements of interest in favor of that approach[75] and recently announced the first criminal indictment for a no poach agreement.[76] The DOJ also recently brought a case against a provider of kidney dialysis services throughout the US alleging that the company violated federal antitrust law by engaging in no poach agreements with competitors, but a jury returned a verdict of not guilty.[77]

c. *Agreements Evaluated Under the Rule of Reason*

435. As explained in Chapter II, all agreements that are not considered as per se violations are presumptively analyzed under the rule of reason. In particular, all vertical agreements, except for certain tying arrangements,[78] are subject to the rule of reason. A vertical agreement is an agreement between parties at different levels of the distribution chain.

436. One type of vertical restraint is a resale price maintenance (RPM) agreement, which limits the resale price of the supplier's product, either by specifying a price floor (minimum RPM)[79] or a price ceiling (maximum RPM).[80] In concluding that RPM agreements are subject to the rule of reason, the US Supreme Court explained that "the

---

71 493 U.S. 411 (1990).

72 *Id.* 416–418.

73 *Id.* 436 n. 19.

74 US Antitrust Agencies, *Antitrust Guidance for Human Resource Professionals* (Oct. 2016), *available at* https://www.justice.gov/atr/file/903511/download.

75 *See* Statement of Interest of the United States, *In re: Railway Industry Employee No-Poach Antitrust Litig.*, 2:18-mc-00798 (W.D. Pa. Feb. 8, 2019), ECF No. 158; Statement of Interest of the United States, *Seaman, et al. v. Duke University, et al.*, 15-cv-00462 (M.D.N.C. Mar. 7, 2019), ECF No. 325; Corrected Statement of Interest of the United States, *Harris v. CJ Star, LLC*, 2:18-cv-00247 (E.D. Wash. Mar. 8, 2019), ECF No. 38; Corrected Statement of Interest of the United States, *Richmond v. Bergey Pullman Inc.*, 2:18-cv-00246 (E.D. Wash. Mar. 8, 2019), ECF No. 45; Corrected Statement of Interest of the United States, *Stigar v. Dough Dough, Inc.*, 2:18-cv-00244 (E.D. Wash. Mar. 8, 2019), ECF No. 34.

76 DOJ, Press Release, *Health Care Company Indicted for Labor Market Collusion* (Jan. 7, 2021), *available at* https://www.justice.gov/opa/pr/health-care-company-indicted-labor-market-collusion.

77 Dan Papscun, *DaVita, Ex-CEO Found Not Guilty in DOJ's No-Poaching Case*, BLOOMBERG LAW (Apr. 16, 2022, 12:19 AM), *available at* https://news.bloomberglaw.com/antitrust/davita-ex-ceo-found-not-guilty-in-dojs-no-poaching-case.

78 *Illinois Tool Works Inc.*, 547 U.S. 28 (adding a market power requirement to plaintiffs required showing).

79 *See Leegin Creative Leather Prod., Inc. v. PSKS, Inc.*, 551 U.S. 877 (2007) (holding the rule of reason analysis applies to minimum RPM claims).

80 *See Khan*, 522 U.S. 3 (holding the rule of reason analysis applies to maximum RPM claims).

primary purpose of the antitrust laws is to protect interbrand competition"[81] and thus, the rule-of-reason inquiry in vertical RPM agreements should be whether the agreement has or will have an anticompetitive or procompetitive effect.[82] It is important to distinguish these resale agreements from unilateral resale policies, which are typically permissible due to the lack of an agreement.[83] Additionally, manufacturers are free to suggest resale prices to retailers as long as there is no coercion.[84] Another type of vertical agreement, a consignment agreement, in which a company retains title to goods and dictates the price charged by the consignee, is lawful if it is a bona fide consignment.[85] Other types of vertical price fixing agreements include, for example, rebates,[86] advertising programs,[87] and national accounts.[88] Finally, in addition to the vertical restraints concerning price, nonprice restraints, such as exclusive dealing arrangements (e.g., where a manufacturer prevents its distributors from selling its competitors' products)[89] and territorial or customer restrictions, are also evaluated under the rule of reason.[90]

437. In addition to vertical agreements, joint ventures or competitor collaborations[91] where the parties integrate in such a way that "hold[s] the promise of increasing

---

81 Interbrand competition refers to competition between different suppliers or brand, as opposed to intra-brand competition, which refers to competition between resellers of the same brand of products.

82 *Id.* 15.

83 *United States v. Colgate*, 250 U.S. 300 (1919) (holding a manufacturer has the right to announce price policies unilaterally and refuse to do business with distributors that refuse to comply with suggested prices policies); *see also United States v. Parke, Davis & Co.*, 362 U.S. 29, 43 (1960) (narrowing *Colgate*'s holding that an agreement exists when "the producer secures adherence to his suggested prices by means which go beyond his mere declination to sell to a [consumer] who will not observe his announced policy"); *Monsanto*, 465 U.S. 752 (holding the termination of a price-cutting distributor after complaints from adhering distributors does not in and of itself establish the termination resulted from a vertical conspiracy).

84 *See, e.g., Isaksen v. Vermont Casting, Inc.*, 825 F.2d 1158 (7th Cir. 1987) (adhering to minimum prices suggested in operating manual does not establish agreement to adhere); *see also Gray v. Shell Oil Co.*, 469 F.2d 742, 748 (9th Cir. 1972) (noting the distinction "between 'coercion' on the one hand and 'exposition, persuasion and argument' on the other").

85 *United States v. General Electric. Co.*, 272 U.S. 476 (1926) (upholding the consignment arrangement as it was an agency contract and a principle is not capable of conspiring with its agent under Section 1); *Simpson v. Union Oil Co. of California*, 377 U.S. 13, 21 (1964) (reaffirming that price maintenance is lawful in bona fide consignments plans, but finding so-called consignment plan not a bona fide consignment pan as it was a "cover" for "fixing prices through many retail outlets").

86 *See, e.g., Checker Motors Corp. v. Chrysler Corp.*, 405 F.2d 319 (2d Cir. 1969) (affirming district court ruling that manufacturer's direct to consumer rebate plan did not violate Section 1 when it left dealers free to sell at their own prices).

87 *See, e.g., In re Compact Disc Min. Advertised Price Antitrust Litig.*, 216 F.R.D. 197 (D. Me. 2003) (cooperative advertising program which conditioned advertising benefits and funds on adhering to minimum advertised price).

88 *See, e.g., Ryko Mfg. Co. v. Eden Servs.*, 823 F.2d 1215 (8th Cir. 1987) (upholding national accounts program where distributor acted merely as an agent); *see also Mularkey v. Holsum Bakery, Inc.*, 146 F.3d 1064 (9th Cir. 1998) (upholding national account program under the rule of reason). Under a national accounts program, certain large customers receive significant volume discounts from the prices that the seller recommends that its distributors charge. *See Ryko Mfg. Co.*, 823 F.2d 1219.

89 *See, e.g., United States v. Dentsply Int'l, Inc.*, 399 F.3d 181, 185 (3d Cir. 2005); *E&L Consulting Ltd. v. Doman Indus. Ltd.*, 472 F.3d 23, 29 n. 4 (2d Cir. 2006).

90 *Continental T.V., Inc. v. GTE Sylvania Inc.*, 433 U.S. 36 (1977) (noting the procompetitive benefits to interbrand competition from territorial or customer restrictions); *see also Ezzo's Invs. v. Royal Beauty Supply*, 243 F.3d 980 (6th Cir. 2001) (applying rule of reason to distribution limitation).

91 US Antitrust Agencies, *Antitrust Guidelines for Collaborations Among Competitors* (the Collaboration Guidelines) 2 (Apr. 2000), *available at* https://www.ftc.gov/sites/default/files/attachments/press-releases/ftc-doj-issue-antitrust-guidelines-collaborations-among-competitors/ftcdojguidelines.pdf ("Competitor collaborations involve one or more business activities, such as research and development, production, marketing, distribution, sales or purchasing.").

a firm's efficiency and enabling it to compete more effectively"[92] are typically analyzed under the rule of reason. Relatedly, joint purchasing agreements are generally evaluated under the rule of reason.[93] The US Antitrust Agencies previously issued, though have since withdrawn, guidance and statements recognizing that such agreements can have competitive effects.[94]

438. Agreements to exchange price or other information are also subject to the rule of reason.[95] As explained by the Supreme Court: "The exchange of price data and other information among competitors does not invariably have anticompetitive effects; indeed such practices can in certain circumstances increase economic efficiency and render markets more, rather than less, competitive."[96] In assessing these agreements, courts consider the type of information exchanged and the exchange's impact on competition.[97] Although these information exchanges are examined under the rule of reason, proof that competitors have exchanged such information may be considered as evidence in a per se illegal, horizontal price fixing case.[98]

d. *Hybrid Approaches to the Antitrust Standard of Review*

439. Finally, as described in Chapter II, courts can also apply the so-called quick look standard to specific categories of agreements. In *NCAA v. Board of Regents*,[99] the US Supreme Court discussed a quick look analysis. The case involved a challenge to a National Collegiate Athletic Association (NCAA) rule on the number of games member schools could televise and an agreement between the NCAA and broadcasters which guaranteed a minimum price for the broadcast rights to games.[100] Rejecting the lower courts' application of the per se rule to the restraint, the US Supreme Court held that while the restraint at issue is of the type that is normally subject to per se analysis, that analysis was improper because the case "involve[d] an industry in which horizontal restraints on competition are essential if the product is to be available at all."[101] The Court further held that the plaintiff need not prove market power because when a restraint is a naked restriction,

---

92 *Copperweld Corp. v. Independence Tube Corp.*, 467 U.S. 752, 768 (1984); *see also Dagher*, 547 U.S. 7 (finding rule of reason applies to joint venture as a single entity that sells gasoline "under two different brands at a single, unified price").

93 *See, e.g.*, *Northwest Wholesale Stationers*, 472 U.S. 284 (upholding purchasing cooperative between competing stationery retailers under the rule of reason).

94 *See, e.g.*, Collaboration Guidelines, *supra* n. 91, Chapter IV; US Antitrust Agencies, *Statement of Antitrust Enforcement Policy in Health Care* (Aug. 1996) (Statement of Antitrust Enforcement (Withdrawn)), *available at* https://www.justice.gov/atr/page/file/1197731/download.

95 *See, e.g.*, *United States v. Citizens & S. Nat'l Bank*, 422 U.S. 86, 113 (1975) ("[T]he dissemination of price information is not itself a per se violation of the Sherman Act.").

96 *United States v. United States Gypsum Co.*, 438 U.S. 422, 441 n. 16 (1978).

97 *Id.* ("A number of factors including most prominently the structure of the industry involved and the nature of the information exchanged are generally considered in divining the procompetitive or anticompetitive effects of this type of interseller communication.").

98 *See, e.g.*, *In re Flat Glass*, 385 F.3d 368–69 (holding "a finder of fact could reasonably infer that the flat glass producers used the information to implement collusive price increases; that is, 'the exchanges of information had an impact on pricing decisions'").

99 *Id.*

100 *Id.* 91–94.

101 *Id.* 101.

"no elaborate industry analysis is required to demonstrate the anticompetitive character of [the] agreement."[102]

440. The Supreme Court revisited the quick look analysis in *FTC v. Indiana Federation of Dentists*,[103] a case which challenged an agreement between dentists to refuse to provide patient X-rays to dental insurers to evaluate claims.[104] There, reversing the Seventh Circuit, the US Supreme Court found that the claims did not require market analysis because the agreement produced actual detrimental effects.[105] By contrast, the Supreme Court reversed application of the quick look standard in a case involving restrictions on price and quality advertising adopted by the California Dental Association.[106] The Court held the rule of reason applied because the advertising restrictions "might plausibly be thought to have a net procompetitive effect" and thus, "the obvious anticompetitive effect that triggers abbreviated analysis has not been shown."[107] The Supreme Court also refused to apply the quick look standard in *FTC v. Actavis, Inc.*,[108] a case involving a so-called "reverse payment" patent litigation settlement discussed further below in Section II.

2. EU Framework for Evaluating Concerted Conduct

A. *Evaluating Legality of Agreements*

441. Article 101(1) TFEU prohibits agreements between undertakings, decisions by associations of undertakings, and concerted practices which have as their object or effect the restriction of competition. These prohibitions are intended to catch all forms of collusion.[109] A precise characterization of the nature of the undertakings' co-operation does not alter the analysis to be carried out under Article 101 TFEU.[110]

442. Hence, Article 101(1) TFEU refers to all agreements and concerted practices between independent undertakings that distort competition in the market.[111] A genuinely unilateral measure, adopted by an undertaking without the express or implied participation of another undertaking, is not covered by Article 101(1) TFEU.[112] If the undertaking holds a dominant position, however, such conduct may be subject to Article 102 TFEU.[113]

---

102 *Id.* 109 (internal quotation marks and citation omitted).

103 476 U.S. 447 (1986).

104 *Id.* 449–51.

105 *Id.* 460–61.

106 *California Dental Ass'n*, 526 U.S. 756.

107 *Id.* 771, 778.

108 570 U.S. 136 (2013).

109 Case C-49/92 P, *Commission v. Anic Partecipazioni*, ECLI:EU:C:1999:356, ¶131 (July 8, 1999).

110 Case C-238/05, *Asnef-Equifax v. Ausbanc*, ECLI:EU:C:2006:734, ¶32 (Nov. 23, 1999).

111 Case C-194/14 P, *AC-Treuhand AG v. Commission*, ECLI:EU:C:2015:717, ¶¶35–36 (Oct 22, 2015).

112 Case 107/82, *AEG-Telefunken AG v. Commission*, ECLI:EU:C:1983:293, ¶38 (Oct 25, 1983); Joined Cases 228/82 and 229/82, *Ford-Werke Aktiengesellschaft v. Commission*, ECLI:EU:C:1984:80, ¶16 (Feb 28, 1984); Case T-43/92, *Dunlop Slazenger v. Commission*, ECLI:EU:T:1994:79, ¶56 (July 7, 1994),; Case T-368/00, *General Motors Nederland BV v. Commission*, ECLI:EU:T:2003:275, ¶¶58, 79 (Oct. 21, 2003).

113 *See* Chapter V.

a. *Agreement Between Two or More Undertakings*

443. Under Article 101 TFEU, an agreement requires a meeting of the minds between at least two parties. This requirement thus excludes purely unilateral action. Moreover, the ECJ has held that two or more legally separate entities can be treated as a single undertaking for competition law purposes if their relationship justifies treating them as a single economic unit.[114] In this situation, agreements between two or more legally separate entities will usually be regarded as an internal allocation within a corporate group, rather than an agreement between independent undertakings.

444. An agreement between a parent company and a subsidiary or between two companies which are under the common control of a third does not fall within Article 101(1) TFEU if the companies form a single economic unit within which the subsidiary has no real freedom to determine its course of action in the market.[115] Hence, legal entities that are part of the same economic unit cannot compete with one another and cannot give rise to an "agreement between undertakings" under Article 101(1) TFEU.[116]

445. For instance, in *Christiana & Nielsen*, the European Commission concluded that a market-sharing agreement between a company and its wholly owned subsidiary was outside the scope of Article 101 TFEU because there was no competitive relationship between the two companies that could be restricted. The ECJ followed the European Commission's approach, ruling that Article 101 TFEU does not apply to a parent-subsidiary relationship when the subsidiary, although having separate legal personality, enjoys no economic independence.[117]

446. Where a parent company holds all or almost all of the shares of a subsidiary, there is a rebuttable presumption that the subsidiary is controlled by the parent and that they therefore form a single economic unit.[118] The ECJ has also ruled that the joint control of a subsidiary by two parent companies does not preclude the existence of an economic unit comprising only one of the two parent companies and the subsidiary concerned, even in the situation where that parent company's proportion of the share capital is lower than the proportion of the other parent company.[119]

447. In *Gosme/Martell DMP*, however, the European Commission considered an agreement between Martell and DMP, the latter being a joint subsidiary owned 50%

---

114 Case 48/69, *ICI v. Commission*, ECLI:EU:C:1972:70, ¶140 (July 4, 1972); Case T-9/99, *HFB and Others v. Commission*, ECLI:EU:T:2002:70, ¶61 (Mar. 20, 2002); Case T-66/99, *Minoan Lines SA v. Commission*, ECLI:EU:T:2003:337, ¶¶122, 129 (Dec. 11, 2003).

115 Case T-102/92, *Viho Europe BV v. Commission*, ECLI:EU:T:1995:3, *upheld* (Jan. 12, 1995), Case C-73/95 P, *Viho Europe BV v. Commission*, ECLI:EU:C:1996:405, ¶¶16–18 (Oct. 24, 1996).

116 Case COMP/IV/22.548, *Christiani & Nielsen* (June 18, 1969).

117 Case 22/71, *Béguelin Import Co v. Import Export Sa GL*, ECLI:EU:C:1971:113, ¶8 (Nov. 25, 1971); Case 48/69, *ICI*, ECLI:EU:C:1972:70, ¶132–134 (July 14, 1972); Case 15/74, *Centrafarm BV v. Sterling Drug Inc.*, ECLI:EU:C:1974:114, ¶41 (Oct. 31, 1974); Case T-71/03, *Tokai Carbon Co. Ltd. v. Commission*, ECLI:EU:T:2005:220, ¶59 (June 15, 2005).

118 Case T-470/13, *Merck KGaA v. Commission*, ECLI:EU:T:2016:452, ¶¶433–434 (Sept. 8, 2016); Case C-440/11 P, *Commission v. Stichting Administratiekantoor Portielje*, ECLI:EU:C:2013:514, ¶¶38–45 (July 11, 2013); Case C-521/09 P, *Elf Aquitaine v. Commission*, ECLI:EU:C:2013:644, ¶¶56–59 (Oct. 1, 2013); Case T-56/09, *Saint-Gobain Glass France and Others v. Commission*, ECLI:EU:T:2014:160, ¶210 (Mar. 27, 2014); Case T-354/94, *Stora Kopparbergs Bergslags v. Commission*, ECLI:EU:T:1998:104, ¶80 (May 14, 1998).

119 Case C-628/10 P, *Alliance One International Inc. v. Commission*, ECLI:EU:C:2012:479, ¶101 (July 19, 2012).

by Martell and 50% by Piper-Heidsieck. The European Commission found that Martell and DMP were independent undertakings. The European Commission considered that at the time, Martell was not in a position to control the commercial activity of DMP because the parent companies each held 50% of the capital and voting rights of DMP; half the supervisory board members represented Martell shareholders and half Piper-Heidsieck shareholders; DMP distributed brands not belonging to its parent companies; Martell and Piper-Heidsieck products were invoiced to customers on the same document; and DMP had its own sales force and it alone concluded the conditions of sale with its customers.[120]

448. The conduct of a joint venture may be imputed to its parent companies where those parent companies exercise decisive influence over the joint venture's strategic business decisions[121] based on the economic, organizational and legal links between them.[122] It is irrelevant that the parent company is unaware of the infringing conduct or that the joint venture has its own legal personality.[123] In addition, the conduct of a joint venture may be imputed to only one parent company where only that parent company, to the exclusion of the others, exercises decisive influence over the joint venture.[124]

b. *Existence of an Agreement*

449. The fact that an agreement is partially[125] or never[126] implemented is irrelevant to the analysis of whether an agreement existed for the purpose of Article 101(1) TFEU.[127] The way the parties' meeting of the minds is manifested is also irrelevant as long as it constitutes the expression of the parties' joint intention[128] to act in a specific way.[129]

450. The concept of intent is interpreted very broadly by European courts. An infringement of competition rules warranting the imposition of a fine can be committed

---

120 Case COMP/IV/32.186, *Gosme/Martell-DMP*, ¶30 (1991).

121 Case COMP/38629, *Chloroprene Rubber* ¶¶420–422 (2007); *See also*, Case T-77/08, *Dow Chemical Co. v. Commission*, ECLI:EU:T:2012:47, ¶¶73–89 (Feb. 2, 2012).

122 Case C-179/12 P, *Dow Chemical Co. v. Commission*, ECLI:EU:C:2013:605, ¶¶64–65 (Sept. 26, 2013); *See also*, Case COMP/IV/30.320, *Optical Fibres*, (*EEC Treaty*) (1986), where the European Commission treated JVs in the UK, France and Germany as a separate undertaking and held that the arrangements were likely to restrict competition between them; Corning's interest in each JV was 50% in the UK and Germany and 40% in France. Each JV was technologically dependent on Corning. Corning had certain veto rights (but not voting control), and actively participated in the management.

123 Case T-76/08, *Du Pont de Nemours & Co. v. Commission*, ECLI:EU:T:2012:46, ¶¶75–80 (Feb. 2, 2012); Case T-77/08, *Dow Chemical Co.*, ECLI:EU:T:2012:47, ¶¶91–103 (Feb. 2, 2012); *See also*, Case COMP/F/38.443, *Rubber Chemicals* ¶¶420–440 (2005), suggesting that a full-function joint venture could be presumed to be independent from its parent companies.

124 Case T-541/08, *Sasol v. Commission*, ECLI:EU:T:2014:628, ¶49 (July 11, 2014).

125 Case COMP/39181, *Candle Waxes* ¶¶299–301 (2008); Case T-558/08, *Eni SpA v. Commission*, ECLI:EU:T:2014:1080, ¶¶132–133, (Dec 12, 2014).

126 Case COMP/C.37.750/B2, *French Beer* ¶64 (2004).

127 Case T-240/07, *Heineken Nederland BV v. Commission*, ECLI:EU:T:2011:284, ¶45 (June 16, 2011).

128 Case T-41/96, *Bayer AG v. Commission*, ECLI:EU:T:2000:242, ¶62 (Oct. 26, 2000); Case C-74/04 P, *Commission v. Volkswagen AG*, ECLI:EU:C:2006:460, ¶37 (July 13, 2006).

129 Case T-7/89 *Hercules Chemicals NV v. Commission*, ECLI:EU:T:1991:75, ¶256 (Dec. 17, 1991); *See also* Case 41/69, *ACF Chemiefarma v. Commission*, ECLI:EU:C:1970:71, ¶112 (July 15, 1970); Case T-44/02 OP, *Dresdner Bank AG v. Commission*, ECLI:EU:T:2006:271, (Sept. 27, 2006).

either intentionally or negligently.[130] The General Court underlined that it is not necessary that the undertaking concerned have actual knowledge that it infringed EU competition rules. It is sufficient that the undertaking "could not have been unaware that the object of its conduct was the restriction of competition."[131] Even though the intention of the parties is not necessary for a finding of infringement, the European Commission can consider their intention when considering the anti-competitive nature of the concerned practices.[132]

451. An agreement is not confined to cover only legally-binding contracts.[133] An agreement may be written or oral[134] and so-called informal "gentlemen's agreements" are captured within the meaning of Article 101(1) TFEU.[135] The existence of an agreement may be shown by direct documentary evidence, such as a written contract[136] or circulars sent to the other party.[137] An agreement may also be established by inference from the conduct of the parties[138] or from surrounding circumstances.[139] An agreement can also be inferred from the continuing business relationship between the parties.[140] Moreover, a series of connected agreements that pursue the same overall objective can be considered as one agreement.[141]

452. The fact that a party may have been pressured, coerced, or threatened to agree does not affect the existence of an agreement within the meaning of Article 101(1) TFEU.[142] If a party faces such pressure, coercion, or threats, cases have determined that it should complain to the competent competition authority instead of capitulating by taking part in the infringement.[143]

453. An agreement may be made on the undertakings' behalf by its employees despite the ignorance of senior management[144] even if the employee acts contrary to

---

130 Council Regulation 1/2003 of Dec. 16, 2002 on the implementation of the rules on competition laid down in Articles 81 and 82 of the Treaty, 2003 OJ (L 1) 1.

131 Case T-141/89, *Tréfileurope v. Commission*, ECLI:EU:T:1995:62, ¶176 (Apr. 6, 1995); Case T-15/89, *Chemie Linz v. Commission*, ECLI:EU:T:1992:37, ¶350 (Mar. 10, 1992).

132 Case T-491/07, *CB v. Commission*, ECLI:EU:T:2012:633, ¶¶125, 251 (Nov. 29, 2012); Case C-67/13 P, *CB v. Commission*, ECLI:EU:C:2014:2204, ¶54 (Sept. 11, 2014).

133 Case 209/78, *Van Landewyck Sarl v. Commission*, ECLI:EU:C:1980:248, ¶¶85–91 (Oct. 29, 1980).

134 Case T-7/89 *Hercules Chemicals NV*, ECLI:EU:T:1991:75, ¶256 (Dec. 17, 1991).

135 Case COMP/V/37.614/F3, *Interbrew and Alken-Maes*, ¶¶247 and 248 (Dec. 5, 2001); Case T-48/02, *Brouwerij Haacht v. Commission*, ECLI:EU:T:2005:436 (Dec. 6, 2005); Case COMP/E-1/37.512, *Vitamins* ¶¶554 (2001); Case T-53/03, *BPB Plc v. Commission*, ECLI:EU:T:2008:254, ¶82 (July 8, 2008).

136 Case 41/69, *ACF Chemiefarma*, ECLI:EU:C:1970:71, (July 15, 1970).

137 Case 32/78, 36/78, 82/78, *BMW Belgium SA v. Commission*, ECLI:EU:C:1979:191, ¶¶28–30 (July 12, 1979).

138 Case C-277/87, *Sandoz Prodotti Farmaceutici SpA v. Commission*, ECLI:EU:C:1990:6 (Jan 11, 1990).

139 Case 28/77, *Tepea*, ECLI:EU:C:1978:133, ¶¶17–57 (July 12, 1979); Case 32/78, 36/78, 82/78, *BMW Belgium SA*, ECLI:EU:C:1979:191 (July 12, 1979).

140 COMP/Case IV/31.503, *Konica* (Dec. 18, 1987).

141 Case T-25/95, *Cimenteries CBR v. Commission*, ECLI:EU:T:2000:77, ¶¶4019–4058 (Mar. 15, 2000).

142 Case COMP/IV/29.146, *BMW Belgium* (Dec. 23, 1977); Case 32/78, 36/78, 82/78, *BMW Belgium SA*, ECLI:EU:C:1979:191, ¶¶35–37 (July 12, 1979).

143 Case T-141/89, *Tréfileurope*, ECLI:EU:T:1995:62, ¶58 (Apr. 6, 1995); *See also*, Case C-189/02 P, *Dansk Rørindustri AS v. Commission*, ECLI:EU:C:2005:408, ¶¶132–152 (June 28, 2015); Case T-59/99, *Ventouris Grp. Enters. SA v. Commission*, ECLI:EU:T:2003:334, ¶90 (Dec. 11, 2003); Case T-71/03, *Tokai Carbon Co. Ltd.*, ECLI:EU:T:2005:220, ¶77 (June 15, 2005); Case T-33/05, *Spanish Raw Tobacco v. Commission*, ECLI:EU:T:2011:24, ¶217 (Feb. 3, 2011).

144 Case 100/80, *Musique Diffusion Française SA v. Commission*, ECLI:EU:C:1983:158, ¶97 (June 7, 1983); Case COMP/IV/32.725, *Viho/Parker Pen*, ¶16 (July 15, 1992).

express instructions.[145] For instance, if a company director attended meetings where cartel activity took place, acting contrary to instructions does not affect the undertaking's liability for the cartel.[146]

454. The fact that parties cooperate informally to restrict competition may nonetheless give rise to a concerted practice. Therefore, an undertaking that attends meetings passively or by courtesy is still liable under Article 101(1) TFEU if agreements of an anticompetitive nature are reached during those meetings and the undertaking did not publicly distance itself from what was discussed.[147]

c. *Concerted Practices*

455. A concerted practice covers every type of contact between competitors that may lead to uniform behavior in the market, even if the concerted practice does not result in a proper agreement, such as a written or verbal contract. Participating in meeting with competitors and sharing or receiving commercially sensitive information, even when participants may not eventually reach an agreement regarding their future conduct is sufficient to characterize a concerted conduct.[148] This stems from the concept inherent in EU competition rules, according to which each economic operator must determine independently the policy which it intends to adopt on the market. Although this requirement of independence does not deprive market players of the right to adapt themselves intelligently to the existing and anticipated conduct of their competitors, it does, however, strictly preclude any direct or indirect conduct between such operators, the object or effect whereof is either to influence the conduct on the market of an actual or potential competitor or to disclose to such a competitor the course of conduct which they themselves have decided to adopt or contemplate adopting on the market.[149]

456. In *Anic Partecipazioni*, the ECJ stated that a concerted practice will be held to exist where two or more undertakings act together, behave in the market pursuant to those collusive practices, and there is a relationship of cause and effect between the collusion and the conduct in the market.[150] It is for the undertakings concerned to prove that the concerted action did not have any influence whatsoever on its own conduct in the market.[151]

457. It is not necessary to distinguish between agreements and concerted practices for Article 101(1) TFEU to apply.[152] The purpose of having the terms "agreement" and "concerted practice" in Article 101 TFEU is to cover all types of arrangements in which undertakings accept a limitation of their freedom of action.[153]

---

145 Case T-56/99, *Marlines SA v. Commission*, ECLI:EU:T:2003:333, ¶60 (Dec. 11, 2003).

146 Case T-53/03, *BPB Plc*, ECLI:EU:T:2008:254, ¶360, 431 (July 8, 2008).

147 Case T-83/08, *Denka Chemicals v. Commission*, ECLI:EU:T:2012:48, ¶¶62–63 (Feb. 2, 2012).

148 Case C-49/92 P, *Anic Partecipazioni*, ECLI:EU:C:1999:356, (July 8, 1999).

149 Case T-7/89 *Hercules Chemicals NV*, ECLI:EU:T:1991:75, (Dec. 17, 1991).

150 *Id.* ¶¶255–256; Case C-49/92 P, *Anic Partecipazioni*, ECLI:EU:C:1999:356, ¶118 (July 8, 1999).

151 Case C-199/92 P, *Hüls AG v. Commission*, ECLI:EU:C:1999:358, ¶167 (July 8, 1999).

152 Case C-49/92 P, *Anic Partecipazioni*, ECLI:EU:C:1999:356, ¶112, 131 (July 8, 1999); Case C-8/08, *T-Mobile Netherlands BV v. Raad van bestuur van de Nederlandse Mededingingsautoriteit*, ECLI:EU:C:2009:343, ¶23 (June 4, 2009).

153 Case C-49/92 P, *Anic Partecipazioni*, ECLI:EU:C:1999:356, ¶112 (July 8, 1999).

For instance, in *Fresh Del Monte*,[154] the General Court rejected an argument that the European Commission had failed to find a meeting of minds between producers or the existence of a common course of conduct because the conduct at stake constituted a concerted practice, not an agreement. The concept of concerted practice is important where there is insufficient evidence of an actual agreement.

458. Although agreements and concerted practices are conceptually different, there is no rigid distinction between the two. In cartel cases, the European Commission often states that there is an agreement or a concerted practice, without deciding which one. For instance, in *PVC*, the European Commission determined that the parties to the cartel had participated in an agreement and/or a concerted practice[155] and the General Court upheld the European Commission stating that the European Commission cannot be expected to classify the infringement precisely.[156] Moreover, in *HFB Holding*, the General Court clarified that the dual characterization of a behavior as both an agreement and a concerted practice does not require, simultaneously and cumulatively, proof that each factual piece of the behavior presents the constituent elements both of an agreement and of a concerted practice; instead, the dual characterization refers to the existence of a "complex whole" comprising a number of factual elements, some of which have been characterized as agreements and others as concerted practices.[157]

459. A concerted practice will usually be inferred if direct or indirect contact between two or more undertakings is documented and the undertakings in question remain active in the market.[158] However, in *Suiker Unie*[159] the ECJ made clear that Article 101(1) TFEU precludes any direct or indirect contact between undertakings the object or effect of which is either to influence future market conduct or to disclose future intentions.

460. Hence, just like agreements, collusion may take the form of direct or indirect contact between undertakings through meetings, or disclosure of future intentions, whether oral or written.[160] In *Cimenteries*,[161] the General Court held that the concept of a concerted practice implies the existence of "reciprocal contacts" and that such contacts exist where one competitor discloses its future intentions or conduct in the market to another, whether this sharing of information is requested or not.[162]

---

154 Case T-587/08, *Fresh Del Monte Produce Inc. v. Commission*, ECLI:EU:T:2013:129, ¶300 (Mar. 14, 2013).

155 Case T-305/94, *Limburgse Vinyl Maatschappij (LVM) v. Commission*, ECLI:EU:T:1999:80, (Apr. 20, 1999). *See also*, Case COMP/IV/33.708, *British Sugar* (1998); on appeal: Case T-202/98, *Tate & Lyle Plc v. Commission*, ECLI:EU:T:2001:185, (July 12, 2001).

156 Case T-305/94, *Limburgse Vinyl Maatschappij (LVM)*, ECLI:EU:T:1999:80, ¶696 (Apr. 20, 1999); Case T-186/06, *Solvay SA v. Commission*, ECLI:EU:T:2011:276, ¶¶90–92 (June 16, 2011); Case T-191/06, *FMC Foret SA v. Commission*, ECLI:EU:T:2011:277, ¶¶102–104 (June 16, 2011); Case T-83/10, *Riva Fire v. Commission*, ECLI:EU:T:2014:1034, ¶¶154–155 (Dec. 9, 2014).

157 Case T-9/99, *HFB and Others*, ECLI:EU:T:2002:70, ¶187 (Mar. 20, 2002); Case C-49/92 P, *Anic Partecipazioni*, ECLI:EU:C:1999:356, ¶132–33 (July 8, 1999).

158 Case 29/83 and 30/83, *CRAM and Rheinzink v. Commission*, ECLI:EU:C:1984:130, (Mar. 28, 1984).

159 Case 40/73, *Suiker Unie UA v. Commission*, ECLI:EU:C:1975:174, ¶174 (Dec. 16, 1975).

160 Case T-202/98, *Tate & Lyle Plc*, ECLI:EU:T:2001:185, ¶¶54 *et seq.* (July 12, 2001); Case COMP/E-1/37.152, *Plasterboard* ¶¶471–477 (2002); on appeal, Case 29/83 and 30/83, *CRAM and Rheinzink*, ECLI:EU:C:1984:130, (Mar. 28, 1984); Case T-53/03, *BPB Plc*, ECLI:EU:T:2008:254, ¶¶135–155 (July 8, 2008).

161 Case T-25/95, *Cimenteries CBR*, ECLI:EU:T:2000:77, (Mar. 15, 2000).

162 *Id.* ¶¶1849–1850.

It is thus not necessary to show that an undertaking has formally undertaken or committed to adopt a particular conduct. It is sufficient that, by its statement of intention, the competitor eliminated or reduced uncertainty about the conduct expected from it in the market.[163]

461. In a highly concentrated oligopolistic market, the exchange of commercial information between competitors in preparation for an anticompetitive agreement suffices to prove the existence of a concerted practice where the information enables operators to know the market positions and strategies of their competitors.[164]

462. The fact that only one of multiple competing undertakings reveals its intentions is not sufficient to exclude the possibility of a concerted practice.[165] In *Tate & Lyle*[166] the General Court held that there had been a concerted practice at meetings when only one undertaking notified its competitors of its future pricing intentions. The General Court found that the information supplied was not otherwise readily accessible market data and the meetings allowed the participants to become aware of that information more simply, rapidly, and directly.

463. In the same vein, the presumption that the undertakings take account of the information exchanged with their competitors applies when they act together on a regular basis over a long period.[167] Such a presumption even applies if the concerted action is the result of a meeting held by the participating undertakings on a single occasion rather than of a course of conduct.[168]

B. *Hardcore Cartels in the Life Sciences Sector*

464. Anticompetitive practices considered most harmful are called "hardcore cartels." These cartels involve two or more competing undertakings, businesses, or individuals intentionally limiting or reducing competition. In its 1998 Recommendation, the Organization for Economic Co-operation and Development (OECD) described hardcore cartels as: "anticompetitive agreement[s], anticompetitive concerted practice[s], or anticompetitive arrangement[s] by competitors to fix prices, make rigged bids (collusive tenders), establish output restrictions or quotas, or share or divide markets by allocating customers, suppliers, territories, or lines of commerce."[169]

465. The term "cartel" is used to describe an agreement or other form of co-operation between two or more actual or potential competitors which has the object or effect of reducing competition between them regarding prices, markets, customers, and/or products. Arrangements involving price fixing, market sharing, the exchange of confidential information, and/or collective boycotts are regarded

163 *Id.* ¶1852.

164 Case C-455/11 P, *Solvay SA v. Commission*, ECLI: EU:C:2013:796, ¶¶39–40 (Dec. 5, 2013); *see also*, Case T-655/11, *FSL Holdings v. Commission*, ECLI:EU:T:2015:383, ¶¶391, 458 (June 16, 2015).

165 Case T-202/98, *Tate & Lyle Plc*, ECLI:EU:T:2001:185, ¶¶54 *et seq.* (July 12, 2001). *See also*, COMP/AT.39850, *Container Shipping* ¶¶32–47 (2016).

166 Case T-202/98, *Tate & Lyle Plc*, ECLI:EU:T:2001:185, ¶60 (July 12, 2001).

167 Case C-49/92 P, *Anic Partecipazioni*, ECLI:EU:C:1999:356, ¶121 (July 8, 1999).

168 Case C-8/08, *T-Mobile Netherlands BV*, ECLI:EU:C:2009:343, ¶59 (June 4, 2009).

169 OECD, Recommendation of the Council Concerning Effective Action Against Hard Core Cartels, COM (1998) 35 final, 3 (Mar. 25, 1998), *available at* https://one.oecd.org/document/C(98)35/FINAL/en/pdf.

as *hardcore* restrictions of competition falling under the prohibition of Article 101(1) TFEU irrespective of their effects on the market.

466. Although the number of precedents regarding hardcore restrictions between competitors is relatively limited within the life sciences industry, competition authorities still have had the opportunity to review anticompetitive agreements between competitors, both at the EU and Member States level.

a. *Pricing Agreements*

467. An arrangement or concerted practice restricting prices is generally prohibited under EU antitrust rules. Among pharmaceutical suppliers, price fixing agreements are rare due to the extensive national price regulation of the sector in most EU Member States, as well as the fact that originator drugs are often highly differentiated except as compared to generics.

468. Nevertheless, the European Commission and NCAs have issued many decisions regarding pricing cartels in the life sciences industry.

469. In the *Vitamins* case,[170] eight pharmaceutical companies were fined for participating in eight distinct secret price-fixing cartels affecting several vitamin products. The participants in each of the "sub-cartels" corresponding to each type of vitamin allegedly fixed prices, implemented common price increases, and issued similar price announcements. In addition, the cartel members allegedly set up a scheme to monitor and enforce their agreements and participated in regular meetings to implement the agreement.[171] The European Commission found that the collusive arrangements in the various vitamins were not spontaneous or haphazard developments, but were planned, conceived, and directed by the same persons at the most senior levels of the concerned undertakings. The price increases for the great majority of the different vitamins were often announced and made on the same occasion. The principal aspects of the agreements and arrangements, which have been characterized as restrictions of competition by the European Commission, were: market allocation and market share quotas, concerted price increases, setting target and minimum prices, collusion on the implementation of those price increases in the different markets, adaptation of the cartelists' individual conduct and pricing in order to ensure the maintenance of the agreed quotas, and in some cases, arranging for "compensation" to adjust actual sales to the quotas, and allocation of the business of specific customers.

470. Given the continuity and similarity of method, the European Commission considered it appropriate to treat the complex agreements covering the different vitamins in the same procedure. The European Commission held that the agreements affecting the vitamins individually had the object and effect of restricting competition in the

---

170 Case COMP/E-1/37.512, *Vitamins* ¶554 (2001); Case T-15/02, *BASF AG v. Commission*, ECLI:EU:T:2006:74, (Mar. 15, 2006) and Case T-26/02, *Daiichi Pharmaceutical Co. Ltd. v. Commission*, ECLI:EU:T:2006:75, (Mar. 15, 2006). Notably the General Court upheld the findings and the analysis of the European Commission on the practices at stake but either reduced or annulled depending on the findings the leader and the instigator markup applied by the European Commission to BASF for some of the practices.

171 Case COMP/E-1/37.512, *Vitamins* ¶¶172–188; 250–254; 275–278; 311–316; 336–337; 415–419; 467–470; 497–505 (2001).

community and the EEA. Market sharing and price fixing were found to restrict competition within the meaning of both Article 101(1) TFEU by their very nature, and each of the horizontal arrangements had the essential characteristics of the prohibition set forth in Article 101(1) TFEU.

471. In the *Methylglucamine* case,[172] the European Commission found the cartelists entered into a cartel to fix prices for methylglucamine.[173] The participants had meetings every year that allegedly started with an informal exchange of information between company officials responsible for the distribution and marketing of methylglucamine. During these meetings, each participant allegedly shared their sales data and turnover figures from the previous year,[174] agreed on the percentage increase and the list price of methylglucamine that would be applied to small customers during the coming year, and agreed on the individually negotiated prices applicable to larger customers. As a result, the cartelists' list prices were practically the same.[175] The European Commission found the cartelists had implemented a complex collusive arrangement, through specific agreements or concerted practices, complementing the basic agreement on price fixing and market sharing by allocation of individual customers, pursuing the same common purpose of eliminating competition between them.[176]

472. The French *Subutex* case[177] is an example of how a cartel in the pharmaceutical sector can impact generic entry. The French Competition Authority (*Autorité de la concurrence* (FCA)) fined the licensor and the licensee of the specialty drug Subutex for having entered into an agreement a few months before entry of a competitor's generic drug in the market. The purpose of the agreement between the licensor and licensee of Subutex was to disparage the generics of Subutex to strengthen the pharmacists' loyalty towards the originator drug. The strategy was jointly designed but implemented by the licensee only, as the licensor was not directly active in the market.[178]

473. More precisely, the first branch of the anticompetitive agreement aimed at "[d]elaying/[d]iscouraging" generic entry by challenging bioequivalence and raising "health issues" with health professionals.[179] The parties agreed that the licensee's com-

---

172 Case COMP/E-2/37.978, *Methylglucamine* (2002).

173 Methylglucamine is a chemical substance used in X-ray analyses.

174 Case COMP/E-2/37.978, *Methylglucamine* ¶¶76–78 (2002).

175 *Id.* ¶¶83–85.

176 The European Commission considered that the complex collusive arrangements had the object and effect of restricting competition by directly or indirectly fixing sales prices and market shares. The collusive arrangements and mechanisms adopted by the producers allegedly were ultimately aimed at fixing prices and removing any competition on price. The European Commission stated that the cartelists breached Article 101(1) TFEU by exchanging price and customers' sensitive information. The cartelists were found to have colluded on prices and price increases and adapted their individual conduct and pricing to ensure the maintenance of the agreed market sharing. The European Commission found that by participating in regular meetings and having other contacts to agree the above restrictions, the cartelists were able to easily implement and modify these restrictions as required.

177 FCA, Decision No. 13-D-21, *Schering-Plough* (Dec. 18, 2013).

178 The FCA also fined the licensee alone on the basis of Article 102 TFEU prohibiting abuses of dominant position, for a disparagement behavior toward the generic of Subutex, Buprenorphine Arrow, and for having the implemented loyalty rebates in favor of certain pharmacists, without any justified economic consideration, with the sole aim of saturating their shelves and blocking the generic's access to the market.

179 FCA, Decision No. 13-D-21, *Schering-Plough* ¶¶101 *et seq.* (Dec. 18, 2013).

munication would emphasize the differences between the originator drug and the generics in order to instill doubts in the minds of doctors and pharmacists and avoid substitution of Subutex with a generic drug during patients' treatment.[180] In combination with this first branch and in order to further delay the entry of Subutex generics into the market, the licensor and licensee agreed on a pricing strategy to minimize the generics' penetration to pharmacies and customer loyalty programs through direct sales.[181]

474. The Paris Court of Appeal upheld the FCA findings and stated that if economic operators that are facing entry in the market of a competing product are entitled to adopt a strategy to defend their market shares, they cannot implement practices that artificially distort free competition. Therefore, the implementation of a strategy aimed at delaying the arrival of generic drugs into the market, which, after the expiry of patents, makes it possible to re-establish competition that was previously non-existent, constitutes a particularly harmful practice.

475. In *Nomeco/TMJ*,[182] the Danish Competition Authority found that the two largest wholesalers of pharmaceutical products had entered into an anticompetitive agreement where they coordinated prices and other trading conditions, including the conditions set for the return of pharmaceutical specialties between wholesalers and manufacturers and between wholesalers and pharmacies. Since, as a result of the Danish pharmaceutical regulation, many of the normal parameters of competition such as price and quality were already reduced, the authority found that it was all the more important to maintain the few remaining competition parameters. Therefore, the agreement allegedly impaired competition by impacting the overall level of service and resulting in cost increases for the manufacturers.

476. In *Alcyon*,[183] the FCA found that three wholesalers took part in several cartels regarding the distribution of veterinary products. The cartelists allegedly agreed to profit from the health emergency caused by the rapid spread of bluetongue disease in French cattle by allegedly agreeing on the level of costs they would submit to the government regarding the distribution of vaccines during three vaccination campaigns.[184] In particular, the FCA found that the wholesalers trade association played a pivotal role in the conduct as it disseminated amongst its members the calculation method used to overestimate their costs and allegedly used its influence to convince distributors not to decrease prices.

477. In *Federfarma Teramo*,[185] the Italian Competition Authority (*Autorità Garante della Concorrenza e del Mercato* (AGCM)) fined a pharmacist trade association for fixing the retail prices of OTC pharmaceutical products via a circular detailing the maximum discounts applicable to each product. The AGCM relied on a copy of the circular which included a prospectus listing the maximum discounts applicable to 250 OTC pharmaceuticals. The circular was shared among all the members of the

180 *Id.* ¶¶107, 121, 440 *et seq.*

181 *Id.* ¶¶131, 468 *et seq.*

182 KFST (Copenhagen), *Nomeco and Tjellesen Max Jenne*, 12/07423 LTA/MEF (Nov. 26, 2014).

183 FCA, Decision No. 18-D-15, *Alcyon France SA* (July 26, 2018).

184 *Id.* ¶¶76, 173–184.

185 AGCM, Case I684, Decision No. 18421, *Federfarma Teramo-Sconti sui Prezzi al Pubblico* (May 29, 2008).

trade association. The AGCM found that the trade association circular amounted to an association of undertakings with an anticompetitive objective.

b. *Agreements Involving Market Sharing or Output Restrictions*

478. Outside pricing agreements, the European Commission and NCAs also take a particularly strict view of practices which can "share markets or sources of supply," "limit or control production… or investment," or "limit or control… markets."[186]

479. Agreements that restrict output or limit production are typically considered part of a wider cartel to fix prices or share markets because, in the absence of such restrictions on output, market forces would undermine the price-fixing arrangements by driving down prices to their competitive levels.

480. In the *Vitamins* case,[187] in addition to price fixing, the cartelists also allegedly allocated sale quotas to stabilize their respective worldwide market shares.[188] If one of the cartelists sold more than its allocated quota, the others set corrective measures where the overselling company "would have to slow down sales to enable the others to catch up."[189] In some cases, "if at the end of the year a producer was substantially ahead of its quota, it had to purchase vitamins from the others in order to compensate them for the corresponding shortfall in their allocation."[190] The European Commission considered that the significant increase in the price of vitamin C had to be interpreted in light of the fact that the cartel members agreed on such market share allocation as well as a reporting and monitoring system.

481. In the *Methylglucamine* case,[191] the cartelists entered into an agreement with the primary goal of maintaining a 50% market share *status quo* in the worldwide market for methylglucamine.[192] In addition to fixing prices and price levels, the cartelists agreed not to compete for each other's customers to prevent customers from switching to another supplier.[193] To prevent customer switching, the cartelists agreed that they would respond to a price query from a customer attributed to another cartelist by quoting their list prices, which were higher than the prices actually negotiated with their respective customers.[194] The European Commission considered that the implementation of price-fixing agreements should be analyzed as part of an overall plan for market sharing.

482. In *Alcyon*,[195] the FCA found that three wholesalers concluded a "non-aggression" pact to freeze out competition and allocate customers for the distribution of veterinary drugs. Allegedly, there were "non-aggression" pacts between the market leader and the third-largest player, on the one hand, and the third and second-largest player, on the other. By not soliciting customers from each other for

---

186 TFEU, art. 101.
187 Case COMP/E-1/37.512, *Vitamins* (2001).
188 *Id.* ¶164.
189 *Id.* ¶196.
190 *Id.*
191 Case COMP/E-2/37.978, *Methylglucamine* (2002).
192 *Id.* ¶88 *et seq.*
193 *Id.* ¶96.
194 *Id.* ¶¶90–97.
195 FCA, Decision No. 18-D-15, *Alcyon France SA* (July 26, 2018).

nearly 3 years (for the first agreement) and 2 months (for the second agreement), the agreements were considered to have limited these companies' commercial independence and restricted competition in the market.

483. In *Andreae Noris Zahn*,[196] the German Federal Cartel Office found that seven individuals and their respective companies entered into anticompetitive agreements to get back to their original market positions after the end of a competitive "discount war" in the wholesale market for pharmaceutical products. The competitors compared the situation before and after the "discount war" with the objective of reallocating customers that had switched suppliers during the competitive phase, and agreed to completely stop new customer acquisition. The authority found that this arrangement should be analyzed as a quota cartel bordering on a price-fixing cartel.

484. In the Spanish case *Colegio Farmacéuticos*,[197] the intervention of a public body in the practices at stake did not prevent the characterization of a cartel by the Spanish Competition Authority (*Comisión Nacional de los Mercados y la Competencia* (CNMC)). The commission ruled that the co-operation agreement between the Regional Health Service of Castilla-La Mancha (SESCAM) and the regional Professional Association of Pharmacists, through which the latter established a rotation system for pharmacies to distribute pharmaceutical products to healthcare centers and care homes in Castilla La-Mancha that did not allow patients to choose the pharmacy they purchased from, had to be considered as a market-sharing agreement.

485. Similarly, in *Ordre des pharmaciens de Basse-Normandie*,[198] the FCA found that a regional professional Order for the pharmacists that asked retirement homes to buy from the nearest pharmacies rather than those located farther away, even though the latter may be more competitive, breached Article 101(1) TFEU. The FCA considered that the pressure exerted by the Order was a concerted action having as its object and effect the distortion of competition that could not have been justified by the aim of ensuring an adequate "territorial network" of pharmacies to respond to the needs of the population.

486. Finally, in the Italian *Lucentis* case,[199] the AGCM analyzed an alleged agreement between Roche and Novartis, which allegedly intended to discourage and limit the off-label use of Roche's cancer drug (Avastin) in the treatment of eye diseases where Novartis was the market leader with Lucentis, as a form of market sharing between the parties.

487. The AGCM considered that Novartis and Roche colluded to avoid competition from Avastin in the treatment of eye diseases by artificially differentiating Avastin from Lucentis, even though the two drugs derived from the same molecule and would allegedly constitute equivalent treatments. The arrangement was allegedly

---

[196] German Federal Cartel Office, Case No. B3-129/03, *Andrae Noris Zahn AG, Sanacorp Pharmahandel AG, Phoenix Pharmahandel Aktiengesellschaft & Co. KG and Gehe Pharma Handel GmbH* (Nov. 26, 2006).

[197] CNMC, Decision No. 639/08, *Colegio Farmacéuticos Castilla-La Mancha* (Apr. 22, 2009).

[198] FCA, Decision No. 09-D-17, *Ordre des pharmaciens de Basse-Normandie* (Apr. 22, 2009).

[199] AGCM, Case I760, Decision No. 24823, *Roche-Novartis/Farmaci Avastin e Lucentis* (May 27, 2014).

intended to raise concerns about the safety of Avastin used in ophthalmology to shift demand towards the more expensive Lucentis. The competition authority found that such conduct falls within the prohibition in Article 101(1) TFEU as a market allocation that was mutually beneficial to both parties, since Novartis would have increased its profits from the sale of Lucentis and Roche, in turn, would have benefitted from the royalties paid by Novartis to its subsidiary Genentech, as the licensor of Lucentis.

c. *Bid Rigging*

488. Bid rigging covers any behavior designed to distort the bidding process. Through bid rigging, competing bidders decide beforehand who should win the tender, instead of competing to submit the most attractive offer. Bid rigging cartels include a wide range of practices, ranging from cover bids, bid suppression, and bid rotation to classic market allocation.

489. In *Kemofarmacija,*[200] the Slovenian Competition Authority found that four pharmaceutical wholesalers rigged bids in public procurement tenders by public pharmacies to preserve their market shares. The authority found that the four undertakings submitted mostly identical offers in terms of prices and rebates and considered that, although wholesale prices of medicines for human use are set as legally binding maximum prices, this should not prevent suppliers from offering lower prices or discounts. Thus, by submitting identical offers, the wholesalers prevented free competition in the market and end-users of the medicine from benefiting from competitive rebates, in violation of Article 101(1) TFEU.

490. In *Hungaropharma,*[201] the Hungarian Competition Authority found that three pharmaceutical wholesalers, with the active collaboration of two consultant companies, influenced the public procurement of medicines by harmonizing their prices prior to the submission of their offers and sharing the market amongst themselves. The public buyer relied on an external expert who, with the help of another consulting company, organized the collusion between the parties. The authority found that both the wholesalers and the two consulting companies manipulated the procurement notice and, prior to the submission of the offers, set their respective prices in consideration of the prices of the others resulting in a market-sharing scheme.

491. In *Prodotti Disinfettanti,*[202] the AGCM found that nine suppliers of antiseptic and disinfectants rigged bids launched by the public health system through the creation of a common entity. The authority alleged that the cartelists exchanged information prior to each tender. and concerted their behavior in relation to the bid prices to be submitted in the course of the tenders through a system that eliminated any uncertainty as to the final assignee of a particular contract, in breach of Article 101(1) TFEU.

---

200 Slovenian Competition Authority, Case No. 62157, *Kemofarmacija, Salus, Farmadent and Gopharm* (Oct. 14, 2013).

201 Hungarian Competition Authority, Case No. Vj/28/2013, *Hungaropharma* (Sept. 15, 2015).

202 AGCM, Case I/639, Prov. No. 15393, *Prodotti disinfettanti* (Apr. 26, 2006).

492. Finally, in *Advanced Accelerator Applications Ibérica*,[203] the CNMC fined the two main competitors active in the market in Spain for the supply of radiopharmaceutical fluorodeoxyglucose for bid rigging. The conduct consisted of an agreement to deliberately lose bids to supply radiopharmaceuticals to hospitals, as part of a geographic market sharing agreement assigning specific hospitals to each cartelist. Subsequently, the companies subcontracted services to each other at prices significantly lower than those charged to the hospitals. The European Commission found that this behavior allowed competitor to be awarded contracts at substantially higher prices than those at which their proximity to the customers would have allowed them to bid, knowing for a fact that their competitor would not behave competitively.

II. Agreements related to patents

1. Introduction to Patent Concerns under Antitrust/Competition Law

493. The pharmaceutical sector is one of the most research-intensive industries. Pharmaceutical companies devote substantial resources to research and innovation, with the aim of discovering new molecules or processes that may establish new treatments or refine existing ones. The OECD thus estimated in 2019 that "on average across OECD countries, the industry spent nearly 12% of its gross value added on R&D. This is almost as high as in the electronics, optical and air and spacecraft industries, and considerably higher than across manufacturing as a whole."[204]

494. The cost of developing a new drug has been the subject of debate, with recent estimates ranging from US$314 million[205] to US$2.8 billion.[206] The trend is nonetheless for research costs to increase in the sector. In the words of the OECD, "expenditure on R&D in the pharmaceutical industry in OECD countries grew by 14% in real terms between 2010 and 2016."[207] Conversely, patents contribute to roughly 70% to 80% of overall revenues of pharmaceutical companies.[208]

495. Due to these costs, pharmaceutical companies typically file patents to protect the IP of their drugs and to recoup the investment made during the R&D phase. Patent rights are not self-enforcing. Every patent holder must enforce its rights against generic competitors, including by taking legal action. Patent lawsuits can either result in an infringement judgment, whereby the infringing generic is blocked

---

203 CNMC, Case No. S/0644/18, *Advanced Accelerator Applications Ibérica* (Feb. 2, 2021).

204 OECD, *Health at a Glance 2019: OECD Indicators*, OECD PUBLISHING 214 (2019), *available at* https://read.oecd-ilibrary.org/social-issues-migration-health/health-at-a-glance-2019_fc8b43f4-en#page1.

205 Kavisha Jayasundara et al., *Estimating the clinical cost of drug development for orphan versus non-orphan drugs*, 14 ORPHANET J. RARE DIS. (Jan. 10, 2019), *available at* https://ojrd.biomedcentral.com/articles/10.1186/s13023-018-0990-4#citeas.

206 Joseph A DiMasi et al., *Innovation in the pharmaceutical industry: new estimates of R&D costs*, J. HEALTH ECON. (Feb. 12, 2016), *available at* https://pubmed.ncbi.nlm.nih.gov/26928437/

207 OECD, *Health at a Glance 2019: OECD Indicators*, *supra* n. 204, Chapter IV.

208 *Driving Innovation: Drug Patents vs. Prizes*, DRUG PATENT WATCH (June 7, 2022), *available at* https://www.drugpatentwatch.com/blog/driving-innovation-drug-patents-vs-prizes/.

from marketing its drug until the patent expires, or in a judgment that the patent is invalid or has not been infringed, which de facto opens the market to the generic.

496. Parties to a pharmaceutical patent dispute may also decide to settle their case out of court. Patent settlement agreements cover all sorts of commercial agreements, formal or informal, aimed at settling disputes on actual or potential issues such as patent infringement or validity. These include so-called *reverse payment agreements* whereby a patent holder pays a generic company to settle a potential patent challenge.

2. Evaluation of Agreements Involving Patents Under US Law

A. *General Considerations*

497. US antitrust and patent law may sometimes be in tension. Antitrust law, among other goals, seeks to encourage equal market access, prevent monopolization, and foster consumer welfare through lower prices. Patent law, on the other hand, protects exclusivity and encourages innovation. By offering periods of exclusivity for inventions and discoveries, patent law ensures that innovators have the necessary resources to fund future R&D projects. While the grant of a patent may reward innovators with exclusivity for advances in medicine, courts have found that in certain situations patent restrictions may be used in ways that reduce or harm competition in violation of the antitrust laws.

498. A patent provides its owner with a bundle of rights as a matter of law, including the rights: (1) to exclude others from selling infringing products, (2) to decide which, and how many (if any), persons can practice the patented innovation, and (3) to choose the financial terms on which the patent owner is willing to allow them to do so. Despite these rights, antitrust concerns may still arise in circumstances involving pharmaceutical patent licensing and the settlement of pharmaceutical patent disputes. For example, antitrust laws may condemn a patent holder that seeks to impose license terms extending beyond the term of its patent monopoly. This use of a patent might raise antitrust concerns because the specific restraint imposed by the license extends beyond the term of the licensor's lawful patent monopoly.

499. Even when a restraint supposedly falls within the scope of a licensor's lawful patent claims, the US Supreme Court has carved out an exception for patent litigation settlement agreements that contain a "reverse payment" (sometimes called "pay for delay"). That is, when a brand name pharmaceutical manufacturer settles a patent dispute with a generic challenger, it may be unlawful for the patent holder to make a large and "unjustified" payment in exchange for the generic's agreement to drop its patent challenge and remain off the market for some period of time even if the agreement allows for entry prior to the expiration of the patent.[209] Among other things, the Court observed that there is nothing in the Patent Act allowing a patent holder to pay off an alleged infringer.

---

209 *Actavis*, 570 U.S. 170.

500. In sum, while patents provide a legal right to exclude to patent owners, the antitrust laws may limit the use of that patent in ways that unreasonably restrain competition in the relevant market, particularly in ways not contemplated in the Patent Act. This section first examines certain patent licensing arrangements and their treatment under US antitrust laws. It then explains the Supreme Court's decision in *FTC v. Actavis* and the development of antitrust law surrounding "reverse payment" patent litigation settlements in the US.

B. *Patent Licensing Agreements*

a. *The Rights of Patent Holders*

501. In exchange for disclosing their innovations to the public, patent holders are entitled to specific property rights. First, a patent holder has "the right to exclude others from making, using, offering for sale, or selling the invention throughout the United States" during the term of the patent.[210] This right to exclude is protected by statute and is essential to the purpose of the patent grant, providing an incentive to innovate and to share innovations with the public.[211] Second, a patent holder has a statutory right to determine whether anyone may practice the innovation described in the patent and to limit the number of persons who may do so even to the exclusion of the patent holder itself. The Patent Act specifically gives a patent holder the right to "grant and convey an exclusive right under his application for patent, or patents, to the whole or any specified part of the United States."[212]

502. This statutory right to grant an exclusive license necessarily allows for situations in which there is only one firm that may practice the patented innovation.[213] Notwithstanding potential effects on competition, patent holders are not obligated to license the patent to anyone or even to practice the patent themselves. It is "settled doctrine" that a patent holder "has no obligation either to use [the patent] or to grant its use to others."[214] Third, patent holders have the right to be compensated for the use of their patented innovation and may set the financial terms on which others may practice the patent, including by demanding a royalty. "While a

---

210 35 U.S.C. § 154(a)(1); *see also* U.S. C. art. I, ¶8, cl. 8 (granting Congress the power "[t]o promote the progress of science and useful arts, by securing for limited times to authors and inventors the exclusive right to their respective writings and discoveries"); *Actavis,* 570 U.S. 136, 147 ("[A] valid patent excludes all except its owner from the use of the protected process or product." (quoting *United States v. Line Material Co.,* 333 U.S. 287, 308 (1948))).

211 *See* FTC, To Promote Innovation: The Proper Balance of Competition and Patent Law and Policy, 1–2 (Oct. 2003), *available at* https://www.ftc.gov/sites/default/files/documents/reports/promote-innovation-proper-balance-competition-and-patent-law-and-policy/innovationrpt.pdf ("Patent policy encourages prospective inventors to invest time and money in inventions, because a patent's grant of the exclusive right to make, sell, and use the invention for a certain period of time can allow inventors to realize returns sufficient to encourage the initial investments.").

212 *See* 35 U.S.C. § 261.

213 *See, e.g., Genentech, Inc. v. Eli Lilly & Co.,* 998 F.2d 931, 949 (Fed. Cir. 1993) (explaining that "the grant of an exclusive license is a lawful incident of the right to exclude provided by the Patent Act"); *United States v. Westinghouse Elec. Corp.,* 648 F.2d 642, 647 (9th Cir. 1981) ("The right to license [a] patent, exclusively or otherwise, or to refuse to license at all, is 'the untrammeled right' of the patentee.").

214 *Hartford-Empire Co. v. United States,* 323 U.S. 386, 432–33, (1945); *see also Yagoozon, Inc. v. Kids Fly Safe,* No. 14-040, 2014 WL 3109797, at *8 (D.R.I. July 8, 2014) (noting "[i]t is not misuse of patent rights for a patentee to deal only with those with whom it pleases"); DOJ & FTC Antitrust IP Guidelines for the Licensing of Intellectual Property § 2.2 (2017) ("Nor does such market power impose on the intellectual property owner an obligation to license the use of that property to others."), *available at* https://www.justice.gov/atr/IPguidelines/download.

patent lasts, the patentee possesses exclusive rights to the patented article – rights he may sell or license for royalty payments if he so chooses."[215]

503. The FTC and DOJ recognize that IP licensing can significantly benefit competition.[216] IP is a single component of many in the production process, and a patent holder must be able to adequately manage the additional components to realize the commercial value that the patent provides.[217] In many circumstances, it is more efficient for the owner of the patent to license its rights to other firms that are able to effectively manage the production and commercialization process. This effective integration can benefit consumers by expediting the commercialization process and reducing costs.[218]

504. While patent licensing is recognized as procompetitive, there may be instances where it can lessen competition in an industry and raise antitrust concerns. The US Antitrust Agencies have published guidelines with examples of potentially problematic licensing arrangements.[219] For example, a license might divide the market among firms that otherwise would have competed using different technologies and therefore could adversely affect the market for a specific good.[220] Additionally, where there are two actual or potential competitors involved in R&D for a specific product, a license by one to the other might reduce competition for the development of that product because it effectively merges those two companies.[221] Specifically, the US agencies are most concerned with firms in a horizontal relationship – that is, but for the licensing arrangement, those that would have been actual or potential competitors in a relevant market.[222] The evaluation of the antitrust implications of a patent license is a fact-intensive process that requires a detailed understanding of the market at issue and the business motivations of the parties to the transaction. Although the agency guidelines are not binding on the agencies or US courts, they provide guideposts for how to limit antitrust risk when entering into patent licensing arrangements.

b. *Analysis of Certain Patent Licensing Restrictions Under the Rule of Reason*

505. The first question when analyzing anticompetitive restraints in patent licensing arrangements is whether the restraints merely reflect rights given to the patent holder by Congress in the Patent Act. If so, that is the end of the analysis.[223] There is no role for antitrust analysis in such situations.

---

215 *See Kimble v. Marvel Entm't., LLC*, 576 U.S. 446, 451 (2015).

216 *See, e.g.*, DOJ & FTC Antitrust IP Guidelines, *supra* n. 214, Chapter IV, 5–7

217 *Id.* 5.

218 *Id.*

219 *Id.*

220 *Id.* 7.

221 *Id.*

222 *Id.*

223 *See United States v. Studiengesellschaft Kohle, m.b.H.*, 670 F.2d 1122, 1127–28 (D.C. Cir. 1981) ("[T]he conduct at issue is illegal if it threatens competition in areas other than those protected by the patent, and is otherwise legal. The patentee is entitled to exact the full value of his invention but is not entitled to endanger competition in other areas by manipulating his patent monopoly."); *USM Corp. v. SPS Techs., Inc.*, 694 F.2d 505, 513 (7th Cir. 1982) ("Patent licensing agreements between competitors are sometimes struck down under antitrust law, of course, but only upon proof of an anticompetitive effect beyond that implicit in the grant of the patent."); *SCM Corp. v. Xerox Corp.*, 645 F.2d 1195, 1206 (2d Cir. 1981) ("[W]e hold that where a patent has been

506. Restraints that may have potential anticompetitive effects beyond those contemplated by the Patent Act, are commonly analyzed under the rule of reason. This analysis requires a plaintiff to first show that the license is likely to have anticompetitive effects or harm competition. If this burden is met, the defendant must come forward with procompetitive justifications for the restraint. If these justifications exist, the plaintiff can show that the restraint is unnecessary to achieve the procompetitive goal or that less restrictive alternatives exist.[224] Even so, some licensing arrangements are so plainly anticompetitive that they are treated as per se unlawful, and as a result, analysis by a court is unnecessary to determine whether they harm competition.[225] The FTC and DOJ advocate for rule-of-reason treatment when the license in question "can be expected to contribute to an efficiency-enhancing integration of economic activity" such as the combination of IP with production capability.[226] When a license does not create an efficiency benefit, the agencies advocate for per se treatment.[227]

507. The following section analyzes specific restraints in licensing arrangements that the federal enforcement agencies have expressed concern may harm competition.

c. *Competitive Effects and Potential Harm*

(1) Patent Licensing Agreements in Consolidated Markets or that Result in Market Foreclosure

508. An important consideration when evaluating a licensing arrangement is the structure of the specific market at issue and whether the license tends to reduce competition or foreclose access beyond what is inherent in the rights granted to patent holders in the Patent Act. The federal enforcement agencies focus on the "degree of concentration in, the difficulty of entry into, and the responsiveness of supply and demand to changes in price in the relevant markets."[228] For example, when parties to a licensing arrangement are in a vertical relationship, concerns may arise in certain circumstances if the license tends to foreclose access to or increases a competitor's costs in obtaining important inputs in that market.[229] Alternatively, the US Antitrust Agencies have expressed concern that certain restraints in a vertical license might facilitate coordination among entities in a horizontal relationship.[230] For example, licensees that are competitors in a market and are subject to the same restriction in a license may be

---

lawfully acquired, subsequent conduct permissible under the patent laws cannot trigger any liability under the antitrust laws."); *see also Precision Instrument Mfg. Co. v. Auto. Maint. Mach. Co.*, 324 U.S. 806, 816 (1945) ("A patent is an exception to the general rule against monopolies and to the right to access to a free and open market.").

224 *See* DOJ & FTC Antitrust IP Guidelines, *supra* n. 214, Chapter IV, 16–17 (explaining that "[t]he Agencies' general approach in analyzing a licensing restraint under the rule of reason is to inquire whether the restraint is likely to have anticompetitive effects and, if so, whether the restraint is reasonably necessary to achieve procompetitive benefits that outweigh those anticompetitive effects.").

225 *See, e.g., FTC v. Super. Ct. Trial Lawyers Ass'n*, 493 U.S. 411, 433 (1990); *Nat'l Soc. of Prof'l Eng'rs v. United States*, 435 U.S. 679, 692 (1978).

226 *See* DOJ & FTC Antitrust IP Guidelines, *supra* n. 214, Chapter IV, 17.

227 *Id.* 19–20.

228 *Id.*

229 *Id.* 20.

230 *Id.*

able to coordinate pricing because of the common restraint. In sum, the risk of these concerns is heightened in markets that are concentrated or have high barriers to entry.[231]

(2) Exclusive Licenses

509. Special concerns also arise in situations where a patent holder grants an exclusive license to exercise the patent. The Patent Act specifically provides patent owners with the right to grant exclusive licenses, which limit the ability of the licensor to license others and to potentially use the technology itself. The US Antitrust Agencies have stated that antitrust concerns related to exclusive licenses only arise "if there is a horizontal relationship among licensors, or among licensees, or between the licensor and its licensee(s)."[232] Specific examples of licensing arrangements that give rise to antitrust concerns are "cross-licensing by competitors that collectively possess market power, grant backs, and acquisitions of intellectual property rights."[233] As explained below, however, exclusive licenses in these contexts only give rise to potential antitrust concerns where they have an exclusionary effect beyond that inherent in the patent – for example, by consolidating the rights to actual or potential competing technologies in a manner that increases market power.[234] Non-exclusive licenses that do not contain restraints on the conduct of the licensor or licensee do not typically present antitrust concerns.[235] However, the US Antitrust Agencies have warned that "[a] non-exclusive license may have the effect of exclusive licensing if it is structured so that the licensor is unlikely to license others or to practice the technology itself."[236]

510. Because of these concerns, some exclusive licenses related to pharmaceutical patents must be submitted to the US Antitrust Agencies for review. In general, under the HSR Act, certain mergers and acquisitions must be reported to the FTC and the DOJ. Due to concerns about the potential effects of exclusive licenses, the FTC issued amendments to the premerger notification rules that clarify when the licensing of a pharmaceutical patent is reportable to the FTC as an asset sale under the HSR Act (*see* Chapter III).

511. A patent holder's exercise of its rights is not transformed into an antitrust violation merely because it might exclude competitors or otherwise affect competition. To the contrary, the possibility of such exclusion is inherent in the nature of the patent grant. It has been settled law for more than a century that even the grant of an exclusive license that allows only a single entity to sell a patented product does not, by itself, violate the antitrust laws.[237] Exclusive licenses are "[o]ne of

---

231 *Id.* 21.

232 *Id.*

233 *Id.*

234 *See, e.g., United States v. New Wrinkle, Inc.*, 342 U.S. 371, 380 (1952) (holding that an agreement to pool patents and fix prices is illegal).

235 *Id.*

236 *Id.* 22; *see also FTC v. Endo Pharms. Inc.*, 596 F. Supp. 3d 115, 124 (D.D.C. 2022) (holding that the FTC plausibly alleged an exclusive license even when the patentee could practice the technology itself).

237 *See, e.g., Bement v. Nat'l Harrow Co.*, 186 U.S. 70, 94 (1902) ("There is nothing which violates the act [*i.e.*, the Sherman Act] in the agreement that plaintiff would not license any other person than the defendant to manufacture or sell any harrow of the peculiar style and construction then used or sold by the defendant."); *Cook Inc. v. Boston Scientific Corp.*, 333 F.3d 737, 740 (7th Cir. 2003) ("[T]here is no argument that Angiotech would have violated antitrust law or been guilty of patent misuse had it granted an exclusive, nonassignable license."); *Instructional*

the most common forms of licensing" and, as noted above, expressly permitted by the Patent Act.[238] For an exclusive license to violate the antitrust laws, it must restrict competition beyond the lawful exclusivity granted by patent rights.[239] For example, courts have held that an exclusive license may violate the antitrust laws where the patent holder uses it to obtain royalties beyond the life of the patent.[240] Or, it might be unlawful, under certain circumstances, for the patent holder to condition exclusivity on "the licensee's agreement to purchase, use, or sell, or not to purchase, use, or sell, another article of commerce not within the scope of his patent monopoly."[241] Finally, anticompetitive concerns could arise when the patent holder imposes license terms that "extend the term of his monopoly beyond that granted by law."[242] The common thread running through all of these examples is that the restriction at issue is more likely to be subject to antitrust scrutiny when it falls outside of the exclusionary scope inherent in the grant of a patent.

512. The D.C. Circuit recently reaffirmed these principles in *FTC v. Endo Pharms.*[243] In that case, the court upheld an order dismissing the FTC's complaint challenging an exclusive patent license because the FTC failed to explain how the challenged agreement "meaningfully differs from a standard exclusive license," because there were no allegations that the agreement "created anticompetitive effects greater than that authorized by settled law and precedent," and because the FTC had not pointed to "any aspect of the [agreement] that might justify further antitrust scrutiny."[244] The court noted, however, that "[i]n a future case, the Commission is free to plead that a licensing agreement results in unjustifiable competitive

---

Sys. Dev. Corp. v. Aetna Cas. & Sur. Co., 817 F.2d 639, 644 (10th Cir. 1987) ("Exclusive licensing of a patent, copyright, or trademark is not a violation of § 1 of the Sherman Act so long as the agreement does not extend beyond marketing arrangements reasonably necessary to effectuate the rights granted."); *Miller Insituform, Inc. v. Insituform of N. Am., Inc.*, 830 F.2d 606, 608 (6th Cir. 1987) ("[A] patentee is free to control licensing for the exclusive use of its patent without running afoul of the prohibitions against monopoly contained in the Sherman Act."); *Rail-Trailer Co. v. ACF Industries, Inc.*, 358 F.2d 15, 16–17 (7th Cir. 1966) ("[A] patentee may… grant an exclusive license for the manufacture of the patented device, which license serves to exclude the patentee himself from engaging in the manufacture of the device, and which action, without more, does not constitute an illegal restraint of trade or violation of the anti-trust laws."); *Staley v. Gilead Scis., Inc.*, No. 19-02573, 2020 WL 1032320, at *19 (N.D. Cal. Mar. 3, 2020) (explaining that an "exclusive license without more is not an antitrust violation); *In re Aggrenox Antitrust Litig.*, 94 F. Supp. 3d 224, 245 (D. Conn. 2015) ("[P]atent holders may legally grant exclusive licenses and… the particular restraint on competition such agreements represent is an exception to antitrust prohibition and expressly permissible by statute. That is not disputed.").

238 *See* Roger M. Milgrim & Eric E. Bensen, Milgrim on Licensing, ¶15.08 (2020); 35 U.S.C. § 261; *see also* Herbert Hovenkamp et al., IP and Antitrust, An Analysis of Antitrust Principles Applied to Intellectual Property Law, ¶21.07a (3d ed. 2013) ("Since exclusive licenses are expressly permitted by the intellectual property provisions, a simple exclusive license must be regarded as immune from antitrust challenge.").

239 *See, e.g., USM Corp. v. SPS Techs., Inc.*, 694 F.2d 505, 513 (7th Cir. 1982) ("Patent licensing agreements between competitors are sometimes struck down under antitrust law, of course, but only upon proof of an anticompetitive effect beyond that implicit in the grant of the patent."); *United States v. Studiengesellschaft Kohle, m.b.H.*, 670 F.2d 1122, 1131 (D.C. Cir. 1981) ("The law is settled that S.K. could legally have licensed Hercules alone to use the patented process… This lesser restraint, which has fewer anticompetitive effects than a lawful exclusive license, gives the Ziegler arrangement an important badge of reasonableness.").

240 *See, e.g., Zila, Inc. v. Tinnell*, 502 F.3d 1014 (9th Cir. 2007); *Scheiber v. Dolby Labs.*, 293 F.3d 1014 (7th Cir. 2002).

241 *See Zenith Radio Corp. v. Hazeltine Research, Inc.*, 395 U.S. 100, 136 (1969).

242 *See id.*; *see also Staley v. Gilead Sciences, Inc.*, 446 F. Supp. 3d 578 (N.D. Cal. 2020) (denying motion to dismiss when exclusive patent licenses allegedly prohibited competition after expiration of the patents at issue).

243 No. 22-5137, 2023 WL 5490337, at *4 (D.C. Cir. Aug. 25, 2023).

244 *Id.* at *5-6.

harms, so long as it explains how those harms exceed what the Patent Act and settled precedent permit."[245]

(3) Tying and Package Licensing

513. Patent holders sometimes license multiple pieces of IP together in a single license. While such licenses can be procompetitive, such as when multiple IP items must be used together, they can also be viewed as a form of anticompetitive tying under the antitrust laws.[246]

(4) Minimum Resale Price Maintenance

514. Licensors can also condition licenses on licensees' agreement to charge a minimum resale price for a product incorporating the licensed technology. Vertical agreements incorporating minimum resale price restrictions are evaluated under the rule of reason, while horizontal restraints (which function like a horizontal price-fixing cartel) are per se illegal.[247] Potential procompetitive justifications for vertical RPM restraints include stimulating interbrand competition by limiting intrabrand competition, limiting reseller free-riding, and facilitating market entry.[248]

(5) Field of Use Restrictions

515. Another common restrict in patent licenses is a field of use restriction, where a patent holder limits the scope of the patent rights to a defined area or application. For example, a licensor could permit one licensee to use a patent for commercial purposes but require another licensee to only use the patent for noncommercial purposes.[249] Field of use restrictions are generally analyzed under the rule of reason and are only found to be illegal if they are used to "extend the patent into areas not protected by the patent monopoly."[250]

(6) Licensing Safety Zones

516. Recognizing that licensing arrangements may encourage innovation and increase competition, the US Antitrust Agencies created a "safety zone" that provides certainty to parties to licensing arrangements. The agencies will not challenge a patent licensing restraint if "(1) the restraint is not facially anticompetitive and (2) the licensor and its licensees collectively account for no more than twenty percent of each relevant market significantly affected by the restraint."[251] Importantly, the agencies have emphasized that a patent license's failure to fall within the scope of the safety zone does not make it automatically anticompetitive: "Indeed,

---

245 *Id.* at *6.

246 *See* DOJ & FTC Antitrust IP Guidelines, *supra* n. 214, Chapter IV, 28–29; *see also Hearing Components, Inc. v. Shure, Inc.*, No. 9:07-CV-104, 2009 WL 815526, *1 (E.D. Tex. Mar. 26, 2009) (discussing package licensing as a potential form of anticompetitive "patent misuse").

247 DOJ & FTC Antitrust IP Guidelines, *supra* n. 214, Chapter IV, 27–28.

248 *See, e.g., Leegin Creative Leather Prod., Inc. v. PSKS, Inc.*, 551 U.S. 877, 889–92 (2007).

249 *See Gen. Talking Pictures Corp. v. W. Elec. Co.*, 304 U.S. 175, 181, *aff'd on reh'g*, 305 U.S. 124 (1938).

250 *United States v. Studiengesellschaft Kohle, m.b.H.*, 670 F.2d 1122, 1133 (D.C. Cir. 1981); *see also Carter v. Variflex, Inc.*, 101 F. Supp. 2d 1261, 1265–66 (C.D. Cal. 2000) ("Courts analyze field of *1266 use restrictions under the rule of reason to assess their anticompetitive effects.").

251 DOJ & FTC Antitrust IP Guidelines, *supra* n. 214, Chapter IV, 24–25.

it is likely that the great majority of licenses falling outside the safety zone are lawful and procompetitive."[252] Instead of drawing a bright line between licensing agreements that are procompetitive and anticompetitive, the safety zone is designed to provide patent owners with certainty as to the licensing agreements that are unproblematic.

517. In sum, under US law, patent licensing arrangements are generally analyzed under the rule of reason. As a threshold matter, to determine whether a licensing restriction is potentially subject to antitrust scrutiny under the rule of reason, courts and the US Antitrust Agencies must assess whether the challenged restraint falls outside the scope of the inherent exclusionary effect of a patent grant. Horizontal license agreements, as opposed to vertical agreements, are more likely to raise antitrust concerns, especially when the licenses' restriction falls outside of the bounds of the patent holder's right to exclude.

C. *Patent Litigation Settlements*

518. The regulatory framework that governs the marketing and sale of pharmaceutical products in the US[253] can create an incentive for manufacturers of brand and generic drugs to settle patent infringement litigation in ways that allegedly delay generic competition. Known as "pay-for-delay" or "reverse payment" settlements, antitrust issues may arise when a brand and generic drug manufacturer settle patent infringement litigation and the patent holder makes a payment to the patent defendant.

(1) The *Actavis* Decision and the Historical Background of Reverse Payment Settlements

519. Because of the unique regulatory structure created by Hatch-Waxman,[254] some brand-name manufacturers and generic challengers have resolved patent disputes by including a "reverse payment" in the settlement agreement. In the typical reverse payment settlement, the generic challenger agrees to drop its challenge to the validity of the brand manufacturer's patents by settling underlying patent litigation. In exchange, the brand makes a payment to the generic, whether it be in the form of cash, an agreement not to market an authorized generic, or a variety of other valuable business arrangements. The brand also often provides the generic with a license to enter the market early (i.e., before the expiration of the brand's patents). The payment is considered a reverse payment because instead of a patent defendant paying to settle the patent litigation, the patent plaintiff pays the defendant.

520. Prior to 2013, different circuits within the US Courts of Appeals were split as to whether patent settlements that contained reverse payments were permissible under the antitrust laws. The Federal Circuit, Second Circuit, and Eleventh Circuit found these settlements permissible if they were within the scope of the patent

---

252 *Id.*

253 *See* Chapter I.

254 *See* Chapter I, Section II.2.B.

(that is, they excluded competition for no longer than the life of the patent and no more broadly than the claims of the patent), while the Third and Sixth Circuits adopted a presumption that they were not.[255]

521. The Supreme Court decided in *FTC v. Actavis, Inc.* that reverse payment settlements could sometimes violate the antitrust laws.[256] In *Actavis*, Solvay Pharmaceuticals owned the NDA and patents that covered brand name AndroGel.[257] Actavis and Paddock Laboratories filed ANDAs that sought FDA approval to market generic equivalents, and both manufacturers filed Paragraph IV certifications claiming that Solvay's patents were invalid or not infringed by their generic versions.[258] Solvay sued Actavis and Paddock for patent infringement.[259] Although the FDA eventually approved Actavis' ANDA, it did not enter the market. Solvay, Actavis, and Paddock entered into a settlement agreement resolving the patent litigation.[260] As part of this settlement, Actavis agreed not to enter the market with its generic product until 65 months prior to the expiration of Solvay's patent in exchange for a cash payment and a license to market and promote branded Androgel.[261] In total, Solvay agreed to pay an estimated $19–30 million dollars to Actavis annually.[262]

522. In 2009, the FTC filed a lawsuit against all settling manufacturers. The FTC claimed that Actavis and Solvay violated Section 5 of the FTC Act by "unlawfully agreeing to share in Solvay's monopoly profits, abandon their patent challenges, and refrain from launching their low-cost generic products to compete with AndroGel for nine years."[263] The district court dismissed the complaint for failure to plausibly state an antitrust violation.[264] The Eleventh Circuit affirmed that decision and held that absent fraud or sham litigation in acquiring a patent, a reverse payment settlement agreement is immune from antitrust scrutiny "so long as its anticompetitive effects fall within the scope of the exclusionary potential of the patent."[265] The US Supreme Court granted certiorari to resolve the split in the US Courts of Appeals over whether settlement agreements containing reverse payments could be subject to antitrust attack.

523. The US Supreme Court reversed the Eleventh Circuit and held that "reverse payment settlements… can sometimes violate the antitrust laws" even if they are within the exclusionary scope of the patent.[266] The Court explained that this "form

---

255 *Compare In re Ciprofloxacin Hydrochloride Antitrust Litig.*, 544 F.3d 1323 (Fed. Cir. 2008) (holding that settlement agreements containing reverse payments were generally immune from antitrust scrutiny) *and In re Tamoxifen Citrate Antitrust Litig.*, 466 F.3d 187 (2d Cir. 2006) (similar) *with In re K-Dur Antitrust Litig.*, 686 F.3d 197, 214–218 (3d Cir. 2012) (holding that pharmaceutical settlement agreements containing reverse payments were presumptively unlawful); *In re Cardizem CD Antitrust Litig.*, 332 F.3d 896, 915 (6th Cir. 2003) (refusing to dismiss complaint alleging anticompetitive reverse payment).

256 *Actavis*, 570 U.S. 136.

257 *Id.* 144.

258 *Id.*

259 *Id.* 145.

260 *Id.*

261 *Id.*

262 *Id.*

263 *Id.*

264 *In re Androgel Antitrust Litigation (No. II)*, 687 F. Supp. 2d 1371, 1379 (N.D. Ga. 2010).

265 *FTC v. Watson Pharmaceuticals, Inc.*, 677 F.3d 1298, 1312 (11th Cir. 2012).

266 *Actavis*, 570 U.S. 141.

of settlement is unusual" and that "there is reason for concern that settlements taking this form tend to have significant adverse effects on competition."[267]

524. In reaching this conclusion, the US Supreme Court rejected the Eleventh Circuit's "scope of the patent" test. Under this test, a settlement agreement would not be subject to antitrust scrutiny so long as the settlement agreement fell within the legitimate scope of Solvay's patents' exclusionary potential.[268] Thus, if the settlement agreement's exclusionary terms were not greater than the term of Solvay's patent exclusivity, there could be no antitrust violation. The US Supreme Court held that this test was not appropriate because it assumes that the patents are valid or not infringed, and only a "valid patent excludes all except its owner from the use of the protected process or product."[269] However, in patent litigation, "[t]he patent … may or may not be valid, and may or may not be infringed" and an invalidated patent carries no exclusionary right."[270] As a result, the Supreme Court explained that "it would be incongruous to determine antitrust legality by measuring the settlement's anticompetitive effects solely against patent law policy, rather than by measuring them against procompetitive antitrust policies as well."[271]

525. The Court noted five considerations leading to its holding that "a reverse payment, where large and unjustified, can bring with it the risk of significant anticompetitive effects."[272] First, "the specific restraint at issue has the 'potential for genuine adverse effects on competition.'"[273] Reverse payments may allow the brand pharmaceutical manufacturer to divide the market, splitting monopoly profits between the brand and generic, and resulting in higher prices to consumers.[274] Second, in some situations, the anticompetitive consequences of reverse payment settlement agreements will sometimes be unjustified.[275] A reverse payment may amount to no more than the cost of litigation saved through the settlement or reflect compensation for other services that the generic has promised to perform.[276] In these situations, there is not the same concern that the brand manufacturer is using monopoly profits to prevent generic entry.[277] But these potential justifications alone do not justify the dismissal of a lawsuit. Third, "where a reverse payment [settlement] threatens to work unjustified anticompetitive harm, the patentee likely has the power to bring about that harm in practice."[278] Fourth, antitrust actions involving reverse payments are not administratively unfeasible.[279] Most courts would not have to rule on the validity of the brand's patents because "[a]n unexplained large reverse payment itself would normally suggest that the patentee has serious

---

267 *Id.* 147–48.
268 *Id.* 148.
269 *Id.* 147.
270 *Id.*
271 *Id.* 148.
272 *Id.* 147, 158.
273 *Id.* 153 (quoting *Indiana Federation of Dentists,* 476 U.S. 460–461).
274 *Id.* at 153–154.
275 *Id.* 156.
276 *Id.*
277 *Id.*
278 *Id.* 157.
279 *Id.*

doubts about the patent's survival."[280] Fifth, subjecting reverse payments to antitrust scrutiny does not discourage settlements. Parties to patent disputes are free to settle in other ways, "for example, by allowing the generic manufacturer to enter the patentee's market prior to the patent's expiration, without the patentee paying the challenger to stay out prior to that point."[281] These considerations, taken as a whole, outweigh the "strong consideration" of "the desirability of settlements."[282]

526. Importantly, the Court also held that the rule of reason should apply to reverse payment cases. While FTC urged the Court to hold that reverse payments are presumptively unlawful and to apply a "quick look" approach, the Court declined to do so given the complexities associated with the pharmaceutical industry and the potential for procompetitive justifications.[283]

(2) Reverse Payment Framework

527. In the years following *Actavis,* the lower courts have struggled to consistently apply the rule of reason in analyzing reverse payment settlement agreements. Generally, however, a plaintiff is required to present evidence that a brand name patent holder made a payment to a generic manufacturer. The payment must be "large" and "unjustified" in the sense that it exceeds anticipated future litigation costs and lacks any other convincing justification. The size of the payment may be indicative of anticompetitive intent – a large payment would lack economic sense unless the brand name patent holder was concerned about the validity of its patents.

(a) Lawful Settlements

528. Patent settlements are commonplace and in general do not raise antitrust concerns.[284] The US Supreme Court's decision in *Actavis* did not alter this understanding. Instead, the Court addressed a specific, narrow category of patent settlement agreements that could present a unique type of anticompetitive harm: one where a brand patentholder sues a generic defendant for patent infringement, then "agree[s] to pay the defendants many millions of dollars to stay out of its market."[285]

529. Acknowledging that there is a strong public policy favoring settlements, the Court made clear that settlements with no "reverse payment" and an entry date prior to patent expiration would not create antitrust liability.[286] For example, the Court explained that "allowing the generic manufacturer to enter the patentee's market prior to the patent's expiration" was a "commonplace" form of settlement that would

---

280 *Id.*

281 *Id.* 158.

282 *Id.*

283 *Id.* 159.

284 *See Standard Oil Co., Ind. v. United States*, 283 U.S. 163, 171 (1931) ("Where there are legitimately conflicting claims or threatened interferences, a settlement [of a patent dispute] by agreement, rather than litigation, is not precluded by the [Sherman] Act.").

285 *Actavis,* 570 U.S. 147.

286 *See In re Humira (Adalimumab) Antitrust Litig.*, 465 F. Supp. 3d 811, 839 (N.D. Ill. 2020) ("To avoid deterring settlements because of exposure to antitrust liability, the [*Actavis*] Court noted an important exception. Parties remain free to settle on other terms.").

not attract antitrust scrutiny.[287] And the Court recognized that this type of settlement actually benefits competition.[288] Thus, a settlement agreement that does not involve a payment from the brand to the generic and allows a generic manufacturer to enter the patentee's market prior to the patent's expiration would not raise the same concerns.

(b) "Large and Unjustified" Payments

530. *Actavis* was concerned with "large and unjustified" payments. While the US Supreme Court did not set a threshold amount for what constituted a "large" payment, it does require a payment that exceeds reasonably anticipated litigation costs and lower courts have followed this approach.[289] While lower courts have also declined to define an exact threshold amount that will constitute a "large" payment, decisions provide examples of payment sizes that are problematic.[290] At the pleading stage, a plaintiff is required to plead information sufficient to estimate the value of the reverse payment.[291] A plaintiff is typically not required to provide precise figures and calculations to survive a motion to dismiss.[292]

(i) Non-Cash Payments

531. The *Actavis* decision explicitly involved cash payments from a patent holder to a generic challenger and did not address whether a non-cash payment raised antitrust concerns. As the law surrounding reverse payments has developed, lower courts have held that non-cash payments flowing from a brand manufacturer to a generic challenger can constitute a "large and unjustified payment." While a few decisions following *Actavis* found that only cash payments could constitute such a payment,[293] the vast majority of lower courts to address the issue have confirmed that non-cash payments can be equally problematic.[294] Arguments to the contrary

---

287 *Actavis*, 570 U.S. 158.

288 *Id.* 154 ("We concede that settlement on terms permitting the patent challenger to enter the market before the patent expires would also bring about competition, again to the consumer's benefit.").

289 *Id.* 170; *see, e.g.*, *In re Opana ER Antitrust Litig.*, 162 F. Supp. 3d 704, 719 (N.D. Ill. 2016) (holding that reverse payment had been adequately pled because the amount of litigation costs saved by brand name manufacturer had the case proceeded were a small fraction of the actual payment); *United Food and Commercial Workers Local 1776 & Participating Employers Health and Welfare Fund v. Teikoku Pharma USA, Inc.*, 74 F. Supp. 3d 1052 (N.D. Cal. 2014) (holding that plaintiffs allegations that there was a large and unjustified payment were plausible when the payment at issue had no rational connection to and far exceeded anticipated litigation costs).

290 *Impax Lab'ys, Inc. v. Fed. Trade Comm'n*, 994 F.3d 484, 494 (5th Cir. 2021), *cert. denied*, 142 S. Ct. 712, 211 L. Ed. 2d 400 (2021) (holding that $102 million dollar payment was large and unjustified); *In re Wellbutrin XL Antitrust Lit. Indirect Purchaser Class*, 868 F.3d 132, 162 (3d Cir. 2017) (finding that $233 million paid to three generic manufacturers was a large payment under *Actavis*); *In re Nexium (Esomeprazole) Antitrust Litig.*, 842 F.3d 34, 50, 54 (1st Cir. 2016) (jury finding that a $300-$690 million payment constituted a large payment).

291 *In re Loestrin 24 Fe Antitrust Litig.*, 814 F.3d 538, 552 (1st Cir. 2016).

292 *See id.*

293 *See, e.g.*, *Loestrin 24 Fe Antitrust Litig.*, 45 F. Supp. 3d 180 (D.R.I. 2014), *vacated*, 814 F.3d 538 (1st Cir. 2016).

294 *See, e.g.*, *King Drug Co. of Florence, Inc. v. SmithKline Beecham Corp.*, 791 F.3d 388, 403–04 (3d Cir. 2015) (explaining that non-cash payment constituted a large and unjustified payment under *Actavis*); *In re Actos End Payor Antitrust Litig.*, No. 13-cv-9244(RA), 2015 WL 5610752, at *13 (S.D.N.Y. Sept. 22, 2015) ("This Court shares the majority view that *Actavis's* holding is not limited to payments made in cash."); *In re Aggrenox Antitrust Litig.*, 94 F. Supp. 3d 243 ("A settlement agreement may be very simple or tremendously complex, and it may involve all manner of consideration; and if, when viewed holistically, it effects a large and unexplained net transfer of value from the patent holder to the alleged patent-infringer, it may fairly be called a reverse-payment settlement."); *United Food & Commercial Workers*, 74 F. Supp. 3d 1069–70 (rejecting argu-

have been dismissed as prioritizing form over substance.[295] Payments may take many forms and still result in a considerable transfer of value from a brand to a generic manufacturer. As a result, courts will take a detailed look at the specific alleged payment to determine whether there was a large and unjustified transfer of value from the brand manufacturer to the generic challenger.

(ii) No-Authorized Generic (AG) Agreements

532. One kind of alleged non-cash payment that has been at issue in reverse payment litigations is an agreement by the brand manufacturer not to introduce an authorized generic version of the branded product during the generic first-filer's 180-day exclusivity period. Often referred to as "No-AG" agreements, these arrangements may confer significant value to the first-filer generic. During the 180-day exclusivity period, no other ANDA filer may enter the market with a generic version of the RLD. But this rule does not bar the patentholder from introducing its own generic version of its brand product that competes with the generic first filer during the exclusivity period. According to a 2006 study, generic prices were 16% lower following the entry of an authorized generic.[296] By agreeing to forego the opportunity to enter the market with an authorized generic, the patentholder creates a monopoly in the generic market and transfers the profits it would have made from its authorized generic. Some No-AG agreements have been called "more anticompetitive than a large cash payment for delay."[297]

533. Recognizing this concern, lower courts have consistently held that explicit and de facto No-AG agreements may constitute an illegal reverse payment under *Actavis*.[298] These courts have emphasized that *Actavis* did not intend to draw a formal line between cash and non-cash forms of payment, and that "No-AG" agreements can often be worth substantial amounts of money to the generic challenger.[299] Indeed, the Third Circuit recently found that a No-AG commitment was worth more than $500 million to the generic challenger.[300] While a plaintiff is not required to prove the exact value that the No-AG agreement confers to the generic challenger at the

---

ment that reverse payments can only be made in cash because "[t]here are many plausible methods by which plaintiffs may calculate the value of non-monetary terms"); *In re Effexor XR Antitrust Litig.*, No. 11-5479 (PGS) (LHG), 2014 WL 4988410, *19 (D.N.J. Oct. 6, 2014) ("The common use of the term payment is described as something given to discharge a debt or obligation and does not require the payment to be in the form of money.").

295 *In re Loestrin 24 Fe Antitrust Litig.*, 814 F.3d 550 (explaining that "this approach is consistent with antitrust law, which has consistently prioritized substance over form").

296 *See* FTC, *Authorized Generics: An Interim Report* (2009), *available at* https://www.ftc.gov/reports/authorized-generics-interim-report-federal-trade-commission.

297 Phillip E. Areeda (late) & Herbert Hovenkamp, Antitrust Law: An Analysis of Antitrust Principles and Their Applications, ¶ 2045. (Fourth and Fifth Editions, 2023 Cum. Supp. 2018–2023).

298 *Impax Lab'ys*, 994 F.3d 494 (explaining that promise not to market an AG constituted valuable consideration to the generic challenger); *King Drug Co. of Florence*, 791 F.3d 405 (holding that "No-AG" payment constituted a reverse payment under *Actavis*); *In re Loestrin 24 Fe Antitrust Litig. (Loestrin III)*, 261 F. Supp. 3d 307, 333 (D.R.I. 2017) (explaining that a "No-AG" agreement constituted a reverse payment because it constituted a transfer of value to the settling generic company); *In re Amitiza Antitrust Litig.* , No. CV 21-11057-RGS, 2022 WL 17968695, *4 (D. Mass. Dec. 27, 2022) (refusing to dismiss claims alleging a *de facto* No-AG agreement); *In re Xyrem (Sodium Oxybate) Antitrust Litig.*, 555 F. Supp. 3d 829, 855 (N.D. Cal. 2021) ("Plaintiffs plausibly allege the existence of an implicit or de facto no-AG agreement.").

299 *FTC v. AbbVie Inc*, 976 F.3d 327, 353 (3d Cir. 2020), *cert. denied sub nom.* 141 S. Ct. 2838 (2021).

300 *In re Lipitor Antitrust Litig.*, 868 F.3d 231, 260 (3d Cir. 2017).

pleading stage, it is required to demonstrate that the payment "is plausibly large."[301] The overwhelming majority of courts to address this issue have found that allegations of a No-AG agreement are sufficient to constitute a payment that is plausibly large.

(iii) "Side Deals"

534. There are many other ways that parties might choose to structure the compensation attached to a settlement agreement. So-called "side deals" may arise in the context of pharmaceutical patent litigation settlements, meaning that the settling parties contemporaneously enter into another kind of agreement with the patent settlement. Antitrust plaintiffs and enforcers have argued that these separate agreements, entered at the same time as the patent settlement, can constitute a "payment" under *Actavis*. The FTC has referred to "side deals" as one of the "most pernicious and common forms of reverse payments"[302] because while side deals may be unrelated to the case (and patent) at issue, they can still result in a significant transfer of value from the patent holder to the generic challenger.

535. For example, in *FTC v. AbbVie Inc*, the Third Circuit found that a supply arrangement for a separate drug included in a patent litigation settlement between a patent holder and a generic could constitute a large and unjustified payment.[303] In exchange for settling existing patent litigation involving the drug Androgel, AbbVie (the patent holder) agreed to sell Teva a supply of TriCor for a four-year term.[304] Teva had previously entered into a settlement agreement that allowed it to enter the TriCor market, but it had struggled to enter the market because it had not received FDA approval.[305] The court found that this supply agreement, while unrelated to the product in the existing litigation, was a large and unjustified payment under *Actavis*.[306] The payment was "large" because the supply of TriCor was extremely valuable to Teva and allowed it to capitalize on the 180-day exclusivity period that it earned as first filer.[307] The payment was found to be "unjustified" because AbbVie allegedly had no incentive to increase generic competition in the relevant market and the deal would result in a loss of $100 million in TriCor sales.[308] In holding that this constituted a reverse payment, the Third Circuit made clear that the inclusion of a separate business agreement does not shield a settlement from antitrust scrutiny.[309] Holding such would "elevate[] form over substance" because companies "could avoid liability for anticompetitive reverse payments simply by structuring them as two separate agreements."[310] In the end,

---

301 *Id.*

302 FTC, Press Release, *FTC Enters Global Settlement to Resolve Reverse-Payment Charges against Teva* (Feb.19, 2019), *available at* https://www.ftc.gov/news-events/news/press-releases/2019/02/ftc-enters-global-settlement-resolve-reverse-payment-charges-against-teva.

303 *AbbVie*, 976 F.3d 357.

304 *Id.*

305 *Id.*

306 *Id.*

307 *Id.* (explaining that Teva would allegedly make $175 million on generic TriCor sales during the exclusivity period).

308 *Id.*

309 *Id.* 358.

310 *Id.*

the Third Circuit explained that regardless of the form the alleged payment takes, the relevant inquiry should focus on whether something of large value passed from the patent holder to the generic challenger.[311]

536. Another potential type of side deal is an agreement to settle separate litigation in exchange for settlement in the pending lawsuit.[312] This type of arrangement can be highly beneficial to the parties and promotes the public policy towards settling disputes out of court.[313] Courts, however, have taken inconsistent approaches to whether the settlement of a separate case can constitute a reverse payment under *Actavis*. In the Third Circuit's decision in *Lipitor*, a brand patent holder and first-to-file generic manufacturer settled a patent dispute related to brand Lipitor. As part of the settlement, the parties resolved a separate dispute related to the brand manufacturer's Accupril product where the patent holder agreed to release its Accupril claims against the generic maker.[314] The Third Circuit found that this qualified as a reverse payment: "[T]he patent holder['s] ... alleged agreement to release the Accupril claims, therefore, 'was an inducement – valuable to both it and [the generic] – to ensure a longer period of supra-competitive monopoly profits based on [the Lipitor patent, which was] at risk of being found invalid or not infringed.'"[315] In *In re Humira (Adalimumab) Antitrust Litigation*, however, a district court found that a patent settlement agreement that provided for delayed US entry in exchange for early entry in the European market did not constitute a reverse payment:

> The European deals were early entry settlements of the kind that did not worry the Court in *Actavis*... The transfer of value, as large as it was, did not have the hallmarks of an unjustified and otherwise inexplicable payment because the package either increased competition or preserved an anticompetitive status quo... The effect of the payment was to increase, not restrain competition by bringing competitors into the market when patents otherwise prohibited the competition... There is also a broader reason to uphold these agreements under antitrust review: encouraging patent litigants to settle worldwide patent disputes. Any early entry date in one region could always be considered a transfer of value in return for a later entry date in another region.[316]

(c) Accelerator Provisions

537. Plaintiffs have also challenged settlement agreements that contain accelerator provisions. An accelerator clause is a common settlement term that "ensure[s] that if a generic or authorized generic began marketing its product before that date,

---

311 *Id.* 358–59.

312 *See In re Lipitor Antitrust Litig.*, 868 F.3d 253 (holding that plaintiffs had pled a reverse payment agreement based on brand's settlement of case with generic company in exchange for a settlement in a different case).

313 *See, e.g.*, *In re Humira*, 465 F. Supp. 3d 841 ("There is also a broader reason to uphold these agreements under antitrust review: encouraging patent litigants to settle worldwide patent disputes").

314 *In re Lipitor Antitrust Litig.*, 868 F.3d 244.

315 *Id.* 253–54.

316 *In re Humira*, 465 F. Supp. 3d 840–841.

the licensed generic could also enter without further delay."[317] Such provisions can function like "most favored entry" provisions – if one manufacturer begins marketing its product, then other manufacturers' entry dates are "accelerated" so that they, too, can enter earlier.[318]

538. Some courts have found that accelerator provisions can function as anticompetitive reverse payments under *Actavis* when they are structured such that they transfer value from the brand to a generic.[319] For example, in *In re HIV Antitrust Litigation*, the accelerator provision was structured as a "most favored entry plus" provision: as part of a settlement between the brand and the generic, the brand agreed to give the generic 180 days of exclusivity ahead of the entry date of any other manufacturer.[320] According to the plaintiffs, the brand and generic would have negotiated an earlier settlement date for the generic absent this provision, so the accelerator clause represented a payment from the brand to the generic.[321] The court denied the defendants' motion for summary judgment, holding that the jury must balance the procompetitive benefits of the accelerator provision against the anticompetitive effects under the rule of reason.[322]

539. Accelerator provisions can also raise anticompetitive concerns outside of the *Actavis* framework. In *Value Drug Company v. Takeda Pharmaceuticals*, for example, the court denied defendants' motion to dismiss a plaintiff's claim that a brand conspired with generics to order market entry and restrict output because the accelerator provisions in its settlement agreements could function as "cartel enforcement mechanism[s]" by "threatening 'reversion to competitive behavior' – i.e., immediate entry by [the generic co-conspirators] – if certain market events were to occur."[323]

540. These divergent outcomes show that decisions on whether the settlement of separate litigation qualifies as a reverse payment are a fact-specific inquiry and not amenable to bright line rules. As a result, the lower courts continue to conduct the detailed inquiry that *Actavis* required – determining whether the alleged payment was large and "unjustified" and exceeded the value of avoided litigation expenses.[324]

---

317 *In re Actos End Payor Antitrust Litig.*, No. 13-CV-9244 RA, 2015 WL 5610752, *15 (S.D.N.Y. Sept. 22, 2015), *aff'd in part, vacated in part*, 848 F.3d 89 (2d Cir. 2017).

318 *See In re HIV Antitrust Litig.*, No. 19-CV-02573-EMC, 2023 WL 3088218, *2 (N.D. Cal. Feb. 17, 2023) (stating that the "MFE/MFEP provision is essentially an acceleration provision" because it "it provided that, if Gilead were to give another manufacturer a license to enter the market and that manufacturer's entry date was earlier than the one that had been given to Teva, then Teva's entry date would be accelerated so that it would be 180 days earlier than the one given to the manufacturer").

319 *See id.*; *In re Xyrem (Sodium Oxybate) Antitrust Litig.*, 555 F. Supp. 3d 829, 860 (N.D. Cal. 2021) ("Accordingly, like other courts analyzing acceleration clauses at the motion to dismiss stage, the Court holds that acceleration clauses plausibly cause anticompetitive harm as part of an alleged reverse payment scheme."); *In re Sensipar (Cinacalcet Hydrochloride Tablets) Antitrust Litig.*, No. CV 19-1460-LPS, 2020 WL 7022364, *6 (D. Del. Nov. 30, 2020) ("The Court agrees with Plaintiffs that the acceleration provision, too, could be proven to constitute value transferred.").

320 *In re HIV Antitrust Litig.*, 2023 WL 3088218, *2.

321 *Id.*

322 *Id.* 41.

323 *Value Drug Co. v. Takeda Pharms., U.S.A., Inc.*, No. CV 21-3500, 2022 WL 952896, at *5 (E.D. Pa. Mar. 30, 2022) (quoting *In re Xyrem*, 555 F. Supp. 3d 860).

324 *Actavis*, 570 U.S. 170.

541. Courts apply the rule of reason to determine whether a payment from a brand to a generic to resolve patent litigation violates the antitrust laws. The payment must be "large and unjustified" in the sense that it exceeds the value of expected litigation costs. A payment need not be cash – courts typically look to whether there was a large transfer of value from the brand to the generic, regardless of the form it takes. Among other types of payments, No-AG agreements, certain side business deals, and accelerator provisions have been found to constitute large and unjustified payments. Overall, courts must undertake a fact-intensive inquiry that involves a detailed analysis of the industry, the product, and the specific payment at issue to determine the legality of a reverse payment patent litigation settlement.

3. Evaluation of Agreements Involving Patents Under EU Law

A. *Patent Licensing Agreements*

a. *Introduction*

542. Licensing agreements can be defined as contracts by which the licensor grants the licensee an IP right to use the protected work or technology to produce or to sell a product, in exchange for payment to the rights holder. While licensing agreements are generally lawful under EU antitrust rules, they can still attract scrutiny from European competition authorities.

543. Patent licensing agreements may vary in form and scope. In particular, the licensor can confer on the licensee an exclusive, sole, or non-exclusive right to exploit the protected work or technology. Under EU law, an exclusive license is understood as a commitment from the licensor not to grant a license to another company to exploit the protected work or technology in the relevant product and geographic market, as well as not to exploit itself the protected work or technology in these markets. A sole license refers to the situation in which the licensor undertakes not to license another company the right to exploit the protected work or technology in the product and geographic market conceded, although the licensor itself may exploit it in the market. A non-exclusive license means that the licensor does not commit to any of the two above-mentioned obligations.

544. Licensing agreements can be included in other forms of collaboration agreements. For instance, licensing agreements where undertakings agree to jointly exploit the results of joint R&D are analyzed as R&D agreements under EU rules (*See*Section III.2.B). Licensing agreements can also be distinguished from other types of agreements, such as co-manufacturing, co-promotion, and co-marketing agreements (*See* Section III.2.D below). The present section focuses on patent licensing agreements in which one undertaking grants another the right to exploit its patented results of research, including the transfer of know-how, patents, and copyrights used for the production of contract products.

545. Licensing agreements involve both horizontal and vertical relationships between companies. When the practice involves cross-licensing between companies that compete at the same level of the value chain, the agreement is horizontal in nature. In other circumstances, the licensing can be analyzed as a vertical

relationship. In both cases, the technology transfer agreement (TTBER)[325] primarily governs.[326]

546. Licensing agreements are not per se anticompetitive. But competition risks may arise from the contractual obligations in the licensing agreements. For instance, the licensor may limit the licensee's freedom to set prices or impose exclusive grant back provisions, which would guarantee that all improvement made to the licensed technology by the licensee benefit the licensor. The licensor and licensee may also agree on market or customer allocations by restricting passive sales into certain territories or to certain customers. Licensors may include non-challenge clauses in the licensing agreement to prevent the licensee from challenging the validity of their IP rights.

547. This section examines the antitrust issues that may arise from licensing agreements through the lenses of EU competition law.

b. *Exemption under the TTBER*

548. The European Commission considers most license agreements as procompetitive because they allow holders of IP rights to recoup their R&D costs while simultaneously allowing technology and know-how to spread more widely.[327] They are therefore generally exempted from the prohibition of anticompetitive agreements under the TTBER. Like any other agreement, however, a license which may affect trade between Member States and prevent, restrict, and distort competition to an appreciable extent is liable to infringe Article 101(1) TFEU.

(1) Application of the TTBER

(a) Scope of application

549. Technology transfer agreements concern the licensing of technology rights. The European Commission considers that such agreements will usually improve economic efficiency and should be deemed procompetitive as they can reduce duplication of R&D, strengthen the incentive for the initial R&D, spur incremental innovation, facilitate diffusion, and generate product market competition. As the likelihood of procompetitive effects outweighing any anticompetitive effects is significant, the TTBER defines categories of technology transfer agreements which the European Commission sees as normally satisfying the conditions laid down in Article 101(3) TFEU.[328] The TTBER thus defines the conditions under which such agreements may benefit from a safe harbor and be exempted from the prohibition rule contained in article 101(1) TFEU. Agreements that benefit from the block exemption are legally valid and enforceable. However, the benefit of the exemption may be withdrawn by the European Commission and the NCAs where they find that the agreement has effects incompatible with Article 101(3) TFEU.

---

325 Commission Regulation 316/2014 of Mar. 21, 2014, on the application of Article 101(3) TFEU to categories of technology transfer agreements (TTBER).

326 Licensing agreements can also give rise to issues under the rules governing abuses of dominance, which are covered in Chapter V.

327 European Commission Communication and Guidelines on the application of Article 101 TFEU of the Treaty on the Functioning of the European Union to technology transfer agreements (the EU Guidelines on Technology Transfer Agreements), 2014 OJ (C 89) 3, ¶9.

328 Commission Regulation 316/2014 (the TTBER), *supra* n. 325, Chapter IV.

550. According to Article 1(1)(c), the application of the TTBER is subject to three conditions:[329]

- the *existence of a technology transfer agreement*, i.e., a technology rights licensing agreement (including a patent licensing agreement) for the purpose of the production of contract products by the licensee or its subcontractor(s) or an assignment of technology rights between two undertakings for the same purpose where part of the risk associated with exploitation of the technology remains with the assignor;
- which is *entered into between two undertakings*;[330] and
- concerns *the production or sale of the contract products*, i.e., the production or sale of goods or services that either integrate or are produced with the use of the licensor's technology (a pure R&D subcontracting agreement is not covered by the TTBER).

(b) The safe harbor

551. For the purpose of assessing whether a licensing agreement can benefit from the safe harbor provided by the TTBER, the relevant markets in which the parties to the agreement operate must be defined.

552. The position of the parties needs to be assessed both in the relevant market(s) for the licensed technology rights and the relevant market(s) for the contract products. While the relevant product markets consist of the contract product and its substitutes, the relevant technology markets comprise the IP that is licensed and its close substitutes for the production of the same goods. As far as patents are concerned, there is often only one technology available and no substitute. But this is not always the case: in the *Servier* case, Servier acquired (or tried to acquire) the exclusive rights to several competing technologies for producing perindopril.[331] The European Commission found that this acquisition formed part of Servier's overall strategy to delay generic entry.

553. Regarding product markets, the licensee's market share is calculated based on the licensee's sales of products incorporating the licensor's technology and competing products, which means the total sales of the licensee on the product market in question.

554. In technology markets, market shares can usually be calculated based on technology's share of total licensing income from royalties. However, because of the practical difficulties in calculating a licensor's market share based on royalty income, it can be calculated based on the sales of products incorporating the licensed technology in downstream product markets. This means that the licensor's market share is to be calculated based on the sales of the licensor and all its licensees of products incorporating the licensed technology.

555. If the technology is new and did not generate any sales in the preceding calendar year, a zero market share is assigned. Even though the threshold is exceeded when sales commence, the safe harbor will continue to apply for two consecutive calendar years following the year when the threshold was exceeded.

---

329 TTBER, art. 1(1)(c).

330 It seems that the TTBER excludes from its scope multilateral contracts, but a special set of rules has been included in its related guidelines regarding multilateral contracts involving technology pools. *See id.* ¶244 *et seq.*

331 Case COMP/AT/39612, *Perindopril (Servier)* (2014).

556. Once the relevant markets have been defined, it is necessary to determine whether the parties would have been actual or potential competitors in the absence of the agreement. Generally, a licensing agreement between competitors may raise bigger issues than those between non-competitors. The European Commission's guidelines on the TTBER[332] indicate that:

- For products markets, companies will be considered actual competitors if they are both active in the same relevant markets and, in the absence of the license, participate without infringing on the IP rights of the other party. And companies will be considered as potential competitors if they are likely to enter that market in response to a small but permanent price increase and would be able to do so without infringing on the IP rights of the other party.
- In technology markets, if the parties are already licensing out substitutable technology rights, or if the licensee is already licensing out its technology rights and the licensor enters the technology market by granting the licensee a license for competing technology rights, the parties are considered actual competitors. And the companies will be considered potential competitors if they hold substitutable technologies and the licensee is not licensing out its own technology, provided it would be likely to do so in the case of a small but permanent increase in technology prices.

557. As for the safe harbor itself, pursuant to Article 2 and 3 of the TTBER, licensing agreements may benefit from an exemption if they meet the following market share thresholds:

- for agreements between competitors, the TTBER applies provided that the combined market share of the parties does not exceed 20% on the relevant market(s);
- for agreements between non-competitors, the TTBER applies provided that the market share of each of the parties does not exceed 30% on the relevant market(s).

(c) Prohibition of hardcore restrictions

558. Article 4 of the TTBER provides for two sets of hardcore restrictions which, if present in a licensing agreement, will deprive the agreement from the benefit of the exemption. The TTBER distinguishes between hardcore restrictions for competing undertakings from those for non-competing undertakings.

559. For agreements between competing undertakings, the exemption shall not apply when:

- the agreement directly or indirectly restricts a party's ability to determine its prices when selling products to third parties;[333]
- the agreement includes output limitations, except in the following cases:
  - limitations on the output of contract products imposed on the licensee in a non-reciprocal agreement (i.e., an agreement where only one of the parties is licensing its technology rights to the other party or where, in the case of

[332] EU Guidelines on Technology Transfer Agreements, *supra* n. 327, Chapter IV.

[333] Commission Regulation 316/2014 (the TTBER), *supra* n. 325, Chapter IV, art. 4(1)(a).

cross-licensing, the licensed technologies rights are not competing technologies and the rights licensed cannot be used for the production of competing products); or

- limitations imposed on only one of the licensees in a reciprocal agreement (i.e., a cross-licensing agreement where the licensed technologies are competing technologies or can be used for the production of competing products).[334]

- the agreement allocates markets or customers, except in the following cases:[335]
  - when a non-reciprocal agreement contains an obligation on the licensor and/or the licensee not to produce the licensed technology rights within the exclusive territory reserved for the other party and/or not to sell actively and/or passively into the exclusive territory or to the exclusive customer group reserved for the other party;
  - when a non-reciprocal agreement contains a restriction of active sales by the licensee into the exclusive territory or to the exclusive customer group allocated by the licensor to another licensee, provided the latter was not a competing undertaking of the licensor at the time of the conclusion of its own license;
  - when there is an obligation on the licensee to produce the contract products only for its own use provided that the licensee is not restricted in selling the contract products actively and passively as spare parts for its own products; or
  - when in a non-reciprocal agreement, there is an obligation on the licensee to produce the contract products only for a particular customer, where the license was granted in order to create an alternative source of supply for that customer.
- the agreement restricts the licensee's ability to exploit its own technology rights or restricts the ability of any of the parties to the agreement to carry out R&D, unless such restriction is indispensable to prevent the disclosure of the licensed know-how to third parties.[336]

560. Regarding undertakings that are not competitors, the exemption shall not apply to agreements which:
- directly or indirectly restrict a party's ability to determine its prices when selling products to third parties; however, it is possible to impose maximum sale prices or recommended prices, provided that the prices do not amount to a fixed or minimum sale price as a result of pressure from, or incentives offered by, any of the parties;[337]
- contains a restriction of the territory into which, or of the customers to whom, the licensee may passively sell the contract products, except in the following cases:[338]
  - the agreement restricts passive sales into an exclusive territory or to an exclusive customer group reserved for the licensor;

[334] *Id.* art. 4(1)(b).
[335] *Id.* art. 4(1)(c).
[336] *Id.* art. 4(1)(d).
[337] *Id.* art. 4(2)(a).
[338] *Id.* art. 4(2)(b).

   - the agreement contains an obligation to produce the contract products only for the licensee's own use provided that the licensee is not restricted in selling the contract products actively and passively as spare parts for its own products;
   - the agreement contains an obligation to produce the contract products only for a particular customer, where the license was granted in order to create an alternative source of supply for that customer;
   - the agreement restricts sales to end users of wholesalers;
   - the agreement restricts sales to unauthorized distributors by members of a selective distribution system.
- restrict active or passive sales to end users by licensees which are members of a selective distribution system, and which operate at the retail level. However, the agreements may prohibit such members from operating out of an unauthorized place of establishment.[339]

561. Hardcore restrictions are considered as particularly egregious; as a result, not only are agreements that contain hardcore clauses deprived of the benefit of the block exemption, but such arrangements are generally considered unsuitable for an individual exception under Article 101(3) TFEU either (*see* Section 2 below). The TTBER Guidelines state: "Moreover, the European Commission considers that in the context of individual assessment it is unlikely that hardcore restrictions of competition fulfil the four conditions of Article 101(3) TFEU."[340]

(d) Excluded restrictions

562. Pursuant to Article 5 of the TTBER, the block exemption shall not cover the following types of obligations:
- *Exclusive Grant Backs*, i.e., any direct or indirect obligation imposed on the licensee to grant back an exclusive license or to assign back rights, in whole or in part, to the licensor (or to a third party designated by him) for the new improvement or the new applications of the licensed technology that the licensee could have developed.
- *Non-challenge Clauses*, i.e., any direct or indirect obligation on a party to an agreement not to challenge the validity of IP rights held by the other party in the Union (termination of the technology transfer agreement is still possible in the case of an exclusive license and if the licensee challenges the validity of any of the licensed technology rights).
- If the undertakings are non-competitors, limitation on the licensee's use or development of its own technology or limitation of the ability of any of the parties to carry out R&D (unless necessary to prevent disclosure of know-how to third parties).

563. In that case, contrary to hardcore restrictions, the whole agreement would still be exempted under the TTBER, except for these specific provisions.

---

339 *Id.* art. 4(2)(c).

340 EU Guidelines on Technology Transfer Agreements, *supra* n. 327, Chapter IV, ¶95.

c. *Analysis under Article 101 TFEU*

564. Where the market share threshold is exceeded or the licensing agreement cannot benefit from the block exemption under the TTBER for any other reason, there is no presumption of illegality, except in the case of hardcore restrictions. In that case, the agreement must be individually assessed under Article 101 TFEU.

(1) Assessment under Article 101(1) TFEU

565. In order to assess whether a licensing agreement infringes Article 101(1) TFEU, it must be determined, using a counterfactual test, how competition would occur in the absence of the agreement, considering the nature of the agreement; the existence of express or implicit restraints; the market position of the parties, competitors, and buyers of the licensed products; the barriers to entry; the existence of brand loyalty; the maturity of the technology in the market; the impact of innovation; and the potential cumulative effects created by a network of licensing agreements.

566. If a licensing agreement restricts actual or potential competition that would have existed without the agreement or the contractual restraints, it is caught under the prohibition of Article 101(1) TFEU. The likely impact of the licensing agreement on inter-technology competition and intra-technology competition must be considered. For inter-technology competition, an agreement involving, for instance, the cross-licensing of rights between competitors might prevent each of them from gaining a technological advantage over the other. Intra-technology competition might be reduced if the agreement imposes territorial restraints on licensees or facilitates collusion between the licensees (e.g., RPM by the licensees).

567. The Guidelines on the TTBER mention several potential restrictions that can result from licensing agreements, including:

   - *Royalty Obligations*. Provisions in a licensing agreement that concern the payment of royalties for the use of protected technologies will not normally have restrictive effects, whether the agreement is concluded between competitors or not. However, there are some instances where the European Commission shows concern with some royalty arrangements, especially between competitors. For instance, in the case of a licensing agreement between competitors, the European Commission considers that reciprocal running royalties, i.e., calculated based on the sales, in which the license does not provide for the integration of complementary technologies or does not have the purpose of achieving another procompetitive aim, is a hardcore price-fixing restriction.[341]
   - *Exclusive Licensing*. If the parties are not competitors, the licensing agreement with exclusivity is unlikely to fall under the prohibition of Article 101(1) TFEU unless an already dominant licensee obtains an exclusive license to one or more competing technologies. On the other hand, reciprocal exclusive licensing between competitors is considered a hardcore restraint pursuant to Article 4(1)(c) of the TTBER.[342]

---

341 *Id.* ¶¶184 *et seq.*

342 *Id.* ¶¶190 *et seq.*

- *Sales Restrictions*. Restrictions among non-competitors generally do not raise issues, unless the licensor individually has a significant market power and a series of similar agreements concluded by other licensors result in a cumulative effect, the sales restriction could be caught by Article 101(1) TFEU.[343]
- *Output Restrictions*. Output restrictions for licenses between non-competitors are block exempted up to the market share threshold of 30% of both licensor and licensee. Above this threshold, the main anticompetitive risk is a reduction of intra-technology competition between licensees. Anticompetitive effects will thus depend on the market position of the licensor and the licensee and the extent to which the output limitation prevents the licensee from satisfying demand for the products incorporating the licensed technology. As for licenses between competitors, the TTBER provides that reciprocal output restrictions are treated as a hardcore restriction. If the license is not reciprocal, the agreement may restrict competition if the parties have significant market power, unless the licensor's technology is substantially better than the licensee's technology and the output limitation substantially exceeds the output of the licensee prior to the conclusion of the agreement.[344]
- *Field of Use Restrictions*. Field of use restrictions limit the license to one or more technical fields of application or one or more product markets or industrial sectors. They are to be differentiated from customer restrictions, even though a technical field of use restriction may correspond to certain groups of customers within a product market. The main competitive concern related to field of use restrictions is the risk that the licensee ceases to be a competitive force outside the licensed field of use, which is greater with cross licensing and asymmetrical field of use restrictions (risk of market-sharing arrangement amounting to a hardcore restriction). For field of use restrictions on licensees in agreements between non-competitors, the licensor is normally also entitled to grant sole or exclusive licenses to different licensees limited to one or more fields of use.[345]
- *Captive Use Restrictions*. Captive use restrictions can be defined as an obligation on the licensee to limit its production of the licensed product to the quantities required for the production of its own products and for the maintenance and repair of its own products. In the case of licenses between competitors and where prior to the conclusion of the agreement, the licensee was not an actual or likely potential supplier of components to other producers, the agreement may result in serious negative market effects when the licensor has significant market power on the component market. In the case of licenses between non-competitors, there are two main competitive risks: a restriction of intra-technology competition in the market for the supply of inputs and an exclusion of arbitrage between

---

343 *Id.* ¶197 *et seq.*

344 *Id.* ¶¶204 *et seq.*

345 *Id.* ¶¶208 *et seq.*

licensees enhancing the possibility for the licensor to impose discriminatory royalties on licensees.[346]

- *Tying and Bundling.* Tying or bundling occurs when the licensee interested in one technology is forced or receives strong incentives to buy a license for another technology or purchase a product at the same time. Regardless of whether the parties are competitors, the main restrictive effects of tying are foreclosure of competing suppliers of the tied product, the maintenance of the licensor's market power through the creation of barriers to entry, or the increase of royalties by the licensor. However, tying may also give rise to efficiency gains when for instance the tied product is necessary for a technically satisfactory exploitation of the licensed technology or to ensure that production under the license conforms to quality standards respected by the licensor and other licensees.[347]
- *Non-compete Obligations.* Obligations on the licensee not to use third-party technologies which compete with the licensed technologies may entail risks of foreclosure against third-party technologies or collusion between licensors, when several licensors use a non-compete clause in separate agreements (i.e., in the case of cumulative use). However, non-compete obligations may also produce procompetitive effects by promoting dissemination of technology through a reduction of the risk of misappropriation of the licensed technology, in particular know-how.[348]
- *Most Favored Licensee Clauses.* A clause obliging the licensor to grant the licensee the most favorable terms it may have granted to another licensee may be captured by Article 101(1) TFEU if it leads to uniformity of pricing.[349]

(2) Analysis under Article 101(3) TFEU

568. If the agreement infringes Article 101(1) TFEU but cannot benefit from an exemption under the TTBER, an individual assessment of the licensing agreement is necessary to determine if it can benefit from an individual exemption under Article 101(3) TFEU. In that case, the Guidelines on the TTBER still provide useful indications as to how these agreements should be assessed.

569. In general, an individual exemption will apply if efficiency gains are proven, i.e., the agreement contributes to promoting technical or economic progress, under the following conditions:

   - The agreement must produce objective economic benefits. License agreements can bring together complementary technologies to create new or improved products or lower the costs of production for existing products. A licensing agreement may also bring about potential synergies between the respective technologies of the licensor and the licensee which enables the licensee to attain a cost/output configuration which he could not attain otherwise. At the distribution stage, licensing agreements can bring about efficiencies in the form of cost savings or the provision of valuable services to consumers. Efficiency

---

346 *Id.* ¶¶216 *et seq.*

347 *Id.* ¶¶221 *et seq.*

348 *Id.* ¶¶226 *et seq.*

349 *Id.* ¶118.

gains can also be found in agreements where technology owners assemble a technology package by bringing together technologies which are then licensed to third parties. This technology package might reduce transaction costs for the licensees. Procompetitive effects might also be found in a licensing agreement whereby the parties agree not to assert their IP rights against each other. In sectors in which there are numerous IP rights the parties need to navigate through, the licensing agreement thus enables them to develop their technology on their side without the risk of infringement claims.[350]

- The restriction must be indispensable to the attainment of these objectives. In that respect, the parties need to demonstrate that seemingly realistic and significantly less restrictive alternatives would be significantly less efficient. The Guidelines on the TTBER indicate that in the case of simple licensing between two parties it is generally not necessary to go beyond an examination of whether individual restraints are indispensable. Normally, there is no less restrictive alternative to the license agreement.[351]
- The efficiency gains must be passed on to consumers. This condition means that consumers of the products under the license must at least be compensated for the negative effects of the agreement. This is the case if the licensing agreement leads to a change in the cost structure of the companies concerned which gives them an incentive to reduce prices to consumers or if the agreement allows the consumers to obtain a new or improved product, even though there is a price increase.[352]
- The agreement must not afford the parties the possibility of eliminating competition with respect to a substantial part of the products or technology at issue. This condition requires an analysis of the remaining competitive pressures in the market and the impact of the agreement on these sources of competition.[353]

B. *Patent Litigation Settlements*[354]

a. *Introduction*

570. Due to the specificity of the EU regulatory framework, there is no exclusivity period for the first filer generic. Therefore, a patent settlement agreement does not have the same effect on the EU market as it does in the US. In the EU, the anticompetitive effects are more limited, whereas in the US, the regulatory landscape has led to contested settlement agreements between brand manufacturers and generic entrants.

571. In the EU, patent rights do not impede the regulatory marketing authorization of generic pharmaceuticals, nor does the regulatory marketing authorization of a challenger generic prevent the regulatory marketing authorization of the subsequent generic drugs.

---

350 *Id.* ¶176.

351 *Id.* ¶177.

352 *Id.* ¶178.

353 *Id.* ¶179.

354 Although this chapter focuses on the analysis of pay-for-delay agreements from a cartel perspective, it should be noted that this type of conduct may also, under European law, fall under the prohibition of abuse of dominance when the originator holds such a position. *See* Chapter V.

572. However, generic drugs could still face patent infringement lawsuits by originators in the EU. It is thus crucial to reconcile two conflicting imperatives: the necessity of patent protection with the need for competition in the market.

573. In the *Servier* case, the General Court stated:

> It is possible that the provisions of Article 101 TFEU may apply if the use of one or more patents, in concert between undertakings, were to lead to the creation of a situation which may come within the concepts of agreements between undertakings, decisions of associations of undertakings or concerted practices within the meaning of Article 101(1) TFEU.[355]

574. More particularly, concerning patent settlement agreements, it added:

> For the purposes of reconciling patent law and competition law in the particular context of settlements between parties to a patent dispute, a balance must be struck between, on the one hand, the need to allow undertakings to make settlements, the increased use of which is beneficial for society and, on the other hand, the need to prevent the risk of misuse of settlement agreements, contrary to competition law, leading to entirely invalid patents being maintained and, especially in the medicinal products sector, an unjustified financial burden for public budgets.[356]

575. Other NCAs have made the same observation. The CMA stated in the *Aspen* case that pay-for-delay agreements raise "complex questions of judgement as to the right balance between two conflicting public interests: in rewarding innovation via a temporary monopoly right, and in price competition."[357]

576. The EU, NCAs, and the ECJ have tried to draw a line between those two conflicting interests through developing case law that distinguishes between patent settlement agreements that:

- involve a reverse payment instrumental to the finding of an acceptable and legitimate solution of settlement for both parties; or
- substitute the uncertainty inherent to the patent litigation for certainty through a significant transfer of value.[358]

b. *Categories of Patent Settlements*

577. Doctrine and European competition authorities have categorized patent settlement agreements depending on whether they may hinder generics' entry into the market or not.

578. From that perspective, the European Commission distinguishes between so-called "Category A" agreements, which do not limit the generic's entry into the market, and "Category B" agreements, which do limit a generic's entry. It further sorts out Category B

---

355 Case T-691/14, *Servier SAS e.a. v. Commission*, ECLI:EU:T:2018:922, ¶242 (Dec. 12, 2018).

356 *Id.* ¶252.

357 CMA, Case No. 50455, *Anticompetitive agreement with respect to fludrocortisone acetate 0.1 mg tablets* (hereinafter, Case No. 50455, *Anticompetitive agreement*), ¶8.16 (2020).

358 Amalia Athanasiadou, *Patent Settlements in the Pharmaceutical Industry Under US Antitrust and EU Competition Law, Delaying Generic Entry in the EU*, 75 INT'L COMPETITION L. SERIES 328 (2018).

agreements depending on whether they contain a value transfer from the originator manufacturer to the generic manufacturer ("Category B.II") or not ("Category B.I").[359]

(1) Agreements that do not restrict the generic's ability to market its own products and thus do not raise competition issues ("Category A")

579. Category A agreements "should be unproblematic from a competition law perspective, as they allow immediate market entry by the generic company with its own product."[360]

580. However, the European Commission notes that this type of agreement might still fall under competition law scrutiny for unilateral conduct by the originator company, which might have caused generic delay (*see* Chapter V).

581. More generally, when assessing these agreements, competition authorities must find the right balance between facilitating generic entry to lower the price of pharmaceutical products and protecting the investments of the originator in order to promote innovation.

582. For instance, in the *Lundbeck* case, in 2003, Lundbeck concluded a patent settlement with Neolab. In 2002, Neolab launched generic citalopram in the UK market and Lundbeck started infringement proceedings. Neolab lodged a counterclaim that Lundbeck's crystallization patent was invalid. Lundbeck eventually settled with Neolab, which still had an interest and a serious chance in obtaining damages from Lundbeck through a finding of invalidity of Lundbeck's crystallization patent. Lundbeck thus agreed to pay Neolab its incurred damages in exchange for Neolab releasing Lundbeck from any claim for damages. Lundbeck in turn released Neolab from any claims under its patents for past sales and future sales until a certain date, reserving its patent rights for the period afterwards. The European Commission found that the agreement did not restrict Neolab's ability to market its own product and was therefore deemed unproblematic.[361]

(2) Agreements that limit generic entry and raise competition issues ("Category B")

583. Some patent settlements in the pharmaceutical sector may prove to be problematic from a competition law standpoint, as stated in the European Commission's Pharmaceutical Sector Inquiry – Final Report.[362] Settlements that may result in delaying generic entry in exchange for a value transfer (e.g., a payment) from the originator manufacturer to the generic manufacturer ("Category B.II.") are under particular scrutiny. Settlements that restrict entry beyond the patent's exclusionary zone may also raise antitrust issues, although in more limited cases ("Category B.I.").

---

359 European Commission SWD, Pharmaceutical Sector Inquiry – Final Report (the Pharmaceutical Sector Inquiry – Final Report) ¶741 *et seq.* (July 8, 2009), *available at* https://ec.europa.eu/competition/sectors/pharmaceuticals/inquiry/staff_working_paper_part1.pdf.

360 European Commission, Eighth Report on the Monitoring of Patent Settlements (Jan.–Dec. 2016) (hereinafter Eighth Report on the Monitoring of Patent Settlements), ¶15 (Mar. 9, 2018), *available at* https://ec.europa.eu/competition/sectors/pharmaceuticals/inquiry/patent_settlements_report8_en.pdf.

361 Case COMP/AT/39226, *Lundbeck*, ¶¶164, 639 (2013).

362 Pharmaceutical Sector Inquiry – Final Report, *supra* n. 359, Chapter IV, 269.

(a) Agreements that delay generic entry in return for value transfer ("Category B.II.")

(i) Non-challenge and non-compete clauses

584. Non-challenge and non-compete clauses constitute the most straightforward competitive restraints in patent settlement agreements.

585. A *non-challenge clause* explicitly recognizes the validity of the originator manufacturer's patent and states that the generic manufacturer will not challenge the validity of that patent.

586. Through a *non-compete clause*, the generic manufacturer undertakes that it will refrain from entering the market until the patent expires.

587. In that respect, in the *Cephalon* case, the European Commission analyzed both a non-compete and a non-challenge commitment and found they breached EU competition rules.[363]

588. Generic entry can also be limited through a straightforward licensing agreement: if the patent settlement agreement provides that the originator manufacturer will grant a license for certain patent rights to the generic manufacturer, the agreement will be considered as limiting the generic entry even though it allows the licensee to enter the market with the originator drug because, through the terms of the negotiated license agreement, the originator manufacturer controls the market entry of its competitor. As a result, the generic manufacturer is unable to compete in the market without constraints, as required under competition law standards.[364]

(ii) Value transfers

589. The European Commission distinguishes between monetary transfers and commercial side deals.

   – Monetary transfers (e.g., payment of a sum of money, investment, purchase of an asset)

     Value transfers involved in patent settlements include monetary transfers, which can take several forms.

     A *direct monetary transfer* (e.g., payment of a lump sum) from the originator company to the generic company is the most obvious value transfer. For instance, in the *Lundbeck* case, Lundbeck incentivized the generic manufacturers not to enter the market through direct payments – sometimes presented as the sum Lundbeck would have to deposit were it to proceed with a patent infringement action.[365] In the UK *Aspen* case, Amilco received a 30% share of the increased price that Aspen could charge for the fludrocortisone acetate tablets thanks to the patent settlement agreement.[366]

     Consideration in a patent settlement agreement can also take the form of an *investment* from the originator in the generic manufacturer's business.

---

363 Case COMP/AT/39686, *Cephalon* (2020).

364 Pharmaceutical Sector Inquiry – Final Report, *supra* n. 359, Chapter IV, 269.

365 Case COMP/AT/39226, *Lundbeck*, ¶¶164, 639 (2013).

366 Case No. 50455, *Anticompetitive agreement, supra* n. 357, Chapter IV.

For instance, in the *Cephalon* case, the originator manufacturer Cephalon purchased from Teva a non-exclusive, worldwide license to Teva's modafinil-related IP rights.[367]

A monetary transfer of value can equally involve the *purchase of an asset*. As an example, in the *Lundbeck* case, the originator manufacturer agreed to buy back the generic's citalopram stock.[368]

- Commercial side deals (e.g., distribution agreements)

  The originator manufacturer can also offer commercial side deals, in which a commercial benefit is granted to the generic manufacturer. These commercial side-deals can take various forms, such as distribution agreements or patent licenses on other products.

  In the *Lundbeck* case, for example, a generic manufacturer concluded a distribution agreement with Lundbeck with guaranteed profits in exchange for not entering the market with its own product.[369]

  In the *Cephalon* case, Teva benefited from a package of commercial side deals. First, Cephalon granted Teva a license to access clinical data that enabled the latter to gain time to obtain the necessary regulatory approvals for another medicine.[370] Second, Teva was appointed as Cephalon's exclusive distributor for modafinil in the UK. Finally, Cephalon committed to purchase the modafinil API from Teva.

- License agreement or non-assert clause under which the originator agrees not to seek to enforce patent or IP rights against the generic manufacturer

  A value transfer could also entail the award to the generic manufacturer of a *license* that allows it to enter the market.

  Similarly, a *non-assert clause*, in which the originator manufacturer agrees not to sue the generic manufacturer for patent infringement, allowing the generic medicine to enter the market despite the lack of a license, might technically be considered a value transfer.

  In that respect, Cephalon committed to granting Teva a non-exclusive license to manufacture and sell its generic modafinil product in the US as of 2011 and in other markets (including the EEA) as of 2012. It also committed to do the same with respect to the provision of modafinil API for finished pharmaceutical products that have modafinil as an active ingredient.[371]

(b) Agreements that contain restrictions exceeding the scope of the patent ("Category B.I")

590. Category B.I. agreements should not be problematic from a competition law perspective, except if they are concluded outside the exclusionary zone created by the patent (its geographic scope, its period of protection, or its exclusionary

---

367 Case COMP/AT/39686, *Cephalon* (2020).

368 Case COMP/AT/39226, *Lundbeck*, ¶¶441 (2013).

369 *Id.*

370 Case COMP/AT/39686, *Cephalon* (2020).

371 *Id.* ¶453.

scope) or if they involve a patent which the patent holder knows does not meet the patentability criteria (e.g., patents granted based on misleading or incomplete information).

591. The European Commission assessed these Category B.I. agreements in its 2009 Sector Inquiry and found that in almost all these settlement agreements, the validity of the originator company's patent and the patent infringement by the generic company were recognized by a court decision prohibiting the latter from marketing its generic product until after patent expiry. The generic company chose to accept the court ruling(s) as final, rather than appeal. It also recognized the validity of the originator company's patent(s) and/or agreed not to challenge validity in the future, and undertook not to enter the market or to stop marketing its own product until after the expiry of the patent(s).[372]

592. In that case, if the originator manufacturer obtains the generic's commitment not to enter a market that is wider than the territory that is protected by the patent, there is a chance that the related settlement agreement can be considered anticompetitive.

593. The same rationale applies to restrictions that fall outside the period of protection of the patent. For instance, in the *Servier* case, generic manufacturers committed not to enter the market until 2021, well after the expiry of Servier's process patents in 2008, and that was found to be anticompetitive.[373]

594. Finally, patent settlement agreements that contain restrictions exceeding the scope of the patent, i.e., when the generic's activity is outside the exclusionary scope of the patent and therefore should not be affected by it, can be deemed anticompetitive, as the patent holder cannot legitimately prevent non-infringing competitors from entering the market.

595. In the *Lundbeck* case, generic manufacturer Merck KG (GUK) committed not to launch citalopram products based on Natco's API, on the basis that Natco's API might be infringing Lundbeck's patent. The European Commission, however, found that: "Lundbeck did not have the power under patent law to conclude by itself on the exclusionary scope of its own patents and unilaterally decide that Natco citalopram would be infringing."[374]

c. *Analysis under EU Competition Law Provisions of Patent Settlement Agreements*

596. Competition Commissioner Margrethe Vestager stated in 2020, "it is illegal if pharmaceutical companies agree to buy-off competition and keep cheaper medicines out of the market. Even when their agreements are in the form of patent settlements or other seemingly normal commercial transactions."[375] On that basis, the European Commission has had the opportunity to review many patent settlement deals.

---

372 Pharmaceutical Sector Inquiry – Final Report, *supra* n. 359, Chapter IV, 275.

373 Case COMP/AT/39612, *Perindopril (Servier)*, ¶317 (2014).

374 Case COMP/AT/39226, *Lundbeck*, ¶¶768 (2013).

375 European Commission, Press Release IP/20/2220, *Antitrust: Commission fines Teva and Cephalon €60.5 million for delaying entry of cheaper generic medicine* (Nov. 26, 2020).

597. Patent settlement agreements were identified by the European Commission as warranting special attention from competition authorities in its Pharmaceutical Sector Inquiry – Final Report.[376] As such, they have been the subject of a continued monitoring by the European Commission since 2009. Eight annual reports have been published by the European Commission between 2010 and 2018 to better understand and identify settlements that delay generic entry and harm consumers in violation of EU law.[377]

598. This monitoring relates to the significant increase of patent settlement agreements in the EU in the early 2000s: 22% of the settlements from 2000 to 2008 involved Category B.II agreements (which restricted the generic's entry in the market and involved a value transfer).[378] In the years following the first sector inquiry, however, patent settlements decreased from 22% in 2009 to 11% in 2016.[379] This reduction was due, according to the European Commission, to "the increased awareness of companies and their legal advisors regarding the question whether such agreements might attract competition law scrutiny" and the "the fact that the European Commission announced a continued monitoring of patent settlements" as well as "the ongoing competition proceedings in the *Servier* and *Lundbeck* cases [that] might have had a deterrent effect."[380]

599. European decisional practice and case law on patent settlements have indeed developed dramatically in recent years, including through two enlightening rulings by the ECJ on pay-for-delay agreements in 2020[381] and 2021.[382]

600. Pharmaceutical companies now have a clearer framework against which to examine the agreements they may wish to conclude with an originator or generic manufacturer. First, companies must assess the existence of potential competition with the other party to the agreement. Second, they must determine whether the agreement at stake may entail a restriction of competition by object or by effect.

(1) Existence of potential competition between the originator and the generic producer

601. The framework to establish whether the originator and the generic manufacturer are (at least) potential competitors was established by the ECJ in its *GSK (Paroxetine)* ruling on January 30, 2020[383] and clarified in its *Lundbeck* ruling on March 25, 2021.[384] The standard required to establish potential competition is considered to be low and thus favorable to competition authorities and claimants.[385]

---

376 Pharmaceutical Sector Inquiry – Final Report, *supra* n. 359, Chapter IV.

377 Eighth Report on the Monitoring of Patent Settlements, *supra* n. 360, Chapter IV, ¶1.

378 Pharmaceutical Sector Inquiry – Final Report, *supra* n. 359, Chapter IV, ¶762.

379 Eighth Report on the Monitoring of Patent Settlements, *supra* n. 360, Chapter IV, ¶49.

380 European Commission, Second Report on the Monitoring of Patent Settlements (Jan.–Dec. 2010), ¶35 (July 6, 2011), *available at* https://ec.europa.eu/competition/sectors/pharmaceuticals/inquiry/patent_settlements_report1.pdf.

381 Case C-307/18, *Generics (UK) Ltd and Others v. Competition and Markets Authority*, ECLI:EU:C:2020:52, ¶38 (Jan. 30, 2020).

382 Case C-591/16 P, *Lundbeck v. Commission*, ECLI:EU:C:2021:243, (Mar. 25, 2021).

383 Case C-307/18, *Generics (UK) Ltd and Others*, ECLI:EU:C:2020:52, (Jan. 30, 2020).

384 Case C-591/16 P, *Lundbeck*, ECLI:EU:C:2021:243, (Mar. 25, 2021).

385 Walid Chaiehloudj, *Pay For Delay Agreements: An overview of EU and US Case Law*, E-COMPETITIONS Pay-for-delay agreements, May 2021, art. No. 99337.

602. In *GSK (Paroxetine)*, the CMA assessed patent settlement agreements concluded between GlaxoSmithKline (GSK) and two generic companies, Alpharma Limited and Generics UK, which had challenged GSK's patent regarding paroxetine, a prescription-only drug used to treat depressive and anxiety-related disorders, sold by GSK under the brand name Seroxat. In a 2016 decision, the CMA found that these agreements breached Article 101 TFEU and the equivalent prohibition under Chapter I of the UK Competition Act 1998, and imposed fines totaling £44.99 million on the parties to the agreements.[386]

603. GSK and the generic manufacturers appealed the CMA decision before the UK Competition Appeal Tribunal (CAT). The CAT stayed the proceedings and referred a request for a preliminary ruling to the ECJ in March 2018. Among the issues to be ruled upon by the ECJ was the question of whether the generic manufacturers could be considered potential competitors of GSK for the supply of paroxetine, even though their ability to enter the market for paroxetine was subject to the outcome of the court proceedings relating to the validity of GSK's patent.

604. The ECJ recalled that agreements between undertakings can only be prohibited if they have a negative and appreciable effect on competition within the internal market. This requires, with respect to horizontal agreements between originators and generic producers, a showing that the parties are in competition with each other, at least potentially.

605. The ECJ ruled that to assess whether a generic company not yet present in a market can be viewed as a potential competitor to the originator, it must be determined if there are real and concrete possibilities of the former entering that market and competing with the latter. Accordingly, to assess patent settlement agreements which have the effect of temporarily foreclosing a generic manufacturer, it must be determined *in concreto* whether there would have existed, absent these agreements, real and concrete possibilities for the generic company to enter that market and compete with the incumbent. The ECJ explained that:

> Such a criterion means that there can be no finding of a potential competitive relationship as an inference merely from the purely hypothetical possibility of such entry or even from the mere wish or desire of the manufacturer of generic medicines to enter the market. Conversely, there is no requirement that it must be demonstrated with certainty that manufacturer will in fact enter the market concerned and, a fortiori, that it will be capable, thereafter, of retaining its place there.[387]

606. The ECJ indicated that the assessment of potential competition had to be carried out with regard to the structure of the market, including the specific features of the pharmaceutical sector, the relevant economic and legal context, and the facts of the specific case at hand. In this regard, the court noted that regulatory constraints apply to the pharmaceutical sector, including notably the marketing

---

386 CMA, Case No. CE-9531/11, *Paroxetine* (2016). The CMA also found that GSK held a dominant position in the market for paroxetine and abused that position by entering into agreements with the generic manufacturers.

387 Case C-307/18, *Generics (UK) Ltd and Others*, ECLI:EU:C:2020:52, ¶38 (Jan. 30, 2020).

authorizations required to put new drugs in the market, as well as the existence of patents, which the ECJ said should be granted a "high level of protection."[388]

607. In practice, the ECJ ruled that the referring court should consider the following criteria:

- First, at the time when the agreement was concluded, whether the generic manufacturer had taken sufficient preparatory steps to enable it to enter the relevant market within such a period of time as would impose competitive pressure on the originator.

  The ECJ specified that such steps could include, e.g., applying for the required administrative authorizations for the marketing of a generic version of the drug at stake, manufacturing a stock of that generic drug (either through its own production facilities or through supply contracts concluded with third parties), or undertaking the legal steps to challenge the originator's patent. According to the ECJ:

  > Such steps permit the conclusion that a manufacturer of generic medicines has a firm intention and an inherent ability to enter the market of a medicine containing an active ingredient that is in the public domain, even when there are process patents held by the manufacturer of originator medicines.[389]

- Second, whether the market entry of the generic company faced barriers to entry that can be considered insurmountable. In this regard, the ECJ held that the existence of a patent protecting the manufacturing process of an active ingredient that is in the public domain could not, as such, be regarded as an insurmountable barrier. Much to the contrary, it considered that the generic manufacturer's readiness to challenge the validity of that patent and to take the risk, upon entering the market, of being subject to infringement proceedings brought by the patent holder argued in favor of the existence of competition between the two undertakings. The ECJ added that:

  > The genuineness of [the patent] dispute, particularly when it is the subject of court proceedings, far from precluding the existence of any competition between them, rather constitutes evidence of the existence of a potential competitive relationship between them.[390]

  More generally, this means that each time a patent is in the public domain, the ECJ is likely to consider that potential competition exists. Some have argued that, consequently, "all settlements based on a secondary patent therefore become suspect."[391]

- Third, whether additional subjective factors could confirm the generic manufacturer's "firm intention" and "inherent ability" to enter the market. On this point, the ECJ ruled that the conclusion of a patent settlement itself

---

[388] *Id.* ¶¶41, 137.

[389] *Id.* ¶44.

[390] *Id.* ¶52.

[391] Walid Chaiehloudj, *Pay For Delay Agreements: An overview of EU and US Case Law,* E-COMPETITIONS Pay-for-delay agreements, May 2021, art. No. 99337.

constitutes a strong indication that a competitive relationship existed between the generic producer and the originator. The greater the transfer of value from the originator to the generic company, in exchange for a delay in the latter's market entry, the stronger the indication.

608. *Lundbeck (Citalopram)*. The ECJ clarified its reasoning in the *Lundbeck* case in 2021. Lundbeck held patents for the API antidepressant citalopram and had developed, initially, two processes to produce the API, which were protected in a number of European countries until 2003. Over time, Lundbeck developed other production processes for which it also obtained adequate patents.

609. Between 2002 and 2003, Lundbeck concluded six patent settlement agreements with four undertakings active in the production and/or sale of generic medical products, namely Merck KG (or Generics UK, its subsidiary, hereafter "GUK"), Alpharma, Arrow and Ranbaxy, to delay the launch of their version of the drug once the basic patent expired. Consequently, on June 19, 2013, the European Commission imposed a €94 million fine on the Danish pharmaceutical group for having restricted the market entry of these four generic manufacturers in exchange for payment in various forms, including: direct payment of a lump sum, purchase of the generic citalopram stock and guaranteed profits in a distribution agreement.[392] The European Commission also imposed fines totaling €52.2 million on the four generic competitors.

610. Lundbeck and the generic manufacturers appealed the European Commission's decision, which the General Court upheld on September 8, 2016.[393] The case was then brought before the ECJ.

611. Before the ECJ, Lundbeck argued that the European Commission erred in law in finding that the manufacturers of generic medicines that had concluded the agreements at issue were at least potential competitors of Lundbeck at the time those agreements were concluded. According to Lundbeck, the introduction of generic medicines that infringe on other parties' IP rights cannot be considered an expression of potential competition under Article 101(1) TFEU.

612. The ECJ dismissed this ground of appeal following the analysis grid set in the *GSK* case, discussed above. It recalled that to assess whether an undertaking that is not yet present in a market is a potential competitor, it must be determined whether there are "real and concrete possibilities of [it] joining that market" and competing with the incumbent.[394]

613. In that respect and with regard to pay-for-delay agreements, the structure of the market and the economic and legal context within which market players operate should be analyzed. In particular, one ought to consider the regulatory constraints that are characteristic of the life sciences sector, the IP rights and the patents held by the originators relating to one or more processes for the manufacture of an active ingredient that is in the public domain, and determine whether there would have existed, in the absence of those agreements, "real and concrete possibilities for those undertakings to enter that market" and compete with the incumbent.

---

392 Case COMP/AT/39226, *Lundbeck*, ¶¶164, 639 (2013).

393 Case T-472/13, *Lundbeck v. Commission*, ECLI:EU:T:2016:449, (Sept. 8, 2016).

394 Case C-591/16 P, *Lundbeck*, ECLI:EU:C:2021:243, ¶54 (Mar. 25, 2021).

614. Following the criteria set in *GSK*, in order to characterize these real and concrete possibilities to enter the market, the ECJ:

- Examined if the generic manufacturer had a "firm intention and inherent ability to enter the market," by assessing whether, at the time those agreements were concluded, the generic manufacturers had taken "sufficient preparatory steps" to enable them to enter the market concerned within a period short enough to create competitive pressure on the originator manufacturer.
- Assessed the existence of potential competition between an originator manufacturer and a generic manufacturer "at the time when the settlement agreement in respect of the process patent dispute between them was concluded." The ECJ clarified that evidence relating to events subsequent to the conclusion of a settlement agreement and, in particular, relating to the outcome of the patent dispute which had justified the conclusion of that agreement (in this case, documents indicating how the generic manufacturers perceived the strength of Lundbeck's new process patents when the agreements in question were concluded) cannot be taken into consideration to assess whether the parties to that agreement were potential competitors at the time when it was concluded.[395]
- Confirmed whether the market entry of the generic manufacturers "would have met barriers to entry that are insurmountable." In that respect, the existence of a patent which protects the manufacturing process of an active ingredient that is in the public domain cannot be considered as an insurmountable barrier, regardless of its presumed validity since "that presumption sheds no light, for the purposes of applying Articles 101 and 102 TFEU, on the outcome of any dispute in relation to the validity of that patent."[396] Even though a patent exists, a manufacturer of generic medicines who has a firm intention and an inherent ability to enter the market, shows a readiness to challenge the validity of such a patent, and takes the risk of being subject to infringement proceedings brought by the patent holder, can be characterized as a potential competitor. The ECJ further added that "it is not for the competition authority concerned to carry out a review of the strength of the patent at issue or of the probability of a dispute between the patent holder and a manufacturer of generic medicines being brought to an end with a finding that that patent is valid and has been infringed."[397]
- Considered "additional factors," including the conclusion of a patent settlement agreement between the generic manufacturers and the originator manufacturer at a time when the former was not present in the market concerned. According to the ECJ, the factors to be considered can either be *objective*, such as the investments already made, the steps taken in order to obtain a marketing authorization and the supply contracts concluded with the generic manufacturers' API suppliers,[398] *or subjective* – provided that they are not

---

395 *Id.* ¶68.
396 *Id.* ¶58.
397 *Id.* ¶60.
398 *Id.* ¶78.

decisive for the purpose of the assessment of the real and concrete possibilities to enter the market.[399] In the latter case, the perception by the originator manufacturer of the risk that generic manufacturers present to its commercial interests can be taken into account in the analysis, if that perception affected the conduct in the market of the originator manufacturer.[400]

615. Consequently, in this instance, confirming the General Court's decision, the ECJ ruled as follows:

- It was not for the European Commission to decide on the validity of the patent held by Lundbeck, i.e., to provide definitive proof that the citalopram, which the manufacturers of generic drugs intended to market, did not infringe Lundbeck's new process patents, since the existence of such patent did not preclude a finding that there was potential competition between Lundbeck and the generic manufacturers.
- Neither did such a patent constitute an insurmountable barrier for the generic manufacturers, which were both willing and ready to enter the citalopram market, and which had already made considerable investments to that end at the time the agreements were concluded. Notably, the ECJ took the fact that Lundbeck's original patents had expired and that other processes of production of generic citalopram existed, which did not infringe Lundbeck's patents, into account.
- In the absence of insurmountable barriers to entry, the fact that a generic manufacturer did not hold a marketing authorization when it concluded its agreement with the originator manufacturer cannot preclude all potential competition between the two. The ECJ indicated that steps taken by each of the generic manufacturers concerned with a view to obtaining a marketing authorization for the drugs at stake constituted relevant indications of their firm intention and inherent ability to enter the market, and thus established the existence of potential competition between them and Lundbeck.
- It is not necessary to demonstrate with certainty – as had already been mentioned in the *GSK* case – that the manufacturers of generic medicines would have entered the market and that this entry would inevitably have been successful, but only that those manufacturers had real and concrete possibilities in that respect.[401]

616. Further, the parties had argued that recital 29 of the Guidelines on the application of Article 101 TFEU to technology transfer agreements prevented them from being considered potential competitors since "[i]n principle, the parties to an agreement are not considered competitors if they are in a one-way or two-way blocking position."[402] A one-way blocking position is when a technology

---

399 *Id.* ¶74.

400 *Id.* ¶76.

401 Case C-307/18, *Generics (UK) Ltd and Others*, ECLI:EU:C:2020:52, ¶38 (Jan. 30, 2020).

402 EU Guidelines on Technology Transfer Agreements, *supra* n. 327, Chapter IV, ¶29. ("In principle, the parties to an agreement are not considered competitors if they are in a one-way or two-way blocking position. A one-way blocking position exists where a technology right cannot be exploited without infringing upon another valid technology right, or where one party cannot be active in a commercially viable way on the relevant market

right cannot be exploited without infringing upon another valid technology right, or where one party cannot be active in a commercially viable way on the relevant market without infringing the other party's valid technology right. The ECJ ruled that a one-way blocking position could not be applied to pay-for-delay agreements and is subject to exceptions, since in practice, there will be cases where there is no certainty whether a particular technology right is valid and infringed.

617. *Servier (Perindopril).* Although the standard set by the ECJ is low, a generic manufacturer cannot, in all cases, be considered as a potential competitor of the originator manufacturer.

618. In the *Servier* case, the European Commission had sanctioned Servier and, inter alia, Hungarian generic manufacturer Krka for having entered into anticompetitive agreements in relation to the supply of the antihypertensive drug perindopril, including a patent settlement agreement.[403]

619. However, the General Court annulled the fines imposed on Servier and Krka for that specific portion of the alleged infringement after concluding that there was no restriction of competition by effect.[404] It notably found that the European Commission had not established that, in the absence of the agreements, Krka would probably have entered the relevant markets and thus had not shown that it was a potential competitor.[405] In its analysis, the European Commission indeed failed to take into account that Servier owned a patent that could be considered valid and the importance of this factor for a generic company when assessing the risks of market entry. The General Court reminded that generic company's recognition or non-recognition of the validity of the patent in question or its perception of the strength of that patent is decisive when determining whether it is likely to enter the market at risk. In the case at stake, the General Court considered that the European Commission did not properly account for the effects that the patent in question and Krka's recognition of its validity could have on the assessment of Krka's likely behavior in the absence of an agreement.[406]

(2) Existence of a restriction of competition by object or effect

620. While the European Commission and the NCAs tend to consider patent settlement agreements as per se restrictions or restrictions by object, the ECJ has adopted a more balanced approach, based on a case-by-case analysis.

---

without infringing the other party's valid technology right. This is, for instance, the case where one technology right covers an improvement of another technology right and the improvement cannot be legally used without a license of the basic technology right. A two-way blocking position exists where neither technology right can be exploited without infringing upon the other valid technology right or where neither party can be active in a commercially viable way on the relevant market without infringing the other party's valid technology right and where the parties thus need to obtain a license or a waiver from each other. However, in practice there will be cases where there is no certainty whether a particular technology right is valid and infringed.").

403 Case COMP/AT/39612, *Perindopril (Servier)* (2014).

404 Case T-691/14, *Servier SAS e.a.*, ECLI:EU:T:2018:922, ¶1234 (Dec. 12, 2018).

405 *Id.* ¶1160.

406 *Id.* ¶¶1145–1161.

(a) Overview of the EU approach

621. The European Commission has initially taken a strict approach that patent settlements and other pay-for-delay arrangements may be analyzed as by-object restrictions (*see* Chapter II regarding the notion of restriction by object).

622. According to the European Commission, if:

> The limitations on entry in question are not achieved through the strength of the patent, but through inducements from the originator undertaking to the generic undertaking aligning previously competing interests, then a restriction of competition by object may exist, including when the limitations in question exceed the substantive scope of the patent.[407]

623. In its *Lundbeck* case, the European Commission devised a three-pronged test to identify agreements showing such characteristics. It found that even if patent settlement agreements are within the applicable patents' temporal, territorial, and substantive scope, some agreements have the potential to restrict competition by their very nature on account of three criteria:[408]

- the generic manufacturer and the originator manufacturer are at least potential competitors;
- the generic manufacturer commits itself to limit, for the duration of the agreement, its independent efforts to enter one or more EEA markets with generic products; and
- the agreement includes a transfer of value from the originator manufacturer which substantially reduces the incentives of the generic manufacturer to independently pursue its efforts to enter one or more EEA markets with the generic product (an exclusion payment).

624. The European Commission considered that these agreements were "restrictions of competition by object" since they "were by their very nature injurious to the proper functioning of normal competition."[409]

625. That approach was again used in subsequent cases, most notably *Servier.*[410]

626. However, this approach has not been confirmed by the ECJ. Contrary to the European Commission, the ECJ considers that pay-for-delay agreements do not necessarily constitute restriction of competition by object in all cases. The ECJ holds that a case-by-case analysis must be carried out to determine whether the agreement is a per se restriction. The standard for the assessment was set out in the *GSK* preliminary ruling[411] and further clarified in appeal in the *Lundbeck* case.[412]

627. Based on these two cases, the position of the ECJ can be summarized as follows:

- Settlement agreements can be anticompetitive only if the involved companies are (at least) potential competitors.

---

407 Case COMP/AT/39226, *Lundbeck*, ¶¶659 (2013).

408 *Id.*

409 *Id.* ¶¶821, 871, 959, 1010, 1084, 1171.

410 Case COMP/AT/39612, *Perindopril (Servier)* (2014).

411 Case C-307/18, *Generics (UK) Ltd and Others*, ECLI:EU:C:2020:52, (Jan. 30, 2020).

412 Case C-591/16 P, *Lundbeck*, ECLI:EU:C:2021:243, (Mar. 25, 2021).

- Analyzing such agreements requires a determination of whether the generic would have entered into the market without the pay-for-delay settlement.
- Classification of the agreement as a restriction of competition "by object" is not self-evident. A restriction by object is only characterized if the value transfer cannot have any other explanation than the commercial interest of both the holder of the patent and the party allegedly infringing the patent not to engage in competition on the merits. A case-by-case analysis is thus necessary. Moreover, any restrictions by effect must be analyzed based on a prospective analysis of the market in the absence of the concerted practice (counterfactual). Some authors have considered that this grid of analysis is "impracticable" and leads to significant legal uncertainty. The anticompetitive object of the patent settlement agreement is characterized by demonstrating it has been concluded only to impede competition, yet this demonstration implies determining the intention of the parties in a patent dispute context. Moreover, the authors note that only caricatured patent settlement agreements, i.e., with disproportionately large value transfers, could qualify as restriction by object under the reasoning of the ECJ.[413]
- Proven procompetitive effects capable of raising a reasonable doubt that a settlement agreement causes a sufficient degree of harm to competition can exclude a characterization of a restriction by object.

(b) Key cases

628. *Lundbeck (Citalopram)*. In its 2013 *Lundbeck* case, the European Commission held that patent settlements can be compatible with Article 101 TFEU in two instances:
   - When the reverse payment is instrumental to the finding of an acceptable and legitimate solution of settlement for both parties:
     - The existence of a reverse payment in the context of a patent settlement is not always problematic, particularly when: (i) that payment is linked to the strength of the patent, as perceived by each of the parties, (ii) it is necessary in order to find an acceptable and legitimate solution in the eyes of the two parties and (iii) it is not accompanied by restrictions intended to delay the market entry of generics.[414]
   - When the agreement is reached without inducement and the settlement's restrictions do not go beyond the protection given by patent law:
     - When in a patent dispute a settlement is reached without inducement on the basis of each party's assessment of the probability of a patent being held valid and infringed by a court, such a patent settlement will normally not infringe Article 101(1) TFEU of the Treaty if the agreed limitations on the behavio[r] of the generic undertaking do not go beyond the rights granted by patent law.[415]

---

413 Walid Chaiehloudj, *Pay For Delay Agreements: An overview of EU and US Case Law*, E-COMPETITIONS Pay-for-delay agreements, May 2021, art. No. 99337.

414 Case COMP/AT/39226, *Lundbeck*, ¶¶638, 639 (2013), *see also* the appeal, Case T-472/13, *Lundbeck*, ECLI:EU:T:2016:449, ¶350 (Sept. 8, 2016).

415 Case COMP/AT/39226, *Lundbeck*, ¶638 (2013).

629. However, the European Commission found that patent agreements that do not fall under one of these two categories can restrict competition by object when they meet the three criteria listed in Section A above. Analyzing each of these criteria, the European Commission found that in Lundbeck's case, the generic manufacturers' acceptance of the limitations placed on their commercial autonomy by the patent settlement agreements was achieved not in consideration of the strength of Lundbeck's patents, but through the significant transfer of value from Lundbeck to the generic manufacturers. It was therefore considered that these limitations should be regarded as by-object restrictions of competition within the meaning of Article 101(1) TFEU.

630. The General Court upheld the European Commission's findings on appeal.[416] The ECJ eventually also rejected Lundbeck's arguments, although it did so based on a more nuanced assessment of the existence of a restriction by object.

631. Before the ECJ, Lundbeck's criticism of the General Court's judgment was two-fold: first, it challenged the characterization of the agreements in question as restrictions by object and, second, it questioned the methodology used to arrive at that conclusion, specifically the absence of a counterfactual test.

632. On the first criticism, the ECJ recalled that the concept of a restriction by object can only apply to agreements between undertakings which show, considering their content and objectives, and the economic and legal context, a sufficient degree of harm to competition so that it is not necessary to assess their effects, "since some forms of coordination between undertakings can be regarded, by their very nature, as being harmful to the proper functioning of normal competition."[417]

633. By reference to the *GSK* case (*see* below), the ECJ reiterated that patent settlement agreements cannot be considered as restrictions by object in all cases. Such agreements must only be seen as restrictions by object:

> When it is plain from the[ir] examination [...] that the transfers of value provided for *by it* cannot have any explanation other than the commercial interest of both the holder of the patent at issue and the party allegedly infringing the patent not to engage in competition on the merits, since agreements whereby competitors deliberately substitute practical cooperation between them for the risks of competition can clearly be characteri[z]ed as "restrictions by object."[418]

634. In order to conduct such an examination, one must examine if the net gain of the value transfer from the originator manufacturer to the generic manufacturer is significant enough to act as an incentive for the latter to refrain from entering the market and not to compete on the merits with the originator manufacturer on a case-by-case basis. The net gain of the value transfer need not be greater than the profits expected by the originator manufacturer from the patent proceedings if they were to be successful.[419]

---

416 Case T-472/13, *Lundbeck*, ECLI:EU:T:2016:449, (Sept. 8, 2016).

417 Case C-591/16 P, *Lundbeck*, ECLI:EU:C:2021:243, ¶112 (Mar. 25, 2021).

418 *Id.* ¶114.

419 *Id.* ¶115.

635. The ECJ found that, in this instance, several elements confirmed that the value transfer acted as an incentive to prevent the generic manufacturer from competing on the merits with Lundbeck:

- The patent settlement agreement effectively kept the generic manufacturer outside of the markets concerned.
- The parties were in dispute over whether Lundbeck's patent was sufficiently strong to prevent them from entering the market, which shows that it is not the patent alone, but, in reality, the value transfer from the patent settlement agreement, which constituted the decisive criterion triggering their commitment not to enter the market.
- The lump sums paid to the generic manufacturers had apparently been calculated taking into consideration the profit or turnover which they expected to make, had they entered the market, for the duration of the patent settlement agreement.
- These lump sums were sizeable enough to lead the generic manufacturers to accept the constraints of the patent settlement agreement, even though they had made considerable efforts to prepare their market entry and they did not intend, absent the settlement, to desist from those efforts because of Lundbeck's new process patents.
- Lundbeck did not provide any justification for these transfers of value by demonstrating the existence of any other consideration or proven and legitimate commitments by the generic manufacturers.

636. The arguments raised by Lundbeck did not call that conclusion into question, according to the ECJ.

637. In particular, Lundbeck's second criticism relied on the following statement in the *GSK* ruling:

> When the agreement at issue is one which has the effect of temporarily keeping an undertaking outside a market, it must be determined whether there would have existed, in the absence of that agreement, real and concrete possibilities for that undertaking to enter that market and compete with the undertakings established in that market.[420]

638. Thus, Lundbeck argued that an examination of the counterfactual scenario was necessary in any competitive analysis of a restriction – be it by object or effect – to establish the causal link between the practice and the restriction in question.

639. The ECJ however found that an examination of the counterfactual scenario, which has the purpose of drawing out the *effects* of a collusive practice when the analysis of that practice does not reveal a sufficient degree of harmfulness for it to qualify as a restriction by object, is not required to characterize a restriction by *object*.[421]

640. The ECJ ultimately dismissed Lundbeck's appeal on March 25, 2021.

641. *Johnson & Johnson (Fentanyl).* In 2013, the European Commission fined Johnson & Johnson and Novartis €16 million for having concluded an anticompetitive

---

420 Case C-307/18, *Generics (UK) Ltd and Others*, ECLI:EU:C:2020:52, ¶37 (Jan. 30, 2020).

421 Case C-591/16 P, *Lundbeck*, ECLI:EU:C:2021:243, (Mar. 25, 2021).

agreement in relation to the supply of the generic painkiller Fentanyl.[422] This case slightly differs from the others mentioned in the present chapter as the agreement at stake was not a patent settlement agreement (at the time of the parties' agreement, Johnson & Johnson's patent protection had expired). Instead, the parties signed a co-promotion agreement, which provided strong incentives for the generic not to enter the market through monthly payments that exceeded the profits the generic expected to obtain from the sales of its generic product. The European Commission concluded that the agreement was anticompetitive by object. In order to determine whether the co-promotion agreement had the potential to restrict competition by its very nature, the European Commission explained that it took into account the following elements: the fact that the generic undertaking limited, for the duration of the agreement, its independent efforts to enter the market with its generic product and the fact that the agreement was related to as transfer of value from the originator which substantially reduced the incentives of the generic to independently pursue its efforts to enter the market with its generic product.[423] In that regard, the European Commission concluded that the co-promotion agreement included a non-entry mechanism, which provided strong incentives for Novartis not to enter the Dutch market for the duration of the agreement. If Novartis entered the Dutch market, it would have lost the considerable monthly payments from Johnson & Johnson, which exceeded what Novartis expected to earn if it launched the product and which was considerably less than what Johnson & Johnson expected to lose if Novartis entered the market. Besides, the analysis of the European Commission seemed to show that the parties' intentions confirmed the objective elements of the analysis and that both parties acted in full knowledge of the objective of the agreement, designed to ensure that Novartis was kept out of the market and that Johnson & Johnson could maximize its profits for sales of the originator product as long as the agreement was in force and share these supra-competitive profits with Novartis.[424]

642. *Servier (Perindopril)*. One year later, in 2014, the European Commission fined Servier and five generic rivals for having entered into anticompetitive agreements in relation to the supply of the antihypertensive drug perindopril, including patent settlement agreements from 2005 to 2007. It also imposed a €41.3 million fine on Servier for abuse of its dominant position in the market for perindopril API technology.

643. Although, the European Commission reiterated its per se analysis[425] and used the three-pronged test already applied in the *Lundbeck* case, it seemed to adopt a more flexible approach. After having first proceeded to establish, through an analysis of each individual patent settlement agreement, "whether the content,

---

422 Case COMP/AT/39685, *Fentanyl* (2013).

423 *Id.* ¶219.

424 *Id.* ¶¶222, 223.

425 Case COMP/AT/39612, *Perindopril (Servier)*, ¶1134 (2014) ("However, the European Commission considers that, depending on the specific circumstances of the case, a patent settlement agreement by which a generic company accepts restrictions on its ability and incentives to compete in return for a value transfer (either in the form of significant sums of money or another significant inducement) can be a restriction of competition by object contrary to Article 101 TFEU of the Treaty.").

objectives, and legal and economic context of the patent settlement agreement concluded between Servier and the generic company constitutes a restriction by object," it complemented its analysis with an additional evaluation of the likely restrictive effects.[426]

644. The European Commission concluded that the five agreements could be characterized as restrictions by object and that they were likely to entail restrictive effects on competition.[427] Particularly with respect to the agreements concluded with Krka, the European Commission considered that the parties entered into an agreement akin to market sharing, whereby Krka essentially renounced its ability to compete through non-challenge and non-compete obligations in 18 out of 20 Member States, including the two biggest worldwide markets for Servier, and received a sole license in seven Member States, considered to belong to Krka's core markets, as economic inducement. The European Commission considered that the conclusion of these agreements amounted to a single and continuous restriction of competition by object.[428]

645. Continuing with an analysis of the effects of the agreements, the European Commission also found that in the absence of the non-challenge clause in the patent settlement agreement, Krka would have remained a prominent potential competitor to Servier through its challenge to the validity of the patent.[429]

646. The European Commission's decision imposing fines totaling €427.7 million (including fines for abuse of dominance – *see* Chapter V) was appealed in front of the General Court and upheld on the existence of a violation of Article 101 TFEU in December 2018.[430] However, the Court annulled the fines imposed on Servier and Krka under their agreements by concluding that, on this point, there was no restriction of competition by object and by effect.[431]

647. As for the allegation of restriction by object, the Court considered that the European Commission had not established the existence of a reverse payment resulting from the granting of a license at an abnormally low price and which, since it is not intended to compensate for the costs inherent in the settlement of a dispute, constitutes an inducement. The European Commission was thus not entitled to find that there was a restriction of competition revealing a sufficient degree of harm to be classified as a restriction by object.

648. As for the alleged restrictions by effect, the Court noted that the European Commission had not established that, in the absence of the agreements: (i) Krka would probably have entered the relevant markets, and that (ii) the continuation of the proceedings brought by Krka against the patent would probably, or even plausibly, have led to a more rapid or more complete invalidation of that patent.[432] The case is currently under appeal before the ECJ.

---

426 *Id.* ¶1211.

427 *Id.* ¶¶5.2.2.5, 5.3.2.5, 5.4.2.5, 5.5.3.5.5, 5.6.2.5.

428 *Id.* ¶1812.

429 *Id.* ¶1834.

430 Case T-691/14, *Servier SAS e.a.*, ECLI:EU:T:2018:922, ¶407 (Dec. 12, 2018).

431 *Id.* ¶1234. The Court also annulled the fine imposed on Servier for abuse of dominance. *See* Chapter V.

432 *Id.* ¶¶1160, 1203.

649. *Teva (Cephalon).* In 2020, the European Commission fined Teva and several generic manufacturers €60.5 million for having concluded patent settlements aimed at delaying market entry of a cheaper generic version of Cephalon's drug treating sleep disorders, modafinil, for several years after Cephalon's main patents expired.[433]

650. Cephalon incentivized Teva not to enter the market with a cheaper version of modafinil in exchange for a number of commercial side deals, including Cephalon's purchase of a license held by Teva, granting Teva access to clinical data, appointing Teva as Cephalon's exclusive distributor for modafinil in the UK, Cephalon's commitment to buy the modafinil API from Teva, and lump sum payments.

651. The European Commission held that the settlement agreement constituted a restriction by object. Indeed, Teva committed to stay out of the modafinil market (through non-compete and non-challenge clauses) not because of the perceived strength of Cephalon's patents but because of the substantial value transfer from Cephalon, mainly stemming from the commercial side deals which Teva could not have achieved outside the context of the patent settlement agreement.

652. The value transfer served to reward Teva for staying out of the modafinil markets and for not independently competing with its generic product. The settlement agreement thus was akin to a market exclusion agreement in which the potential competitor is rewarded for not competing and which, therefore, is a restriction of competition by its very nature.[434]

653. The delayed entry of Teva into the market meant that prices for modafinil were not pushed down. The European Commission considered that the agreement in question caused substantial harm to EU patients and the healthcare systems by keeping prices high for that medicine.

654. However, this case confirms the slight change of approach initiated by the European Commission in the *Servier* case compared to the *Lundbeck* case: although patent settlement agreements can be considered per se restrictions, an analysis of the restrictive effects can also be carried out.[435] The European Commission concluded nonetheless in the *Cephalon* case that the settlement agreement's likely effects on competition were appreciable. A counterfactual test concluded that there was less competition in the market when the settlement agreement was in force. The restrictions contained in the agreement (non-compete and non-challenge clauses) prevented Teva from selling modafinil products in the EEA and this resulted in removing Teva as a potential competitor. It replaced the uncertainty of Teva's entry into the market with the certainty of Teva's non-entry into the market. Moreover, Cephalon could more generally preserve its market power: without the agreement, Teva could have succeeded in invalidating Cephalon's patents so that not only Teva itself, but also other generic companies could have entered the modafinil markets, thereby undermining Cephalon's market power and its ability to maintain high prices. The European Commission noted: "While generally patent

---

433 Case COMP/AT/39686, *Cephalon* (2020).

434 *Id.* ¶1017.

435 *Id.* ¶1019.

settlements can be legitimate, we believe that the settlement agreement between Teva and Cephalon was not."[436]

655. The Commission's decision was upheld on appeal. In a judgment of 18 October 2023,[437] the General Court rejected Teva's arguments regarding the characterization of a restriction by object as well as the existence of plausible explanations for the complex contractual arrangements entered into between Cephalon and Teva other than the interest of both parties not to engage in competition on the merits. The General Court, considering that the entry in the modafinil market of Cephalon's main competitive force was delayed as a result of the agreements, also rejected Teva's argument that the restrictions had no anticompetitive effect.

656. *GSK (Paroxetine).* In the context of a preliminary ruling referred by the CAT, the ECJ had the opportunity to explain the criteria to determine whether a settlement agreement related to a dispute between the holder of a pharmaceutical patent and a manufacturer of generic medicines infringes EU competition law.

657. The ECJ stated that a patent settlement agreement between an originator manufacturer and a generic manufacturer, which are potential competitors, whereby the latter commits not to enter the market and not to pursue patent proceedings challenging the validity of the originator patent for the duration of the settlement agreement, and in consideration of which the generic manufacturer receives value transfers, can be considered a restriction by object:

- if it is clear that the net gain stemming from the value transfers to the generic "can have no other explanation than the commercial interest of the parties to the agreement not to engage in competition on the merits";[438]
- *unless* the settlement agreement in question is backed by proven procompetitive effects capable of raising a reasonable doubt that it causes a sufficient degree of harm to competition.

658. Eventually, the CAT issued its final decision in the *GSK* case in May 2021 and applied the ECJ's guidance to the settlement agreements at issue. It upheld the CMA's finding of an infringement of both Articles 101 and 102 TFEU.[439] Regarding Article 101 TFEU, the CAT confirmed that the generic manufacturers were potential competitors of GSK and that the agreements in question restricted competition by effect and in principle by object since the generic manufacturers only concluded the settlement agreements once the value transfers offered by GSK were inducement enough not to enter the market.

659. *Aspen.* Finally, it is worth mentioning one of the most important cases decided by the CMA, the *Aspen* (fludrocortisone) case.

660. In July 2020, the CMA fined the sole UK supplier of fludrocortisone acetate tablets, Aspen, and two generic manufacturers, Amilco and Tiofarma, a total of

---

436 European Commission, Press Release IP/20/2220, *Antitrust: Commission fines Teva and Cephalon €60.5 million for delaying entry of cheaper generic medicine* (Nov. 26, 2020).

437 Case T-74/21, *Teva Pharmaceutical Industries Ltd and Cephalon Inc.*, ECLI:EU:T:2023:651 (Oct. 18, 2023).

438 Case C-307/18, *Generics (UK) Ltd and Others*, ECLI:EU:C:2020:52, ¶111 (Jan. 30, 2020) (emphasis added).

439 CAT, Case Nos. 1251-1255/1/12/16, *GlaxoSmithKline*, [2021] CAT 20, (2021). *See* Chapter V for a discussion of the abuse of dominance.

£2.3 million (and secured an £8 million payment for the NHS, in accordance with a settlement agreed with the parties) for having concluded an anticompetitive agreement for the supply and distribution of fludrocortisone in the UK.[440] Under the terms of this agreement, both generic manufacturers agreed to stay out of the market; in exchange, Amilco received a 30% share of the increased prices that Aspen could charge on fludrocortisone, while Tiofarma was given the right to be the sole manufacturer of the fludrocortisone acetate tablets for direct sale in the UK.

661. In analyzing this case, the CMA first assessed the legal and economic context relevant to the agreement in light of the European Commission's precedents. In particular, the CMA emphasized the specifics of the *Aspen* case, as Aspen is not an originator manufacturer but acquired a marketing authorization for fludrocortisone acetate tablets decades after the original patent had expired.[441]

662. The CMA considered that Aspen, Amilco, and Tiofarma were potential competitors and that the agreement concluded had the object of preventing, restricting and/ or distorting competition in the market for the supply of fludrocortisone in the UK. The CMA considered:

- the legal and economic context, particularly: (i) that for 26 years no competing fludrocortisone acetate tablets product had been supplied in the UK, (ii) Aspen was the sole UK supplier of these tablets at the time the parties entered the agreement, and (iii) Tiofarma and Amilco, working together, were potential competitors of Aspen in the relevant market; and
- its content and objectives, notably the fact that the generic manufacturers committed not to enter the market concerned for the duration of the agreement, thereby preventing competition between the parties and, in consideration, received significant value transfers of a pecuniary and non-pecuniary nature.[442]

663. The CMA considered that the characterization of an infringement by object "must be adopted when it is plain from the assessment of the agreement at issue that the transfer of value provided under the agreement cannot have any explanation other than the commercial interest of both [parties] not to engage in competition on the merits."[443]

664. Moreover, the CMA added that "where there is no 'genuine dispute' relating to a patent underlying an agreement involving payments from an incumbent to a potential entrant, therefore, it is more straightforward to conclude (if the evidence supports this) that the agreement is a market sharing or market exclusion agreement."[444]

665. The CMA nonetheless analyzed the effects of the pay for delay agreement and found that it had the effect of notably delaying the likely independent launch of Amilco and Tiofarma's drug until the end of the agreement and artificially increasing the price for fludrocortisone acetate tablets up to 1800%.[445]

---

440 Case No. 50455, *Anticompetitive agreement, supra* n. 357, Chapter IV.
441 *Id.* ¶8.17.
442 *Id.* ¶8.93.
443 *Id.* ¶8.119.
444 *Id.* ¶8.116.
445 *Id.* ¶1.13.

III. Competitor collaborations

666. The life cycle of a medical product can be broken down into several phases, including R&D, manufacturing, and commercialization, which may often be pursued in collaboration with other pharmaceutical companies, either to share costs or expertise. Thus, the life sciences sector is characterized by the prevalence of R&D, joint manufacturing, co-promotion, co-marketing, and distribution agreements.

667. Horizontal agreements are agreements entered into between actual or potential competitors. Two companies are treated as actual competitors if they are active in the same relevant market. A potential competitor is a company that would, in the absence of the agreement and in case of a small but permanent increase in relative prices, be likely within a short period of time to undertake the necessary additional investments or other necessary switching costs to enter the relevant market in which the incumbent is active. Co-operation agreements between non-competitors that are active in the same product market but in different geographic markets are also generally considered as horizontal agreements.

1. Evaluation of Competitor Collaborations under US Law

A. *General Considerations*

668. As described in Section I above, certain agreements between competitors can be condemned as per se illegal under US antitrust law, such as price fixing, bid rigging, or market allocation agreements. Such agreements will be condemned regardless of whether the participants purport to describe the arrangement as a "joint venture."[446] But there are many kinds of collaborations among competitors that are lawful under US antitrust law, including joint ventures, agreements involving R&D, joint manufacturing, marketing or promotional arrangements, and more.

669. Bona fide competitor collaborations are generally evaluated under the "rule-of-reason" framework, which requires a careful look at whether (or to what extent) the agreements reduce or promote competition in various markets. Such collaborations enjoy rule-of-reason treatment because courts and US Antitrust Agencies have recognized their potential to promote competition and benefit consumers.[447]

670. The US Antitrust Agencies jointly issued the Collaboration Guidelines laying out the general principles that US Antitrust Agencies apply when evaluating potential collaborations.[448] Initially, agencies consider the "nature of the agreement," including its purpose and whether it may have harmed competition.[449]

---

446 *See, e.g.*, *Timken Roller Bearing Co. v. United States*, 341 U.S. 593, 598 (1951) ("Nor do we find any support in reason or authority for the proposition that agreements between legally separate persons and companies to suppress competition among themselves and others can be justified by labeling the project a 'joint venture.' Perhaps every agreement and combination to restrain trade could be so labeled.").

447 *Copperweld*, 467 U.S. 768 ("Other combinations, such as … joint ventures …, hold the promise of increasing a firm's efficiency and enabling it to compete more effectively. Accordingly, such combinations are judged under the rule of reason …").

448 *See* Collaboration Guidelines, *supra* n. 91, Chapter IV.

449 *See id.* 10.

671. If the competitive implications are not clear from an initial review, the agencies will conduct a more in-depth review evaluating several key factors. First, the agencies will assess the market shares of the participants and level of market concentration to assess whether the agreement may create or increase market power.[450] Second, the agencies will assess whether the participants have the "ability and incentive to compete independently."[451] Third, the agencies will examine whether potential market entry would be timely, likely, and sufficient to deter or counteract any anti-competitive harms.[452] Finally, if the investigation "indicates anticompetitive harm, the Agencies examine whether the relevant agreement is reasonably necessary to achieve procompetitive benefits that likely would offset anticompetitive harms."[453]

672. US Antitrust Agencies have also identified so-called safety zones, which are guidelines to help assess whether certain competitor collaborations are unlikely to draw antitrust challenge. These safety zones do not apply to agreements that would otherwise be considered per se illegal or subject to a merger analysis.[454] Subject to those caveats, "[a]bsent extraordinary circumstances," US Antitrust Agencies will "not challenge a competitor collaboration when the market shares of the collaboration and its participants collectively account for no more than 20% of each relevant market in which competition may be affected."[455]

B. *Joint Ventures*

673. A "joint venture" is a broad term that encompasses many kinds of potential collaborations in which separate companies pool resources to pursue some common business goal such as making or selling a product, sometimes with the creation of a formal joint venture legal entity. As with most potential collaborations among corporate entities, joint ventures are not immune from US antitrust laws.[456]

674. Joint ventures among competitors carry potential antitrust risks. The US Antitrust Agencies may investigate research joint ventures, production joint ventures, and joint-purchasing arrangements, among other types of collaborations. Joint ventures may raise more significant antitrust concerns when the participants have a high combined market share.[457] Both courts and agencies may be especially concerned about restrictions in collaboration agreements that may impact competition outside the scope of the collaboration and that are not reasonably necessary to achieve the arrangement's procompetitive effects.[458]

675. Even if there is no direct agreement to reduce competition outside of the collaboration, information obtained by the participants through a collaboration sometimes can have spillover effects that can facilitate coordination or otherwise reduce competition between the participants. In certain circumstances, these spillover

---

450 *See id.* 17–18.

451 *See id.* 19.

452 *See id.* 21–23.

453 *See id.* 11–12.

454 *See id.* 26.

455 *Id.*

456 *American Needle, Inc.*, 560 U.S. 199 ("[J]oint ventures have no immunity from antitrust laws").

457 See Collaboration Guidelines, *supra* n. 91, Chapter IV, ¶3.33.

458 *Id.* 4.

effects can outweigh the procompetitive effects of the collaboration. Companies entering competitor collaborations can reduce antitrust risk by limiting the participants' access to competitively sensitive information from the other party or the joint venture. That process can involve limiting the types of information that are shared (e.g., the parties may decide not to share customer-specific or forward-looking pricing information) or creating firewalls between employees involved in the collaboration and those with responsibility for making competitive decisions for their respective companies.

C. *Research and Development Agreements*

676. Certain kinds of research collaborations may also benefit from the terms of the National Cooperative Research and Production Act (NCRPA), which was the first antitrust statute to address joint R&D collaboration.[459] The NCRPA limits the damages available to plaintiffs challenging the legality of certain kinds of joint ventures[460] under US antitrust law and guarantees the application of the rule of reason standard.[461] The NCRPA, however, does not extend to many activities that may be deemed harmful to competition, including the exchange of cost information or allocating markets.[462]

---

459 *See* 15 U.S.C. §§ ¶4301–4306.

460 *Id.* ¶4301(6) (defining covered joint venture as "any group of activities, including attempting to make, making, or performing a contract, by two or more persons for the purpose of (A) theoretical analysis, experimentation, or systematic study of phenomena or observable facts, (B) the development or testing of basic engineering techniques, (C) the extension of investigative findings or theory of a scientific or technical nature into practical application for experimental and demonstration purposes, including the experimental production and testing of models, prototypes, equipment, materials, and processes, (D) the production of a product, process, or service, (E) the testing in connection with the production of a product, process, or service by such venture, (F) the collection, exchange, and analysis of research or production information, or (G) any combination of the purposes specified in subparagraphs (A), (B), (C), (D), (E), and (F), and may include the establishment and operation of facilities for the conducting of such venture, the conducting of such venture on a protected and proprietary basis, and the prosecuting of applications for patents and the granting of licenses for the results of such venture.").

461 *Id.* ¶4302.

462 *Id.* ¶4301(b) (excluding from definition of joint venture "(1) exchanging information among competitors relating to costs, sales, profitability, prices, marketing, or distribution of any product, process, or service if such information is not reasonably required to carry out the purpose of such venture, (2) entering into any agreement or engaging in any other conduct restricting, requiring, or otherwise involving the marketing, distribution, or provision by any person who is a party to such venture of any product, process, or service, other than – (A) the distribution among the parties to such venture, in accordance with such venture, of a product, process, or service produced by such venture, (B) the marketing of proprietary information, such as patents and trade secrets, developed through such venture formed under a written agreement entered into before June 10, 1993, or (C) the licensing, conveying, or transferring of intellectual property, such as patents and trade secrets, developed through such venture formed under a written agreement entered into on or after June 10, 1993, (3) entering into any agreement or engaging in any other conduct – (A) to restrict or require the sale, licensing, or sharing of inventions, developments, products, processes, or services not developed through, or produced by, such venture, or (B) to restrict or require participation by any person who is a party to such venture in other research and development activities, that is not reasonably required to prevent misappropriation of proprietary information contributed by any person who is a party to such venture or of the results of such venture, (4) entering into any agreement or engaging in any other conduct allocating a market with a competitor, (5) exchanging information among competitors relating to production (other than production by such venture) of a product, process, or service if such information is not reasonably required to carry out the purpose of such venture, (6) entering into any agreement or engaging in any other conduct restricting, requiring, or otherwise involving the production

677. More generally, it is not unusual for competitor collaborations to entail joint R&D. US antitrust law recognizes that such agreements are often procompetitive and, even apart from the ventures automatically subject to rule-of-reason treatment under the NCRPA, will be analyzed under the rule of reason. US enforcement agencies, however, have alleged that "Joint R&D agreements... can create or increase market power or facilitate its exercise by limiting independent decision making or by combining in the collaboration, or in certain participants, control over competitively significant assets or all or a portion of participants' individual competitive R&D efforts."[463] The overarching competitive concern is that even an R&D collaboration "may injure consumers by reducing innovation below the level that otherwise would prevail, leading to fewer or no products for consumers to choose from, lower quality products, or products that reach consumers more slowly than they otherwise would" or might "injure consumers by reducing the number of independent competitors in the market for the goods, services, or production processes derived from the R&D collaboration, leading to higher prices or reduced output, quality, or service."[464] These potential concerns are heightened when certain market circumstances are present, such as when the collaboration participants already hold market power over an existing market product, when the underlying R&D efforts are between firms that have existing IP in the space, or when regulatory barriers limit the ability of other market participants to "catch up" with the collaboration's R&D efforts.[465] If the R&D is geared towards a product that cannot adequately be assessed in the context of an existing product market, the agencies may assess the competitive impact in a "Research and Development Market."[466]

D. *Manufacturing Collaborations*

678. As with R&D collaborations, US Antitrust Agencies recognize that production and manufacturing arrangements can be procompetitive by allowing participants to combine complementary technologies and potentially create new consumer products that would not otherwise be produced.[467] But manufacturing collaborations that involve agreements on output levels or the price of the manufactured product may create a risk of anticompetitive harm, especially where the collaboration reduces two entities' ability or incentive to otherwise market competing products.[468]

(other than the production by such venture) of a product, process, or service, (7) using existing facilities for the production of a product, process, or service by such venture unless such use involves the production of a new product or technology, and (8) except as provided in paragraphs (2), (3), and (6), entering into any agreement or engaging in any other conduct to restrict or require participation by any person who is a party to such venture, in any unilateral or joint activity that is not reasonably required to carry out the purpose of such venture.").

463 See Collaboration Guidelines, *supra* n. 91, Chapter IV, 14.

464 *See id.*

465 *See id.* 15.

466 *Id.* 11–12 (discussing agencies' approach to R&D Markets).

467 *Id.* 13.

468 *See id.*

E. *Co-Promotion and Co-Marketing Collaborations*

679. US antitrust law recognizes that co-promotion and co-marketing agreements may be procompetitive where they allow participants to combine complementary assets in a way that allows products to more efficiently reach the marketplace.[469] But as with manufacturing arrangements, marketing collaborations that involve competitors jointly agreeing on price, output, or other competitive significant variables can raise concerns about potential anticompetitive harm. These concerns can be magnified if the collaboration undermines the participants' incentives to compete independently, such as by reducing the participants' incentives to engage in comparative advertising.[470]

680. Co-promotion and co-marketing agreements, like other joint ventures or competitor collaborations, are generally analyzed under the rule of reason. The Collaboration Guidelines explain how the agencies evaluate these agreements. To evaluate whether an agreement is a legitimate competitor collaboration entitled to rule-of-reason treatment, an agency or court will look first to whether the agreement integrates the resources of the companies to develop potential efficiencies. For example, a joint marketing or promotion agreement might result in the combination of complementary assets that permits the participants to commercialize products faster or more efficiently. These types of arrangements are likely to be considered lawful under a rule-of-reason analysis where the procompetitive benefits outweigh the likely anticompetitive effects. If, however, the arrangement will merely make it easier for the participants to exercise market power or increase prices, or if the potentially anticompetitive effects outweigh the efficiency-enhancing aspects of the arrangement, the arrangement may violate antitrust laws.

681. The FTC has challenged co-promotion and co-marketing agreements between brand-name and generic pharmaceutical companies in connection with patent settlements.[471] Private plaintiffs have also challenged these agreements on similar grounds.[472] In this context, a potential concern is that a co-promotion or co-marketing agreement might be one way for the brand company to surreptitiously transfer value to the allegedly infringing generic as an alleged payment to delay generic entry.

F. *Joint Lobbying Efforts and Noerr-Pennington Immunity*

682. Sometimes individuals or entities will join together to petition the government to take a certain action which results in eliminating or restraining competition.[473] The US Supreme Court doctrine of *Noerr-Pennington* immunity can shield such activity from antitrust liability.[474] The immunity applies to petitioning of all

---

469 *See id.* 14.

470 *See id.*

471 *See Impax Lab'ys, Inc.*, 994 F.3d 484.

472 *See, e.g.*, *In re Opana ER Antritrust Litig.*, 162 F. Supp. 3d 713; *In re Aggrenox Antitrust Litig.*, 94 F. Supp. 3d 243; *In re Niaspan Antitrust Litig.*, 42 F. Supp. 3d 735, 744 (E.D. Pa. 2014).

473 Companies can petition the government in their individual capacity as well, but this chapter is focused on §1 of the Sherman Act.

474 The immunity gets its name from two Supreme Court cases: *Eastern R.R. Presidents Conf. v. Noerr Motor Freight*, 365 U.S. 127 (1961) and *United Mine Workers of Am. v. Pennington*, 381 U.S. 657 (1965).

branches of government – judicial, executive, and legislative.[475] In determining whether the immunity applies, courts consider the "source, context and nature of the anticompetitive restraint at issue."[476] While the doctrine is often referred to as an immunity, most courts have concluded that *Noerr-Pennington* is an affirmative defense.[477]

683. *Noerr-Pennington* immunity has its roots in *Eastern R.R. Presidents Conference v. Noerr Motor Freight*,[478] where the Court found antitrust immunity for a publicity and lobbying campaign by a group of railroads to influence legislation which would be unfavorable to the trucking industry.[479] *Noerr* pointed to two reasons for its holding: (1) "To hold that the government retains the power to act in [its] representative capacity and yet hold, at the same time, that the people cannot freely inform the government of their wishes would impute to the Sherman Act a purpose to regulate, not business activity, but political activity, a purpose which would have no basis whatever in the legislative history of that Act"; and (2) "such a construction of the Sherman Act would raise important constitutional questions."[480] Thereafter, in *United Mine Workers of America v. Pennington*,[481] the US Supreme Court extended the immunity to the petitioning of the executive branch when it held that large coal producers and a union's efforts to influence the Secretary of Labor to set a high minimum wage in their industry and place restrictions on nonunion producers, which made it difficult for small coal producers to compete.[482] Later, in *California Motor Transport Co. v. Trucking Unlimited*,[483] the US Supreme Court extended *Noerr-Pennington* to efforts to influence the courts.[484]

---

475 *Eastern R.R. Presidents*, 365 U.S. 127 (extending immunity to legislative branch); *United Mine Workers of Am.*, 381 U.S. 657 (extending immunity to the executive branch); *California Motor Transp. Co. v. Trucking Unlimited*, 404 U.S. 508 (1972) (extending immunity to the judiciary and administrative agencies).

476 *Allied Tube & Conduit Corp. v. Indian Head, Inc.*, 486 U.S. 492, 499 (1988).

477 *See, e.g.*, *We, Inc. v. City of Phila.*, 174 F.3d 322, 326 (3d Cir. 1999). While affirmative defenses are generally waived if not raised in first responsive pleading, courts have held that *Noerr-Pennington* is not waived if it is raised within a reasonable time and other party is not prejudiced. *See, e.g.*, *Bayou Fleet v. Alexander*, 234 F.3d 852, 860 (5th Cir. 2000).

478 *Eastern R.R. Presidents*, 365 U.S. 127.

479 *Id.* 129–32.

480 *Id.* 137–38.

481 381 U.S. 657.

482 *Id.* 671 ("Joint efforts to influence public officials do not violate the antitrust laws even though intended to eliminate competition.").

483 In *California Motor Transport Co.*, the plaintiffs, highway carriers operating in California, alleged that defendants, competing carriers, conspired "to institute state and federal proceedings to resist and defeat applications by [plaintiffs] to acquire operating rights or to transfer those rights." 404 U.S. 509. The US Supreme Court first held that *Noerr-Pennington* immunity applies to petitioning the courts, but then held that the allegations in this case fell within the sham exception to the immunity. *Id.* 516.

484 In the context of petitioning in the adjudicative process, courts have held that *Noerr-Pennington* immunity applies to settlement agreements negotiated with government officials, *see, e.g.*, *A.D. Bedell Wholesale Co. v. Philip Morris Inc.*, 263 F.3d 239, 252 (3d Cir. 2001), to meetings between creditors to discuss acceptable terms in court proceedings, *see, e.g.*, *United Airlines v. U.S. Bank N.A.*, 406 F.3d 918, 921 (7th Cir. 2005), and to pre-suit demand letters, *see, e.g.*, *Sosa v. DIRECTV, Inc.*, 437 F.3d 923, 935–38 (9th Cir. 2006). Conversely, courts have generally held *Noerr-Pennington* does not apply to settlement agreements between private parties. *See, e.g.*, *In re Cardizem CD Antitrust Litig.*, 105 F. Supp. 2d 618, 635–44 (E.D. Mich. 2000), *aff'd*, 332 F.3d 896 (6th Cir. 2003). Courts are split on whether *Noerr-Pennington*

684. There are limits to the scope of *Noerr-Pennington* immunity. The US Supreme Court has found *Noerr-Pennington* not to apply to efforts to influence private standard-setting organizations where the antitrust injury resulted from the private body's adoption of the standards and not the government.[485] The US Supreme Court has also held that boycotts to achieve non-economic ends are protected under *Noerr-Pennington*,[486] while economically motivated boycotts are not protected.[487]

685. Likewise, there are a number of express exceptions to *Noerr-Pennington* immunity.[488] First, there is the sham exception.[489] "The 'sham' exception to *Noerr* encompasses situations in which persons use the government *process* – as opposed to the *outcome* of that process – as an anticompetitive weapon."[490] In *California Motor Transport Co. v. Trucking Unlimited*,[491] the Supreme Court applied the sham exception for the first time, finding that defendants' "pattern of baseless, repetitive claims" was not protected under *Noerr-Pennington*.[492] Later, in *Professional Real Estate Investors v. Columbia Pictures Industries (PRE)*,[493] the US Supreme Court established a two-part test to determine when litigation is a sham. First, a plaintiff must show that the underlying suit is "objectively baseless in the sense that no reasonable litigant could realistically expect to succeed on the merits."[494] If a suit is objectively baseless, courts then evaluate whether the underlying suit "conceal[s] an attempt to interfere *directly* with the business relationship of a competitor through the use [of] the governmental *process* – as opposed to the *outcome* of that process – as an anticompetitive weapon."[495] US Courts of Appeals are split over the correct analysis to apply to series or patterns of petitioning, with the Second, Third, Fourth, and Ninth Circuits holding that the two-step analysis from *PRE* applies to a single sham

---

applies to petitioning of foreign governments. *Compare Coastal States Mktg., Inc. v. Hunt*, 694 F.2d 1358, 1364–67 (5th Cir. 1983) (extending *Noerr-Pennington* to petitioning of foreign governments), *with Occidental Petroleum Corp. v. Buttes Gas & Oil Co.*, 331 F. Supp. 92, 107–08 (C.D. Cal. 1971) (holding *Noerr-Pennington* did not apply to petitioning of foreign governments).

485 *Allied Tube & Conduit Corp.*, 486 U.S. 492.

486 *NAACP v. Claiborne Hardware Co.*, 458 U.S. 886 (1982) (applying *Noerr-Pennington* to civil conspiracy claim by white merchants whose businesses were boycotted by the NAACP).

487 *FTC v. Superior Court Trial Lawyers Ass'n*, 493 U.S. 411 (1990) (holding *Noerr-Pennington* did not apply where the members of attorney association who provided court-appointed representation to indigent defendants boycotted after being denied a pay increase because the alleged restraint of trade, the anticompetitive boycott, was the means by which the defendants attempted to influence the government).

488 One situation for which the Supreme Court has refused to recognize an exception is conspiracies with public officials. *City of Columbia v. Omni Outdoor Advert.*, 499 U.S. 365, 382 (1991).

489 *Eastern R.R. Presidents*, 365 U.S. 144 ("There may be situations in which a publicity campaign, ostensibly directed toward influencing governmental action, is a mere sham to cover what is actually nothing more than an attempt to interfere directly with the business relationships of a competitor and the application of the Sherman Act would be justified.").

490 *City of Columbia*, 499 U.S. 380 (finding sham exception *Noerr-Pennington* immunity did not apply to billboard company who petitioned government to enact city ordinances which restricted new billboards and therefore prevented plaintiff from constructing new billboards).

491 404 U.S. 508.

492 *California Motor Transport Co.*, 404 U.S. 513.

493 508 U.S. 49 (1993).

494 *Id.* 60 (explaining that sham lawsuit cannot exist where there is probable cause to sue).

495 *Id.* 60–61 (internal quotation marks and citations omitted).

petition, while *California Motor Transport* applies to cases in which there are a series of sham petitions.[496]

686. The second exception is the ministerial exception. Courts have held that *Noerr-Pennington* immunity does not apply to situations where "the government acts in a merely ministerial or non-discretionary capacity in direct reliance on the representations made by private parties."[497] Courts have held that companies' tariff and rate filings with government regulators are not protected by *Noerr-Pennington* because such actions are not petitioning activity.[498] Similarly, courts have held that the FDA's listing of patents in the Orange Book is a ministerial act.[499]

687. Third, there is the misrepresentation exception. Making misrepresentations or false statements in the process of petitioning can eliminate the applicability of *Noerr-Pennington* immunity.[500] While the Supreme Court has not directly ruled on the issue,[501] lower courts have found the misrepresentation exception does not apply in the case of purely political contexts but does apply in administrative or court contexts.[502]

688. Finally, there is the commercial exception, which involves situations in which the government acts as a private participant in the marketplace.[503] Many courts, however, have declined to apply this exception.[504]

2. Evaluation of Competitor Collaborations under EU Law

A. *General Considerations*

689. The types of horizontal agreements which are considered most likely to result in procompetitive effects are covered by block exemption regulations: the R&D Block

---

496 *See PrimeTime 24 Joint Venture v. NBC*, 219 F.3d 92, 101 (2d Cir. 2000) (denying defendants *Noerr-Pennington* protection where they initiated a large volume of signal-strength challenges, affecting a satellite provider); *Hanover 3201 Realty, LLC v. Village Supermarkets, Inc.*, 806 F.3d 162, 179–83 (3d Cir. 2015) (finding defendants engaged in sham petitioning based on four petitions, including administrative and court challenges to permit applications, despite limited success on some petitions); *Waugh Chapel South, LLC v. UFCW Union Local 27*, 728 F.3d 354, 365 (4th Cir. 2013) (denying union defendants *Noerr-Pennington* protection where they filed 14 challenges to a commercial real estate and succeeded on only one of the challenges, thus suggesting a policy of initiating sham litigation); *USS-POSCO Indus. v. Contra Costa Cnty. Bldg. & Constr. Trades Council*, 31 F.3d 800 (9th Cir. 1994) (finding *Noerr-Pennington* protection where defendants were successful in 15 out of 29 lawsuits).

497 *In re Buspirone Patent & Antitrust Litig.*, 185 F. Supp. 2d 365, 369 (S.D.N.Y. 2002).

498 *See, e.g., Litton Sys., Inc. v. AT&T Co.*, 700 F.2d 785, 807 (2d Cir. 1983) (explaining the "mere *incident* of regulation – the tariff filing requirement" is not protected by *Noerr-Pennington*).

499 *See, e.g., In re Buspirone Patent & Antitrust Litig.*, 185 F. Supp. 2d 365 (listing of patent is ministerial and therefore not protected by *Noerr-Pennington*).

500 *In re Union Oil Co.*, 138 FTC 1 (2004) (finding Unocal was not entitled to *Noerr-Pennington* immunity for its misrepresentations to the California Air Resources Board).

501 *See Professional Real Estate Investors*, 508 U.S. 61 n. 6 ("We need not decide here whether and, if so, to what extent *Noerr* permits the imposition of antitrust liability for a litigant's fraud or other misrepresentations.").

502 *See In re Union Oil Co.*, 138 FTC 26 (surveying lower courts decisions and concluding "the weight of lower court authority, spanning more than thirty years, has recognized that misrepresentations may preclude application of *Noerr-Pennington* in less political arenas than the legislative lobbying at issue in *Noerr* itself").

503 *See, e.g., George R. Whitten, Jr. v. Paddock Pool Builders, Inc.*, 424 F.2d 25, 33 (1st Cir. 1970) (holding *Noerr-Pennington* immunity "for efforts to influence public officials in the enforcement of laws does not extend to efforts to sell products to public officials acting under competitive bidding statutes").

504 *See e.g., In re Airport Car Rental Antitrust Litig.*, 693 F.2d 84, 88 (9th Cir. 1982) (holding "[t]here is no commercial exception to *Noerr-Pennington*"); *Greenwood Utils. Comm'n v. Mississippi Power Co.*, 751 F.2d 1484, 1505 n. 14 (5th Cir. 1985) (noting "there should be no commercial exception to *Noerr-Pennington*").

Exemption Regulation[505] and the Specialization Block Exemption Regulation[506] (together, the "Horizontal Block Exemption Regulations").

690. Under the Horizontal Block Exemption Regulations, agreements between competitors that do not reach a certain level of market shares on the relevant market(s) may benefit from a safe harbor, provided that they do not contain certain clauses, known as "hardcore restrictions."[507] Hardcore restrictions are considered to be particularly egregious. Not only are agreements that contain hardcore clauses deprived of the benefit of the block exemption, but such arrangements are also generally considered unsuitable for an individual exception under Article 101(3) TFEU (*see* Chapter II).

691. The Horizontal Block Exemption Regulations also provide that certain types of provisions be excluded from the benefit of the exemption ("excluded restrictions"): contrary to hardcore restrictions, the rest of the agreement may still be exempted but terms pertaining to that restriction will not.

692. Although the Horizontal Block Exemption Regulations create a safe harbor, this does not mean that agreements which cannot be exempted (e.g., when the combined market share of the competing parties exceeds the relevant thresholds) have necessarily restrictive effects on competition. Agreements that do not benefit from the block exemption must therefore be assessed under Article 101 TFEU.

693. Agreements that have the ability to restrict competition normally fall under Article 101(1) TFEU. However, under Article 101(3) TFEU, agreements between undertakings that fall under the prohibition of Article 101(1) TFEU and do not benefit from the block exemption may still benefit from an individual exemption where:

- they contribute to improving the production or distribution of goods or to promoting technical or economic progress;
- they allow consumers a fair share of the resulting benefit;
- they do not impose restrictions on the companies concerned that are not indispensable to the attainment of these objectives; and
- they do not afford such companies the possibility of eliminating competition in respect of a substantial part of the products in question (*see* Chapter II).

694. The European Commission has issued Horizontal Guidelines, which provide the guiding principles to analyze the legality of these arrangements under Articles 101(1) and 101(3) TFEU.[508]

695. The Horizontal Guidelines observe that horizontal co-operation agreements can lead to substantial economic benefits by combining complementary activities, skills or assets, sharing risk, saving costs, increasing investments, enhancing product

---

505 Commission Regulation 2023/1066 of June 1, 2023 on the application of Article 101(3) TFEU to certain categories of research and development agreements (the R&D Block Exemption Regulation).

506 Commission Regulation 2023/1067 of June 1, 2023 on the application of Article 101(3) TFEU to certain categories of specialization agreements (the Specialization Block Exemption Regulation).

507 The mechanism is similar to that of the TTBER analyzed in Section 2 above.

508 European Commission, Guidelines on the applicability of Article 101 TFEU to horizontal co-operation agreements (the EU Horizontal Guidelines), 2023 OJ (C 259) 1.

quality and variety or accelerating innovation.[509] However, horizontal co-operation agreements could also give rise to competition concerns where the parties agree to fix prices or output, share markets, or where the co-operation enables the parties to maintain or increase their market power.

696. Article 101 TFEU requires a balanced assessment of the pro- and anticompetitive effects of horizontal co-operation agreements. The Horizontal Guidelines provide a grid of analysis for the main types of horizontal co-operation agreements, i.e., R&D agreements, production agreements including subcontracting and specialization agreements, purchasing agreements, commercialization agreements, standardization agreements including standard contracts, and information exchanges.

697. The most common types of horizontal co-operation agreements are treated in the Horizontal Guidelines, irrespective of their formalization. These agreements may in some instances result in the creation of a joint venture between the parties. Joint ventures (*see* Chapter III for more details on joint ventures from the perspective of merger control) which are not full function[510] must be analyzed as collaboration agreements between competitors under EU antitrust rules, and therefore assessed pursuant to Article 101 TFEU. Full-function joint ventures, on the other hand, are assessed under merger control rules and Regulation 139/2004.

698. The Horizontal Guidelines also must be read in conjunction with the European Commission guidelines on the application of Article 81(3) of the Treaty.[511] Under the Horizontal Guidelines, which were issued by the European Commission to help analyze cooperation between competitors, irrespective of the nature of that cooperation, an agreement can be complex, encompassing several phases of a product life cycle and thus several types of the above-mentioned agreements.[512] All the chapters of the Horizontal Guidelines pertaining to the different parts of the complex co-operation may be relevant. However, where there is conflicting evidence, it may be necessary to determine the center of gravity of these complex agreements which will prevail for the entire co-operation. To determine the center of gravity and the necessary framework, two factors should be taken into account: the starting point of the co-operation (e.g., if an agreement involves R&D and joint production of the results, the center of gravity likely would be deemed to be the R&D phase if the latter could not take place without the success of the former) and the degree of integration of the different function combined in the agreement (e.g., using the prior example, if the agreement provided for a full integration in the area of production and only a partial integration of some R&D activities, the center of gravity of the co-operation likely would be the joint production).[513]

---

[509] *Id.* ¶20.

[510] As per the criteria set by the European Commission Notice on the control of concentrations between undertakings. *See* Council Regulation 139/2004 of Jan. 20, 2004 on the control of concentrations between undertakings (the EU Merger Regulation), 2004 OJ (L 24) 1.

[511] European Commission Notice – Guidelines on the application of Article 81(3) of the Treaty, 2004 OJ (C 101) 8.

[512] EU Horizontal Guidelines, *supra* n. 508, Chapter IV, ¶¶6, 7.

[513] *See id.*

699. Although not covered in the Horizontal Guidelines, when conducting an assessment of horizontal co-operation agreements under Article 101 TFEU, it must also be determined if trade between Member States is affected to an appreciable extent. Moreover, the application of Article 101 TFEU to co-operation agreements does not exclude parallel application of Article 102 TFEU. Sector-specific rules might also apply to horizontal co-operation agreements.

B. *R&D Agreements*

a. *Introduction*

700. R&D is defined by the European Commission as:

> The acquisition of know-how relating to products, technologies or processes and the carrying out of theoretical analysis, systematic study or experimentation, including experimental production, technical testing of products or processes, the establishment of the necessary facilities and the obtaining of IP rights for the results.[514]

701. The pharmaceutical industry is heavily regulated and frequently involves R&D agreements.[515] Although R&D is highly encouraged throughout numerous EU initiatives,[516] it is a sufficiently important parameter of life sciences competition that R&D agreements can also restrict competition in certain instances.

702. In life sciences related sectors, the European Commission therefore analyzes competition not only between existing and future products, but also with respect to innovation efforts. In *Bayer/Monsanto*,[517] the European Commission introduced the concept of "innovation spaces," which encompasses all substitutable discovery targets for R&D efforts on which the undertakings compete. Although this concept has only been used in merger control so far,[518] it could also apply to the assessment of horizontal co-operation arrangements.

703. The intensity of R&D activity often varies between originator and generic companies. While originator companies heavily invest in R&D – their products are often patent-protected – generic companies which offer medicines that replicate originator drugs invest comparatively less. One study in Europe showed that R&D spending amounted to 17% of originator companies' worldwide turnover from prescription drugs, almost as much as marketing and promotion operations (23%) and manufacturing (21%). On the other hand, generic companies spent only 7% of their turnover on R&D compared to 51% for manufacturing and 13% for marketing.[519]

---

514 Commission Regulation 2023/1066 (R&D Block Exemption Regulation), *supra* n. 505, Chapter IV, art. 101(3).

515 European Commission SWD, Evaluation of the Horizontal Block Exemption Regulations (May 6, 2021), 17, tbl. 2.

516 *See* for instance, the European Commission's DG Research and Innovation, EU Research and innovation Strategic Plan 2020–2024 (Oct. 20, 2020) *available at* https://commission.europa.eu/documents_en?f%5B0%5D=document_title%3AEU%20Research%20and%20innovation%20Strategic%20Plan or the EU research and innovation funding program until 2027 ("Horizon Europe"), which is the EU key funding program for research and innovation with a budget of €95.5 billion (*available at* https://research-and-innovation.ec.europa.eu/funding/funding-opportunities/funding-programmes-and-open-calls/horizon-europe_en).

517 Case COMP/M.8084, *Bayer/Monsanto* (2018).

518 Case COMP/M. 7932, *Dow/DuPont* (2017).

519 Pharmaceutical Sector Inquiry – Final Report, *supra* n. 369, Chapter IV, 48.

704. R&D activities in the pharmaceutical sector can either relate to fundamental innovation (the discovery of new medicines) or incremental innovation, i.e., the improvement or novel use of existing medicinal products. The European Commission's Pharmaceutical Sector Inquiry – Final Report notes that R&D agreements in the pharmaceutical sector "may vary in form and scope and range from the outsourcing of certain R&D activities to the joint improvement of existing products or technologies or to the co-operation concerning the research or development of completely new medical products."[520]

705. For the R&D Block Exemption Regulation,[521] R&D agreements are those between two or more parties that relate to the conditions under which those parties pursue:
   - joint R&D of contract products or contract technologies and joint exploitation of the results of that R&D;
   - joint exploitation of the results of R&D of contract products or contract technologies jointly carried out pursuant to a prior agreement between the same parties;
   - joint R&D of contract products or contract technologies excluding joint exploitation of the results;
   - paid-for R&D of contract products or contract technologies (i.e., R&D that is carried out by one party and financed by a financing party) and joint exploitation of the results of that R&D;
   - joint exploitation of the results of paid-for R&D of contract products or contract technologies pursuant to a prior agreement between the same parties; or
   - paid-for R&D of contract products or contract technologies excluding joint exploitation of the results.[522]

706. More specifically, two main types of agreements can be distinguished depending on the organization of the joint activities carried out under a R&D agreement, which are either: (1) carried out by a joint team, organization or undertaking or jointly entrusted to a third party and considered joint R&D agreements, or (2) allocated between the parties by way of specialization in the context of R&D or exploitation. This type of agreement is qualified as specialization in the context of R&D.

707. Moreover, for the R&D Block Exemption Regulation to apply, joint R&D must be the main purpose of the agreement rather than ancillary. R&D agreements might be exempted under the R&D Block Exemption Regulation. The Horizontal Guidelines provide additional guidance as to the interpretation of the R&D Block Exemption Regulation as well as to the assessment of these agreements under Article 101 TFEU.

708. R&D may also include a technology transfer, which allows for the licensing or cross-licensing of certain IP rights (*see* Section II.3.A above). In this case the TTBER might apply.

709. R&D agreements should be distinguished from standardization agreements, which have as their primary objective the definition of technical or quality requirements

---

520 *Id.* ¶1249.

521 Commission Regulation 2023/1066 (R&D Block Exemption Regulation), *supra* n. 505, Chapter IV, art. 101(3).

522 *Id.* art. 1.

with which current or future products, production processes, services, or methods may comply. So far, standardization agreements have had little relevance for the life sector.

b. *Relevant Markets for R&D Collaborations*

710. The definition of the relevant markets in R&D agreements is more specific than for other types of agreements.

(1) Market Definition

711. The R&D Block Exemption Regulation defines the relevant product market as the market for the products capable of being improved, substituted, or replaced by the contract products. This regulation also defines relevant technology markets, i.e., the markets for the technologies or processes capable of being improved, substituted, or replaced by the contract technologies.[523]

712. *Product markets.* If the R&D cooperation agreement relates to the development of products that will improve or substitute existing products (i.e., competition in the market), the market(s) for those existing products or technologies are relevant for the assessment. Existing product markets may also be relevant for the assessment where the R&D agreement relates to products that will *replace* existing products (i.e., competition for the market). This is the case in particular when innovation may result in an entirely new product which creates its own new product market – for example, a new vaccine for a previously incurable disease.

713. If the R&D agreement concerns an *important input item* of a final product, the impact of the agreement may need to be assessed not only in the market for the component but also in the market for the final product (if the input item is technically or economically a key element of the final product and if the parties have market power with respect to the final product). For instance, if the relevant market is an existing product which the R&D only seeks to improve, the market share will be calculated based on the current sales value of the existing products.

714. *Technology markets.* As for technology markets, if the IP rights are marketed separately from the products to which they relate, the relevant technology market must also be defined. The relevant technology market consists of the technology (IP) that is sold or licensed and technologies that are regarded as substitutable by licensees. Where an R&D agreement concerns the development of technologies that will improve, substitute or replace existing technologies, the markets for those existing technologies are relevant markets for the Article 101 TFEU assessment.

715. *Early innovation efforts.* While the previous version of the Horizontal Guidelines distinguished, within new product markets, between situations where it is possible to identify at an early stage competing R&D poles, i.e., R&D activities aimed at creating new products that, if successful, will be at least somewhat substitutable,

---

523 *Id.* art. 1(16), (17).

and situations in which the innovative efforts in an industry are not clearly structured and do not allow the identification of R&D poles,[524] the current Horizontal Guidelines generally mention that "in some cases, undertakings may cooperate on R&D that is not closely related to a specific product or technology. The results of such early innovation efforts may ultimately serve multiple purposes and, in the longer term, feed into various products or technologies."[525] In that case, in order to assess the competitive position of the parties, it may be necessary to take into account factors such as the nature and scope of the innovation efforts, the objectives of the various lines of research, the specialization of the different teams involved or the results of the past innovation efforts of the undertakings concerned. This may require the use of specific metrics, for example, the level of R&D expenditure, or the number of patents or patent citations.[526]

(2) Calculation of Market Shares

716. *Product markets.* As regards market shares, if the R&D concerns a new product market aimed at replacing an existing product, market shares may be calculated based on the current sales value of the existing products. Consequently, the R&D Block Exemption Regulation bases its exemption on the market share in the relevant market for the products capable of being improved, substituted, or replaced by the contract products.

717. If the R&D concerns a new product which will create new demand, the Horizontal Guidelines indicate that a calculation of market shares based on sales is not possible.[527] The R&D Block Exemption Regulation therefore considers this type of agreement between non-competitors to be exempted irrespective of market shares.[528]

718. *Technology markets.* In the case of technology markets, the market share of a technology licensor is calculated on the basis of the sales by the licensor and all its licensees of products incorporating the licensed technology, as a share of all sales of competing products, irrespective of whether the competing products are produced using the technology that is being licensed. This methodology is used due to the general difficulty of obtaining reliable royalty income data and because calculations based on actual royalty income may underestimate a technology's position on the market.[529]

719. *Early innovation efforts.* As with new products that will create a new market, where the R&D agreement concerns innovation efforts that are, at the time when the R&D agreement is entered into, not yet closely related to a specific product or technology, market shares are impossible to determine and the R&D Block Exemption Regulation will apply irrespective of the market share thresholds.[530]

---

524 European Commission, Guidelines on the applicability of Article 101 TFEU to horizontal co-operation agreements, 2011 OJ (C 11) 1, ¶119 *et seq.*

525 EU Horizontal Guidelines, *supra* n. 508, Chapter IV, ¶133.

526 *Id.* ¶134.

527 *Id.* ¶99.

528 *Id.* ¶99.

529 *Id.* ¶96.

530 *Id.* ¶99.

c. *Safe Harbor of the R&D Block Exemption Regulation.*

720. To benefit from the safe harbor under the R&D Block Exemption Regulation, an R&D agreement must imperatively meet three conditions and pass a market share test.[531]

721. First, the parties must have full access to the final results of the R&D, including IP rights and know-how, for the purposes of further R&D and exploitation, as soon as they become available. Access rights may, however, be limited in two situations: (i) where the parties limit their rights of exploitation, in particular by specializing (e.g., restrictions on territories or customers); or (ii) research institutes, academic bodies, and specialized companies providing R&D as a service may agree to limit their use of the results for further research only.

722. Second, if the agreement provides only for joint R&D or paid-for R&D, without joint exploitation, each party must be granted access to the pre-existing know-how of the other party that is indispensable to exploit the results. Reasonable compensation is allowed.

723. Third, if the agreement provides for joint exploitation, it might only pertain to results which are protected by IP rights or constitute know-how and which are indispensable for the manufacture of the contract products or the application of the contract technologies.

724. If the above conditions are met, the exemption then depends on the parties' market shares:[532]

- If the parties are not actual or potential competitors, the exemption shall apply regardless of their market shares, for the duration of the R&D agreement and for 7 years after the product or technology entry in the market (if the results are jointly exploited).
- If the parties are actual or potential competitors, the exemption only applies for the above-mentioned period if, at the time the R&D agreement was entered into, the combined market share of the parties does not exceed 25% in the relevant product or technology market. For paid-for R&D and agreements pertaining to the exploitation of the results of paid-for R&D, the combined market share of the party financing the R&D and all the parties with which this financing party has concluded R&D agreements in relation to the same contract products or technologies cannot exceed 25%.

725. The exemption will continue to apply after that period provided the combined market share of the parties remains under the 25% threshold. The scope of the exemption is large and covers ancillary restrictions, such as the assignment or licensing of IP rights to one of the parties or the joint venture created for the purpose of the R&D.[533] If such provisions are not considered ancillary, the TTBER might apply (see Section 2 above).[534]

---

531 Commission Regulation 2023/1066 (R&D Block Exemption Regulation), *supra* n. 505, Chapter IV, arts. 3, 4, 5, 6.

532 *Id.* art. 6.

533 *Id.* art. 2(3).

534 Commission Regulation 316/2014 (the TTBER), *supra* n. 325, Chapter IV.

726. Following the European Commission's evaluation of the previous version of the Horizontal Block Exemption Regulations, which found the 25% threshold was subject to several criticisms, notably the absence of a threshold for non-competitors, the complexity of market shares calculation, and the view that the threshold was too low,[535] the R&D Block Exemption Regulation now applies to R&D agreements related to entirely new products and early innovation efforts without any market share threshold (*see* b.(2) above).

d. *Hardcore and Excluded Restrictions*

727. Article 8 of the R&D Block Exemption Regulation provides a list of "hardcore" restrictions that will deprive the agreement from the benefit of the exemption:[536]

- the restriction of the freedom of the parties to carry out R&D independently or in co-operation with third parties in a field unconnected with that to which the R&D agreement relates or, after the completion of the joint R&D or the paid-for R&D, in the field to which it relates or in a connected field;
- the limitation of output or sales, except for:
  - the setting of production targets where the joint exploitation of the results includes the joint production of the contract products;
  - the setting of sales targets where the joint exploitation of the results includes the joint distribution of the contract products or the joint licensing of the contract technologies, either carried out by a joint team, organization or undertaking or jointly entrusted to a third party;
  - practices constituting specialization in the context of exploitation; and
  - the restriction of the freedom of the parties to manufacture, sell, assign or license products, technologies or processes which compete with the contract products or contract technologies during the period for which the parties have agreed to jointly exploit the results;
- the fixing of prices when selling the contract product or when licensing the contract technologies to third parties, with the exception of the fixing of prices charged to immediate customers or the fixing of license fees charged to immediate licensees where the joint exploitation of the results includes the joint distribution of the contract products or the joint licensing of the contract technologies, either carried out by a joint team, organization or undertaking or jointly entrusted to a third party;
- the restriction of the territory in which, or of the customers to whom, the parties may passively sell the contract products or license the contract technologies, with the exception of the requirement to exclusively license the results to another party;
- the requirement not to make any, or to limit, active sales of the contract products or contract technologies in territories or to customers that have not been exclusively allocated to one of the parties by way of specialization in the context of exploitation;

---

535 European Commission, Evaluation of the Horizontal Block Exemption Regulations, *supra* n. 515, Chapter IV, 46.

536 Commission Regulation 2023/1066 (R&D Block Exemption Regulation), *supra* n. 505, Chapter IV, art. 8.

- the requirement to refuse to meet demand from customers in the parties' respective territories, or from customers otherwise allocated between the parties by way of specialization in the context of exploitation, that would market the contract products in other territories within the internal market;
- the requirement to make it difficult for users or resellers to obtain the contract products from other resellers within the internal market.

728. In addition, the R&D Block Exemption Regulation provides for two types of excluded restrictions:[537]

- *No-challenge clauses,* which can concern either the obligation not to challenge the validity of pre-existing IP rights held by the parties in the internal market and which are relevant to the R&D or the obligation not to challenge, after the expiry of the R&D agreement, the validity of IP rights held by the parties that protect the results of the R&D. However, it is possible to provide in the R&D agreement for a termination clause in the event of such a challenge.
- *Obligation not to grant licenses to third parties to manufacture the contract products* or to apply the contract technologies, unless: (i) the agreement provides for the exploitation of the results of the joint R&D or paid-for R&D by at least one of the parties, and (ii) such exploitation takes place in the internal market vis-à-vis third parties. This exception guarantees that the results of the R&D co-operation can benefit third parties and not only the parties to the agreement.

e. *Analyzing R&D Agreements under Article 101 TFEU*

729. For R&D agreements that do not fall under the safe harbor of the R&D Block Exemption Regulation, the main competition concerns that may arise are the following, they may: (1) slow down or reduce innovation, leading to fewer or inferior products in terms of quality, reaching the market later than they would otherwise, (2) reduce competition between the parties outside the scope of the agreement, for instance by increasing the likelihood of anticompetitive coordination and resulting in higher prices, or (3) foreclose other players from the market when the co-operation involves a company with significant market power for a key technology and where there is exclusive exploitation of the results of the R&D.

(1) Restriction of competition by object

730. R&D agreements are not generally considered as restrictions by object (*see* Chapter II on by-object restrictions). However, if R&D agreements are used to engage in a disguised cartel, e.g., by giving the parties the opportunity to engage in price fixing, output limitation, or market sharing practices, they could restrict competition by object.[538]

---

[537] *Id.* art. 9.

[538] EU Horizontal Guidelines, *supra* n. 508, Chapter IV, ¶¶141–142.

(2) Restriction of competition by effect

731. To assess the potential effects on competition of R&D agreements, relevant factors include the effect on innovation, the parties' combined market share, concentration ratios, number of players or innovators, and entry conditions.

732. R&D agreements generally are not likely to restrict competition in certain instances:

- *Pure R&D agreements* which do not include joint exploitation of possible results by means of licensing, production, and/or marketing (those agreements may only cause competition issues if the competition in innovation is appreciably reduced and leaves only a limited number of credible R&D competing poles) or agreements relating to co-operation at a rather early stage, far removed from the exploitation of possible results.
- *R&D agreements between non competitors or co-operation for which the parties are not able to carry out the necessary R&D independently* (with respect to their assets, know-how and resources), where the parties will not be considered potential competitors and the agreement will normally not have any restrictive effects.
- *R&D co-operation with outsourcing of previously captive R&D*, where R&D is carried out by specialized companies, research institutes, or similar entities which are not active in the exploitation of the results. Although such agreements often include transfer of know-how or exclusivity of supply clauses, they are not considered to be restrictions by effect because the parties are viewed as complementary rather than competitors.

733. R&D agreements are most likely to give rise to restrictive effects where the parties have market power in an existing relevant market, or, where competition with respect to innovation is appreciably reduced.[539] In particular, hardcore restrictions (e.g., those restricting freedom of the parties to carry out R&D independently or in connection with third parties in another domain or after the term of the agreement, limitation of output or sales, price fixing, territory restrictions) are at greatest risk of generating anticompetitive effects.[540]

734. Restrictive effects in situations where R&D agreements aim to improve an existing product or technology can be distinguished from those where they are directed at an entirely new product or technology, including early innovation efforts.[541]

735. In the first case, possible effects can be identified in the relevant market for the existing product or technology. In existing markets, however, effects on prices, output, product quality, product diversity, or innovation are only likely if the parties together hold a strong position, entry is difficult, and few other innovative activities can be identified. And if R&D only affects a minor component of a final product, the consequences on competition for the final items, if any, may be limited.

736. If the R&D is directed at the replacement of an existing product or technology, possible anticompetitive effects include delaying the development of the replacing

---

539 *Id.* ¶145.
540 *Id.* ¶141.
541 *Id.* ¶¶147–151.

product or technology. They are more likely to occur where the parties have market power on the existing product or technology market and are also the only undertakings engaged in R&D relating to a replacement for the existing product or technology. A similar effect can arise if a major player in an existing market cooperates with a smaller player or a potential competitor who is just about to emerge with a product or technology that may jeopardize the incumbent's position.

737. R&D agreements that provide for joint exploitation of the results of the R&D have a greater potential to restrict competition, although it depends again on whether one or more of the parties has market power. For instance, in the case *Pasteur Merieux/ Merck*, the European Commission analyzed the notified agreements underpinning the creation of a joint venture between the two companies, to which they would entrust their activities in the sector of vaccines for human use and in certain related sectors, within the EEA territory. The European Commission concluded that, by limiting the parties' ability to license their vaccines and vaccine technology to third parties for use in the EEA, other than through the JV, the agreements had appreciably restricted competition.[542] On the other hand, if the joint exploitation is carried out solely by means of licensing to third parties, restrictive effects such as foreclosure are unlikely.

738. As regards the second case, R&D agreements aiming to develop an entirely new product or technology or related to early innovation efforts are, in principle, unlikely to give rise to restrictive effects on competition, prices, or output in existing markets and the assessment must take into account that the outcome of R&D is by nature uncertain. However, this conclusion might be nuanced in the certain situations, especially if the R&D agreement brings together independent R&D efforts that are at a stage that is close to the launch of the new product or technology. In that case, restrictive effects may result directly from the coordination of the parties' R&D efforts, irrespective of whether the R&D agreement contains restrictions on the parties' ability to carry out R&D independently or with third parties. For example, the R&D agreement may lead one or more of the parties to abandon its R&D project and pool its capabilities with those of the other parties.

(3) Analyzing R&D Agreements under Article 101(3) TFEU

739. The Horizontal Guidelines indicate that "the assessment of restrictive agreements under Article 101 TFEU is made within the actual context in which they occur and on the basis of the facts existing at any given point in time."[543] In the context of R&D agreements, this means that it could be necessary to consider *ex ante* investments as well as the time to recoup those investments to assess these four conditions.

740. On the other hand, if the agreement results in an irreversible event (i.e., if once it has been implemented, the *ex ante* situation cannot be re-established), the assessment of efficiency gains must be made only based on facts at the time of its implementation. For example, in cases where parties agree to abandon their individual R&D activity, the agreement might not be incompatible with Article 101 TFEU if enough third

---

542 Case COMP/IV/34.776, *Pasteur Merieux-Merck*, ¶70 (1994).

543 EU Horizontal Guidelines, *supra* n. 508, Chapter IV, ¶163.

parties are competing with similar R&D projects and even if those projects fail in the future. However, the prohibition of Article 101 TFEU may apply to other parts of the agreement where there is no irreversibility. If, for example, the agreement also provides for joint exploitation, Article 101 TFEU may apply to that part of the agreement if, due to subsequent market developments, the agreement gives rise to restrictive effects on competition and no longer satisfies the conditions of Article 101(3) TFEU taking due account of *ex ante* sunk investments.[544]

741. By combining complementary skills and assets, many R&D agreements may bring about efficiency gains by resulting in more rapid development of improved or new products and technologies, leading to a wider dissemination of knowledge and thus leading to further innovation, and/or giving rise to cost reductions.

742. In the *KSB/Goulds/Lowara/ITT* case, the European Commission thus found that "under Article [101](3) a mere contribution to the promotion of technical or economic progress is required."[545]

743. Article 101(3) TFEU prohibits restrictions that go beyond what is required to realize the efficiency gains obtained by an R&D agreement. In the *Matra Hachette v. Commission* case, the General Court indicated that it must be established "that any adverse effects on competition resulting from the project are proportionate to the contribution made by it to economic or technical progress."[546] This means that there must not have been less restrictive means to attain the efficiency gain. However, this requirement can be easily attained. The European Commission stated in *Asahi/Saint Gobain* that the requirement could be satisfied if the agreement leads to beneficial results more quickly, efficiently and cost-effectively, even if the parties could have carried the R&D independently.[547]

744. In addition, an R&D agreement's efficiency gains must be passed on to consumers to the extent that such efficiency gains outweigh any restrictive effects on competition. The Horizontal Guidelines indicate that this pass-on to consumers is more likely if the R&D agreement results in the combination of complementary skills and assets. But if the parties' co-operation is based on similar skills and assets, it is likely that the R&D agreement could eliminate the R&D activity of one of the parties partly or entirely, which may be not benefit consumers.[548]

745. In assessing the likeliness of the efficiency gains being passed on to consumers, the market power of the parties is considered: the higher the market power, the less likely the efficiency gains will benefit consumers to the extent that they balance the restrictive effects on competition of the R&D agreement.

746. No individual exemption can be granted for agreements which might eliminate competition for the products or technologies in question. If enough competitors remain in the market, there will be no elimination of competition. The European Commission indicated in *Fujitsu AMD Semiconductor* that this element is met if

---

544 *Id.* ¶¶165–167.

545 Case COMP/91/38, *KSB/Goulds/Lowara/ITT*, ¶26 (1990).

546 Case T-17/93, *Matra Hachette SA v. Commission*, ECLI:EU:T:1994:89, ¶135 (July 15, 1994).

547 Case COMP/IV/33.863, *Asahi/Saint-Gobain*, ¶28 (1994).

548 EU Horizontal Guidelines, *supra* n. 508, Chapter IV, ¶¶159–161.

the parties do not acquire a dominant position as a result of the agreement.[549] In *Pasteur Mérieux-Merck*, the European Commission went further and found the element could be met if potential competition remained.[550]

C. *Manufacturing Agreements*

747. Manufacturing or production agreements vary in form. They may involve the creation of a joint venture. A full-function joint venture must be appraised under the relevant merger rules. A non-full function joint venture, however, is assessed under Article 101 TFEU. These agreements could also involve less structured forms of co-operation such as subcontracting arrangements.[551]

748. The relationship between parties to a manufacturing agreement can be either horizontal or vertical. There are three general types of production or manufacturing agreements:

   - Joint production agreements, where the parties commit to jointly producing certain medical products, APIs, or other semi-finished products.
   - Specialization agreements, where the parties agree that one or both will stop manufacturing a final medical product or a certain input and buy it from the other party, which agrees to produce and supply the product. When the agreement is reciprocal, the parties each agree to stop producing different products and to purchase them from the other party.
   - Subcontracting agreements, where a party allows another party to handle the manufacturing of a final medical product or a specific input. Subcontracting agreements may also be entered into to augment production, in which case the contractor entrusts the subcontractor with the production of a good continuing its own production of the same good.

749. In life sciences, CMO agreements are common. CMO agreements are a type of subcontracting arrangement where a company focuses its efforts on R&D or marketing and outsources the manufacturing of the drug.

750. Manufacturing agreements may be exempted under the Specialization Block Exemption Regulation.[552] Agreements that do not benefit from the block exemption must be assessed under Article 101 TFEU.

a. *Application of the Specialization Block Exemption Regulation*

751. The Specialization Block Exemption Regulation covers unilateral and reciprocal specialization agreements, as well as joint production agreements. This regulation establishes a threshold of 20% of the combined market share of the parties, below which agreements will be presumed to be compatible provided other conditions are met.

752. Subcontracting agreements and other horizontal production agreements that do not constitute specialization agreements are not covered by the block exemption.

---

549 Case COMP/IV/34.891, *Fujitsu AMD Semiconductor*, ¶45 (1994).

550 Case COMP/IV/34.776, *Pasteur Mérieux-Merck*, ¶97 (1994).

551 For the EU, the Council Regulation 139/2004 (EU Merger Regulation), *supra* n. 510, Chapter IV.

552 Commission Regulation 2023/1067 (Specialization Block Exemption Regulation), *supra* n. 506, Chapter IV, art. 101(3).

However, they are unlikely to harm competition when their combined market share does not exceed 20%. In this case, the European Commission considers that the agreement is likely to fulfill the conditions of Article 101(3) TFEU.[553]

753. The exemption provided for in the Specialization Block Exemption Regulation also covers ancillary restrictions, such as the assignment or licensing of IP rights to one or more parties.

754. The exemption will not apply to specialization agreements which directly or indirectly have as their object or effect any of the following restrictions:
   - the fixing of prices when selling the products to third parties, with the exception of the fixing of prices charged to immediate customers in the context of joint distribution;
   - the limitation of output or sales except for:
     - provisions on the agreed amount of products in the context of unilateral or reciprocal specialization agreements or the setting of the capacity and production volume in the context of a joint production agreement; and
     - the setting of sales targets in the context of joint distribution; or
     - the allocation of markets or customers.

755. The exemption can be withdrawn by the European Commission and the Member States competition authorities where they find that an agreement has effects that are incompatible with the conditions of Article 101(3) TFEU (e.g., where the market is very concentrated and competition is already weak).[554]

b. *Assessment under Article 101(1) TFEU*

756. If the parties' combined market share exceeds the threshold set forth by the Specialization Block Exemption Regulation or if the block exemption is unavailable, the manufacturing agreement could still be considered as having no significant restrictive effects if the market is considered dynamic. For instance, a manufacturing agreement may be permitted in a market in which entry is frequent and market positions change rapidly.

757. Generally, the main competition concerns that can arise from manufacturing agreements are:[555]
   - The direct limitation of competition between the parties with respect to output levels, quality, or price. This is particularly true in joint production agreements.
   - Coordination between the parties and collusive outcome, i.e., when the parties, as suppliers, coordinate their behavior leading to increased prices or reduced output, quality, variety or innovation. The Horizontal Guidelines find that this risk arises when the parties have market power or where the market has

553 EU Horizontal Guidelines, *supra* n. 508, Chapter IV, ¶231.

554 *See* Commission Regulation 2023/1067 (Specialization Block Exemption Regulation), *supra* n. 506, Chapter IV, at Recital 15; Council Regulation No. 1/2003, *supra* n. 130, Chapter IV, 205.

555 EU Horizontal Guidelines, *supra* n. 508, Chapter IV, ¶¶218–220.

certain characteristics, e.g., where the agreement increases the proportion of costs the parties have in common or involves an anticompetitive exchange of commercially sensitive information.

- Foreclosure of third parties in a related market where one of the parties has a strong market position. For instance, a joint production agreement in an upstream market might lead to higher prices of a key component of a downstream product, leading indirectly to higher costs for the downstream product. This could force a downstream competitor out of the market and enable the parties to the joint production agreement to increase their downstream market power and downstream prices.

758. As a general principle, agreements that limit output or share markets or customers are considered as restricting competition by their nature. However, there are two exceptions concerning manufacturing agreements:[556]

- if the limitation of output directly concerns the manufacturing agreement and the other parameters of competition are not eliminated, the manufacturing agreement will not be deemed anticompetitive by object; or
- if there is a joint distribution of the jointly manufactured products, the Horizontal Guidelines consider price fixing not to be anticompetitive by object.

759. Other relevant factors to determine whether the agreement infringes Article 101 TFEU include the concentration ratio in the market, whether the parties are close competitors, and the number of market participants. Even if the market shares of the parties and the concentration ratio are high, restrictive effects might still be unlikely in situations where the market is dynamic, i.e., barriers to entry or expansion are low and market positions change frequently.

760. Assessments of anticompetitive effects may also include the ability of customers to switch suppliers, the extent of spare capacity in the industry, whether competitors are likely to increase supply if prices increase, whether one of the parties to the agreement is an important competitive force, and the number and intensity of the links between competitors in the market (e.g., other co-operation agreements).

761. To assess whether a manufacturing agreement is likely to result in anticompetitive effects, the counterfactual situation that would prevail in the absence of the agreement must be analyzed:

- If the manufacturing agreement concerns a new market, it is unlikely to have restrictive effects on competition.[557]
- Direct limitation of the competition between the parties can arise in industries where production is the key activity (e.g., by affecting quality and/or range of products or innovation).[558]
- Anticompetitive foreclosure of third parties in a related market might also be a result of the agreement, especially where the contractual product is a

---

556 *Id.* ¶223.

557 *Id.* ¶227.

558 *Id.* ¶238.

key input in a downstream product and the co-operation enables the parties to raise the costs of their competitors in the downstream market.[559]

- A collusive outcome might result from the parties' increased market power, combined with commonality of costs between the parties or with an exchange of commercially sensitive information. A manufacturing agreement is more likely to lead to a collusive outcome if the parties already had, prior to the agreement, a high proportion of common variable costs.[560]

762. Manufacturing agreements can include commercialization functions, such as joint distribution or joint marketing. These arrangements may carry a higher risk of restrictive effects on competition because they are closer to consumers and could lead to the joint fixing of prices.[561]

c. *Analysis under Article 101(3) TFEU*

763. Manufacturing agreements can bring about efficiency gains resulting in cost savings through economies of scope and scale, better production technologies or ability to launch new products, or increased quality and variety by combining complementary skills and know-how, inter alia.[562]

764. Restrictions such as limitation of output or price fixing (except if the agreement involves joint commercialization) would not be considered indispensable and are therefore considered harmful to competition, however.[563]

765. Consumers are also unlikely to gain from cost savings resulting from output reduction or market allocation, compared to the cost-efficiencies resulting from economies of scope and scale. Moreover, the European Commission considers that parties are more likely to pass through variable cost savings to consumers than fixed cost savings. In general, parties with a stronger position in the market are viewed as less likely to pass through efficiency gains to consumers.[564]

766. Finally, a manufacturing agreement may result in spillover effects (i.e., side effects of an agreement between two companies which affect competition between them in another relevant market than the one covered by the agreement) in neighboring markets (upstream or downstream markets). The assessment of the manufacturing agreement would cover these spillover markets.[565]

D. *Co-Promotion and Co-Marketing Collaborations*

767. Under the Pharmaceutical Sector Inquiry – Final Report,[566] co-promotion agreements can be defined as the joint commercialization of a specific medical product under one single trademark. Co-marketing agreements involve the commercialization of a specific medical product by multiple parties under separate trademarks.

---

559 *Id.* ¶238.
560 *Id.* ¶240.
561 *Id.* ¶239.
562 *Id.* ¶248.
563 *Id.* ¶251.
564 *Id.* ¶¶252–255.
565 *Id.* ¶257.
566 Pharmaceutical Sector Inquiry – Final Report, *supra* n. 359, Chapter IV, 426.

Co-promotion and co-marketing agreements are frequent in the life sciences sector. They are often used by companies to commercialize their products in a territory where they lack the infrastructure to support local commercialization and/or, in case of co-marketing more specifically, as a means to have a better coverage of the market, through the use of second brands.

768. Co-promotion and co-marketing agreements are part of the wider category of "commercialization agreements," which cover the commercialization of a final medical product through co-operation between pharmaceutical companies for the sale, distribution and/or promotion of their products. These agreements can vary widely in scope, from joint selling agreements involving the joint determination of all commercial aspects related to the sale of the product to more limited agreements, which address only one specific commercialization function: distribution, after-sales services or advertising for instance.

769. Commercialization agreements can be vertical (one company supplies the other), horizontal (both parties market the product), or both. They can encompass several other forms of co-operation, such as exploitation of R&D, joint production, or specialization. The Horizontal Guidelines require a determination as to the "cent[er] of gravity" of the agreement.[567]

770. To assess a commercialization agreement, the relevant product and geographic market directly concerned by the co-operation must be defined. Moreover, the agreement might affect neighboring markets horizontally or vertically related to the market directly concerned by the co-operation. In such cases, those neighboring markets also need to be defined.

771. The main competition concerns that may arise from commercialization agreements are:

- price fixing,
- output limitation, which can be facilitated, because the parties can agree on the volume of products to be put in the market, therefore restricting supply;
- geographic or customer allocation: the Horizontal Guidelines mention this concern may arise where the parties' production plants are located in different geographic markets or where the agreements are reciprocal;[568] and
- such agreements may lead to exchange of commercially sensitive information relating to some aspects of the co-operation (commonality of costs) or other unrelated aspects, and result in a collusive outcome.

772. Agreements limited to joint selling may carry significant concerns as they usually have the purpose of coordinating the pricing policies of competing manufacturers or service providers. These agreements may not only preclude price competition between the parties on substitute products, but they may also impose quotas on the parties, within the framework of a system for allocating orders. As a result, such agreements are likely to limit competition by object. The Horizontal Guidelines indicate that even when the joint selling agreement is non-exclusive, i.e., where

---

567 EU Horizontal Guidelines, *supra* n. 508, Chapter IV, ¶320.

568 *Id.* ¶324.

the parties have the possibility to sell individually outside the agreement, it could lead to a coordination of the prices charged by the parties.[569]

773. Market allocation may be another risk of restriction by object when the parties are active in different geographic markets. In a reciprocal distribution agreement to distribute each other's products, the parties might deliberately allocate markets or customers to eliminate actual or potential competition between them. In a non-reciprocal agreement, the risk of market allocation is less pronounced. The Horizontal Guidelines consider that it is, however, necessary to assess whether the non-reciprocal agreement constitutes the basis for a mutual understanding to avoid entering each other's markets.[570]

774. The Horizontal Guidelines indicate that generally, commercialization agreements are not likely to give rise to competition issues if they are objectively necessary "in order to allow a party to enter a market that it could not have entered independently, or that it could not have entered with a smaller number of parties than those that take part in the cooperation, for example, because of the costs involved."[571]

775. Some reciprocal distribution arrangements may also have restrictive effects on competition, depending on whether the agreement is objectively necessary for the parties to enter each other's markets. The Horizontal Guidelines indicate that if the agreement reduces the independence of one of the parties with regard to the decision to enter or not enter the other parties' market(s), by limiting its incentives to do so, it is likely to give rise to restrictive effects on competition. The risk of restrictive effects is less pronounced for non-reciprocal agreements.[572]

776. As in other contexts, only commercialization agreements between competitors with sufficient market power will be deemed to restrict competition. On the other hand, the Guidelines indicate that if the combined market share of the parties is below 15%:

- the parties are unlikely to yield sufficient market power for the agreement to have restrictive effects on competition, unless such agreement contains hardcore restrictions of competition;
- in any case, it is likely that the agreement fulfills the conditions for an individual exemption under Article 101(3) TFEU. The doctrine has often considered this second affirmation as the existence of a blurred frontier between the safe harbor and the need to demonstrate efficiency gains: in some instances, where the parties' combined market share approaches 15%, although remaining below that threshold, it might be necessary to fulfill the conditions of Article 101(3) TFEU for the agreement to be individually exempted.

777. If the combined market share of the parties is above the safe harbor, the Horizontal Guidelines consider the agreement will have a likely impact on the market and its effects on competition must be assessed.

---

569 *Id.* ¶330.
570 *Id.* ¶332.
571 *Id.* ¶326.
572 *Id.* ¶327.

778. In general, joint commercialization involves the exchange of sensitive commercial information (e.g., marketing strategy, pricing). This can lead to a collusive outcome within and outside the co-operation with negative effects that need to be assessed in light of the overall effects of the agreement. For instance, it is unlikely that an exchange of pricing information is necessary in a joint advertising agreement.

779. Moreover, joint commercialization agreements are likely to give rise to restrictive effects "if [they increase] the parties' commonality of variable costs to a level which is likely to lead to a collusive outcome."[573]

780. This risk depends on the characteristics of the market and the market power of the parties: commonality of costs increases the risk of collusive outcome notably if the commercialization costs account for a large proportion of the variable costs of the product concerned (high marketing costs, for instance, compared to the overall price of the product).

781. Commercialization agreements between undertakings that fall under the prohibition of Article 101 TFEU and do not benefit from the safe harbor may nevertheless benefit from an individual exemption under Article 101(3) TFEU (*see* Section III.2. above).

782. Price fixing generally is not justified unless it is indispensable for the integration of other marketing functions and generates substantial efficiencies. This question is decisive for agreements that involve price fixing or market allocation, which would otherwise be considered restrictions of competition by object unless indispensable.

783. The Horizontal Guidelines also underline that savings resulting from the elimination of costs that were inherently part of the competition, without any integration of economic activities, cannot be regarded as efficiencies. For instance, a decrease in transportation costs resulting from customer allocation, when the logistical system of the parties is not actually communalized, cannot be considered an efficiency.

784. Efficiency gains must be proved by the parties, for instance, in the form of the contribution of the parties to significant capital, technology or other assets, as well as reduced duplication of resources and facilities.

785. The criterion pertaining to the absence of elimination of competition needs to be analyzed both on the relevant product markets but also on spillover markets.

786. With respect to co-promotion and co-marketing agreements more specifically, these are generally considered to be procompetitive. However, they may still entail restrictions of competition and, in practice, the level of risk is more important with co-marketing agreements than with co-promotion agreements, as the former are more likely to facilitate market sharing or price fixing arrangements and, as such, more exposed to antitrust scrutiny.

787. Indeed, in the case of co-promotion, the co-promoter will only engage in promotion activities on behalf of the marketing authorization holder, which will continue to book the sales. It is therefore accepted, in the context of co-promotion agreements, that the parties align on the strategy for the promotion and distribution of the product and that the marketing authorization holder controls such strategy.

---

573 *Id.* ¶336.

However, the parties must refrain from exchanging information or coordinating their behavior for products outside of the scope of their collaboration.

788. By contrast, in the context of a co-marketing agreement, each party is responsible for the commercialization of the product and, although certain aspects of the collaboration can be agreed or entrusted to one party only (e.g., regulatory authorizations, manufacturing), both parties independently sell the product, in competition one with the other. This implies greater caution and certain limits with respect to the determination of the strategy for the commercialization of the products. In practice, precedents are scarce and there is limited guidance from the authorities, with the notable exception of one case in Italy concerning a co-marketing agreement between Novartis and Italfarmaco for long-acting somatostatin products (marketed respectively under the brands Sandostatina LAR and Longastatina LAR). In this case, the AGCM imposed commitments on the parties with respect to certain provisions contained in their agreement which were considered to raise competition concerns.[574] The AGCM found that the agreement, as originally construed, provided for the exchange of commercially sensitive information and conferred on Novartis the right to control the commercial and promotional strategy of its co-marketer, Italfarmaco, through various means such as the validation of promotional documents, the imposition on Italfarmaco of obligations in terms of financial and human resources to perform the agreement and the imposition of a minimum market share to be achieved by Italfarmaco. The agreement also contained a non-compete clause preventing Italfarmaco from distributing similar drugs to the one subject of the co-marketing. The parties submitted commitments to address the AGCM's concerns, including removing the minimum market share clause, removing Novartis' control over Italfarmaco's promotional strategy, which thus no longer had to be aligned on that of Novartis, and limiting the exchange of information solely to data strictly necessary for the correct performance of the co-marketing agreement, thereby preserving the competition between the parties on the market. The obligation imposed on Italfarmaco to dedicate sufficient resources to the co-marketing agreement and the non-compete clause, however, were not modified as they were considered justified and proportionate in the context of a co-marketing agreement.

IV. Vertical agreements

789. Both US and European antitrust laws cover agreements that are entered into by companies that are not competitors but that are active at a different level of the supply chain – so-called "vertical agreements." While enforcers generally acknowledge that vertical agreements are less likely to result in restrictions of competition compared to horizontal agreements between actual or potential competitors, they can nevertheless give rise to specific competition issues that are addressed differently on both sides of the Atlantic. In particular, the European Commission and the NCAs in the EU have taken a more stringent overall approach to vertical restrictions than their US counterparts.

---

574 AGCM, Case No. I770, *ARCA/Novartis-Italfarmaco* (June 4, 2015).

1. Evaluation of Vertical Agreements under US Law

A. *General Considerations*

790. As with horizontal agreements between competitors, vertical agreements are generally evaluated under Section 1 of the Sherman Act (as noted above) and generally assessed under the rule of reason that allows a flexible inquiry into the competitive effect of the agreement at issue.[575] The rule of reason involves an analysis of the market at issue, including whether the agreement is likely to increase market power and whether new entry is likely.[576] If concerns are identified, the rule of reason can then entail weighing the agreement's reasonableness and procompetitive benefits against any alleged harm to competition.

B. *Distribution Arrangements*

791. Exclusive dealing arrangements, exclusive distribution arrangements, and distribution restrictions (e.g., territorial or customer restraints) are examples of distribution agreements subject to antitrust scrutiny.

792. Exclusive dealing arrangements may involve a supplier requiring a customer to purchase all of its products from the supplier, in the process precluding the customer from buying (or reselling) products from the supplier's competitors. Such arrangements are generally lawful given recognition that exclusive dealing arrangements can benefit competition in a variety of ways, such as providing more certainty for the parties involved and potentially improving product quality.[577] But such arrangements can raise concerns if they operate to substantially foreclose competition in a particular market. Foreclosure analysis generally requires a showing that the parties involved in the exclusive dealing arrangement have a sufficiently strong market position such that there are no alternatives for competing suppliers.

793. Distribution contracts may involve territorial or customer restraints, such as a distributor agreeing to sell a supplier's product only in a particular geographic area or to a particular category of customers. As with exclusive dealing arrangements, such restraints have recognized procompetitive benefits, such as allowing suppliers to have better control over their products or encouraging distributors (or retailers) to invest more in reselling the product if they have related exclusive rights to sell in a particular area or to certain customers. Conversely, such arrangements may raise antitrust concerns if they reduce or eliminate competition among suppliers or among distributors.

---

575 *See, e.g., Ramsey v. National Ass'n of Music Merchants, Inc.*, 798 F.3d 1186 (9th Cir. 2015) ("Vertical agreements… are analyzed under the rule of reason, whereby courts examine 'the facts peculiar to the business, the history of the restraint, and the reasons why it was imposed,' to determine the effect on competition in the relevant product market." (quoting *Nat'l Soc'y of Professional Eng'rs v. United States*, 435 U.S. 679, 692 (1978)).

576 *See, e.g., Leegin Creative Leather Prod., Inc. v. PSKS, Inc.*, 551 U.S. 877, 886 (2007) (describing the rule of reason and noting that "[a]ppropriate factors to take into account include specific information about the relevant business and the restraint's history, nature, and effect" as well as "[w]hether the businesses involved have market power").

577 *See Continental T.V., Inc.*, 433 U.S. 54 ("Vertical restrictions promote interbrand competition by allowing the manufacturer to achieve certain efficiencies in the distribution of his products. These 'redeeming virtues' are implicit in every decision sustaining vertical restrictions under the rule of reason.").

C. *Resale Price Maintenance*

794. RPM or vertical price restraints are arrangements where manufacturers place limits on the prices that distributors or retailers can set for certain goods or services. These arrangements can be categorized as either minimum RPM, wherein a price floor is set, or maximum RPM, wherein a price ceiling is set.

795. For many decades, RPM was considered per se illegal in the US.[578] In 1997, however, the US Supreme Court acknowledged that "vertical maximum price fixing 'may have procompetitive interbrand effects'"[579] and found that the rule-of-reason analysis applies to maximum RPM agreements.[580] In 2007, in *Leegin Creative Leather Products v. PSKS, Inc.*,[581] the Court held that all vertical minimum RPM agreements should be analyzed under the rule of reason. The Court explained that the "reasons upon which *Dr. Miles* relied [in 1911] do not justify a per se rule" and that "economics literature is replete with procompetitive justifications for a manufacturer's use of RPM."[582] In applying the rule of reason, the Court explained certain factors are relevant to the inquiry, such as: (1) "the number of manufacturers that make use of the practice in a given industry," (2) "the source of the restraint" – i.e., whether the impetus was the retailer or the manufacturer, and (3) whether the dominant manufacturer or retailer has market power.[583]

796. With RPM now subject to the rule of reason, companies have obtained greater flexibility at the national level to design procompetitive agreements.[584] Nevertheless, companies should be aware that minimum RPM agreements remain per se illegal under some state laws.[585] Companies worried about being subject to the rule of reason or state law per se rules can use alternatives to RPM agreements, such as unilateral action or policies that suggest resale prices.[586]

D. *Tying and Bundling*

797. A tying arrangement is "an agreement by a party to sell one product but only on the condition that the buyer also purchases a different (or tied) product, or at least

---

578 *See, e.g.*, *Dr. Miles Med. Co. v. John D. Park & Sons Co.*, 220 U.S. 373 (1911) (holding vertical price fixing is per se illegal); *see also Albrecht v. Herald Co.*, 390 U.S. 145 (1968) (holding maximum RPM arrangements should be evaluated under the rule of reason); *Leegin Creative Leather Prods.*, 551 U.S. 877 (holding minimum price maintenance arrangements should be evaluated under the rule of reason).

579 *State Oil Co.*, 522 U.S. 14 (quoting *Alt. Richfield Co. v. USA Petroleum Co.*, 495 U.S. 328, 343 n. 13 (1990)). The Court further noted that the concern from *Albrecht* "that maximum price fixing could be used to disguise arrangements to fix minimum prices," "can be appropriately recognized and punished under the rule of reason." *Id.* 17. The Court concluded that there is "insufficient economic justification for per se invalidation of vertical maximum price fixing… [N]ot only because it is difficult to accept the assumptions underlying *Albrecht*, but also because *Albrecht* has little or no relevance to ongoing enforcement of the Sherman Act." *Id.* 18.

580 *Id.* 22 (noting "rule-of-reason analysis will effectively identify those situations in which vertical maximum price fixing amounts to anticompetitive conduct").

581 551 U.S. 877.

582 *Id.* 878, 889 (explaining ways minimum RPM can increase interbrand competition).

583 *Id.* 897–98.

584 *See, e.g.*, *In re Nine West Grp. Inc.*, 2008 FTC LEXIS 53 (May 6, 2008) (modifying pre-*Leegin* consent order to allow Nine West to engage in RPM agreements).

585 *See, e.g.*, Md. Code Ann., Com. Law, ¶11-204 (explicitly prohibiting minimum RPM).

586 *See, e.g.*, *Gray*, 469 F.2d 748.

agrees that he will not purchase that product from any other supplier."[587] Bundling is a separate but similar concept, in that it refers to instances in which the products are sold together in fixed proportions, and are analyzed under the tying framework when customers cannot purchase the products separately.[588] Bundled rebating agreements (also known as bundled loyalty discounts), where customers receive discounts for purchasing multiple products together from the same producer, may also be found to have anticompetitive effects similar to tying arrangements.[589]

798. Early decisions on tying arrangements held the arrangements to be per se illegal.[590] While the per se standard still nominally applies, the US Supreme Court's "strong disapproval of tying arrangements has substantially diminished."[591] Thus, a plaintiff must make additional showings under the per se standard.[592] To prove a tying arrangement per se unlawful under Section 1 of the Sherman Act,[593] the plaintiff must show: (1) two separate products or services, (2) that the two products are tied together or customers are coerced, (3) that the seller possesses sufficient market power in the tying product market sufficient to coerce acceptance of the tied product, and (4) that the tying arrangement affects a substantial volume of commerce.[594] Some courts have also required proof that the tie has anticompetitive effects,[595] and others have considered whether there was a business justification for the tie.[596] Furthermore, where the conditions for per se unlawfulness have not been met, a tying arrangement can still be considered unlawful under the rule of reason.[597]

799. In showing the first element of per se tying arrangement, involving two separate products, the inquiry "turns not on the functional relation between the [products], but rather on the character of the demand for the[m]."[598] Thus, to have two separate

---

587 *Northern Pac. Ry. Co.*, 356 U.S. 5–6.

588 Bundling discounts are also often challenged under Section 2.

589 *See LePage's Inc. v. 3M*, 324 F.3d 141, 155 (3d Cir. 2003) (en banc) (comparing bundled rebates to tying); *Cascade Health Sols. v. PeaceHealth*, 515 F.3d 883, 897 (9th Cir. 2008) (explaining that "it is evident that bundled discounts, while potentially procompetitive by offering bargains to consumers, can also pose the threat of anticompetitive impact by excluding less diversified but more efficient producers").

590 *See, e.g., Northern Pac. Ry. Co.*, 356 U.S. 5–7 (noting tying arrangements are "among the practices which the courts have heretofore deemed to be unlawful in and of themselves").

591 *Illinois Tool Works Inc.*, 547 U.S. 35.

592 *Id.*; *see also PSI Repair Servs., Inc. v. Honeywell, Inc.*, 104 F.3d 811, 815 n. 3 (6th Cir. 1997) (noting that the per se and rule of reason have merged in the case of tying arrangements).

593 Tying arrangements can also be challenged under § 2 of the Sherman Act, §3 of the Clayton Act, and §5 of the FTC Act.

594 Tying cases may list three or four elements a plaintiff must prove, but the essence of the elements is the same. *See, e.g., Paladin Assocs., Inc. v. Montana Power Co.*, 328 F.3d 1145, 1159 (9th Cir. 2003); *Gordon v. Lewistown Hosp.*, 423 F.3d 184, 214 (3d Cir. 2005); *United States v. Microsoft Corp.*, 253 F.3d 34, 85 (D.C. Cir. 2001); *Suture Express, Inc. v. Owens & Minor Distrib., Inc.*, 851 F.3d 1029, 1037 (10th Cir. 2017).

595 *See, e.g., Wells Real Estate, Inc. v. Greater Lowell Bd. of Realtors*, 850 F.2d 803, 815 (1st Cir. 1988) (finding "tying claim must fail absent any proof of anticompetitive effects in the market for the tied product").

596 *See, e.g., United States v. Jerrold Elecs. Corp.*, 187 F. Supp. 545, 557–58 (E.D. Pa. 1960) (finding tie-in justifiable for a limited period of time during the development period of the new industry), *aff'd*, 365 U.S. 567 (1961).

597 *See Microsoft Corp.*, 253 F.3d 94–95 (rejecting application of per se tying liability and remanding for evaluation under the rule of reason).

598 *Jefferson Parish Hosp. Dist. No. 2 v. Hyde*, 466 U.S. 2, 19 (1984) (holding anesthesiology services separate from other hospital services).

products "there must be sufficient consumer demand so that it is efficient for a firm to provide [them] separately."[599] In applying this test, courts have held the following, for example, to be separate products: credit card services and debit card services,[600] vehicles and vehicles advertising,[601] and state-specific bar review courses and multistate bar review courses.[602] By contrast, courts have held the following, for example, not to be separate products: marketable and hard-to-market vehicles,[603] a single family residence and the leased property on which the residence was built,[604] and mortgage financing and an attorney's fees pursuant to a mortgage finance transaction.[605]

800. The second element a plaintiff must prove is that the seller conditioned purchase of both products. Most courts require plaintiffs to show coercion.[606] Simply encouraging and attempting to persuade do not constitute coercion.[607] Thus, where the buyer has the option to purchase the products separately or together as a bundle, and the option to purchase the products separately is economically feasible, there is no illegal tying.[608]

801. The third element a plaintiff must prove is that the seller has "sufficient economic power with respect to the tying product to appreciably restrain free competition in the market for the tied product."[609] The US Supreme Court has made clear that "sufficient economic power" exists only when the seller has market power in the tying market.[610] "Market power is the power 'to force a purchaser to do something that he would not do in a competitive market' and often takes the form of a seller's ability 'to raise price and restrict output.'"[611] Market power is found when the seller possesses a large share in the tying market or where the seller offers a unique product that competitors cannot provide.[612]

---

599 *Eastman Kodak Co. v. Image Technical Services, Inc.*, 504 U.S. 451, 462 (1992) (finding service and parts for the maintenance of photocopiers and micrographic equipment constituted separate products).

600 *In re Visa Check/Mastermoney Antitrust Litig.*, 297 F. Supp. 2d 503 (E.D.N.Y. 2003), *aff'd sub nom.*, *Wal-Mart Stores, Inc. v. Visa U.S.A., Inc.*, 396 F.3d 96 (2d Cir. 2005).

601 *Dauro Adver., Inc. v. GMC*, 75 F. Supp. 2d 1165 (D. Colo. 1999).

602 *Park v. Thomson Corp.*, No. 05-2931, 2007 U.S. Dist. LEXIS 2001, *9–10 (S.D.N.Y. Jan. 11, 2007).

603 *Southern Pines Chrysler-Plymouth, Inc. v. Chrysler Corp.*, 826 F.2d 1360, 1363 (4th Cir. 1987).

604 *Souza v. Estate of Bishop*, 821 F.2d 1332, 1335–36 (9th Cir. 1987).

605 *Amey, Inc. v. Gulf Abstract & Title, Inc.*, 758 F.2d 1486, 1503 (11th Cir. 1985).

606 *See, e.g.*, *Paladin Assocs., Inc.*, 328 F.3d 1159 ("Essential to the second element of a tying claim is proof that the seller *coerced* a buyer to purchase the tied product."); *Aquatherm Indus., Inc. v. Florida Power & Light Co.*, 145 F.3d 1258, 1263 (11th Cir. 1998) (affirming dismissal of tying arrangement claim because "the essential element of coercion on the part of the product seller is absent completely from the facts presented").

607 *See, e.g.*, *Paladin Assocs., Inc.*, 328 F.3d 1160 (noting "[o]ur sister circuits have held that evidence of 'mere sales pressure' does not constitute evidence of coercion").

608 *See, e.g.*, *id.* 1159–60.

609 *Northern Pac. Ry. Co.*, 356 U.S. 2.

610 *Illinois Tool Works Inc. v. Indep. Ink, Inc.*, 547 U.S. 28, 42–43 (2006) (rejecting the presumption that a patent confers market power).

611 *Suture Express, Inc. v. Owens & Minor Distrib., Inc.*, 851 F.3d 1029, 1039 (10th Cir. 2017) (quoting *Jefferson Parish Hosp. Dist. No. 2 v. Hyde*, 466 U.S. 2, 14 (1984) and *Eastman Kodak Co. v. Image Technical Services, Inc.*, 504 U.S. 451, 464 (1992)); *see also Suture Express*, 851 F.3d 1039 ("Without power in the tying market, we would expect that a customer would not feel obliged to take the tie, as he could simply go elsewhere to buy the tying and tied products separately.").

612 *Jefferson Parish Hosp. Dist. No. 2 v. Hyde*, 466 U.S. 2, 17 (1984).

802. To prove the fourth and final element, a plaintiff must show the tying arrangement has a substantial effect on interstate commerce.[613] The US Supreme Court has explained that "the controlling consideration is simply whether a total amount of business, substantial enough in terms of dollar-volume so as not to be merely *de minimis*, is foreclosed to competitors by the tie."[614] "[T]he relevant figure is the total volume of sales tied by the sales policy under challenge, not the portion of this total accounted for by the particular plaintiff who brings suit."[615] The US Supreme Court has held amounts as low as $60,800 to be substantial.[616]

803. Even where the plaintiff makes out the per se elements, courts may look at the additional element of anticompetitive effect in the tied product market,[617] or consider whether there are any business justifications[618] and consequently find that the tying arrangements are not per se illegal.

2. Vertical Agreements under EU Law

A. *Definition of a Vertical Agreement*

804. In addition to prohibiting certain horizontal agreements, the prohibition set forth in Article 101(1) TFEU covers any agreement that would unduly distort the production, circulation, and distribution of goods and services along a given production or value chain, including vertical agreements between undertakings operating at different levels of a production or value chain.

805. Regulation on the application of Article 101(3) TFEU to categories of vertical agreements and concerted practices[619] (the VBER) defines a vertical agreement as:

> An agreement or concerted practice between two or more undertakings, each of which operates, for the purposes of the agreement or the concerted practice, at a different level of the production or distribution chain, and relating to the conditions under which the parties may purchase, sell or resell certain goods or services.[620]

806. Thus, vertical agreements relate to the conditions under which their parties, i.e., the supplier and the buyer, may purchase, sell, or resell certain goods or services. Vertical agreements relating to all final and intermediate goods and services are

---

613 *Northern Pac. Ry. Co. v. United States*, 356 U.S. 1, 11 (1958) (explaining tying arrangement must affect a "not insubstantial amount of interstate commerce" (internal quotation marks and citation omitted)).

614 *Fortner Enters., Inc. v. U.S. Steel Corp.*, 394 U.S. 495, 501 (1969).

615 *Id.* 502.

616 *United States v. Loew's, Inc.*, 371 U.S. 38, 49 (1961).

617 *See, e.g., E & L Consulting Ltd. v. Doman Indus. Ltd*, 472 F.3d 23, 31–32 (2d Cir. 2006) (explaining plaintiffs must show anticompetitive effects as an element of their tying claim).

618 *See, e.g., Collins Inkjet Corp. v. Eastman Kodak Co.*, 781 F.3d 264, 271 (6th Cir. 2015) (explaining a "defendant is still permitted to argue as a sort of affirmative defense that its tying arrangement has procompetitive effects, or, alternatively, has a valid business justification"); *see also Mozart Co. v. Mercedes Benz of N.A., Inc.*, 833 F.2d 1342, 1348–51 (9th Cir. 1987) (affirming jury's finding that the only feasible way to control the quality of Mercedes replacement parts was the use of the tying arrangement).

619 Commission Regulation 2022/720 of May 10, 2022 on the application of Article 101(3) TFEU to categories of vertical agreements and concerted practices (the VBER), 2022 OJ (L 134) 4.

620 *Id.* art. 1.1(a).

covered. A vertical agreement can also be found in situations where: (i) the supplier is both a manufacturer and distributor of goods, while the buyer is only a distributor and not also a competing undertaking at the manufacturing level, or (ii) the supplier is a provider of services operating at several levels of trade, while the buyer operates at the retail level and is not a competing undertaking at the level of trade where it purchases the contract service.[621] This covers so-called "dual distribution," i.e., cases where a supplier distributes its products or services to customers both directly and through third-party distributors.

807. For Article 101 TFEU to apply to vertical agreements, the agreement or concerted practice must be between two or more undertakings, within the meaning of EU competition law. Vertical agreements with final consumers not operating as undertakings do not fall under Article 101(1) TFEU, as that provision applies only to agreements between undertakings, decisions by associations of undertakings, and concerted practices of undertakings.

808. However, Article 101 TFEU will generally not apply to an agency agreement where the principal and its agent are considered for the purposes of the agreement to constitute one undertaking. The determining factor in defining an agency agreement for the application of Article 101 TFEU is the financial or commercial risk borne by the agent in relation to the activities for which it has been appointed as an agent by the principal. Thus, the agreement will be qualified as an agency agreement if the agent does not bear any, or bears only insignificant, risks in relation to the contracts concluded or negotiated on behalf of the principal, in relation to market-specific investments for that field of activity, and in relation to other activities required by the principal to be undertaken on the same product market. Where the agent bears one or more of the relevant risks, the agreement between agent and principal does not constitute an agency agreement for the purpose of applying Article 101 TFEU. In that situation, the agent will be treated as an independent undertaking and the agreement between agent and principal will be subject to Article 101 TFEU as any other vertical agreement.[622]

809. In the case of agency agreements, the selling or purchasing function of the agent forms part of the principal's activities. Since the principal bears the commercial and financial risks related to the selling and purchasing of the contract goods and services, all obligations imposed on the agent in relation to the contracts concluded or negotiated on behalf of the principal fall outside Article 101 TFEU.[623]

810. However, since the agent is a separate undertaking from the principal, the provisions which concern the relationship between the agent and the principal may infringe upon Article 101(1) TFEU. Therefore, a provision preventing the principal from appointing other agents to a given type of transaction, customer or territory, or a provision preventing the agent from acting as an agent or distributor

---

621 *Id.* arts. 1(1)(c) & 2(4); *see also* Commission Notice – Guidelines on Vertical Restraints, SEC (2010) 411 final, ¶¶27–28, 94.

622 *See* Commission Communication, Guidelines on Vertical Restraints (the Vertical Guidelines), 2010 OJ (C 130) 1, ¶¶13–17.

623 *See id.* ¶¶18–21.

of undertakings which compete with the principal, may fall within the scope of Article 101(1) TFEU.

811. An agency agreement may also fall within the scope of Article 101(1) TFEU where it facilitates collusion. That could, for instance, be the case when multiple principals use the same agents while collectively preventing others from using these agents, or when they use the agents to collude on marketing strategy or to exchange sensitive market information between the principals.

812. Finally, Article 101 TFEU does not apply to unilateral conduct.[624] To qualify as an agreement within the meaning of Article 101 TFEU, it is sufficient that the parties have expressed their joint intention to conduct themselves in the market in a specific way.[625] In the case of a vertical agreement, there are two ways in which acquiescence to a particular unilateral policy can be established. First, the acquiescence can be deduced from the powers conferred upon the parties in a general agreement drawn up in advance.[626] Secondly, in the absence of such an explicit acquiescence, competition authorities can show the existence of tacit acquiescence.[627] It is then necessary to show, first, that one party requires explicitly or implicitly the co-operation of the other party for the implementation of its unilateral policy and, second, that the other party complied with that requirement by implementing that unilateral policy in practice.[628]

B. *Presumption of Validity of Vertical Agreements*

813. Vertical agreements are generally considered less harmful than horizontal agreements. They may nonetheless raise barriers to entry, soften competition or facilitate collusion among buyers or suppliers, and create obstacles to market integration. In its Vertical Guidelines, the European Commission considers that:

> For most vertical restraints, competition concerns can only arise if there is insufficient competition at one or more levels of trade, that is, if there is some degree of market power at the level of the supplier or the buyer or at both levels. Vertical restraints are generally less harmful than horizontal restraints and may provide substantial scope for efficiencies.[629]

---

624 Case 107/82, *AEG-Telefunken AG*, ECLI:EU:C:1983:293, (Oct 25, 1983); Cases 228/82 and 229/82, *Ford-Werke Aktiengesellschaft*, ECLI:EU:C:1984:80, ¶16 (Feb. 28, 1984); Case T-43/92, *Dunlop Slazenger*, ECLI:EU:T:1994:79, ¶56 (July 7, 1994); Case T-368/00, *General Motors Nederland BV*, ECLI:EU:T:2003:275, ¶¶58, 79 (Oct. 21, 2003).

625 Case T-41/96, *Bayer AG*, ECLI:EU:T:2000:242, ¶62 (Oct. 26, 2000); Case C-74/04 P, *Volkswagen AG*, ECLI:EU:C:2006:460, ¶37 (July 13, 2006); Case T-7/89, *Hercules Chemicals NV*, ECLI:EU:T:1991:75, ¶256 (Dec. 17, 1991); *see also* Case 41/69, *ACF Chemiefarma*, ECLI:EU:C:1970:71, (July 15, 1970).

626 Vertical Guidelines, *supra* n. 622, Chapter IV, ¶25; *see, e.g.*, Case C-277/87, *Sandoz*, ECLI:EU:C:1990:6, (Jan 11, 1990) and Case C-279/87, *Tipp-Ex GmbH & Co. KG v. Commission*, ECLI:EU:C:1990:57, (Feb. 8, 1990). *See also*, Case T-368/00, *General Motors Nederland BV*, ECLI:EU:T:2003:275, (Oct. 21, 2003).

627 Vertical Guidelines, *supra* n. 622, Chapter IV, ¶25; Case C-74/04 P, *Volkswagen AG*, ECLI:EU:C:2006:460, ¶37 (July 13, 2006).

628 Vertical Guidelines, *supra* n. 622, Chapter IV, ¶25; Case T-41/96, *Bayer AG*, ECLI:EU:T:2000:242, (Oct. 26, 2000).

629 European Commission, Memo/138, *Antitrust: Commission Adopts Revised Competition Rules for Vertical Agreements* (Apr. 20, 2010), *available at* https://ec.europa.eu/commission/presscorner/detail/en/MEMO_10_138.

814. Due to the lesser degree of harm caused by vertical agreements, the VBER presumes that restrictions of competition included in vertical agreements are compatible with competition law under certain conditions. The exemption will be granted to a vertical agreement in its entirety only if: (i) the parties' respective market shares are below 30% in each of their respective market, and (ii) the agreement does not contain any hardcore restrictions. When an agreement contains a so-called "excluded restriction" and the parties' respective market shares are below 30%, the exemption will not apply to this restriction only, without prejudice of the rest of the arrangement.[630]

815. The life sciences industry is by nature subject to many IP issues, and vertical agreements often include provisions relating to those rights. In principle, agreements related to IP fall outside the scope of the VBER. However, Article 2(3) of the VBER presumes that the exemption shall apply to agreements related to IP where five conditions are satisfied:[631]

- the IPR provisions must be part of a vertical agreement under which the parties purchase, sell or resell goods or services. The exemption will not apply to an agreement concerning the assignment or licensing of IPRs for the manufacture of goods, or a pure licensing agreement;[632]
- the IPRs must be assigned to, or licensed for use by, the buyer. The exemption will not apply where the IPRs are provided by the buyer to the supplier or, in a subcontracting agreement where the supplier transfers know-how to a subcontractor;[633]
- the IPR provisions must not constitute the primary object of the agreement;[634]
- the IPR provisions must be directly related to use, sale or resale of goods or services by the buyer or its customers.[635] The IPR provisions will normally concern the marketing of the contract goods or services; and
- the IPR provisions for the contract goods or services must not contain restrictions of competition having the same object as vertical restraints which are not exempted under the VBER.[636]

816. In general, the assignment or license is covered by the VBER when the use or sale of goods or services can be performed more effectively in combination with the use of the IP rights. The main IP rights which are likely to be able to meet this requirement are trademarks, know-how and copyright.[637] Certain IP agreements that do not meet the requirements of Article 2(3) will benefit from the TTBER.

817. In the context of vertical relationships, the relevant market with respect to the supplier is the market in which it sells the contract products to the buyer. With

---

630 VBER, *supra* n. 619, Chapter IV, TFEU arts. 4 and 5.
631 Case COMP/C2-38, *Telenor* ¶196 (2003).
632 Vertical Guidelines, *supra* n. 622, Chapter IV, ¶33.
633 *Id.* ¶34.
634 *Id.* ¶35.
635 *Id.* ¶36.
636 *Id.* ¶37.
637 *Id.* ¶38–45.

respect to the buyer, the relevant market is the market in which the buyer purchases the contract products.[638]

818. Where a vertical agreement involves three parties, each operating at a different level of trade, each party's market share must be 30% or less to benefit from the presumption of compatibility with Article 101 TFEU. These market share thresholds apply throughout the duration of the agreement and are not only assessed at the time of its conclusion. For instance, in an agreement between a supplier, a wholesaler and a retailer, the market shares of the supplier and the wholesaler in their respective downstream markets must not exceed 30% and the market share of the wholesaler and the retailer must not exceed 30% in their respective purchase markets in order to benefit from the safe harbor.

819. The European Commission considers that if an agreement does not benefit from an exemption because the market share thresholds of 30% are exceeded, it does not raise any presumption that the agreement falls within the scope of the prohibition of Article 101(1) TFEU or does not fulfill the conditions of Article 101(3) TFEU. In general, sufficient anticompetitive effects for the purpose of the application of Article 101(1) TFEU are only likely to occur when at least one of the parties has or obtains some degree of market power and the agreement contributes to the creation, maintenance or strengthening of that market power or allows the parties to exploit such market power.

C. *Prohibition of Hardcore Restrictions*

820. Although vertical agreements are generally considered less harmful to competition, the European Commission considers that hardcore restrictions fall within the prohibition of Article 101(1) TFEU and cannot be automatically exempted, even if the parties to a vertical agreement have only limited market power. Hardcore restrictions include:[639]

- The imposition of a fixed or minimum resale price. The obligation for the buyer to charge a fixed or minimum resale price is known as RPM and is considered a hardcore restriction. RPM includes not only the setting of a fixed or minimum resale price, but also the imposition of constraints on the grant of discounts, the determination of the buyer's resale margin, and other measures restricting the buyer's flexibility in deciding its resale price.[640] On the other hand, recommended or maximum prices will not be considered to infringe competition if prices are truly recommended or maximum and it is genuinely possible for the reseller to determine its retail price. However, such recommendations will not be covered "where they lead, directly or by indirect or concealed means, to the fixing of a retail price or the imposition of a minimum sale price by the supplier."[641]

---

638 *Id.* ¶¶87–95.

639 VBER, *supra* n. 619, Chapter IV, art. 4.

640 Vertical Guidelines, *supra* n. 622, Chapter IV, ¶48.

641 Case C-506/07, *Lubricantes y Carburantes Galaicos SL v. GALP Energía España SAU*, ECLI:EU:C:2009:504, ¶4 (Sept. 3, 2009).

In practice, RPM has consistently been considered a violation of Article 101(1) TFEU by the European Commission and the European courts.[642] RPM has been condemned both in cases where a single supplier agrees with its purchasers that they will not resell below a certain price[643] and in cases where groups of suppliers agree to impose resale prices on their purchasers.[644] RPM encompasses not only the setting of a fixed or minimum resale price, but also indirect means leading to RPM such as the imposition of limitations on the grant of discounts,[645] fixing the buyer's resale margin, and other measures restricting the buyer's freedom in determining its resale price.[646] Various measures are considered "supportive" of direct or indirect price fixing in the sense that they make the price fixing more effective.[647] These include arrangements where the supplier adopts means that help to identify price-cutting distributors (such as a price monitoring system[648]). However, the use of such supportive measures does not in itself lead to RPM.[649]

The European Commission however acknowledges that RPM can lead to efficiency and a rise in interbrand competition in some rare and specific conditions, for instance when applied for a limited time when a new product is introduced to the market or when a coordinated, short-term low-price campaign will benefit consumers.[650] RPM may also be procompetitive when it encourages retailers to provide services that would not be given in normal circumstances. However, these conditions are rarely met in practice.

- Any restriction concerning the territory into which or the customers to whom a buyer may sell the contract goods or services. Hence, any restriction impeding the supply of goods by a distributor located in one Member State to a customer located in another Member State is considered a hardcore restriction. Agreements aimed at prohibiting or limiting parallel trade are targeted

---

642 Case 243/83, *Binon & Cie SA v. AMP*, ECLI:EU:C:1985:284, ¶16–17 (July 3, 1985).

643 Case COMP/IV/27.010, *Deutsche Philips GmbH* (1973); Case COMP/IV/35.679, *Novalliance/Systemform* (1996); Case COMP/IV/36.516, *Nathan-Bricolux* (2000); Case COMP/AT/40.182, *Pioneer* (2018); Case COMP/AT/40469, *Denon & Marantz* (2018); Case COMP/AT/40465, *Asus* (2018); Case COMP/AT/40181, *Philips* (2018).

644 Cases 43/82 and 63/82, *VBVB and VBBB v. Commission*, ECLI:EU:C:1984:9, (Jan. 17, 1984); Case COMP/IV/27.393, COMP/IV/27.394, *Publishers Association v. Commission* (1988), on appeal, Case T-66/89, *Publishers Association v. Commission*, ECLI:EU:T:1992:84, (July 9, 1992).

645 *See* Case COMP/IV/30.174, *Vimpoltu* (1983) (fixing of maximum discount); Case COMP/IV/30.937, *Pronuptia* (1986) (obligation not to harm the brand image of the supplier through pricing level); Case COMP/36.516, *Nathan-Bricolux* (2000) (ban on discounts, rebates or sales that can damage the supplier's brand); Case COMP/35.918, *JCB* (2000) (fixing of uniform discounts across a distribution system); Case COMP/36.264, *Mercedes-Benz* (2001) (agreement on a maximum rate of 3% for discounts).

646 Vertical Guidelines, *supra* n. 622, Chapter IV, ¶48; *see also* Case COMP/IV/26.912, *Hennessy-Henkell* (1980) (buyer required to set price between maximum and minimum level); Case COMP/IV/28.748, *AEG-Telefunken* (1982) (payment by supplier of a bonus to buyers demonstrating good conduct on prices); Case COMP/IV/35.679, *Novalliance/Systemform* (1966) (obligation on buyer to inform supplier of prices and discount rates); Case COMP/37.975, *PO/Yamaha* (2003) (eligibility for bonus conditional on rebates not exceeding 15% of the recommended retail price).

647 Vertical Guidelines, *supra* n. 622, Chapter IV, ¶48.

648 *See* Case COMP/AT/40.182, *Pioneer*, ¶155 (2018); Case COMP/AT/40469, *Denon & Marantz*, ¶95 (2018); Case COMP/AT/40181, *Philips*, ¶64 (2018).

649 Vertical Guidelines, *supra* n. 622, Chapter IV, ¶48.

650 *Id.* ¶225.

by such restriction, whether they take the form of a simple instruction to dealers to cease exporting[651] or are simply imposed through a common understanding between the parties not to export[652] even if such understanding is not included in a formal written agreement. Article 101(1) TFEU applies irrespective of whether the supplier takes active steps to enforce it,[653] and even if the agreement contains a clause stating that the ban is inapplicable if prohibited by law.[654]

821. However, the parties to the agreement may still restrict:[655]

- Active sales[656] by the buyer into the exclusive territory or to an exclusive customer group reserved to the supplier or allocated by a buyer party to the agreement to a territory or a customer group which has been allocated exclusively to another buyer or which the supplier has reserved to itself. A territory or customer group is exclusively allocated when the supplier agrees to sell his product only to one distributor for distribution in a particular territory or to a particular customer group and the exclusive distributor is protected against active selling into his territory or to his customer group by all the other buyers of the supplier inside the EU territory, irrespective of sales by the supplier. The supplier is allowed to combine the allocation of an exclusive territory and an exclusive customer group. This protection of exclusively allocated territories or customer groups must, however, permit passive sales to such territories or customer groups.
- Sales to end users by a buyer operating at the wholesale level of trade. The exception allows a supplier to structure its distribution network by

---

651 Case T-368/00, *General Motors Nederland BV*, ECLI:EU:T:2003:275, ¶¶146 *et seq.*, *upheld* (Oct. 21, 2003), Case C-551/03 P, *Opel/General Motors Nederland BV v. Commission*, ECLI:EU:C:2006:229, (Apr. 6, 2006), the Court considered that a distribution agreement "clearly manifests the will to treat export sales less favorably than national sales and thus leads to a partitioning of the market in question."

652 *See* related Cases COMP/35.587, *Video Games*, COMP/35.706, *Nintendo Distribution* and COMP/36.321, *Omega* (2002), where written agreements from which express export ban had been removed thereafter proceeded on the "shared understanding" that dealers would not export.

653 *See* Case COMP/IV/31-741, *Sandoz* (1987), *appeal dismissed*, C-277/87, *Sandoz*, ECLI:EU:C:1990:6, (Jan 11, 1990); *see also*, Case 19/77, *Miller International Schallplatten GmbH v. Commission*, ECLI:EU:C:1978:19, ¶7 (Feb. 1, 1978); Case T-175/95, *BASF Lacke & Farben AG v. Commission*, ECLI:EU:T:1999:99, ¶156 (May 19, 1999); Case T-176/95, *Accinauto SA v. Commission*, ECLI:EU:T:1999:100, ¶123 (May 19, 1999).

654 Case COMP/IV/30.809, *John Deere*, ¶¶24–29 (1984).

655 VBER, *supra* n. 619, Chapter IV; TFEU 2022 OJ (L 134) 4, art. 4(b), and Vertical Guidelines, *supra* n. 622, Chapter IV, ¶¶51–59.

656 Vertical Guidelines, *supra* n. 622, Chapter IV, ¶51 ("Active sales mean actively approaching individual customers by for instance direct mail, including the sending of unsolicited e-mails, or visits; or actively approaching a specific customer group or customers in a specific territory through advertisement in media, on the internet or other promotions specifically targeted at that customer group or targeted at customers in that territory. Advertisement or promotion that is only attractive for the buyer if it (also) reaches a specific group of customers or customers in a specific territory, is considered active selling to that customer group or customers in that territory." Whereas "'Passive' sales mean responding to unsolicited requests from individual customers including delivery of goods or services to such customers. General advertising or promotion that reaches customers in other distributors' (exclusive) territories or customer groups but which is a reasonable way to reach customers outside those territories or customer groups, for instance to reach customers in one's own territory, are passive sales. General advertising or promotion is considered a reasonable way to reach such customers if it would be attractive for the buyer to undertake these investments also if they would not reach customers in other distributors' (exclusive) territories or customer groups.").

keeping the wholesale and retail levels separate. A ban on direct supplies by a wholesaler to end consumers should not distort competition, since it merely reflects the separation of functions between wholesaler and retailer.[657]

- Sales by the members of a selective distribution system to unauthorized distributors within a reserved territory.
- The buyer's ability to sell components, supplied for the purposes of incorporation, to customers who would use them to manufacture the same type of goods as those produced by the supplier.
- Any restriction on the ability of members of a selective distribution system to resell the goods to end users or other members of the network. Dealers in a selective distribution system cannot be restricted with regards to the users to whom they may sell or the purchasing agents acting on behalf of those users, except to protect an exclusive distribution system operating elsewhere. Within a selective distribution system, the dealers should be free to sell, both actively and passively, to all end users, both offline and online. Within the territory where the supplier operates a selective distribution network, this system may not be combined with exclusive distribution, as that would lead to a hardcore restriction of active and passive sales by the dealers. Similarly, the agreement cannot prevent or restrict the active or passive sale of the contract products between the members of the selective distribution network. Selected distributors must remain free to purchase the contract products from other appointed distributors within the network, operating either at the same or at a different level of trade. Hence, selected distributors cannot be forced to purchase the contract products exclusively from a given source.
- Any restriction that prevents end users, independent repairers, and service providers from obtaining spare parts directly from the manufacturer of those spare parts.

D. *Excluded Restrictions*

822. A vertical agreement may also contain clauses considered as "excluded" by the VBER. Although these excluded restrictions do not benefit from the exemption, this does not affect the application of the exemption to the other provisions of the agreement.

823. Excluded restrictions include:
   - Any direct or indirect non-compete obligation for a period exceeding 5 years or an indefinite period.
   - Any direct or indirect obligation or restriction on the buyer as regards the manufacture, purchase, distribution, or sale that applies after the termination of the agreement.
   - Any direct or indirect obligation on members of a selective distribution system not to sell specified brands of particular competing suppliers.

---

657 Case 26/76, *Metro SB-Großmärkte GmbH & Co. KG v. Commission*, ECLI:EU:C:1977:167, ¶¶28–29 (Oct. 25, 1977).

E. *Vertical Restraints in the Life Sciences Sector*

824. To the extent that the parties to a vertical agreement have respective market shares exceeding the 30% thresholds or if a vertical agreement contains one or more hardcore restrictions, it will not be exempted by the VBER and will fall within the scope of Article 101(1) TFEU.

825. From an EU standpoint, decisional practice and case law concerning vertical agreements in the life sciences sector is mainly focused on parallel trade issues. Some national competition agencies have also sanctioned RPM issues in the past.

a. *Fixed or Minimum Resale Price Issues*

826. In the life sciences sector, fixed or minimum resale prices have rarely been an issue given the fact that prices are usually regulated at the Member State level. Some NCAs nevertheless have applied Article 101 TFEU in cases involving RPM or price-fixing issues between wholesalers and pharmacies.

827. In *Hungaropharma*, the Hungarian Competition Authority held that an agreement between a wholesaler and pharmacies restricting resale prices was illegal per se.[658] The case concerned a straightforward RPM arrangement, where the pharmacies agreed on resale prices in the agreements concluded with the wholesaler, Hungaropharma. Due to the wording and context of the arrangement, the authority did not accept Hungaropharma's defense that these were actually maximum prices. It also rejected the argument that the RPM arrangement was not harmful to consumers, as it found the agreement was was aimed at reaching discount price levels below the market price.

828. In *Bayer Vital*, the German Competition Authority condemned indirect RPM, whereby Bayer Vital anticompetitively influenced the resale prices of non-prescription medicines sold in pharmacies. In Germany, pharmacies can set their own prices for non-prescription pharmaceuticals (unless, in exceptional cases, costs are reimbursed by health insurance funds). The German Competition Authority found that Bayer Vital intentionally influenced the sales price of pharmacies by granting pharmacies extra discounts for premium positioning and complying with price recommendations. Bayer Vital concluded target agreements with several pharmacies in which they were promised an additional discount for "positioning Bayer products as premium products." To obtain this "partnership bonus," the pharmacies had to essentially observe Bayer Vital's non-binding price recommendation; time-limited price campaigns were tolerated, but not permanently low prices.[659]

b. *Territorial and Parallel Trade Issues*

829. The very foundation of the EU is based on the development of a single market, where goods and services can move freely to the benefit of European customers.

---

658 Márton Horányi, *The Hungarian Competition Council prohibits restrictive clauses in cooperation agreements between a wholesaler of pharmaceutical products and pharmacies (Hungaropharma)*, E-COMPETITIONS Dec. 2008, art. No. 26200.

659 Bundeskartellamt, Press Release, *Bundeskartellamt Imposes Fine Against Bayer Vital* (May 28, 2008).

The European Commission and European Courts therefore have a history of adversity to geographical limitations and other measures that may stifle parallel trade.[660]

830. Article 101 TFEU catches territorial restrictions that directly or indirectly form part of an agreement between two or more undertakings.[661]

831. Article 101 TFEU prohibits absolute territorial protections, i.e., situations where a supplier structures its distribution system in such a way that each reseller is protected, in its territory, from any competition by resellers established in other territories. This arrangement commonly prohibits resellers from making any sale (including passive sales) outside its territory. The ECJ considers that export bans have as their object the restriction of competition; anticompetitive effects therefore do not need to be demonstrated to find infringement of Article 101 TFEU.[662]

832. More generally, the European Commission considers in its Guidelines that:

> The objective of Article 101 is to ensure that undertakings do not use agreements – in this context, vertical agreements – to restrict competition in the market to the detriment of consumers. Assessing vertical restraints is also important in the context of the wider objective of achieving an integrated internal market. Market integration enhances competition in the EU. Companies should not be allowed to re-establish private barriers between Member States where State barriers have been successfully abolished.[663]

(1) Existence of an Agreement

833. However, Article 101(1) TFEU only apples if there is a "concurrence of wills" between the supplier and its authorized resellers as to the restriction of parallel importations. A unilateral measure cannot be qualified as an agreement on the sole ground that the partner on whom the measure is imposed continues its commercial relations with the supplier. It is necessary to prove, for each measure at issue, that it was specifically the subject of a concurrence of wills, which cannot be overarching, general, or assumed.[664] Thus, companies have a degree of freedom to take steps to restrict export of their products, provided such action is purely unilateral and does not form part of an express or implicit agreement or under standing with their distributors.

834. An agreement can however be found when one of the parties is so dependent on the other that it has little choice but to accept the other's wishes. In *BMW Belgium*, the ECJ ruled that a circular to dealers, which was signed by the recipients, constituted an agreement within the meaning of Article 101 TFEU. BMW's Belgian subsidiary had sent a circular to its Belgian dealers to halt exports to

---

660 *See, e.g.*, Joined Cases 56/64 and 58/64, *Établissements Consten S.à.R.L. and Grundig-Verkaufs-GmbH v. Commission*, ECLI:EU:C:1966:41, (July 13, 1966).

661 Article 102 TFEU may also apply to purely unilateral conducts that restrict or impede parallel trade, when implemented by a manufacturer or supplier that is dominant in the market for the contract products. *See* Chapter V.

662 *Id.*; Case T-62/98, *Volkswagen AG v. Commission*, ECLI:EU:T:2000:180, ¶¶178–196 (July 6, 2000).

663 Vertical Guidelines, *supra* n. 622, Chapter IV, ¶7.

664 Case T-41/96, *Bayer AG*, ECLI:EU:T:2000:242, ¶67–69 (Oct. 26, 2000), *upheld* by Case C-2/01 P, *Bayer AG v. Commission*, ECLI:EU:C:2004:2, ¶¶101, 118 (Jan. 6, 2004).

Germany, which were made attractive by the higher German prices, compared to the controlled prices on cars in Belgium. The ECJ found that the dealers had agreed to BMW's request to stop exports, albeit reluctantly, thus entering into an agreement which supplemented their regular contractual relationship.[665]

835. In *Volkswagen*,[666] the European Commission fined Volkswagen, together with its Audi and Autogerma subsidiaries, for concluding allegedly anticompetitive agreements with their Italian dealers. The suppliers had developed a strategy to prevent customers from Germany and Austria from buying new cars in Italy for immediate re-export, by implementing a set of measures including a restrictive margin and bonus policy, restrictions of supply on the Italian market, restrictions on cross-deliveries, and termination of dealer contracts. The General Court affirmed the European Commission's decision, finding that the effects of the export restrictions did not need to establish for the application of Article 101 TFEU, if it can be demonstrated that the object of the measures is to restrict competition.[667] The ECJ upheld the General Court's judgment, confirming that the European Commission was entitled to find that the rule according to which dealers' sales bonus took into account sales outside the contract territory only up to a certain limit infringed Article 101 TFEU. The ECJ held that imposing a limit on the volume of export sales on which the dealer could earn a bonus was susceptible to inducing dealers to sell in their contract territory and therefore made it more difficult for German and Austrian consumers to find an Italian dealer prepared to sell them cars.[668]

836. In *Bayer*, due to a substantial price differential between France and Spain on the one hand and the UK on the other, French and Spanish wholesalers of Bayer's medicine started re-exporting Adalat to the British market, undercutting UK distributors. In response, Bayer introduced a policy of restricting the quantities supplied to its French and Spanish wholesalers according to the level of their previous orders. Bayer argued that its policy was purely unilateral. However, the European Commission concluded that the policy constituted one of the aspects of an agreement designed to partition national markets. On appeal, the General Court annulled the European Commission's decision that an export ban had been tacitly incorporated into Bayer's distribution agreements.[669] Conducting an evaluation of the evidence, the Court found, first, that Bayer had not sought to monitor the conduct of individual wholesalers or to make supply conditional on the final destination of the products; and, second, that the wholesalers attempted to obtain additional supplies so that they could continue exporting to customers in the UK. On appeal the ECJ held that to find that an agreement has been concluded by tacit acceptance:

> It is necessary that the manifestation of the wish of one of the contracting parties to achieve an anticompetitive goal constitute an invitation to the other party, whether express or implied, to fulfil that goal jointly, and that

---

665 Joined Cases 32/78, 36/78, 82/78, *BMW Belgium SA*, ECLI:EU:C:1979:191, ¶¶28–36 (July 12, 1979); *see also*, Case T-9/92, *Automobiles Peugeot SA v. Commission*, ECLI:EU:T:1993:38, ¶63 (Apr. 22, 1993).

666 Case COMP/IV/35.733, *Volkswagen* (1998).

667 Case T-62/98, *Volkswagen AG*, ECLI:EU:T:2000:180, (July 6, 2000).

668 Case C-338/00, *Volkswagen AG v. Commission*, ECLI:EU:C:2003:473, (Sept. 18, 2003).

669 Case T-41/96, *Bayer AG*, ECLI:EU:T:2000:242, (Oct. 26, 2000).

applies all the more where, as in this case, such an agreement is not at first sight in the interests of the other party, namely the wholesalers.[670]

837. In *Opel/General Motors*,[671] however, the Courts considered that the existence of an agreement had not been demonstrated by some of the practices implemented by the supplier.

838. The European Commission had originally fined Opel for implementing a strategy that aimed at restricting or preventing the sale of new cars in the Netherlands to non-resident customers. Dealers had been told that the number of cars which they were expected to sell on the basis of their dealer contract should be sold principally within the Netherlands, thereby limiting the scope for export sales. Furthermore, by way of direct instructions given by its District Managers to a number of exporting dealers, and on the basis of subsequent commitments received from a number of these dealers to stop all export sales, Opel ensured a substantial reduction of exports. Finally, Opel operated a number of sales campaigns, which each contained a provision that bonus payments would be refused if dealers carried out sales to non-resident end consumers.

839. On appeal, the General Court stated that "in the absence of agreements between undertakings, a unilateral act by one undertaking without the express or tacit participation of another does not fall within [Article 101(1) TFEU]."[672] It considered that the implementation, purely internally, of a policy aiming to restrict parallel exports cannot be considered as an anticompetitive agreement, as long as the supplier did not ask distributors to comply with this policy, as the case may be under threat of a sanction. Therefore, if a circular is neither signed by the recipients, followed by a change in their behavior nor effectively enforced by the supplier, it remains a unilateral declaration of intent.[673]

840. However, the General Court upheld the European Commission's finding that Opel's exclusion of the sales made outside the contract territory from the calculation of bonuses should be considered an infringement by object of Article 101 TFEU.[674]

841. In the life sciences sector, and particularly in the pharmaceutical market, significant price differences between Member States (due to regulated prices for medicines and pharmaceutical products in many of them) have made parallel trade and territorial restraints a specific issue. Parallel trade in the life sciences industry generally entails purchasing pharmaceutical products in one Member State and reselling them in another at a higher price, benefiting from the price gap between the export and import countries.

842. Parallel trade restrictions can take a variety of forms from direct export bans to indirect measures designed to make export more difficult or less attractive, such as refusal to supply, limitation of supply, referral obligations, differential pricing,

---

670 Case C-2/01 P, *Bayer AG*, ECLI:EU:C:2004:2, ¶102 (Jan. 6, 2004).

671 Case COMP/36.653, *Opel* (2000), *on appeal*, Case T-368/00, *General Motors Nederland BV*, ECLI:EU:T:2003:275, (Oct. 21, 2003), *upheld by* Case C-551/03 P, *Opel/General Motors Nederland BV*, ECLI:EU:C:2006:229, (Apr. 6, 2006).

672 Case C-551/03 P, *Opel/General Motors Nederland BV*, ECLI:EU:C:2006:229, ¶58 (Apr. 6, 2006).

673 Case T-368/00, *General Motors Nederland BV*, ECLI:EU:T:2003:275, ¶78–88 (Oct. 21, 2003).

674 *Id.* ¶¶100–106.

product differentiation, and restrictions on warranty terms and the provision of after-sales warranty services.[675]

(2) Direct Prohibition of Exports Restrictions

843. The prohibition on exports from one Member State to another constitutes an obstacle to the achievement of the EU single market and prevents any actual competition within this single market in respect of the products affected by that prohibition.

844. The first EU pharmaceutical case that concerned a direct export ban is *Johnson & Johnson*,[676] in which three subsidiaries of Johnson & Johnson Inc. imposed restrictions on dealers in the UK and in Germany, hindering exports of pregnancy tests. All subsidiaries' price lists included the condition "export prohibited except by prior arrangement." The European Commission found that export bans, which were included in the price lists applied by the subsidiaries for the sale of their products to pharmaceutical dealers, formed an essential part of the sale contracts between each company and its dealers and could therefore be considered as agreements between undertakings within the meaning of Article 101 TFEU.[677] Their provisions restricted competition within the single market since they prevented buyers in the UK and Germany from reselling the products of the concerned subsidiaries to other countries.[678]

845. In *Sandoz*,[679] although no written general contract existed between Sandoz and its customers, the European Commission considered that the continuous commercial relationship between Sandoz and its customers constituted an agreement under Article 101 TFEU. It found that Sandoz's commercial invoices, which were stamped with the phrase "export forbidden," formed an integral part of the agreement on which Sandoz and its customers based their transactions. As a consequence, the European Commission considered that wholesalers had essentially accepted this export prohibition provision, so that the export restriction was not a unilateral action taken by Sandoz against its distributors, but rather a bilateral arrangement to minimize parallel trading. The European Commission deemed the export prohibition provision to be illegal under competition law and fined Sandoz.

846. In *Bayer*,[680] to prevent the volumes of Adalat destined for France and Spain (where the product was less expensive) from being re-exported to the UK (where the product was more expensive), Bayer reduced the quantities of Adalat it supplied to its Spanish and French distributors and refused to supply wholesalers who were engaged on both the local and international markets. In response, the wholesalers concerned reduced their orders to a certain level to give Bayer the impression that they were responding to its stated intention to cover only the needs of their traditional market, while at the same time continuing to try to obtain additional volumes of Adalat, which were destined for export through various subterfuges, including

---

675 Vertical Guidelines, *supra* n. 622, Chapter IV, ¶50.
676 Case COMP/IV/29.702, *Johnson & Johnson* (1980).
677 *Id.* ¶28.
678 *Id.* ¶¶29–33.
679 Case COMP/IV/31-741, *Sandoz* (1987).
680 Case COMP/IV/34.279/F3, *Adalat* (1996).

indirectly placing orders through small wholesalers. The European Commission fined Bayer for implementing a supply quota system for its drug Adalat considering that there was an agreement between Bayer and its wholesalers, as Adalat's quota policy was part of their ongoing commercial relationship. The European Commission held that to limit parallel trade from lower priced countries, Bayer refused to supply wholesalers with the full amounts they requested. The European Commission further considered that customers' acquiescence and their long-term course of dealing with Bayer established the existence of a prohibited agreement under Article 101 TFEU.

847. However, on appeal, the General Court disagreed with the European Commission and found that a unilateral policy restricting parallel exports implemented by a supplier shall not be seen as an anticompetitive agreement when (i) the exporting wholesalers are not penalized and (ii) wholesalers actually tried to circumvent the measures put in place by their supplier to attempt to continue exporting.[681] The General Court further held that the mere continuation of commercial relations with the supplier when it adopts a new policy, which is implemented unilaterally, does not amount to tacit acquiescence to that policy where the distributors' de facto conduct is contrary to that policy.[682] Finally, the General Court dismissed the European Commission's argument that parallel imports would eventually lead to price harmonization in the pharmaceutical industry as "devoid of all foundation."[683]

(3) Dual Pricing Restrictions

848. Dual pricing practices consist of manufacturers charging different prices to wholesalers depending on the final destination of the product. Hence, if the wholesaler sells the product in the domestic market, it pays a lower price compared to the situation where the product is to be exported, thereby making exports less profitable.

849. In *Organon*,[684] Organon notified the European Commission of a new pricing scheme for its contraceptive pills. Before changing the price scheme of its contraceptive pills, Organon used to apply a discount of 12.5% on all products supplied to its customers irrespective of their final destination. The new price regime differentiated between those pills to be sold in the UK and those intended for export. Only the former ones could further benefit from the 12.5% discount rate. Organon informed all British wholesalers with export activities of these new price conditions. In fact, wholesalers could only receive the rebate if they were able to prove that the relevant orders were destined for the local market and that they would not be reexported. Wholesalers with distribution activities mainly on the sole British market were also invited by letter not to supply products at the British price including the rebate to other wholesalers which may reexport these products. The European Commission found that the new price regime, which formed part of continuous business relations

---

681 Case T-41/96, *Bayer AG*, ECLI:EU:T:2000:242, ¶73 *et seq.* (Oct. 26, 2000), *upheld by* Case C-2/01 P, *Bayer AG*, ECLI:EU:C:2004:2, (Jan. 6, 2004).

682 Case T-41/96, *Bayer AG*, ECLI:EU:T:2000:242, ¶173 (Oct. 26, 2000).

683 *Id.* ¶181.

684 European Commission, Press Release IP/95/1345, *Contraceptive Pills: Commission Puts an End to Discriminatory Pricing Practices Between the United Kingdom and The Netherlands* (Dec. 5, 1995), *available at* https://ec.europa.eu/commission/presscorner/detail/en/IP_95_1345.

between Organon and its wholesalers constituted a serious infringement of competition rules in that it created a discrimination in the prices of the products according to their geographical destination. For the European Commission, the discriminatory pricing behavior of Organon had important effects, particularly on the sales of these contraceptive pills in the Netherlands. In this country, one of the pills of Dutch origin was not fully reimbursed by the social security scheme, while the British version of the pill, given its lower price, was fully reimbursable. Dutch consumers could take advantage of this price difference by opting for the UK version of the pill, which relieved them from paying an extra amount above the reimbursement price. Organon eventually informed the European Commission that it was withdrawing the new price regime, which the European Commission had opposed, and that the previous price conditions would continue to apply. At the time, the European Commission suspended its proceedings and reserved the right to examine Organon's forthcoming pricing system with the competition rules.

850. In 2001, the European Commission adopted a decision against *Glaxo SA,*[685] the Spanish subsidiary of GSK, which had decided to introduce new sales conditions as an attempt to discourage parallel trade. This new pricing mechanism involved a two-tier system, whereby medicines financed by the funds of the Spanish social security or by Spanish public funds that were then sold within Spain were charged at a lower price than medicines destined for markets outside Spain. Essentially, depending on the eventual geographical location, different prices were charged for the same drug. GSK notified the European Commission about the change in sales conditions in the hopes of receiving negative clearance or an individual exception under Article 101(3) TFEU. However, the European Commission found that the sale restrictions amounted to an export prohibition and dual pricing with the goal of restricting competition. As a result, the agreement reached with the Spanish wholesalers to implement the pricing structure was in violation of Article 101 TFEU and revoked by the European Commission without imposing any fine on GSK.

851. Following an appeal by GSK of the European Commission's decision, the General Court ruled that the European Commission had failed to properly examine the arguments and evidence put forward by the supplier to justify the dual pricing scheme under Article 101(3) TFEU.[686] The General Court acknowledged that the pharmaceutical industry's unique characteristics were important to the legal and economic framework in which efficiencies must be considered under Article 101(3) TFEU. The General Court found that the European Commission had failed to thoroughly examine GSK's claims in that regard, as it did not conduct adequate research into the efficiency loss associated with parallel trading, the magnitude of that loss, or the efficiency gain associated with dual pricing to justify its

---

685 Cases COMP/IV/36.957/F3, *Glaxo Wellcome* (notification); COMP/IV/36.997/F3, *Aseprofar & Fedifar* (complaint); COMP/IV/37.121/F3, *Spain Pharma* (complaint); COMP/IV/37.138/F3, *BAI* (complaint); COMP/IV/37.380/F3, *EAEPC* (complaint) (May 8, 2001).

686 Case T-168/01, *GlaxoSmithKline Services Unlimited v. Commission*, ECLI:EU:T:2006:265, ¶¶275 *et seq.* (Sept. 27, 2006) and Joined Cases C-501/06 P, C-513/06 P, C-515/06 P and C-519/06 P, *GlaxoSmithKline Services Unlimited v. Commission*, ECLI:EU:C:2009:610, ¶104 (Oct. 6, 2009).

conclusions. GSK's factual arguments and evidence on the structure of R&D investments, the peculiarities of R&D finance, and the impact of parallel trade on R&D and sector regulation also were not sufficiently evaluated by the European Commission. The Court held that the European Commission could not abstain from examining whether dual pricing could give rise to a gain in efficiency for interbrand competition, given, in particular, that:

> [I]n the medicines sector the effect of parallel trade on competition is ambiguous, since the gain in efficiency to which it is likely to give rise for intrabrand competition, the role of which is limited by the applicable regulatory framework, must be compared with the loss in efficiency to which it is likely to give rise for interbrand competition, the role of which is central.[687]

852. The ECJ upheld the General Court's findings and emphasized that, to the degree that they were crucial for the conclusion of the analysis, the "nature and specific features" of the sector in question had to be included in an evaluation of efficiencies under Article 101(3) TFEU.[688]

(4) Restrictions Based on the Final Use of the Products

853. The prohibition of Article 101 TFEU will usually apply to obligations that impose limits on the distributor as to the final use or purpose for which the products may be resold, such as solely for medical and not for veterinary purposes in the case of a medication. End-use limitations justified on the basis of public health protection do not fall within Article 101(1) TFEU, however.[689]

854. In *Bayo-n-ox*, Bayer signed agreements with its customers to limit the end purpose of resale of the Bayo-n-ox product, a growth promoter used as an additive in animal nutrition to improve food conversion and daily weight gain. Bayer sent a circular to several customers that specified that the amounts of Bayo-n-ox supplied to each customer were to be used exclusively to cover their own requirements and in their own facilities. The European Commission found that the circulars sent by Bayer invited its customers to confirm their agreement by returning a signed confirmation to Bayer. The European Commission found that the own-use requirement had as its object and effect the prevention of the resale of the Bayo-n-ox by the customers and also its export by them to other Member States. The very wording of the agreement made clear that these customers were to be ruled out as possible sources of supply for Bayo-n-ox. The position of the other actual or potential suppliers was thus artificially reinforced and competition on the supply side restricted. The European Commission therefore dismissed Bayer's argument that the own-use restriction was designed to prevent unauthorized trade

---

687 Case T-168/01, *GlaxoSmithKline Services Unlimited*, ECLI:EU:T:2006:265, ¶296 (Sept. 27, 2006).

688 Joined Cases C-501/06 P, C-513/06 P, C-515/06 P and C-519/06 P, *GlaxoSmithKline Services Unlimited*, ECLI:EU:C:2009:610, ¶103 *et seq.* (Oct. 6, 2009).

689 Case COMP/IV/30.946, *Kathon biocide* (1984); *see also* Commission Notice pursuant to Article 19(3) of Council Regulation 17 concerning an application for negative clearance (IV/30.946 – *Kathon biocide*), *available at* https://eur-lex.europa.eu/legal-content/EN/TXT/PDF/?uri=OJ:C:1984:059:FULL&from=GA; Vertical Guidelines, *supra* n. 622, Chapter IV, ¶60.

and fined Bayer for implementing a vertical agreement aiming at restricting the end purpose of sale of Bayo-n-ox."[690]

(5) Quota Restrictions

855. A product allocation scheme whereby the supplier unilaterally reduces supply to its resellers to a level it considers sufficient for each distributor to satisfy demand within its territory may not infringe Article 101 TFEU, even if this has the effect of restricting parallel trade. However, refusals to supply, limitations of supply or even threats to refuse or to limit supply may infringe Article 101(1) TFEU where the reseller's conduct suggests an "understanding" on its part that it will lose supplies if it resells the product outside its territory.[691]

856. Under a supply quota system, a pharmaceutical company only supplies wholesalers within the limits of predetermined quantities, based on their previous sales.

857. In the French case *Pharma-Lab*,[692] the plaintiffs Pharma-Lab, Pharmajet and Pharmadex denounced practices of quotas or refusal of sale by some twenty pharmaceutical companies against export-only wholesalers,[693] on the one hand (so-called "short liners"), and wholesaler distributors or their exporting subsidiaries on the other, as well as practices of discrimination between wholesaler distributors and exporters, the latter considering themselves to be treated less favorably. According to the plaintiffs, these practices were likely to reveal a horizontal agreement between pharmaceutical companies as well as a vertical agreement between those suppliers and their wholesalers. They argued that the fact that major pharmaceutical companies gradually decreased their deliveries to exporters before eventually stopping these deliveries altogether, while continuing to supply the national wholesaler distributors (even where they delivered for export via their specialist subsidiaries), constituted an export quotas agreement between suppliers and wholesalers that discriminated between exporters and wholesale distributors.

858. However, the FCA observed that the practices of each supplier and the way they developed were not identical, either in terms of the methods employed or the calendar according to which they were implemented. It found that in any case, such similarity in behavior would not alone suffice to prove the existence of any anticompetitive agreement between the pharmaceutical companies, which must be supported by serious, accurate, and corroborating evidence showing real collaboration. Regarding the allegation of discrimination between shortliners and genuine wholesale distributors, the competition authority took the view that this discrimination could not be proven either. Both categories of operator did business on the wholesale pharmaceutical markets under different legal regimes, which may provide justification for them being treated differently: wholesale distributors

---

690 Case COMP/IV/32.026, *Bayo-n-ox* (1989).

691 *See* Case COMP/IV/34.279/F3, *Adalat* (1996); Case T-41/96, *Bayer AG*, ECLI:EU:T:2000:242, (Oct. 26, 2000).

692 FCA, Decision No. 05-D-72, *Pharma-Lab* (Dec. 20, 2005).

693 There were two categories of wholesalers at the time in France. Export-only wholesalers were only allowed to export the medicines outside metropolitan France, taking advantage of the low prices of medicines in France to export drugs to EU Member States with higher prices.

were bound by stringent public service obligation, which was not the case for export-only wholesalers.

859. In *Phoenix Pharma*,[694] the FCA received a complaint by the pharmaceutical wholesale distribution professional association and by wholesaler Phoenix Pharma, concerning practices implemented by several pharmaceutical companies, which had set up quota systems for supplying drugs to wholesale distributors in France. The authority examined the quota systems of six laboratories, which had set up delivery quotas on the French market. The quotas were determined by criteria which were specific to each laboratory and notably took into account the historical purchases of wholesalers. But these systems were characterized by little transparency, a relative rigidity towards wholesalers' business fluctuations and were not favorable to new entrants. The authority, which acknowledged that quota systems had the legitimate aim to rationalize production and optimize medicine distribution with regard to market needs and could be justified in the specific context of the pharmaceutical sector, which is heavily regulated, nonetheless considered that the restrictions imposed by the suppliers should be limited to what is strictly necessary to ensure a reliable and optimal supply of the French market, while maintaining real possibilities of competition between the wholesalers.

860. To meet the competition concerns expressed by the FCA, the pharmaceutical companies amended their supply system of medicines to increase its fluidity, flexibility and transparency. In particular, to objectivize the system, the allocation key with respect to the quantities supplied to each wholesaler, initially based on historical sales, was changed to the market share of each wholesaler on the French market, as published by an independent body, and adjustment mechanisms were introduced in order to take into account variations of demand and serve new entrants, thereby fueling competition. Consequently, deliveries could exceed the quotas initially fixed and new entrants were granted minimum quantities allowing them to start their business activity in satisfactory conditions and effectively compete on the market.[695]

(6) Packaging and Presentation Restrictions

861. Article 101(1) TFEU does not apply to obligations to sell under the supplier's trademarks or to use the supplier's trademarks without modification or addition and only in a suitable manner. However, the use of trademark rights to restrict parallel imports will almost always be prohibited, for instance when they prevent resellers from changing the packaging of the product to comply with the rules applicable in another Member State (change of language, mandatory warnings, etc.).[696] The European Commission found that a distributor's commitment not to contest the validity of the supplier's trademark may violate Article 101(1) TFEU, but only if the mark is sufficiently well known for the restriction on its use to have

694 FCA, Decision No. 07-D-22, *Phoenix Pharma* (July 5, 2007); *see also* FCA, Decision No. 04-D-05, *Phoenix Pharma* (Feb. 24, 2004).

695 *See also* FCA, Decision No. 07-D-45, *Pfizer* (Dec. 13, 2007); Decision No. 07-D-46, *GSK* (Dec. 13, 2007).

696 Joined Cases 56/64 and 58/64, *Établissements Consten S.à.R.L. and Grundig-Verkaufs-GmbH*, ECLI:EU:C:1966:41, (July 13, 1966).

a significant restrictive effect on competition.[697] Nevertheless, where the relabeling or repackaging of a pharmaceutical product may have a negative impact on the product itself or the company's reputation, pharmaceutical companies may have the right to prevent further resale.

862. According to the principle of the EEA-wide exhaustion of trademark rights, the owner of a trademark is not entitled to prohibit its use in relation to goods that have been put in the market in the EEA under the trademark by the owner or with their consent. Also, exhaustion does not apply if there are legitimate reasons for the proprietor to oppose further commercialization of the goods, especially where the condition of the goods is changed or impaired after the goods have been put in the market.

863. This provision has been interpreted by the ECJ in *Bristol-Myers Squibb*, where it held that the trademark owner cannot legitimately oppose the further marketing of a repackaged pharmaceutical product if:

- repackaging is necessary to market the product in the country of importation;
- it does not affect the original condition of the product inside the packaging;
- the new packaging clearly states who repackaged the product and the name of the manufacturer;
- the presentation of the repackaged product is not liable to damage the reputation of the trademark or of its owner; and
- the importer gives notice to the trademark owner before the repackaged product is put on sale, and, on demand, supplies them with a specimen of the repackaged product.

864. In *Paranova*,[698] the appellant challenged these criteria, with a particular focus on the final two elements. The Wellcome Foundation Ltd (Wellcome) owned the Zovirax trademark and registered it in Austria. Zovirax was marketed within the EEA by Wellcome or with its consent. Paranova Pharmazeutika Handels GmbH (Paranova) imported branded Zovirax products from Greece, where they were sold in packs of 70 tablets. To comply with Austrian regulations, Paranova repackaged the products in packs of 60. Paranova's packaging differed from the original in that it included the words "Repackaged and imported by Paranova" in bold type and block capitals on the front, the manufacturer was referred to on the sides and back in normal type and there was a blue band at the edges, as regularly used by Paranova. Paranova informed Wellcome of its intention to market Zovirax in Austria and enclosed color prints of the outer packages, the blister packs, and the instructions for use. Wellcome requested a complete sample of the packaging and that Paranova disclose the state of export and the exact reasons for the repackaging. While Paranova disclosed the reasons for the repackaging (different sizes of packaging), it refused to disclose the state of export or to provide a free sample to Wellcome.

865. Wellcome then sought an injunction to prevent Paranova from marketing Zovirax in packaging with the features described above and without informing the supplier

---

697 Case COMP/IV/32.736, *Moosehead/Whitbread* (1990).

698 Case C-276/05, *The Wellcome Foundation Ltd. v. Paranova Pharmazeutika Handels GmbH*, ECLI:EU:C:2008:756, (Dec. 22, 2008).

of the state of export and precise reasons for the repackaging. The dispute reached the ECJ through a referral. The referring court required clarification from the ECJ as to which elements should be considered decisive in evaluating the conformity of the new packaging to EU rules. In particular, the court asked whether the new packaging should minimize possible adverse effects on trademark rights or whether it would be sufficient to show that the packaging is not liable to damage the reputation of the trademark or that of its proprietor. The ECJ held that where repackaging has been shown to be necessary, the entity repackaging the product only needs to ensure that the presentation of the repackaging is done without damaging the reputation of the trademark or that of its owner. In addition, the parallel importer must provide the trademark owner with all necessary and sufficient information needed to determine whether the repackaging is necessary. This could include information on the state of export but would depend on the circumstances of each case.

866. Going further, in *Orifarm*,[699] the ECJ found that a trademark rights holder cannot oppose the further marketing of a repackaged product only on the grounds that the new packaging does not bear the name of the company that repackaged the product.

---

699 Joined Cases C-400/09, C-207/10, *Orifarm & Paranova v. Merck Sharp & Dohme*, ECLI:EU:C:2011:519, (July 28, 2011).

CHAPTER V

Unilateral Conduct

Gregory Luib and Marion Provost*

* The authors would like to thank Pénélope Agosta, Lucas Leroy, and Kaitlyn Marasi for the very valuable help and contribution to this chapter.

867. This chapter addresses unilateral conduct that can violate the antitrust laws. Section I discusses the key concepts underlying unilateral conduct violations both from a US and European perspective, including the requirements of market power and exclusionary conduct or, in the EU, exploitative conduct, as well as the potential business justifications for otherwise unlawful conduct. Section II addresses the current state of the law with respect to particular types of conduct within the pharmaceutical sector.

I. Key concepts

1. Single-firm Conduct

868. Unilateral, single firm conduct can also give rise to antitrust liability. That is, unlike the joint conduct addressed in the previous chapter, there is no requirement of collusion or other agreement between firms to establish liability under applicable US and European antitrust laws.

869. In the US, unilateral conduct is addressed most often under Section 2 of the Sherman Act ("Section 2"), which prohibits monopolization, attempted monopolization, and conspiracy to monopolize.[1] Section 2's unilateral conduct provisions apply only to firms that already possess monopoly power or have a dangerous probability of achieving monopoly power. Although Section 2 does not require an agreement, and covers purely unilateral conduct, some types of agreements and non-unilateral conduct can also constitute monopolization. For example, conspiracy to monopolize is specifically identified as prohibited conduct in the text of Section 2. In addition, vertical agreements that exclude rivals and serial acquisitions of competitors can constitute unlawful monopolization under certain circumstances.[2]

870. In Europe, Article 102 TFEU prohibits abuses by one or several undertakings of a dominant market position, provided that the conduct affects trade between Member States.[3] The same prohibition can be found in the national laws of each EU Member State, save for the requirement of an effect on trade between Member States.[4]

---

1 The statutory text provides: "Every person who shall monopolize, or attempt to monopolize, or combine or conspire with any other person or persons, to monopolize any part of the trade or commerce among the several States, or with foreign nations, shall be deemed guilty of a felony… " 15 U.S.C. § 2. Although some state antitrust laws include provisions comparable to Section 2, enforcement of such laws is typically harmonized – either by statute or judicial interpretation – with the Sherman Act.

2 *See, e.g., United States v. Microsoft Corp.*, 253 F.3d 34, 62 (D.C. Cir. 2001) (finding Microsoft used restrictive licensing agreements to exclude rival Internet browsers).

3 Article 102 TFEU provides: "Any abuse by one or more undertakings of a dominant position within the internal market or in a substantial part of it shall be prohibited as incompatible with the internal market in so far as it may affect trade between Member States. Such abuse may, in particular, consist in: (a) directly or indirectly imposing unfair purchase or selling prices or other unfair trading conditions; (b) limiting production, markets or technical development to the prejudice of consumers; (c) applying dissimilar conditions to equivalent transactions with other trading parties, thereby placing them at a competitive disadvantage; (d) making the conclusion of contracts subject to acceptance by the other parties of supplementary obligations which, by their nature or according to commercial usage, have no connection with the subject of such contracts." Consolidated version of the TFEU, 2016 OJ (C 202) 1, art. 102.

4 For detailed explanations regarding the condition of an effect on trade between Member States, which determines the application of European law and the jurisdiction of the European Commission and subsequently the EU courts in each individual case, please refer to Chapter II.

871. As detailed in Chapter II, under EU rules, dominance can be enjoyed either by a single firm or collectively. Collective or joint dominance refers to the situation where several firms, because of their structural or contractual links or because of certain specific market conditions, together hold a dominant position in the market. In such cases, because Article 102 TFEU targets unilateral conduct, they are deemed, by virtue of those links, to form a collective entity in the market, and it is that collective entity (and not its members individually) which meets the test of dominance. However, once collective dominance is established, in practice, as the collective entity does not have any legal existence, the analysis focuses on the unilateral conduct of each individual firm forming part of the collective entity to determine whether or not there has been an abuse. Although the line between collective dominance and concerted practices (dealt with under Article 101 TFEU) is blurry insofar as both require two firms (at least) to adopt a common line of action on the market, the difference lies in the absence of agreement in collective dominance cases. However, lack of evidence of a collusion under Article 101 TFEU cannot be overcome by having recourse to the concept of collective dominance under Article 102 TFEU, which targets very specific situations only.

2. Market Power[5]

872. A key concept underlying unilateral conduct violations is the requirement that a firm have a certain degree of market power: monopoly power or a dangerous probability of obtaining monopoly power under Section 2 and a dominant position under Article 102 TFEU. Although most cases involve sellers alleged to have monopoly power or a dominant position, the market power requirement applies to both sellers and buyers. A buyer can indeed have so-called monopsony power over a product or service in a relevant market.[6]

873. Monopoly power under Section 2 is typically defined as "the power to control prices or exclude competition" in a relevant market.[7] Courts often use market share as a proxy in assessing the existence of monopoly power; however, structural features of a market – including most notably barriers to entry – may also be relevant to analyzing a firm's monopoly power.[8] For example, in *American Tobacco Co v. United States*,[9] the Supreme Court held that control of over two thirds of the entire domestic field of cigarettes and over 80% of the field of comparable cigarettes constituted a "substantial monopoly."[10] Similarly, in *United States v. Aluminum Co. of America*,[11] 90% of the market constituted monopoly power.

---

5 See Chapter II for a more detailed discussion of market power.

6 *See* Section I.F below for a more detailed discussion of monopsony.

7 *United States v. E.I. du Pont de Nemours & Co.*, 351 U.S. 377, 391 (1956).

8 *See Broadcom Corp. v. Qualcomm Inc.*, 501 F.3d 297, 307 (3d Cir. 2007), *citing* 2A Phillip E. Areeda (late) & Herbert Hovenkamp, Antitrust Law: An Analysis Of Antitrust Principles And Their Application, ¶531a (5th ed. 2006) ("[M]arket share and barriers to entry are merely surrogates for determining the existence of monopoly power").

9 328 U.S. 781, 797 (1946).

10 *Id.*

11 148 F.2d 416, 429 (2d Cir. 1945).

874. There are no bright-line rules for the market share required to establish monopoly power. However, a share in excess of 70% is typically required to succeed on a Section 2 claim.[12] The market share required to establish monopoly power under Section 2 is greater than the share required to establish market power or harm to competition under Section 1 of the Sherman Act.[13]

875. Although courts typically look to market share as a proxy for the existence of monopoly power, they have also recognized that such power can be proven through direct evidence as well. For example, the US Supreme Court has explained that "proof of actual detrimental effects, such as a reduction of output, can obviate the need for an inquiry into market power."[14]

876. In attempted monopolization cases, where the defendant does not yet have monopoly power, Section 2 requires a showing that the defendant has "a dangerous probability of achieving monopoly power."[15] Typically, the market shares required to succeed in an attempted monopolization claim are lower than those applicable to a monopolization claim.[16]

877. The approach in the EU is different. While there is no such thing as attempted dominance, the concept of dominance under Article 102 TFEU is broader than monopoly power. According to established case law, it refers to "a position of

---

12 *See, e.g.*, *Eastman Kodak Co. v. Image Technical Services, Inc.*, 504 U.S. 451, 481 (1992) (monopoly power can be inferred from 80% market share); *Morgenstern v. Wilson*, 29 F.3d 1291, 1296 n. 3 (8th Cir. 1994) (share of more than 80% sufficient); *Heatransfer Corp. v. Volkswagenwerk, A.G.*, 553 F.2d 964, 981 (5th Cir.1977) (71–76% share sufficient); *Int'l Audiotext Network v. Am. Tel. & Tel. Co.*, 893 F. Supp. 1207, 1217–18 (S.D.N.Y.1994) (70% market share generally adequate at the pleading stage); *but see Broadway Delivery Corp. v. United Parcel Serv. of Am., Inc.*, 651 F.2d 122, 129 (2d Cir. 1981) (noting that a market share between 50% and 70% "can occasionally show market power" with additional evidence); *In re Google Digital Advert. Antitrust Litig.*, No. 21-CV-6841 (PKC), 2022 WL 4226932, *7 (S.D.N.Y. Sept. 13, 2022) (holding that "[a]t the pleading stage, Google's [60%] market share and other relevant market characteristics… permit a plausible inference of monopoly power").

13 *See* Chapter V.I.2.

14 *See FTC v. Indiana Federation of Dentists*, 476 U.S. 447, 460–61 (1986); *Toys "R" Us, Inc. v. FTC*, 221 F.3d 928, 937 (7th Cir. 2000) ("The Supreme Court has made it clear that there are two ways of proving market power. One is through direct evidence of anticompetitive effects. […] The other, more conventional way, is by proving relevant product and geographic markets and by showing that the defendant's share exceeds whatever threshold is important for the practice in the case.").

15 *Spectrum Sports v. McQuillan*, 506 U.S. 447, 456 (1993). Attempted monopolization also requires proof that the defendant has engaged in predatory or anticompetitive conduct with a specific intent to monopolize. *Id.*

16 *See All Star Carts & Vehicles, Inc. v. BFI Canada Income Fund*, 596 F. Supp. 2d 630, 642 (E.D.N.Y. 2009) ("[A] lesser degree of market power is required to be shown to sustain a claim of attempted monopolization than a claim of completed monopolization"); *Virgin Atl. Airways Ltd. v. Brit. Airways PLC*, 872 F. Supp. 52, 64 (S.D.N.Y. 1994) (refusing to dismiss complaint when "the market share figures pleaded… range between 39% and 52% of potentially relevant markets [and] may themselves in certain circumstances demonstrate a dangerous probability of acquiring monopoly power."); *In re Payment Card Interchange Fee & Merch. Disc. Antitrust Litig.*, 562 F. Supp. 2d 392, 402 (E.D.N.Y. 2008) ("MasterCard's assertion that its market share is less than 30% market, while relevant, cannot be dispositive; if the Individual Plaintiffs prove their allegations they may succeed in demonstrating that MasterCard wields monopoly power (or is dangerously likely to acquire it) notwithstanding its limited share of the market."); *M & M Med. Supplies & Serv., Inc. v. Pleasant Valley Hosp., Inc.*, 981 F.2d 160, 168 (4th Cir. 1992) (explaining that "(1) claims of less than 30% market shares should presumptively be rejected; (2) claims involving between 30% and 50% shares should usually be rejected, except when conduct is very likely to achieve monopoly or when conduct is invidious, but not so much so as to make the defendant per se liable; (3) claims involving greater than 50% share should be treated as attempts at monopolization when the other elements for attempted monopolization are also satisfied.").

economic strength enjoyed by an undertaking" on the relevant market which in practice enables it to behave "to an appreciable extent independently of its competitors, customers and ultimately of its consumers."[17]

878. In practice, a number of factors can lead to the conclusion that a firm enjoys significant market power and holds a dominant position in the market. However, the European Commission and European courts mainly rely on market shares to establish dominance, as they constitute the most direct indicator of market power. According to established case law, save in exceptional circumstances, very large market shares are in themselves conclusive evidence of the existence of a dominant position.[18] Besides, in contrast with the situation in the US, under EU law a market share of 50% is generally enough to presume a dominant position on the market.[19]

879. Below 50%, market shares may not be determinative in themselves and other factors must also be taken into account to assess market power and establish dominance under Article 102 TFEU.

880. Market shares below 40% are unlikely to lead to the finding of a dominant position.[20] However, there may be cases where a market share even below 40% may be enough to characterize dominance, in particular where the dominant undertaking's market share is well-above that of its closest competitor. For example, in *British Airways*, the European Commission found that the airline was dominant in the market with a market share of 39.7% because British Airways' market share, despite being limited, was over 2.2 times the combined share of its four largest rivals in the market and more than seven times larger than that of its closest competitor.[21]

881. Finally, other factors including barriers to entry or countervailing buyer power may also be taken into account when assessing market power, particularly when market shares are not themselves conclusive.

3. Exclusionary Conduct

882. Maintaining a monopoly or a dominant market position is not in itself unlawful. The US Supreme Court has noted the important incentive that obtaining a monopoly position provides for other firms to innovate or otherwise take on the monopolist: "To safeguard the incentive to innovate, the possession of monopoly power will not be found unlawful unless it is accompanied by an element of anticompetitive conduct."[22]

883. In addition to monopoly power, therefore, Section 2 requires proof that the defendant has acquired, enhanced, or maintained that power through the use of exclusionary

---

17 Case 27/7, *United Brands Company and United Brands Continentaal BV v. Commission*, ECLI:EU:C:1978:22, ¶65 (Feb. 14, 1978). This definition has been highlighted in the European Commission Communication, Guidance on the Commission's enforcement priorities in applying Article 82 of the EC Treaty to abusive exclusionary conduct by dominant undertakings, 2009 OJ (C 45) 2. *Id.* ¶10.

18 Case 85/76, *Hoffmann-La Roche & Co. v. Commission*, ECLI:EU:C:1979:36, ¶41 (Feb. 13, 1978); Case C-62/86, *AKZO Chemie BV v. Commission*, ECLI:EU:C:1991:286, ¶60 (July 3, 1991)).

19 Case C-62/86, *AKZO Chemie BV*, ECLI:EU:C:1991:286, ¶60 (July 3, 1991).

20 European Commission Communication, *supra* n. 17, Chapter V, ¶14.

21 Case COMP/AT IV/D-2/34.780, *Virgin/British Airways*, ¶88 (1999); confirmed by Case T-219/99, *British Airways v. Commission* ECLI:EU:T:2003:343, ¶211 (Dec. 17, 2003).

22 *Verizon Communications v. Law Offices of Curtis v. Trinko*, LLP, 540 U.S. 398, 407 (2004).

conduct. This requirement is typically characterized as conduct other than competition on the merits, or conduct "distinguished from growth or development as a consequence of a superior product, business acumen, or historic accident."[23] Also, the Sherman Act does not prohibit conduct that merely exploits monopoly power, such as charging higher prices; the conduct must have an exclusionary effect.

884. Because aggressive competition and exclusionary conduct often resemble each other, application of this requirement is one of the more complicated issues in US antitrust law. As a result, courts have struggled to develop a single, broadly applicable standard for assessing allegedly exclusionary conduct. As discussed below, courts have fared better in developing workable standards for particular types of conduct, including, for example, predatory pricing, certain exclusive dealing arrangements, refusals to deal, and abusive litigation.

885. A dominant position is not in itself an offense under EU law either.[24] Only the abuse of such dominant position is prohibited. According to well-established case law, dominant firms are under a "special responsibility not to allow [their] conduct to impair genuine undistorted competition on the common market."[25] This does not mean that a dominant firm cannot protect its own commercial interests but, in doing so, it must always act within the limits of competition on the merits. The ECJ notably recalled this principle in *Generics UK*, stating that:

> When the intention of a manufacturer of originator medicines holding a dominant position is to protect its own commercial interests, in particular by defending its patents, and to guard itself against the competition of generic medicines, that alone does not justify resorting to practices that fall outside the scope of competition on the merits.[26]

886. The notion of abuse under Article 102 TFEU is very broad. It targets any type of conduct where the dominant firm has recourse to methods different from those which govern normal competition and, as a result of which, the degree of competition still existing on the market or the growth of that competition is hindered. Under EU law, abusive conduct can take two forms: exclusionary conduct and exploitative conduct.

887. In broad terms, in contrast to exclusionary conduct where the dominant firm seeks to exclude its competitors from the market, exploitative abuse refers to the situation where the dominant firm uses its market power to reap off trading benefits it would not have had otherwise and distort competition, be it on its own market or on an upstream, downstream or neighboring market, at the expense of its suppliers, customers or competitors and, ultimately, of consumers.[27] Examples of exploitative conduct notably include excessive pricing and discrimination cases.

---

23 *Id.* (quoting *United States v. Grinnell Corp.*, 384 U.S. 563, 570–71 (1966)).

24 Case 322/81, *NV Nederlandsche Banden Industrie Michelin v. Commission*, ECLI:EU:C:1983:313, ¶57 (Nov. 9, 1983).

25 *Id.*; Case C-52/09, *Konkurrensverket v. TeliaSonera Sverige AB*, ECLI:EU:C:2011:83, ¶24 (Feb. 17, 2011); Case C-413/14 P, *Intel v. Commission*, ECLI:EU:C:2017:632, ¶135 (Sept. 6, 2017); Case C-307/18, *Generics (UK) Ltd and Others v. Competition and Markets Authority*, ECLI:EU:C:2020:52, ¶153 (Jan. 30, 2020).

26 Case C-307/18, *Generics (UK) Ltd and Others*, ECLI:EU:C:2020:52, ¶152 (Jan. 30, 2020).

27 Case 27/7, *United Brands Company and United Brands Continentaal BV*, ECLI:EU:C:1978:22, ¶249 (Feb. 14, 1978).

888. In practice, the emphasis of the European Commission's and NCAs' enforcement activity has traditionally been on exclusionary conduct, including in the pharmaceutical sector. However, Article 102 TFEU(a) and (c) provide a basis for the authorities to tackle exploitative conduct by a dominant firm and the European Commission specified in its Guidance on the European Commission's enforcement priorities in applying Article 82 of the EC Treaty (now Article 102 TFEU)[28] that it may decide to intervene in relation to exploitative practices, particularly where the protection of consumers and the proper functioning of the market cannot otherwise be adequately ensured. In the pharmaceutical sector, this is exemplified by the recent concerns expressed by several European competition authorities and growing interest in excessive pricing cases.

4. Anticompetitive Effect

889. Unilateral conduct cases require the showing that the challenged conduct had an anticompetitive effect – that is, harm to competition and therefore harm to consumers.[29] There are no per se illegal unilateral conduct violations, in contrast with certain types of joint conduct, such as price fixing, bid rigging, and market division.

890. Under Section 2, the requirement of harm to competition is typically addressed as part of the analysis of the allegedly exclusionary conduct and/or as part of the analysis of whether the plaintiff has suffered what is called "antitrust injury" – an injury flowing from a harm to competition as opposed to just an injury to the particular plaintiff. Courts require a showing of harm to market-wide competition, rather than harm to a particular competitor.[30] But competitors can sue when that conduct in addition to harming competition generally also impaired or eliminated the ability of rivals to compete.[31] In *United States v. Microsoft*, for example, the Court condemned Microsoft's agreements licensing Windows to Original Equipment Manufacturers (OEMs) because it found these provisions had the anticompetitive effect of preventing OEMs from pre-installing a rival browser.[32] Although Microsoft entered into these agreements with OEMs, the agreements had the effect of harming competition for Internet browsers and limiting consumer choice.[33]

891. The Supreme Court has been careful to distinguish between unlawful monopoly power and "growth or development as a consequence of a superior product, business acumen, or historic accident."[34] As a result, courts will only find anticompetitive effects sufficient to establish liability under Section 2 if the exclusion

---

28 European Commission Communication, *supra* n. 17, Chapter V.

29 *See Am. Key Corp. v. Cole Nat'l Corp.*, 762 F.2d 1569, 1579 n. 8 (11th Cir.1985) ("Harm to competition is a necessary element of all private antitrust suits under §§ 1 and 2 of the Sherman Act…").

30 *See* Chapter VI, Section I.5.A; *see also Brunswick Corp. v. Pueblo Bowl-O-Mat, Inc.*, 429 U.S. 477, 488 (1977) ("The antitrust laws… were enacted for the protection of competition not competitors.").

31 *See United States v. Microsoft Corp.*, 253 F.3d 34 66 ("Microsoft's conduct, through something other than competition on the merits, [had] the effect of significantly reducing usage of rivals' products and hence protecting its own operating system monopoly").

32 *Id.* 61–62.

33 *Id.*

34 *United States v. Grinnell Corp.*, 384 U.S. 563, 571 (1966).

amounts to something other than competition on the merits. For example, the exclusion of less efficient competitors through aggressive competition by a monopolist will not in all cases result in liability under Section 2.[35]

892. In principle, there is no per se infringement under Article 102 TFEU. Therefore, the characterization of an abuse normally requires the demonstration of an anticompetitive effect. This was made clear by the ECJ already in the *Hoffmann-La Roche* case, where the Court defined the concept of abuse as relating to the situation where the conduct of the dominant firm "has the effect" of hindering competition.[36] The effect-based approach was subsequently recalled in several judgments of the ECJ.[37] Furthermore, in the Guidance on the European Commission's enforcement priorities in applying Article 82 of the EC Treaty (now Article 102 TFEU), the European Commission embraced the principle of the effect-based approach, saying that it will normally only intervene under Article 102 TFEU where the conduct under review "is likely to lead to anticompetitive foreclosure," i.e., when, as a result of the alleged abusive conduct, actual or potential competitors are eliminated from the market or prevented from accessing supplies or the market.[38] This guidance has been partly amended on March 27, 2023, pending the adoption of new guidelines in 2025, in order to take into account the evolution of case law, the experience gained in applying Article 102 TFUE as well as market developments since 2008, in particular those related to the digitalization of the economy.[39] The major change brought by the amendments to the guidance is the broadening of the European Commission's scope of intervention. The European Commission's intervention will indeed no longer be limited to cases resulting in the full exclusion or marginalization of competition but will now also extend to conduct capable of weakening competition, thereby hampering the competitive structure of the market to the advantage of the dominant firm and to the detriment of consumers.

893. In practice, the assessment of abusive conduct is complex. First, because the applicable standard of proof does not require the demonstration of an actual effect on competition, it is sufficient for the European Commission to demonstrate that the conduct at stake has the capability of or is likely to hinder competition. In this respect, the General Court recently recalled that the European Commission is not required to identify actual exclusionary effect insofar as such requirement would go against the well-established principle that "the categorization of a practice as abuse within the meaning of Article 102 TFEU cannot be altered because the practice at issue has ultimately not achieved the desired result."[40] Second, in early cases, a formalistic

---

35 *See United States v. Syufy Enterprises*, 903 F.2d 659, 669 (9th Cir. 1990) ("[A]n efficient, vigorous, aggressive competitor is not the villain antitrust laws are aimed at eliminating.").

36 Case 85/76, *Hoffmann-La Roche & Co.*, ECLI:EU:C:1979:36, ¶91 (Feb. 13, 1978).

37 *See, e.g.*, Case C-209/10, *Post Danmark A/S v. Konkurrenceradet*, ECLI:EU:C:2012:172, ¶24 (Mar. 27, 2012); Case C-457/10 P, *AstraZeneca AB v. Commission*, ECLI:EU:C:2012:770, ¶74 (Dec. 6, 2012).

38 European Commission Communication, *supra* n. 17, Chapter V, ¶20.

39 European Commission Communication, Amendments to the Communication from the European Commission Guidance on the European Commission's enforcement priorities in applying Article 82 of the EC Treaty to abusive exclusionary conduct by dominant undertakings, COM (2023) 1923 final (Mar. 27, 2023), and its annex.

40 Case T-612/17, *Google Alphabet (Google Shopping) v. Commission*, ECLI:EU:T:2021:763, ¶442 (Nov. 10, 2021).

approach largely prevailed over the test based on actual or potential effects. For example, in *Michelin II*, the General Court acknowledged that the European Commission did not examine the specific effects of the discount systems applied by Michelin; however, it upheld the European Commission's approach because in this case "the seriousness of the infringement was established by reference to the nature and the object of the abusive conduct."[41] And while there has been a clear shift of approach in the last decade, with more consideration being given to economic arguments, as exemplified by the ECJ's judgment in *Intel*,[42] the enforcement practice sometimes still reflects some inconsistency. The European Commission's change of approach regarding its enforcement priorities, as described above, will also pave the way for more cases to be brought under Article 102 TFEU and, although the principle remains that of an effect-based approach, the European Commission's amended guidance may be perceived as an attempt to lower the applicable standard of proof.

894. In addition, certain behaviors are still presumed to have an anticompetitive effect, meaning in practice that only limited consideration will be given to the actual effects of the practice by competition authorities. For example, this is true for predatory pricing: the ECJ considers that, when a dominant firm sells below its average variable costs,[43] its conduct can be presumed unlawful under Article 102 TFEU.

5. Business Justification

895. A final consideration in monopolization and abuse of dominance cases is the business justification, if any, for the allegedly unlawful conduct.

896. Under Section 2, after a plaintiff establishes an anticompetitive effect from a monopolist's conduct, the defendant may identify one or more legitimate business justifications for its otherwise exclusionary conduct.[44] If the defendant establishes a legitimate, non-pretextual justification for its conduct, the burden shifts back to the plaintiff to rebut that claim.[45] To be considered legitimate, a justification must be procompetitive, efficiency-enhancing, or otherwise grounded in competition on the merits.[46] In addition, courts assess whether there are any alternative courses of action – other than the defendant's conduct – with less competitively restrictive

41 Case T-203/01, *Manufacture française des pneumatiques Michelin v. Commission*, ECLI:EU:T:2003:250, ¶258 (Sept. 30, 2003).

42 Case C-413/14 P, *Intel*, ECLI:EU:C:2017:632, (Sept. 6, 2017); *see also* Case T-286/09 RENV, *Intel Corp Inc. v. Commission*, ECLI:EU:T:2022:19, (Jan. 26, 2022).

43 *See* below, Section II. 1. B., Predatory pricing; in particular, see Case C-62/86, *AKZO Chemie BV*, ECLI:EU:C:1991:286, (July 3, 1991).

44 *See Morris Commc'ns Corp. v. PGA Tour, Inc.*, 364 F.3d 1288, 1295 (11th Cir. 2004) ("Once the defendant has met its burden to show its valid business justification, the burden shifts to the plaintiff to show that the proffered business justification is pretextual.").

45 *See United States v. Microsoft Corp.*, 253 F.3d 34, 59 (D.C. Cir. 2001) ("If the monopolist asserts a procompetitive justification – a non-pretextual claim that its conduct is indeed a form of competition on the merits because it involves, for example, greater efficiency or enhanced consumer appeal – then the burden shifts back to the plaintiff to rebut that claim.").

46 *Id.*; *see also Mylan Pharms. Inc. v. Warner Chilcott Pub. Ltd. Co.*, 838 F.3d 421, 439 (3d Cir. 2016) (affirming summary judgment of Section 2 claim against defendant accused of anticompetitively "product hopping" to keep generic competitors out of the market because defendant offered legitimate reasons for modifying its

results that could achieve the same procompetitive benefits as the allegedly unlawful conduct.

897. Under Article 102 TFEU, although there is no clause similar to Article 101(3) TFEU (*see* above Chapter IV), dominant firms can also claim that their conduct is objectively necessary or that it produces efficiencies that overcome the anticompetitive effects. This has long been established in EU case law.[47] The European Commission has also acknowledged the possibility for dominant firms to put forward an objective justification or efficiencies to justify its otherwise abusive conduct in its Guidance on the European Commission's enforcement priorities in applying Article 82 of the EC Treaty (now Article 102 TFEU).[48] For example, the courts of the EU have considered that a dominant undertaking is entitled to defend its own commercial interest by meeting competition in order to minimize short run losses resulting from its competitors' actions, provided it is able to demonstrate that its conduct is only in response to low pricing by others.[49]

898. However, the standard of proof is very high. When arguing such a defense, the dominant undertaking needs to show, first, that meeting competition is a suitable way to achieve the protection of its commercial interests and, second, that this legitimate aim could not have been achieved by less anticompetitive means. In practice, the same cumulative conditions set forth under Article 101 TFEU(3) apply to a claim of efficiencies under Article 102 TFEU: (i) the conduct must lead to efficiencies being realized, (ii) there must be no less restrictive means to achieve the realization of those efficiencies, (iii) the efficiencies outweigh the negative effects of the conduct, and (iv) the conduct should not eliminate effective competition.[50] This is why, in practice, objective justifications or efficiencies defense are very rarely admitted.[51]

---

patents, including safety concerns); *Epic Games, Inc. v. Apple, Inc.*, 67 F.4th 946, 986 (9th Cir. 2023) (affirming summary judgment in Apple's favor when it claimed its walled-garden application store ecosystem enhanced security and compensated it for its IP investment in its application store).

47 *See, e.g.*, 27/7, *United Brands Company and United Brands Continentaal BV*, ECLI:EU:C:1978:22, ¶184 (Feb. 14, 1978); Case T-30/89, *Hilti AG v. Commission*, ECLI:EU:T:1991:70, ¶102–119 (Dec. 12, 1991); Case C-209/10, *Post Danmark A/S*, ECLI:EU:C:2012:172, ¶41 (Mar. 27, 2012) ("In particular, such an undertaking may demonstrate, for that purpose, either that its conduct is objectively necessary ... or that the exclusionary effect produced may be counterbalanced, outweighed even, by advantages in terms of efficiency that also benefit consumers.").

48 European Commission Communication, *supra* n. 17, Chapter V, ¶¶28–31.

49 Case 27/7, *United Brands Company and United Brands Continentaal BV*, ECLI:EU:C:1978:22, ¶189–91 (Feb. 14, 1978); Case T-65/89, *BPB Industries Plc and British Gypsum Ltd v. Commission*, ECLI:EU:T:1993:31, ¶69 (Apr. 1, 1993).

50 Case C-209/10, *Post Danmark A/S*, ECLI:EU:C:2012:172, ¶42 (Mar. 27, 2012).

51 To the best of the authors' knowledge, although the principle has many times been recalled in case law, there are no cases in which the European Commission and, subsequently, the European courts have recognized that an abusive conduct was objectively justified or counterbalanced by efficiencies. In *AstraZeneca*, on appeal before the General Court, the company explained its behavior by the fact that it no longer wanted to sell Losec capsules or keep the marketing authorization for this product because it was unnecessarily burdensome, in particular in terms of pharmacovigilance obligations. The General Court did not assess this objective justification on the merits. It simply noted that it was raised for the first time on appeal whereas it should have been put forward during the administrative proceedings before the European Commission. Case T-321/05, *AstraZeneca AB and AstraZeneca plc v. Commission*, ECLI:EU:T:2010:266, ¶685–86 (July 1, 2010).

6. Monopsony

899. Monopsony refers to the situation in which a buyer, rather than a seller, has monopoly power. The economic analysis of monopsony is similar to that of monopoly but in reverse. Therefore, having buyer power alone does not constitute monopsony. Nor does aggressive negotiation to obtain lower prices from suppliers.

900. A firm with a monopsony can exert its power by decreasing demand in a relevant market, thereby depressing prices for an input it purchases below a competitive level. Prices below competitive levels can reduce the suppliers' incentive to produce the input, resulting in lower output, worse quality, or less innovation. Alternatively, a monopsonist can overbid or over-purchase an input to increase prices for its competitors who require the same input. Potential applications of monopsony in the pharmaceutical sector include the purchase of APIs or finished pharmaceutical products.

901. Similar to monopoly claims, to state a monopsony claim under Section 2 of the Sherman Act, a plaintiff must show that the defendant has monopsony power and that it engaged in exclusionary conduct.[52] In *Weyerhaeuser Co. v. Ross-Simmons Hardwood Lumber Co.,* the Supreme Court stated that both monopoly and monopsony conduct should be reviewed using similar standards because anticompetitive conduct on both sides of the market can harm consumers in the form of reduced output or decreased quality.[53] The Supreme Court further reasoned that conduct by a monopsonist and monopolist both involve the "deliberate use of unilateral pricing measures for an anticompetitive purpose."[54] Moreover, these claims both involve firms incurring short-term losses in order to reap supra-competitive profits in the future.[55] Monopsony claims, however, often fail for lack of evidence of anticompetitive effects, such as decreased output or increased prices.

902. Although the focus in EU competition law is on the demand side, and thus on monopoly power rather than monopsony power, buyer power can in theory be a concern under Article 102 TFEU if ultimately it leads to disadvantages for consumers, be it in terms of higher prices, loss of choice or quality, less innovation, etc.

903. However, buyer power is often seen as procompetitive and precedents are scarce in this area.[56] To date, monopsony issues have therefore mostly been dealt with in merger cases rather than under Article 102 TFEU. *British Airways*[57] is nonetheless one of the few notable cases under Article 102 TFEU. British Airways, which at

---

52 *See Weyerhaeuser Co. v. Ross-Simmons Hardwood Lumber Co. Inc.*, 549 U.S. 312, 322 (2007) ("The kinship between monopoly and monopsony suggests that similar legal standards should apply to claims of monopolization and to claims of monopsonization.").

53 *Id.*

54 *Id.*

55 *Id.*

56 *See, e.g.*, Case 298/83, *CICCE v. Commission*, ECLI:EU:C:1985:150, (Mar. 28, 1985), where the ECJ upheld the Commission decision rejecting a complaint based on a monopsony claim for lack of evidence.

57 Case COMP/IV/D-2/34.780, *Virgin/British Airways* (1999), confirmed by Case T-219/99, *British Airways*, ECLI:EU:T:2003:343, (Dec. 17, 2003) and Case C-95/04 P, *British Airways v. Commission*, ECLI:EU:C:2007:166, (Mar. 15, 2007).

the time was the largest airline in the UK, was fined for using its buyer power with travel agents as leverage to reinforce its dominant position in the market for airline tickets. More particularly, British Airways offered bonuses and other incentives to travel agencies to encourage them to favor British Airways over its competitors when selling airline tickets to end customers, thereby reinforcing its dominant position in the downstream market.

904. At the national level, some Member States have introduced specific legislation to deal with buyer power, especially in the retail market. This is for example the case in France where unfair trade practices are sanctioned independently of Article 102 TFEU (or its French equivalent Article L.420-2 of the French Commercial Code), but also in Germany where the concept of relative dominance has been used to grasp potentially unfair practices, including the imposition by a firm with buyer power of unfair purchasing conditions.[58]

II. Types of unilateral conduct violations

905. Unilateral conduct has been and likely will continue to be a significant focus of antitrust enforcement in the pharmaceutical sector. A wide variety of unilateral conduct in the sector – both price- and non-price-related – is scrutinized under the antitrust laws, including in particular Section 2 of the Sherman Act and Article 102 TFEU. Competition laws generally encourage and are designed to foster low prices, but certain types of pricing conduct may be deemed exclusionary, including predatorily low prices, certain types of exclusionary discounts and rebates, excessive pricing, and price discrimination. Non-price conduct that may be challenged includes refusals to deal with competitors or would-be competitors, certain lifecycle management strategies, product disparagement, abuse of IP rights, litigation and regulatory abuses, and acquisitions involving competitors when they fall outside the merger control regime (*see* Chapter III).

1. Pricing Conduct

A. *Predatory Pricing*

906. Predatory pricing is a form of exclusionary conduct that involves a firm setting its price below cost in order to drive competitors from the market in the short run and then recouping its losses by reducing competition and charging supra-competitive prices in the long run. Because setting low prices is the essence of competition, the requirements for establishing liability under a predatory pricing theory are substantial. Mere aggressive pricing – even by a firm with monopoly power – is not sufficient to establish predatory pricing.

---

58 In France, unfair competition practices are dealt with in Section I of Chapter II of Title IV of Book IV of the French Commercial Code. In Germany, the concepts of relative dominance and buyer power have notably been discussed in *EDEKA/Plus-Ubernahme*. In a judgment of Nov. 18, 2015, the Düsseldorf Higher Regional Court annulled a *Bundeskartellamt* decision according to which EDEKA, a large supermarket retailer, had abused its relative dominant position *vis-à-vis* suppliers of sparkling wine in breach of the *Anzapfverbot* provision. The German Supreme Court confirmed the judgment of the Düsseldorf Higher Regional Court, considering that EDEKA had merely used its bargaining power in commercial negotiations.

a. *US Approach*

907. In the US, to prevail on a predatory pricing claim, a plaintiff must demonstrate: (1) pricing "below an appropriate measure of its rival's costs," and (2) a "dangerous probability" of recoupment via supra-competitive prices.[59] The Supreme Court has declined to specify the measure of cost to be used in establishing the first element of predatory pricing. In the absence of such guidance, the lower courts typically have used marginal cost or average variable cost as the appropriate metric.[60] Measuring the defendant's costs, however, is a highly fact-intensive analysis.

908. To establish the recoupment element of predatory pricing, a plaintiff must first show that the below-cost pricing was capable of driving rivals from the market.[61] This requires an analysis of the extent and duration of the alleged predation, as well as the relative financial strengths and incentives of the alleged predator and victim. The recoupment element also requires a showing that the relevant market is susceptible to sustained monopoly pricing following the rivals' exit.[62] Often, characteristics of the relevant market – such as low concentration levels and a lack of meaningful entry barriers – render recoupment unlikely.

909. In the US, allegations of predatory pricing have been asserted against pharmaceutical companies, often combined with other types of pricing conduct including bundled rebating (*see* Chapter V, section IV.1.D). In a series of cases, plaintiffs accused Abbott Laboratories (Abbott) of monopolizing the market for certain HIV drugs. Among the allegations was a claim that Abbott engaged in predatory pricing for its HIV drug, Kaletra, which plaintiffs characterized as a bundled product. Kaletra is a single capsule containing lopinavir (a protease inhibitor) and Norvir (a compound, ritonavir, used to "boost" the effectiveness of lopinavir). Although marketed as a standalone HIV drug, Norvir was found to have greater clinical effectiveness as a booster of other protease inhibitors. In response to Abbott's rivals introducing their own protease inhibitors boosted with Norvir, Abbott allegedly increased the price of Norvir by 400%, thereby increasing the prices of the rival products competing with Abbott's Kaletra. The district court agreed with the plaintiffs that Kaletra represented a bundled product and denied Abbott's summary judgment motion on the predatory pricing claim.[63]

910. In a related case involving the same set of facts, plaintiffs alleged that Abbott engaged in monopoly leveraging, which is using monopoly power in one market

---

[59] *Brooke Grp. Ltd. v. Brown & Williamson Tobacco Corp.*, 509 U.S. 209, 222, 224 (1993).

[60] *See Advo, Inc. v. Philadelphia Newspapers, Inc.*, 51 F.3d 1191, 1198 (3d Cir. 1995) ("As long as a firm's prices exceed its marginal cost, each additional sale decreases losses or increases profits. Such pricing is presumably not predatory."); *Stearns Airport Equip. Co. v. FMC Corp.*, 170 F.3d 518, 532 (5th Cir. 1999) ("Ideally, an inquiry into whether a monopolist had sold his product below cost would look at the true marginal cost… But because the true marginal costs of production are difficult to generate, this Court attempts to estimate them by using average variable costs.").

[61] *Brooke Group*, 509 U.S. 225.

[62] *Id.* 225–26.

[63] *Safeway Inc. v. Abbott Labs.*, 761 F. Supp. 2d 874, 891–92 (N.D. Cal. 2011). Because this case involved a bundled product, the applicable legal test was the discount attribution rule from *Cascade Health Solutions v. PeaceHealth*, 515 F.3d 883 (9th Cir. 2008), *see* Section II.B.b.(2) below, rather than the Brooke Group predatory pricing test.

to obtain a monopoly in another market. According to the plaintiffs, Abbott used its monopoly power in the booster market to raise the price of Norvir, while selling its own boosted protease inhibitor at too low of a price. This allegedly squeezed competing producers of protease inhibitors that depend on Norvir for their boosted effectiveness. On appeal, the Ninth Circuit reversed the district court's denial of Abbott's motion to dismiss, finding that Abbott's conduct was the functional equivalent of a price squeeze.[64] Applying the Supreme Court's decision in *Pacific Bell Telephone Co. v. linkLine Communications, Inc.*,[65] the court found the plaintiffs' claims failed, as they alleged no refusal to deal at the booster level, and no below-cost pricing at the boosted level. Because the plaintiffs failed to allege the first prong of *Brooke Group* (i.e., below-cost pricing), the Ninth Circuit found it unnecessary to reach the second prong (i.e., dangerous probability of recoupment).

b. *EU Approach*

(1) Overview and Legal Test

911. Predatory conduct under EU law refers to the practice whereby a dominant undertaking sets its prices at a below-cost level, meaning that it voluntarily incurs losses or foregoes profits in the short term to force one or more of its competitors out of the market, discipline them, or make it more difficult for future competitors to enter the market, with a view to maintaining or strengthening its market position, thereby causing consumer harm. Predation therefore has two components: first, a sacrifice on the part of the dominant firm which incurs a loss that could have been avoided and, second, an anticompetitive foreclosure effect.

912. The reference test to determine whether a dominant undertaking has engaged in predatory pricing has been defined by the ECJ in the *Akzo* case.[66] In this case, the ECJ established a presumption that prices below average variable costs (i.e., those varying depending on the quantities produced) must be regarded as abusive, the rationale being that, since each sale generates a loss, there can be no other explanation for selling below average variable costs than the elimination of competition. The ECJ further considered that prices below average total costs (i.e., fixed costs plus variable costs) but above average variable costs may constitute an abuse if they are part of a plan for eliminating competition. In other words, when a dominant firm sells below its average total costs, the European Commission can find an infringement only if it adduces additional evidence that this conduct is part of an overall anticompetitive strategy.

913. In its Guidance on the European Commission's enforcement priorities in applying Article 82 of the EC Treaty (now Article 102 TFEU), the European Commission provided further guidance on the situations in which it is more likely to intervene.[67] Generally speaking, the European Commission will take action if consumers risk being harmed by the predatory pricing conduct, that is if it is likely that, in the

---

64 *John Doe I v. Abbott Labs.*, 571 F.3d 930, 935 (2009).

65 555 U.S. 438 (2009).

66 Case C-62/86, *AKZO Chemie BV*, ECLI:EU:C:1991:286, ¶71–72 (July 3, 1991).

67 European Commission Communication, *supra* n. 17, Chapter V, ¶¶63 *et seq.*

long run, the dominant undertaking will increase its prices above competitive level so as to recoup its losses and therefore benefit from the sacrifice it made. However, the European Commission may also intervene in other circumstances, for example if the conduct is likely to prevent or delay a decline in prices that would otherwise have occurred. In addition, the European Commission considers that it is not necessary for competitors to have actually left the market in order to demonstrate anticompetitive foreclosure effects, as it may be that the dominant undertaking is only looking to discipline its existing competitors already present on the market: in such a case, prices below cost level ensure that the dominant firm will maintain its market position by preventing other market players from engaging in vigorous competition on price, to the detriment of consumers. Finally, although not entirely excluded, the European Commission specified that it is very unlikely that predation will create efficiencies.

(2) Key Cases

914. There are only a few precedents of predatory pricing conduct in the pharmaceutical sector, which all concerned prices offered to hospitals in the context of tender procedures. Because tenders are organized at the national level, these cases have all been dealt with by NCAs.

915. In *Napp Pharmaceutial*,[68] the UK Office of Fair Trading (OFT) imposed a 3.2 million pounds fine on Napp for abusive price-cutting after finding that Napp applied a 90% discount in the provision of unstained morphine to hospitals just after its patent expired, so as to make market entry more difficult for generics. In assessing Napp's pricing policy, the OFT applied the *Akzo* test and found that Napp was selling below its average variable cost. Napp argued that sales below cost to hospitals were objectively justified since compensating margins were possible through follow-on sales in the community segment (so-called "source effect"). The OFT rejected this plea and found that the very reason that Napp was able to make significant margins on community sales was that it had been successful in crushing competition in relation to sales to hospitals.[69] On appeal, the CAT confirmed the OFT's finding and held that, as Napp had offered prices below its average variable cost to hospitals, the demonstration of a plan to eliminate competition was not relevant.[70]

916. It is interesting to note that a different approach was taken by the FCA in the *Durogesic* case. In this case, the FCA decided, in 2009, to investigate, among other practices, whether prices close to zero offered by Janssen-Cilag to hospitals in the context of generic entry on the market could constitute an abuse of dominant position.[71] However, the predatory pricing allegation in this case was

---

68 OFT, Case No. CA98/2/2001, *NAAP*, (Mar. 30, 2001), *available at* https://assets.publishing.service.gov.uk/media/555de4bf40f0b669c4000169/napp.pdf, *see* Derek Ridyard, *The UK Competition Authority holds abusive below-cost pricing in the pharmaceuticals sector (Napp)*, E-COMPETITIONS Mar. 2001, art. No. 21109.

69 *Id.*, ¶¶193–196.

70 CAT, Case No. 1001/1/1/01, *Napp Pharmaceutical v. Director General of Fair Trading* (Jan. 15, 2002), *available at* https://www.catribunal.org.uk/cases/10011101-napp-pharmaceutical-holdings-limited-and-subsidiaries.

71 FCA, Decision No. 09-D-28, *Janssen-Cilag* ¶¶149–152 (July 31, 2009); *see also* Anne Wachsmann & Nicolas Zacharie, *Predatory Pricing: The French Competition Authority Rejects the Request for Interim Measures in a Predatory Pricing Case in the Pharmaceutical Sector but Continues its Investigations on the Merits of the*

subsequently dropped during the investigation before the SO was issued.[72] The outcome was different in *GlaxoSmithKline* (GSK), though. In 2007, the FCA fined the laboratory €10 million for alleged predatory pricing in the market for sodic cefuroxime, an antibiotic for systemic use marketed under the trademark Zinnat, widely used at hospitals.[73] The French watchdog found that, upon generic entry, GSK offered very low prices to hospitals (below the transfer price at which it purchased Zinnat from another subsidiary of the GSK group) so as to eliminate competition. According to the FCA, this strategy, which in fact pursued a wider objective, was successful not only because the generic company Flavelab was forced to exit the market but also because, as a result thereof, other competitors of GSK in the market for sodic cefuroxime were dissuaded from developing further generics of GSK's products. Through its aggressive pricing policy, GSK managed to broadly limit competition for its portfolio of products in the hospital market.

917. The FCA's decision was however subsequently set aside on appeal, on the ground that the FCA had failed to characterize an infringement of Article 102 TFEU and Article L. 420-2 of the French Commercial Code.[74] The Paris Court of Appeal approved the FCA insofar as it concluded that GSK sold below its costs and won several tenders on the market for sodic cefuroxime. However, the dominance had not been established in this market, where GSK originally faced competition from several players, but in another market, for injectable acyclovir, where GSK marketed Zovirax. According to the Paris Court of Appeal, contrary to the situation in *Akzo*, where the European Commission established the dominance of Akzo on a neighboring but intrinsically linked market to that on which Akzo engaged in predation, in the present case the markets for sodic cefuroxime, on the one hand, and injectable acyclovir, on the other hand, only shared general characteristics of hospital markets but were not intertwined. This lack of relation between the dominated market and the non-dominated one in which GSK offered low prices led the Paris Court of Appeal to consider that the commercial policy of GSK on Zinnat, which allegedly aimed at building an aggressive reputation, could not have disciplined potential competitors not to enter the market for injectable acyclovir. This conclusion was further supported by the fact that several competitors subsequently successfully launched generics of Zovirax. In 2009, the French Supreme Court confirmed the Paris Court of Appeal's ruling.[75]

918. Despite the partial annulment of the FCA's findings by the Paris Court of Appeal, two important takeaways can be drawn from the GSK case. First, the Paris Court

---

Case (Janssen-Cilag France), CONCURRENCES July 2009, No. 4-2009, art. No. 29270, 117–119.

72 FCA, Decision No. 17-D-25, *Janssen-Cilag* (Dec. 20, 2017).

73 FCA, Decision No. 07-D-09, *GlaxoSmithKline* (Mar. 14, 2007).

74 Laure Schulz & Patricia Perennes, *The Paris Court of Appeal Rebuts the Decision of the Competition Council Regarding Practices in the Market of Distribution of Pharmaceutical Products (GlaxoSmithKline)*, E-COMPETITIONS Apr. 2008, art. No. 19851. *See e.g.*, Marie Koehler de Montblanc, *Abuse of a Dominant Position: The Paris Court of Appeal Calls for Greater Care and Vigilance to be Exercised When Assessing "Predation by Reputation" Claims (GlaxoSmithKline France)*, CONCURRENCES Apr. 2008, No. 3-2008, art. No. 27581.

75 French Supreme Court, Case No. 08-14.503, *GlaxoSmithKline France* (Mar. 17, 2009). *See e.g.*, Anne Wachsmann &, and Bastien Thomas, *Predatory Pricing: The Court of Cassation Upholds the Analysis of the Paris Court of Appeal Regarding the Absence of Predatory Pricing (GlaxoSmithKline France)*, CONCURRENCES Mar. 2009, No. 2-2009, art. No. 26028, 117–118.

of Appeal upheld the FCA's approach in taking into consideration, for the purposes of the predatory price test, the transfer price at which GSK had bought Zinnat from another subsidiary of the group. Absent the disclosure by GSK of its real costs for this product, the Court of Appeal considered, pursuant to the OECD principles applicable at the time,[76] that the transfer price reflected a competitive price similar to the one GSK could have obtained from a third party on the market. Second, the Paris Court of Appeal did not criticize the FCA for having conducted the predatory price test for each individual tender rather than taking into account GSK's prices globally on the French market. It has thus implicitly confirmed the FCA's finding that, in case of tender procedures, competition happens for each specific tender and the existence of a predatory price should therefore be assessed on a case-by-case basis.

B. *Discount and Rebate Policies*

919. The contractual relationships among manufacturers, wholesalers, and other third parties in the distribution of pharmaceutical products often provide for various types of discounts and rebates, which can take many different forms (e.g., based on loyalty, exclusivity, volume, or bundling of products/services). While these practices are common, they can also have antitrust implications.

a. *Types of Discounts and Core Issues*

920. Granting discounts or rebates to a trading partner is a common commercial practice in all sectors. Discounts and rebates are generally beneficial to buyers as they pay a lower price on their purchases and can have efficiency enhancing effects, even when implemented by a monopolist or dominant firm. However, in some cases, discount and rebate policies can have the potential to exclude rivals from the market or foreclose access to the market.

921. While it is not possible to categorize each and every type of discount, especially because their potential anticompetitive effects depend on a wide range of factors and circumstances, which require a case-by-case analysis, a broad distinction can be made between unconditional and conditional rebates.

922. On the one hand, unconditional rebates generally correspond to quantity rebates (i.e., volume-based) granted to customers for every purchase, without any other condition, resulting in a lower average unit price for purchasers buying larger quantities of products. Unconditional rebates usually reflect economies of scale on the part of the supplier, which are shared with customers, and are therefore procompetitive or competitively neutral.

923. On the other hand, conditional rebates are those which reward a customer's purchasing behavior, i.e., they are only granted provided that the customer meets certain conditions, for example buying a minimum volume over a certain period of time or a certain share of its demand from the supplier. In practice, conditional rebates can take many different forms. The most common are loyalty rebates

---

[76] OECD, *Transfer Pricing Guidelines for Multinational Enterprises and Tax Administrations*, OECD PUBLISHING (1995, last updated in 2010), *available at* https://www.oecd.org/ctp/transfer-pricing/transfer-pricing-guidelines.htm.

(including exclusivity rebates) and multi-product rebates (also referred to as bundling or tying arrangements).

924. Loyalty rebates reward the fidelity of the customer: the more the customer purchases from the supplier over a certain period of time, the better price it will get in exchange. Exclusivity rebates are an extreme form of loyalty rebates where the customer is required to purchase all or most of its needs from the same supplier. Loyalty rebates are often granted on a retroactive basis, meaning that, above a certain threshold, the discount will retroactively apply on all the customer's purchases. Otherwise, they are deemed incremental, i.e., the discount only applies to purchases made above a certain threshold.

925. Volume discounts, which result in better prices for larger purchases, generally have not been found to be unlawful. Because they do not involve any loyalty or exclusivity requirements, volume discounts typically are deemed procompetitive or competitively neutral.

926. Bundling or tying is another common commercial practice. A distinction can be made between pure bundling, where the products are only available together and mixed bundling, where the products are sold separately but the customer will pay a lower price if it buys them together (also referred to as multi-product rebates).

927. When implemented by a monopolist or dominant firm, loyalty rebates and tying arrangements can have a foreclosure effect and therefore be anticompetitive. The enforcement approach is different in the US, where an effect-based analysis has always prevailed, and in the EU, where a stricter stance has traditionally been taken. However, EU law has recently tended to converge toward a more effect-based approach.

b. *Enforcement Approach and Key Cases in the US*

(1) Loyalty and Exclusivity Rebates

928. Loyalty and exclusivity rebates have been challenged under theories of predatory pricing and exclusive dealing. Exclusive dealing occurs when a manufacturer limits a distributor from purchasing inputs from other firms.[77] Exclusive dealing can be anticompetitive where it forecloses a substantial portion of the relevant market,[78] although there are often procompetitive reasons for entering into exclusive arrangements such as supply assurance, price stability, recouping investments, and more.[79] Therefore, courts analyze exclusive dealing claims under the rule of reason.[80]

---

77 *See* FTC, *Exclusive Dealing or Requirements Contracts*, *available at* https://www.ftc.gov/advice-guidance/competition-guidance/guide-antitrust-laws/dealings-supply-chain/exclusive-dealing-or-requirements-contracts (defining exclusive dealing and noting it is judged under a rule of reason standard accounting for procompetitive and anticompetitive effects).

78 *Barr Lab'ys, Inc. v. Abbott Lab'ys*, 978 F.2d 98, 110–11 (3d Cir. 1992) (summarizing the law of exclusive dealing and upholding an exclusivity contract).

79 *See ZF Meritor, LLC v. Eaton Corp.*, 696 F.3d 254, 270 (3d Cir. 2012) (listing the potential procompetitive benefits of exclusivity).

80 *See, e.g.*, *McWane, Inc. v. FTC.*, 783 F.3d 814, 833 (11th Cir. 2015) (applying rule of reason to exclusive dealing program); *Fraser v. Major League Soccer, L.L.C.*, 284 F.3d 47, 68 (1st Cir. 2002) (citation omitted) ("Such agreements are not inherently unlawful; they are judged primarily by considering, in addition to competitive or efficiency justifications, any actual or threatened adverse effects on competition.").

929. Under the predatory pricing theory,[81] courts apply a price-cost test to analyze the challenged discounts, first looking at whether prices for a given product fall below an appropriate cost to produce it, and second looking at whether the discounting firm had a "dangerous probability" of recouping its investment in its below-cost prices. In *ZF Meritor, LLC v. Eaton Corp.*, the Third Circuit held that characterization of a rebate arrangement as exclusive dealing, rather than predatory pricing, does not foreclose the use of the price-cost test, which still applies where price is the main method of exclusion.[82] The plaintiffs in *ZF Meritor* alleged exclusionary effects from rebate pricing as well as anti-competitive provisions in contracts themselves; plaintiffs "presented considerable evidence" that the defendant was a monopolist and wielded that power to "effectively force every direct purchaser... to enter into restrictive long-term agreements..."[83] While in *ZF Meritor*, price was not the primary form of exclusion, other courts continue to follow the rule that exclusive dealing claims can sometimes be addressed with the price-cost test.[84]

930. As an alternative to the price-cost test does not apply to the challenged rebating strategies, particularly where pricing is not the main means of exclusion, US courts may apply a rule-of-reason analysis comparable to the one used in assessing exclusive dealing claims, as explained above. To prevail under this rule-of-reason analysis, a plaintiff must show that "it [is] probable that performance of the contract will foreclose competition in a substantial share of the line of commerce affected."[85] Because the exclusive dealing claims in *ZF Meritor* did not primarily involve pricing, the court provided several factors to consider in evaluating the legality of exclusive dealing agreements, including: (1) whether the defendant has significant market power or there has been substantial market foreclosure, (2) the duration of any contract and the ability of customers to terminate an agreement, (3) the likely or actual anticompetitive effects of the agreement in light of any procompetitive effects, (4) whether the defendant's behavior was coercive, and (5) whether exclusive dealing is used by competitors of the defendant.[86] In this case, the defendant "possessed monopoly power," there was evidence of use of coercion, a lack of entrants pointed to high entry barriers, foreclosure was substantial, agreements were not short-term and contained numerous anticompetitive provisions, and procompetitive effects paled in comparison to these anticompetitive ones.[87] The Third Circuit therefore found that there was sufficient evidence to uphold a jury finding of liability.[88]

---

81 *See* Section II.1.A. above.

82 696 F.3d 273, 275 (noting that the price-cost test has been applied "regardless of the way in which the plaintiff cast its grievance, because pricing itself operated as the exclusionary tool.").

83 *Id.* 277.

84 *See, e.g., Eisai Inc. v. Sanofi-Aventis U.S., LLC*, No. CIV.A. 08-4168 MLC, 2014 WL 1343254, *26 (D.N.J. Mar. 28, 2014), aff'd, 821 F.3d 394 (3d Cir. 2016) ("The Court finds that price is the predominant mechanism of exclusion under Sanofi's practices, and thus, the price-cost test applies.").

85 *Tampa Elec. Co. v. Nashville Coal Co.*, 365 U.S. 320, 327 (1961). *See also* Section II(B)(b)(1) below, for further explanation of exclusive dealing law in this context.

86 696 F.3d 271–72, 279, 281.

87 *Id.* 283–89.

88 *Id.* 303.

931. Two recent cases – each involving EpiPens – featured challenges to Mylan's rebating and discounting practices. Each of them demonstrates the highly fact-intensive nature of challenges to rebating practices in the life sciences field. The courts examined factors such as rebate contract duration, the operation of specific anticompetitive provisions, ease of termination, and tangible effects on pricing and competitive strategy. First, in *In re EpiPen (Epinephrine Injection, USP) Mktg., Sales Practices & Antitrust Litig.*, the district court granted summary judgment to Mylan under a rule-of-reason standard.[89] Although the court found that Mylan had significant market power, it declared this factor "not dispositive" and instead focused on others such as the duration and ease of termination of the contracts at issue.[90] Specifically, the court found that the rebate contracts were "short-term and easily terminable," with several lasting two-and-a-half years or less and containing 90-day clauses for termination without cause. The facts also demonstrated that rebate agreements were frequently renegotiated and terminated early, showing that the agreements did not exclude competition.[91] The court also held that the exclusivity-based discounts were not unlawful, relying on the facts that payors sent bid requests to both Mylan and the plaintiff manufacturers, some payors simply chose to cover only one product, smaller rebates were still available for agreements that were not exclusive, and others switched between covering EpiPen and its competitors.[92]

932. Second, *In re EpiPen Direct Purchaser Litigation* involved similarly fact-intensive analysis by the court, even at the motion to dismiss stage. There, the district court refused to dismiss claims by drug wholesalers that Mylan engaged in a bribery and kickback scheme with pharmacy benefit managers (PBMs) involving rebates on its EpiPen product.[93] The plaintiffs alleged that Mylan tied its rebates and administrative fees to PBMs to the wholesale acquisition cost of EpiPens, such that as the list price increased, so did the benefits to the PBMs and Mylan.[94] The district court found that bribery can be a violation of the Sherman Act when it "is directed toward suppressing competition in the market generally." The court denied Mylan's motion to dismiss.[95] The court further found that Mylan controlled "nearly the whole market" and was able to maintain a stable market share despite "huge price increases." As a result, the court found that anticompetitive conduct was plausibly alleged and the claims could continue.[96]

933. Government enforcers also continue to review rebating practices based on de facto exclusive dealing theories, as seen by the FTC's ongoing monopolization case against Surescripts.[97] The FTC complaint alleged that Surescripts used exclusivity and loyalty rebates to maintain its monopolies in two complementary markets: routing electronic prescriptions and determining eligibility for prescriptions

---

89 507 F. Supp. 3d 1289 (D. Kan. 2020), *aff'd*, No. 21-3005, 2022 WL 3009140 (10th Cir. July 29, 2022).

90 *Id.* 1344.

91 *Id.* 1354.

92 *Id.* 1347–48.

93 *In re EpiPen Direct Purchaser Litig.*, No. 20-cv-0827, 2021 WL 147166 (D. Minn. Jan 15, 2021).

94 *Id.* *8-*9.

95 *Id.* *25.

96 *Id.*

97 Complaint for Injunctive and Other Equitable Relief, *FTC v. Surescripts*, LLC, No. 1:19-cv-01080 (D.D.C. 2019).

(together, "e-prescribing").[98] By including such rebates in its customer contracts, the FTC alleged, Surescripts, with its 95%-plus share in each market, was able to foreclose competitors from entering the relevant markets through an "anticompetitive web of exclusive contracts."[99] The district court denied Surescripts' motion to dismiss.[100] The case is ongoing, demonstrating how enforcers and plaintiffs alike analyze how provisions with potential anticompetitive effects operate in tandem with one another.

(2) Bundled Discounts

934. Under US antitrust law, a tying arrangement is one in which: (1) there are two products, (2) the two products are tied together or customers are coerced such that the customer must take the tied product from the supplier not because of preference but in order to have access to the tying product, (3) the supplier has substantial economic power over the tying product, (4) there is an anticompetitive effect, and (5) a not insubstantial volume of commerce is affected.[101] Courts have reached different conclusions regarding the plausibility of antitrust challenges to bundled pricing arrangements.

935. Bundled discounts are often examined as de facto tying arrangements on the theory that conditioning the discount for a product on the purchase of another product effectively creates a tie. The Third Circuit, for example, applied such an analysis in *LePage's Inc. v. 3M*, where plaintiff LePage's alleged that 3M employed bundled discounts and associated contracts to violate Section 2 by monopolizing he market for lower-priced transparent tape.[102] The court applied a tying theory because analyzing bundled discounts under a standard price cost analysis for predatory pricing could yield inconsistent results: a bundled discount may have aggregate prices above cost, but could still foreclose portions of the market to competitors who do not have similarly diverse products to bundle.[103] A monopoly in one product line, bundled with rebates in product lines where a company does not have a monopoly, could therefore create anticompetitive effects and force out competitors who, due to their lack of similar product lines, have no chance to compete.[104] This was the case in *LePage's*, where the court examined the impacts of 3M's rebates and concluded that a jury could reasonably find that 3M wielded its monopoly in transparent tape, backed by their expansive product catalog, to squeeze out LePage's.[105]

936. However, not all courts agree with this analysis, and some prefer to apply the price-cost test. For instance, in *Cascade Health Solutions v. PeaceHealth*,[106] the Ninth

---

98 *Id.* *1-*3.

99 *Id.* *14.

100 *FTC v. Surescripts, LLC*, 424 F. Supp. 3d 92, 104 (D.D.C. 2020).

101 Tying is discussed in greater detail in Chapter IV.

102 324 F.3d 141, 144, 147 (3d. Cir. 2003).

103 Accordingly, the court rejected 3M's argument that "a company's pricing action is legal if its prices are not below its costs" and restated that "a monopolist will be found to violate § 2 of the Sherman Act if it engages in exclusionary or predatory conduct without a valid business justification." *Id.* 152.

104 *Id.* 155 (citing *SmithKline Corp. v. Eli Lilly & Co.*, 575 F.2d 1056 (3d Cir. 1978)).

105 *Id.* 157.

106 515 F.3d 883, 899–900 (9th Cir. 2008).

Circuit critiqued the standard established by *LePage's*, stating it "could protect a less efficient competitor at the expense of consumer welfare" because bundling discounts can allow buyers to "get more for less" and sellers to realize savings that result from selling multiple products to one customer, rather than selling one product individually. Therefore, the *LePage's* standard may miss instances where bundled discounts "constitute competition on the merits."[107] The Ninth Circuit thus declined to follow *LePage's*, concluding that it did not provide a sufficiently clear standard for companies to understand when their discounts are legal or illegal. The court instead held that the exclusionary conduct element of a Section 2 claim cannot be satisfied by reference to bundled discounts unless the discounts result in prices that are below an appropriate measure of the defendant's costs.[108] Under the Ninth Circuit's rule, if the discount given on the entire bundle of products is allocated to only the competitive product or products in the bundle and the competitive product or products were sold below the average variable cost of producing them under that allocation, then the bundled discount is predatory and anticompetitive.[109]

937. In *Pfizer Inc. v. Johnson & Johnson*,[110] the district court denied a motion to dismiss, holding that Pfizer had plausibly alleged antitrust injury in its complaint challenging Johnson & Johnson's conduct involving, among other things, bundled rebates for its product Remicade (infliximab), for which Pfizer had a competing biosimilar, Inflectra. In particular, Pfizer alleged that Johnson & Johnson bundled rebates across multiple products, including ones for which Pfizer has no competing products, and effectively based its rebates on the bundling of existing patients (i.e., incontestable demand) and new patients (i.e., contestable demand).[111] The court held that Johnson & Johnson's multi-product bundle, on its own, did not raise any antitrust concern, finding that Pfizer failed to allege that it could not offer its own multi-product bundle.[112] The court, however, rejected Johnson & Johnson's argument that bundling contestable and incontestable demand for the same product cannot constitute an antitrust violation and found that bundling incontestable and contestable demand could foreclose competition for new patients.[113] That is, if the market of existing Remicade patients were truly incontestable and inelastic, the court found, new infliximab patients and their insurers would be deprived of the ability to make a meaningful choice between Remicade and its biosimilars. The court allowed the case to proceed to discovery to determine the legality of Johnson & Johnson's conduct and the parties ultimately reached a settlement.

938. In contrast, the district court granted the defendant's motion to dismiss in *Shire US, Inc. v. Allergan, Inc.*[114] In doing so, the court observed that bundled rebates are not

---

107 *Id.* 899.

108 The court cited Supreme Court precedent as a forceful suggestion that "we should not condemn prices that are above some measure of incremental cost." *Id.* 901–02 (citing *Brooke Grp. Ltd. v. Brown & Williamson Tobacco Corp.*, 509 U.S. 209, 223 (1993) and *Weyerhaeuser Co. v. Ross-Simmons Hardwood Lumber Co. Inc.*, 549 U.S. 312, 325 (2007)).

109 515 F.3d 903.

110 333 F. Supp. 3d 494 (E.D. Pa. 2018).

111 *Id.* 498–500.

112 *Id.* 503–04.

113 *Id.*

114 375 F. Supp. 3d 538 (D.N.J. 2019).

inherently anticompetitive and the analysis of such rebates is highly fact-specific. In this case, Allergan, the maker of Restasis, bundled rebates across multiple products when negotiating with Medicare Advantage Part D plans for placement of Restasis on their formularies.[115] Shire, the maker of competing drug Xiidra, alleged that these bundled rebates made it impossible for Shire to offer discounts that compete with the bundled rebates provided by Allergan, because by bundling the rebates Allergan could offer Restasis at a price below its average variable cost. The court first rejected Shire's market definition of Medicare Part D as too narrow, finding that the relevant market includes all persons or entities to whom a supplier can reasonably sell.[116] The court further found that the complaint failed to demonstrate anticompetitive conduct because the contracts governing the rebates were short-term (i.e., lasting only one year) and open to annual competitive bidding.[117] In addition, according to the court, Allergan did not have a monopoly over the other drugs it bundled with Restasis, and Shire failed to allege that it has no other available products it could bundle with Xiidra to compete with Restasis.[118]

939. In sum, US courts take differing approaches to bundled discounting practices depending on their perceived threat level to competition, evaluating many cases through the lens of tying.

(3) Rebate Walls

940. A recent report by the FTC to Congress addressed so-called rebate walls.[119] The report defined a rebate wall as "a situation in which a dominant pharmaceutical manufacturer uses rebate strategies in its contracts with third party payors to maintain market power, by giving its products preferred status in drug formularies, and to prevent sales of competing products."[120] This phenomenon purportedly occurs with rebates that are conditioned on formulary access or a market share requirement, which prevent third-party payers from being able to switch patients to a lower-priced alternative by providing the payers with strong incentives to block patient access to lower-priced drugs. According to the FTC report, rebate walls may be challenged under exclusive dealing, bundling, or tying theories of harm. To date, neither the FTC nor any private litigant has pursued the rebate wall theory. On the other hand, rebating competition for formulary position is also often used as evidence of competition. For example, in *In re Intuniv Antitrust Litig.*, the district court found that rebating practices suggested competition with non-stimulant drugs in the ADHD treatment market.[121]

c. *Enforcement Approach and Key Cases in the EU*

941. Antitrust liability of a dominant firm implementing a conditional discount or rebate policy can be established quite easily under Article 102 TFEU. This is because,

---

115 *Id.* 542–45.

116 *Id.* 547.

117 *Id.* 558. This analysis is similar to the analysis of agreement duration in exclusive dealing cases.

118 *Id.* 557.

119 FTC, Report on Rebate Walls (May 2021), *available at* https://www.ftc.gov/system/files/documents/reports/federal-trade-commission-report-rebate-walls/federal_trade_commission_report_on_rebate_walls_.pdf.

120 *Id.* 1.

121 496 F. Supp. 3d 639, 666 (D. Mass. 2020).

for a long time, particularly for exclusivity rebates, applying economics-based tests was not considered necessary in the EU. Despite some evolution in the past ten years and very recently with the *Intel* case, the effect-based approach is still being navigated and not yet consistently applied. Furthermore, in its Communication amending the Guidance on the European Commission's enforcement priorities in applying Article 82 of the EC Treaty (now Article 102 TFEU),[122] the European Commission does not exclude that, in a case where no exclusionary effect can be characterized, a discount policy could still be found abusive if it merely affects the structure of competition. The amendments introduced by the European Commission thus open up the possibility for a potential discretionary deviation of an effect-based approach, to the benefit of a more formalistic approach.

(1) Early Cases

942. In the early cases, the European Commission and the European courts adopted rather formalistic reasoning. In the landmark *Hoffmann-La Roche* case, the ECJ ruled that:

> An undertaking which is in a dominant position on a market and ties purchasers[,] even if it does so at their request[,] by an obligation or promise on their part to obtain all or most of their requirements exclusively from the said undertaking abuses its dominant position within the meaning of Article 86 [now Article 102 TFEU] of the Treaty, whether the obligation in question is stipulated without further qualification or whether it is undertaken in consideration of the grant of a rebate.
>
> The same applies if the said undertaking, without tying the purchasers by a formal obligation, applies, either under the terms of agreements concluded with these purchasers or unilaterally, a system of fidelity rebates, that is to say discounts conditional on the customer's obtaining all or most of its requirements[,] whether the quantity of its purchases be large or small[,] from the undertaking in a dominant position.[123]

943. This is because, according to the ECJ, exclusivity or fidelity rebates intended to give the purchaser incentives to obtain all or most of its requirements from the dominant firm are not economically justified but rather, "are designed to deprive the purchaser of or restrict his possible choices of sources of supply and to deny other producers access to the market."[124]

944. In *Michelin I*, the discount policy implemented by Michelin was characterized by the use of sales targets with progressive discount rates but did not require customers to enter into an exclusive dealing arrangement with Michelin or purchase all or most of their requirements from it. The ECJ considered that:

> In deciding whether Michelin NV abused its dominant position in applying its discount system[,] it is therefore necessary to consider all the

---

[122] European Commission Communication COM (2023) 1923 final, *supra* n. 39, Chapter V.

[123] Case 85/76, *Hoffmann-La Roche & Co.*, ECLI:EU:C:1979:36, ¶89 (Feb. 13, 1978).

[124] *Id.* ¶90.

circumstances, particularly the criteria and rules for the grant of the discount, and to investigate whether, in providing an advantage not based on any economic service justifying it, the discount tends to remove or restrict the buyer's freedom to choose his sources of supply, to bar competitors from access to the market, to apply dissimilar conditions to equivalent transactions with other trading parties or to strengthen the dominant position by distorting competition.[125]

945. It was concluded that the characteristics of Michelin's discount system, in particular the long reference period over which target sales could be achieved and the lack of transparency of the system, coupled with Michelin's very strong market share compared to that of competitors, had the effect of preventing customers from selecting freely their supplier or change suppliers, making it more difficult for Michelin's competitors to access the market.

946. From these founding judgments, a traditional distinction was drawn between three categories of rebates.[126] At one end of the spectrum, pure quantity rebates are presumed to be lawful.[127] At the other end of the spectrum, exclusivity rebates are presumed to be unlawful. The third category includes all other types of discounts and rebates, which are neither pure quantity rebates nor akin to exclusivity rebates; these rebates are subject to a case-by-case analysis in light of all relevant circumstances.

947. Rebate schemes that specifically target certain customers have also been considered anticompetitive. In this respect, a volume-based discount scheme with different bands can still be caught by Article 102 TFEU if it is structured in such a way that only some customers will benefit from the highest discount rates, compared with competitors, without this situation being justified by the volume of business they bring to the supplier or by economies of scale they allow the supplier to achieve.[128]

948. Finally, bundling, also referred to as multi-product rebates, can under certain circumstances infringe Article 102 TFUE. This is notably the case when the grant of the rebate is conditional upon the buyer purchasing as part of the bundle a product which faces competition in order to benefit from a discount on another product for which the supplier is dominant in the market and which would otherwise not be discounted. For example, in *Hoffmann-La Roche*, the ECJ noted that a system of rebates which applied provided that the buyer purchased all its vitamins requirements from Roche was abusive because it induced clients to purchase different groups of vitamins from Roche in order to benefit from the rebate scheme whereas some vitamins, which belonged to separate product markets, could have been

---

125 Case 322/81, *NV Nederlandsche Banden Industrie Michelin*, ECLI:EU:C:1983:313, ¶73 (Nov. 9, 1983).

126 *See also* Case T-286/09, *Intel Corp Inc. v. Commission*, ECLI:EU:T:2014:547, ¶¶74 *et seq.* (June 12, 2014).

127 *Id.* ¶75 ("First, quantity rebate systems ('quantity rebates') linked solely to the volume of purchases made from an undertaking occupying a dominant position are generally considered not to have the foreclosure effect prohibited by Article 82 of the EC Treaty [now Article 102 TFEU]. If increasing the quantity supplied results in lower costs for the supplier, the latter is entitled to pass on that reduction to the customer in the form of a more favo[r]able tariff. Quantity rebates are therefore deemed to reflect gains in efficiency and economies of scale made by the undertaking in a dominant position.").

128 Case C-163/99, *Portugal v. Commission*, ECLI:EU:C:2001:189, ¶52 *et seq.* (Mar. 29, 2001). In this case, the various bands in the discount scheme had been selectively determined so that the highest discount rates in Portuguese airports would be reserved to Portuguese airlines, resulting in a discrimination with other airlines.

purchased from competitors.[129] In doing so, Roche "[made] the conclusion of contracts subject to acceptance by the other parties of supplementary obligations which, by their nature of according to commercial usage, have no cone[ct]ion with the subject of such contracts," in violation of Article 102 TFEU. Bundling practices in the pharmaceutical sector were also sanctioned in France (*see* (3) below).

(2) Evolution towards a more effect-based approach in the assessment of discount and rebate policies

949. In its Guidance on the European Commission's enforcement priorities in applying Article 82 of the EC Treaty (now Article 102 TFEU), the European Commission initiated a move toward a more effect-based assessment of conditional rebates schemes. The European Commission notably introduced the "as-efficient competitor" test as a relevant tool to assess whether a discount system implemented by a dominant firm is actually capable of hindering expansion or preventing entry from equally efficient competitors, by making it more difficult for them to compete for the contestable share of the market, that is the proportion of a customer's purchase requirements that can realistically be switched to a competitor.[130] According to the European Commission, where the effective price that competitors would have to offer is below their average avoidable cost (AAC), as a general rule the rebate scheme should be considered as being capable of foreclosing even equally efficient competitors. Where the effective price is between AAC and long-run average incremental cost (LRAIC), the European Commission will investigate whether other factors point to the conclusion that entry or expansion even by equally efficient competitors is likely to be affected.[131]

950. However, this guidance is not binding on European courts and for many years they stood by the traditional legal test, which considered a discount policy anti-competitive if it merely had the capability of having a foreclosure effect. That test did not require demonstrating the likelihood of an actual effect on competition. For example, in *Tomra*,[132] the General Court recalled that, according to settled case law, it is sufficient for the purposes of Article 102 TFEU to demonstrate that the abusive conduct "tends to restrict competition or, in other words, that the conduct is capable of having that effect." Therefore, enforcing the traditional formalistic approach derived from the early cases, the General Court considered that the analysis of the effects of the commercial prices offered by Tomra conducted by the European Commission was not core to the finding of an infringement of Article 102 TFEU but merely aimed at complementing such finding.

951. Similarly, in *Post Danmark II*, despite a tentative recognition of an effect-based approach, the ECJ recalled that, out of principle, a rebate scheme that tends to make it more difficult for customers to switch suppliers produces an anticompetitive exclusionary effect; therefore, while the as-efficient competitor test is a useful

---

129 Case 85/76, *Hoffmann-La Roche & Co.*, ECLI:EU:C:1979:36, ¶110–111 (Feb. 13, 1978).

130 European Commission Communication, *supra* n. 17, Chapter V, ¶¶23–27, 41.

131 *Id.* ¶44.

132 Case T-155/06, *Tomra Systems ASA v. Commission*, ECLI:EU:T:2010:370, ¶286 *et seq.* (Sept. 9, 2010); confirmed by Case C-549/10 P, *Tomra Systems ASA*, ECLI:EU:C:2012:221, (Apr. 19, 2012).

tool for the purposes of assessing whether pricing conduct is abusive, it is not a necessary condition to conclude that Article 102 TFEU has been infringed.[133]

952. However, more recently, the ECJ paved the way in the *Intel* judgment for a change of approach towards a more effective inclusion of economic-based tests in the assessment of discount and rebate policies implemented by dominant firms in the EU.

953. In its 2009 decision,[134] the European Commission had primarily relied on settled case law to conclude that Intel's exclusivity discounts offered to OEMs for its Central Processing Units (CPUs) met the conditions of the *Hoffmann-La Roche* case and thus constituted an abuse of dominant position. However, the European Commission decided to also conduct an economic analysis of the capability of Intel's rebate scheme to foreclose as efficient competitors, applying the principles set forth in its Guidance on the European Commission's enforcement priorities in applying Article 82 of the EC Treaty (now Article 102 TFEU). The European Commission concluded that Intel's conditional rebates and payments had a loyalty-inducing effect on several key OEMs and on a major retailer, and thus significantly reduced the ability of equally efficient competitors to compete for the sale of their own CPUs, thereby resulting in a loss of choices for consumers and lower incentives to innovate.

954. The European Commission's decision was confirmed by the General Court on appeal.[135] Setting aside the European Commission's guidance and relying on previous case law, the General Court found that it is not necessary to examine the circumstances of the case to conclude that an exclusivity rebate is illegal and that, even in the case of rebates falling within the third category (i.e., rebates that are neither purely quantitative nor akin to an exclusivity rebate), for which an assessment of all the relevant circumstances is warranted, it is nonetheless not a prerequisite to conduct an as-efficient competitor test.[136]

955. On further appeal before the ECJ, Intel pointed to errors of law in the General Court's reasoning, arguing that the General Court failed to take into account all the relevant circumstances of the case to assess the alleged anticompetitive effect of Intel's discount policy, including as regards the relevance of the as-efficient competitor test. In a landmark judgment of September 6, 2017, the ECJ set aside the General Court's judgment.[137] While it recalled the principles established in *Hoffmann-La Roche*, the Court decided to further clarify its case law in situations where the dominant undertaking submits evidence to the European Commission that its conduct was not capable of restricting competition. In that case, the Court found that the European Commission is required to assess whether the practice is capable of foreclosing market access of as efficient competitors and, if so, whether the negative effects can be either objectively justified or outweighed by efficiency gains. Therefore, in that case, where the European Commission had conducted an

---

133 Case C-23/14, *Post Danmark A/S v Konkurrenceradet*, ECLI:EU:C:2015:651, (Oct. 6, 2015).

134 Case COMP/C-3/37.990, *Intel* (2009).

135 Case T-286/09, *Intel Corp Inc.*, ECLI:EU:T:2014:547, (June 12, 2014).

136 *Id.* ¶¶143–144.

137 Case C-413/14 P, *Intel*, ECLI:EU:C:2017:632, (Sept. 6, 2017).

in-depth analysis of the effects of Intel's discount policy based on the as-efficient competitor test, which was central to its conclusion regarding the anticompetitive nature of the conduct, the General Court could not simply dismiss this assessment and ignore Intel's line of arguments in that regard to rely only on the legal test applicable to exclusivity rebates.

956. The case was therefore referred back to the General Court. In a very recent judgment of January 26, 2022,[138] the latter partially annulled the European Commission's 2009 decision, considering that the case law only establishes a mere presumption that certain discount schemes, by their very nature, may be assumed to have restrictive effects on competition. This does not relieve the European Commission from establishing in all cases to the requisite legal standard of proof that the practices are capable of restricting competition. The General Court considered that, in conducting that analysis against Intel, the European Commission made errors and thus failed, in light of all the relevant circumstances of the case, to establish that each of the rebates granted by the dominant undertaking were actually likely to have a foreclosure effect.

957. This ruling marks an important shift in the reasoning of European courts, which seem to finally depart from their traditional formalistic approach in favor of a stricter effect-based analysis, although the new guidance issued by the European Commission in 2023 does not necessarily align with this evolution.[139]

(3) Key Cases in the Pharmaceutical Industry

958. With the exception of *Hoffmann-La Roche*,[140] which involved anticompetitive exclusivity arrangements with several purchasers of vitamins, discount and rebate schemes implemented by pharmaceutical companies have mostly been analyzed at the level of Member States, probably owing to the national dimension of markets in this sector. The main cases will be discussed below.

959. In France, three decisions are noteworthy. The first one involved a bundle implemented by Lilly: when faced with generic competition on the market for Vancomycine, Lilly decided to grant hospitals a rebate on another product, Dobrutex, for which it still had a monopoly, on the condition that the hospitals would continue to purchase Vancomycine from Lilly rather than turning to competitors.[141] In this case, the FCA (*Autorité de la concurrence*, formerly *Conseil de la concurrence*) considered that Lilly's conduct had an anticompetitive object insofar as the bundling had the effect of dissuading hospitals from obtaining at least part of their requirements for Vancomycine from Lilly's competitors, despite the fact that the latter offered lower prices than Lilly, thereby amounting to a fidelity rebate. In addition, according to the FCA, the discount granted on Dobrutex as part of the bundle was artificial and discriminatory against hospitals which only purchased Dobrutex and could not, in such a case, benefit from the discount.

---

138 Case T-286/09, RENV, *Intel Corp Inc.*, ECLI:EU:T:2022:19, (Jan. 26, 2022).

139 European Commission Communication COM (2023) 1923 final, *supra* n. 39, Chapter V.

140 Case 85/76, *Hoffmann-La Roche & Co.*, ECLI:EU:C:1979:36, ¶41 (Feb. 13, 1978).

141 FCA, Decision No. 96-D-12, *Lilly France* (Mar. 5, 1996), confirmed by Paris Court of Appeal, Judgment of May 6, 1997, and French Supreme Court, Case No. 97-15195, (June 15, 1999).

960. The second case concerned a discount scheme implemented by Sandoz, with a rebate applying on the total turnover generated by hospitals with Sandoz on the condition that they purchased certain drugs from Sandoz, for which Sandoz faced competitors on the market; failure to purchase said drugs resulted in the loss of the rebate.[142] Relying on the ECJ's approach in *Hoffmann-La Roche*, the FCA found that Sandoz's discount policy, insofar as it aimed at tying hospitals to ensure their fidelity, had an anticompetitive object.

961. The third case involved volume rebates granted by Schering-Plough to pharmacists on their purchases of Subutex, with progressive discount rates depending on the quantities purchased (5.5% for an order of 70 boxes, 8% for an order of 200 boxes, and 10% for an order 350 boxes), shortly before the generics market entry.[143] The objective of this discount policy was to incentivize pharmacists to make larger orders of Subutex with a view to overload their shelves and foreclose market access for generic companies, as pharmacies have limited stocks. They were thus deemed contrary to Article 102 TFEU.

962. In the UK, in 2019 the CMA closed its investigation against Merck, Sharp and Dohm Limited (MSD) for an alleged abuse of dominant position under Article 102 TFEU in the supply of blockbuster drug Remicade (infliximab) to the National Health Service (NHS), on the basis that there were no grounds for action. In that case, after the patent for Remicade expired in 2015, MSD introduced a discount scheme linking the level of discount offered to each Trust (i.e., a group of hospitals and healthcare professionals) to the total volume of Remicade purchased by Trusts within one region or sub-region. MSD's rebate scheme included a series of bands, with a volume threshold and associated price for each band, and in practice was construed so that the total purchases of Remicade in each region or sub-region would amount to at least 94% of MSD's estimate of total infliximab demand for that region or sub-region.[144] Although the CMA found that MSD's discount scheme was implemented with the intention to exclude biosimilars from the market, the CMA nonetheless concluded, in light of the factual circumstances in its possession, that this discount scheme was in fact not likely to have an exclusionary effect because, at the time the rebate scheme was introduced, the switch to biosimilars was in fact more important than what MSD had anticipated (either because some Trusts were less cautious than MSD had assumed or took a longer-term view of the costs and benefits of biosimilars).

963. Finally, although not specifically targeting an anticompetitive discount scheme, the Romanian Competition Authority sanctioned Roche Romania in 2020 with fines amounting to €12.8 million for having designed and implemented an abusive commercial strategy on the market for oncological products in Romania.[145]

---

142 FCA, Decision No. 03-D-35, *Sandoz* (July 24, 2003), confirmed by Paris Court of Appeal, Judgment of Mar. 30, 2004, No. BOCCRF, 2004-06, NOR: ECOC0400200X, and French Supreme Court, Case No. 04-13910, (June 28, 2005).

143 FCA, Decision No. 13-D-21, *Schering-Plough* ¶¶405 *et seq.* (Dec. 18, 2013).

144 CMA, Case No. 50236, *Remicade, No Grounds for Action Decision* (2019).

145 Romanian Competition Council, Press Release, *The Competition Council Sanctioned Roche Romania with Fines of 12,8 Million Euro* (Jan. 23, 2020), *available at* https://www.consiliulconcurentei.ro/wp-content/uploads/2020/04/amenda_roche_ian_2020_english.pdf.

In Romania, in order to avoid the monopolization of a market, the law provides that a manufacturer must supply its drugs to at least three distributors, which can then compete against the manufacturer in tender procedures. However, the Romanian Competition Council found that with respect to certain of its cancer drugs, Roche offered them to hospitals at a price lower than that offered to distributors, thereby committing a "margin squeeze." In the context of the public procurement procedures, the implementation of such margin-squeeze price strategy has eliminated the possibility of intrabrand competition for hospital supply, under the national oncology program.[146]

C. *Excessive Pricing*

964. Excessive pricing as an infringement of competition law targets the charging of a price which is considered to be unreasonably high and, as such, unfair. While in the US complaints about monopoly prices have so far been unsuccessful, in the EU several pharmaceutical firms have recently been condemned under Article 102 TFEU, which provides the legal basis for tackling alleged unfair pricing behaviors in the form of excessive pricing.

a. *US Approach*

965. Excessive pricing, by itself, is not unlawful under federal antitrust law. The Supreme Court has on multiple occasions condoned the charging of even monopoly prices. In *linkLine*, the Court noted that "antitrust law does not prohibit lawfully obtained monopolies from charging monopoly prices."[147] Similarly, in the *Trinko* case, the Court observed that charging monopoly prices not only is "not unlawful," but "it is an important element of the free-market system." The ability to charge such prices, "at least for a short period," incentivizes the risk taking "that produces innovation and economic growth."[148]

966. The US Antitrust Agencies explained the rationale against pursuing excessive pricing as an antitrust violation in a 2018 submission to an OECD roundtable on pharmaceutical prices:

> U.S. antitrust law does not recognize excessive pricing as an antitrust violation in and of itself, thus allowing legitimate market participants acting independently to set their prices as high as they choose. This policy choice stems from the legislature's determination that ultimately competition will produce not only lower prices, but also better goods and services. Additionally, the policy reflects the difficulty in identifying what prices are excessive and concerns that antitrust enforcement against excessive pricing may chill incentives to compete and innovate in the first place and interfere with the proper functioning of markets.[149]

---

146 OECD, Annual Report on Competition Policy Developments in Romania for 2019, ¶42 (Nov. 9, 2020), *available at* https://one.oecd.org/document/DAF/COMP/AR(2020)50/en/pdf.

147 *Pacific Bell Telephone Co. v. linkLine Communications, Inc.*, 555 U.S. 454.

148 *Verizon Communications v. Law Offices of Curtis V. Trinko, LLP*, 540 U.S. 398, 407 (2004).

149 OECD Note by the United States, *Excessive Pricing in Pharmaceutical Markets*, ¶38, 13 (Nov. 28, 2018), *available at* https://www.ftc.gov/system/files/attachments/us-submissions-oecd-2010-present-other-international-competition-fora/excessive_prices_in_pharmaceuticals_united_states.pdf.

967. Although the FTC and the DOJ have not yet pursued antitrust enforcement against firms simply charging high prices for pharmaceuticals (or any other product), states have sought to enact laws targeting high prices in the pharmaceutical sector. To date, such attempts have failed. For example, the Washington, D.C. City Council enacted a law in 2005 prohibiting any patented drug from being sold in the District for an "excessive price" – a term not specifically defined in the legislation, which provided for both public and private enforcement, as well as a wide array of remedies, including fines and treble damages. A pre-enforcement challenge to the act succeeded, with the Federal Circuit Court of Appeals holding that the act was "contrary to the goals established by Congress in the patent laws" and thus preempted by federal patent law.[150]

968. In 2017, Maryland passed a law prohibiting pharmaceutical manufacturers or wholesalers (but not retailers selling directly to consumers) from engaging in "price gouging in the sale of an essential off-patent or generic drug." The statute defined price gouging as "an unconscionable increase in the price of a prescription drug," with unconscionable increase defined as an increase that is "excessive and not justified by the cost of producing the drug or the cost of appropriate expansion of access to the drug to promote public health." The Fourth Circuit, however, struck down the law as "unconstitutional under the dormant commerce clause because it directly regulates transactions that take place *outside Maryland*."[151] As the court explained, "the Act effectively seeks to compel manufacturers and wholesalers to act in accordance with Maryland law outside of Maryland. This it cannot do."[152] Further, if other states were to enact similar statutes, such a regime "would impose a significant burden on interstate commerce involving prescription drugs."[153]

969. Most recently, New York initiated investigations into price increases for several drugs relating to COVID-19 conditions. A newly formed Office of Pharmacy Benefits within the New York Department of Financial Services "commenced investigations under Section 111 of the Insurance Law into anomalously large spikes in the prices of six drugs that occurred during the COVID-19 pandemic, under circumstances determined to warrant further investigation."[154] According to the press release announcing the investigations, if the agency finds that illegal conduct occurred or that a price increase was not justified, such conclusions will be memorialized in a report by the newly formed Drug Accountability Board, and referrals to other relevant legal authorities may be made. To date, New York has not publicly announced the results of these investigations.

970. Although liability for excessive pricing, including price gouging, has not been imposed on market participants in the pharmaceutical sector, companies operating in this space should be mindful of the attention garnered by substantial increases

---

150 *Biotechnology Industry Org. v. District of Columbia*, 496 F.3d 1362, 1374 (Fed. Cir. 2007).

151 *Association for Accessible Medicines v. Frosh*, 887 F.3d 664, 666, 671, 674 (4th Cir. 2018) (emphasis in original).

152 *Id.* 672.

153 *Id.* 670.

154 New York Department of Financial Services, Press Release, *Governor Cuomo Announces Investigations into Prescription Drug Price Spikes Connected to the COVID-19 Pandemic* (Jan. 21, 2021), *available at* https://www.dfs.ny.gov/reports_and_publications/press_releases/pr202101212.

in drug prices. Such price increases can draw the attention of both federal and state enforcers, with the potential for long and costly investigations – even in the absence of an enforcement action. When initiating a significant price increase, companies will benefit from documenting the benefits of the drug at issue, the R&D expenditures incurred in developing the drug, and the cost savings to the health care system generally from the drug.

b. *EU Approach*

(1) Overview and Legal Test

971. The legal basis for excessive pricing as an infringement of EU competition law is Article 102(a) TFEU, which prohibits the imposition, within the internal market, of "unfair purchase or selling prices or other unfair trading conditions."

972. For many years, there was a certain reluctance to make use of that provision against allegedly high prices imposed by dominant firms, the rationale being that, in such a case, the market will correct itself. However, over the last few years, both the European Commission and NCAs have shown a renewed and growing interest in pursuing excessive pricing cases in the pharmaceutical sector, with enforcement clearly being on the rise since 2016. The basic theory of harm is that, in some cases, pharmaceutical companies use their market power to significantly increase the price of old but critical drugs, without any objective justification, thereby making huge profits that do not reward any specific risk-taking, investment or other improvement to the benefit of the patients.

973. Although other methodologies are available,[155] the reference test for determining whether a price is unfair within the meaning of Article 102 TFEU was established by the ECJ in its landmark *United Brands* judgment.[156] Under the two-limb test set out by the Court, it should first be determined whether the difference between the costs incurred by the dominant firm and the price actually charged is excessive and, if so, whether the price that has been imposed is either unfair in itself or when compared to competing products. The European Commission recalled in the *Aspen* case that the two conditions of the second limb of the test (unfair in itself or when compared to competing products) are alternative and not cumulative.[157]

974. In practice, the European Commission is mindful that although it is sometimes necessary to take action in the field of excessive pricing, this should not undermine innovation. As underlined by Margrethe Vestager, Executive Vice-President and Commissioner in charge of competition, there is a difference between charging a high price for a drug as a reward for innovation, and charging an excessive and thus unfair price, which cannot be objectively justified. Accordingly, "when we [the European Commission] do take action against excessive prices, we need

---

155 Case 27/7, *United Brands Company and United Brands Continentaal BV*, ECLI:EU:C:1978:22, ¶253 (Feb. 14, 1978); Case COMP/AT/40394, *Aspen*, ¶83 (2021). *See* for the application of a comparator test based on the comparison of prices between geographic markets Case C-177/16, *AKKA/LAA v. Konkurences Padome*, ECLI:EU:C:2017:689 (Sept. 14, 2017).

156 Case 27/7, *United Brands Company and United Brands Continentaal BV*, ECLI:EU:C:1978:22, ¶252 (Feb. 14, 1978).

157 Case COMP/AT/40394, *Aspen*, ¶82 (2021); *see also* Order of the ECJ, C-159/08 P, *Isabella Scippacercola and Ioannis Terezakis v. Commission*, ECLI:EU:C:2009:188, ¶47 (Mar. 25, 2009).

to make sure we're not taking away the rewards that encourage businesses to innovate."[158] This explains why, for example, the European Commission has consistently declined to investigate complaints of excessive pricing against Gilead in relation to the price of its drug Sovaldi, a breakthrough medicine indicated for the treatment of hepatitis C. Despite the very high cost of this treatment for health systems, the price charged by Gilead was considered to be a reward for innovation and, in the European Commission's view, it was up to national regulatory bodies to use their economic bargaining power to contain the price of Sovaldi for EU patients.[159]

975. The general enforcement policy in Europe, both at the European Commission and Member States level, is therefore to limit interventions of competition authorities in the field of excessive pricing to situations where a clear market failure has been identified. Hence, although not a condition for the finding of an infringement under Article 102 TFEU, one of the common features of the recent cases is that the price hikes imposed by pharmaceutical firms: (i) concerned rather old, off-patent drugs, often treating limited patient populations with no alternative on the market, and (ii) were generally accompanied by other abusive conduct such as threats of or actual delisting of products or other retaliation measures on health authorities.

(2) Key cases

976. There are three key European cases regarding excessive pricing in the pharmaceutical sector: *Aspen*, *Leadiant* and *Pfizer/Flynn*. Other notable cases include *CD Pharma* in Denmark and several decisions in the UK (most of which have been adopted before Brexit).

977. *Aspen*. Following a 2016 ruling from the AGCM sanctioning Aspen with a fine of €5.2 million for having charged excessive prices for some essential off-patent cancer drugs (Cosmos drugs),[160] and concerns expressed by several other Member States, the European Commission opened a formal investigation against the company in May 2017 for an alleged abuse of dominant position in the form of excessive pricing, covering all Member States except Italy. But instead of conducting a full-blown probe against Aspen, the European Commission chose to accept commitments from Aspen, which were made binding upon the company by a decision of April 15, 2021. In doing so, the European Commission avoided the characterization of an infringement of Article 102 TFEU and hedged itself against a potential challenge of its decision before European courts.

978. In its preliminary assessment, the European Commission expressed concerns that Aspen devised a pan-European strategy to impose, without any objective

---

158 Margrethe Vestager, Speech, *Protecting Consumers from Exploitation* (Nov. 21, 2016), *available at* https://ec.europa.eu/commission/commissioners/2014-2019/vestager/announcements/protecting-consumers-exploitation_en.

159 European Parliament, P-008636/2014, *Parliamentary Question, Answer Given by Ms. Vestager on Behalf of the European Commission* (Dec. 23, 2014), *available at* https://www.europarl.europa.eu/doceo/document/P-8-2014-008636-ASW_EN.html.

160 AGCM, Case A480, Decision No. 26185, *Incremento Prezzo Farmaci Aspen* (Sept. 29, 2016), *upheld* by the Regional Administrative Court for Latium, First Chamber Judgement, Case No. 12806/2016, *Aspen Pharma Trading Ltd and Others v. Autorità Garante della Concorrenza e del Mercado* (July 6, 2017), *available at* https://en.agcm.it/en/media/press-releases/2018/7/alias-2502.

justification, significant price increases on national health systems for the Cosmos drugs. This strategy was based on three pillars:

- first, a sequenced implementation throughout the EU in order to circumvent the purpose and functioning of the external reference pricing system, which allows national health authorities to fix the price of a given drug by taking into account the price of that same drug in other Member States;
- second, retaliation measures to overcome the potential resistance of national health authorities, including threats of or, in some cases, actual de-listings and withdrawals of the concerned drugs from the market; and
- third, the implementation of a stock allocation system that prevented, or at least limited, parallel trade between Member States.

979. According to the European Commission's preliminary findings, Aspen derived unusually large profits from the price increases, achieving margins ranging between 70% and 90%. By comparison, prior to 2012, Aspen's margins reached a maximum of 40–50% and the median margins of comparators (i.e., companies selling drugs having a similar profile to that of the product concerned) was on average less than 50%. In addition, the European Commission reached the preliminary conclusion that there were no legitimate reasons justifying the price increases imposed by Aspen, since the latter reflected neither any specific risk-taking nor innovation, investment, or material improvement in the products. The European Commission also took into account the fact that Aspen, which was aware of the critical importance of the drugs for patients and the absence of any real alternative (given that Aspen had managed to maintain very high market shares across all Member States, even in those Member States where it faced competition), used this as leverage against health authorities to impose price increases that it may not have otherwise obtained.

980. To remedy the European Commission's concerns, Aspen offered a series of commitments, which the latter accepted and made binding pursuant to Section 1, Article 9 1 of Regulation 1/2003.[161] Such commitments consist of:

- reducing the net prices for each of the products concerned in all Member States by, on average, 73%, with the new prices corresponding to maximum prices for the next 10 years; these price reductions were to apply retroactively from October 2019, with Aspen having to reimburse national health systems the difference in price for the transitory period between October 2019 and the actual implementation of the price decrease; and
- supplying the products for at least 5 years and then, for an additional period of 5 years, either continue to do so or, should Aspen decide to discontinue the commercialization in one or several Member States, give a 12 months' notice to health authorities and make the marketing authorization available for sale to any interested third party.

981. *Leadiant.* Since 2018, Leadiant has faced several complaints for excessive pricing in relation to the price of its CDCA-based orphan drug, used for the treatment

[161] Case COMP/AT/40394, *Aspen* (2021).

of a rare disease, *cerebrotendineous xanthomatosis* (CTX). The first complaint was brought in the Netherlands, followed by complaints in Belgium, Italy, and Spain. To date, the Dutch and Italian competition authorities have imposed fines on Leadiant. The investigation is still ongoing in Spain, where the Spanish regulator recently refused commitments offered by Leadiant. Belgium declined to investigate.

982. In the Netherlands, the ACM imposed a fine on Leadiant in July 2021, amounting to €19.5 million. The ACM found that, following its acquisition of CDCA-based drug from another manufacturer in 2008, Leadiant implemented a sequenced strategy to impose several significant price increases: first, Leadiant increased the original price from €46 for a pack of 100 capsules to €885; then, after CDCA was declared an orphan drug, Leadiant set the price at €3,103. Eventually, when Leadiant was granted a marketing authorization for a second CDCA-based drug – which did not materially differ from the original one – it discontinued the first drug and the new treatment for CTX reached €14,000 in the Netherlands.

983. In Italy, the AGCM fined Leadiant €3.5 million in May 2022. The AGCM found that, since 2017, Leadiant had been charging an excessive price of approximately €15,500 per pack to the Italian National Health Service, which was only reduced in December 2019, after the opening of the investigation. The AGCM noted that Leadiant implemented a complex strategy, including a dilatory and obstructive behavior during negotiations with the AIFA.[162]

984. *Pfizer / Flynn (UK)*. In a decision of December 7, 2016, Pfizer and Flynn Pharma were fined by the CMA 84.2 million and 5.2 million pounds, respectively.[163] The CMA found that an overall price increase of 2,600% imposed by Pfizer and Flynn Pharma on a mature anti-epileptic drug, Epanutin (phenytoin capsules) constituted an abuse of dominance by both Pfizer, as manufacturer and supplier of the drug, and Flynn Pharma, as marketing authorization holder and distributor. The CMA made this finding despite the fact that the resale price was ultimately lower than the price of other anti-epilepsy drugs, notably phenytoin tablets.

985. In 2018, the CMA's decision was quashed by the CAT.[164] The latter considered that the CMA failed to correctly apply the *United Brand* test because "it did not appropriately consider what was the right economic value for the product at issue; and it did not take sufficient account of the situation of other, comparable products, in particular of the phenytoin sodium tablet," sold at a lower price. In 2020, the Court of Appeal upheld for the most part the ruling of the CAT.[165] While it recalled that competition authorities benefit

---

162 AGCM, Decision No. A524, *Leadiant Biosciences/Farmaco per la cura della Xantomasi erebrotendinea* (May 31, 2022), *available at* https://www.agcm.it/dotcmsCustom/getDominoAttach?urlStr=192.168.14.10:8080/41256297003874BD/0/5F6041FF7929D043C125849B0046F058/$File/p27940.pdf.

163 CMA, Decision No. CE/9742-13, *Unfair pricing in respect of the supply of phenytoin sodium capsules in the UK* (Dec. 7, 2016), *available at* https://assets.publishing.service.gov.uk/media/594240cfe5274a5e4e00024e/phenytoin-full-non-confidential-decision.pdf.

164 CAT, Case Nos. 1275-1276/1/12/17, *Flynn Pharma Ltd and Pfizer Inc. v. CMA*, [2018] CAT 11, ¶4 (June 7, 2018).

165 UK Court of Appeal, Case No. C3/2018/1847 & 1874, *CMA v. Flynn Pharma Limited and Pfizer Inc.*, [2020] EWCA Civ 339, (Mar. 10, 2020).

from a certain freedom when defining the method they see fit to establish the excessiveness of a price, the Court noted that these authorities should take into consideration the methods and evidence brought forward by the parties in their defense. Following the Court of Appeal's ruling, the case has been remitted to the CMA, where it is still pending following the issuance of a new SO in August 2021.

986. *Other cases*. In addition to these three major cases, Italian company CD Pharma was sanctioned in Denmark for having abused its dominant position as exclusive distributor of Syntocinon, a drug given to pregnant women for the induction of labor, by imposing excessive prices on a wholesaler, Amgros, which had no alternative source of supply.[166]

987. In the UK, where the CMA has been particularly active, three other decisions were recently adopted. First, following two statements of objections issued in December 2016 and August 2017 respectively, the CMA fined Auden McKenzie and Actavis UK (now Accord-UK) 260 million pounds on July 15, 2021 for imposing excessive prices on the NHS for hydrocortisone tablets, used in the treatment of adrenal insufficiency, and paying their competitors to stay out of the market.[167] The decision has been appealed to the CAT.

988. Second, on July 29, 2021, Advanz and its previous owners (two private equity firms) were fined over 100 million pounds for having imposed a 1,110% increase in the price of liothyronine tablets used to treat thyroid deficiency.[168] The CMA's decision has also been appealed to the CAT.

989. In both cases, the companies used the "flaws" of the law to exit the regulated market and freely set high prices for medicines that they knew were indispensable to patients.

990. Finally, in December 2020, the CMA closed an investigation, two months after its launch, against Essential Pharma by accepting commitments offered by the company. Essential Pharma supplies two treatments for bipolar disorder based on lithium carbonate: Priadel and Camcolit. The CMA suspected Essential Pharma of an abuse of dominant position in the market for lithium carbonate medicines because Essential Pharma considered withdrawing Priadel from the UK market to either secure a price increase for that drug or force the switch of patients to the more expensive Camcolit. To remedy the CMA's concerns, the company committed to ensure the continuity of the supply of Priadel in the national market for the next 5 years.

---

166 Danish Competition Council, Decision, No. DIPS-14/08469, *CD Pharma* (Jan. 31, 2018), *confirmed* by Danish Competition Appeals Tribunal, Decision No. KL-2-2018, *CD Pharma AB v. Competition Council* (Nov. 29, 2018), and further *upheld* by Maritime and Commercial High Court, No. BS-3038/2019-SHR, *CD Pharma AB v. Competition Council* (Mar. 2, 2020).

167 CMA, Press Release, *CMA Finds Drug Companies Overcharged NHS* (July 15, 2021), *available at* https://www.gov.uk/government/news/cma-finds-drug-companies-overcharged-nhs. Auden McKenzie/Actavis UK, Waymade and AMCo were also found to have infringed the UK equivalent of Article 101 TFEU by entering into agreements whose object was to prevent competition on the hydrocortisone tablets market.

168 CMA, Press Release, *CMA Fines Pharma Firm Over Pricing Of Crucial Thyroid Drug* (July 29, 2021), *available at* https://www.gov.uk/government/news/cma-fines-pharma-firm-over-pricing-of-crucial-thyroid-drug.

D. *Price Discrimination*

991. Price discrimination broadly refers to the conduct where a supplier charges different prices to similarly situated customers or offers the same price to differently situated customers. Whereas in the US the prohibition of price discrimination is not limited to monopolies but applies to all firms if it injures competition, in the EU the approach is different: price discrimination is generally not prohibited unless it constitutes an abuse of a dominant position.

a. *US Approach*

992. Discrimination in prices charged to different customers is not likely to give rise to a Section 2 violation, but may violate the Robinson-Patman Act (RP Act), which applies to all firms, not just monopolists.[169] The federal antitrust agencies have not brought a price discrimination suit in over two decades, and the trend in the courts has been to narrow the scope of the RP Act. Nonetheless, private litigants continue to pursue price discrimination as an unlawful form of unilateral conduct.

993. To prevail on a price discrimination claim under the RP Act's Section 2(a), a plaintiff must show four elements: "(1) the relevant sales were made in interstate commerce; (2) the products sold were of the same grade and quality; (3) that [the seller] discriminated in price as between [the plaintiff] and another purchaser; and (4) the discrimination had a prohibited effect on competition."[170] When a sale or contract includes both tangible goods and intangible rights or services, it is covered by the RP Act if the dominant nature or purpose is the sale of tangible products.[171] The RP Act in Section 2(f) also bars buyers from knowingly inducing or receiving price discrimination, and Sections 2(b), 2(c), and 2(d) effectively bar price discrimination through commissions and brokerages, facilities for processing or sale, or the furnishing of services or facilities connected to goods.[172]

994. Importantly, the act only proscribes price discrimination if it threatens to or does injure competition. There are three so-called lines of injury addressed by the act: (1) primary line injury (affecting competition at the level of the seller and its competitors), (2) secondary line injury (affecting competition at the level of the seller's customers), and (3) tertiary line injury (affecting competition at the level of the purchaser's customers).

995. There are several affirmative defenses to a claim of price discrimination. A good-faith effort to meet a competitor's low price is an absolute defense to otherwise discriminatory pricing, which is known as the meeting competition defense.[173]

---

169 The Robinson-Patman Act is codified in statute at 15 U.S.C. § 13.

170 *See, e.g., Nicolosi Disrib., Inc. v. FinishMaster, Inc.*, No. 18-CV-03587-BLF, 2019 WL 8883851, *4 (N.D. Cal. Aug. 26, 2019) (collecting cases).

171 *See, e.g., Innomed Labs, LLC v. ALZA Corp.*, 368 F.3d 148, 156 (2d Cir. 2004) (finding RP Act applicable to distribution and supply agreement that gave Innomed the semi-exclusive right to distribute ALZA's patented pharmaceutical products, in return for up-front, royalty, and supply payments).

172 *See* 15 U.S.C. § 13.

173 *See Standard Oil Co. v. Fed. Trade Comm'n*, 340 U.S. 231, 249–50 (1951) ("[I]t is a complete defense to a charge of price discrimination for the seller to show that its price differential has been made in good faith to meet a lawful and equally low price of a competitor."); *Alan's of Atlanta, Inc. v. Minolta Corp.*, 903 F.2d 1414, 1419 (11th Cir. 1990) (internal citations omitted) ("This defense is the so-called 'meeting competition

Another affirmative defense is a price differential justified by either differences in the cost to manufacture, sell, or deliver the products[174] or changing market conditions.[175] These justified differential defenses both emerge from the text of the RP Act[176] and have been elaborated on by various courts.[177]

996. In addition, if a defendant can show that the same prices were functionally available to the plaintiff, the price discrimination claim will fail.[178] Moreover, the RP Act allows functional discounts, or discounts provided for the value of services performed by the buyer for the seller.[179] While the Act does not itself reference functional discounts, the US Supreme Court established this defense in *Texaco Inc. v. Hasbrouck*, codifying the "practice of the Federal Trade Commission" of "permitting legitimate functional discounts."[180] Functional discounts are a defense against RP Act price discrimination claims unless the discount is given for services not done at all or the discount's amount greatly exceeds the cost or value of the service.[181]

997. Price discrimination suits in the pharmaceutical sector have largely been unsuccessful. Retail pharmacies have sued pharmaceutical manufacturers, arguing that they discriminated against the pharmacies and in favor of other customers, including pharmaceutical benefit managers (PBMs) and other payers.[182]

---

defense.' It allows a seller to rebut a *prima facie* case of price discrimination, and therefore avoid liability, by showing that its discriminatory actions were taken in good faith to counter the actions of a competitor. In effect, it gives a seller the right to economic 'self-defense.'").

174 *See Texaco Inc. v. Hasbrouck*, 496 U.S. 543, 552 n. 6 (1990) (quoting 15 U.S.C. § 13(a), which states in part "[t]hat nothing herein contained shall prevent differentials which make only due allowance for differences in the cost of manufacture, sale, or delivery resulting from the differing methods or quantities in which such commodities are to such purchasers sold or delivered.").

175 The RP Act states that "nothing herein contained shall prevent price changes from time to time where in response to changing conditions affecting the market for or the marketability of the goods concerned, such as but not limited to actual or imminent deterioration of perishable goods, obsolescence of seasonal goods, distress sales under court process, or sales in good faith in discontinuance of business in the goods concerned." 15 U.S.C. § 13(a). This defense is not limited to the particular scenarios described in the RP Act, but "is limited to circumstances which are similar to those named in the statute." *Comcoa, Inc. v. NEC Telephones, Inc.*, 931 F.2d 655, 661 (10th Cir. 1991) (holding that the defense applies to obsolescence of non-seasonal goods).

176 *See* 15 U.S.C. § 13(b) ("Upon proof being made, at any hearing on a complaint under this section, that there has been discrimination in price or services or facilities furnished, the burden of rebutting the prima-facie case thus made by showing justification shall be upon the person charged with a violation of this section…").

177 *See Bookends & Beginnings LLC v. Amazon.com, Inc.*, No. 21-CV-02584 (VF), 2022 WL 18144916, at *22 (S.D.N.Y. Aug. 24, 2022), report and recommendation adopted, No. 1:21-CV-2584-GHW-VF, 2022 WL 4586213 (S.D.N.Y. Sept. 29, 2022) (discussing various defenses to the RP Act); *Sw. Paper Co., LLC v. Hansol Paper*, No. CV 12-8721 CAS (RZX), 2013 WL 11238487, *3–*6 (C.D. Cal. Apr. 15, 2013) (same).

178 *See Cap. Ford Truck Sales, Inc. v. Ford Motor Co.*, 819 F. Supp. 1555, 1568 (N.D. Ga. 1992) (stating as a requirement for an RP Act claim that the discount not be "functionally available" to the plaintiff on equal terms).

179 *See Coal. for a Level Playing Field, L.L.C. v. AutoZone, Inc.*, 813 F. Supp. 2d 557, 566–67 (S.D.N.Y. 2011) (noting that plaintiffs' proposed amended complaint failed under this defense because discounts were based on "a different mix of distribution, warehousing, marketing, and promotional services to parts manufacturers" and it was likely that in different contracts, bargaining led to different contract terms and "lawful discounts for the different functions chain retailers perform.").

180 *Texaco*, 496 U.S. 562–63.

181 *Coal. For A Level Playing Field*, 737 F. Supp. 2d 211 (citing 14 Herbert Hovenkamp, Antitrust Law: An Analysis of Antitrust Principles and Their Application ¶2333, 108 (1999)).

182 *See, e.g.*, *Drug Mart Pharmacy Corp. v. Am. Home Prod. Corp.*, 472 F. Supp. 2d 385, 390 (E.D.N.Y. 2007), amended, No. 93-CV-5148, 2007 WL 4526618 (E.D.N.Y. Dec. 20, 2007) (exemplifying such a claim); *In re Direct Purchaser Insulin Pricing Litig.*, No. 320CV3426BRMLHG, 2021 WL 2886216, *4,

998. Pharmaceutical manufacturers have brought unsuccessful lawsuits against other manufacturers for price discrimination, arguing that discounts to favored customers[183] or the sale of both branded and generic versions of a drug at different prices[184] violated the RP Act.

999. Price discrimination claims against pharmaceutical manufacturers, PBMs, and other payers often fail due to a lack of demonstrated harm to competition, as opposed to harm to individual competitors. For example, the Second Circuit affirmed summary judgment for a defendant pharmaceutical manufacturer, finding that "plaintiffs could not generate evidence tending to show that they lost more than a *de minimis* number of customers to the favored purchasers, indicating that competition was not substantially harmed or threatened by the price difference in question."[185]

b. *EU Approach*

1000. Price discrimination between customers can be caught by Article 102 TFEU. Traditionally, a distinction has been made between: (i) horizontal discrimination (also referred to as primary line discrimination), the purpose of which is to foreclose competitors by targeting actual or potential customers with selective price reductions or other favors, and (ii) vertical discrimination (also referred to as secondary line discrimination), whose objective is to favor a trading partner in an upstream or downstream market, thereby conferring a competitive advantage on the latter.[186]

1001. In practice, discount and rebate schemes targeting more specifically certain customers have regularly been found discriminatory and sanctioned because of their actual or potential exclusionary effect. For example, in *Hilti*, the company was sanctioned for offering selective price reductions and other advantageous conditions to the main customers of its competitors.[187]

1002. Secondary line discrimination, which is directly targeted by Article 102(c), prohibits the application by a dominant firm of "dissimilar conditions to equivalent transactions with other trading parties, thereby placing them at a competitive

*8 (D.N.J. July 9, 2021) (dismissing RP Act Section 2(C) claims alleging that PBM practices around insulin led to price increases for insulin); *Cash & Henderson Drugs, Inc. v. Johnson & Johnson*, 799 F.3d 202, 206 (2d Cir. 2015).

183 *See, e.g.*, *Barr Labs., Inc. v. Abbott Labs.*, 978 F.2d 98, 109–10 (3d Cir. 1992) (affirming summary judgment for defendant, finding that its sales to drug warehouse chains did not amount to price discrimination).

184 *See, e.g.*, *Eon Labs Manufacturing v. Watson Pharms., Inc.*, 164 F. Supp. 2d 350, 362 (S.D.N.Y. 2001) (dismissing plaintiff's price discrimination claim challenging defendant's simultaneous sale of a branded drug and an authorized generic thereof).

185 *Cash & Henderson Drugs*, 799 F.3d 210 (2d Cir. 2015); *see also Klamath-Lake Pharm. Ass'n v. Klamath Med. Serv. Bureau*, 701 F.2d 1276 (9th Cir. 1983) (affirming dismissal of price discrimination claim by pharmacy association against health care provider that had purchased drugs from a manufacturer at a discount for failing to establish the discount substantially injured competition).

186 This distinction has been made by several NCAs in the EU (*e.g.*, France or Denmark) and *upheld* by Advocate General Mengozzi in *Post Danmark A/S* (*see* Opinion of Advocate General Mengozzi delivered on May 24, 2011, C-209/10, *Post Danmark A/S*, ECLI:EU:C:2012:172, ¶46 (Mar. 27, 2012)).

187 Case COMP/IV/30.787 and 31.488, *Hilti* (1987), confirmed on appeal by Case T-30/89, *Hilti AG*, ECLI:EU:T:1991:70, (Dec. 12, 1991) and Case C-53/92 P, *Hilti AG v. Commission*, ECLI:EU:C:1994:77 (Mar. 2, 1994). *See also Hoffmann-La Roche* and *Michelin* cases cited in Section II.A.1 above.

disadvantage." Secondary line discrimination has rarely been recognized as an abuse.[188] That is because, according to the ECJ, when a dominant firm treats its business partners differently, competition is not necessarily distorted:

> ...the mere presence of an immediate disadvantage affecting operators who were charged more, compared with the tariffs applied to their competitors for an equivalent service, does not, however, mean that competition is distorted or is capable of being distorted.[189]

1003. Therefore, "[i]t is only if the behavio[r] of the undertaking in a dominant position tends, having regard to the whole of the circumstances of the case, to lead to a distortion of competition between those business partners that the discrimination between trade partners which are in a competitive relationship may be regarded as abusive."[190]

1004. In the pharmaceutical sector more specifically, two national cases are of relevance. First, in 2006, the Latvian Competition Authority fined AGA SIA, a producer and trader of medical gas, for abusing its dominant position through price discrimination. AGA SIA enjoyed significant market power in the market for medical gas in Latvia, with a market share consistently above 40%, as well a monopolist position in the market for bottled compressed medical gas. The competition authority found that AGA SIA has applied discriminatory prices for medical gas amongst its customers without any economic justification.[191] Second, also in 2006, the Maltese Competition Authority fined the National Blood Transfusion Services (NBTS) for having discriminated against private clinics when selling blood products. Indeed, while as a result of a national regulation, private clinics had to pay for the products, public hospitals were able to obtain all their requirements free of charge. The Maltese Competition Authority considered that this regulation had the effect of placing the private clinics at a competitive disadvantage and therefore entailed a restriction of competition.[192]

2. Non-pricing Conduct

1005. Non-pricing conduct encompasses a wide range of practices, from refusal to deal to so-called "product hopping," misuse of IP rights and many more, such as abusive

---

188 In the early years, the ECJ notably tackled geographic price discrimination insofar as the latter constitutes a restriction to free movement of goods within the internal market. In *United Brands*, the Court upheld the European Commission's finding that the application of different prices across Member States, coupled with a contractual prohibition of parallel imports, constitutes an abuse of dominant position insofar as this policy led to "[a] rigid partitioning of national markets." *See* Case 27/7, *United Brands Company and United Brands Continentaal BV*, ECLI:EU:C:1978:22, ¶232–34 (Feb. 14, 1978). However, charging different prices across Member States does not always amount to an abuse if the price differences can be objectively justified by variations in the conditions of competition and the intensity of competition. Case T-83/91, *Tetra Pak v. Commission*, ECLI:EU:T:1994:246, ¶160 (Oct. 6, 1994); Case COMP/AT.40026, *Velux*, ¶45 (2008).

189 Case C-525/16, *MEO – Serviços de Comunicações e Multimédia SA v. Autoridade da Concorrencia*, ECLI:EU:C:2018:270, ¶26 (Apr. 19, 2018).

190 *Id.* ¶27.

191 Competition Council of the Republic of Latvia, Case No. p/04/04/8, *AGA SIA* (Sept. 7, 2006); *see also* Andra Rubene, *The Latvian Competition Authority Fines the Medical Gas Monopolist for the Application of an Unfair and Discriminating Price (AGA SIA)*, E-COMPETITIONS Sept. 2006, art. No. 12435.

192 Phyllis Aquilina, *The Maltese Competition Authority Upheld as Abusive The Commercial Practices of a Private Hospital and Quashes Subsidiary Legislation Stipulating Prices of Blood Products Supplied to Private Medical Undertakings (Malta's National Blood Transfusion Service)*, E-COMPETITIONS Oct. 2006, art. No. 16288.

litigation or disparagement practices. While it may be legitimate to engage in these practices when the objective is to protect a firm's own legitimate commercial interests, these practices may also violate Section 2 and/or Article 102 TFEU in certain circumstances. Here again, the approach to each specific type of conduct in the US and in the EU is not necessarily aligned.

A. *Refusal to Deal*

a. *US approach*

(1) Core Issues

1006. As a general rule, a company has no duty to help or deal with its rivals.[193] However, there are limited situations in which an exception may be made to this general rule. The US Supreme Court, for example, has held that certain circumstances, such as ceasing an existing and profitable course of dealing with a competitor, may give rise to a duty to cooperate with a competitor. In *Aspen Skiing Co. v. Highland Skiing Corp.*, the owner of a major facility for downhill skiing in Aspen, Colorado brought suit against the owner of the three other major Aspen ski facilities challenging the discontinuation of a jointly offered interchangeable six-day "all-Aspen" lift ticket.[194] From 1962 to 1977, the companies offered the all-Aspen, 6-day ticket, which allowed skiers to use one interchangeable pass for a one-week period.[195] Profits were then split according to the number of visits to each mountain.[196] In 1978, the defendant withdrew from the all-Aspen lift ticket and offered passes featuring only its mountains.[197] The defendant further refused to sell the plaintiff any lift tickets to its three facilities, either at a discount or at retail value, which made it extremely difficult for the plaintiff to market its own ski package, limited to its single facility, to replace the joint offering.[198]

1007. In assessing whether the defendant's conduct was an unlawful refusal to deal under Section 2, the Supreme Court acknowledged that "even a firm with monopoly power has no general duty to cooperate… with a competitor."[199] The Court further stated that the "right to refuse to deal with other firms" is not "unqualified" and that noncooperation can have "evidentiary significance"[200] The Court then reasoned that because the defendant made an important change in distribution of a long-time ski pass, which reduced the quality of the ski ticket for consumers, adversely impacted the plaintiff's ability to compete, and was not supported by a valid business justification such as efficiency, the refusal to cooperate with a competitor was unlawful under Section 2.[201]

---

193 *Aspen Skiing Co. v. Aspen Highlands Skiing Corp.*, 472 U.S. 585, 600, 105 S. Ct. 2847, 2856, 86 L. Ed. 2d 467 (1985) (explaining that the trial court correctly instructed the jury that "a firm possessing monopoly power has no duty to cooperate with its business rivals").

194 *Id.*

195 *Id.* 589.

196 *Id.*

197 *Id.* 592.

198 *Id.* 593.

199 *Id.* 600.

200 *Id.* 600, 601.

201 *Id.* 605–611.

1008. The Supreme Court revisited its approach to refusals to deal in *Verizon Communications, Inc. v. Law Offices of Curtis Trinko, LLP.*[202] There, the Court explained that it was "cautious" to recognize exceptions to the idea that the antitrust laws generally permit a monopolist to refuse to cooperate with rivals, noting that *Aspen Skiing* is "at or near the outer boundary of § 2 liability."[203] The Court further distinguished the facts in *Aspen Skiing*. First, unlike Aspen Skiing Company in which the defendant was engaged in a long-time course of dealing with its competitor, Verizon had not voluntarily engaged in a course of dealing with its rivals. Second, while Aspen Skiing Company refused to sell to its competitor even at the retail price, Verizon refused to sell at the regulated, cost-based price. Finally, unlike the ski lift tickets in *Aspen Skiing*, the services that Verizon had allegedly refused to provide were not otherwise available to the public.

1009. In both *Aspen Skiing* and *Trinko*, the Supreme Court was cautious about expanding antitrust liability for other refusals to cooperate, including under what is called the essential facilities doctrine. The essential facilities doctrine was first named by the D.C. Circuit in *Hecht v. Pro-Football*[204] and was most clearly expressed in the Seventh Circuit's *MCI Communications v. AT&T.*[205] Under the essential facilities doctrine, a firm in control of a facility essential to its competitors is required to provide reasonable access to the facility if possible.[206] To establish a violation under this doctrine, a plaintiff must prove four elements: (1) control of the essential facility by a monopolist, (2) a competitor's inability practically or reasonably to duplicate the essential facility, (3) denial of the use of the facility to a competitor, and (4) the feasibility of providing the facility.[207]

1010. The Supreme Court has neither recognized nor repudiated this doctrine. In *Aspen Skiing*, the Court appeared to condone the doctrine when it stated that antitrust laws do not impose duties to deal on monopolists.[208] In *Trinko*, however, the Court chose not to address the essential facilities doctrine stating that "[w]e have never recognized [the essential facilities] doctrine… and we find no need either to recognize it or to repudiate it here."[209] Although *Trinko* narrowed *Aspen Skiing* as "at or near the outer boundary of § 2 liability,"[210] it likely left the essential facilities doctrine in effect until the Supreme Court definitely rules otherwise. As a result, many lower courts continue to recognize the essential facilities doctrine.[211]

---

202 540 U.S. 398 (2004).

203 *Id.* 409.

204 570 F.2d 992 (D.C. Cir. 1977) ("The essential facility doctrine, also called the 'bottleneck principle,' states that 'where facilities cannot practicably be duplicated by would-be competitors, those in possession of them must allow them to be shared on fair terms. It is illegal restraint of trade to foreclose the scarce facility.").

205 708 F.2d 1081, 1132 (7th Cir. 1983).

206 *Id.*

207 *Id.* 1132–33.

208 *Aspen Skiing Co.*, 472 U.S. 600 ("[E]ven a firm with monopoly power has no general duty to engage in a joint marketing program with a competitor.").

209 *Verizon Commc'ns Inc.*, 540 U.S. 411.

210 *Id.* 409.

211 *See, e.g., Aerotec Int'l, Inc. v. Honeywell Int'l, Inc.*, 836 F.3d 1171, 1185 (9th Cir. 2016) ("Although the Supreme Court has never recognized the doctrine… we have continued to treat it as having a basis in § 2 of the Sherman Act."); *MetroNet Servs. Corp. v. Qwest Corp.*, 383 F.3d 1124, 1129 (9th Cir. 2004) (finding that "denial of access to an essential facility violates Section 2 because control of an essential facility can 'extend

1011. Following the Court's *Trinko* decision, lower courts have rejected refusal-to-deal claims in situations in which there was no voluntary prior course of dealing between the parties or there was a legitimate business justification for the refusal to deal, including for example where the refusal increased the defendant's short-term profits.[212] Conversely, courts have allowed refusal-to-deal claims to proceed where plaintiffs have shown the defendant changing or eliminating a prior course of dealing or acting contrary to its own short-term economic interest in refusing to deal with a competitor.[213]

1012. Specific types of refusals to deal that have recently received attention in the pharmaceutical sector include the refusal to supply product samples to potential generic competitors to allow them to perform testing for purposes of their generic applications based on REMS or other restrictive distribution practices, as well as so-called data blocking. REMS are sometimes required by the FDA when a drug presents certain safety concerns that require restrictions beyond standard post-approval monitoring. REMS programs can involve restrictions on distribution or certain requirements relating to patient testing or provider enrollment, all of which are referred to as elements to assure safe use, or ETASU.

1013. If a generic manufacturer wishes to bring a new generic drug to market, it must file an ANDA.[214] To submit an ANDA, the generic company must provide data showing that its generic drug is bioequivalent to a previously approved branded drug, often referred to as the RLD. To prove bioequivalence, generic companies must engage in testing protocols comparing its drug to the RLD, which requires the use of certain amounts of the RLD. With certain types of REMS programs, a generic manufacturer typically is unable to acquire the drug from a wholesaler or distributor – it needs to be acquired directly from the branded drug company.

---

monopoly power from one stage of production to another'"); *Laurel Sand & Gravel, Inc. v. CSX Transp., Inc.*, 924 F.2d 539, 544 (4th Cir. 1991) (recognizing essential facilities claim of a railroad company against national railroad for denial of access to trackage rights); *Advanced Health–Care Servs., Inc. v. Radford Cmty. Hosp.*, 910 F.2d 139, 150–51 (4th Cir. 1990) (recognizing the essential facilities doctrine for a hospital's denial of a medical equipment supplier's access to patients); *Twin Laboratories, Inc. v. Weider Health & Fitness*, 900 F.2d 566, 568–69 (2d Cir. 1990) ("As the word 'essential' indicates, a plaintiff must show more than inconvenience, or even some economic loss; he must show that an alternative to the facility is not feasible."); *MCI Communications Corp.*, 708 F.2d 1132–33 (establishing four-party test for finding essential facility liability); *Hecht v. Pro-Football, Inc.*, 570 F.2d 982, 992 (D.C. Cir. 1977) (recognizing essential facilities doctrine).

212 *See e.g., Four Corners Nephrology Assocs. v. Mercy Med. Ctr.*, 582 F.3d 1216, 1221, 1225 (10th Cir. 2009) (affirming summary judgment because "even a putative monopolist[] has 'no antitrust duty to deal with its rivals'"); *In re Adderall XR Antitrust Litig.*, 754 F.3d 128, 136 (2d Cir. 2014) (holding plaintiff "failed to allege facts that would place this case within *Aspen Skiing's* narrow exception to the 'long recognized right… to freely exercise his own independent discretion as to parties with whom he will deal.'"); *Transhorn, Ltd. v. United Techs. Corp.*, 502 F.3d 47, 52 (2d Cir. 2007) (holding that refusal to deal did not support actual and attempted monopolization claims for failure to allege a prior course of dealings); *North Star Gas Co. v. Pacific Gas & Elec. Co.*, 2016 WL 5358590, *24 (N.D. Cal. 2016) (dismissing ¶2 refusal-to-deal claim that was based on facts "materially almost identical" to *Trinko*).

213 *Altitude Sports & Ent., LLC v. Comcast Corp.*, No. 19-CV-3253-WJM-MEH, 2020 WL 8255520, *10 (D. Colo. Nov. 25, 2020) (refusing to dismiss refusal to deal claim when there was a prior course of dealing); *Steward Health Care Sys., LLC v. Blue Cross & Blue Shield of Rhode Island*, 311 F. Supp. 3d 468, 491 (D.R.I. 2018) (refusing to grant summary judgment for defendant on refusal to deal claim without a prior course of dealing and noting that the law "impose[s] a duty on Blue Cross to compete fairly, and specifically to not forego short term profits for the purpose of blocking competition and maintaining a monopoly").

214 *See* Chapter I.

1014. In applying the general principle that even a monopolist has no duty to deal with its competitors, manufacturers of branded drugs may be reluctant to sell samples of their drugs to would-be generic competitors so that they can conduct bioequivalence studies. With the REMS in place, the brand manufacturer may have the additional concern of ensuring the REMS and accompanying ETASU are followed, both out of concern for patient safety and to ensure they are meeting their regulatory obligations.[215] Generic manufacturers, meanwhile, argue that without the ability to buy the drug from the branded manufacturer, they cannot develop and obtain approval for their generic products under the ANDA process, foreclosing them from competing with the branded manufacturers.[216]

1015. In 2019, the US Congress enacted the CREATES Act.[217] The Act includes a provision allowing drug developers to sue RLD manufacturers if they refuse to sell them samples for testing purposes. For products under REMS with ETASU, the drug developer must seek what is called a covered product authorization from the FDA confirming that its proposed testing complies with applicable safety guidelines. Once a generic developer completes this (and other steps required under the CREATES Act), it may purchase drug samples from the RLD manufacturer.

1016. Another aspect of REMS programs is the single shared system REMS (SSSR). Once generic companies begin filing ANDAs, the FDA may require the brand and generic manufacturers to cooperate on a shared REMS program. In rare cases, some plaintiffs have argued that a brand drug manufacturer has failed to cooperate with a generic drug developer in the development of an SSSR, causing an anticompetitive delay in generic entry.[218] Such conduct includes failing to negotiate with the generic manufacturer in good faith, refusing to meet or negotiate with the generic manufacturer at all, and making unreasonable demands on generic manufacturers in exchange for their participation in the SSSR. Because participation in an FDA-imposed SSSR is required, preventing generics from participating therein could present a hurdle to receiving approval of their ANDAs and marketing their drugs.[219] Despite this, liability on this ground is rare.[220]

---

215 *See Mylan Pharms. Inc. v. Celgene Corp.*, No. CV 14-2094, 2018 WL 11299447, *3 (D.N.J. Oct. 3, 2018) (internal citations and quotations omitted) (stating that REMS are meant to ensure that prescription drugs' benefits outweigh their risks and that ETASU requirements seek to reduce risks for patients).

216 *See In re Suboxone (Buprenorphine Hydrochloride and Naloxone) Antitrust Litigation*, 64 F. Supp. 3d 665, 687 (E.D. Pa., 2014) (noting that plaintiffs alleging that abuse of the REMS/SSSR process kept generic drugs off the market).

217 Further Consolidated Appropriation Act, 2020, PL 116-94, Dec. 20, 2019, 133 Stat 2534 ¶610 (CREATES Act incorporated into appropriations bill).

218 *In re Suboxone (Buprenorphine Hydrochloride & Nalaxone) Antitrust Litig.*, 421 F. Supp. 3d 12, 30 (E.D. Pa. 2019), *aff'd sub nom. In re Suboxone (Buprenorphine Hydrochlorine & Naloxone) Antitrust Litig.*, 967 F.3d 264 (3d Cir. 2020) ("Plaintiffs allege that Reckitt used the SSRS as a means to undermine and delay generic entry by feigning cooperation in the SSRS development process.").

219 *In re Suboxone (Buprenorphine Hydrochloride & Nalaxone) Antitrust Litig.*, 421 F. Supp. 3d 12, 27 (E.D. Pa. 2019), aff'd sub nom. *In re Suboxone (Buprenorphine Hydrochlorine & Naloxone) Antitrust Litig.*, 967 F.3d 264 (3d Cir. 2020) ("[t]he FDA will withhold ANDA approval until such time that an appropriate REMS has been created… The FDA can also require that ANDA sponsors coordinate with the manufacturer of the branded counterpart drug for the purposes of creating a Single Shared REMS program…").

220 *See, e.g., In re Suboxone (Buprenorphine Hydrochloride & Naloxone) Antitrust Litig.*, 64 F. Supp. 3d 665, 688 (E.D. Pa. 2014), on reconsideration in part sub nom. I*n re Suboxone (Buprenorphine Hydrochloride & Nalaxone) Antitrust Litig.*, No. 13-MD-2445, 2015 WL 12910728 (E.D. Pa. Apr. 14, 2015) (dismissing claim of SSRS abuse because the generic drugmaker was not completely precluded from filing an ANDA).

1017. Finally, data blocking is a tactic that was briefly addressed in the FTC's recent case against Martin Shkreli and Vyera Pharmaceuticals (discussed below). In their contracts with distributors of the drug Daraprim, the defendants required the distributors to agree not to provide sales data to data aggregators such as IQVIA and Wolters Kluwer. When available, this market data allows potential generic competitors to evaluate the market size for a drug by giving them accurate information on sales. Although data blocking was not addressed in detail in the FTC case, because that provision of the agreement was not found to impede entry, it is a potential area of focus for the FTC and private plaintiffs in the future.

(2) Key Cases

1018. As noted above, a notable recent case involving a refusal to deal in the pharmaceutical sector is the FTC's lawsuit against Martin Shkreli and Vyera Pharmaceuticals.[221] After his company acquired the rights to Daraprim (pyrimethamine), Shkreli moved the drug from an open retail distribution system, in which it could be made available through general retail pharmacies, to a closed system, making it available only through five distributors and specialty pharmacies.[222] Under the applicable distribution agreements, the distributors were restricted to selling Daraprim to only specified customers. The distributors were also required to get written approval to sell to someone not already on the preapproved customer list. The defendants also limited the number of bottles of Daraprim that could be sold at any given time and closely monitored sale quantities, at one point buying back the drug from a pharmacy at twice the price originally paid, because the defendants believed the pharmacy was going to sell them to a company that provides RLDs to would-be generic competitors for bioequivalence testing.

1019. In addition to restricting access to Daraprim to prevent generic manufacturers from having access to the RLD, Shkreli and Vyera allegedly signed a supply agreement to prevent other manufacturers from purchasing the API for Daraprim.[223] The API is necessary for manufacturing the drug and must be purchased from an FDA-approved manufacturer. The defendants entered an exclusive distribution agreement with two major international API manufacturers, prohibiting them from selling the Daraprim API to other US drug manufacturers, thereby preventing them from developing a generic version of the drug.[224]

1020. The district court ruled that the defendants had monopolized the pyrimethamine market in violation of Section 2, as well as violating Section 1 through unreasonable restraints of trade.[225] The court found that the defendants had maintained their monopoly through their anticompetitive conduct, and that there were no patient safety-related concerns justifying the distribution restrictions they had put in place.[226] Because Daraprim previously had been subject to open distribution

---

221 *FTC v. Shkreli*, 581 F. Supp. 3d 579 (S.D.N.Y. Jan. 14, 2022).

222 *Id.* 602–05.

223 *Id.* 634–35.

224 *Id.* 636–37.

225 *Id.* 629, 643.

226 *Id.* 633–34 ("Shkreli offered no evidence, however, that patients were assisted in any of these ways.").

without any serious side effects requiring specialty pharmacy monitoring or support, the court concluded that the defendants' justifications for the conduct were pretextual. Notably, Shkreli was found individually liable on the antitrust claims, and the district court issued an injunction banning him for life from participation in the pharmaceutical industry.[227]

1021. In *In re Suboxone (Buprenorphine Hydrochloride and Naloxone) Antitrust Litigation*,[228] Reckitt Benckiser, the manufacturer of Suboxone, was accused of delaying the approval of ANDAs for generic Suboxone by feigning its participation in the shared REMS process. Plaintiffs alleged that Reckitt made "unnecessary, unprecedented, and unreasonable demands" as a condition precedent to generic manufacturer participation in the SSSR for Suboxone.[229] Reckitt sought an upfront agreement that all manufacturers would share the costs of product liability in potential future lawsuits and refused to share non-public information about its REMS. The FDA acknowledged it could not force Reckitt to disclose information on its REMS and said the generics could create an SSSR without the information. Reckitt refused to cooperate, and two days before the proposed SSSR was submitted, argued an important element of the REMS had been omitted and refused to sign, leading the generics to seek a waiver for approval of a generic-only SSSR.[230]

1022. Reckitt argued that the plaintiffs' REMS-based claim should be dismissed because even a monopolist has no duty to deal with its competitors.[231] The court first noted that: "*Linkline* and *Trinko* undermine Plaintiffs' position, as the Supreme Court has unequivocally stated that statutes and regulations requiring cooperation between competitors do not create an antitrust duty to deal."[232] The court further found that the generics were "capable of submitting an SSSR without Reckitt's involvement, and ultimately did just that."[233] The court acknowledged that if the SSSR process is manipulated in such a way as to completely prevent a generic company from filing an ANDA, antitrust liability may attach. However, the court found that was not the case in this matter and granted Reckitt's motion to dismiss the plaintiffs' REMS claim.[234]

1023. *Mylan Pharmaceuticals, Inc. v. Celgene Corp.*,[235] centered on Celgene's drugs Thalomid and Revlimid, and Mylan's alleged inability to obtain samples to develop generic versions of those drugs. Mylan alleged that Celgene had used the REMS programs for the two drugs as a pretext to prevent Mylan from acquiring samples to conduct bioequivalence studies.[236] Celgene moved for summary judgment. The court first reiterated the Supreme Court's ruling in *Trinko* on refusals to deal.[237] The court then discussed the timeline of Celgene's

---

227 *Id.* 643.

228 64 F. Supp. 3d 665 (E.D. Pa. 2014).

229 *Id.* 675.

230 *Id.* 675–76.

231 *Id.* 679.

232 *Id.* 687.

233 *Id.* 688.

234 *Id.*

235 No. 14-2094, 2018 WL 11299447 (D.N.J. 2018).

236 *Id.* *1.

237 *Id.* *8.

alleged refusal to sell samples to Mylan. Mylan argued that FDA approval of its bioequivalence protocols was not necessary for Celgene to sell samples outside the REMS program, and that Celgene's insistence on this approval was anticompetitive, citing the fact that Celgene provided samples for use in clinical trials without subjecting the recipients to FDA review of their protocols. The court, however, found that the clinical trials required enrollment in one of the REMS-required safety monitoring programs,[238] and, on summary judgment, held that based on the undisputed facts it was objectively reasonable for Celgene to require FDA approval of Mylan's testing protocols before selling Mylan samples of either Thalomid or Revlimid.[239]

1024. The court, however, reached a different conclusion regarding Celgene's alleged delay tactics after Mylan received FDA approval of its testing protocols.[240] After it received such approval, Mylan asked Celgene to sign a straightforward confidentiality agreement, which took roughly six months to negotiate.[241] Celgene also indicated to Mylan that it was reviewing the supplemental information Mylan provided to Celgene, but Celgene did not in fact review such information. Two months after signing the confidentiality agreement, Celgene sent Mylan an indemnification agreement to negotiate, while also requesting a copy of the bioequivalence study protocols and evidence concerning Mylan's insurance coverage.[242] The court found that this extended timeline created issues of fact that should be put to a jury and declined to grant summary judgment on Celgene's post-FDA approval conduct.

1025. In another case also based on Thalomid, *Lannett Co. v. Celgene Corp.*,[243] the Eastern District of Pennsylvania denied defendant Celgene's motion to dismiss. Lannett alleged that Celgene denied them access to Thalomid in violation of FDA requirements, leaving Lannett unable to bring their generic product to the market.[244] Over a series of months, Celgene allegedly imposed "onerous and unreasonable requests" for information from Lannett as a prerequisite to obtaining samples.[245] Lannett filed for injunctive relief, which the court dismissed for lack of ripeness.[246] Following this dismissal, Celgene allegedly continued to refuse to provide samples to Lannett despite satisfying the FDA's requirements.[247] In its motion to dismiss, Celgene argued that pursuant to *Trinko*, the complaint should be dismissed because Lannett failed to allege any prior course of dealing with Celgene and therefore lacked any duty to deal with Lannett.[248] However, the court denied Celgene's motions to dismiss without comment and the case later settled.

---

238 *Id.* *14–*15.
239 *Id.* *12.
240 *Id.* *29.
241 *Id.* *18.
242 *Id.* *19.
243 Decision on Motion to Dismiss, No. 08-cv-3920 (E.D. Pa. Mar. 30, 2011).
244 Compl., No. 08-cv-3920, *2 (E.D. Pa. Mar. 30, 2010).
245 *Id.* *10.
246 *Id.* *12.
247 *Id.* *13–*14.
248 Celgene Motion to Dismiss, No. 08-cv-3920, *2, *9-*10 (E.D. Pa. May 28, 2010).

1026. Finally, in *Natco v. Gilead*, the District of Minnesota court granted Gilead's motions to dismiss Sherman Act claims for failure to state a claim. Natco sued based on Sections 1 and 2 of the Sherman Act as well as under state law, claiming that Gilead denied repeated requests to purchase samples of a drug as part of a "scheme designed to preclude access."[249] The court held that Gilead was simply complying with FDA restrictions on distribution without a prescription, and that Natco would have been able to obtain samples from a certified physician, leading to the conclusion that Natco failed to state an actionable Section 2 claim.[250] The court also dismissed Natco's Section 1 claim because Natco failed to specify facts supporting the existence of a conspiracy or agreement, a fundamental element of a Section 1 claim.[251]

b. *EU approach*

(1) Core Issues

1027. Refusal to deal may constitute an abuse under Article 102 TFEU only in exceptional circumstances. Indeed, similar to the US, there is a generally recognized principle in EU law that any company, even in a situation of dominance, has the right to choose its trading partners.[252] Thus, a refusal to deal may constitute an infringement of Article 102 TFEU only if it has a foreclosure object of effect or prevents the emergence of a competitor in the market.

1028. In its Guidance on its enforcement priorities in applying Article 82 of the EC Treaty (now Article 102 TFEU) to abusive exclusionary conduct by dominant undertakings, the European Commission explained that the concept of refusal to supply covers a broad range of practices, such as a refusal to supply products to existing or new customers, refusal to license IP rights, including when the license is necessary to provide interface information, or refusal to grant access to an essential facility or network. It further indicated that it would consider these practices as an enforcement priority if all the following circumstances are present: (i) the refusal relates to a product or service that is objectively necessary to be able to compete effectively in a downstream market, (ii) the refusal is likely to lead to the elimination of effective competition in the downstream market, and (iii) the refusal is likely to lead to consumer harm.[253]

1029. In practice, cases criticizing a refusal to deal are rather scarce under EU law and many of them were in fact dealt with under the essential facilities doctrine. However, there have been a few cases over the years where refusals to deal have been considered anticompetitive. For example, in *Commercial Solvents*, the ECJ

---

[249] *Natco Pharma Ltd. v. Gilead Scis., Inc.*, No. CV 14-3247 (DWF/JSM), 2015 WL 5718398, *2 (D. Minn. Sept. 29, 2015).

[250] *Id.* *5.

[251] *Id.* *7.

[252] Case 238/87 *Volvo v. Veng*, ECLI:EU:C:1988:477, ¶8 (Oct. 5, 1988); Joined Cases C-241/91 P and C-242/91 P, *Radio Telefis Eireann (RTE) and Independent Television Publications Ltd (ITP) v. Commission*, ECLI:EU:C:1995:98, ¶49 (Apr. 6, 1995); Case C-418/01, *IMS Health GmbH v. NDC Health GmbH*, ECLI:EU:C:2004:257, ¶34 (Apr. 29, 2004); Case T-201/04 *Microsoft Corp. v. Commission*, ECLI:EU:T:2007:289, ¶¶319, 330, 331 (Sept. 17, 2007).

[253] European Commission Communication, *supra* n. 17, Chapter V, ¶¶78–81.

considered that a quasi-monopoly, which decides to reserve raw materials to its own production of derivatives and therefore refuses to supply a customer on the downstream market, which is itself a manufacturer of these derivatives, risks eliminating all competition from that customer and abuses its dominance.[254] To the contrary, a refusal justified by technical or commercial requirements cannot normally be considered abusive.[255]

1030. In the pharmaceutical sector, a refusal to deal is often motivated by the protection of the pharmaceutical firm's commercial interests, more particularly its willingness to prevent parallel trade, that is exports from one Member State to another Member State, which can affect its profitability.

1031. It should be noted that, traditionally, competition authorities have always severely sanctioned unilateral conduct that directly or indirectly has the effect of impeding parallel trade by creating artificial barriers to the free movement of goods and services within the EU. Indeed, as these practices result in market partitioning, they are generally considered as being inherently harmful to competition and thus, as having an anticompetitive object.[256]

1032. However, both the ECJ and NCAs have recognized the specificity of the markets in the pharmaceutical sector, which are highly regulated. Therefore, prices of pharmaceutical products might differ dramatically across Member States. Against this background, intermediary buyers (generally wholesalers) have tried to take advantage of this situation by purchasing drugs in the Member States where the prices set by the regulators are lower and reselling them in other Member States where the regulated price is higher, thereby making a profit, to the detriment of the manufacturer and without any benefit to the customers or to the social security entities paying for the drugs.[257]

1033. To address this situation, some competition authorities have recognized that pharmaceutical companies may use quota systems for certain drugs, thereby limiting the quantities available on a national market, or refuse to sell, including to existing customers, if they suspect parallel trade.

(2) Key Cases

1034. Although parallel trade restrictions have often been sanctioned under Article 101 TFEU,[258] a restriction of parallel trade may also constitute an abusive refusal to deal under Article 102 TFEU.

1035. In its judgment of September 16, 2008 (*Syfait II*), the ECJ held that the practice of a dominant undertaking aiming at avoiding all parallel exports can be caught by

---

[254] Cases 6/73 and 7/73, *Istituto Chemioterapico Italiano and Commercial Solvents v. Commission*, ECLI:EU:C:1974:18, ¶25 (Mar. 6, 1974).

[255] Case C-418/01, *IMS Health GmbH*, ECLI:EU:C:2004:257, ¶38 (Apr. 29, 2004); Case 311/84, *SA Centre belge d'études de marché – Télémarketing v. CLT et IPB*, ECLI:EU:C:1985:394, ¶26 (Oct. 3, 1985).

[256] Joined Cases C-501/06 P, C-513/06 P, C-515/06 P and C-519/06 P, *GlaxoSmithKline Services Unlimited v. Commission*, ECLI:EU:C:2009:610, ¶59 (Oct. 6, 2009).

[257] Joined Cases C-468/06 to C-478/06, *Sot. Lélos kai Sia EE and Others v. GlaxoSmithKline AEVE Farmakeftikon Proïonton, formerly Glaxowellcome AEVE*, ECLI:EU:C:2008:504, ¶¶35–36 (Sept. 16, 2008).

[258] Case T-450/05, *Peugeot*, ECLI:EU:T:2009:262, ¶46 (July 9, 2009); *see also* Case C-551/03 P, *Opel/General Motors Nederland BV v. Commission*, ECLI:EU:C:2006:229, ¶67 (Apr. 6, 2006). *See* Chapter IV for more details.

Article 102 TFEU.[259] In this case, drawing from the conclusions of the *Commercial Solvent* case, the Court established that:

> [T]he refusal by an undertaking occupying a dominant position on the market of a given product to meet the orders of an existing customer constitutes abuse of that dominant position under Article 82 EC where, without any objective justification, that conduct is liable to eliminate a trading party as a competitor.[260]

1036. These practices, "by partitioning the national markets, neutralize the benefits of effective competition in terms of the supply and the prices that those exports would obtain for final consumers in the other Member States."[261]

1037. Having said that, considering the pharmaceutical sector specifically, the Court ruled that a dominant undertaking may counter commercial threats posed by an undertaking wishing to be supplied with significant quantities intended for parallel export.[262] While it cannot cease to meet the ordinary orders of an existing customer solely because that customer exports part of the quantities to other Member States, a pharmaceutical company can refuse to meet extraordinary orders. Extraordinary orders correspond to those where the quantities requested are "out of all proportion to those previously sold by the same wholesalers to meet the needs of the market in that Member State."[263] In practice, it is for the national courts to ascertain whether the orders are ordinary or extraordinary. For the purpose of this assessment, two factors must be taken into account: (i) the size of the orders in relation to the requirements of the market in the first Member State, and (ii) the size of the orders in relation to the previous business relations between the manufacturer and the wholesalers concerned.[264]

1038. In certain Member States, NCAs have also addressed quota systems and restrictions of parallel trade. In a decision of December 20, 2005, the FCA considered that pharmaceutical firms could, without committing an abuse of dominance, oppose parallel exports by refusing to supply exporters who had no activity in the national territory and were simply reselling at a profit, drugs purchased in bulk at a regulated price.[265]

1039. In a subsequent commitments decision issued on July 5, 2007, the FCA addressed more particularly the quota systems implemented by four pharmaceutical companies for the supply of drugs to wholesalers in France. First, the FCA found that each pharmaceutical company could be considered in a dominant position towards wholesalers on its own portfolio of drugs. Indeed, wholesalers in the pharmaceutical sector are under strict regulatory obligations, including the obligation to: (i) maintain at all time stocks amounting to at least 9/10

---

259 Joined Cases C-468/06 to C-478/06, *Sot. Lélos kai Sia EE and Others*, ECLI:EU:C:2008:504, ¶66 (Sept. 16, 2008).

260 *Id.* ¶34.

261 *Id.* ¶66.

262 *Id.* ¶71.

263 *Id.* ¶¶71, 76.

264 *Id.* ¶76.

265 FCA, Decision No. 05-D-72, *GlaxoSmithkline (GSK) and Others* (Dec. 20, 2005).

of all available pharmaceutical specialties, and (ii) supply pharmacies within 24 hours of their orders; they have therefore no choice but to purchase drugs from each and every pharmaceutical company to be able to meet their obligations and pharmacies' demand. Second, the FCA acknowledged that the quota systems pursue a legitimate aim to optimize the production and distribution of pharmaceutical products, taking into account the specificity of the pharmaceutical sector. Third, the FCA nevertheless expressed concerns that the quota systems at stake, which were characterized by a low level of transparency and a certain degree of rigidity over time – as allocations were calculated based on the sales history of each wholesaler – could restrain effective competition in the market, including by hindering the entrance of new participants. According to the FCA, any restriction imposed on the wholesalers should therefore be limited to what is strictly necessary to ensure that the domestic market is correctly supplied, while maintaining genuine possibilities of competition between the wholesalers. To address the FCA's concerns, the targeted pharmaceutical companies offered to modify their allocation systems to guarantee an effective supply of the domestic market while still allowing wholesalers more flexibility to maintain a certain level of competition, as well as a greater transparency towards wholesalers on the functioning of the quota systems.[266] Two other pharmaceutical companies which already operated quota systems where the quantities between wholesalers were objectively allocated, also took commitments before the FCA in two subsequent decisions of December 13, 2007 in order to integrate more flexibility in their systems.[267]

1040. A similar stance was adopted in Belgium. In the *Bofar* case, Bofar, a pharmaceutical wholesaler, filed a complaint against nine pharmaceutical companies for abuse of dominance following their refusals to supply products. In parallel, Bofar also requested an injunctive relief that, on an interim basis, the pharmaceutical companies be required to resume supplying the products at stake. The Prosecutor rejected the request for interim measures on the ground that the pharmaceutical companies' refusal to supply did not *prima facie* amount to an abuse of dominance. In reaching this conclusion, the Prosecutor took into account the specificities of the pharmaceutical markets and Bofar's status as an export distributor, *i.e.*, one which does not possess the required licenses to distribute products in Belgium and planned to benefit from the nationally fixed prices in order to resell products in other Member States. More specifically, the Prosecutor built his reasoning on Advocate-General Jacobs' Opinion in *Syfait I*,[268] holding that a refusal to supply an export wholesaler can be legitimately justified by the protection of pharmaceutical companies' commercial interests and does not constitute an abuse of a dominant position. Following an appeal by Bofar, the Belgian Competition Council upheld the decision of the Prosecutor on April 2, 2009, affirming the view that it was not evident that there was a *prima facie* infringement of Article 102 TFEU and/or Article 3 of the

266 FCA, Decision No. 07-D-22, *Phoenix Pharma* (July 5, 2007).

267 FCA, Decision No. 07-D-45, *Pfizer* (Dec. 13, 2007); Case No. 07-D-46, *GSK* (Dec.13, 2007).

268 Opinion of Advocate General Jacobs, C-53/03, *Synetairismos Farmakopoion Aitolia & Akarnanias (Syfait) and Others v. GlaxoSmithKline Plc and GlaxoSmithKline AEVE*, ECLI:EU:C:2004:673, (Oct. 28, 2004).

Belgian Law on the Protection of Economic Competition.[269] Following the interim measures proceedings, the case was eventually dismissed on the merits.

1041. An application of the principles laid down in *Syfait II* can be found in the Romanian *Roche* case. SC Relad International SRL (Relad), a distributor, lodged a complaint against its supplier SC Roche Romania SRL (Roche). It alleged that Roche had abused its dominant position by, among other things, refusing to supply the products ordered by Relad. In assessing whether Roche's practice amounted to an abuse of dominant position, the Romanian Competition Authority applied the test established in *Syfait II*. In particular, the Romanian Competition Authority examined whether the refusal to supply was motivated by an attempt to prevent parallel trade. Relad's orders were compared to those of the other distributors, and it was found that Roche's supplies had steadily increased following growing demand and increased budget allocations in the healthcare system. Finding no infringement, the Romanian Competition Authority closed the investigation.[270]

1042. However, in a more recent case, the Romanian Competition Authority fined GSK for failure to observe commitments in the context of an abuse of dominance probe relating to the supply of drugs on the domestic market.[271] While GSK had committed to supply enough quantities of the products concerned for 2 years in order to ensure that domestic demand would be met, it stopped marketing 3 versions of Seretide before the end of the 2-year deadline, leading to the removal of these products from the national list of reimbursed products.

B. *Allegedly Anticompetitive Innovation*

1043. The practice of pharmaceutical companies introducing changes to existing medications – often with accompanying IP right protections – is sometimes referred to in the industry as being part of "Life Cycle Management" or, pejoratively by antitrust plaintiffs or enforcers, as "product hopping." In practice, such changes may take various forms such as reformulation, modification of the galenic form (e.g., from capsules to tablets), modification of the non-active ingredients, or combination of two or more active ingredients that had previously been marketed separately.

1044. From a legal perspective, the development of a new and improved formulation of a drug is not, in and of itself, anticompetitive.[272] To the contrary, drug innovation

---

269 Belgian Competition Authority, Decision No. 2009-V/M-04, Case No. MEDE-V/M-07/0038, *Bofar* (Apr. 2, 2009); *see also* Carmen Verdonck & Louise Depuydt, *The Belgian Prosecutor Refuses a Request for Preliminary Measures in a Pharmaceutical "Refusal To Supply" Case (Bofar)*, E-COMPETITIONS Mar. 2008, art. No. 21834.; Jacques Derenne, Mariëtte Swart & Cédric Kaczmarek, *The Belgian Competition Authority Confirms Refusal by the Competition Auditor to Adopt Interim Measures Following Alleged Abuse Of Dominance by 10 Pharmaceutical Companies Concerning Pharmaceuticals Parallel Imports (Bofar)*, E-COMPETITIONS Apr. 2009, art. No. 26216.

270 Alexandr Svetlicinii, *The Romanian Competition Authority Follows Case Law Precedent and Finds No Abuse Of Dominance on the Pharmaceuticals Distribution Market (Roche)*, E-COMPETITIONS May 2013, art. No. 54944.

271 *See* Romanian Competition Council, Press Release, *The Competition Council Sanctioned GlaxoSmithKline SRL with Fine of 11.9 Million Lei* (Aug. 2020), *available at* https://www.vbb.com/media/Insights_Articles/amenda_GSK_aug_2020_english.pdf.

272 *See Allied Orthopedic Appliances Inc. v. Tyco Health Care Grp. LP*, 592 F.3d 991, 1000–01 (9th Cir. 2010) (holding that a medical technology improvement "facilitate[d] the introduction of new types of sensors with added capabilities at less cost to customers" and correspondingly refusing to find antitrust liability at the summary judgment stage). *See also* C-457/10 P, *AstraZeneca AB*, ECLI:EU:C:2012:770, (Dec. 6, 2012).

is generally immune from the antitrust laws. However, there are circumstances in which such innovation, when accompanied by other actions that could be considered coercive or exclusionary, may be deemed anticompetitive.[273]

a. *US Approach*

(1) Core Issues

1045. One of the first US cases to allege so-called "anticompetitive innovation" was *Berkey Photo, Inc. v. Eastman Kodak Co.*,[274] in which the Second Circuit ultimately held that Kodak's introduction of an arguably superior film, even if it undermined competition, did not create an antitrust cause of action unless there was some form of coercion involved.[275] Notably, the court found that consumers were not coerced to purchase Kodak's new film "especially since Kodak did not remove any other films from the market when it introduced the new one."[276] As discussed in more detail below, whether conduct that accompanies innovation constitutes coercion is a fact-specific inquiry

1046. Balancing the introduction of a particular innovation against its potential exclusionary effects can be a struggle for courts. While a patent grant shows innovation, it does not show an innovation's value or usefulness to the market. Usually, an innovation's value is determined by ordinary market forces like supply and demand. But where the introduction of a new innovation is accompanied by the withdrawal of an old potential substitute (sometimes referred to as a "hard product" hop – as opposed to a "soft product hop" in which the old product is left on the market to compete with the new), consumers may be ***coerced*** into buying the new product even they would have preferred to purchase the old product. This potentially exclusionary conduct, usually not the innovation itself, is the focus of antitrust litigation and enforcement actions. That said, "soft" hopping generally does not give rise to liability because consumers still have a choice.[277]

1047. The execution of a hard "hop" is not, however, dispositive. As discussed below, at least one court has deemed it necessary to balance "the important public interest in encouraging innovation in the pharmaceutical industry with [its] obligations to protect consumers and to ensure fair competition under the antitrust laws."[278] It further noted, however, that courts should remain "wary both of second-guessing Congress's legislative judgment and of turning courts into tribunals over innovation sufficiency."[279]

---

273 *See, e.g.*, *Mylan Pharms. Inc. v. Warner Chilcott Pub. Ltd. Co.*, 838 F.3d 421, 439 (3d Cir. 2016) (allowing replacement of a drug with a new formulation where producer Warner Chilcott showed "non-pretextual purposes for their various product changes" but noting that "we do not rule out the possibility that certain insignificant design or formula changes, combined with other coercive conduct, could present a closer call with respect to establishing liability.").

274 603 F.2d 263 (2d Cir. 1979).

275 *Id.* 287 ("If a monopolist's products gain acceptance in the market, therefore, it is of no importance that a judge or jury may later regard them as inferior, so long as that success was not based on any form of coercion.").

276 *Id.*

277 *See Walgreen Co. v. AstraZeneca Pharms. L.P.*, 534 F. Supp. 2d 146, 152 (D.D.C. 2008) (finding no antitrust injury where the initial drug at issue remained on the market, "available as a consumer choice either by prescription or over-the-counter" because the new formulation simply outcompeted generic substitutes).

278 *Mylan Pharms.*, 838 F.3d 440.

279 *Id.*

(2) Key Cases

1048. In general, US case law on this issue distinguishes between the introduction of new products and ancillary actions which allegedly interfere with the operation of the market, as represented by customer choice. The development of a new product is not usually problematic; issues arise with the inhibition of or interference with this choice.

1049. In *In re Suboxone (Buprenorphine Hydrochloride and Naloxone) Antitrust Litigation*,[280] the district court addressed whether product hopping can constitute an antitrust violation or whether, as the defendant argued, it was simply the pro-competitive development and marketing of a new product. The court ultimately held that "due to market characteristics unique to the pharmaceutical industry," some of the plaintiffs' claims plausibly alleged antitrust violations and could not be dismissed.[281]

1050. The court first noted that, because ordinarily innovation will also inflict harm upon competitors, courts should not condemn a product change unless they are relatively confident that the conduct in question is anticompetitive.[282] The court held, however, that a monopolist's introduction of a new product can be exclusionary when accompanied by certain practices, and that the test is not foreclosure of the market entirely but "whether the challenged practices bar a substantial number of rivals or severely restrict the market's ambit."[283] The court framed the question of product hopping as whether the introduction of a new product was accompanied by other wrongful conduct that would harm competition and prevent consumer choice. The plaintiffs' product-hopping allegations – including the defendant's removal of the older product and allegedly false statements disparaging the product – were sufficient to allege exclusionary conduct under Section 2 because these measures "could plausible coerce patients and doctors to switch."[284]

1051. The Second Circuit became the first appellate court to analyze product hopping in *New York ex rel. Schneiderman v. Actavis PLC.* (hereinafter "*Namenda*")[285] The case involved Actavis's actions relating to its Alzheimer's drug, Namenda. When Namenda IR, a twice-daily drug, was nearing the end of its patent exclusivity period, Actavis introduced Namenda XR, a once-daily drug. The State of New York alleged that, during this period, Actavis began to pull all of Namenda IR from the market, forcing a switch to Namenda XR and preventing generic manufacturers from benefitting from state drug substitution laws that would have

---

280 64 F. Supp. 3d 665.

281 *Id.* 672.

282 *Id.* 679–80.

283 *Id.* 680, 683 (quotation and citation omitted).

284 *Id.* 682. Other early product-hopping cases include: *Walgreen.*, 534 F. Supp. 2d 151 (dismissing a case alleging attempted monopolization because "there is no allegation that AstraZeneca eliminated any consumer choices. Rather, AstraZeneca... introduced a new drug to compete with already-established drugs – both its own and others' – and with the generic substitutes for at least one of the established drugs") and *Abbott Labs. V. Teva Pharm. USA, Inc.*, 432 F. Supp. 2d 408, 430 (D. Del. 2006) (denying motion to dismiss complaint alleging antitrust violations where the defendants introduced new drug formulations and withdrew the prior versions whose exclusivity period would soon expire).

285 787 F.3d 638 (2d Cir. 2015).

allowed pharmacists to automatically substitute generic versions of Namenda IR, but would not allow generic substitution for Namenda XR. A district court granted a preliminary injunction preventing the removal of Namenda IR from the market before generic entry, and the Second Circuit upheld this decision.

1052. The Second Circuit examined Actavis's conduct under a theory of attempted monopolization. Namenda IR and XR were the only two drugs in their class on the market, which, according to the court, established Actavis's monopoly power.[286] Turning to Actavis's conduct, the court noted that, although product innovation generally benefits consumers, product redesign is anticompetitive when it coerces consumers and impedes competition.[287] Like the court in *Suboxone*, the Second Circuit stated that product withdrawal alone is not anticompetitive, but when combined with some other conduct it can be coercive to consumers.[288] Actavis, the court said, engaged in a "hard switch" of both introducing a new product and withdrawing an old one.[289] The court found that Actavis's procompetitive justifications were pretextual (based on the available documentary evidence), without closely analyzing whether the procompetitive justifications would outweigh the anticompetitive harms.[290] The court concluded that the combination of withdrawing a successful drug from the market and introducing a reformulated version of that drug forced patients to switch to the new version and impeded generic competition. Without a procompetitive justification, the court ruled that this conduct violated Section 2.[291]

1053. In *Mylan Pharmaceuticals*,[292] the Third Circuit distinguished the Second Circuit's ruling in *Namenda* and upheld a grant of summary judgment in defendant Warner Chilcott's favor. The Third Circuit first found that Mylan failed to show that Warner Chilcott had monopoly power, as a high level of interchangeability and cross-elasticity of demand existed between the product subject to the alleged product hop, Doryx, and other tetracyclines prescribed to treat acne. Warner Chilcott's share of the larger relevant market never exceeded 18%, according to the court.

1054. The court then addressed Warner Chilcott's alleged conduct, finding that the *Namenda* case was factually distinguishable because it involved attempts to avoid a patent cliff (abrupt drop in sales following patent expiry) that were not present in the case before it.[293] Mylan, unlike the generic manufacturers in *Namenda*, had a period of over 20 years to produce a generic version of Doryx, had 180 days of exclusive rights to market its generic Doryx once it received approval, sold its generic product for a higher price than branded Doryx for a period of time, and made profits from its sale of generic Doryx.[294] As a result, the court held

286 *Id.* 651–52.
287 *Id.* 652–53.
288 *Id.* 653.
289 *Id.* 654.
290 *Id.* 658.
291 *Id.* 663.
292 838 F.3d 421.
293 *Id.* 439.
294 *Id.* 438–39.

that Mylan was not foreclosed from the market.[295] In addition, the Third Circuit identified "strong" evidence of non-pretextual purposes for Warner Chilcott's various product changes, including adverse patient reactions and shelf-life stability problems with the older version of Doryx, as well as evidence that Warner Chilcott introduced various dosages of the drug in response to actions of competitors and therefore affirmed summary judgment for Warner Chilcott.[296]

1055. In *In re Asacol Antitrust Litigation*,[297] the district court evaluated allegations of product hopping after Warner Chilcott acquired both Asacol and Asacol HD. Asacol was prescribed for mild to moderately active ulcerative colitis, while Asacol HD was only approved for moderately active ulcerative colitis.[298] Asacol's patent was set to expire, so Warner Chilcott made efforts via marketing to switch patients from Asacol to Asacol HD.[299] Both drugs remained on the market, and there was limited switching from Asacol to Asacol HD.[300] Warner Chilcott then introduced a new drug called Delzicol and stopped selling Asacol altogether.[301]

1056. The court held there was no hard hop from Asacol to Asacol HD because the products were sold side by side for several years and further noted that "product introduction" alone is not anticompetitive.[302] The plaintiffs argued that the marketing practices encouraging the switch from Asacol to Asacol HD were still coercive to consumers, but the court called this a soft switch, with both products still on the market, maintaining consumer choice.[303] The court dismissed the product hop claim involving Asacol HD, but permitted the one involving Delzicol to move forward, since Warner Chilcott removed Asacol from the market upon Delzicol's introduction, creating a hard switch.[304]

b. *EU Approach*

1057. The EU acknowledged in its Pharmaceutical Sector Inquiry – Final Report that pharmaceutical firms that have invested large resources in R&D for a successful product have obvious economic incentives in focusing on incremental innovation for their top selling products.[305] As such, the mere introduction by a dominant firm of an upgraded version of a drug, be it through a new formulation, mode of administration, or other improvement, is not enough to amount to an abuse of dominance.

1058. Product hopping as an infringement of competition law therefore requires other conditions to be met, in particular the demonstration of a strategy on the part of the dominant firm to exclude rivals by encouraging, before or upon competitors'

---

295 *Id.* 438.

296 *Id.* 439–41.

297 233 F. Supp. 3d 247 (D. Mass. 2017).

298 *Id.* 255.

299 *Id.* 268.

300 *Id.* 269.

301 *Id.* 257.

302 *Id.* 268.

303 *Id.* 269.

304 *Id.* 269–70.

305 European Commission SWD, Pharmaceutical Sector Inquiry – Final Report (the Pharmaceutical Sector Inquiry – Final Report), ¶995 (July 8, 2009), *available at* https://ec.europa.eu/competition/sectors/pharmaceuticals/inquiry/staff_working_paper_part1.pdf.

entry on the market, the switch of patients from the first-generation to the second-generation product. In this respect, both the nature of the incremental innovation in terms of the benefits it brings to patients and the timing of that innovation play a critical role in the assessment of the conduct. Therefore, while it is legitimate for a pharmaceutical company to minimize the erosion of its sales when faced with generic or biosimilar entry, the launch of a second-generation product as an instrument to redirect demand towards that new product and make market penetration more difficult for competitors of the first-generation product may, under certain circumstances, be considered abusive.

1059. The leading case in this area is *AstraZeneca*. In 2005, the European Commission found that AstraZeneca abused its dominant position by selectively withdrawing the marketing authorizations for Losec capsules in certain Member States where it faced generic entry in order to force the switch of patients to a new tablet version, Losec MUPS.[306] According to the European Commission, it emerged from AstraZeneca's internal documents that this strategy pursued a double objective: first, to delay generic entry and, second, to prevent parallel trade of the original Losec capsules.[307] In light of the regulatory framework applicable at the time of the practices,[308] the withdrawal of the marketing authorization of Losec capsules prevented generic manufacturers from relying on the clinical trials conducted for this product when applying for their own marketing authorization, thereby significantly delaying generic entry.

1060. On appeal, AstraZeneca attempted to explain its behavior by the fact that it no longer had an interest in selling capsules and that maintaining the marketing authorization for this product obliged it to comply with onerous pharmacovigilance obligations. However, the General Court rejected this argument and broadly confirmed the European Commission's decision. It did reduce AstraZeneca's fine because the European Commission had failed to prove that the deregistration of the marketing authorizations for Losec capsules in Denmark and Norway prevented parallel imports in these countries.[309] On further appeal before the ECJ, the latter acknowledged that maintaining a marketing authorization imposes onerous pharmacovigilance obligations on its owner, which can in theory constitute an objective justification for the deregistration of said marketing authorization.[310] However, since this objective was not reflected in the company's internal documents, the Court concluded, in light of all the other relevant circumstances of the case, that it was unlikely that the withdrawal of the marketing authorization for Losec capsules was indeed justified by the costs of pharmacovigilance obligations.[311]

---

306 Case COMP/A.37.507/F3, *AstraZeneca* (2005).

307 *Id.* ¶256.

308 At the time, under Council Directive 65/65 of Jan. 26, 1965 on the approximation of provisions laid down by Law, Regulation or Administrative Action relating to proprietary medicinal products, 1965 OJ (L 22) 369, the abridged procedure for generic products, allowing generic manufacturers to rely on clinical data already submitted for the reference product, was available provided that the marketing authorization for the reference drug was still marketed. *See id.* ¶¶259–262.

309 Case T-321/05, *AstraZeneca AB and AstraZeneca plc*, ECLI:EU:T:2010:266, ¶840–861 (July 1, 2010).

310 Case C-457/10 P, *AstraZeneca AB*, ECLI:EU:C:2012:770, ¶135 (Dec. 6, 2012).

311 *Id.* ¶136.

1061. The reasoning of the Court is also interesting with regard to the impact of the regulatory framework on the competition law analysis. The Court ruled that the mere withdrawal of Losec capsules and, in parallel, the introduction of Losec MUPS was not sufficient to conclude to an abuse of dominance on the part of AstraZeneca since such conduct was not in and by itself capable of delaying or preventing generic entry and parallel trade. But in light of the regulatory framework that applied at the time of the practices, it is the deregistration of the marketing authorizations for Losec capsules which in fact fell short of competition on the merits and was thus found anticompetitive.[312]

1062. It should be noted that, since that judgment, the regulatory framework has been amended in order to allow generic manufacturers to rely on the clinical data for the reference product even if the marketing authorization for such product has been deregistered by the originator company.[313] Consequently, as long as generics of a first-generation product are not denied the possibility to enter the market, it is not entirely clear whether a hard switch (whereby the first-generation product is withdrawn from the market as was the case in AstraZeneca) and, *a fortiori*, a soft switch (whereby the first and second-generation products both remain available on the market) would still be considered as abusive product hopping under Article 102 TFEU. Having said that, the characterization of an abuse cannot be ruled out and, in practice, the conclusion in any given case may vary depending on the legal and economic context as well as the specific circumstances in which the conduct took place. Against this background, pharmaceutical companies should bear in mind that the internal documents of the dominant undertaking, insofar as they generally reflect the commercial strategy and objective pursued by the product hopping, will play a key role in the conclusion that competition authorities are likely to reach.

1063. Another example of alleged "product hopping" is the UK *Gaviscon* case.[314] In 2011, the OFT fined Reckitt Benckiser 10.2 million pounds for an abuse of dominant position following the implementation of a strategy designed to delay generic entry, consisting of replacing Gaviscon Original Liquid with a new, patented version of the same medicine, Gaviscon Advance. As in *AstraZeneca*, the UK regulatory framework was key in the OFT's finding of infringement.[315] Indeed, in the UK, when a patent expires and a "generic name" is assigned for a given active ingredient, general practitioners can search on the NHS software for the name of the branded product and then provide patients with an "open" prescription under the generic name of the product. Pharmacies can thus choose whether to deliver the branded product or a generic version to patients. In the present case, the OFT found that Reckitt Benckiser had planned to withdraw its first-generation product before a generic name for this product was assigned. In doing so, Reckitt Benckiser ensured that, when searching for the name "Gaviscon," doctors would

---

312 *Id.* ¶121.

313 Generic marketing authorization's procedure is developed in Chapter I, Section 2.A.

314 OFT, Case No. CA98/02/2011, *Gaviscon* (Apr. 12, 2011); *see* ECN Brief, *The UK OFTC Finds That a Medicine Producer Abuses Its Dominant Position and Imposes a Fine of £10 200 000* (Reckitt Benckiser), E-COMPETITIONS Apr. 2011, art. No. 37888.

315 However, to the best of our knowledge, the UK regulatory framework was not amended following the OFT decision.

have no choice but to prescribe Gaviscon Advance Liquid. Therefore, according to the OFT, the withdrawal could not be regarded as "normal competition" but was motivated by a desire to hinder the development of generic competition. Moreover, the OFT found that, at the time of the withdrawal, Reckitt Benckiser could foresee that its conduct was likely to restrict competition compared to a situation where the first-generation of Gaviscon would have been kept on the market, alongside the new version.

C. *Use and Abuse of IP Rights and Regulatory Processes*

1064. IP rights allow the holders of those rights to lawfully exclude competitors and others from the market. Exclusion through IP rights is generally lawful and in fact is the reward for innovating and securing those rights. This type of exclusion is different from exclusionary conduct based on a misuse of IP rights, which may constitute a violation of US and European antitrust laws.

1065. Antitrust issues can arise in connection with the acquisition, exploitation, and enforcement of IP rights, including patents, trademarks, copyright, and other similar rights. In the US, antitrust theories of harm based on the abuse or misuse of IP rights are often asserted as counterclaims in infringement actions. Abuses of IP rights and regulatory processes can include variations of sham litigation, committing fraud to obtain a patent, creating anticompetitive patent thickets, and misusing patents to seek rights not granted under the patent. In the EU, although a breach of Article 102 TFEU can be raised as a defense in patent litigation, in practice the abuse or misuse of IP rights is usually pursued and sanctioned independently by competition authorities, when such conduct results in at least potential exclusionary effects against rival firms.

a. *US Approach*

(1) *Noerr-Pennington* Doctrine and Sham Litigation

1066. Under the *Noerr-Pennington* doctrine,[316] petitions by private parties to courts and administrative agencies generally are protected from antitrust liability. In certain circumstances, however, the use of litigation or a regulatory process against a competitor can violate Section 2. An important exception to *Noerr-Pennington* immunity involves sham petitioning – that is, the filing of a sham lawsuit or administrative proceeding. This exception applies both to involvement in litigation as well as in regulatory proceedings. The sham exception is often litigated in the pharmaceutical sector, including in cases in which a branded drug manufacturer is alleged to have delayed competition by filing sham infringement lawsuits against generic drug manufacturers, filing sham citizen petitions with the FDA, and fraudulently listing patents in the FDA's Orange Book.[317]

---

316 The doctrine is named after two Supreme Court cases: *Eastern Railroad Presidents Conference v. Noerr Motor Freight*, 365 U.S. 127 (1961) and *United Mine Workers of America v. Pennington*, 381 U.S. 657 (1965). The Supreme Court held in *Noerr* that the use of a publicity campaign to influence government action was not reachable under the Sherman Act. *Noerr*, 365 U.S. 145. In *Pennington*, the Supreme Court applied this doctrine to a labor union seeking a minimum wage increase, even where their intent was to eliminate competition. *Pennington*, 381 U.S. 669–70.

317 Sham citizen petitions and Orange Book listings are addressed below in this section.

1067. In *Professional Real Estate Investors, Inc. v. Columbia Pictures Industries, Inc. (PRE)*,[318] the Supreme Court set out a two-prong test for determining when petitioning activity qualifies as a sham. Under the first prong, a plaintiff must show the petitioning activity is "objectively baseless." A claim is objectively baseless if no reasonable litigant could have anticipated success on the merits. If the petitioning activity is found to be objectively baseless, the court next considers whether the petition "conceal[s] an attempt to interfere *directly* with the business relationship of a competitor through the use [of] the governmental *process* – as opposed to the *outcome* of that process – as an anticompetitive weapon."[319] In other words, there must be a subjective intent to interfere with a competitor's business via the petitioning process, regardless of the anticipated outcome of the petitioning.

1068. The standard established by *PRE* makes it challenging to demonstrate litigation is a sham.[320] *PRE* explains that if there is "a reasonable belief that there is a chance that a claim will be held valid upon adjudication" the first *PRE* prong – objective baselessness – is not satisfied.[321] In the context of patent litigation, there is a "presumption of patent validity and the burden [is] on the patent challenger to prove invalidity by clear and convincing evidence."[322] As a result, "it will be a rare case in which a patentee's assertion of its patent in the face of a claim of invalidity will be so unreasonable as to support a claim that the patentee has engaged in sham litigation."[323] Even after meeting the high standard of the first prong, the plaintiff must further show that the defendant's subjective motivation in bringing the lawsuit was a bad-faith attempt to thwart competition.

1069. Cases alleging sham litigation in defense in the pharmaceutical sector often survive motions to dismiss or summary judgment,[324] although courts have dismissed some cases prior to trial.[325] In *FTC v. AbbVie, Inc.*,[326] the Third Circuit addressed

---

318 508 U.S. 49 (1993).

319 *Id.* 60–61 (internal quotation marks and citations omitted).

320 *See, e.g., FTC v. AbbVie, Inc.*, 976 F.3d 327, 361 (3d Cir. 2020) ("Generally, a plaintiff seeking to show the sham litigation exception faces 'an uphill battle.'") (quoting *In re Wellbutrin XL Antitrust Litig. Indirect Purchaser Class*, 868 F.3d 132, 147 (3d Cir. 2017)); *Tyco Healthcare Grp. LP v. Mutual Pharm. Co., Inc.*, 762 F.3d 1338, 1346 (Fed. Cir. 2014) ("Only if the exacting standards of *PRE* are satisfied will the patentee lose its Noerr-Pennington immunity in [the patent litigation] setting.").

321 *PRE*, 508 U.S. 62–63 (internal quotation marks and citations omitted).

322 *Tyco Healthcare*, 762 F.3d 1345.

323 *Id.*

324 *See, e.g., In re Loestrin 24 Fe Antitrust Litig.*, 433 F. Supp. 3d 274, 314–15 (D.R.I. 2019) (finding sufficient evidence of both objective and subjective baselessness for plaintiffs' sham litigation claim to survive summary judgment); *In re Ranbaxy Generic Drug Application Antitrust Litig.*, 2019 U.S. Dist. LEXIS 205849, *29–30 (D. Mass. 2019) (finding sham petitioning exception sufficiently alleged where defendants used the tentative approval stage of the ANDA approval process "to secure exclusivity while awaiting final approval to bar competition"); *Takeda Pharm. Co. v. Zydus Pharms.*, 2018 U.S. Dist. LEXIS 213473, *16 (D.N.J. 2018) (holding that Takeda's decision to file a lawsuit in response to a Paragraph IV certification letter from Zydus was not *per se* reasonable, such that *Noerr* immunity automatically applies); *In re Wellbutrin SR Antitrust Litig.*, 749 F. Supp. 2d 260, 263–66 (E.D. Pa. 2010) (permitting plaintiffs' sham litigation claim to survive summary judgment and holding entire lawsuit need not be a sham for purposes of the sham exception to *Noerr*).

325 *See, e.g., In re Lantus Direct Purchaser Antitrust Litig.*, 284 F. Supp. 3d 91, 110 (D. Mass. 2018) (dismissing sham litigation claims for lack of evidence that patent infringement action filed in response to Paragraph IV certification was objectively baseless).

326 976 F.3d 327 (3d Cir. 2020).

claims by the FTC that AbbVie had engaged in sham litigation with respect to its AndroGel product. The Third Circuit reversed the district court's ruling that AbbVie's litigation against a potential supplier of a generic version of AndroGel was objectively baseless, pointing to support for the litigation in the patent prosecution record.[327] Having reversed on objective baselessness, the Third Circuit declined to address the subjective motivation prong of *PRE*.[328] The court, however, affirmed the district court's decision that AbbVie's litigation against a second potential generic competitor was objectively baseless, finding that the potential competitor had sufficiently amended its ANDA application to remove it from the scope of the patent at issue.[329] The court also upheld the lower court's finding of an anticompetitive motivation for AbbVie's patent lawsuit.[330]

1070. Some courts have held that the *PRE* test does not apply in sham litigation cases involving multiple lawsuits – that is, *PRE* applies only to cases involving a single lawsuit or proceeding. Courts instead have turned to the Supreme Court's decision in *California Motor Transport v. Trucking Unlimited*, in which the Court found the defendants' "pattern of baseless, repetitive claims" were not protected under *Noerr-Pennington*.[331] For example, the Ninth Circuit has held that *PRE* and *California Motor Transport* address different situations: "When dealing with a series of lawsuits, the question is not whether any one of them has merit – some may turn out to, just as a matter of chance – but whether they are brought pursuant to a policy of starting legal proceedings without regard to the merits and for the purpose of injuring a market rival."[332] The Second, Third, and Fourth Circuits have similarly allowed Section 2 liability to be based on a pattern of petitioning without applying *PRE*.[333] The First and Seventh Circuits, however, have required the application of the *PRE* test to each sham petition in a series.[334] For example, in *In re Humira (Adalimumab) Antitrust Litigation*, the district court held that, because more than half of the defendants' PTO applications resulted in patents, the allegations about its "petitioning of the PTO are not plausible acts of sham petitioning."[335]

(2) Abuse of FDA Citizen Petitions

1071. Another application of the sham exception that arises with some frequency in the pharmaceutical sector involves the abuse of FDA citizen petitions. Citizen petitions provide an avenue for public input into the FDA's drug approval process. Any

---

327 *Id.* 366.

328 *Id.*

329 *Id.* 368.

330 *Id.* 371.

331 404 U.S. 508, 513, 516 (1972) (involving allegations that defendant highway carriers conspired to file state and federal proceedings to oppose plaintiffs' applications to obtain carrier rights).

332 *USS-POSCO Indus. v. Contra Costa County Building & Construction Trades Council*, 31 F.3d 800, 810–11 (9th Cir. 1994).

333 *See Primetime 24 Joint Venture v. NBC*, 219 F.3d 92, 101 (2d Cir. 2000); *Hanover 3201 Realty, LLC v. Village Supermarkets, Inc.*, 806 F.3d 162, 178–81 (3d Cir. 2015); *Waugh Chapel South, LLC v. United Food & Commercial Workers Union Local 27*, 728 F.3d 354, 363–64 (4th Cir. 2013).

334 *See Puerto Rico Tel. Co. v. San Juan Cable LLC*, 876 F.3d 767, 772 (1st Cir. 2017); *U.S. Futures Exch., LLC v. Bd. Of Trade of the City of Chicago, Inc.*, 953 F.3d 955, 965 (7th Cir. 2020).

335 465 F. Supp. 3d 811, 830 (N.D. Ill. 2020), *aff'd sub nom. Mayor & City Council of Baltimore v. AbbVie Inc.*, 42 F. 4th 709 (7th Cir. 2022).

individual or company may file a citizen petition concerning scientific or legal issues regarding drug products, whether they are under review by the FDA or have already been approved. The citizen petition process provides the FDA with an avenue through which it can receive concerns regarding drug products it reviews. However, the process also can be abused by firms seeking to delay approval of competing products. Several Section 2 claims have focused on branded drug manufacturers' filing of one or more citizen petitions with the FDA that have allegedly resulted in delay in the approval of competing generic products.

1072. Although citizen petitions are regarded as petitioning of the government and therefore generally protected under the *Noerr-Pennington* doctrine, filing sham citizen petitions with the FDA can trigger the sham exception to *Noerr* and potentially subject the petition filer to Section 2 liability. As the Second Circuit observed, although administrative filings, such as citizen petitions, are "less susceptible than lawsuits to the sham exception, [they] still carry the potential for antitrust liability."[336] Under *PRE*, to prove an FDA citizen petition is a sham, a plaintiff must demonstrate that the petition is objectively baseless and that the petitioner's subjective motivation in filing the petition was to use the process as an anticompetitive weapon. Objective baselessness – typically the focus of courts' analysis of sham citizen petition claims – is assessed at the time at which the petition was filed.[337]

1073. It is challenging for defendants to win dismissal of sham citizen petition claims at either the motion to dismiss or summary judgment stages. Several courts have held that the issue of whether a citizen petition is a sham is generally a question of fact properly reserved for the jury.[338] As one district court noted, a court should only rule on the objective baselessness prong as a matter of law where there is "no dispute over the predicate facts" of the underlying petition.[339] To the extent sham citizen petition claims get dismissed prior to trial, lack of evidence showing the petition delayed generic entry is one basis for such dismissals.[340]

1074. Courts reviewing allegedly sham citizen petitions have focused on certain factors in deciding whether the petitions qualify for *Noerr* immunity. One factor is the timing of the citizen petition. One court focused on the timing of the petition in denying a defendant's motion to dismiss, noting that the defendant had waited until six months prior to the generic competitor's scheduled market entry, even though the drug was in development for 6 years and the parties had litigated the patent

---

336 *In re DDVAP Direct Purchaser Antitrust Litig.*, 585 F.3d 677, 686 (2d Cir. 2009).

337 *See, e.g.*, *In re Wellbutrin XL Antitrust Litig. Indirect Purchaser Class*, 868 F.3d 148–49; *In re Restasis (Cyclosporine Ophthalmic Emulsion) Antitrust Litig.*, 333 F. Supp. 3d 135, 154 (E.D.N.Y. 2018).

338 *See, e.g.*, *In re Lipitor Antitrust Litig.*, 868 F.3d 273; *In re EpiPen (Epinephrine Injection, USP) Mktg., Sales Practices & Antitrust Litig.*, 336 F. Supp. 3d 1256, 1307 (D. Kan. 2018); *In re Restasis (Cyclosporine Ophthalmic Emulsion) Antitrust Litig.*, 333 F. Supp. 3d 154–55; *In re Suboxone (Buprenorphine Hydrochloride and Naloxone) Antitrust Litig.*, 64 F. Supp. 3d 665, 689 (E.D. Pa. 2014); *In re Flonase Antitrust Litig.*, 795 F. Supp. 2d 300, 310 (E.D. Pa. 2011).

339 *In re Flonase Antitrust Litig.*, 795 F. Supp. 2d 310.

340 *See, e.g.*, *In re Wellbutrin XL Antitrust Litig.*, Civil Action Nos. 08-2431 (direct), 08-2433 (indirect), 2012 WL 1657734, *25, 30 (E.D. Pa. 2012) (granting summary judgment for defendant where plaintiffs failed to show citizen petition delayed ANDA approval).

infringement suit for 3 years before the petition's filing.[341] The filing of the petition on the day after a court ruled that the ANDA filer did not infringe the patents covering a branded drug similarly played a substantial part in a court's decision to reverse summary judgment on the subjective baselessness prong of *PRE*.[342]

1075. Another factor considered by the courts is the FDA's response to the citizen petition at issue. As observed by the Federal Circuit in reversing summary judgment for a petition filer, "[p]articularly probative of whether the citizen petition was reasonable is the FDA's response, which denied the petition in terms indicating that, in the FDA's view, it was wholly without merit."[343] Similarly, allegations that the FDA found the citizen petition "had no convincing evidence" and lacked "any basis" for its arguments have been deemed sufficient to survive a motion to dismiss.[344] Further, statements by the FDA in related litigation that the agency's need to evaluate and respond to unsuccessful portions of a citizen petition delayed its approval of an ANDA precluded summary judgment on the issue of causation.[345] Further, the FDA's characterization of a citizen petition as "complex" and the fact that the FDA took several years to assess the petition does not necessarily preclude a finding of objective baselessness.[346] However, to survive a motion to dismiss on objective baselessness requires more than just a showing that the FDA rejected a petition on the same day that it approved the ANDA addressed by the petition.[347]

1076. Another factor in assessing allegedly sham citizen petitions is the extent to which such petitions succeed in the relief they seek. Successful petitions, by definition, are not shams under *PRE*.[348] In contrast, one court denied a defendant's motion to dismiss where "[m]uch of the relief sought was not even available to the FDA to grant."[349] Another court denied defendants summary judgment where it was "clear" that the defendants "were fully aware that the relief they requested in their [p]etition was contrary to FDA law and practice."[350]

1077. There is disagreement in the courts on how to treat petitions with mixed results or partial success at the FDA.[351] One court has held that a citizen petition is not

---

341 *In re EpiPen Antitrust Litig.*, 336 F. Supp. 3d 1307–08.

342 *Tyco Healthcare*, 762 F.3d 1348; *see also In re Suboxone Antitrust Litig.*, 64 F. Supp. 3d 689 (observing that the FDA made a referral to the FTC and noted that the timing of the petition and related conduct by the defendant in relation to the expected entry of generic competition "cannot be ignored").

343 *Tyco Healthcare*, 762 F.3d 1347.

344 *In re DDVAP Direct Purchaser Antitrust Litig.*, 585 F.3d 686, 694 (reversing dismissal of sham citizen petition claim).

345 *In re Prograf Antitrust Litig.*, 2014 WL 4745954, *7 (D. Mass. 2014).

346 *In re Lipitor Antitrust Litig.*, 868 F.3d 273–74 (reversing dismissal of sham citizen petition allegations).

347 *Apotex Inc. v. Acorda Therapeutics, Inc.*, 823 F.3d 51, 62 (2d Cir. 2016) (affirming dismissal of sham citizen petition claim).

348 *See, e.g., In re Wellbutrin XL Antitrust Litig.*, 2012 WL 1657734, *24 ("A successful effort to influence government action… certainly cannot be characterized as a sham.") (quoting *PRE*, 508 U.S. 58).

349 *In re Suboxone Antitrust Litig.*, 64 F. Supp. 3d 690.

350 *Louisiana Wholesale Drug. Co. v. Sanofi-Aventis*, No. 07 CV 7343(HB), 2008 WL 4580016, *5 (S.D.N.Y. 2008).

351 *See, e.g., In re Wellbutrin XL Antitrust Litig.*, 2012 WL 1657734, *28 (finding it unnecessary to address the question and noting that "[t]he parties have not pointed to, and this Court has not found, binding authority on the issue of whether petitions with a mix of sham and non-sham requests can be considered objectively baseless as a whole").

a sham if at least one claim in the petition has objective merit.[352] Another court found that the FDA's denial of every substantive (as opposed to procedural) request in each of a filer's three petitions by itself is insufficient to plausibly allege the objective baselessness of the petitions – although such denial was sufficient when combined with the lack of a reasonable expectation that the FDA would agree to the bioequivalence standard sought by the filer.[353]

1078. Finally, in a decision interpreting the FTC Act, the Third Circuit affirmed the dismissal of a complaint brought by the FTC 5 years after the defendant had filed the last of a series of citizen petitions with the FDA. The court held that the FTC's allegations of "long-past conduct" were insufficient under Section 13(b) of the FTC Act to demonstrate that the defendant "is violating" or "is about to violate" the law, threshold requirements for the agency to bring an action under Section 13(b).[354]

(3) Improper Orange Book Listings

1079. A final example of "sham" activity in the pharmaceutical sector that may violate Section 2 is the baseless filing of patents in the FDA's Orange Book. To gain approval for a new drug, a manufacturer must identify all patents that claim the drug or a method of using the drug in its NDA.[355] All such patents are listed by the FDA in the Orange Book, known formally as "Approved Drug Products with Therapeutic Equivalence Evaluations." Then, to obtain FDA approval for a generic version of an approved drug before patent expiration, a generic company must certify that there is no valid patent listed in the Orange Book that will be infringed by marketing of the generic product or that any patents listed in the Orange Book are invalid, unenforceable, or not infringed (known as a Paragraph IV certification). If the generic applicant files and serves a Paragraph IV certification, it triggers a right for the branded company to sue and, if it does so within 45 days, a 30-month stay on ANDA approval.[356]

1080. Allegations that a branded drug company knowingly submitted false information to the FDA for listing in the Orange Book, allowing the branded company to obtain a 30-month stay of generic approval, may be sufficient to state a Section 2 claim.[357] As with FDA citizen petitions, courts often refuse to dismiss claims of baseless Orange Book listings at the motion to dismiss or summary judgment stage.[358] And it should be noted that, although Orange Book cases typically involve the listing of patents that

---

352 *In re Flonase Antitrust Litigation*, 795 F. Supp. 2d 311–12.

353 *In re Restasis Antitrust Litig.*, 333 F. Supp. 3d 156 (denying defendant's motion to dismiss).

354 *FTC v. Shire Viropharma, Inc.*, 917 F.3d 147, 156, 160 (3d Cir. 2019).

355 The statute requires the NDA applicant to list any patent which "claims the drug for which the applicant submitted the application" or which "claims a method of using such drug" if "a claim of patent infringement could reasonably be asserted if a person not licensed by the owner of the patent engaged in the manufacture, use, or sale of the drug." 21 U.S.C. § 355(b)(1).

356 For more details, *see generally* Chapter I, Section II.2.B.

357 *See, e.g., In re Lipitor Antitrust Litig.*, 868 F.3d 231, 271–72 (3d Cir. 2017); *In re DDVAP Direct Purchaser Antitrust Litig.*, 585 F.3d 677, 694 (2d Cir. 2009); *In re Remeron Antitrust Litig.*, 335 F. Supp. 2d 522, 531 (D.N.J. 2004); *In re Buspirone Patent Litig.*, 185 F. Supp. 2d 363, 369–76 (S.D.N.Y. 2002).

358 *See, e.g., In re Loestrin 24 FE Antitrust Litig.*, 433 F. Supp. 3d, 315 (denying summary judgment motion); *In re Buspirone Patent Litig.*, 185 F. Supp. 2d 376 (denying motion to dismiss); *Warner Lambert Co. v. Purepac Pharm. Co.*, 2000 WL 34213890, *7 (D.N.J. 2000) (same).

should not be listed, at least one case has addressed the failure to timely list the required patents in the Orange Book in an attempt to extend the patent holder's monopoly.[359]

1081. Courts have taken different approaches to addressing claims of baseless Orange Book listings. Some courts have assessed whether the plaintiff has sufficiently pleaded that the listing meets the elements of the sham exception to *Noerr*.[360] Where plaintiffs have alleged both that the patents at issue were obtained by fraud on the PTO (*Walker Process* fraud claims, *see* Section (4) below) and that the listing of those patents in the Orange Book was baseless, some courts have simply applied their *Walker Process* fraud determination to the Orange Book claim.[361] That is, if there is sufficient evidence to move forward on a *Walker Process* fraud claim, there is also sufficient evidence to state a claim for fraudulent listing of the same patents in the Orange Book.

1082. Some courts have focused on the elements of the statute governing Orange Book listings in assessing Section 2 claims. For example, in *In re Lantus Direct Purchaser Antitrust Litig.*, the Third Circuit ruled that a plaintiff sufficiently alleged that a defendant's Orange Book listing was an "improper means" of maintaining its monopoly power where the listed patent claimed neither the drug nor a method of using the drug named in the NDA.[362] The court rejected the defendant's argument that the drug delivery system (an injection pen) addressed by the listed patent qualifies as a "dosage form," which under FDA regulations is a "drug product," which in turn is a "drug."[363]

1083. In *In re Actos End-Payor Antitrust Litig.*,, the court focused on whether listed patents were the types of patents that must be listed in the Orange Book. NDA applicants are required to describe a patent as a drug product patent if it claims the NDA drug at issue. NDA applicants are further required to describe a patent as a method-of-use patent if it claims a method of using the NDA drug. Because the claims of the patents at issue did not literally read on the drug for which the NDA was submitted, the court ruled that the plaintiffs plausibly alleged that the defendant's listing of the patents as drug product patents in the Orange Book was inaccurate and violated Section 2.[364]

1084. Finally, because the FDA does not perform an independent review of whether patents listed in the Orange Book are valid or infringed, some courts have held that listing patents in the Orange Book does not constitute petitioning of the government and is therefore not immune from the antitrust laws under *Noerr*.[365]

---

359 *See In re Remeron Antitrust Litig.*, 335 F. Supp. 2d, 530–32 (denying motion to dismiss allegations that defendant failed to list patent in Orange Book within required 30-day period from patent approval date).

360 *See, e.g.*, *Warner Lambert*, 2000 WL 34213890, *6 (finding complaint sufficiently alleged fraud exception to *Noerr*).

361 *See, e.g.*, *In re Lipitor Antitrust Litig.*, 868 F.3d 271–72; *In re DDVAP Direct Purchaser Antitrust Litig.*, 585 F.3d 694; *In re Loestrin 24 FE Antitrust Litig.*, 433 F. Supp. 3d, 315.

362 *In re Lantus Direct Purchaser Antitrust Litig.*, 950 F.3d 1, 7–8 (1st Cir. 2020).

363 *Id.* 7.

364 *See In re Actos End-Payor Antitrust Litig.*, 417 F. Supp. 3d 352, 369–70 (S.D.N.Y. 2019); *see also Organon Inc. v. Mylan Pharms.*, 293 F. Supp. 2d 453, 459–60 (D.N.J. 2003) (finding defendant had "a reasonable basis" under then existing FDA statute and regulations for Orange Book listing).

365 *See, e.g.*, *Organon*, 293 F. Supp. 2d, 458–59 (noting that the FDA's action in listing the patent at issue in the Orange Book "was not an independent governmental determination, but rather a purely ministerial function"); *In re Buspirone Patent Litig.*, 185 F. Supp. 2d, 372–73 (characterizing a fraudulent Orange Book listing as "much closer to the filing of a tariff than to genuine acts of petitioning the government").

(4) *Walker Process* Fraud

1085. *Walker Process* fraud is a standalone theory of harm under Section 2 of the Sherman Act. Such fraud occurs when an innovator attempts to enforce a patent obtained by committing fraud before the PTO. In the Supreme Court case from which the cause of action gets its name, *Walker Process Equipment, Inc. v. Food Machinery & Chemical Corp.*,[366] the Court held that proof that the patentee obtained the patent "by knowingly and willfully misrepresenting facts to the Patent Office" is sufficient to strip the patentee of its exemption from the antitrust laws and therefore give rise to a claim under Section 2, provided the other elements of a monopolization claim are satisfied.[367]

1086. To prevail on a *Walker Process* claim, an antitrust plaintiff must establish that the defendant procured the relevant patent by knowing and willful fraud on the PTO or (in the case of an assignee) that the defendant maintained and "enforced the patent with knowledge of the fraudulent manner in which it was obtained"[368] – in addition to the elements required to prove monopolization or attempted monopolization. In an attempted monopolization claim based on *Walker Process* fraud, the plaintiff must show some conduct on the part of the defendant to enforce the fraudulently obtained patent.

1087. To prove the fraud element of a *Walker Process* claim, a plaintiff typically must show the same elements underlying a common-law fraud claim, including: "(1) a false representation of a material fact was made, (2) with the intent to deceive, (3) which induced the deceived party to act in justifiable reliance on the misrepresentation, and (4) which caused injury that would not otherwise have occurred."[369]

1088. Although *Walker Process* claims are typically asserted as counterclaims by defendants in patent infringement suits, a *Walker Process* claim "is a separate cause of action from a patent declaratory judgment action … governed by principles of antitrust law," including the requirement of demonstrating antitrust standing (i.e., injury of the type the antitrust laws were meant to address) and damages.[370] Like other fraud claims, *Walker Process* claims are subject to *the* heightening pleading requirements of Rule 9(b) of the Federal Rules of Civil Procedure, under which plaintiffs are required to allege "with particularity the circumstances constituting fraud."[371]

1089. Inequitable conduct before the PTO is a related defense to patent infringement claims. Previously, inequitable conduct was considered by the courts as insufficient to establish *Walker Process* fraud because inequitable conduct required a less demanding

---

366 382 U.S. 172 (1965). In *Walker Process*, as a counterclaim in a patent infringement action, the defendant alleged the plaintiff had procured the patent by filing a false oath to the PTO that concealed a fact that made the invention unpatentable.

367 *Id.* 172, 177.

368 *Id.* 179.

369 *C.R. Bard, Inc. v. M3 Sys., Inc.*, 157 F.3d 1340, 1364 (Fed. Cir. 1998).

370 *Ritz Camera & Image, LLC v. SanDisk Corp.*, 700 F.3d 503, 508 (Fed. Cir. 2012).

371 *Medimmune, Inc. v. Genentech, Inc.*, 427 F.3d 958, 967 (Fed. Cir. 2005) ("Like all fraud-based claims, *Walker Process* allegations are subject to the pleading requirements of Fed. R. Civ. P. 9(b)."). Federal Rule of Civil Procedure 9(b) provides in relevant part: "In alleging fraud or mistake, a party must state with particularity the circumstances constituting fraud or mistake." Fed. R. Civ. P. 9(b).

standard regarding intent and materiality.[372] The Federal Circuit – the court to which most *Walker Process* decisions are appealed – has since ruled that the evidentiary standards for these two defenses are the same.[373] As a result, a showing of inequitable conduct before the PTO is likely sufficient to make out a *Walker Process* fraud claim.

1090. *Walker Process* fraud claims sometimes implicate the *Noerr-Pennington* doctrine, which shields certain acts of petitioning the government – including patent infringement lawsuits – from antitrust scrutiny. Although the Supreme Court has declined to address the relationship between *Noerr-Pennington* and *Walker Process*,[374] the Federal Circuit has held that *Walker Process* and the sham exception to *Noerr-Pennington* "provide alternative legal grounds on which a patentee may be stripped of its immunity from the antitrust laws; both legal theories may be applied to the same conduct."[375]

(5) Patent Thickets

1091. A patent thicket is a collection of overlapping patent rights in a particular field of technology that an innovator must "cut" through in order to commercialize a product. A patent thicket can be owned by a single company or multiple companies. Concerns have been raised about pharmaceutical firms obtaining numerous, often weak patents – including after their products have been approved by the FDA – to deter the entry of generics or biosimilars.

1092. A recent decision addressed what the court described as a "new kind of antitrust claim" one challenging a pharmaceutical firm's patent thicket relating to its approved product and its conduct surrounding the thicket.[376] The plaintiffs alleged that AbbVie maintained its monopoly over adalimumab (including Humana and its biosimilars) and thereby violated Section 2 by "obtaining and asserting 'swaths of invalid, unenforceable, or noninfringed patents without regard to the patents' merits.'"[377] AbbVie allegedly was able to delay biosimilar entry by "repeatedly and aggressively asserting [its] patent thicket during a lengthy, detailed regulatory process (and subsequent infringement litigation)."[378] The allegedly unlawful conduct took place in multiple venues, including patent prosecutions and *inter partes* review proceedings before the PTO, the biologic licensing process before the FDA, and patent infringement actions in federal district court.

---

372 *See, e.g., Nobelpharma AB v. Implant Innovations, Inc.*, 141 F.3d 1059, 1069 (Fed. Cir. 1998) ("Consistent with the Supreme Court's analysis in *Walker Process*,... we have distinguished 'inequitable conduct' from *Walker Process* fraud, noting that inequitable conduct is a broader, more inclusive concept than the common law fraud needed to support a *Walker Process* counterclaim."); *Dippin' Dots, Inc. v. Mosey*, 476 F.3d 1337, 1346 (Fed. Cir. 2007) (upholding finding of inequitable conduct, but reversing finding of Walker Process fraud).

373 *Therasense, Inc. v. Becton, Dickinson & Co.*, 649 F.3d 1276, 1290–91 (Fed. Cir. 2011) (*en banc*) ("tight[ening] the standards for finding both intent and materiality in order to redirect [the inequitable conduct] doctrine that has been overused to the detriment of the public").

374 *See Professional Real Estate Investors v. Columbia Pictures Industries*, 508 U.S. 49, 61 n.6 (1993) (declining to decide whether *Noerr* permits "the imposition of antitrust liability for litigant's fraud or other misrepresentations").

375 *Nobelpharma*, 141 F.3d, 1071. The *Noerr-Pennington* doctrine and the sham exception thereto are discussed in greater detail in Section II.2.D below.

376 *In re Humira (Adalimumab) Antitrust Litig.*, 465 F. Supp. 3d 811, 826 (N.D. Ill. 2020).

377 *Id.* 827 (quoting plaintiffs' complaint).

378 *Id.*

1093. In addressing this novel claim, the court noted that it was not grounded in either *Walker Process* fraud, anticompetitive acquisition of patents, or sham patent litigation (*see* Section D. below on sham litigation). The court nonetheless found that the vast majority of the alleged conduct is immunized from antitrust scrutiny as lawful petitioning of the government, and "what's left are a few sharp elbows thrown at a sophisticated competitor participating in regulated patent and biologic-drug regimes."[379] The court also distinguished AbbVie's conduct from patent pooling – the intentional acquisition of a large number of patents – which does not involve petitioning the government. Finally, the court ruled that, even if AbbVie's nonimmunized conduct were sufficient to make out a standalone Section 2 claim, the complaint failed for lack of antitrust injury "because it is not plausible that AbbVie's nonimmunized conduct intimidated the other defendants into delaying the launch of their biosimilars (or otherwise caused any antitrust injury)."[380] The court therefore dismissed the plaintiffs' patent thicket claim. On appeal, the Seventh Circuit affirmed dismissal of the claim, finding that plaintiffs were unable to overcome *Noerr* immunity, had not relied on *Walker Process*, and otherwise failed to make out a Section 2 claim.[381]

(6) Patent Misuse

1094. Patent misuse is an affirmative defense to an action to enforce patent rights, including both infringement actions and contract actions seeking to collect royalties under a patent license. If patent misuse is shown, it will preclude enforcement of the patent until the misuse is "purged."[382] Although patent misuse cannot be the basis for a standalone Section 2 claim, federal antitrust standards generally guide courts' decisions as to what type of conduct qualifies as patent misuse.[383] At the same time, courts have found patent misuse in circumstances in which the challenged conduct did not rise to the level of an antitrust violation, which typically requires more exacting proof.

1095. The Federal Circuit has explained that patent misuse will only be found where the patent owner's conduct expands the physical or temporal scope of the patent at issue and where anticompetitive effects in a relevant market are established.[384] Courts typically engage in a rule-of-reason analysis of conduct alleged to be patent misuse.[385]

1096. Courts have found patent misuse in a wide variety of conduct, including compelling a patent licensee to take unwanted licenses to different patents,[386] compelling a

---

379 *Id.* 834.

380 *Id.* 835.

381 *Mayor & City Council of Baltimore v. AbbVie Inc.*, 42 F.4th 709, 712–14 (7th Cir. 2022).

382 *C.R. Bard, Inc. v. M3 Sys.*, 157 F.3d, 1372.

383 Congress has amended the Patent Act to exclude certain types of conduct from qualifying as patent misuse. For example, 1988 amendments to the act imposed a market power requirement for tying arrangements to constitute patent misuse. *See* 35 U.S.C. § 271(d)(5).

384 *Princo Corp. v. International Trade Comm'n*, 616 F.3d 1318, 1340 (Fed. Cir. 2010).

385 *See, e.g.*, *Windsurfing Int'l v. AMF, Inc.*, 782 F.2d 995, 1001–02 (Fed. Cir. 1986); *USM Corp. v. SPS Techs., Inc.*, 694 F.2d 505, 511–12 (7th Cir. 1982).

386 *See, e.g.*, *Hazeltine Research v. Zenith Radio Corp.*, 388 F.2d 25, 33–35 (7th Cir. 1967), *aff'd in part & rev'd in part*, 395 U.S. 100 (1969); *Koninklijke Philips N.V. v. Cinram Int'l*, 2013 U.S. Dist. LEXIS 76163, *21–27 (S.D.N.Y. 2013).

patented process licensee to purchase unpatented products to use in the process,[387] collecting royalties from multiple parties for the same patents used in the same product,[388] compelling royalty payments regardless of the licensee's use of the patent,[389] placing restrictions on the purchase or sale of goods outside a patent monopoly,[390] and seeking licenses that extend the patentee's rights beyond the statutory life of the patent.[391]

b. *EU Approach*

1097. Over the years, the ECJ has developed case law in relation to the exercise of IP rights by their proprietor and the compatibility thereof with competition rules. Generally speaking, while it is not disputed that the existence of rights conferred by a patent or another IP right to its owner are not inherently challengeable under antitrust rules, the exercise of those rights, if misused, can give rise to conduct contrary to the competition rules and, when that happens, must be penalized.[392]

1098. Under Article 102 TFEU more specifically, it follows from the precedents of the ECJ and NCAs that strategies of dominant firms intended to delay generic entry by artificially prolonging the protection conferred by their IP rights, be it through the communication of false information to patent offices (*AstraZeneca*) or the filing of divisional patents (*Pfizer*), may give rise to an abuse of dominant position. Furthermore, although primarily sanctioned under Article 101 TFEU (*see* Chapter IV), pay-for-delay strategies can also be caught by Article 102 TFEU (*Servier* and *GSK Paroxetine*).

1099. Finally, alongside the misuse of IP rights, the misuse of a regulatory process can also give rise to abusive conduct. To the contrary, vexatious litigation (equivalent to sham litigation in the US), is very rarely recognized as an abuse.

(1) Misrepresentations Before Patent Offices

1100. *AstraZeneca* is the first case in the EU in which the European Commission, followed by the General Court and the ECJ, assessed the question of misuse of IP rights in the pharmaceutical sector.[393] In this case, the European Commission fined AstraZeneca €60 million for two distinct types of abusive conduct, one of which consisted in instrumentalizing patent offices by providing them with false information in order to unduly prolong AstraZeneca's IP rights and delay generic entry of AstraZeneca's blockbuster drug Losec.

---

387 *See, e.g.*, *B.B. Chem. Co. v. Ellis*, 314 U.S. 495, 497–98 (1942).

388 *See, e.g.*, *PSC Inc. v. Symbol Techs.*, 26 F. Supp. 2d 505, 510–11 (W.D.N.Y. 1998).

389 *See, e.g.*, *Hazeltine Research v. Zenith Radio Corp.*, 395 U.S. 100, 133–40 (1969).

390 *See, e.g.*, *M. Eagles Tool Warehouse, Inc. v. Fisher Tooling Co.*, 2007 U.S. Dist. LEXIS 23636, *63–64 (D.N.J. 2007).

391 *See, e.g.*, *Rocform Corp. v. Acitelli-Standard Concrete Wall*, 367 F.2d 678, 681 (6th Cir. 1966).

392 Case T-691/14, *Servier SAS e.a. v. Commission*, ECLI:EU:T:2018:922, ¶241 (Dec. 12, 2018); *see also* Case C-457/10 P, *AstraZeneca AB*, ECLI:EU:C:2012:770, (Dec. 6, 2012) where the same logic prevailed. *See also*, outside of the pharmaceutical sector, Joined Cases C-241/91 P and C-242/91 P, *Radio Telefis Eireann (RTE) and Independent Television Publications Ltd (ITP)*, ECLI:EU:C:1995:98, ¶50 (Apr. 6, 1995); Case T-201/04, *Microsoft Corp.*, ECLI:EU:T:2007:289, ¶691 (Sept. 17, 2007).

393 Case COMP/A.37.507/F3, *AstraZeneca* (2005); confirmed by Case T-321/05, *AstraZeneca AB and AstraZeneca plc*, ECLI:EU:T:2010:266, (July 1, 2010), and Case C-457/10 P, *AstraZeneca AB*, ECLI:EU:C:2012:770, (Dec. 6, 2012).

1101. Beyond the product hopping behavior described in Section B above, AstraZeneca had also applied for supplementary protection certificates (SPCs) before several national patent offices across the EU to extend the duration of the exclusive right attached to its patent for omeprazole, the active ingredient of Losec, a drug indicated for the treatment of gastrointestinal conditions. The European Commission found that the company was granted those SPCs on an irregular basis, as the information provided to patent offices in support of AstraZeneca's application and subsequently in response to questions raised by some of those patent offices or in the context of legal proceedings brought by competitors in certain Member States to invalidate those SPCs, was erroneous.[394] As a result of this conduct, AstraZeneca was able to keep generic manufacturers away from the market. In characterizing the abuse, the European Commission took into account the fact that the patent offices instrumentalized by AstraZeneca only had a limited degree of discretion in assessing the information provided.

1102. On appeal, the General Court upheld the European Commission's decision and noted that:

> ...the European Commission applied Article 82 EC [now Article 102 TFEU] correctly in taking the view that the submission to the patent offices of objectively misleading representations by an undertaking in a dominant position which are of such a nature as to lead those offices to grant it SPCs to which it is not entitled or to which it is entitled for a shorter period, thus resulting in a restriction or elimination of competition, constitute[s] an abuse of that position.[395]

1103. The General Court further specified that "the misleading nature of representations made to public authorities must be assessed on the basis of objective factors."[396] Consequently, the deliberate nature of the conduct or the good faith or bad faith of the dominant firm are irrelevant to the characterization of the abuse. In other words, it is sufficient that the information provided to regulatory bodies be false or misleading to conclude that Article 102 TFEU was violated.

1104. Finally, it should be noted that, pursuant to the standard legal test regarding anti-competitive effects, it is not necessary to prove that the conduct had an actual effect on competition, the potentiality of such effect being sufficient to conclude that there was an abuse. In the *AstraZeneca* case, the General Court not only disregarded the fact that some authorities were able to detect that the information they had received was false and/or that some competitors had successfully challenged the SPCs granted to AstraZeneca but, validating the European Commission's approach, considered that AstraZeneca's behavior was "objectively of such a nature as to restrict competition"; therefore "the question whether [AstraZeneca's conduct was] abusive in nature [could not] depend on the contingencies of the reactions of third parties."[397] On further

---

394 Case COMP/A.37.507/F3, *AstraZeneca* ¶626 *et seq.* (2005). *See also* Case T-321/05, *AstraZeneca AB and AstraZeneca plc*, ECLI:EU:T:2010:266, ¶305–07 (July 1, 2010).

395 Case T-321/05, *AstraZeneca AB and AstraZeneca plc*, ECLI:EU:T:2010:266, ¶361 (July 1, 2010).

396 *Id.* ¶356.

397 *Id.* ¶360.

appeal before the ECJ, the latter confirmed that, in the presence of a global strategy to exclude generic manufacturers from the market, "the existence of an abuse is not affected by the fact that that strategy did not succeed in some countries," if the European Commission has correctly established that the misleading representations made by AstraZeneca were likely to result in the irregular obtainment of SPCs.[398] Thus, although the judgment does not clearly say so, it stems from the positions taken by the General Court and the ECJ that the misrepresentations made by AstraZeneca were so intrinsically likely to restrict competition that it was not necessary to consider their anticompetitive effects. It should finally be noted that, although with respect to proceedings under Article 101 TFEU, the ECJ recently confirmed in a preliminary ruling that the provision of misleading information to health professionals, health authorities and the public in general constitutes a restriction of competition by object.[399]

(2) Divisional Patents

1105. Divisional patents derive from an earlier patent application (referred to as the parent patent), which includes more than one invention; divisional patents aim at partitioning the inventions included under the parent patent to protect each one individually.[400] Their purpose is to remedy the lack of unity of invention of the parent patent. Procedurally, divisional patent applications are independent from the parent application but, if granted, the divisional patent will have the same expiry date as the parent patent.[401]

1106. In January 2012, the AGCM fined Pfizer €10.6 million for an abuse of dominant position related to divisional patents. The AGCM found that Pfizer had designed and implemented a complex strategy based on the filing of divisional patents to obstruct the entry of generic versions of its blockbuster drug Xalatan, a treatment based on the active ingredient *latanoprost* indicated for the treatment of glaucoma.[402]

1107. First, to circumvent the expiration date of its basic patent in September 2009, Pfizer filed a divisional patent in June 2002, which was awarded in 2006. Even though the divisional patent had the same expiration date as the basic patent, i.e., September 2009, it allowed Pfizer to file for an SPC with the Italian Office of Patents and Trademarks. An SPC was granted in 2009, allowing Pfizer to take advantage of a temporary extension of the main patent's protection until July 2011. Then, Pfizer submitted an application for a six-month pediatric extension of the SPC, which extended its patent protection until January 2012. Second, in parallel, Pfizer pressured and threatened generic manufacturers with legal action to discourage them from entering the market prior to the expiration of Pfizer's patent protection.

---

398 Case C-457/10 P, *AstraZeneca AB*, ECLI:EU:C:2012:770, ¶111 (Dec. 6, 2012).

399 Case C-179/16, *F. Hoffmann-La Roche Ltd and Others v. Autorità Garante della Concorrenza e del Mercato*, ECLI:EU:C:2018:25, (Jan. 23, 2018).

400 EPO, European Patent Guide, s. 5.8; *see also* Medicines for Europe, Position Paper, *The issue of abuses of divisional patent application* (Mar. 2021), *available at* https://www.medicinesforeurope.com/wp-content/uploads/2021/04/Medicines-for-Europe-Position-Paper-on-Divisional-Patents-Mar-2021.pdf.

401 Pharmaceutical Sector Inquiry – Final Report, *supra* n. 305, Chapter V, ¶273.

402 AGCM, Decision No. A431, *Pfizer* (Jan. 11, 2012); *see* Stefano Grassani, *The Italian Competition Authority Sanctions Company for Abuse Of Dominance Challenging Divisional Patent Filing in the Visual Glaucoma Drugs Industry Resting on Effects-Based Approach (Pfizer)*, E-COMPETITIONS Jan. 2012, art. No. 42839.

1108. The AGCM concluded that Pfizer had abused its dominant position by creating a climate of legal uncertainty with an exclusionary intent, which has resulted in, among other things, a delay in the market entry of generics for at least seven months and the maintenance of a de facto monopoly for Pfizer.

1109. However, in September 2012, the Administrative Court of Lazio annulled the AGCM's decision[403] on the ground that Pfizer had only exercised its legitimate right to apply for a divisional patent, and that the AGCM had failed to demonstrate a strategy to impede market access.

1110. In February 2014, the Council of State annulled the judgment of the Administrative Court of Lazio and reaffirmed the AGCM's decision.[404] The Council of State emphasized that it is not necessary to question whether Pfizer lawfully requested or obtained the divisional patent and the SPC. Rather, the question is whether Pfizer exercised the rights derived from its patent with an anticompetitive intent and in a manner that diverges from the right's fundamental purpose, resulting in the delay in market entry of Xalatan's alternatives.

1111. For a long time, this case was the only one regarding an alleged misuse of IP rights based on the exercise of the prerogatives conferred by those rights in accordance with patent law. It has notably been criticized for violating the rule of law, the principle of legal certainty, and undermining the patent system.[405]

1112. However, further guidance in this area is now expected from the European Commission. In October 2022, the European Commission sent a SO to Teva,[406] alleging that the company artificially extended its market monopoly for its drug Copaxone by strategically filing and withdrawing divisional patents in order to create legal barriers and uncertainty for generic companies. The basic theory of harm is that, because of Teva's strategy, generic companies were forced, each time Teva filed for a new divisional patent, to multiply challenges in court of the concerned patents and to either delay their entry on the market or decide to launch at risk.

(3) Pay-for-delay as an Abuse of Dominance

1113. According to settled case law, the same conduct may constitute an infringement of both Articles 101 and 102.[407] (*See* also Chapter IV.) In the recent years, this principle has notably been applied in the context of pay-for-delay cases.

---

403 Italian Administrative Court of First Instance, Case No. 7467/2012, *Pfizer* (Sept. 3, 2012); *see, e.g.*, Sara Lembo, *The Italian Administrative Court of First Instance Quashes the Competition Authority's Decision Against a Pharmaceutical Company for Misuse of a Patent (Pfizer)*, E-COMPETITIONS Sept. 2012, art. No. 49151.

404 Italian Council of State, Case No. 09181/2012, *Pfizer* (Jan. 14, 2014); *see, e.g.*, Silvia Pietrini, *Abuse of Rights: The Italian Supreme Administrative Court Allows the Appeal of the Competition and Market Authority Regarding an Abuse of Rights Committed by a Dominant Undertaking (Pfizer)*, CONCURRENCES Jan. 2014, No. 2-2014, art. No. 66046, 210–211.

405 *See* Damien Geradin, *When Competition Law Analysis Goes Wrong – The Italian Pfizer/Pharmacia Case*, SOCIAL SCIENCE RESEARCH NETWORK (Feb. 10, 2014), *available at* https://papers.ssrn.com/sol3/papers.cfm?abstract_id=2393383.

406 European Commission, Press Release IP/22/6062, *Antitrust: Commission sends Statement of Objections to Teva over misuse of the patent system and disparagement of rival multiple sclerosis medicine* (Oct. 10, 2022) *available at* https://ec.europa.eu/commission/presscorner/detail/en/IP_22_6062.

407 *See, e.g.*, Case T-51/89, *Tetra Pak Rausing SA v. Commission*, ECLI:EU:T:1990:41, (July 10, 1990).

1114. In July 2014, the European Commission imposed fines totaling €427.7 million on Servier and five generic manufacturers – Niche/Unichem, Matrix (now part of Mylan), Teva, Krka and Lupin – for concluding a series of reverse payment patent settlements aimed at protecting Servier's bestselling blood pressure medicine, perindopril, from generic competition in the EU (*see* above Chapter IV).[408] In addition to a violation of Article 101 TFEU, the European Commission found that Servier, which was allegedly dominant in the market, had also infringed Article 102 TFEU. Faced with the expiry of its patent protection after 15 years of exclusivity, Servier implemented a comprehensive strategy to protect its market position by all means. First, Servier was accused of creating a "maze of patents"[409] and influencing regulatory standards to modify the parameters for generic entry.[410] Second, the European Commission considered that Servier "pursued a targeted exclusionary strategy" based on the removal of all competitive threats, in particular through numerous technology acquisitions and pay-for-delay agreements.[411]

1115. However, in an important judgment of December 12, 2018, the General Court partially annulled the European Commission's decision and substantially reduced Servier's fine on the ground that the European Commission had erred in law in defining the relevant product market and concluding that Servier has a dominant position.[412] The case is currently pending before the ECJ.[413]

1116. It should nonetheless be noted that the ECJ has already confirmed, in the context of a recent preliminary ruling in the *Generics UK* case that when a dominant firm enters a pay-for-delay agreement to exclude rivals, it not only violates Article 101 TFEU but, in certain circumstances, can also abuse its dominant position in breach of Article 102 TFEU.[414]

1117. In February 2016, the CMA imposed fines totaling 44.99 million pounds on GSK, Generics UK, and Alpharma for several competition law infringements. First, the CMA condemned GSK for having entered into "pay-for-delay" agreements with its competitors. Additionally, the CMA found that GSK's conduct in making payments to its competitors to induce them to delay their efforts to enter the UK paroxetine market independently of GSK, also constituted an abuse of dominance.[415]

1118. In April 2016, the CAT referred several questions for a preliminary ruling to the ECJ. Among these questions, the CAT notably asked the ECJ to clarify whether the strategy of a dominant undertaking of entering into settlement agreements to preclude the risk of unrestricted generic entry, insofar as such settlement agreements concern a process patent for the production of an active ingredient, could

---

408 Case COMP/AT/39612, *Perindopril (Servier)* (2014).

409 Expression used in Servier's internal documents referring to its patenting strategy consisting in filing as many blocking patents as possible. The patents covered all aspects associated with the molecule, its synthesis, production processes, polymorphic forms until establishing a dense network of patents around Perindopril.

410 *Id., see* ¶2793.

411 *Id.*

412 Case T-691/14, *Servier SAS e.a.*, ECLI:EU:T:2018:922, ¶¶1419–1482 (Dec. 12, 2018).

413 Pending Cases C-176/19 P, *Commission v. Servier and Others* and C-201/19 P, *Servier and Others v. Commission.*

414 Case C-307/18, *Generics (UK) Ltd and Others*, ECLI:EU:C:2020:52, (Jan. 30, 2020).

415 CMA, Case No. CE-9531/11, *Paroxetine* (2016).

constitute an abuse of dominance.[416] The ECJ's answer was positive. However, the Court stated that, in circumstances such as those in the case at hand, there can only be an abuse of dominance if separate effects on competition can be identified, i.e., if the dominant firm's unilateral strategy is capable of producing effects going beyond those resulting from the anticompetitive agreements:

> Article 102 TFEU must be interpreted as meaning that the strategy of a dominant undertaking, the holder of a process patent for the production of an active ingredient that is in the public domain, which leads it to conclude, either as a precautionary measure, or following the bringing of court proceedings challenging the validity of that patent, a set of settlement agreements which have, at the least, the effect of keeping temporarily outside the market potential competitors who manufacture generic medicines using that active ingredient, constitutes an abuse of a dominant position within the meaning of Article 102 TFEU, provided that that strategy has the capacity to restrict competition and, in particular, to have exclusionary effects, going beyond the specific anticompetitive effects of each of the settlement agreements that are part of that strategy, which it is for the referring court to determine.[417]

1119. In May 2021, the CAT upheld the CMA's decision but reduced the fine.[418] Regarding the abuse of dominance, the CMA considered the ECJ's judgment and concluded that there was indeed an abuse:

> A conscious strategy of seeking to prevent unrestricted generic products coming onto the market, put into effect by making a series of agreements with each of the first three generic companies to threaten entry, 'has the capacity' to have an overall anticompetitive effect beyond that of each agreement considered in isolation.[419]

(4) Abuse of Regulatory Procedures

1120. The approach of the ECJ is quite different when the allegations involve a potential misuse of regulatory procedures, including misrepresentations made by dominant firms to regulatory bodies. It should be noted that the criteria laid down in *ITT Promedia* has expressly been rejected as irrelevant in the context of alleged abuses of regulatory procedures, "since those criteria relate to a possibly abusive exercise of the right to bring legal proceedings against a competitor."[420]

1121. The landmark European case in this area is *AstraZeneca*,[421] in which the ECJ held that an undertaking with a dominant position cannot use regulatory procedures to distort competition. In this case, the European Commission found that AstraZeneca

---

[416] *Id.* ¶21.

[417] Case C-307/18, *Generics (UK) Ltd and Others*, ECLI:EU:C:2020:52, ¶172 (Jan. 30, 2020).

[418] CAT, Case Nos. 1251-1255/1/12/16, *GlaxoSmithKline*, [2021] CAT 20, (2021).

[419] *Id.* ¶104.

[420] Case T-321/05, *AstraZeneca AB and AstraZeneca plc*, ECLI:EU:T:2010:266, ¶363 (July 1, 2010).

[421] *Id.*; *see* Case C- 457/10 P, *AstraZeneca AB*, ECLI:EU:C:2012:770, (Dec. 6, 2012).

had provided false information to several national patent offices in order to obtain SPCs for its drug Losec, thereby artificially prolonging its exclusivity on the market (*see* Section C. above).[422]

1122. Relying on the principles laid down in *AstraZeneca*, the FCA has sanctioned Janssen-Cilag, on the one hand, and Roche and Novartis, on the other hand, in two distinct cases because they unduly interfered with the regulatory process of health authorities in France, through the dissemination of allegedly alarmist or misleading messages to these authorities.

1123. *Janssen-Cilag*. The first case concerned Janssen-Cilag's allegedly unfounded intervention before the *Agence nationale de sécurité du médicament et des produits de santé* (AFSSAPS, now the ANSM) regarding the marketing authorization that had been granted to Ratiopharm, a manufacturer of a generic version of its Durogesic drug, and the subsequent inscription of that pharmaceutical specialty on the list of generics, which allows pharmacists to automatically substitute the originator drug for generics.

1124. According to the FCA's findings, in the context of the Mutual Recognition Procedure, Ratiopharm's specialties, which had been approved as generics of Durogesic by the European Commission, could not be denied generic status in France and had to be registered on the list of generics by the ANSM. Against this background, the FCA considered that Janssen-Cilag's repeated interventions before the ANSM to question the bioequivalence of Ratiopharm's generics and therefore implicitly challenge the European Commission's decision (which could not be set aside by the ANSM) were legally unfounded and thus constituted an abusive intervention in the decision-making process of that health authority. In particular, the FCA noted that, while it is legitimate for pharmaceutical companies to discuss scientific topics with health authorities and share concerns about potential risks to the public health, a dominant firm "cannot unduly intervene in the decision-making process of a health authority by presenting to the latter arguments likely to encourage it to adopt a decision contrary to the applicable legal framework."[423]

1125. The FCA's decision was broadly upheld on appeal. However, Janssen-Cilag's fine was reduced to €21 million by the Paris Court of Appeal because, contrary to the FCA's interpretation, the Court considered that Janssen's goal was not to challenge Ratiopharm's marketing authorization (which had been approved by the European Commission under the Mutual Recognition Procedure) but only the registration of its product as a generic version of Durogesic in France.

1126. The French Supreme Court dismissed Janssen's further appeal on June 1, 2022. In its judgment, the Supreme Court confirmed for the first time that the FCA can review the communications of dominant pharmaceutical firms with health authorities insofar as they may form the basis of an abusive conduct. However, the Supreme Court indirectly set an important limit on the FCA's jurisdiction – noting that the FCA cannot substitute its appraisal to that of the health authorities

---

422 Case T-321/05, *AstraZeneca AB and AstraZeneca plc*, ECLI:EU:T:2010:266, ¶305–07 (July 1, 2010).

423 FCA, Decision No. 17-D-25, *Janssen-Cilag* ¶435 (Dec. 20, 2017).

when it comes to examining scientific issues. In that case, the Supreme Court nonetheless approved the Court of Appeal's findings that Janssen did not enter into a scientific debate before the ANSM but raised a legal point which it knew, or ought to have known, was not legitimate (the ANSM being legally bound to register Ratiopharm's specialties on the list of generics pursuant to the European Commission's decision).

1127. *Roche/Novartis*. In the French *Roche/Novartis* case, the FCA, whose decision was subsequently overturned on appeal, had initially fined the two pharmaceutical companies a record €444 million for an alleged abuse of collective dominance in the French market for the treatment of wet macular degeneration (AMD), an ophthalmic condition affecting mainly the elderly, notably through alleged misleading communications to the health authorities on the risks associated with the off-label use of Avastin for the treatment of wet AMD.[424]

1128. Whereas the AGCM in Italy had found Novartis and Roche liable for an anti-competitive agreement under Article 101 TFEU (*see* Chapter IV), the FCA found that Novartis, which markets Lucentis, a drug considered at the time of the practices as the reference treatment from wet AMD, and Roche, which sells Avastin, a cancer treatment that can also be used off-label (and subject to several manipulations) for the treatment of wet AMD, could be considered as collectively dominant in the French market for the treatment of that disease. The assessment of the FCA relied on the fact that: (i) both Lucentis and Avastin were originally developed by a subsidiary of Roche, Genentech, which licensed the products to Novartis, on the one hand, and its parent company Roche, on the other hand, based on their respective experience in each sector (ophthalmology and oncology, respectively), and (ii) Novartis held a minority, non-controlling participation in Roche.

1129. On that basis, two abuses were sanctioned: on the one hand, the FCA found that Novartis alone engaged in a structured communication campaign targeted toward health professionals and the public in general to disparage the off-label use of Avastin (*see* Section II.2.E below); on the other hand, the FCA found that Novartis and Roche adopted alarmist, and sometimes even misleading, communications targeted towards health authorities, exaggerating the risks associated with the off-label use of Avastin to discourage any initiative by these authorities to issue an administrative authorization for the off-label use of Avastin in the eyes. According to the FCA, this second part of the communication strategy was intended to instill doubt regarding the safety profile of Avastin when used to treat wet AMD and therefore block or at least delay their initiatives.

1130. In particular, despite the distinction made by the Supreme Court in the *Janssen-Cilag* case between scientific and legal communications, the FCA in this matter assessed the content of the scientific discussion between Roche and Novartis, on the one hand, and the health authorities, on the other hand, and found that the arguments presented by the two pharmaceutical companies did not faithfully reflect the state of the science at the time.

---

424 FCA, Decision No. 20-D-11, *Roche/Novartis* (Sept. 9, 2020); overturned by Paris Court of Appeal, div. 5 Ch. 5–7, Judgment of Feb. 16, 2023, No. 2020/14632.

1131. The FCA's findings were completely overturned on appeal. In a judgment of February 16, 2023,[425] the Paris Court of Appeal, while confirming the FCA's jurisdiction to assess Roche and Novartis' communications with the health authorities in the context of an intense scientific debate, disagreed with the assessment made by the FCA of these communications. The Paris Court of Appeal considered that, in a context of intense scientific debate on the safety of Avastin used off-label in ophthalmology which raised a question of general interest, Roche and Novartis' communications relied on a sufficient factual basis and presented the results of the comparative studies on the safety and efficiency of the two medicines in a faithful and measured manner.[426] As such, they were both objective and proportionate and could therefore not, contrary to the FCA's findings, be regarded as abusive. It should however be noted that the Paris Court of Appeal only analyzed Roche and Novartis' communications that took place before 2012 because it found that there was a legal impediment for the off-label prescription of Avastin for the treatment of wet AMD as of December 2011, thereby rendering Avastin and Lucentis not substitutable as of this date and thus belonging to distinct product markets. Although they were not specifically assessed by the Paris Court of Appeal, which has therefore not decided on their legality, the same principles (objectivity and proportionality) should apply to determine whether the post-2011 communications of Roche and Novartis could have been abusive.

1132. It is worth noting that, just a few days before the judgment of the Paris Court of Appeal, the Belgian Competition Authority fined Novartis €2.8 million for having adopted a misleading and alarmist communication before the Belgian health authorities in the period between November 2013 and end of 2015.[427] The Belgian Competition Authority found that, during this period, Novartis continued to warn ophthalmologists, hospitals and the regulator about the risks of an off label use of Avastin despite the fact that new comparative studies had been published in 2014 and no longer supported the existence of a scientific uncertainty concerning the off-label use of Avastin.[428]

(5) Vexatious Litigation

1133. As a principle, a company exercising its rights before the courts is presumed to act lawfully. This is because, according to the ECJ, a company's ability to exercise its rights would be jeopardized if it were possible to allege a violation of competition law against a legal or natural person that initiates an action in court or before a regulatory body to safeguard its rights.[429] Therefore, although this ability is not without limits and, in exceptional circumstances, may trigger antitrust liability under Article 102 TFEU, in practice it is very difficult to characterize an abuse.

---

425 Paris Court of Appeal, div. 5 Ch. 5–7, Judgment of Feb. 16, 2023, No. 2020/14632.

426 *Id.* ¶388.

427 Belgian Competition Authority, Decision No. ABC-2023-P/K-02, *ABC* (Jan. 23, 2023).

428 *Id.* ¶¶84–86, referring to Case C-179/16, *F. Hoffmann-La Roche Ltd and Others*, ECLI:EU:C:2018:25, ¶92 (Jan. 23, 2018).

429 Ioannis Lianos & Pierre Regibeau, *"Vexatious"/"Sham" Litigation in EU and US Antitrust Law: A Mechanism Design Approach*, (CLES UCL, Research Paper No. 1, 2017), *available at* https://papers.ssrn.com/sol3/papers.cfm?abstract_id=3076073.

1134. Two cumulative conditions, interpreted strictly, need to be met: first, the action cannot reasonably be considered as an attempt to establish the rights of the undertaking concerned and can therefore only serve to harass the opposite party and second, it is conceived in the framework of a plan whose goal is to eliminate competition.[430] In other words:

> The fact that unmeritorious litigation is instituted does not in itself constitute an infringement of Article [102] of the Treaty unless it has an anticompetitive object. Equally, litigation which may reasonably be regarded as an attempt to assert rights vis-à-vis competitors is not abusive, irrespective of the fact that it may be part of a plan to eliminate competition.[431]

1135. Practically speaking, the legal action brought by the dominant firm must be: (i) knowingly groundless, and (ii) intended to exclude a competitor from the market.

1136. In *ITT Promedia*, a dispute arose between ITT Promedia, whose main business was the publication of commercial telephone directories, and Belgacom, who enjoyed a monopoly on the Belgian market for voice telephony services and was also responsible for granting access to the data needed for the production, sale and distribution of directories. Before the Belgian courts, ITT Promedia challenged Belgacom's refusal to give it access to the data under fair, reasonable, and non-discriminatory terms. Belgacom filed counterclaims against ITT Promedia alleging that the latter violated Belgian legislation concerning commercial practices and economic competition as well as Article 86 of the EC Treaty (now Article 102 TFEU). ITT Promedia subsequently lodged a complaint before the European Commission alleging that Belgacom had abused its dominant position by initiating vexatious litigation against it. The European Commission rejected this complaint because Belgacom's counterclaims were not manifestly unfounded and because ITT Promedia had not demonstrated that Belgacom's goal was to eliminate competition from the market.

1137. The General Court upheld the European Commission's approach. Regarding the first criterion, the General Court noted that:

> It is not a question of determining whether the rights which the undertaking concerned was asserting when it brought its action actually existed or whether that action was well founded, but rather of determining whether such an action was intended to assert what that undertaking could, at that moment, reasonably consider to be its rights.[432]

1138. In other words, unmeritorious litigation does not itself constitute an infringement of Article 102 TFEU if the claimant considers at the time of bringing its action that it is lawfully defending its rights, irrespective of the chances of success of its action. Evidence to the opposite is very difficult to demonstrate and explains why, in practice, vexatious litigation is almost never recognized as an abuse of dominant position in Europe.

---

430 Case T-111/96, *ITT Promedia NV v. Commission*, ECLI:EU:T:1998:183, (July 17, 1998).

431 *Id.* ¶56.

432 *Id.* ¶73.

1139. These principles were subsequently applied in two cases. In *Protégé International*, the General Court upheld the European Commission's decision to dismiss Protégé's complaint against Pernot Ricard. The complaint alleged that Pernot Ricard abused its dominant position by initiating allegedly vexatious litigation against Protégé after Protégé registered the whiskey brands "Wild Geese, Wilde Geese Rare Irish Whiskey and Wild Geese Irish Soldiers and Hereos." Pernot Ricard had alleged that Protégé's registration of these brands risked confusion with its American brand, "Wild Turkey." Protégé considered Pernot Ricard's concerns to be unfounded because the brands could not be seriously mistaken and claimed that Pernot Ricard's aim was in fact to harass its competitor in order to delay its entry into the market. However, the European Commission, upheld by the General Court, found that objective elements, including the use of the term "wild" and the fact that both products were whiskeys, suggested that Pernot Ricard had reasonable grounds for its action against Protégé even though its action was ultimately unsuccessful.[433] The General Court stated that it is only when the absence of legal grounds is obvious, and known by the claimant, that the first criterion of the legal test for vexatious litigation is fulfilled. The General Court further noted that, in the case at hand, Protégé had failed to demonstrate that Pernot Ricard's litigation was meant to harass Protégé and that the litigation was part of a strategy to eliminate competition.

1140. In *Agria Polska v. Commission*,[434] the principles established in *ITT Promedia* were raised by several applicants who went bankrupt as consequence of prior litigation engaged against them for parallel trade. In this case, Agria Polska and other companies, active in the sale of plant protection products, had been subject to administrative and criminal proceedings by plant protection products manufacturers and distributors, based on alleged infringements of Articles 101 and 102. Agria Polska considered that the proceedings launched against it were abusive and thus brought the case before the European Commission, alleging vexatious litigation and referring to the criteria set forth in *ITT Promedia*. The European Commission rejected the complaint without examining the *ITT Promedia* conditions, considering there was a low likelihood of establishing an infringement of Article 102 TFEU on the part of the plaintiffs in the administrative and criminal proceedings as it may be legitimate in the context of parallel trade, for producers and distributors of plant protection products to inform the competent national authorities of possible infringements by their competitors of the national provisions in force, given the risks for their reputation and of adverse effects on the original condition of the products.[435]

1141. The Spanish case against MSD España could be regarded as a rare example of vexatious litigation. In October 2022, MSD España and its parent company were sanctioned €38.9 million for having allegedly abused its dominant position in the market for contraceptive vaginal rings.[436] The CNMC alleged MSD España withheld information from the Spanish courts in the context of actions

---

433 Case T-119/09, *Protégé International Ltd v. Commission*, ECLI:EU:T:2012:421, ¶¶55–57 (Sept. 13, 2012).

434 Case T-480/15, *Agria Polska sp. zo.o v. Commission*, ECLI:EU:T:2017:339, (May 16, 2017), confirmed by Case C-373/17 P, *Agria Polska sp. zo.o v. Commission*, ECLI:EU:C:2018:756, (Sept. 20, 2018).

435 T-480/15, *Agria Polska sp. zo.o.*, ECLI:EU:T:2017:339, ¶47 (May 16, 2017).

436 CNMC, Decision No. S/0026/19, *MSD* (Oct. 21, 2022).

to enforce its patent rights for Nuvaring against the manufacture and marketing of a competing vaginal ring. The CNMC argued that, by withholding factual and technical information from the courts, MSD España, whose objective was not to protect its patents rights, unduly obtained injunctive relief delaying the marketing and sale by Insud Pharma of Ornibel by at least four months. This decision is under appeal.

D. *Product Disparagement*

1142. Disparagement in the sphere of competition law can be broadly defined as the unfair criticism of another company, its products, or its services with a view toward gaining a competitive advantage over that company. While in the US disparagement is unlikely to give rise to a violation of Section 2, except in exceptional circumstances, the risk is much greater under Article 102 TFEU as disparagement is seen as a form of unfair competition. Thus, when a dominant firm disparages competing products, such conduct is considered to fall outside the scope of competition on the merits.

a. *US Approach*

1143. Generally, a company's communications regarding its own products are unlikely to lead to liability under Section 2. As described by one court, "[a]dvertising that emphasizes a product's strengths and minimizes its weaknesses does not, at least unless it amounts to deception, constitute anticompetitive conduct violative of § 2."[437] That is because truthful and non-misleading commercial speech is typically protected by the First Amendment. The same principle applies to communications, statements, or advertising informing consumers about the weaknesses or disadvantages of competing products. Disparagement of rival products is often seen as part of the competitive process. Communications, statements, or advertisements about competing products that are false or misleading, however, can violate Section 2 under certain circumstances.[438] In such cases, the concern is that false or misleading statements restrict consumers' access to true and complete information, which may exclude competitive products from the market.

1144. Courts have taken three distinct approaches to product disparagement claims under Section 2. Under the first, most restrictive approach, some courts have ruled out Section 2 liability altogether for false advertising, reasoning that such advertising enhances, rather than harms, competition.[439]

1145. Under the second approach, false advertising is presumed to have a *de minimis* effect on competition and does not violate Section 2. That presumption, however, can be rebutted by a plaintiff by satisfying a six-factor test. The advertising must be: "(1) clearly false, (2) clearly material, (3) clearly likely to induce reasonable reliance, (4) made to buyers without knowledge of subject matter, (5) continued

---

437 *Berkey Photo*, 603 F.2d 287–88.

438 False or misleading advertising is also assessed under Section 43(a) of the Lanham Act, 15 U.S.C. § 1125(a). The Lanham Act analysis is beyond the scope of this publication.

439 The Fifth and Seventh Circuits have adopted this approach. *See Retractable Techs. v. Becton Dickinson & Co.*, 842 F.3d 883, 895 (5th Cir. 2016); *Sanderson v. Culligan Int'l Co.*, 415 F.3d 620, 623–24 (7th Cir. 2005).

for prolonged periods, and (6) not readily susceptible of neutralization or other offsets by rivals."[440]

1146. Two recent cases from the pharmaceutical sector applied the *de minimis* approach. In *Genus Lifesciences Inc. v. Lannett Company, Inc.*, the district court granted Lannett's motion to dismiss Genus's false advertising-based Section 2 claim.[441] Genus claimed that Lannett falsely advertised its cocaine hydrochloride solution, C-Topical, claiming that it was grandfathered as a preliminary NDA product, as FDA approved, as a generic version of Genus' competing product, as a branded drug pursuant to an NDA, and as having a topical route of administration. The court found that Genus had satisfied the first four *de minimis* factors: falsity, materiality, reasonable reliance, and lack of subject matter knowledge. However, Genus had failed to satisfy the fifth (prolonged period of advertising) and sixth (not susceptible to neutralization) factors. The court focused on the latter factor, finding that Genus failed to allege why an advertising campaign touting its competing product as the only FDA-approved cocaine hydrochloride product would not be successful, or why any efforts to tell its customers that C-Topical is unapproved or that its route of administration is misleading would fail. As a result, "Genus has failed to plead more than *de minimis* effect on competition from Lannett's false statements."[442]

1147. In *In re EpiPen (Epinephrine Injection, USP) Mktg., Sales Practices & Antitrust Litig.*, the district court granted summary judgment to Mylan on Sanofi-Aventis's false advertising claims under Section 2, finding that Sanofi had failed to satisfy three of the six *de minimis* factors.[443] The court found that a Mylan-funded study did not falsely state that the two companies' epinephrine drugs – Mylan's EpiPen and Sanofi's Auvi-Q – were not bioequivalent. Rather, the study found that the delivery of epinephrine was not bioequivalent because Mylan's product was absorbed more quickly upon delivery. Nor did Mylan falsely suggest in marketing materials that payers' decisions to exclude Sanofi's product from their formularies were grounded in safety concerns. Rather, Mylan truthfully stated that payers made their coverage decisions based on financial and clinical recommendations. The court also found no factual dispute as to whether Mylan's statements continued for prolonged periods or were not readily susceptible to neutralization by Sanofi. Regarding the latter factor, the court noted that Sanofi is "one of the world's largest pharmaceutical companies" and no reasonable jury could infer "that Sanofi's Auvi-Q marketing efforts were incapable of responding to Mylan's marketing of EpiPen."[444]

---

440 *American Prof'l Testing Serv. v. Harcourt Brace Jovanovich Legal & Prof'l Pubs.*, 108 F.3d 1147, 1152 (9th Cir. 1992). The Second, Sixth, Ninth, Tenth, and Eleventh Circuits have adopted this approach. *See National Ass'n of Pharm. Manufacturers, Inc. v. Ayerst Labs.*, 850 F.2d 904, 916 (2d Cir. 1988); *American Council of Certified Podiatric Physicians & Surgeons v. American Bd. of Podiatric Surgery, Inc.*, 323 F.3d 366, 370 (6th Cir. 2003); *American Professional Testing Service*, 108 F.3d 1152; *Lenox MacLaren Surgical Corp. v. Medtronic, Inc.*, 762 F.3d 114, 1126–28 (10th Cir. 2014); *Duty Free Americas, Inc. v. Estee Lauder Cos.*, 797 F.3d 1248, 1268–69 (11th Cir. 2015).

441 378 F. Supp. 3d 823, 842 (N.D. Cal. 2019). Dechert represented the defendants in this matter.

442 *Id.*

443 507 F. Supp. 3d 1289, 1362 (D. Kan. 2020).

444 *Id.* 1361–62. *See also Eon Labs*, 164 F. Supp. 2d 361 (rejecting Section 2 claim based on alleged monopolist's inclusion of mislabeled product inserts where purchaser only saw the information after opening properly labeled drug packaging and the inaccurate information in the inserts was limited to the product name).

1148. The third approach to false advertising under Section 2 involves a case-by-case analysis of the defendant's statements to determine whether they had an anti-competitive effect.[445] In *Eisai, Inc. v. Sanofi-Aventis US, LLC*, the Third Circuit held that, "[w]hile false or deceptive statements may violate the antitrust laws in 'rare' circumstances, at minimum, a plaintiff must show that such statements induced or were likely to induce reasonable reliance by consumers."[446] The court noted that Eisai identified only a handful of examples of hospitals that decided not to switch to its product, Fragmin, after the hospitals' representatives attended presentations by Sanofi or its consultants. Even if those examples were sufficient to establish reasonable reliance, according to the court, Eisai failed to demonstrate that it could not have corrected Sanofi's misstatements by supplying the hospitals with accurate information.

b. *EU Approach*

1149. According to settled case law of the ECJ, any pharmaceutical company, even a dominant one, can employ a strategy to minimize the erosion of its sales when facing generic or biosimilar entry. Doing so is legitimate and considered part of the normal competitive process. However, an important limit to that principle is that dominant firms cannot act outside the scope of competition on the merits.[447]

1150. Against this background, disparagements of generics by originators can in theory be considered abusive. Although the case was related to an Article 101 TFEU violation, the ECJ took a very strict approach regarding disparagement in its *Hoffman-La Roche* preliminary ruling of 2018, considering that the dissemination, in a context of scientific uncertainty, of misleading information relating to the adverse effects of Avastin used off-label constitutes a restriction of competition by object.[448] Insofar as the objective behind the alleged abusive communications would be the same, i.e., exclusion of a rival drug from the market, the same reasoning could be followed under Article 102 TFEU.

1151. However, up until the opening of two recent investigations by the European Commission against Teva and Vifor Pharma, respectively, for an alleged disparagement of competing products,[449] disparagement as a violation of Article 102 TFEU had only been condemned by the FCA, which has a strong track-record of enforcement in this field, both in and outside the pharmaceutical industry. In the pharmaceutical sector, the FCA has sanctioned the disparagement of generics in four different cases

---

445 The Third, Eighth, and D.C. Circuits have adopted this approach. *See West Penn Allegheny Health Sys. Inc. v. UPMC*, 627 F.3d 85, 109–10 (3d Cir. 2010); *International Travel Arrangers, Inc. v. Western Airlines, Inc.*, 623 F.2d 1255, 1267 (8th Cir. 1980); *Caribbean Broadcasting Sys., Ltd. v. Cable & Wireless P.L.C.*, 148 F.3d 1080, 1087 (D.C. Cir. 1998).

446 821 F.3d 394, 407 n.40 (3d Cir. 2016) (citations omitted).

447 *See, e.g.*, Case C-457/10 P, *AstraZeneca AB*, ECLI:EU:C:2012:770, ¶129 (Dec. 6, 2012).

448 Case C-179/16, *F. Hoffmann-La Roche Ltd and Others*, ECLI:EU:C:2018:25, (Jan. 23, 2018).

449 *See* European Commission, Press Release IP/21/1022, *Antitrust: Commission opens formal investigation into possible anticompetitive conduct of Teva in relation to a blockbuster multiple sclerosis medicine* (Mar. 4, 2021), *available at* https://ec.europa.eu/commission/presscorner/detail/en/ip_21_1022; European Commission, Press Release IP/22/3882, *Antitrust: Commission opens investigation into possible anticompetitive disparagement by Vifor Pharma of iron medicine* (June 20, 2022), *available at* https://ec.europa.eu/commission/presscorner/detail/en/ip_22_3882.

since 2013: *Plavix, Subutex, Durogesic* and, most recently, *Avastin/Lucentis*. It is worth noting that it has adopted a progressively stricter approach in its review of the communications made by dominant firms, not only towards healthcare professionals but also towards health authorities and the public in general.

(1) Key Cases

1152. In *Plavix*,[450] the FCA imposed a €40.6 million fine to Sanofi for relaying misleading information to healthcare professionals on alleged differences between Plavix and Sanofi's own generic, on the one hand, and the generic versions of other manufacturers, on the other hand, in order to delay the latter's market penetration to the benefit of its own products. Plavix, whose active ingredient is clopidogrel, is indicated for both the prevention of severe atherothrombotic events and for the treatment of acute coronary syndrome (ACS). At the time of the practices, it was one of the blockbusters of the pharmaceutical industry representing a major cost for the French health system under its reimbursement regime (€625 million per year).

1153. In its communications, Sanofi emphasized the difference of therapeutic indications between Plavix and the generics (as the latter were not authorized for the treatment of ACS) as well as a difference in the salts used as an excipient in Plavix and its generics. These differences resulted from the fact that the salts used in Plavix and the ACS indication was still patent protected. While Sanofi's statements were based on objective facts, Sanofi suggested that the difference in salts was the reason for the difference in therapeutic indications, leading healthcare professionals to believe that there was a medical obstacle to substitution for the treatment of ACS, whereas it in fact resulted from a purely legal obstacle.

1154. According to the FCA, this communication campaign, which only lasted for five months, had the objective and effect of instilling in healthcare professionals an unjustified doubt as to the quality and safety of generics, leading doctors to favor the prescription of Plavix and pharmacists to deliver either Plavix or Sanofi's own generic (which used the same salts as the originator drug and was the only generic indicated for ACS) to the patients. The FCA underlined that the anticompetitive effect of Sanofi's communication campaign was reinforced by the risk aversion of healthcare professionals, their limited knowledge of the regulatory framework, including marketing authorization procedures, as well as their general distrust towards generics at the time of the practices.

1155. The FCA's decision was upheld by the Paris Court of Appeal and subsequently, the French Supreme Court. In its judgment, the Supreme Court notably approved the Paris Court of Appeal for finding that Sanofi had portrayed the objective differences between Plavix and its generics in "an inappropriate and ambiguous" light, thereby abusing its right to communicate on the active ingredient and the therapeutic indications of its drug. The Supreme Court also approved the Paris Court of Appeal's finding that the effects of Sanofi's communication campaign lasted longer than the five-month infringement period.

---

450 FCA, Decision No. 13-D-11, *Sanofi-Aventis* (May 14, 2013) confirmed by the Paris Court of Appeal, div. 5 Ch. 5–7, Judgment of Dec. 18, 2014, No. 2013/12370 and the Supreme Court, Commercial Chamber, Judgment of Oct. 18, 2016, No. 15-10384.

1156. In *Subutex*,[451] the FCA fined Schering-Plough €15.3 million for having implemented a disparagement campaign against Arrow's generic version of its blockbuster drug Subutex, a substitution treatment for opioid drug dependence based on buprenorphine. The drug was available in the form of tablets for oral administration but the existence of a misuse involving the dissolution of tablets for intravenous injections had been reported. The FCA found that Schering-Plough instrumentalized the risk of intravenous injections by drug addicts to encourage healthcare professionals not to substitute Subutex for Arrow's generic, pointing out differences in the excipients of the two products and an alleged higher solubility of the generic, without such allegations being supported by medical studies. The FCA noted that the disparagement campaign, combined with the discounts offered to pharmacists (*see* above Section A.), was successful as it led doctors to prescribe Subutex and specify on their prescriptions that it was "non substitutable" in 67% of cases. In addition, pharmacists had stocked up on Subutex and were less inclined to substitute it for a generic version, even when the prescription did not contain the mention "non substitutable."

1157. In *Durogesic*,[452] Janssen-Cilag (a company of the Johnson & Johnson group) was fined €25 million (later reduced to €21 million on appeal) for two distinct but related types of abusive conduct: first, an improper comparison between its product, Durogesic, a powerful opioid analgesic indicated for the treatment of severe chronic pain and its generics and, second, an unfounded intervention before the health authorities (regarding the latter, *see* above Section D.), both forming part of a complex strategy to delay generic entry and protect Janssen's position on the market.

1158. Regarding the disparagement, Janssen highlighted the atypical nature of Durogesic's generics, as the generic patches differed in size and quantity of active ingredient compared to Durogesic patches. Janssen also questioned the abridged procedure for the delivery of marketing authorizations to generics, which only requires the production of bioequivalence studies. Finally, Janssen distorted the content of the warning letter issued by the ANSM, which focused on the narrow therapeutic margin of fentanyl and on the risks associated with the switch of patients from one specialty to another in the course of their treatment. In its communication, Janssen however chose to only highlight the risk associated with the switch of patients treated with Durogesic to a generic version, thereby conveying a truncated and, thus, misleading message to healthcare professionals.

1159. As a result of this disparagement campaign, doctors and pharmacists were wrongly led to believe that there was a problem of efficacy and innocuity with the generics of Durogesic, which could potentially be dangerous for patients' health.

---

451 FCA, Decision No. 13-D-21, *Schering-Plough* (Dec. 18, 2013), confirmed by Paris Court of Appeal, div. 5 Ch. 5–7, Judgment of Mar. 26, 2015, No. 2014/0330 and Supreme Court, Commercial Chamber, Judgment of Jan. 11, 2017, No. 15-17134.

452 FCA, Decision No. 17-D-25, *Janssen-Cilag* ¶531 (Dec. 20, 2017), partially confirmed by Paris Court of Appeal, div. 5 Ch. 5–7, Judgment of July 11, 2019, No. 2018/01945. *See* Anne Wachsmann & Nicolas Zacharie, *Denigration: The Paris Court of Appeal Largely Upholds the Condemnation by the French Competition Authority of a Pharmaceutical Company for an Abuse of Its Dominant Position Having Delayed and Then Limited Generic Entry (Janssen-Cilag, Johnson & Johnson)*, CONCURRENCES July 2019, No. 4-2019, art. No. 92309, 99–101.

1160. In *Avastin/Lucentis*,[453] one of the two infringements sanctioned by the FCA concerned a structured disparagement campaign implemented by Novartis in order to favor the sale of its blockbuster drug Lucentis, a revolutionary treatment for wet age macular degeneration (AMD), against the off-label use of Avastin (the other infringement is addressed in Section D. above). Novartis was fined almost €254 million for that infringement alone.

1161. In this case, contrary to the three above-mentioned precedents of the FCA, Novartis's alleged abusive communication did not target a generic product, which by definition has the same active ingredient as the originator drug and is therefore bioequivalent to the latter, but instead targeted Avastin, a cancer drug that had similar characteristics to Lucentis when used in the eye, without however being bioequivalent.

1162. Faced with the off-label use of Avastin for the treatment of wet AMD and in a context of scientific uncertainty regarding the safety of Avastin used in the eye, Novartis designed and implemented a structured communication campaign emphasizing the differences between Lucentis and Avastin, the risks associated with the off-label use of Avastin in the eye and the fact that Lucentis, on the other hand, was specifically authorized for the treatment of wet AMD. In its communication, Novartis relied on a series of scientific studies establishing the non-inferiority of Avastin in terms of efficacy but leaving open the question of its safety compared to that of Lucentis to instill doubt as to the off-label use of Avastin. The FCA found that Lucentis selectively presented the results of the scientific studies, insisting specifically on the side-effects of Avastin and the risks associated with its injection in the eye, with a view to preserve the sales of Lucentis. In doing so, Novartis would have abused the collective dominant position it allegedly held with Roche on the market and, therefore, violated Article 102 TFEU (*see* Section D. above regarding the collective dominant position of Novartis and Roche).

1163. However, as mentioned above (*see* Section D), the FCA's decision was completely overturned on appeal. In its judgment of February 16, 2023,[454] the Paris Court of Appeal first stated that the standard of proof cannot be the same when the communications, such as in the case at stake, do not concern generics but another originator drug, because the bioequivalence of the drugs is not established. Second, it considered that Novartis' communications were limited to objective findings, did not contain any erroneous assertions, and were not lacking in moderation or prudence.[455] Therefore, as Novartis' speech was factually based and did not exceed the limit of Novartis' freedom of speech,[456] it did not amount to abusive disparagement.

(2) Takeaways for the Assessment of Communications by Dominant Pharmaceutical Firms

1164. Important takeaways can be drawn from these precedents. First, disparagement as a violation of Article 102 TFEU is not limited to communications on generics but, as shown by the *Avastin/Lucentis* case and the European Commission's ongoing

453 FCA, Decision No. 20-D-11, *Roche/Novartis* (Sept. 9, 2020).
454 Paris Court of Appeal, *supra* n. 425, Chapter V.
455 *Id.* ¶426.
456 *Id.* ¶450.

investigation into Vifor Pharma, may potentially extend to any competing product. With respect to off-label use, the ECJ specified in a preliminary judgment of January 23, 2018 concerning the Italian *Avastin/Lucentis* case that, for the purposes of market definition, a drug used off-label can be included in the relevant market provided that there is "a sufficient degree of interchangeability" with the on-label drug, which must be objectively assessed in light of all the circumstances of the case (*see* above Chapter II).[457] Consequently, although to date there is no precedent concerning the disparagement of biosimilars, the communications of dominant pharmaceutical firms on biologic drugs and their biosimilars are not exempt from potential antitrust liability under Article 102 TFEU.

1165. Second, disparagement is not limited to the provision of false information on a competing product or company but includes any alarmist or misleading communication that is capable, given the risk aversion of healthcare professionals, of influencing their behavior, be it at the stage of prescribing a drug or at the stage of delivering it to a patient. In practice, as exemplified in the French precedents, disparagement can take many forms: dissemination of false or truncated information, ambiguous messaging, incomplete or subjective presentation of scientific studies, emphasis on the risks associated with a certain treatment without any objective or scientific evidence supporting this assertion, etc. In broad terms, any communication that lacks objectivity, clarity and is not fully exhaustive can be deemed abusive under Article 102 TFEU. Against this very strict approach, great caution is required from pharmaceutical companies when elaborating their promotional materials and training their sales force on the key messages to be conveyed to healthcare professionals, particularly before the loss of their exclusivities and more generally upon the arrival of competitors on the market.

1166. Third, as is often the case in antitrust investigations, internal documents play an important role in the authorities' assessment of a conduct and its rationale. Caution is therefore also required in the preparation of those internal documents. Furthermore, regarding product disparagement, the reactions of third parties to the communication campaign is often key to assess the effects of the conduct. In all the French cases, the FCA gathered testimony from healthcare professionals in the course of its investigation and sometimes based a substantial part of its analysis on it.

E. *Acquisitions*

1167. Finally, mergers and acquisitions of competing firms or products can be challenged as unlawful under US and EU antitrust laws under certain circumstances.

a. *US Approach*

1168. In the US, although transactions are typically reviewed under Section 7 of the Clayton Act, a merger or acquisition that creates or maintains monopoly power can satisfy the conduct element of Section 2 of the Sherman Act.[458]

457 Case C-179/16, *F. Hoffmann-La Roche Ltd and Others*, ECLI:EU:C:2018:25, ¶51 (Jan. 23, 2018).

458 *United States v. Grinnell Corp.*, 384 U.S. 563, 567, 576 (1966).

1169. There are two notable cases brought by the FTC alleging monopolization via acquisition in the pharmaceutical sector. In 2008, the FTC sued Ovation Pharmaceuticals, Inc. (now Lundbeck, Inc.), challenging Ovation's acquisition of the drug NeoProfen from Abbott. The FTC's complaint alleged that NeoProfen was the only competitor to Ovation's Indocin, which is used to treat patent ductus arteriosus, a potentially fatal congenital heart defect affecting premature infants. The FTC alleged that Ovation increased the price of Indocin thirteen-fold immediately following its acquisition of NeoProfen.[459] The district court dismissed the FTC's complaint on market definition grounds, finding that the two products competed in separate markets, a determination upheld by the Eighth Circuit.[460]

1170. In 2017, the FTC challenged and reached a settlement regarding Mallinckrodt ARD Inc.'s (Mallinckrodt) acquisition of the US rights to develop the drug Synacthen, which, according to the FTC, allowed Mallinckrodt to illegally maintain its monopoly over therapeutic adrenocorticotropic hormone (ACTH) drugs used to treat infantile spasms, a rare seizure disorder affecting infants. According to the complaint, Synacthen, which was approved to treat infantile spasms outside the US, was a competitive threat to Mallinckrodt's Acthar product, the only FDA-approved ACTH drug. The FTC alleged that Mallinckrodt's acquisition of Synacthen prevented another bidder from launching it in the US, thereby maintaining Mallinckrodt's monopoly over ACTH drugs.[461] Mallinckrodt agreed to pay $100 million and grant a license to develop Synacthen to a licensee approved by the FTC to settle the case.[462]

b. *EU Approach*

1171. In the early years, absent a merger control regime in the EU, the ECJ allowed mergers and acquisitions to be challenged under Article 102 TFEU. In *Continental Can*, the European Commission fined a company for abuse of dominance because one of its subsidiaries had acquired approximately 80% of the shares of a rival firm, with the effect of "practically eliminating competition" in the market for packaging products.[463] The European Commission's decision was subsequently annulled by the ECJ on the ground that the European Commission had not substantiated the elimination of competition. Nevertheless, the ECJ did not challenge the basic principle that a merger or an acquisition can amount to an abuse of dominant position.

---

459 Complaint, *FTC v. Ovation Pharms., Inc.*, Civ. No. 08-6379 (D. Minn. Dec. 16, 2008).

460 *FTC v. Lundbeck, Inc.*, 650 F.3d 1236 (8th Cir. 2011).

461 Complaint, *FTC v. Mallinckrodt ARD Inc.*, Civ. No. 1:17-cv-00120 (D.D.C. Jan. 15, 2017).

462 FTC, Press Release, *Mallinckrodt Will Pay $100 Million to Settle FTC, State Charges It Illegally Maintained its Monopoly of Specialty Drug Used to Treat Infants* (Jan. 18, 2017), *available at* https://www.ftc.gov/news-events/news/press-releases/2017/01/mallinckrodt-will-pay-100-million-settle-ftc-state-charges-it-illegally-maintained-its-monopoly. In addition, in 2015, the FTC entered a consent order with Cardinal Health settling charges that Cardinal monopolized 25 local markets for the sale and distribution of low-energy radiopharmaceuticals through, among other things, acquisitions of two competing radio pharmacies. Under the settlement, Cardinal agreed to pay $26.8 million in disgorgement of ill-gotten gains. *See* Final Order and Stipulated Permanent Injunction, *FTC v. Cardinal Health, Inc.*, No. 15-cv-3031 (S.D.N.Y. 2015).

463 Case COMP/IV/26 811, *Europemballage Corporation and Continental Can Company Inc.* (Decision 72/21/CEE, Dec. 9, 1971); annulled by Case 6/72, *Europemballage Corporation and Continental Can Company Inc.*, ECLI:EU:C:1973:22, (Feb. 21, 1973).

1172. Since then, the EU has adopted its merger control regime. In principle, mergers and acquisitions can only be challenged by third parties as part of the merger control review process. Indeed, Article 21 of the EU Merger Regulation provides that Regulation 1/2003 (among others), which relates to the application of Articles 101 and 102, shall not apply to concentrations within the meaning of Article 3 of the EU Merger Regulation, "except in relation to joint ventures that do not have a Community dimension and which have as their object or effect the coordination of the competitive behavior of undertakings that remain independent."[464]

1173. Some companies have nonetheless attempted on rare occasions to challenge a merger under Article 102 TFEU. In this respect, although not in the pharmaceutical sector, two recent cases brought respectively before the French and Italian competition authorities are worth mentioning.

1174. In Italy, the Administrative Tribunal of Lazio recently overturned a decision of the AGCM that had applied Article 102 TFEU to sanction an acquisition made by a dominant firm.[465] In 2020, the AGCM found that Eventim had abused its dominant position on the market for ticket sales for live concerts of pop music by implementing a multi-faceted strategy including, among others, the acquisition of four important national promoters of live concerts of pop music. On appeal, the Administrative Tribunal of Lazio annulled the AGCM's decision because the acquisitions were part of a legitimate business objective, not an exclusionary strategy. In addition, the Tribunal referred to Article 21 of the EU Merger Regulation to consider that it was not possible for the AGCM to apply Article 102 TFEU in the context of an acquisition as this would amount to disregarding the provisions of the EU Merger Regulation.

1175. In France, the FCA rejected a complaint by Towercast against the incumbent operator TDF for an alleged abuse of dominance resulting from TDF's acquisition of Itas. The FCA held that, absent a specific abusive conduct unrelated to the merger, a merger or an acquisition cannot, in and by itself, constitute a violation of Article 102 TFEU.[466]

1176. Towercast however lodged an appeal before the Paris Court of Appeal, which referred a question to the ECJ for a preliminary ruling, essentially asking whether the existence of the EU Merger Regulation now precludes the application of Article 102 TFEU to a concentration. In a ruling of March 16, 2023,[467] following the opinion of Advocate General Kokott,[468] the ECJ considered that the EU Merger Regulation, which is a piece of secondary legislation, cannot preclude the applicability of the Treaty itself, including Article 102 TFEU. Therefore, when a concentration has escaped *ex-ante* merger control, it may subsequently be challenged on the basis of Article 102 TFEU, provided, of course, that an abusive conduct can be characterized. In this respect, the ECJ clarified in its judgment

---

464 Council Regulation 139/2004 of Jan. 20, 2004 on the control of concentrations between undertakings (the EU Merger Regulation), 2004 OJ (L 24) 1, art. 21.

465 Administrative Tribunal of Lazio, Decision No. 3334, *Eventim* (Mar. 24, 2022).

466 FCA, Decision No. 20-D-01, *TDF Itas* (Jan. 16, 2020).

467 Case C-449/21, *Towercast*, ECLI:EU:C:2023:207, (Mar. 16, 2023).

468 Opinion of Advocate General Kokott, C-449/21, *Towercast*, ECLI:EU:C:2022:777, (Oct. 13, 2022).

that the simple strengthening of the acquirer's dominant position through the implementation of the concentration is insufficient to characterize an abuse, and that it must be demonstrated that, by means of the acquisition, the dominant undertaking significantly restricts competition on the market.

1177. In a context where the European Commission is especially keen to catch killer acquisitions (*see* Chapter III), this judgment is of significant importance insofar as it further expands the toolbox of the authorities and enlarges their scope of intervention, thereby increasing risk and legal uncertainty for companies. While officials of the European Commission have confirmed, off the record, that cases under Article 102 TFEU should remain exceptional, the possibility that, in very specific circumstances, a merger or an acquisition that has escaped merger control be subsequently successfully challenged under Article 102 TFEU can no longer be excluded.

CHAPTER VI

Private enforcement

Steven Bizar and Marion Provost*

* The authors would like to thank Lucas Leroy and Agnese Nadalini for their very valuable help and contribution to this chapter.

1178. Private enforcement in the context of antitrust cases refers to the situation where private litigants bring a case against a defendant alleging a breach of competition law and seeking an injunction and/or claiming damages as a result. While in the US private enforcement has traditionally been a common route to enforce antitrust rules, in the EU it is a much more recent development. Furthermore, in the EU, private enforcement is still mostly perceived as a complementary tool to public enforcement, rather than an alternative (although it can be, in case of stand-alone actions).

1179. In addition, the procedural framework and substantive provisions differ on both sides of the Atlantic. A classic illustration is the absence of discovery or treble damages in the EU. In fact, when establishing a framework for the private enforcement of Articles 101 and 102 TFEU, the EU sought to avoid what it perceived as pitfalls in the US system.

I. US private enforcement

1180. In the US, private actions for antitrust enforcement have a long history, starting with the passage of the Clayton Act in 1914.[1] This section will explain the statutory framework within which private actions can be brought, the various types of private actions, and the procedural and substantive issues that arise in the context of such actions.

1. Statutory Framework for Private Enforcement in the US

A. *Sherman Act*

1181. In 1890, Congress passed the Sherman Act amid fears that the country's economic power would fall into a limited number of hands.[2] The Act reflected an attempt by Congress to "prevent further concentration [of power] and to preserve competition among a large number of sellers."[3] Since then, the Sherman Act has become the primary federal law prohibiting anticompetitive practices. The Sherman Act does not in itself grant a private right of action, but Section 4 of the Clayton Act allows certain private parties to seek damages and injunctive relief for violations of the Sherman Act.[4] Importantly, in such actions plaintiffs can seek recovery for the entire amount of damages attributable to multiple defendants from any one of the defendants, which is known as joint and several liability.

a. *Section 1 Claims: Combinations, Contracts, or Conspiracies (Joint Conduct) in Restraint of Trade*

1182. As developed in Chapter IV, Section 1 of the Sherman Act generally prohibits "[e]very contract, combination in the form of trust or otherwise, or conspiracy, in restraint of trade or commerce among the several States, or with foreign

---

1 15 U.S.C. §§ 12–27.

2 15 U.S.C. §§ 1–2. For more information, *see* Chapter II. *United States v. Von's Grocery Co.*, 384 U.S. 270, 274 (1966).

3 *Id.*

4 *In re Publ'n Paper Antitrust Litig.*, 690 F.3d 51, 62 (2d Cir. 2012).

nations."[5] The language of Section 1 is expansive as any contract or commercial transaction will, to a certain degree, restrain trade. A literal reading of Section 1 would prohibit almost all agreements and "would outlaw the entire body of private contract law."[6] After the Sherman Act was enacted, courts faced the challenge of construing the Act so that it was consistent with Congress's objective of promoting competition while balancing the parties' right to enter into contracts, which naturally involve some degree of restraint of trade. Courts overcame this challenge by interpreting the Sherman Act to only prohibit agreements that unreasonably restrain trade.[7] Therefore, Section 1 of the Sherman Act prohibits an agreement between two or more entities that unreasonably restrains trade and has an effect on interstate commerce.[8]

1183. To establish an unlawful agreement under Section 1 of the Sherman Act, a plaintiff must first prove that two separate economic entities entered into an agreement. Unilateral and independent action is not proscribed under Section 1 of the Sherman Act because only when two separate entities come together and enter into an agreement can they "bring together economic power that was previously pursuing divergent goals."[9] The Supreme Court has, for example, held that an entity can refuse to deal with another party "as long as it does so independently," because independent conduct is not prohibited by Section 1 of the Sherman Act.[10]

1184. The Supreme Court has also determined that certain entities are not separate under the Sherman Act and, therefore, are not capable of entering into agreements for purposes of the Act.[11] For example, a corporation and its wholly owned subsidiary are not considered separate entities under the Sherman Act, and thus cannot enter into an unlawful agreement to restrain trade.[12] A corporation and its wholly owned subsidiary possess "complete unity of interest" because the "corporate actions" are guided by one "corporate consciousness[]," as the subsidiary acts to advantage the parent company and sole shareholder.[13]

1185. In addition, an essential element in proving a violation of Section 1 of the Sherman Act is showing the existence of an agreement. A plaintiff can prove that there was an agreement through direct or circumstantial evidence. Direct evidence is evidence from which no inference is required to establish the existence of an

---

5 15 U.S.C. § 1. For additional information, *see* Chapter IV.

6 *Nat'l Soc'y of Pro. Eng'rs v. United States*, 435 U.S. 679, 687–88 (1978); *see also Chicago Bd. of Trade v. United States*, 246 U.S. 231, 238 (1918) ("But the legality of an agreement or regulation cannot be determined by so simple a test, as whether it restrains competition. Every agreement concerning trade, every regulation of trade, restrains. To bind, to restrain, is of their very essence.").

7 *Nat'l Soc'y of Pro. Eng'rs*, 435 U.S. 690.

8 *Id.*; *see also Standard Oil Co. v. United States*, 221 U.S. 1, 31 (1911).

9 *Copperweld Corp. v. Independence Tube Corp.*, 467 U.S. 752, 769 (1984).

10 *Monsanto Co. v. Spray-Rite Serv. Corp.*, 465 U.S. 752, 761 (1984); *Schwimmer v. Sony Corp. of Am.*, 677 F.2d 946, 952 (2d Cir. 1982) ("Proof of joint or concerted action is required; proof of unilateral action does not suffice."); *see also Fisher v. Berkeley*, 475 U.S. 260, 266 (1986) ("Even where a single firm's restraints directly affect prices and have the same economic effect as concerted action might have, there can be no liability under § 1 in the absence of agreement.").

11 *Copperweld*, 467 U.S. 769.

12 *Id.*

13 *Id.*, 771.

agreement.[14] Examples of direct evidence include a signed, written agreement, or admissible testimony that there was an agreement.[15]

1186. Parties, however, do not have to enter into a written agreement to violate Section 1, as circumstantial evidence indicating that the parties shared a "conscious commitment" to an unlawful course of action, is sufficient.[16] Antitrust law, however, limits the inferences that can be drawn from certain types of ambiguous circumstantial evidence – that is, evidence that is as consistent with unilateral conduct as with an agreement. For example, parallel business conduct itself is not sufficient to establish a violation of Section 1. Even "conscious parallelism," where parties in a concentrated market take action in the marketplace taking into account the actual or anticipated actions of their competitors, is not unlawful under the Sherman Act.[17] Parallel conduct by itself does not show an agreement because the parties' conduct, while similar in form or proximate in time, could also be the product of unilateral decision-making based on an awareness of how competitors might respond given past history or a shared recognition of common market realities.[18] To prove concerted action, a plaintiff must also provide some additional proof – often referred to as "plus factors" – that the parallel conduct stemmed from an agreement or a meeting of the minds.[19]

b. *Section 2 Claims: Monopolization and Attempted Monopolization (single firm conduct)*

1187. As developed in Chapter V, Section 2 of the Sherman Act makes it unlawful to "monopolize, or attempt to monopolize… any part of the trade or commerce among the several states, or with foreign nations."[20] Section 2 prohibits both individual firm's monopolization or attempts to monopolize and an agreement to monopolize. To win a monopolization suit under Section 2, a plaintiff must show that the defendant: (1) possesses "monopoly power in the relevant market," and (2) willfully acquired or maintained "that power as distinguished from [its] growth or development as a consequence of a superior product, business acumen, or historic accident."[21] To establish an attempt to monopolize, a plaintiff must show [attempt elements]. To establish a defendant's liability under Section 2, it is not sufficient for a plaintiff to show that the defendant has monopoly power or a dangerous probability of acquiring such power.[22] Instead, a plaintiff must show that the defendant acted to willfully acquire or maintain that power through exclusionary means instead of procompetitive behavior.[23]

---

14 *See, e.g., Am. Chiropractic Ass'n v. Trigon Healthcare, Inc.*, 367 F.3d 212, 226 (4th Cir. 2004) (explaining that "direct evidence… is 'explicit and requires no inferences to establish the proposition or conclusion being asserted.'").

15 *See, e.g., United States v. Topoco Assocs., Inc.*, 405 U.S. 596, 601–06 (1972).

16 *Monsanto Co.*, 465 U.S. 764.

17 *Bell Atl. Corp. v. Twombly*, 550 U.S. 544, 553–54 (2007) (quotation marks omitted).

18 *Id.*

19 *Id.*

20 15 U.S.C. § 2. For more detail, *see* Chapter V.

21 *United States v. Grinnell Corp.*, 384 U.S. 563, 570–71 (1966); *see also T. Harris Young & Assocs., Inc. v. Marquette Elecs., Inc.*, 931 F.2d 816, 823 (11th Cir. 1991).

22 *Ne. Tel. Co. v. Am. Tel. & Tel. Co.*, 651 F.2d 76, 84–85 (2d Cir. 1981); *Berkey Photo, Inc. v. Eastman Kodak Co.*, 603 F.2d 263, 275 (2d Cir. 1979); *Viamedia, Inc. v. Comcast Corp.*, 951 F.3d 429, 451 (7th Cir. 2020).

23 *Grinnell*, 384 U.S. 571; *see also, e.g., Aspen Skiing Co. v. Aspen Highlands Skiing Corp.*, 472 U.S. 585, 595–96 (1985).

1188. Although Section 2 of the Sherman Act does not explicitly use the term "market," courts have consistently found that this notion is intrinsic in a monopolization claim because "[i]t is impossible to monopolize a market that does not exist."[24] Two factors are important to determine a relevant product market: (1) whether a product is interchangeable with alternate products, and (2) "the cross-elasticity of demand," meaning whether "consumers will change their consumption of one product in response to a price change in another."[25] Stated simply, the concept of cross-elasticity of demand refers to whether a customer faced with a price increase for product A will seek to purchase product B instead. If so, then product A and product B may be seen as part of the same product market. The test for whether products are interchangeable nonetheless requires a somewhat mechanical application by a court, as the court must determine whether a product can be easily substituted with another product based on their functionality. Instead, the test for cross-elasticity of demand requires a more detailed and complex economic analysis usually provided by an expert witness.

1189. An examination of monopoly power also entails an assessment of whether the defendant is able to exert its power in a specific geographic area or region. The inquiry into the relevant geographic market is an inquiry into the appropriate geographic area where plaintiffs could seek alternative products if the defendant were to raise its prices.[26]

1190. Once the relevant product and geographic markets are established, a court must determine whether a defendant has improperly acquired "monopoly power" within those relevant markets, or has a dangerous probability of doing so. The Supreme Court has defined monopoly power as "the power to control prices or exclude competition" within the relevant market.[27] Courts often use a defendant's market share as the tool to determine whether the defendant possesses monopoly power.[28] Plaintiffs can also establish a defendant's monopoly power if the defendant has controlled price in the relevant market or has successfully excluded or foreclosed possible competitors from the market.[29]

1191. In an attempted monopolization claim under Section 2, a plaintiff need not prove actual possession of monopoly power but rather that there exists "a dangerous probability of actual monopolization, which has generally required a definition of the relevant market and examination of market power."[30] Compared to a monopolization claim, where the defendant must possess monopoly power and a general intent to exclude competitors,[31] in an attempted monopolization claim a defendant

---

24 *Collins v. Associated Pathologists, Ltd.*, 844 F.2d 473, 480 (7th Cir. 1988); *see also*, *Standard Oil Co. v. United States*, 221 U.S. 1, 61 (1911) ("The commerce referred to by the words 'any part,' construed in the light of the manifest purpose of the statute, has both a geographical and a distributive significance; that is, it includes any portion of the United States and any one of the classes of things forming a part of interstate or foreign commerce.").

25 *Eastman Kodak Co. v. Image Technical Services, Inc.*, 504 U.S. 451, 469 (1992).

26 *United States v. Philadelphia Nat'l Bank*, 374 U.S. 321, 359 (1963); *see* Chapter II.

27 *United States v. E.I. du Pont de Nemours & Co.*, 351 U.S. 377, 391–92 (1956).

28 *Eastman Kodak Co.*, 504 U.S. 481 ("Respondents' evidence that Kodak controls nearly 100% of the parts market and 80% to 95% of the service market, with no readily available substitutes, is, however, sufficient to survive summary judgment under the more stringent monopoly standard of § 2.").

29 *McWane, Inc. v. FTC*, 783 F.3d 814, 832 (11th Cir. 2015).

30 *Spectrum Sports, Inc. v. McQuillan*, 506 U.S. 447, 455 (1993).

31 *Tops Mkts., Inc. v. Quality Mkts., Inc.*, 142 F.3d 90, 101 (2d Cir. 1998); *Spectrum Sports*, 506 U.S. 457; *Times-Picayune Publ'g Co. v. United States*, 345 U.S. 594 (1953).

must have engaged in anticompetitive activities with the specific intent to acquire a monopoly by eliminating the competition. Anticompetitive activities can take many forms from below cost of predatory pricing to licensing practices.[32]

B. *State Antitrust, Unfair Competition, and Consumer Protection Claims, and State Common Law Claims*

1192. Individual states have enacted their own antitrust laws, and a plaintiff can bring a private enforcement action at the state level seeking to enforce state antitrust laws. Many states mirror the federal antitrust laws; however, the federal laws are only the floor and states can and have established stricter laws, i.e., statutes that are even broader in application than federal law. In addition, plaintiffs often seek passive claims under state common law, including claims for violation of antitrust common law – when it exists – and other causes of action, such as unjust enrichment.

C. *Statute of Limitations*

1193. In general, antitrust actions must be commenced within 4 years after the case of action accrued.[33] However, determining the functional length of a statute of limitations can be complicated by various factors, including the effect of on-going conduct,[34] when the plaintiffs began suffering injury,[35] and actions that toll the running of the limitations period.[36]

2. Bases for Federal Jurisdiction

1194. A plaintiff can bring a case in federal court if the court has personal and subject matter jurisdiction.[37] Personal jurisdiction relates to whether the court "may adjudicate the rights of particular persons regarding a particular claim."[38] For a court to exercise personal jurisdiction, a defendant must have some contact with the state where the court is located, meaning a defendant must avail itself of the forum or take actions that have an effect in the forum to justify the exercise of jurisdiction over it.[39] Additionally, a defendant can only be made a party by proper service

---

32 *Brooke Grp. Ltd. v. Brown & Williamson Tobacco Corp.*, 509 U.S. 209, 222, 226 (1993) (finding that there are two prerequisites to prove predatory pricing, first the plaintiff "must prove that the prices complained of are below an appropriate measure of its rival's costs," second, the plaintiff must prove a "probable recoupment and injury to competition"); *Lorain J. Co. v. United States*, 342 U.S. 143 (1951) (unilateral refusal to deal claim); *Broadcom Corp. v. Qualcomm Inc.*, 501 F.3d 297 (3d Cir. 2007) (unlawful licensing practices).

33 15 U.S.C. § 15b; *see Berkey Photo, Inc. v. Eastman Kodak Co.*, 603 F.2d 263, 295 (2d Cir. 1979) ("By statute, 15 U.S.C. § 15b, a four-year period of limitations applies in private antitrust suits.")

34 *Humana, Inc. v. Celgene Corp.*, 2022 WL 1237883 (D.N.J. Apr. 27, 2022) (holding that ongoing actions enforcing alleged conspiracy – specifically, refusing to sell samples of drugs to generic producers and suing some for patent infringement – could toll statute of limitations).

35 *See In re Glumetza Antitrust Litig.*, 611 F. Supp. 3d 848, 862 (N.D. Cal. 2020) (holding, in an alleged reverse payment case, that "each continuing violation (i.e., each new sale) merely triggered the statute of limitations anew for that act.")

36 *Id.* (agreeing with plaintiffs that "defendants' fraudulent concealment of their settlement agreement, specifically the No-AG provision, tolled the statute of limitations").

37 I Moore's Manual – Federal Practice and Procedure ¶5.01 (2022).

38 *Id.*

39 *See e.g., In re New Motor Vehicles Canadian Exp.*, 307 F. Supp. 2d 145 (D. Me. 2004), *order amended*, 2004 WL 1571617 (D. Me. Apr. 20, 2004); *In re Vitamins Antitrust Litig.*, 120 F. Supp. 2d 58 (D.D.C. 2000).

of process (*see* Section C. below).[40] By comparison, subject matter jurisdiction grants federal courts the power to hear and adjudicate a case.[41] Federal courts, compared to state courts, are courts of limited jurisdiction and thus, can only hear cases arising under federal law (federal question jurisdiction) or in which there is a diversity of citizenship among the parties (diversity jurisdiction).

A. *Federal question jurisdiction*

1195. Federal courts have subject matter jurisdiction over cases arising under federal law. Notably, Section 4 of the Clayton Act states that:

> Any person who shall be injured in his business or property by reason of anything forbidden in the antitrust laws may sue therefor in any district court of the United States in the district in which the defendant resides or is found or has an agent, without respect to the amount in controversy, and shall recover threefold the damages by him sustained, and the cost of suit, including a reasonable attorney's fee.[42]

1196. This section of the Clayton Act is "a vehicle for private enforcement of the antitrust laws"[43] and in short, it is what permits private plaintiffs to bring suits under the Sherman Act in federal court.

B. *Diversity Jurisdiction and the Class Action Fairness Act as the basis for suing for State Law Violations in Federal Court*

1197. Congress also has provided that federal courts have diversity jurisdiction over cases that do not arise under federal law "but that involve citizens of different states, or citizens of the United States and aliens or foreign subjects, provided that the amount in controversy exceeds $75,000."[44] Therefore, plaintiffs can bring an action to federal court, even if the claim does not arise out of federal law, as long as they can meet these two threshold elements: (1) complete diversity, and (2) an amount in controversy that exceeds $75,000. In 2005, Congress enacted the Class Action Fairness Act (CAFA) which substantially expanded federal diversity jurisdiction over class action cases by relaxing the complete diversity requirement for certain cases. Under CAFA, a federal court has diversity jurisdiction over class actions claims where "'any member' of a class of plaintiffs is a citizen of a different state than the defendant," and if the aggregate amount in controversy "across all class members exceeds $5 million."[45] CAFA thus serves as a vehicle and the basis for some indirect purchasers to sue in federal court, on a class-wide basis, for violations of state antitrust and unfair competition laws.

---

40 *Zenith Radio Corp. v. Hazeltine Rsch, Inc.*, 395 U.S. 100, 110 (1969); *see also In re Polyester Staple Antitrust Litig.*, No. 3:03CV1516, 2008 WL 906331 (W.D.N.C. Apr. 1, 2008).

41 I Moore's Manual, *supra* n. 37, Chapter VI, ¶5.03.

42 15 U.S.C. § 15.

43 *Cargill, Inc. v. Monfort of Colo., Inc.*, 479 U.S. 104, 109 (1986).

44 I Moore's Manual, *supra* n. 37, Chapter VI, ¶5.03; 28 U.S.C. § 1332.

45 Phillip E. Areeda (late) & Herbert Hovenkamp, Antitrust Law: An Analysis of Antitrust Principles and Their Applications, ¶ 331. (Fourth and Fifth Editions, 2023 Cum. Supp. 2018–2023).

C. *Supplemental jurisdiction*

1198. Federal courts can also exercise supplemental jurisdiction over state law claims that are not within the court's original jurisdiction if those claims are related to claims over which the court has original jurisdiction and the court determines that it would be efficient, convenient, and fair to exercise jurisdiction over the state law claims.[46] Indirect purchasers often use supplemental jurisdiction to bring antitrust damages claims in federal court by bringing a claim for injunctive relief under federal law, then persuading the court to exercise supplemental jurisdiction over their state law antitrust claims.[47]

D. *Service of Process: The extraterritorial application of the US Antitrust laws to conduct abroad that has an effect in the US*

1199. As noted above, to adjudicate a claim against a defendant, a federal court must also have personal jurisdiction over that defendant, regardless of whether it is a person or a corporation. Whether a federal court has personal jurisdiction over a defendant requires a statutory and constitutional due process inquiry, and a federal court may not exercise personal jurisdiction until the defendant has been properly served.[48]

1200. The Clayton Act provides for different rules to serve a corporation and to establish jurisdiction over the corporate defendant. The Clayton Act states that "[a]ny suit, action, or proceeding… against a corporation may be brought not only in the judicial district whereof it is an inhabitant, but also in any district wherein it may be found or transacts business; and all process in such cases may be served in the district of which it is an inhabitant, or wherever it may be found."[49] Therefore, the Clayton Act explicitly permits extraterritorial service of process, and courts have also allowed service to a defendant's facility whether in the US or abroad.[50]

3. Types of Lawsuits

A. *Single Plaintiff Lawsuits*

1201. Private antitrust action may involve antitrust claims asserted by a single plaintiff or multiple plaintiffs against one or more defendants. To bring a claim, a party must have standing to bring an antitrust suit, meaning the party must have suffered antitrust injury.[51] Courts have defined an antitrust injury as an "injury of the type the antitrust laws were intended to prevent and that flows from that which makes defendants' acts unlawful."[52] Under the Clayton Act, not every person who was distantly harmed by an antitrust violation can bring a claim. The law focuses

---

46 1 Moore's Manual, *supra* n. 37, Chapter VI, ¶5.90.

47 *See* Section I.3.B.a below, for a discussion of limitations on indirect purchasers' ability to bring federal antitrust damages claims.

48 *Id.* ¶6.01.

49 15 U.S.C. § 12; 15 U.S.C. § 22.

50 15 U.S.C. § 22.

51 *See* Chapter II, Section I.1.B.

52 *Brunswick Corp. v. Pueblo Bowl-O-Mat, Inc.*, 429 U.S. 477, 489 (1977); *Zenith Radio Corp. v. Hazeltine Rsch., Inc.*, 395 U.S. 100, 125 (1969).

on ensuring that the plaintiff is the proper party to bring the suit and address the wrong, not a party too remote from the injury. Moreover, the injury to the plaintiff(s) must flow from a harm to competition or the competitive process. The antitrust laws are intended to protect competition as a whole, not just individual competitors.[53] At the same time, there is no specific or right number of plaintiffs needed to bring suit. For example, under the Clayton Act, only one plaintiff with antitrust standing is required to bring a claim for a Sherman Act violation.

B. *Class Action Lawsuits*

1202. When more than one person or entity has suffered harm from Sherman Act violations, the group can seek to bring their claims in a class or representative action. There are two major advantages for plaintiffs to bring a claim through a class action. First, the class action mechanism may conserve judicial resources, as it will adjudicate actions that could be brought by similarly situated plaintiffs in one single proceeding. Second, the mechanism enables individual plaintiffs to bring a claim when they have small damages that would not otherwise justify the cost of litigation. For a group of plaintiffs to properly bring a case as a class, they must prove several elements for the court to certify the class. Under Rule 23 of the Federal Rules of Civil Procedure (Fed. R. Civ. P. 23), one or more member of the class can pursue the case on behalf of the whole class if

> the class is so numerous that joinder of all members is impracticable; (2) there are questions of law or fact common to the class; (3) the claims or defenses of the representative parties are typical of the claims or defenses of the class; and (4) the representative parties will fairly and adequately protect the interests of the class.[54]

1203. After meeting these four prerequisites, plaintiffs must satisfy at least one additional element under Fed. R. Civ. P. 23(b).[55] In antitrust actions, plaintiffs typically must establish that "(1) questions of law or fact common to class members must predominate over any questions affecting only individual members;" or "(2) the class action must be superior to other available methods for the fair and efficient adjudication of the matter."[56] Courts have broad discretion in determining whether a class meets the requirements for certification and a decision to certify a class must be supported by specific findings given the importance of the certification decision to the conduct of the litigation.[57] Even after a class of plaintiffs is certified, the district court retains "broad discretion in determining whether to modify or even decertify a class" while appellate courts may vacate or reverse an improvidently granted certification decision.[58]

---

53 *Brunswick*, 429 U.S. 488.

54 Fed. R. Civ. P. 23(a).

55 Fed. R. Civ. P. 23(b).

56 *Id.*; *see also In re Compact Disc Minimum Advertised Price Antitrust Litig.*, 216 F.R.D. 197, 205 (D. Me. 2003).

57 *Comcast Corp. v. Behrend*, 569 U.S. 27 (2013); *Amchem Prod., Inc. v. Windsor*, 521 U.S. 591 (1997); *In re Hydrogen Peroxide Antitrust Litig.*, 552 F.3d 305 (3d Cir. 2008), as amended (Jan. 16, 2009).

58 *In re Titanium Dioxide Antitrust Litig.*, 962 F. Supp. 2d 840, 861 (D. Md. 2013) (quoting *Wu v. MAMSI Life & Health Ins. Co.*, 256 F.R.D. 158, 162 (D. Md. 2008)). For the ability of appellate courts to vacate improperly granted certification decisions, *see, e.g.*, *Comcast Corp. v. Behrend*, 569 U.S. 27, 34 (U.S., 2013) (overturning improper class certification in an antitrust class action suit).

The available remedies and ability to recover damages may depend on whether the plaintiffs are direct or indirect purchasers.

a. *Direct Purchaser Plaintiffs*

1204. Direct Purchaser Plaintiffs are customers who bought directly from the defendant in the lawsuit. The Clayton Act grants these direct purchaser plaintiffs the right to sue a defendant for violations of the antitrust laws.[59]

b. *Indirect Purchaser Plaintiffs: Illinois-Brick and Hanover Shoe*

1205. Under the Clayton Act, indirect purchaser plaintiffs generally do not have standing to being a federal antitrust claim seeking damages, although they can sue for injunctive relief and may be able to sue for damages under certain state antitrust laws. This interpretation stems from the Supreme Court's decision in *Hanover Shoe* and was further developed in *Illinois-Brick* and *ARC America*.[60]

1206. In *Hanover Shoe*, the Supreme Court explained that a buyer who is illegally overcharged by the seller has a right to recover from the seller, and the buyer retains this right even when the buyer "maintains his own price but takes steps to increase his volume or to decrease other costs."[61] The Court reasoned that the buyer maintains their right to recover because they would have made more profits had the seller not illegally overcharged for its goods.[62] However, the Court did not allow the defendant to assert a "passing-on defense," meaning the defendant could not claim that the plaintiff did not suffer any damages because the plaintiff also raised its prices, and thus, passed the overcharge to another buyer. This defense would also undermine the importance of treble damages as the ultimate consumers "would have only a tiny stake in a lawsuit and little interest in attempting a class action. In consequence, those who violate the antitrust laws by price fixing or monopolizing would retain the fruits of their illegality because no one was available who would bring suit against them."[63]

1207. In *Illinois-Brick*, the Supreme Court found that indirect purchasers do not have standing to sue for damages because allowing indirect plaintiffs to seek damages, while not allowing direct purchasers to use a pass-on defense, would create the possibility of double recovery along with costly and lengthy inquiries.[64] The Court explained that allowing the use of passing-on theories would undermine the "effectiveness" of treble damages as it "would transform treble-damages actions into massive efforts to apportion the recovery among all potential plaintiffs that could have absorbed part of the overcharge from direct purchasers to middlemen to ultimate consumers."[65] Notably, CAFA allows indirect purchasers to bring

---

59 *See* Section II.1, Chapter VI.

60 *Hanover Shoe, Inc. v. United Shoe Mach. Corp.*, 392 U.S. 481 (1968); *Illinois Brick Co. v. Illinois*, 431 U.S. 720 (1977); *California v. ARC America Corp.*, 490 U.S. 93 (1989).

61 *Hanover Shoe*, 392 U.S. 489.

62 *Id.*

63 *Id.*, 494.

64 *Illinois Brick*, 431 U.S. 737.

65 *Id.*

a class-action suit under both federal and state statutes, and if they cannot recover damages under the federal statute, they might recover damages under the state statute in those states refuting the *Illinois-Brick* doctrine.[66]

1208. In *ARC America*, the Supreme Court held that federal law did not preempt state laws permitting indirect purchasers from recovering damages for antitrust violations.[67] It explained that "*Illinois Brick* was a decision construing the federal antitrust laws, not a decision defining the interrelationship between the federal and state antitrust laws," and therefore "[t]he congressional purposes on which Illinois Brick was based provide no support for a finding that state indirect purchaser statutes are pre-empted by federal law."[68]

C. *Opt-Out or Direct-Action Plaintiff Lawsuits*

1209. Once a class is established, individual plaintiffs who would fit into the definition of the class have the right to opt out of the class. Class members must be provided notice of the class, and the notice must explain their rights to opt-out of the class.[69] If a class member does not exercise its right to opt-out, it will be bound by the judgement of the class action. On the contrary, if a member chooses to opt-out of the class, it will not be bound by the final judgment and can pursue its own action should it wish to do so.

4. Transfers, MDL and Consolidation

1210. Often multiple antitrust actions based on the same or similar facts are filed against the same defendants. The actions may be filed in the same federal district court or in different courts in different jurisdictions. In such situations, federal courts in the US rely on several important mechanisms to consolidate and coordinate related civil cases to promote efficiency and the interests of justice.

1211. Initially, related civil cases pending in the same federal district court are typically assigned to a single judge to decide whether either the consolidation or coordination of pretrial proceedings is "feasible and is likely to reduce conflicts and duplication[.]"[70] District courts may also transfer cases to another district court "[f]or the convenience of parties and witnesses, in the interest of justice."[71] Where "cases appear to involve common questions of law or fact, and consolidation may tend to reduce cost and delay," the cases may be consolidated.[72] While some cases may be entirely consolidated through trial, partial consolidation also is possible. For example, in some cases consolidation may be limited to pretrial discovery before separate trials on "one or more separate issues, claims, crossclaims, counterclaims, or third-party claims."[73]

---

66 *See e.g., Hyde v. Abbott Labs., Inc.*, 473 S.E.2d 680, 683–84 (1996).

67 *ARC Am. Corp.*, 490 U.S. 105.

68 *Id.*

69 Fed. R. Civ. P. 23(c)(2)(B)(v)(vi).

70 FJC, Manual for Complex Litigation (Complex Litig.), § 20.11 (4th ed. 2004), *available at* https://www.uscourts.gov/sites/default/files/mcl4.pdf.

71 28 U.S.C. § 1404(a).

72 *Id.; see also* Fed. R. Civ. P. 42.

73 Fed. R. Civ. P. 42(b).

1212. Where related civil cases are filed across different federal districts, procedures also exist for those cases to be transferred and consolidated for purposes of pre-trial discovery in a single federal court as part of a Multidistrict Litigation (MDL) proceeding under the authority of the MDL Panel.[74] The MDL Panel consists of seven sitting federal circuit or district court judges who are appointed to serve by the Chief Justice of the US.[75] No two members of the MDL Panel may be from the same federal judicial circuit.[76] Transfers can be initiated either by one of the parties or by the MDL Panel on its own initiative.[77] While MDL cases often consolidate cases from many different federal jurisdictions, MDL treatment can be appropriate for cases involving as few as two federal districts.[78] In all cases, the MDL Panel must evaluate whether the transfer will "eliminate duplication in discovery, avoid conflicting rulings and schedules, reduce litigation cost, and save the time and effort of the parties, the attorneys, the witnesses, and the courts."[79] In other words, cases will be transferred and either consolidated or coordinated for pretrial proceedings to reduce the burden on the litigants, witnesses, and the judicial system.

1213. Once cases are transferred to a single district court by the MDL Panel (the "transferee court"), the transferee court is authorized to exercise "the powers of a district judge in any district for the purpose of conducting pretrial depositions in such coordinated or consolidated [] proceedings."[80] Upon the initial transfer of cases by the MDL Panel, the transferee court will commonly establish a master file for the MDL proceedings and then look to appoint lead or liaison counsel and steering committees to manage the case, both procedurally and substantively.[81] For class action cases in particular, the transferee court may then encourage plaintiffs to file one or more consolidated class action complaints (e.g., for direct and indirect purchaser plaintiffs), set a schedule for briefing and assignment of any motions to dismiss, and encourage the parties to agree upon common discovery protocols, including protocols for the production of electronically stored information (ESI) and proposed protective orders to safeguard against the disclosure of sensitive and proprietary business information.[82] Once the consolidated amended complaint has survived any motion to dismiss and has been answered, the transferee court then will often work with the parties toward entering a case management order and discovery schedule for pretrial proceedings through class certification and summary judgment motion practice.[83]

---

74 28 U.S.C. §§ 1407, 2112; FJC, Complex Litig., *supra* n. 70, Chapter VI, § 20.13.

75 28 U.S.C. § 1407(d).

76 *Id.*

77 FJC, Complex Litig., *supra* n. 70, Chapter VI, § 20.131.

78 *Id.*

79 *Id.*

80 28 U.S.C. § 1407(b).

81 *See, e.g., In re Generic Digoxin and Doxcycline Antitrust Litig.*, MDL No. 2274, Case No. 16-MD-2724, Pretrial Order No. 1 (E.D. Pa. Aug. 15, 2016) (inviting applications for liaison counsel) & Pretrial Order Nos. 2–3 (E.D. Pa. Sept. 8, 2016) (appointing liaison counsel).

82 *See, e.g., In re Generic Digoxin and Doxcycline Antitrust Litig.*, MDL No. 2274, Case No. 16-MD-2724, Pretrial Order No. 5 (E.D. Pa. Nov. 16, 2016).

83 *See, e.g., In re Generic Pharms. Pricing Litig.*, MDL No. 2274, Case No. 16-MD-2724, Pretrial Order No. 105 (E.D. Pa. Oct. 24, 2019).

1214. In theory, the power of the transferee court is limited to pretrial proceedings; the Supreme Court has previously held that the MDL statute does not permit a transferee judge to assign a transferred case to itself for trial and instead requires that the transferee court remand cases back to their original district courts for trial.[84] In practice, however, there are steps that may permit the transferee court to resolve MDL proceedings under certain circumstances.[85] In addition, where appropriate, transferee courts have full authority to terminate cases when deciding dispositive motions, which would make any remand for trial unnecessary.[86]

1215. Of note, however, formal consolidation and coordination of cases through the MDL process is limited to civil cases filed in federal courts.[87] The MDL Panel does not, by contrast, have the authority to transfer or consolidate cases filed in state courts, even where those cases involve common questions of law or fact with federal cases.[88] While state and federal judges may at times seek to coordinate discovery proceedings and timelines for cases that involve common questions, such coordination is ad hoc and not guaranteed between parallel separate state and federal proceedings.[89]

5. Principal Threshold Issues

1216. As a threshold matter, Plaintiffs pursuing private claims in federal court must first establish that both: (A) they have standing to sue under the antitrust laws, and (B) they have adequately pleaded sufficient facts that, if substantiated with evidence, would entitle them to relief under the antitrust laws.

A. *Standing to Sue and Antitrust Injury*

1217. To bring a claim in federal court, every plaintiff must at a minimum establish its constitutional standing to bring suit by showing that three elements are met: (1) an "injury in fact" suffered by the plaintiff, (2) a "causal connection between the injury and the conduct complained of," and (3) the likelihood that the injury will be addressed by a favorable decision.[90] This constitutional doctrine of standing is based on the text of Article III of the US Constitution limiting the jurisdiction of federal courts to "Cases" and "Controversies."[91]

---

84 *See In re Lexecon, Inc. v. Milberg Weiss Bershad Hynes & Lerach*, 523 U.S. 26, 27 (1998) (describing the "straightforward language" of 28 U.S.C. § 1407(f) imposing a "responsibility to remand, which bars recognizing any self-assignment power in a transferee court").

85 *See generally* FJC, Complex Litig., *supra* n. 70, Chapter VI, § 20.132 (describing the use of "bellwether" trials for actions originally filed in the transferee district and the filing of an amended complaint asserting venue in the transferee district, among other potential alternatives).

86 *See id.* ("Although the transferee judge has no jurisdiction to conduct a trial in cases transferred solely for pretrial proceedings, the judge may terminate actions by ruling on motions to dismiss, for summary judgment, or pursuant to settlement, and may enter consent decrees.").

87 FJC, Complex Litig., *supra* n. 70, Chapter VI, § 20.3.

88 Exceptions exist for cases filed in state courts that are either removed to federal court under 28 U.S.C. § 1446 before transfer to the MDL Panel or cases that are transferred from state to federal court through so-called "snap removal" proceedings under 28 U.S.C. § 1441(b)(2).

89 *See* FJC, Complex Litig., *supra* n. 70, Chapter VI, § 20.311 (discussing the types of actions often coordinated between state and federal courts).

90 *Lujan v. Defenders of Wildlife*, 504 U.S. 555, 560–61 (1992).

91 *Id.* 559–60.

1218. Beyond the jurisdictional requirement of constitutional standing, a plaintiff seeking to bring a private action under the antitrust laws also must demonstrate "antitrust standing," a prudential doctrine that the Supreme Court has described as "somewhat different from that of standing as a constitutional doctrine."[92] The Supreme Court has further explained this requirement as follows: "Harm to the antitrust plaintiff is sufficient to satisfy the constitutional standing requirement of injury in fact, but the court must make a further determination whether the plaintiff is a proper party to bring a private antitrust action."[93]

1219. A complaint will satisfy the antitrust standing requirement if it demonstrates both that: (1) the plaintiff suffered an "antitrust injury;" and (2) the plaintiff suffered injury that is directly enough related to the antitrust violation such that it is an "efficient enforcer" to address and remedy the violation.[94]

1220. *Antitrust Injury*. The Supreme Court has defined "antitrust injury" as an "injury of the type the antitrust laws were intended to prevent and that flows from that which makes [the] defendants' acts unlawful."[95] In *Brunswick Corp. v. Pueblo Bowl-O-Mat, Inc.*, for example, three business operators filed a private antitrust suit under the Clayton Act against the acquisition of several financially-distressed competitors by a large manufacturer.[96] The business operators alleged that they were injured by these acquisitions because, had the manufacturer not acquired these businesses, those competitors would have gone out of business and their own income would have increased.[97] Because the Clayton Act only condemns mergers "when they may produce anticompetitive effects," the Supreme Court held that it was "inimical to the purposes of these laws to award damages" for lost "profits they would have realized had competition been reduced."[98] To recover for damages, the Supreme Court held that the "injury should reflect the anticompetitive effect either of the violation or of anticompetitive acts made possible by the violation."[99]

1221. A showing of "antitrust injury" is necessary for all private antitrust actions, including per se violations.[100] In some cases, satisfying this requirement can be relatively straightforward. For example, courts often summarily accept purchaser allegations of overpayments caused by anticompetitive conduct as sufficient to show antitrust

---

92 *Associated Gen. Contractors of Cal., Inc. v. Cal. State Council of Carpenters*, 459 U.S. 519, 535 n. 31 (1983).

93 *Id.*

94 *See, e.g.*, *Palmyra Park Hosp., Inc. v. Phoebe Putney Mem'l Hosp.*, 604 F.3d 1291, 1299 (11th Cir. 2010) ("We employ a two-prong test for antitrust standing under § 4 of the Clayton Act: first, the plaintiff must have alleged an antitrust injury, and second, the plaintiff must be an efficient enforcer of the antitrust laws"); *Port Dock & Stone Corp. v. Oldcastle Ne., Inc.*, 507 F.3d 117, 121 (2d Cir. 2007) ("In addition to injury in fact to the plaintiff's business or property caused by the antitrust violation, 15 U.S.C. § 15, antitrust standing for a private plaintiff requires a showing of a special kind of 'antitrust injury,' as well as a showing that the plaintiff is an 'efficient enforcer' to assert a private antitrust claim.").

95 *Brunswick Corp. v. Pueblo Bowl-O-Mat, Inc.*, 429 US 477, 489 (1977).

96 *Id.* 480–81.

97 *Id.* 484.

98 *Id.* 487–88.

99 *Id.* 489.

100 *See, e.g.*, *In re Cardizem CD Antitrust Litig.*, 332 F.3d 896, 909 n.15 (6th Cir. 2003) ("Our conclusion that the Agreement was a per se illegal restraint of trade does not obviate the need to decide whether the plaintiffs adequately alleged antitrust injury.").

injury with little further discussion.[101] At the same time, such purchasers must at a minimum plausibly allege that any supra-competitive prices were the result of anticompetitive conduct prohibited by the antitrust laws.[102]

1222. Alleged injuries suffered by competitors often receive more scrutiny. At a high level, "a competitor may not claim an injury resulting from competition even when such competition was actually caused by conduct that violates the antitrust laws."[103] Nevertheless, competitors are not foreclosed from showing antitrust injury where their injuries are caused by anticompetitive effects linked to antitrust violations.[104] For example, although competitors cannot bring antitrust claims to remedy injuries caused by increased competition, they may bring claims based on injuries caused by anticompetitive conduct that impairs their ability to compete effectively or excludes them from the marketplace entirely.[105]

1223. In the pharmaceutical sector, long and uncertain product development timelines can at times present challenges for demonstrating antitrust injury. For example, if a plaintiff bases its antitrust claim on delay or exclusion of a new branded or generic product under development, it may have difficulty showing antitrust injury for alleged antitrust violations unless "it can plead its intent and preparedness to enter the market[.]"[106] Where the company has not even sought FDA approval, for example, a court may find a lack of antitrust injury.[107] Similarly, where a potential purchaser plaintiff bases antitrust claims on the alleged delayed entry of a pharmaceutical product, a court may find a lack of antitrust injury if it finds that such entry was not likely or even possible.[108]

---

101 *E.g., In re Nexium Antitrust Litig.*, 777 F.3d 9, 26 (1st Cir. 2015); *In re DDAVP Direct Purchaser Antitrust Litig.*, 585 F.3d 677, 688 (2d Cir. 2009); *In re Warfarin Sodium Antitrust Litig.*, 391 F.3d 516, 531 (3d Cir. 2004).

102 *See, e.g., In re Canadian Import Antitrust Litig.*, 470 F.3d 785, 791 (8th Cir. 2006) ("Plaintiffs allege that they are injured by increased prices for prescription drugs in the United States, which they say result from their inability to import less expensive drugs distributed by Canadian pharmacies. As we have explained, however, the importation of drugs from Canada is prohibited by federal law. The absence of competition from Canadian sources in the domestic prescription drug market, therefore, is caused by the federal statutory and regulatory scheme adopted by the United States government, not by the conduct of the defendants. Consequently, the alleged conduct of the defendants did not cause an injury of the type that the antitrust laws were designed to remedy.").

103 *Andrx Pharms., Inc. v. Biovail Corp. Int'l*, 256 F.3d 799, 812 (D.C. Cir. 2001).

104 *See, e.g., Nat'l Assoc. of Pharm. Mfrs.v. Ayerst Labs.*, 850 F.2d 904, 912–14 (2d Cir. 1988) (holding generic pharmaceutical manufacturer could plausibly suffer antitrust injury from lost sales caused by a branded manufacturer's efforts to discourage pharmacists from dispensing generic prescriptions where those efforts otherwise violated the antitrust laws).

105 *See, e.g., In re Keurig Green Mountain Single-Serve Coffee Antitrust Litig.*, 383 F. Supp. 3d 187, 233 (S.D.N.Y. 2019) (finding antitrust injury when plaintiffs alleged that conduct interfered with their ability to compete).

106 *Andrx Pharms.*, 256 F.3d 815.

107 *See, e.g., Ethypharm SA France v. Abbott Labs.*, 707 F.3d 223, 236–37 (3d Cir. 2013) ("We stress that it is not the general arrangement of manufacturer and distributor that is problematic; it is the fact that Ethypharm cannot sell Antara in the United States because of legal barriers particular to the pharmaceutical market, barriers that Ethypharm chose not to surmount. Ethypharm is literally not a lawful competitor in the United States fenofibrate market, and so it cannot be considered a competitor for purposes of antitrust injury… Accordingly, we conclude that Ethypharm did not suffer antitrust injury because it does not and indeed cannot compete in the United States fenofibrate market, unless and until it acquires the required FDA approval to do so.").

108 *See, e.g., Kroger Co. v. Sanofi-Aventis*, 701 F. Supp. 2d 938, 952–55 (S.D. Ohio 2010) (noting that antitrust injury must directly result from an antitrust violation that is a necessary predicate to its occurrence); *In re Humira (Adalimumab) Antitrust Litigation*, 465 F. Supp. 3d 811, 846 (N.D. Ill. 2020) (stating that "[i]t is not plausible that these agreements prevented an even earlier entry date in the U.S. market for a biosimilar" where strong patent protections blocked entry and therefore that there was no antitrust injury in a drug case alleging that a an agreement between drug manufacturers delayed entry for a biosimilar).

1224. The complex pharmaceutical distribution chains also may create other challenges to showing antitrust injury. In particular, some intermediaries that market or facilitate pharmaceutical products may not be able to establish antitrust injury where they are "not a competitor or a consumer in the market in which trade was allegedly restrained," even if they can show actual business losses attributable to an antitrust violation.[109] In *Barton & Pittinos, Inc. v. SmithKline Beecham Corp.*, for example, the court held that a pharmaceutical marketing company could not show antitrust injury from an alleged conspiracy to restrain competition for a vaccine where the marketing company "lacked the required license to buy, possess, or sell the vaccine" and only worked to "drum up demand for the vaccine" before passing orders along to a supplier.[110] On the grounds that "advertisers and brokers of a good or service are not competitors of companies that actually supply the good or service," the court ultimately held that the pharmaceutical marketing company did not have a cognizable antitrust injury.[111]

1225. *Remoteness.* Beyond showing antitrust injury, a plaintiff seeking to bring private claims under federal antitrust laws also must establish that its injury is direct enough to make the plaintiff an efficient enforcer of the antitrust laws. As described by the Supreme Court, this inquiry looks at the "directness or indirectness" of the asserted injury, where damages are unduly speculative, the potential for duplicative recovery, and the existence of more direct victims who would be more appropriate plaintiffs, among other considerations.[112]

1226. In practice, this remoteness requirement often results in a finding that plaintiffs who are not direct customers or competitors do not have antitrust standing.[113] That said, antitrust standing is not expressly limited to direct market participants, and courts do not always find that the existence of complicated distribution and payment structures in health care and pharmaceutical markets prohibit recovery by the ultimate patient or consumer.[114] Additionally, state law may differ on the question of remoteness.[115]

---

109 *Barton & Pittinos, Inc. v. SmithKline Beecham Corp.*, 118 F.3d 178, 179 (3d Cir. 1997).

110 *Id.* 179–80.

111 *Id.* 184

112 *Associated Gen. Contractors of Cal.*, 499 U.S. 535–46.

113 *See, e.g.*, *Sigmapharm, Inc. v. Mut. Pharm. Co.*, 772 F. Supp. 2d 660, 674–75 (E.D. Pa. 2011) (finding pharmaceutical developer lacked antitrust standing to challenge agreement that allegedly suppressed drug sales in which the developer had a royalty interest), *aff'd*, 454 F. App'x 64 (3d Cir. 2011); *Kaiser Found. v. Abbott Labs.*, No. CV 02-2443-JFW, 2009 U.S. Dist. LEXIS 107512, *9–14 (C.D. Cal. 2009) (finding an alleged injury suffered by a "potential customer of one of Defendant's potential competitors" not the type of "direct" or "proximate" injury that results in antitrust standing).

114 *See, e.g.*, *Blue Shield of Va. v. McCready*, 457 U.S. 465, 479–481 (1982) (finding injury of patient denied reimbursement for psychologist services as a result of alleged conspiracy by payors against psychologists not impermissibly remote where the harm was "clearly foreseeable" and "a necessary step in effecting the ends of the alleged illegal conspiracy"); *In re Warfarin Sodium Antitrust Litig.*, 214 F.3d 395, 401 (3d Cir. 2000) ("Coumadin purchasers were the target of DuPont's antitrust violation. Regardless of the existence of the various links of middlemen, if there were no ultimate consumer of Coumadin, prices charged for the drug by DuPont to distributors, pharmacies, etc., would be irrelevant... It is difficult to imagine a more formidable demonstration of antitrust injury.")

115 *See* Chapter VI, Section I.1.(B), (discussing the different approaches that exist within states regarding remoteness and which potential plaintiffs have standing to sue).

B. *Pleading Standards*

1227. In addition to pleading the basis for antitrust standing, a private plaintiff seeking relief under federal antitrust laws must also file a complaint that contains the following three basic requirements.

No.	Pleading Requirements under Fed. R. Civ. P. 8(a)
1	A "short and plain" statement of the grounds for the court's jurisdiction
2	A "short and plain" statement of the claim showing an entitlement to relief
3	A demand for relief, which may include requests for alternative forms of relief

1228. This "notice pleading" standard only requires that a complaint "contains enough detail to provide a defendant with fair notice of what the… claim is and the grounds upon which it rests."[116]

1229. Even though detailed factual allegations are not necessary at the pleading stage, the Supreme Court has held that a complaint must contain enough factual matter to state a plausible claim. For example, to state a claim under Section 1 of the Sherman Act, the complaint must contain "enough factual matter (taken as true) to suggest that an agreement was made."[117] The facts alleged do not need to show that such an agreement was *probable*, but they must have sufficient detail to suggest that such an agreement was at least *plausible*.[118] Conclusory allegations of an agreement along with evidence of parallel conduct do not suffice unless they are "placed in a context that raises a suggestion of a preceding agreement, not merely parallel conduct that could just as well be independent action."[119] The same plausibility standard also applies to other federal antitrust claims, like allegations of exclusionary conduct or monopolization in violation of Section 2 of the Sherman Act.[120]

6. Principal Vehicles for Raising Dispositive Issues Prior to Trial in Private Antitrust Actions

1230. In US federal courts, there are two principal types of dispositive motions that defendants can make to resolve antitrust litigation short of trial: (A) motions to dismiss, and (B) motions for summary judgment.

A. *Motions to Dismiss*

1231. Upon receipt of a complaint, a defendant has an opportunity to file a motion to dismiss the complaint before filing an answer or other responsive pleading.[121] Defendants may move to dismiss on a variety of grounds, including lack of

---

116 *Silverstrand Invs. v. AMAG Pharms., Inc.*, 707 F.3d 95, 101 (1st Cir. 2013) (internal quotation marks omitted).

117 *Bell Atlantic Corp. v. Twombly*, 550 US 544, 1965 (2007).

118 *Id.*

119 *Id.* 1965–66.

120 *See, e.g., Walgreen Co. v. AstraZeneca Pharms. LP*, 534 F. Supp. 2d 146, 152–53 (D.D.C. 2008) (granting a motion to dismiss where plaintiffs did not plead facts that support a reasonable inference that AstraZeneca engaged in exclusionary conduct prohibited by § 2 of the Sherman Act).

121 *See, generally* Fed. R. Civ. P. 26(b).

subject matter or personal jurisdiction, improper venue, insufficient process or service of process, or the failure to either state a claim upon which relief can be granted or to join a necessary party.[122] A motion to dismiss is intended to shortcut prolonged litigation – and especially protracted discovery – when a complaint is on its face defective or legally deficient. As such, the motion to dismiss is an important safeguard against frivolous or non-meritorious lawsuits that raise no right to relief under the law as pleaded.

1232. When considering a motion to dismiss, a court will generally "accept as true the factual allegations in the Complaint and draw all reasonable inferences in [the] plaintiff's favor."[123] The relevant question for a motion to dismiss is not whether there is sufficient evidence to support the allegations. Instead, the relevant question is whether the allegations in the complaint, if later substantiated with evidence, would support a right to relief under the antitrust laws.

1233. A motion to dismiss is an appropriate vehicle to challenge allegations that do not meet the necessary requirements under the antitrust laws. Courts may grant a motion to dismiss, for example, for lack of antitrust standing or antitrust injury.[124] A court may similarly grant a motion to dismiss for claims that do not satisfy other statutory requirements.[125]

1234. When a district court grants a motion to dismiss, "the decision to grant leave to amend is within the sound discretion of the trial court."[126] While the federal rules require that a "court should freely give leave [to amend] when justice so requires,"[127] "a court may properly deny leave to amend, if an amendment would be futile."[128] That said, courts often do permit the plaintiffs to amend their complaint and such amendment may either address the deficiencies noted in the opinion and avoid a second motion to dismiss or not, in which case the defendants would renew their motion to have the case dismissed.

---

122 *Id.* Federal Rule of Civil Procedure 19 defines required parties as persons subject to service of process and whose joinder will not deprive the court of subject matter jurisdiction if: (A) in that person's absence, the court cannot accord complete relief among existing parties, or (B) that person claims an interest relating to the subject of the action and is so situated that disposing of the action in the person's absence may: (i) as a practical matter impair or impede the person's ability to protect the interest, or (ii) leave an existing party subject to a substantial risk of incurring double, multiple, or otherwise inconsistent obligations because of the interest. Fed. R. Civ. P. 19(1).

123 *Warren Gen. Hosp. v. Amgen Inc.*, 643 F.3d 77, 79–80 (3d Cir. 2011).

124 *See, e.g., id.* (affirming dismissal for lack of antitrust standing); *Ethypharm S.A. France v. Abbott Lab'ys*, 707 F.3d 223, 237 (3d Cir. 2013) (vacating and remanding with instructions to dismiss for lack of antitrust standing); *SigmaPharm, Inc. v. Mut. Pharm. Co.*, 772 F. Supp. 2d 660, 676 (E.D. Pa. 2011) (dismissing for lack of antitrust standing); *But see Value Drug Co. v. Takeda Pharms., U.S.A., Inc.*, No. CV 21-3500, 2022 WL 952896, *8 (E.D. Pa. Mar. 30, 2022) (refusing to dismiss on antitrust standing grounds); *In re Sensipar (Cinacalcet Hydrochloride Tablets) Antitrust Litig.*, No. 2895, 2022 WL 736250, *16 (D. Del. Mar. 11, 2022) (same).

125 *See, e.g., Biocad JSC v. F. Hoffmann-La Roche Ltd.*, 942 F.3d 88, 91–92 (2d Cir. 2019) (upholding dismissal where claims were barred under the Foreign Trade Antitrust Improvements Act); *LifeWatch Servs., Inc. v. Highmark, Inc.*, 509 F. Supp. 3d 356, 368 (E.D. Pa. 2020) (dismissing claims because defendant was immune from federal antitrust liability under the McCarran-Ferguson Act).

126 *In re Bystolic Antitrust Litig.*, 583 F. Supp. 3d 455, 496 (S.D.N.Y. 2022) (citing *Bay Harbour Mgmt., LLC v. Carothers*, 474 F. Supp. 2d 501, 502 (S.D.N.Y. 2007)).

127 Fed. R. Civ. P. 15(a)(2).

128 *In re Zinc Antitrust Litig.*, 155 F. Supp. 3d 337, 384 (S.D.N.Y., 2016).

B. *Motions for Summary Judgment*

1235. A motion for summary judgment is appropriate where "there is no genuine dispute as to any material fact and the movant is entitled to judgment as a matter of law."[129] A party may "file a motion for summary judgment at any time until 30 days after the close of all discovery."[130]

1236. To survive a motion for summary judgment, a plaintiffs must establish that there is a "genuine issue of material fact" as to whether the defendant(s) violated the antitrust laws in a manner that caused the plaintiff "to suffer a cognizable injury."[131] For allegations of conspiracy in particular, a plaintiff "must present evidence 'that tends to exclude the possibility' that the alleged conspirators acted independently."[132] Where the "factual context renders respondents' claims implausible – if the claim is one that simply makes no economic sense – respondents must come forward with more persuasive evidence to support their claim than would otherwise be necessary."[133]

1237. Summary judgment is viewed as "an essential tool in the area of antitrust law because it helps avoid wasteful and lengthy litigation that may have a chilling effect on procompetitive market forces."[134] When considering a motion for summary judgment, the court must "draw all inferences and resolve all ambiguities in favor of the non-moving party[.]"[135]

7. Discovery in Federal Court

1238. Once a complaint in federal court is answered, survives a motion to dismiss, or sometimes even while the motion to dismiss is pending, civil litigation proceeds to discovery. The discovery process allows parties to collect evidence in support of their claims or defenses in advance of trial. This process generally can be broken down separately into fact and expert discovery.

A. *Fact Discovery*

1239. The discovery process generally begins with a conference between the parties in which the parties are expected to attempt in good faith to agree upon a discovery plan.[136] In general, a party to civil litigation "may obtain discovery regarding any nonprivileged matter that is relevant to any party's claim or defense and proportional to the needs of the case[.]"[137]

---

129 Fed. R. Civ. P. 56(a).

130 Fed. R. Civ. P. 56(b).

131 *Matsushita Elec. Indus. Co. v. Zenith Radio Corp.*, 475 U.S. 574, 585–87 (1986).

132 *Id.* 588 (quoting *First Nat. Bank of Ariz. V. Cities Serv. Co.*, 391 U.S. 253, 280 (1968)).

133 *Id.* 587.

134 *Geneva Pharms. Tech. Corp. v. Barr Labs. Inc.*, 386 F.3d 485, 495 (2d Cir. 2004).

135 *Id.* Several courts have addressed motions for summary judgment in antitrust life sciences cases. *See, e.g., In re HIV Antitrust Litig.*, No. 19-CV-02573-EMC, 2023 WL 3088218, *42 (N.D. Cal. Feb. 17, 2023) (granting motion for summary judgment in part and denying it in part); *In re EpiPen (Epinephrine Injection, USP) Mktg., Sales Pracs. & Antitrust Litig.*, No. 17-MD-2785-DDC-TJJ, 2021 WL 2585065 (D. Kan. June 23, 2021) (same); *In re Loestrin 24 Fe Antitrust Litig.*, 433 F. Supp. 3d 274, 333 (D.R.I. 2019) (denying both plaintiffs' and defendants' motions for summary judgment); *In re Suboxone (Buprenorphine Hydrochloride & Naloxone) Antitrust Litig.*, 622 F. Supp. 3d 22, 89 (E.D. Pa. 2022) (denying defendant's motion for summary judgment).

136 *See generally* Fed. R. Civ. P. 26(f).

137 Fed. R. Civ. P. 26(b)(1).

1240. During fact discovery, a party may serve on any other party requests for documents, electronically stored information (including "including writings, drawings, graphs, charts, photographs, sound recordings, images, and other data or data compilations"), and other tangible things that are relevant to any claim or defense.[138] Beyond the discovery of existing documents and information, a party may seek written discovery (typically in the form of interrogatories) and deposition testimony from other parties.[139]

1241. While relevancy is the most basic limit for discovery between parties, a court generally has the discretion to impose limits on the number of depositions and interrogatories beyond those specified in the rules.[140] The Federal Rules of Civil Procedure also prescribe that the court "must limit the frequency or extent of discovery otherwise allowed" where it determines that either "the discovery sought is unreasonably cumulative or duplicative, or can be obtained from some other source that is more convenient, less burdensome, or less expensive" or "the party seeking discovery has had ample opportunity to obtain the information by discovery in the action[.]"[141]

1242. To the extent non-parties may also have relevant information, a party also may request documents and electronically stored information by subpoena.[142] A party may also pursue written discovery and deposition testimony from non-parties by subpoena.[143] In pursuing discovery from non-parties, however, a party seeking discovery from non-parties has an obligation to avoid undue burden or expense.[144] This "undue burden" standard "requires district courts supervising discovery to be generally sensitive to the costs imposed on third parties."[145] For the most part, "courts have consistently held that 'non-party status' is a significant factor to be considered in determining whether the burden imposed by a subpoena is undue," because non-parties "have a different set of expectations' than parties."[146] A party seeking discovery from non-parties accordingly must show a need that is justified by the associated burden; it is not sufficient that the information sought is merely relevant to the litigation or that it may be easier to obtain discovery from the non-party than from an uncooperative party.[147]

B. *Expert Discovery*

1243. Beyond fact discovery, expert discovery is often of paramount importance in antitrust cases. As an initial matter, each party is typically required to identify any witness that it may use to present expert testimony at trial.[148] The timing for

---

138 Fed. R. Civ. P. 34.

139 *See generally* Fed. R. Civ. P. 30.

140 Fed. R. Civ. P. 26(b)(2)(A).

141 Fed. R. Civ. P. 26(b)(2)(C), (i)-(ii).

142 *See generally* Fed. R. Civ. P. 45.

143 *See generally id.*

144 Fed. R. Civ. P. 45(d)(1).

145 *Watts v. SEC*, 482 F.3d 501, 509 (D.C. Cir. 2007) (Kavanaugh, J.).

146 *Rossman v. EN Eng'g, LLC*, 467 F. Supp. 3d 586, 590 (N.D. Ill. 2020).

147 *See id.* 591–92 ("The legitimacy of the subpoena to a non-party is determined by far more than an examination of the relevancy of the materials sought or the fact that it may be simpler for the subpoenaing party to insist on production from a non-party rather than taking reasonable steps to require the non-cooperative party to comply with its basic discovery obligations.").

148 Fed. R. Civ. P. 26(a)(2).

such disclosures can vary depending on the existing discovery schedule and other court orders,[149] but these disclosures are intended to allow parties sufficient notice to conduct discovery into the expert's expected testimony.

1244. A witness may testify as an expert "by knowledge, skill, experience, training, or education" if "the expert's scientific, technical, or other specialized knowledge will help the trier of fact to understand the evidence or to determine a fact in issue" so long as the testimony is based on "sufficient facts or data" and was deduced from "reliable principles and methods" that were "reliably applied" to the facts of the case.[150] The Supreme Court has described this rule as assigning district courts the gatekeeping task of "ensuring that an expert's testimony both rests on a reliable foundation and is relevant to the task at hand."[151]

1245. To assess reliability, the Supreme Court has looked to factors such as whether expert's theory or technique is viewed as "generally accepted" in the scientific community, has been subjected to peer review and publication, can be or has been tested, and has an acceptable known or potential error rate.[152] Beyond reliability, the goal is to ensure a "fit" between the expert testimony and the issues of the case.[153] Courts may, for example, exclude expert testimony in an antitrust case where the expert's methodology "does not distinguish between unlawful and lawful explanations" of the evidence.[154]

1246. In life sciences and pharmaceutical sector cases, parties often will seek expert testimony from economists,[155] industry experts,[156] physicians[157] and, sometimes, patent or regulatory law.[158] Economic experts, for example, may be critical for issues of class certification, market definition, harm to competition, and damages. Industry experts and physicians may also be critical in helping judges or juries resolve questions about market definition; for example, a doctor might testify to market definition questions such as whether one drug is interchangeable with another. In each case, however, parties must demonstrate that the proposed expert analysis is based on sufficient evidence and is the product of reliable principles and methods that are reliably applied and an appropriate fit to the case.[159] Testimony

---

149 Fed. R. Civ. P. 26(a)(2)(D).

150 Fed. R. Evid. 702.

151 *Daubert v. Merrell Dow Pharms., Inc.*, 509 U.S. 579, 597 (1993).

152 *Id.* 593–95.

153 *Id.* 591.

154 *In re Pharm. Benefit Managers Antitrust Litig.*, No. 06-1782, 2017 WL 275398, *18 (E.D. Pa. Jan. 18, 2017).

155 *See, e.g., In re Namenda Direct Purchaser Antitrust Litig.*, 331 F. Supp. 3d 152, 172–75 (S.D.N.Y. 2018) (denying motion to exclude expert testimony from professor of antitrust economics).

156 *See, e.g., In re Neurontin Mktg. and Sales Pracs. Litig.*, 712 F.3d 21, 29–31, 41–45 (1st Cir. 2013) (upholding district court decision to permit expert testimony from a professor at the Harvard School of Public Health presenting analysis to determine whether marketing had a causal effect on prescribing behaviors).

157 *See, e.g., Daubert*, 509 U.S. 583 (evaluating the proposed testimony of a physician and epidemiologist as a well-credentialed expert on the risks from exposure to various chemical substances).

158 *See, e.g., PharmacyChecker.com v. Nat'l Ass'n of Boards of Pharmacy*, No. 19-CV-7577 (KMK), 2023 WL 2973038, *19 (S.D.N.Y. Mar. 28, 2023).

159 *See, e.g., In re Blood Reagents Antitrust Litig.*, 783 F.3d 183, 187–88 (3d Cir. 2015) (holding that antitrust impact analyses and damages models prepared by economic experts must be evaluated for reliability at the class certification stage when offered in support of class certification); *Messner v. Northshore Univ. Health Sys.*, 669 F.3d 802, 812 (7th Cir. 2012) (same).

from even well-qualified experts may be excluded where unduly speculative.[160] Where expert testimony does not meet the required standards, a party may file a so-called *Daubert* challenge to exclude part or all of the expert testimony.[161] When a *Daubert* challenge is filed, the burden is on the proponent of the expert testimony to establish its admissibility by a preponderance of proof.[162]

8. Class Certification

1247. Class certification can be a major fork in the road for any private action that seeks to proceed to a class action trial. If a private action is certified, the potential damages become much more substantial. This dynamic can drive settlement behavior both before and after class certification.

A. *Standard of Review and Practice*

1248. Class certification proceedings require "findings by the court" under a preponderance of the evidence standard and "not merely a 'threshold showing' by a party, that each requirement of Rule 23 is met."[163] In making its findings, "the court must resolve all factual or legal disputes relevant to class certification, even if they overlap with the merits – including disputes touching on elements of the cause of action."[164] In addition, "the court's obligation to consider all relevant evidence and arguments extends to expert testimony, whether offered by a party seeking class certification or by a party opposing it."[165]

1249. Because of the significance of class certification, an evidentiary hearing is often necessary for a district court to fully weigh the available evidence. Courts have held a "district judge may not duck hard questions by observing that each side has some support, or that considerations relevant to class certification also may

---

160 *See, e.g., In re Namenda Direct Purchaser Antitrust Litig.*, 331 F. Supp. 3d 169–72 (excluding industry expert with "30 years in the pharmaceutical industry" whose "credentials certainly qualify her to offer an opinion" where the testimony was not based on sufficient evidence or data); *Aya Healthcare Servs., Inc. v. AMN Healthcare, Inc.*, 613 F. Supp. 3d 1308, 1323 (S.D. Cal. 2020) (excluding expert's opinions even when she was "qualified to testify as a healthcare staffing industry expert" because they were inadmissible).

161 *See, e.g., In re Nexium (Esomeprazole) Antitrust Litig.*, 842 F.3d 34, 52 (1st Cir. 2016) (upholding district court exclusion of an event study that purported to use econometric analysis of stock market data to estimate an objective entry date without a reverse payment that did not "fit the conclusions for which it was offered"); *In re Opana ER Antitrust Litig.*, No. 14 C 10150, 2021 WL 2291067, *29 (N.D. Ill. June 4, 2021) (granting and denying various *Daubert* motions files by plaintiffs and defendants); *In re Loestrin 24 Fe Antitrust Litig.*, 433 F. Supp. 3d 274, 333 (D.R.I. 2019) (same). Courts will deny *Daubert* motions when experts' opinions are reliable, relevant, and helpful to the jury. *See, e.g., In re Androgel Antitrust Litig. (No. II)*, No. 1:09-CV-955-TWT, 2018 WL 2984873, *7 (N.D. Ga. June 14, 2018) (denying defendants' *Daubert* motions); *In re Blood Reagents Antitrust Litig.*, No. 09-MD-2081, 2017 WL 3096168, *12 (E.D. Pa. July 19, 2017) (denying motion to exclude plaintiffs' expert); *In re Wellbutrin XL Antitrust Litig.*, 133 F. Supp. 3d 734, 766 (E.D. Pa. 2015) (same).

162 *See Daubert*, 509 U.S. 592 n. 10. In the US, preponderance of proof means that the court, before admitting evidence, finds that it is "more likely than not" admissible. *See Bourjaily v. U.S.*, 483 U.S. 171, 175 (1987).

163 *In re Hydrogen Peroxide Antitrust Litig.*, 552 F.3d 305, 307 (3d Cir. 2008). Federal Rule of Civil Procedure 23 provides four prerequisites for class certification, (1) a class "so numerous that joinder of all members is impracticable", (2) "questions of law or fact common to the class", (3) "claims or defenses of the representative parties [that] are typical" of the class's claims or defenses, (4) "representative parties [who] will fairly and adequately protect the interests of the class. Fed. R. Civ. P. 23(a). *See also* Chapter VI, Section I.8.B.

164 *Id.*

165 *Id.*

affect the decision on the merits."[166] To the contrary, "[t]ough questions must be faced and squarely decided, if necessary by holding evidentiary hearings and choosing between competing perspectives."[167]

1250. Courts have traditionally bifurcated discovery into separate class certification and merits phases on the theory that narrow class discovery will preserve party resources until and unless a class is certified. In practice, however, the line is often blurred as the proposed class representatives seek – and courts allow – broad class discovery into class certification requirements that overlaps with questions on the merits.[168] Expert testimony can be particularly important at the class certification stage, as regressions often are used to show impact and damages and often come up with a common overcharge. As a result, *Daubert* challenges can be effective in defeating class certification where a plaintiff is relying on expert testimony to show common impact or class certification requirements.[169]

1251. When approaching proposed class definitions, courts generally require that the theory of liability be "limited to the injury caused by the defendants," the class be "definite," and the damages calculations be "limited to injured parties."[170] Plaintiffs are expected to adopt a class definition that "[i]deally… includes no uninjured parties and excludes no injured parties."[171] At the same time, courts have described the task of ensuring that a class is neither over- nor under-inclusive as "more of an art than a science."[172] Because in many cases "it is simply not possible to entirely separate the injured from the uninjured at the class certification stage," a district court may certify a proposed class that "includes… a *de minimis* number of uninjured parties" so long as "it is established that… a mechanism [to separate out the injured and uninjured class members] *can* be identified" at a later stage.[173]

B. *Class Certification Requirements*

1252. Rule 23 of the Federal Rules of Civil Procedure "establishes the legal roadmap courts must follow when determining whether class certification is appropriate."[174] As a threshold matter, the following four factors must each be satisfied:

---

166 *West v. Prudential Secs., Inc.*, 282 F.3d 935, 938 (7th Cir. 2002); *accord Valley Drug Co. v. Geneva Pharms., Inc.*, 350 F.3d 1181, 1188 n.15 (11th Cir. 2003) ("Although the trial court should not determine the merits of the plaintiffs' claim at the class certification stage, the trial court can and should consider the merits of the case to the degree necessary to determine whether the requirements of Rule 23 will be satisfied.").

167 *West,* 282 F.3d 938.

168 FJC, Complex Litig., *supra* n. 70, Chapter VI, § 21.14 ("Courts have recognized that information about the nature of the claims on the merits and the proof that they require is important to deciding certification. Arbitrary insistence on the merits/class discovery distinction sometimes thwarts the informed judicial assessment that current class certification practice emphasizes.").

169 *See, e.g., Behrend*, 569 U.S. 34 (holding that a district court improperly certified a class where the plaintiffs' "model falls far short of establishing that damages are capable of measurement on a class-wide basis"); *In re Blood Reagents Antitrust Litig.*, 783 F.3d 187–88 (holding *Daubert* inquiry necessary where defendant challenged the reliability of plaintiffs' expert's methodologies and the sufficiency of his testimony to satisfy Rule 23).

170 *In re Nexium Antitrust Litig.*, 777 F.3d 9, 18–19 (1st Cir. 2015).

171 *Id.* 22.

172 *Messner*, 669 F.3d 825.

173 *In re Nexium Antitrust Litig.*, 777 F.3d 22, 25, 32 (emphasis in original).

174 *Valley Drug Co.*, 350 F.3d 1187.

No.	Class Certification Prerequisites under Fed. R. Civ. P. 23(a)
1	The class is "so numerous that joinder of all members is impracticable" ("numerosity")
2	Common "questions of law or fact" apply to the class ("commonality")
3	The claims or defenses of class representatives are typical of those of the class ("typicality")
4	Class representatives "will fairly and adequately" protect class interests ("adequacy of representation")

1253. *Numerosity.* In general, when determining whether a class is "so numerous that joinder of all members is impracticable,"[175] the "relevant precedent makes significant distinctions between classes containing more than twenty class members and those containing twenty or fewer."[176] While courts have been reluctant to "specify a 'floor' at which a putative class will fail to satisfy the numerosity requirement," the number of class members can be a "starting point" for the analysis.[177] Other relevant factors considered by district courts include: "(1) judicial economy, (2) geographic dispersion, (3) financial resources of class members, (4) the claimants' ability to institute individual suits, and (5) requests for injunctive relief that could affect future class members."[178] A finding of numerosity must be based on evidence and not speculation; a district court cannot just assume that there are a large number of class members.[179] Numerosity may be a particular challenge in life sciences cases where there are not many buyers at various levels of the distribution chain (e.g., national wholesalers) and where that limited set of buyers purchase large volumes, such that individual suits are more feasible.[180] In addition, numerosity must be met for every proposed class and subclass, which can raise issues with narrowly defined classes. Note that even if a class is denied, individual plaintiffs can still pursue antitrust claims against the defendants.

1254. *Commonality.* To show that "there are questions of law or fact common to the class,"[181] a plaintiff must do more than produce a complaint reciting a list of common questions.[182] Commonality requires a plaintiff to demonstrate that a class action proceeding could find common *answers* to those common questions of law or fact.[183]

---

175 Fed. R. Civ. P. 23(a)(1).

176 *King Drug Co. of Florence, Inc. v. Cephalon, Inc.*, 309 F.R.D. 195, 204 (E.D. Pa. 2015).

177 *In re Modafinil Antitrust Litig.*, 837 F.3d 238, 251 (3d Cir. 2016).

178 *In re Wellbutrin XL Antitrust Litig.*, No. 08-2431, 2011 WL 3563385, *3 (E.D. Pa. Aug. 11, 2011).

179 *Marcus v. BMW of N. Am., LLC*, 687 F.3d 583, 598 (3d Cir. 2012).

180 *See In re Modafinil Antitrust Litig.*, 837 F.3d 238, 258 (3d Cir. 2016) (reversing district court decision certifying class on numerosity grounds); *In re Androgel Antitrust Litig.*, No. 1:09-CV-956-TWT, 2018 WL 3424612, *2 (N.D. Ga. July 16, 2018) (denying proposed class of 33 members on numerosity grounds); *But see In re Opana ER Antitrust Litig.*, No. 14 C 10150, 2021 WL 3627733, *5 (N.D. Ill. June 4, 2021) (certifying class with only 36 members); *In re Intuniv Antitrust Litig.*, No. 1:16-CV-12653-ADB, 2019 WL 4645502, *5 (D. Mass. Sept. 24, 2019) (certifying class with 48 members and collecting cases where courts have certified classes with fewer members).

181 Fed. R. Civ. P. 23(a)(2).

182 *See Wal-Mart Stores, Inc. v. Dukes*, 564 U.S. 338, 349–50 (2011) ("Reciting these questions is not sufficient to obtain class certification… Rule 23 does not set forth a mere pleading standard.").

183 *See id.* 350 (noting a common question "must be of such a nature that it is capable of class-wide resolution – which means that determination of its truth or falsity will resolve an issue that is central to the validity of each one of the claims in one stroke").

At the same time, commonality does not require that all questions of law or fact be identical.[184] For example, some courts have found that variations in state antitrust laws may not be enough to find against a proposed nationwide class that includes state law claims.[185]

1255. *Typicality.* When evaluating whether "the claims or defenses of the representative parties are typical of the claims or defenses of the class,"[186] a district court "must examine 'whether the named plaintiffs' claims are typical, in common-sense terms, of the class, thus suggesting that the incentives of the plaintiffs are aligned with those of the class."[187] Some courts have described the analysis as looking for whether the claims of the class representative are "markedly different" from those of other class members.[188] Typicality does not require that the claims of the class representatives are identical to those of all class members.[189] However, where groups of plaintiffs with significantly different claims are impacted by the same alleged conduct (such as third-party payers and consumers alleging anti-competitive overcharges on purchases of the same pharmaceutical product), the class representatives should "include members from each group."[190]

1256. *Adequacy of Representation.* In determining whether "the representative parties will fairly and adequately protect the interests of the class,"[191] a district court is responsible for "uncover[ing] conflicts of interest between named parties and the class they seek to represent."[192] In particular, a conflict of interest is likely to be found "where the economic interests and objectives of the named representatives differ significantly from the economic interests and objectives of unnamed class members."[193] "If substantial conflicts of interest are determined to exist among a class, class certification is inappropriate."[194] For example, "[a] fundamental conflict exists where some party members claim to have been harmed by the same conduct that benefitted other members of the class."[195] Beyond conflicts of interest, courts evaluating adequacy may evaluate "whether the [class] representatives will adequately prosecute the action."[196]

1257. In addition to each of the four prerequisites of Rule 23(a), class claims must satisfy at least one of the following alternative requirements for class certification.

---

184 *In re Warfarin Sodium Antitrust Litig.*, 391 F.3d 530–31.

185 *See, e.g., id.* 530 ("We agree with the District Court that the fact that there may be variations in the rights and remedies available to injured class members under the various laws of the fifty states in this matter does not defeat commonality and predominance.").

186 Fed. R. Civ. P. 23(a)(3).

187 *In re Niaspan Antitrust Litig.*, 397 F. Supp. 3d 668, 680 (E.D. Pa. 2019) (quoting *In re Blood Reagents Antitrust Litig.*, No. 09-2081, 2015 WL 6123211, *26 (E.D. Pa. Oct. 19, 2015)).

188 *Marcus*, 687 F.3d 598.

189 *In re Warfarin Sodium Antitrust Litig.*, 391 F.3d 531–32.

190 *Id.* 532.

191 Fed. R. Civ. P. 23(a)(4).

192 *Amchem Prods.*, 521 U.S. 625.

193 *Valley Drug Co.*, 350 F.3d 1190.

194 *Id.* 1189.

195 *Id.*

196 *Id.* (quoting *In re HealthSouth Corp. Secs. Litig.*, 213 F.R.D. 447, 460–461 (N.D. Ala. 2003)). *But see Phillips v. Asset Acceptance, LLC*, 736 F.3d 1076 (7th Cir. 2013) ("To question her adequacy is to be unrealistic about the role of the class representative in a class action suit. The role is nominal.").

No.	Alternative Class Certification Requirements under Fed. R. Civ. P. 23(b)
1	Separate actions would risk "inconsistent" or "dispositive" adjudications impairing the claims, interests, or rights of absent class members
2	Class members only seek declaratory or injunctive relief and not individual monetary damages
3	Questions of law or fact common to class members "predominate" over questions affecting individual class members ("predominance") *and* class treatment is "superior to other available methods for fairly and efficiently adjudicating the controversy ("superiority")

1258. Antitrust class actions are typically certified under the last of these alternative requirements – predominance and superiority. Courts have also read an implied ascertainability standard into Rule 23. These factors are discussed below.

1259. *Predominance.* To show that "questions of law or fact common to class members predominate over any questions affecting only individual members,"[197] plaintiffs must show that antitrust impact and injury is capable of "common proof " at trial.[198] By contrast, where it is not possible to determine impact or injury without conducting an individualized inquiry, predominance is not established.[199] For example, where "a market [is] characterized by individual negotiations and a discounted-brand competition strategy," individual issues may instead predominate over common issue and class certification would be unwarranted.[200] A district court must assess the implications of such evidence at the class certification stage even though it also "touches on the merits" of the case.[201] It is important, however, not to confuse questions of injury (or *liability*) with damages. "[W]hen adjudication of questions of liability common to the class will achieve economies of time and expense, the predominance standard is generally satisfied even if damages are not provable in the aggregate."[202] Courts have declined to certify classes in several pharmaceutical antitrust cases on predominance grounds.[203]

1260. *Superiority.* When assessing whether "a class action is superior to other available methods for fairly and efficiently adjudicating the controversy,"[204] the "superiority

---

197 Fed. R. Civ. P. 23(b)(3).

198 *In re Lamictal Direct Purchaser Antitrust Litig.*, 957 F.3d 184, 192–94 (3d Cir. 2020).

199 *Id.*

200 *Id.* 192.

201 *Id.* 194.

202 *Behrend*, 569 U.S. 41; *accord Smilow v. Sw. Bell Mobile Sys., Inc.*, 323 F.3d 32, 40 (1st Cir. 2003) ("Where... common questions predominate regarding liability, then courts generally find the predominance requirement to be satisfied even if individual damages issues remain.").

203 *See, e.g., In re: Lamictal Direct Purchaser Antitrust Litig.*, No. CV 12-995, 2021 WL 2349828, *21 (D.N.J. June 7, 2021); *In re Niaspan Antitrust Litig.*, 464 F. Supp. 3d 678, 715 (E.D. Pa. 2020); *In re Asacol Antitrust Litig.*, 907 F.3d 42, 53 (1st Cir. 2018) (reversing certification of class on predominance grounds); *But see In re Intuniv Antitrust Litig.*, No. 1:16-CV-12653-ADB, 2019 WL 4645502, *11 (D. Mass. Sept. 24, 2019) (certifying class); *In re Namenda Indirect Purchaser Antitrust Litig.*, 338 F.R.D. 527, 576 (S.D.N.Y. 2021) (same); *In re Opana ER Antitrust Litig.*, No. 14 C 10150, 2021 WL 3627733, *5 (N.D. Ill. June 4, 2021) (same).

204 Fed. R. Civ. P. 23(b)(3).

requirement 'asks the court to balance, in terms of fairness and efficiency, the merits of a class action against those of alternative available methods of adjudication.'"[205]

1261. *Ascertainability.* Courts also require that a class be sufficiently "definite," meaning that class membership is defined by objective criteria.[206] Classes that are defined based on subjective criteria, like a class member's state of mind, cannot be certified.[207]

1262. Failure to establish all four prerequisite factors under Rule 23(a) and at least one of the alternative requirements of Rule 23(b) precludes class certification.[208] At the same time, a class action does not need to proceed with just a single class that meets all of these criteria. Instead, "[w]hen appropriate, a class may be divided into subclasses that are each treated as a [separate] class" under the rules.[209] Subclasses may be appropriate for different groups of class members, to handle different state law claims, or where different class members seek different categories of relief (e.g., an injunction versus damages). At the same time, the inclusion of too many subclasses "may indicate that common questions do not predominate" and require the denial of class certification.[210] Similarly, the subdivision of the class raises the risk that sub-classes may not be certified if they do not each meet all class certification prerequisites and at least one of the alternative class certification requirements.

C. *Class Certification Appeals*

1263. Because of its significance to the proceedings and disposition of the case, a private party may petition the court for permission to appeal a district court's decision on class certification within 14 days after the order is entered.[211] This interlocutory appeal, if permitted, does not automatically stay proceedings, unless a stay is ordered by the district court or the appellate court.[212] On appeal, the propriety of class certification will be considered under an abuse of discretion standard.[213]

9. Trial

1264. After discovery has closed and a complaint has survived any motions for summary judgment, private antitrust actions proceed to trial. Recently, relatively few antitrust

---

205 *In re Warfarin Sodium Antitrust Litig.*, 391 F.3d 533–34 (quoting *In re Prudential Ins. Co. Am. Sales Litig.*, 148 F.3d 283, 316 (3d Cir. 1998).

206 *See In re Nexium Antitrust Litigation*, 777 F.3d 9, 19 (1st Cir. 2015) (discussing ascertainability requirement).

207 *See In re Copper Antitrust Litigation*, 196 F.R.D. 348, 352 (W.D. Wis. 2000) ("The proposed class definition[] must not depend on subjective criteria or the merits of the case or require extensive factual inquiry to determine who is a class member.").

208 *Valley Drug Co.*, 350 F.3d 1188.

209 Fed. R. Civ. P. 23(c)(5).

210 FJC, Complex Litig., *supra* n. 70, Chapter VI, § 21.23.

211 Fed. R. Civ. P. 23(f).

212 *Id.*

213 *See Valley Drug Co.*, 350 F.3d 1187 ("We review the district court's grant of class certification for an abuse of discretion"). Abuse of discretion is a standard employed by appellate courts to review lower court decisions. A court abuses its discretion when it decides based on an error of law or a clearly erroneous factual finding, or when it exercises discretion "to an end not justified by the evidence," making "a judgment that is clearly against the logic and effect of the facts as are found." *See Rabkin v. Oregon Health Scis. Univ.*, 350 F.3d 967, 977 (9th Cir. 2003) (quotations and citations omitted).

cases in the pharmaceutical industry have proceeded to trial.[214] One notable exception is *In re Opana ER Antitrust Litigation*, a reverse-payment case in which a jury held that although the defendant possessed market power in the relevant market and entered into a reverse-payment patent settlement, that settlement was not anticompetitive under the rule of reason.[215]

1265. To prepare for trial, it is common for a district court to hold one or more status conferences or pretrial conferences to hear pretrial motions, formulate a trial plan, and ensure the parties are ready for trial. Of note, not all cases that are consolidated or coordinated for discovery proceed to trial together. Instead, the federal rules give a district court broad discretion to "order a separate trial of one or more separate issues, claims, crossclaims, counterclaims, or third-party claims" whether "[f]or convenience, to avoid prejudice, or to expedite and economize" the trial process.[216] Similarly, cases consolidated for discovery purposes by the MDL Panel must generally be returned to their original district court for trial.[217]

1266. Once the parties are ready for trial, defendants in private antitrust actions for damages in the US are entitled to a trial by jury.[218] The jury will include between six and twelve jurors.[219] In general, "the verdict must be unanimous and must be returned by a jury of at least 6 members."[220] To guard against improper conflicts or bias, potential jurors often are asked to complete initial jury questionnaires as part of the jury selection process. The court, and sometimes the litigating parties' counsel, can directly question and vet jurors through a process called *voir dire*. Each party typically has broad discretion to make three peremptory challenges to strike potential jurors, but this discretion is subject to certain limits.[221]

1267. Throughout the trial process, certain key motions may be filed by the parties, including motions *in limine*, motions for judgment as a matter of law, motions for judgment notwithstanding the verdict, and motions for a new trial.

1268. *Motion in Limine.* A motion *in limine* is a procedural mechanism for excluding from the jury evidence that is irrelevant, unreliable, or unduly prejudicial. These

---

214 Three recent examples of trials in the pay-for-delay context are *In re HIV*, *In re Opana*, and *In re Nexium*. *See* Bonnie Eslinger, *Gilead, Teva defeat $3.6B HIV Drug Antitrust Case at Trial*, Law360 (June 30, 2023), *available at* https://www.law360.com/articles/1694505/gilead-teva-defeat-3-6b-hiv-drug-antitrust-case-at-trial; Brendan Pierson, *Endo prevails at trial over Opana purchasers' antitrust claims*, Reuters (July 5, 2022), *available at* https://www.reuters.com/legal/litigation/endo-prevails-trial-over-opana-purchasers-antitrust-claims-2022-07-01/; Brendan Pierson, *U.S. Court upholds AstraZeneca, Ranbaxy win in Nexium antitrust trial*, Reuters (Nov. 21, 2016), *available at* https://www.reuters.com/article/astrazeneca-nexium-appeal/u-s-court-upholds-astrazeneca-ranbaxy-win-in-nexium-antitrust-trial-idUSL1N1DM1W2.

215 *In re Opana ER Antitrust Litigation*, 14-cv-10150, MDL No. 2580, Dkt. 1038 (N.D. Ill. July 1, 2022).

216 Fed. R. Civ. P. 42(b).

217 *See In re Lexecon, Inc. v. Milberg Weiss Bershad Hynes & Lerach*, 523 U.S. 27 (1998) (describing the "straightforward language" of 28 U.S.C. § 1407(f) imposing a "responsibility to remand").

218 *See, e.g., Fleitmann v. Welsbach St. Lighting Co.*, 240 U.S. 27, 29 (1916) ("[W]e agree with the courts below that when a penalty of triple damages is sought to be inflicted, the statute should not be read as attempting to authorize liability to be enforced otherwise than through the verdict of a jury in a court of common law. On the contrary, it plainly provides the latter remedy, and it provides no other.").

219 Fed. R. Civ. P. 48(a).

220 *Id.* 48(b).

221 *See, e.g., SmithKline Beecham Corp. v. Abbott Labs.*, 740 F.3d 471 (9th Cir. 2014) (holding that equal protection principles prohibit discrimination based on sexual orientation in jury selection).

motions typically are argued before trial begins and outside of the presence of the jury. These motions can be important for setting the boundaries of arguments at trial. For example, motions *in limine* can be used to limit or exclude expert testimony that is not supported by sufficient evidence, not based on a reliable methodology, or not relevant to the issues that will be raised at trial.[222]

1269. *Motion for Judgment as a Matter of Law.* At any time before the case is submitted to the jury for deliberation, a party may move for judgment as a matter of law.[223] If the trial court agrees that "a reasonable jury would not have a legally sufficient evidentiary basis" to support any issue required for a party's claim or defense, the court may "grant a motion for judgment as a matter of law against the party on a claim or defense that, under the controlling law, can be maintained or defeated only with a favorable finding on that issue."[224] This motion can be a double-edged sword, as the court has the discretion to decide the issue against the moving party if so warranted. The court also remains free to submit the issue to the jury despite the motion for judgment as a matter of law. If the court does not grant the motion, "the court is considered to have submitted the action to the jury subject to the court's later deciding the legal questions raised by the motion."[225] In this manner, filing a motion for judgment as a matter of law can be critical to parties seeking to preserve the right to later submit a motion for judgment notwithstanding the verdict.[226]

1270. *Motion for Judgment Notwithstanding the Verdict.* Within 28 days after the entry of a jury verdict, a party that previously filed a motion for judgment as a matter of law may renew that motion on the same grounds through a motion for judgment notwithstanding the verdict.[227] If this motion is granted, the court "should disregard any jury determination for which there is no legally sufficient evidentiary basis enabling a reasonable jury to make it. The court may then decide such issues as a matter of law and enter judgment if all other material issues have been decided by the jury on the basis of legally sufficient evidence, or by the court as a matter of law."[228] Therefore, a court granting a motion for judgment notwithstanding the verdict may rule on the case contrary to what the jury has determined.

---

[222] *In re Nexium (Esomeprazole) Antitrust Litig.*, 842 F.3d 54 (holding district court ruling to exclude an expert's testimony that relied only on his general experience and failed to cite "any methodology undergirding his opinions" was not an abuse of discretion); *In re Intuniv Antitrust Litig.*, No. 16-CV-12396-ADB, 2021 WL 10362709, *2 (D. Mass. Mar. 3, 2021) (ruling on 48 separate motions *in limine*); *United Food & Com. Workers Loc. 1776 & Participating Emps. Health & Welfare Fund v. Teikoku Pharma USA*, 296 F. Supp. 3d 1142, 1195 (N.D. Cal. 2017) (ruling on 13 separate motions *in limine*); *AngioDynamics, Inc. v. C.R. Bard, Inc.*, No. 117CV598BKSCFH, 2022 WL 2643583, *1 (N.D.N.Y. July 8, 2022) (addressing both parties' motions *in limine*).

[223] Fed. R. Civ. P. 50(a)(2).

[224] *Id.* 50(a)(1), (B).

[225] *Id.* 50(b).

[226] *See, e.g.*, *González-Bermúdez v. Abbott Labs. PR Inc.*, 990 F.3d 37, 45 (1st Cir. 2021) ("A party certainly must move for judgment as a matter of law under Rule 50(a) at the close of the evidence in order to preserve fully the ability to press a renewed motion for judgment as a matter of law under Rule 50(b) after the verdict."), *aff'd*, 142 S. Ct. 389 (2021).

[227] Fed. R. Civ. P. 50(b).

[228] *Id.* 50, advisory committee's note to 1991 amendment.

1271. *Motion for a New Trial.* Within 28 days after the entry of a jury verdict, a party may also enter a motion for a new trial.[229] Because the rules provide an independent basis for a new trial "for any reason for which a new trial has heretofore been granted in an action at law in federal court,"[230] a party does not need to file a motion for judgment as a matter of law to preserve the right to seek a new trial after a jury verdict.

10. Damages

A. *Availability and Calculation of Damages*

1272. Antitrust damages are intended to place the injured party – whether a single plaintiff or a class of similarly situated persons or entities – in or as near as possible to the position they would have occupied *but for* the wrongful conduct. Although antitrust damages are not intended to punish the wrongdoer, automatic trebling of damages awards, the shifting of attorney's fees and court costs, and joint and several liability could be considered punitive. In addition, antitrust damages, standing alone, are not intended to deter a defendant's wrongful conduct in the future or act as a deterrent to other market participants broadly. Rather, the aim of antitrust damage awards is to compensate the injured party and place that party in the position it otherwise would have occupied[231] absent the unlawful conduct.

1273. There is no one method for calculating antitrust damages. Wide variation in the approach to calculating antitrust damages is not merely accepted but expected. The calculation or measure of antitrust damages should be based on a theory of damages that fits the claim. For example, if the claim is that the defendants, branded and generic pharmaceutical manufacturers, conspired to raise prices by suppressing or delaying generic competition for the branded drug product, then the damages may be the overcharges paid by customers for the branded drug. By way of contrast, if the damage theory is that the defendant engaged in exclusionary conduct that kept the plaintiff from the market, damages might be based on lost sales, or rather the lost net profits on the lost sales.[232]

1274. To recover damages, an antitrust plaintiff must show that the defendant violated the antitrust laws and that the violation caused the plaintiff's injury.[233] Stated differently, a private plaintiff must establish that an antitrust violation occurred (e.g., an unlawful agreement), that it suffered injury as a result of that violation (i.e., injury in fact or impact), and that it is the proper plaintiff (i.e., that it has standing) to sue for damages.[234] The plaintiff must also establish the amount of damages – or quantify its injury. A plaintiff may only recover damages from injuries that are the proximate result of the defendant's or defendants' conduct, but not for injuries that stem from other causes or that are indirect or remote.[235]

---

[229] *Id.* 50(b), 59.

[230] *Id.* 59(a)(A).

[231] American Bar Association, Model Jury Instructions in Civil Antitrust Cases, F-12 (2006).

[232] *Id.* F-13.

[233] *Id.* F-18.

[234] *Associated Gen. Contractors v. Cal. State Council of Carpenters*, 459 U.S. 519, 536 (1983).

[235] *Id.*

1275. While the damages themselves must be traceable to an injury caused by the defendants,[236] plaintiffs are afforded considerable latitude as to the proof of their damages once they have established a violation. In essence, the Supreme Court has expressed its reluctance to allow a defendant who violates the law to avoid damages exposure simply because it is difficult for the plaintiff to calculate the damages it has suffered with precision.[237]

1276. While the approach to calculating damages will vary according to the type of antitrust claim at issue in any particular case, the overarching objective is to conceive of a market absent the challenged conduct – the "but for" world – and to contrast that hypothesized market with the market as it exists. Stated differently, the plaintiff's expert would construct a model that subtracts the "but for" world price (which should have obtained absent the antitrust violation) from the actual world price based on the defendants' transactional sales data to ascertain its baseline (pre-trebling) damages claim. This figure, which can be presented as a percentage or a dollar value, represents the overcharge or the lost net profit attributable to the antitrust violation. For example, in "pay-for-delay" cases where plaintiffs allege that settlement agreements delayed generic entry, plaintiffs typically put forward a damages model that takes the effect of generic entry in the market and "backcasts" it into the past to determine what the effect on price and sales would have been if the generic had entered earlier.[238]

1277. In US pharmaceutical antitrust litigation, economists often rely on econometric and statistical tools, such as multiple regression analysis, in an effort to separate the effect of an alleged price-fixing conspiracy or other unknown conduct from other underlying market factors. These statistical tools are widely used in litigation and have gained acceptance with the courts.[239] In fact, litigants regularly use multiple regression analysis to address questions of impact, harm, and damages in private antitrust cases.[240]

1278. In multiple regression analysis, economists employ the parties' transaction data and seek to explain the movement of a dependent variable (usually the price of a product) using independent or explanatory variables. Economists may also use additional variables to attempt to control for additional market factors that could influence prices. The ultimate object of such an exercise is to identify and quantify the impact of the alleged unlawful conduct by comparing prices in a period free of the unlawful conduct (the so-called benchmark period) with the actual prices (in the alleged conspiracy or cartel period).

---

236 American Bar Association, *supra* n. 231, F-20.

237 American Bar Association, PROVING ANTITRUST DAMAGES: LEGAL AND ECONOMIC ISSUES, 87–89 (3d ed., 2018) (citing *Eastman Kodak Co. v. S. Photo Materials Co.*, 273 U.S. 359 (1927); *Story Parchment Co. v. Paterson Parchment Paper Co.*, 282 U.S. 555 (1931); and *Bigelow v. RKO Radio Pictures*, 327 U.S. 251 (1946)).

238 *See, e.g.*, *In re Glumetza Antitrust Litig.*, 336 F.R.D. 468, 479 (N.D. Cal. 2020) (discussing plaintiffs' expert's backcasting methodology).

239 Daniel Rubinfeld, *Reference Guide on Multiple Regression*, *in* REFERENCE MANUAL ON SCIENTIFIC EVIDENCE, (FJC, 3d ed., 2011).

240 Jonathan Baker and Daniel Rubinfeld, *Empirical Methods in Antitrust Litigation: Review and Critique*, 1 AMERICAN LAW AND ECONOMIC REVIEW, 181–184 (1999).

1279. The aim of this construct is to attempt to identify and isolate the effects of the anticompetitive conduct so that the impact can be measured.[241] In private antitrust litigation this typically is an area of vigorous disagreement and dispute. The focus of the dispute usually is on the assumptions and variables that both sides' experts use when developing their competing models of the "but for" world, whether the models fit the market facts, and whether a particular expert has cherry-picked variables to create an unwarranted and unsupported damages claim. If the model omits material factors, it will incorrectly assign the effects of those missed factors to the conspiracy yielding unreliable and inaccurate results about the effect of the alleged conduct on prices.

1280. Challenges to economic experts' opinion testimony on the issues of impact and damages, as well as the calculation of damages, are common given that the court plays a gatekeeper role to ensure that expert testimony is reliable.[242] A plaintiff often must rely on economic expert opinion testimony to establish impact on the plaintiff and, in class actions and the class of "persons" it seeks to represent. Economists seek to do this through econometric and statistical modelling. Expert opinions for plaintiffs often seek to establish impact and determine the amount of any overcharge (i.e., damages) through means common to the class such as a regression model. A successful challenge to such an opinion offers the tantalizing prospect of defeating the claim in its entirety, because, without a means of establishing impact and damages through common proof, the claim fails. However, as noted above, the threshold for the admissibility of expert opinion testimony is relatively low, since courts often view the issues raised as going to the weight to be given the expert's testimony – a jury question – and prefer to rely on vigorous cross-examination rather than risk reversal by excluding the expert witness altogether.[243] Thus, it is no easy task to mount a successful challenge to expert opinion testimony on class-wide impact and damages, or to otherwise challenge an expert's damages model prior to trial.

1281. Defendants also frequently challenge the availability of certain categories of damage claims. One area of dispute, primarily in reference to Section 1 claims, concerns whether a plaintiff may properly recover for so-called "umbrella damages" – damages based on purchases of a product from one of a defendant's competitors rather than the defendant or its co-conspirators. The theory for recovery rests on the argument that prices for that product would have been affected by the alleged conspiracy across the entire industry since the conduct would have raised prices to customers across the board. Under this theory, non-conspirators take the opportunity presented by the conspirators' supra-competitive pricing to raise their prices without necessarily joining the

---

241 American Bar Association, *supra* n. 237, Chapter VI, 89.

242 *Daubert*, 509 U.S. 579.

243 *In re Korean Ramen Antitrust Litig.*, 281 F. Supp. 3d 892, 931 (N.D. Cal., 2017) ("The inquiry into the admissibility of expert testimony is "a flexible one" where "[s]haky but admissible evidence is to be attacked by cross examination, contrary evidence, and attention to the burden of proof, not exclusion.") (quoting *Primiano v. Cook*, 598 F.3d 558, 564 (C.A.9 (Nev.), 2010)).

alleged cartel. Although the issue has not been resolved by a Supreme Court decision, most federal courts have rejected umbrella damages for Sherman Act Section 1 claims.[244] The issue has come up under state antitrust laws as well, where plaintiffs have argued that even if umbrella damages are not available under federal law, they should be recoverable under state antitrust law. Plaintiffs argue that the reluctance of federal courts to allow umbrella damages under the Sherman Act stems from the Supreme Court's prohibition on the recovery of damages by indirect purchasers – the *Illinois Brick* rule – on the grounds that permitting such damages would greatly complicate the damages phase of already protracted treble damages cases. Plaintiffs reason that since some states permit indirect purchasers to sue for and recover damages under state antitrust law, plaintiffs suing under state statutes should also be able to pursue umbrella damages. Plaintiffs sometimes buttress this argument by pointing to the absence of a harmonization provision (i.e., a provision stating that the state law should be interpreted consistently with the Sherman Act) in state antitrust statutes.

1282. Despite these arguments, most courts applying state antitrust laws have rejected efforts to pursue umbrella damages under state law. "In the absence of any state law authority endorsing umbrella damages claims," courts have found no reason that state laws would or should differ from federal law.[245] Yet there are cases that nonetheless find umbrella damages to be reasonable. In *County of San Mateo v. CSL Ltd.*,[246] for example, a federal magistrate judge determined that umbrella damages are available under California's Cartwright Act, which prohibits unfair trade practices.

B. *Availability of Treble Damages and Attorneys' Fee Awards*

1283. Section 4 of the Clayton Act permits the successful antitrust plaintiff to recover treble damages and attorneys' fees – "threefold the damages by him sustained, and the cost of suit, including a reasonable attorney's fee."[247] While there are provisions that provide for the de-trebling of damages awards in certain cases – such as participation in certain R&D joint ventures under the NCRPA[248] or the DOJ's amnesty program[249] – the double-sided hammer of potential treble damages plus attorneys' fees is intended to deter antitrust violations. The prospect of facing joint and several liability and the absence of a right to contribution by other defendants may add to the deterrent effect of treble damages.

---

244 *In re Processed Egg Prods. Antitrust Litig.*, 312 F.R.D. 124, 144–148 (E.D. Pa. 2015); *In re Skelaxin (Metaxalone) Antitrust Litig.*, No. 1:12-md-2343, 2014 WL 2002887, **7–11 (E.D. Tenn. May 15, 2014); *In re TFT-LCD (Flat Panel) Antitrust Litig.*, MDL No. 1827, 2012 WL 6708866, *6 (N.D. Cal. Dec. 26, 2012), *aff'd*, 637 F. App'x 981 (9th Cir. 2016); *In re Vitamins Antitrust Litig.*, Nos. MISC No. 99-197, 2001 WL 855463, *4 (D.D.C. July 2, 2001); *FTC v. Mylan Labs., Inc.*, 62 F. Supp. 2d 25, 38–40 (D.D.C. 1999).

245 *In re TFT-LCD (Flat Panel) Antitrust Litig.*, MDL No. 1827, 2012 WL 6708866, *7 (N.D. Cal. Dec. 26, 2012). *See also In re Processed Egg Prods.*, 312 F.R.D. 147–149 (denying indirect purchasers' claims for umbrella damages under the laws of 21 states); *Mylan Labs, Inc.*, 62 F. Supp. 2d 38–39, 42 (rejecting umbrella damage claims under the laws of 32 states).

246 No. 10-cv-05686-JSC, 2014 WL 4100602 (N.D. Cal. Aug. 20, 2014).

247 15 U.S.C. § 15.

248 15 U.S.C. §§ 4301–4306.

249 Known as the Antitrust Criminal Penalty Enforcement and Reform Act or ACPERA 15 U.S.C. § 1.

1284. Courts generally refrain from instructing juries on the mandatory trebling of antitrust damages.[250] Thus, agreement or evidence on the trebling of damages generally is inadmissible and could prompt a curative instruction since the jury's sole role is to determine whether the plaintiff was damaged in its business or property and, if so, how much it should recover as a result of the harm it suffered.

1285. The award of attorneys' fees pursuant to the Clayton Act, like the trebling of damages awards, is mandatory.[251] Moreover, "[c]ourts have consistently held that an antitrust plaintiff who receives a favorable verdict, even if that verdict awards only nominal damages, is entitled to seek attorney's fees."[252] "Although in almost all cases an award of compensatory damages will accompany an award of Section 4 attorneys' fees, the latter is not dependent on the former."[253]

1286. Attorneys' fee awards in antitrust cases thus usually turn on what constitutes a reasonable award. As far as determining what amounts to "reasonable," courts generally apply the lodestar method, which has been adjudged "the only reasonably objective basis for valuing an attorney's services."[254] Nonetheless, some courts, especially in cases with a common fund, calculate fees as a percentage of recovery.[255] The commonly used lodestar is the "initial estimate of a reasonable attorney's fee which is properly calculated by multiplying the number of hours expended on the litigation times a reasonable hourly rate.[256] As part of its assessment, the court may also consider the following factors: (1) the time and labor required, (2) the novelty and difficulty of the questions addressed, (3) the skill required, (4) the preclusion of other employment by the attorney owing to work on the case, (5) the attorney's customary fee, (6) whether the fee is fixed by agreement with the client, i.e., meaning the client paid the fee, or contingent, (7) time limitations imposed by the client or circumstances, (8) the amount involved and the results obtained, (9) the experience, reputation and ability of the attorneys, (10) the undesirability of, and challenges presented by, the case, (11) the nature and length of the professional relationship with the client, and (12) awards in similar cases.[257] In short, the district court has wide discretion to determine the fee award, and an appellate court may only overturn its decision if it finds that the award constituted an abuse of discretion.[258]

---

250 *See, e.g., HBE Leasing Corp. v. Frank*, 22 F.3d 41, 46 (2d Cir. 1994) (citing cases).

251 5 U.S.C. § 15.

252 *Gulfstream III Assoc., Inc. v. Gulfstream Aerospace Corp.*, 995 F.2d 414, 418 n.5 (3d Cir. 1993) (citing *U.S. Football League v. N.F.L.*, 887 F.2d 408, 411–12 (2d Cir. 1989), where the court awarded attorneys' fees after the jury awarded $1 in nominal damages).

253 *Id.* 419 (affirming the district court's award of attorneys' fees "even though the trebled verdict was entirely offset by the prior settlements…").

254 *Id.* 421.

255 *Sullivan v. DB Invs., Inc.*, 667 F.3d 273, 330 (3d Cir. 2011) (the percentage of recovery method is "generally favored in common fund cases because it allows courts to award fees from the fund in a manner that rewards counsel for success and penalizes it for failure") (internal quotation marks omitted); *see also Stop & Shop Supermarket Co. v. SmithKline Beecham Corp.*, No. CIV.A. 03-4578, 2005 WL 1213926, *8 (E.D. Pa. May 19, 2005).

256 *Gulfstream III Assoc.*, 995 F.2d 421.

257 *U.S. Football League*, 887 F.2d 408, 413–14 (citing *Johnson v. Georgia Highway Express, Inc.*, 488 F.2d 714, 717–19 (5th Cir. 1974)).

258 *Id.* 414–15.

1287. The Clayton Act also provides for an award of costs. Given the expense of expert work to demonstrate the existence of impact on the plaintiff or the plaintiff class and to quantify damages, the question often arises whether fees for experts are recoverable as costs. The answer is no: the definition of "costs" under the Clayton Act does not include expert witness fees. Thus any amounts paid to expert witnesses are not recoverable under the fee-shifting provisions of the Clayton Act.[259]

C. *Joint and Several Liability*

1288. US antitrust law permits the plaintiff to seek to recover the entire amount of damages caused by multiple defendants from any one of the defendants. This tort law concept of joint and several liability has been a part of antitrust doctrine since soon after the Sherman Act was enacted.[260] Deterrence of unlawful conduct is the primary rationale for joint and several liability. In the same vein, a defendant facing joint and several liability for an antitrust conspiracy has no right of contribution from co-conspirators.[261] The Supreme Court, after examining the antitrust statutes and their legislative history, concluded that Congress had neither expressly nor implicitly intended to create a right of contribution from co-defendants. The Supreme Court declined to craft this right itself, concluding that it lacked the power to do so given the detailed remedial provisions already included in the statutes.[262]

D. *The Effect of Prior Settlements on a Damages Award*

1289. As noted, all defendants are jointly and severally liable for all damages, including any damages that are caused by any settling defendants.[263] The amount paid in settlement by the settling defendant is deducted from the jury verdict but only after trebling.[264]

E. *Use and Legality of Judgement Sharing Agreements Among Defendants*

1290. Given that the US antitrust laws provide for joint and several liability, the automatic trebling of a damages award, and the awards of attorneys' fees to the successful plaintiff, a defendant who wishes to contest liability at trial may face significant risks. In addition, because there is no right of contribution in antitrust cases,[265] a defendant who played an insignificant part in the alleged wrongful conduct – such as a party who joined an existing price-fixing conspiracy late – could find itself

---

259 *Gulfstream III Assocs., Inc. v. Gulfstream Aerospace Corp.*, 789 F. Supp. 1288 (D.N.J. 1992).

260 *See* American Bar Association, 1 Antitrust Law Developments, 756, n. 160 (8th ed., 2017).

261 *See Texas Indus., Inc. v. Radcliff Materials, Inc.*, 451 U.S. 630 (1981); *see* Chapter VI, Section I.10.B.

262 *Id.* 640, 644–45.

263 This rule applies unless the plaintiffs and any settling defendants have agreed in their settlement agreement that any damages associated with a settling defendants' sales of the product in question may be removed from the calculations of overall damages suffered by the plaintiff or the class. Such an agreement sometimes is a condition imposed on the settling defendant by virtue of a judgement sharing agreement. *See infra.*

264 *See Faulkner's Auto Body Ctr., Inc. v. Covington Pike Toyota, Inc.*, 50 F. App'x 664, 670–71 (6th Cir. 2002); *Gulfstream III Assocs.*, 995 F.2d 425; *Burlington Indus. v. Milliken & Co.*, 690 F.2d 380, 392 n.8 (4th Cir. 1982).

265 *Texas Indus., Inc. v. Radcliff Materials, Inc.*, 451 U.S. 630 (1981).

responsible for the entire judgment while other defendants, who may have played a larger role in the wrongful conduct, pay significantly less because they settled with the plaintiffs at an earlier stage in the case. This conundrum – the *in terrorem* risk of a significant and disproportionate judgment – makes it difficult for antitrust defendants to oppose antitrust lawsuits through trial and encourages coerced settlements – where defendants may strike a deal early to avoid the prospect of huge liabilities later.

1291. Judgement sharing agreements are a mechanism that parties have developed to combat the coercive effect of the antitrust damages system by apportioning liability among the defendants based on contract principles.[266] These agreements enable potentially liable co-defendants to contractually allocate liability for any judgment that is entered based on their net share of the sales for which liability is found (after reduction or offset by the amount of any prior settlements). Judgment sharing agreements also permit defendants to settle with plaintiffs prior to trial, but generally require that the settling defendant obtain agreement from the plaintiffs that: (1) the plaintiffs will not seek damages against any non-settling defendants based on the settling defendants' shares of sales, and (2) the plaintiffs not offer proof at trial regarding the amount of the settling party's sales of products released by the settlement.[267]

1292. There are obvious advantages to such agreements for the defendants. Most significantly, a judgment sharing agreement eliminates the non-settling defendants' joint liability for treble damages associated with sales made by the settling defendant or defendants. This is significant because even a defendant with a larger market share may still face a huge exposure if it proceeds to trial owing to the combined market share of sales by the other defendants, including settling defendants. Rather than face the potential liability for trebled damages based on all sales and the entire market, a judgment sharing agreement reduces the non-settling defendants' exposure by requiring that a settling defendant and the plaintiffs remove that settling defendant's share of sales from any damages calculation. This effectively deprives plaintiffs of the leverage they otherwise possess as they seek to sequence settlements among the co-defendants leaving those who refuse a settlement exposed to damages based on the sales of both settling and non-settling defendants.

1293. By apportioning liability among defendants based on market shares, sales volumes, or some other agreed calculus before any judgment is entered, judgment sharing agreements also reduce the uncertainty associated with the prospect of joint and several liability even if no defendants settle. As a result, defendants would have some sense of their overall exposure to damages based on their contractual obligations long before heading into a trial. This predictability may encourage smaller defendants to remain in the case, and contribute to the defense, since they would not face the risk of treble damages for the entire market. At the same time, the certainty about the parameters of damages exposure that a judgment sharing agreement provides may

---

266 *In re Brand Name Prescription Drugs Antitrust Litigation*, No. 94 C 897, 1995 WL 221853 (N.D. Ill., Apr. 11, 1995).

267 *Id.* *3.

enable larger defendants who believe in the merits of their case to contest liability even in the face of the treble damages and joint and several liability.

1294. Not surprisingly, plaintiffs have raised a variety of challenges to the legality of judgment sharing agreements. For example, plaintiffs have argued that judgment sharing agreements should be invalidated because they encourage future violations of law,[268] improperly insure against violations of law,[269] and discourage and prevent settlements.[270] Others have argued that judgement sharing agreements can undermine the deterrence of antitrust violations and stabilize price-fixing cartels.[271] Courts have generally rejected these arguments.[272] One notable exception occurred where the court determined that the "main purpose" and "overall result" of the sharing agreement was to keep defendants "from individually resolving their disputes under the guise of defense cooperation" as well as to discourage the "presentation of relevant and admissible evidence at trial."[273] Where, however, the agreement permits the defendants to settle plaintiffs' claims and apportions liability among the defendants as distinguished from involving a third party not involved in the alleged wrongful conduct in the settlement process, the agreement will be viewed not as insurance against unlawful conduct but rather as a lawful contract to apportion liability.[274] As the court found in a seminal case on the subject:

> Absent a judgment sharing agreement, plaintiffs' attorneys are primed to exploit the immense exposure of the last defendant to settle. The relative culpability of the defendant is no longer pertinent. Instead, a sort of 'game theory' element emerges. Where, as under most judgment sharing agreements, each defendant is responsible for damages relating to its own sales, however, the "game theory" element of the settlement process is eliminated. "[S]ettlement discussions occur on a more rational basis... and settlement is thus promoted."[275]

1295. In upholding judgment sharing agreements, courts have generally opted to facilitate dispositions based on the merits rather than solely based on avoiding the *in terrorem* threat of massive damages exposures.

---

268 *Id.* *2.

269 *Id.* *3.

270 *Id.* **3–4.

271 Christopher R. Leslie, *Judgement Sharing Agreements*, 58 Duke L.J. 747, 749 (2009).

272 *See, e.g.*, *California v. Infineon Techs. AG*, No. C 06-4333, 2007 WL 6197288, *4 (N.D. Cal. Nov. 29, 2007) ("Defendants' agreement does nothing to limit defendants' exposure to joint and several liability in litigation before the court, or to otherwise prevent plaintiff States from seeking a judgement against one or all signatory defendants (or non-signatory defendants for that matter), in accordance with the principles of joint and several liability"); *In re Terazosin Hydrochloride Antitrust Litig.*, No. 99-MDL-1317, 2002 WL 35651678, *2 (S.D. Fla. Aug. 28, 2002) (expressing skepticism of a magistrate judge's order refusing to invalidate a judgment sharing agreement but stating it was not clearly erroneous and that "the majority of commentators tend to view such agreements with guarded approval"); *In re Linerboard Antitrust Litig.*, 292 F. Supp. 2d 631, 637 (E.D. Pa. 2003) (noting the existence of a judgment sharing agreement and applying it when approving a settlement); *Cimarron Pipeline Const., Inc. v. Nat'l. Council on Comp. Ins.*, No. Civ-89-822, 1992 WL 350612, *3 (W.D. Okla. Apr. 10, 1992) (refusing to invalidate a judgment sharing agreement because "[t]here has been simply no persuasive evidence presented that the Defendants' sharing agreement has had a negative impact on settlement negotiations").

273 *In re San Juan Dupont Plaza Hotel Fire Litig.*, 1989 WL 996278, *3 (D.P.R. Sept. 14, 1989).

274 *In re Brand Name Prescription Drug Antitrust Litig.*, 1995 WL 221853 *3, *4.

275 *Id.* *4 (internal citations omitted).

11. Appeal

1296. In federal courts, parties have a right to appeal an adverse decision after a final judgment. In addition, appeal may be possible on a permissive basis at the discretion of the court. In each case, the standard applied will depend upon the questions raised on appeal.

A. *Appeals of a Final Order*

1297. In the US, the final judgment rule ordinarily requires that all claims of error for litigation be raised "in a single appeal following final judgment on the merits."[276] Parties to private antitrust actions generally may file a notice of appeal as a right within 30 days after the entry of a final judgment.[277] For these purposes, an appeal of an order on a motion to dismiss or for summary judgment that disposes of all claims in a lawsuit is considered a final judgment. Certain motions filed after the entry of judgment can extend this period until 30 days from the entry of the order disposing of the final motion.[278] In addition, the time to file a notice of appeal also may be extended if a party moves for an extension within the permissible period or even outside of that window if the party "shows excusable neglect or good cause."[279]

B. *Permissive Appeals*

1298. Beyond the right to appeal a final judgment, parties may seek permission from a district court to file an interlocutory appeal where an order "involves a controlling question of law" that has "substantial ground for difference of opinion" and "an immediate appeal... may materially advance the ultimate termination of the litigation."[280] Where permission is obtained, the court of appeals has discretion over whether to hear the appeal.[281]

C. *Standard of Review*

1299. There are three basic standards of review of district court decisions for any appeal.[282]

1300. Appeals on questions of law are reviewed *de novo*.[283] This standard looks at the legal question anew and does not give deference to the prior court's decision.

---

276 *Firestone Tire & Rubber Co. v. Risjord*, 449 U.S. 368, 374 (1981) (citing 28 U.S.C. § 1291).

277 Fed. R. App. P. 4(a)(1)(A).

278 *Id.* 4(a)(4)(A) (listing motions: (i) for judgment under Rule 50(b), (ii) to amend or make additional factual findings under Rule 52(b), (iii) for attorney's fees under Rule 54, (iv) to alter or amend the judgment under Rule 59, (v) for a new trial under Rule 59, and (vi) for relief under Rule 60).

279 *Id.* 4(a)(5)(A)(ii).

280 28 U.S.C. § 1292(b).

281 *Id.*; *see also* Fed. R. App. P. 4(a)(5).

282 *See Pierce v. Underwood*, 487 U.S. 552, 558 (1988) ("For purposes of standard of review, decisions by judges are traditionally divided into three categories, denominated questions of law (reviewable *de novo*), questions of fact (reviewable for clear error), and matters of discretion (reviewable for 'abuse of discretion')").

283 *See, e.g.*, *Teva Pharms. USA, Inc. v. Novartis Pharms., Corp.*, 482 F.3d 1330, 1336 (Fed. Cir. 2007) ("The determination of whether an actual controversy exists under the Declaratory Judgment Act in a patent case is a question of law that we review de novo.").

1301. Appeals of questions of fact are reviewed for "clear error."[284] Because the trial court as the initial finder of fact is closer to the evidence and witness testimony, this standard provides that the trial court's factual findings are entitled to deference.

1302. Finally, appeals on questions related to discretionary decisions (e.g., class certification, evidentiary rulings) are reviewed for "abuse of discretion."[285] This standard is highly deferential to the trial court, but "[a]n abuse of discretion may be found where the 'district court's decision rests upon a clearly erroneous finding of fact, an errant conclusion of law or an improper application of law to fact.'"[286]

II. EU private enforcement

1303. Although the possibility for victims of infringements of competition law to seek compensation for the harm suffered as a result thereof has always existed in the legal systems of the Member States and has long been recognized as a fundamental right by the ECJ, in practice by contrast with the US, private enforcement, either on a stand-alone or follow-on basis, is still at a rather early stage of development in Europe. In order to foster the development of private actions for damages throughout the EU, which alongside public enforcement constitute an integral part of competition law enforcement, the European Parliament and the Council of the European Union have adopted, upon proposal from the European Commission, the Damages Directive of November 26, 2014, i.e., Articles 101 and 102 TFEU and their national equivalents.[287]

1304. As will be further detailed below, the aim of the EU Damages Directive – which is not specific to the pharmaceutical sector – is to provide a common framework for actions for damages to ensure a level playing field for victims of competition law infringements across the Member States and to facilitate compensation through the establishment of several presumptions, reducing the burden of proof for claimants. However, in practice, some disparities remain among the Member States, and claimants still face some practical hurdles and challenges that need to be overcome. While those are progressively addressed, notably thanks to the guidance of the ECJ, there is still a long way to go before private enforcement in the EU becomes an effective deterrent tool and complement to public enforcement. That being said, private actions for damages are flourishing all over the Member States, including in the pharmaceutical sector, where plaintiffs are often either state entities seeking compensation for the overcharge on health expenses or insurance companies.

---

284 *See, e.g., SmithKline Corp. v. Eli Lilly & Co.*, 575 F.2d 1056, 1062 (3d Cir. 1978) ("To the extent that the court's findings are based on narrative or historical facts, they can only be disturbed on appeal if they are found to be clearly erroneous.").

285 *See, e.g., General Electric Co. v. Joiner*, 522 U.S. 136, 139 (1997) (holding that "abuse of discretion is the appropriate standard" for evaluating a district court's decision to admit or exclude expert testimony).

286 *In re Warfarin Sodium*, 391 F.3d 527 (quoting *In re Gen. Motors Corp. Pick-Up Truck Fuel Tank Prod. Liab. Litig.*, 55 F.3d 768, 783 (3d Cir.1995)).

287 Council Directive 2014/104 of the European Parliament and of the Council of Nov. 26, 2014 on certain rules governing actions for damages under national law for infringements of the competition law provisions of the Member States and of the EU (the EU Damages Directive), 2014 OJ (L 349) 1.

1. The Development of Private Enforcement in the European Union

A. *The Fundamental Right to Compensation for Victims of Anticompetitive Practices*

1305. The direct effect of the provisions of the EU Treaties has long been established by the ECJ. In its landmark judgment *Van Gend en Loos*,[288] the ECJ found that EU law "not only imposes obligations on individuals but is also intended to confer upon them rights"[289] that national courts must safeguard. This principle was reaffirmed in *BRT v. Sabam* regarding the direct effect of Articles 101 and 102 TFEU.[290]

1306. Subsequently, the ECJ recognized the fundamental right for victims of competition law infringements to seek compensation for the harm suffered as a result thereof, as it helps deter anticompetitive conduct and maintain effective competition in the common market. The first expression of this right can be found in *Courage*,[291] where the ECJ held that:

> The full effectiveness of Article 85 of the Treaty [now Article 101 TFEU] and, in particular, the practical effect of the prohibition laid down in Article 85(1) would be put at risk if it were not open to any individual to claim damages for loss caused to him by a contract or by conduct liable to restrict or distort competition.[292]

1307. In *Manfredi*, the ECJ further stated that "any individual can claim compensation for the harm suffered where there is a causal relationship between that harm and an agreement or practice prohibited under Article 81 EC [now Article 101 TFEU]."[293]

1308. While these judgments certainly paved the way for damage claims to be brought by victims of competition law infringements, European competition law enforcement was, historically, mostly left to the public sphere, i.e., competition authorities, be it at the level of the European Commission or at the level of Member States. However, the role of competition authorities is to protect the market, not individual victims of antitrust violations. As such, in the EU, competition authorities do not have the power to award damages, such prerogative lying with the national courts of the Member States only. The Member States are therefore responsible for designating the competent courts and laying down the procedural rules governing actions for damages while considering the principles of equivalence and effectiveness of EU law.[294]

---

288 Case 26/62, *NV Algemene Transport- en Expeditie Onderneming van Gend & Loos v. Netherlands Inland Revenue Administration* ECLI:EU:C:1963:1, (Feb. 5, 1963).

289 *Id.* 12.

290 Case 127/73, *BRT v. Sabam*, ECLI:EU:C:1974:25, ¶16 (Mar. 27, 1974).

291 Case C-453/99, *Courage Ltd. v. Crehan*, ECLI:EU:C:2001:465, (Sept. 20, 2001).

292 *Id.* ¶26; *see also* ¶27; later confirmed by Case C-360/09, *Pfleiderer AG v. Bundeskartellamt*, ECLI:EU:C:2011:389, (June 14, 2011) and Case C-199/11, *Europese Gemeenschap v. Otis NV*, ECLI:EU:C:2012:684, ¶41 (Nov. 6, 2012).

293 Case C-295/04, *Manfredi v. Lloyd Adriatico Assicurazioni SpA*, ECLI:EU:C:2006:461, ¶61 (July 13, 2006); later confirmed by Case C-199/11, *Europese Gemeenschap*, ECLI:EU:C:2012:684, ¶43 (Nov. 6, 2012).

294 This was notably recalled in Case C-295/04, *Manfredi*, ECLI:EU:C:2006:461, ¶62 (July 13, 2006).

1309. In practice, despite the theoretical possibility of seeking compensation for the harm suffered as a result of anticompetitive conduct, very few victims chose to exercise their right and those who did were not always successful. The ineffectiveness of the right to damages was largely due to various legal and procedural hurdles in the Member States' rules governing actions for damages. First, traditional rules of civil liability and procedure were often inadequate for damages actions in the field of competition law. Second, these actions often require complex factual and economic analysis, which are time-consuming and costly. Third, the unavailability of crucial evidence to establish liability to the requisite legal standard of the Member State in which the action was brought often made the risk/reward balance unfavorable for claimants.

B. *The Institutional Initiative: The Green and White papers on Damages Actions*

1310. Faced with the "underdevelopment" of private enforcement in the EU, the European Commission adopted a Green Paper on Damages Actions in 2005 (the Green Paper on Damages Actions).[295] The Green Paper on Damages Actions identified the obstacles for victims to exercise their right to compensation and proposed several options for solving these problems and make private actions for damages a more effective and efficient enforcement tool. The Green Paper on Damages Actions was met with broad interest in the antitrust community and achieved its objective of raising awareness on the right to compensation for victims of competition law infringements, and on the obstacles they face when attempting to enforce their rights, including access to evidence, the standard of proof to establish civil liability as a result of a competition law infringement, the quantification of the harm, and the cost of these actions.

1311. The European Commission then continued its reflection and, in 2008, it published a White Paper on Damages Actions (the White Paper on Damages Actions).[296] Taking into account the findings of the Green Paper on Damages Actions, this document contained a set of recommendations to ensure that victims of competition law infringements have access to genuinely effective mechanisms to obtain full compensation for the harm suffered, around three pillars:

- First, the fundamental right to full compensation, no more, no less, was clearly reaffirmed by the European Commission as well as the contribution of private enforcement to the deterrent effect of competition law.
- Second, the European Commission acknowledged that the legal framework for more effective antitrust damages actions must be based on a genuinely European approach, with balanced measures rooted in the European legal culture and traditions, and
- Third, private enforcement is meant to complement, and not to replace or jeopardize the public enforcement of Articles 101 and 102 TFEU by

---

295 European Commission, Green Paper on Damages actions for breach of the EC antitrust rules, COM (2005) 672 final (Dec. 19, 2005).

296 European Commission, White Paper on Damages actions for breach of the EC antitrust rules, COM (2008) 165 final (Apr. 2, 2008).

the European Commission and the NCAs of the Member States, meaning that some safeguards were needed to preserve the attractivity of certain enforcement tools such as leniency.

1312. The proposed measures and policy choices reflected in the White Paper on Damages Actions form the basis of the EU Damages Directive.

C. *The EU Damages Directive and Subsequent Guidelines*

1313. The EU Damages Directive was formally adopted by the European Parliament and the EU Council on November 26, 2014 and was published in the Official Journal on December 5, 2014. The Member States were required to adapt their national laws and procedures in line with the EU Damages Directive's provisions by December 27, 2016 at the latest.[297] The EU Damages Directive sets out a common framework of both procedural and substantive rules for private actions in the EU that all Member States must observe. However, the EU Damages Directive only provides for a minimum harmonization of the national regimes and each claim must thus still be filed according to the national rules of each jurisdiction. The EU Damages Directive is complemented by soft law instruments whose purpose is to help national jurisdictions in dealing with actions for damages based on infringements of competition law, particularly with respect to the quantification of harm.

a. *The Guiding Principles of the EU Damages Directive*

1314. In its preamble, the EU Damages Directive recalls that Articles 101 and 102 TFEU produce direct effects in relations between individuals and therefore create, for these individuals, obligations and rights which national courts must enforce, including the right for victims to claim damages for the harm caused to them by a violation of these provisions.

1315. However, acknowledging that certain differences exist in the legal and judicial systems of the Member States, the EU Damages Directive only lays down minimum standards for harmonization of private actions for damages, designed to decrease these differences and ensure a level playing field throughout the EU, thereby increasing legal certainty. In practice, this allows Member States to adopt stricter rules, provided however that these do not conflict with the objectives and imperative provisions of the EU Damages Directive. For example, in *Cogeco*, the ECJ considered that the Portuguese rules on limitation periods, according to which an action is time-barred after 3 years without a suspension mechanism for the duration of the competition authority's investigation, were too restrictive.[298]

1316. The guiding principles of the EU Damages Directive revolve around two objectives: on the one hand, addressing the articulation between public and private enforcement; on the other hand, facilitating compensation for victims of anti-competitive practices through the establishment of several legal presumptions regarding the conditions of liability.

---

297 Council Directive 2014/104 (EU Damages Directive), *supra* n. 287, Chapter VI, art. 21(1), 1–19.

298 Case C-637/17, *Cogeco Communications Inc. v. Sport TV Portugal SA*, ECLI:EU:C:2019:263, (Mar. 28, 2019).

1317. First, on the interaction between private and public enforcement, the EU Damages Directive acknowledges the importance of remediating the asymmetry of information by ensuring that claimants, particularly in follow-on damages claims, can request and obtain the disclosure of evidence relevant to their case. Claimants should therefore be able to access, to a certain extent, the European Commission's file or the relevant NCA(s)' file(s). However, this right is not unlimited. National courts should consider the necessity and proportionality of measures that are being contemplated when ordering the disclosure of evidence, including whether certain documents should benefit from partial or total protection. This is the case for evidence containing business secrets or otherwise confidential information which, if disclosed, should be protected appropriately, for example through the redaction of sensitive information or the limitation of disclosure to a closed circle such as a clean team. This is also the case for leniency applications and settlement submissions which, in order to safeguard the attractiveness of cooperation programs, benefit from a total protection, meaning that national courts cannot order their disclosure.

1318. Second, the EU Damages Directive establishes several presumptions and rules that broadly aim at facilitating actions for damages by victims of competition law infringements. In this respect, the EU Damages Directive notably provides that:

- Cartel infringements shall be presumed to cause harm and it is for the defendant to rebut that presumption (Article 17).
- National courts must judicially quantify the harm when it is established that the victim has suffered harm, even if such victim was not itself capable of quantifying its damages (Article 17), provided however that such situation does not result from an inaction of the victim.[299]
- Defendants can invoke a passing-on defense;[300] however, it lies on them to prove, (i) with respect to direct purchasers, that the latter have passed-on the overcharge to their own customers and, (ii) to the contrary, with respect to indirect purchasers, that the direct purchaser, i.e., their supplier, did not pass on the overcharge (Articles 12 to 14).
- In the case of several infringers, they can all be held jointly and severally liable for the harm caused by their conduct; claimants can therefore seek full compensation from any one of them (Article 11).

1319. It should however be noted that the effectiveness of certain rules contained in the EU Damages Directive is still limited in practice today since, pursuant to Article 22, the substantive provisions of the EU Damages Directive shall not apply retroactively (by opposition to the procedural rules which already apply to all actions brought on or after December 26, 2014). This has recently been confirmed by the ECJ in *Volvo and DAF Trucks*, in respect of the presumption according to which cartel infringements cause harm.[301] Consequently, in most

---

299 Case C-312/21, *Tráficos Manuel Ferrer SL v.Daimler AG*, ECLI:EU:C:2023:99, (Feb. 16, 2023).

300 The passing-on defense refers to the argument, often put forward by the defendant in damages claims, that the direct purchaser has not suffered any harm because it transferred the overcharge to its own customers (also referred to as indirect purchasers).

301 Case C-267/20, *AB Volvo & DAF Trucks NV v. RM*, ECLI:EU:C:2022:494, (June 22, 2022).

Member States, the above-mentioned presumptions are still not applicable. By way of example, the French Supreme Court ruled that the presumption provided in Article 13 of the EU Damages Directive according to which direct purchasers have not passed-on overcharges, is not applicable in cases concerning cartel practices implemented before the entry into force of the national legislation implementing the EU Damages Directive because this would be in breach of the principle of non-retroactivity of the substantive provisions of the EU Damages Directive.[302] It is however interesting to note that, in France, in cases where the EU Damages Directive still does not apply, the rule according to which the burden of proving that the overcharge paid by the direct purchaser was not passed on its own customers is jurisprudential and the French Supreme Court could thus, in theory, already shift the burden of proof onto the defendant without, in so doing, applying the law retroactively.

1320. Finally, the EU Damages Directive strongly encourages settlements out of courts. In this respect, Article 18 provides that the five-year limitation to bring an action shall be suspended for the duration of any consensual dispute resolution process. Furthermore, pursuant to Article 19, when a settlement has been reached, the EU Damages Directive requires that the victim reduce its claim for damages by an amount corresponding to the share for which it has already been granted compensation and protects the settling party from contributory claims that would be brought against it by non-settling co-infringers.

b. *Soft Law Instruments*

1321. Alongside the EU Damages Directive, the European Commission has progressively adopted an arsenal of soft law tools (such as guidelines and communications) designed to provide victims and national jurisdictions with specific guidance on the conduct of private enforcement proceedings and the quantification of harm.

1322. In June 2013, the European Commission published a Communication on the quantification of harm in actions for damages based on breaches of Articles 101 and 102 TFEU.[303] The Communication recalls that quantifying the harm is not an exercise directly governed by EU law but by the national laws of the Member States. As such, it is for each Member State to determine the relevant standard of proof and the required degree of precision in showing the harm suffered, including through the establishment of presumptions of a rebuttable or irrefutable nature. It is also for the Member States to determine to what extent and how courts are empowered to make an assessment on the basis of best estimates or to make use of equitable considerations. But whichever the rules that govern quantification of the harm, the Member States must observe the principles of equivalence and effectiveness of EU law.

1323. On the same date, the European Commission also published a practical guide on the quantification of harm to accompany the above-mentioned Communication

---

[302] French Supreme Court, Case No. 21-19.197, *Carrefour/JJSBF* (Oct. 19, 2022).

[303] European Commission Communication, Quantifying harm in actions for damages based on breaches of Article 101 or 102 TFEU of the Treaty on the Functioning of the European Union 2013 OJ (C 167) 7.

(Practical Guide).[304] The Practical Guide, which is much more detailed than the Communication, acknowledges that, once the existence of an infringement and of a causal link between this infringement and the harm suffered by the claimant has been found, determining the amount of damages to be awarded is a difficult exercise that is often challenging for both courts and victims. Therefore, to help national courts with this assessment, the Practical Guide contains general considerations on the quantification of damages, as well as a detailed overview of the various economic methodologies than can be used, both in case of price increases (generally resulting from a cartel infringement) and exclusionary conduct (generally resulting from an abuse of dominance).

1324. In 2019, the European Commission adopted a specific guidance on the passing-on of overcharges.[305] The objective of these guidelines is to provide practical guidance to national courts on how to estimate the passing-on of overcharges to indirect purchasers. They include details on the economic principles that apply in the context of passing-on, the relevant parameters to be taken into account, and the methodologies that can be used to estimate overcharges that have been passed on.

1325. Finally, in 2020, the European Commission issued a Communication on the protection of confidential information by national courts in proceedings for the private enforcement of EU competition law.[306] This Communication provides detailed guidance on issues pertaining to access to evidence and identifies the various measures that can be considered by national courts to protect the confidentiality of some information that needs to be disclosed in the context of private actions for damages.

2. Procedural Issues

1326. Procedural arguments are very often raised by defendants in private enforcement cases, their objective being to see the case dismissed without having to engage in a discussion on its merits. Therefore, in practice, inadmissibility claims based on the lack of standing from the victim to bring a claim or on the relevant limitation period in any given Member State are frequent. On the claimant's side, another important procedural issue concerns access to evidence, including access to the authorities' files in follow-on cases.

A. *Standing*

1327. By way of principle, anyone who has suffered losses as a result of a competition law infringement can claim damages, irrespective of whether they are direct or indirect purchasers.[307] The exercise of the right to sue is governed by national law provisions in the particular jurisdiction in which the action is brought but, pursuant

---

304 European Commission SWD, Practical Guide on Quantifying Harm in Actions for Damages Based on Breaches of Article 101 or 102 TFEU (June 11, 2013).

305 European Commission Communication, Guidelines for national courts on how to estimate the share of overcharge which was passed on to the indirect purchaser (Commission Communication on Guidelines for national courts), 2019 OJ (C 267) 4.

306 European Commission Communication, The protection of confidential information by national courts in proceedings for the private enforcement of EU competition law, 2020 OJ (C 242) 1–17.

307 Case C-295/04, *Manfredi*, ECLI:EU:C:2006:461, (July 13, 2006); *see also* Council Directive 2014/104 (EU Damages Directive), *supra* n. 287, Chapter VI, art. 12(1).

to the EU principle of equivalence, the rules and procedures regarding such actions, when based on Articles 101 and/or 102 TFEU, cannot be less favorable than those governing similar actions resulting from infringements of national law.

1328. The question of standing is rarely raised with respect to direct purchasers. Indeed, a direct purchaser necessarily has standing to bring a claim for damages against its supplier: this is not debatable, and a claim cannot be declared inadmissible on that basis. However, standing should not be confused with the requirement of a causal link. Having standing does not mean that, on the merits, the anticompetitive conduct has caused harm to such direct purchaser, which it is for the latter to establish.

1329. The question is more often raised in relation to indirect purchasers, who do not have a contractual relationship with the undertaking that has infringed competition law and/or who are not active in the market affected by the anticompetitive conduct. In such circumstances, the ECJ has adopted a broad interpretation considering that a direct causal link between the infringement and the harm suffered is not necessary.

1330. In *Kone*,[308] the ECJ held that compensation may be sought in relation to losses suffered by a customer of an undertaking not party to a cartel, but whose prices were nonetheless higher than they would have been absent the cartel because of the umbrella effect of that cartel (i.e., when there is a cartel in a market resulting in increased prices, the non-cartelists follow the market dynamics and thus have a natural tendency to also increase their prices, outside of any coordination). Therefore, although there is no direct relationship with the cartelists, the national laws of the Member States cannot automatically deny the right to sue to a victim of the umbrella effect.

1331. In *Otis*,[309] the ECJ adopted similar reasoning, holding that persons not acting as suppliers or customers in the market affected by the practices can nonetheless claim compensation for the harm suffered as a result of these practices. In the case at hand, which was a follow-on action in the elevator cartel case, the plaintiff was the Province of Upper Austria. The latter sued Otis, one of the cartelists, for damages, on account of the fact that it had provided subsidies, in the form of loans, for the financing of building projects which included the purchase of cartelized products (lifts and escalators) at a price higher than it could have been absent the cartel. The Province of Upper Austria, although not a purchaser of the products, claimed that it suffered loss because of the cartel as the overcharge imposed by the cartelists on their direct customers led to an increase of the loans granted by the Province, whereas the money could have been used more profitably.

B. *Limitation Periods*

1332. Pursuant to Article 10 of the EU Damages Directive, the limitation periods to bring an action for damages should not be less than 5 years. In addition, such limitation periods should not begin to run before the infringement of competition law has ceased and the victim is aware of – or should reasonably be aware of – the

---

308 Case C-557/12, *Kone AG v. OBB-Infrastruktur AG*, ECLI:EU:C:2014:1317, (June 5, 2014).

309 Case C-435/18, *Otis Gesellschaft GmbH v. Land Oberosterreich*, ECLI:EU:C:2019:1069, (Dec. 12, 2019).

infringement, the fact that it caused injury, and the identity of the infringer. Limitation periods should also be suspended or interrupted if a competition authority investigates the conduct to which the action of damages relates.

1333. This provision of the EU Damages Directive has led to some adaptations of the legislative framework in certain Member States, e.g., in Portugal, Spain and Germany where the limitation periods were, before the EU Damages Directive, of a shorter duration. For example, regarding more specifically Germany, the previous limitation period of 3 years under the general provisions of the German Civil Code has been replaced by a general limitation period of 5 years set out in a specific provision in response to Article 10 of the EU Damages Directive.[310] In other countries where the general statute of limitations for civil liability was already in line with the EU Damages Directive (e.g., France, Belgium), specific provisions have nonetheless been introduced in national legislation to take into account certain specificities in damages claims based on a violation of competition law with respect to the starting point of the limitation period and causes of suspension or interruption of the limitation period. In *Cogeco*, which related to a damage claim filed in Portugal by Cogeco following the finding of an abuse of dominance by Sport TV Portugal, the ECJ first noted in a preliminary ruling that the provisions of the EU Damages Directive were not applicable *ratione temporis* to the case since Cogeco's action for damages was brought before the transposition of the EU Damages Directive into Portuguese law. However, the Court held that the combination of (1) a three-year limitation period that starts to run from the date on which the injured party was aware of its right to compensation, even if the party was unaware of the identity of the infringer, and (2) the absence of suspension or interruption of the limitation periods in Portuguese law made it practically impossible for Cogeco to exercise its right to compensation and thus undermined the full effectiveness of EU law.

1334. Despite this, the claim was subsequently rejected by the Lisbon District Court as being time-barred. The court pointed out that the ECJ had disregarded the fact that, even though the statute of limitations was not suspended *ex lege*, Cogeco could have asked for a suspension under Portuguese law, which it did not do.[311]

1335. Very recently, in *Volvo and DAF Trucks*,[312] the ECJ further clarified the temporal applicability of Article 10 of the EU Damages Directive. First, the ECJ held that

---

310 Section 33h of the German Act against Restraints on Competition. The limitation period begins to run at the end of the year in which the claim arose, the infringement ended and the claimant became aware or should have become aware without gross negligence of the circumstances giving rise to the claim. German competition law also provides for a ten-year limitation period, irrespective of the awareness of the claimant or grossly negligent ignorance, which begins 10 years from the time the claim arose, and the infringement was terminated. A thirty-year maximum limitation period was also established, which begins at the latest 30 years after the infringement regardless of any awareness of the claimant. The limitation period may be suspended if: (1) any German competition authority takes investigative measures, (2) the European Commission or another EU Member State's competition authority takes action, (3) or the claimant files a lawsuit for information or disclosure of evidence against the infringer, which subsequently extends the time frame for bringing private enforcement actions in Germany.

311 Charley Connor, *Portuguese Court Rejects ECJ's Cogeco Preliminary Ruling*, GLOBAL COMPETITION REVIEW (Nov. 13, 2020), *available at* https://globalcompetitionreview.com/article/portuguese-court-rejects-ecjs-cogeco-preliminary-ruling.

312 Case C-267/20, *AB Volvo & DAF Trucks NV*, ECLI:EU:C:2022:494, (June 22, 2022).

the provisions of the EU Damages Directive relating to the limitation periods are of a substantive nature and, therefore, they cannot apply retroactively. This is because, according to the ECJ, "unlike procedural time limits, the limitation period, by resulting in the extinction of the legal action, is a matter of substantive law since it affects the enforceability of a subjective right which the person concerned can no longer effectively assert before the courts."[313]

1336. Second, the ECJ recalled that "the existence of an infringement of competition law, the existence of harm, the causal link between that harm and that infringement, and the identity of the perpetrator of the infringement are among the necessary elements which the injured party must have in order to bring an action for damages"[314] and, on this basis, ruled that in this case, only the publication of the European Commission's summary decision provided sufficient information to the victim to be able to effectively seek compensation.

1337. Finally, the ECJ considered that, in circumstances such as those in the case at hand where the infringement occurred before the entry into force of the EU Damages Directive but where the action for damages was brought after the entry into force of the provisions transposing the EU Damages Directive into national law, Article 10 should be regarded as applicable *ratione temporis* "in so far as the limitation period for bringing that action under the old [national] rules had not elapsed before the date of expiry of the time limit for the transposition of the directive."[315] In other words, because Article 10 is considered a substantive provision of the EU Damages Directive that cannot apply retroactively, the relevant limitation period that applied to the claimant in this case was still the old Spanish provision, which provided for a limitation period of one year only. The ECJ held however that the limitation period had not elapsed and the action was not time-barred because the victim only gained sufficient knowledge of the infringement when the European Commission's summary decision was published, which occurred less than a year before the action for damages was introduced.

1338. In France, where the statute of limitations was already aligned with that provided for by the EU Damages Directive, i.e., 5 years, the Paris Court of Appeal traditionally considered that, in cartel cases, the publication of the FCA's decision should be regarded as the starting point for the limitation periods to run insofar as, owing to the secret nature of cartels, a victim, even if it has suspicions, cannot know beforehand with sufficient certainty the nature and scope of the infringement as well as the identity of the infringers.[316]

1339. This principle was recently reaffirmed in the context of an abuse of dominance case in a context where the claimant – the French Social Security – had given

---

313 *Id.* ¶46.

314 *Id.* ¶60.

315 *Id.* ¶79.

316 For recent examples, *see* French Supreme Court, Case No. civ. 19-14.094, *Doux Aliments* (Mar. 31, 2021); French Supreme Court, Case No. 18-16.279, *Franche Comté signaux*, comm., (Jan. 27, 2021); and Paris Court of Appeal, Case No. 19/19448, *JJSBF v. Carrefour*, comm., (Apr. 14, 2021) (confirmed by French Supreme Court, Case No. 21-19.197, comm., (Oct. 19, 2022)); Paris Court of Appeal, Casse No. 19/22293, *Vania v. Carrefour*, comm., (Jan. 5, 2022).

evidence before the competition authority and was therefore aware of the conduct at stake and its potentially anticompetitive character.[317] More particularly, in this case, the French Social Security brought a follow-on damages claim against Sanofi, which had been condemned by the FCA for abusive disparagement of generics of its blockbuster drug Plavix.[318] In first instance, Sanofi successfully argued before the Paris Commercial Court that the claim was time-barred because it was launched on September 12, 2017 whereas the French Social Security, which actively participated to the FCA's investigation, was necessarily aware of the practices long before then and, at the very least, at the latest in September 2011.[319] The Paris Commercial Court indeed noted that, at this time, in response to a request for information of the FCA, the French Social Security had produced an estimate of the losses incurred because of the practices. However, this judgment was overturned on appeal.[320] By contrast to the Paris Commercial Court, the Paris Court of Appeal considered that the French Social Security, although it was aware of the investigation of the FCA, only became aware with certainty of the illegality of Sanofi's conduct when the FCA issued its sanction decision in 2013.

1340. In practice, beyond these theoretical considerations, claimants may have an interest to launch a damage claim in parallel to an on-going investigation of a competition authority, in order to preserve their rights. In such a case, it is possible to request a stay of proceedings pending the outcome of the investigation, which will usually be granted. Not only this may avoid a debate on the limitation periods (especially in abuse of dominance cases) but, in certain cases, it can also encourage an early settlement with the defendant. The defendant may indeed have an interest in settling the claim if this can help its case before the authorities, which may be willing to be more lenient or even, in certain circumstances, to close their investigation without imposing any fine (e.g., if the case is not seen as an enforcement priority, if it is a complicated case in terms of establishing the anticompetitive conduct or if they consider that the private action has had a sufficient deterrent effect on the defendant).

C. *Disclosure and Access to Evidence*

1341. One of the most notable developments brought about by the EU Damages Directive concerns the harmonization of disclosure regimes across Member States. Previously, there was a significant gap between claimant-friendly jurisdictions with sophisticated and well-established disclosure regimes (such as the UK, which was formerly part of the EU) and those where access to evidence held by an adverse party or the competition authority was challenging (notably Germany and the Netherlands). The lack of appropriate disclosure procedures was perceived by EU lawmakers as a barrier to an effective private enforcement of competition law, as it maintained, often to the detriment of claimants, an unjustified asymmetry of information.

---

317 Paris Court of Appeal, Case No. 19/19969, *Sanofi*, comm., (Feb. 9, 2022).

318 *See* Chapter V.

319 Paris Commercial Court, Case No. 2017/053369, *Sanofi* (Oct. 1, 2019).

320 Paris Court of Appeal, Case No. 19/19969, *Sanofi*, comm., (Feb. 9, 2022).

1342. Article 5 and 6 of the EU Damages Directive now deal with access to evidence, whether it is detained by the adverse party, a third party, or included in the file of a competition authority.

1343. While the objective is clearly to facilitate access to evidence with a view to remedy the asymmetry of information between the parties, the EU Damages Directive is also mindful that disclosure should only be ordered on a case-by-case basis, having regard for the principles of necessity and proportionality. In practice, a party seeking to obtain the disclosure of evidence held by another party or a third party should precisely identify the documents or relevant categories of documents to which access is required and justify, for each of them, the reasons why access should be granted.[321] In turn, when assessing requests for disclosure, national courts should make sure that these are proportionate, taking into account the justifications put forward by the requesting party, the relevant factual circumstances of the case, the scope and cost of disclosure, and whether the evidence to which access is required contains confidential information or not.[322] In a recent judgment, the ECJ clarified that the evidence in possession of the defendant or a third party to which access can be requested by the claimant covers evidence that the defendant or the third party needs to create *ex novo* from pre-existing evidence by compiling or classifying information, knowledge or data in its possession, provided however that this exercise is necessary (which is for the claimant to demonstrate) and does not impose an excessive and disproportionate burden on the defendant or the third party from whom the evidence is requested, having regard, in particular, to the legitimate interests and fundamental rights of that party.[323] The ECJ also considered that a national court can order the disclosure of evidence on the basis of Article 5 Section 1 of the EU Damages Directive even if the proceedings have been suspended pending the outcome of the European Commission's investigation. However, in doing so, the national court must ensure that its decision will not unduly interfere with the European Commission's investigation and risk jeopardizing the investigation strategy or the way in which undertakings cooperate with the European Commission. It thus requires that the national court conducts a thorough assessment of the request as regards its relevance, the link between the evidence requested and the damages action, and whether the request is sufficiently precise and proportionate.[324]

1344. Regarding more particularly evidence included in the file of a competition authority, specific additional rules laid down in Article 6 of the EU Damages Directive apply to safeguard the effectiveness of the public enforcement of competition law.[325] Consequently, access to the file of a competition authority should only be granted if no adverse party or a third party is reasonably able to provide the evidence.[326]

---

321 Council Directive 2014/104 (EU Damages Directive), *supra* n. 287, Chapter VI, art. 2.
322 *Id.* ¶3.
323 Case C-163/21, *AD v. PACCAR Inc.*, ECLI:EU:C:2022:863, (Nov. 10, 2022).
324 Case C-57/21, *RegioJet AS v. Ceske Drahy AS*, ECLI:EU:C2023:6, (Jan. 12, 2023).
325 Council Directive 2014/104 (EU Damages Directive), *supra* n. 287, Chapter VI, art. 6, ¶1.
326 *Id.* art. 6, ¶10.

1345. In addition, access to evidence held in the file of a competition authority is limited. First, national courts can only grant access to the following categories of evidence after the competition authority has closed its own proceedings (so-called "grey list"), it being noted that the suspension of such proceedings by a NCA pending the outcome of a parallel investigation by the European Commission does not amount to a closing of the proceedings within the meaning of Article 6 Section 5 of the EU Damages Directives:[327]

- information that was prepared by a natural or legal person specifically for the proceedings of a competition authority;
- information that the competition authority has drawn up and sent to the parties in the course of its proceedings; and
- settlement submissions that have been withdrawn.[328]

1346. The ECJ has recently clarified that, with respect to the above-mentioned categories of evidence, a national court can order the disclosure of evidence and place such evidence under sequestration while postponing its assessment in order to determine whether the evidence fulfills the criteria to be part of the "grey list", to a time when the court has access to such evidence. During the time of examination, the national court must ensure that access to the evidence concerned is not allowed as long as the determination as to whether it belongs to the grey list has not been made and, when such determination is made and the court concludes that the evidence belongs to one of the above categories, as long as the competition authority has not closed its proceedings.[329]

1347. Second, two categories of evidence can never be disclosed in civil litigation (so-called "black list"): leniency statements and settlement submissions.[330] The national court, however, can access leniency statements and settlement submissions upon a reasoned request presented by the claimant and for the sole purpose to ensure that the content of said documents actually correspond to the definition of leniency statements and settlement submissions set forth in Article 2 of the EU Damages Directive.[331] It should be noted that the strict position taken in the EU Damages Directive contrasts with that of the ECJ in *Pfleiderer*.[332] In this case, which dates back to 2011 (i.e., prior to the EU Damages Directive), the ECJ, albeit being conscious that granting a victim access to leniency materials could deter a cartel participant to file for leniency in the first place, tried to reach a balance between the protection of the effectiveness of public enforcement of competition law and the fundamental right to compensation for victims of antitrust violations. The ECJ therefore ruled that a victim could not be precluded from being granted access to documents relating to a leniency procedure involving the perpetrator of the infringement and that it was for the national courts of the Member States, on the basis of their national

---

327 Case C-57/21, *RegioJet AS*, ECLI:EU:C2023:6, (Jan. 12, 2023).
328 Council Directive 2014/104 (EU Damages Directive), *supra* n. 287, Chapter VI, art. 6, ¶5.
329 Case C-57/21, *RegioJet AS*, ECLI:EU:C2023:6, (Jan. 12, 2023).
330 Council Directive 2014/104 (EU Damages Directive), *supra* n. 287, Chapter VI, art. 6, ¶6.
331 *Id.* art. 6, ¶7.
332 Case C-360/09, *Pfleiderer AG*, ECLI:EU:C:2011:389, (June 14, 2011).

laws, to determine the conditions under which such access could be granted or refused by weighing the various interests protected by EU law.

1348. All other type of evidence contained in the file of a competition authority (i.e., evidence that does not fall within one of the above-mentioned categories) can be disclosed at any time during the proceedings before the national court.[333] Consequently, the ECJ held that disclosure of evidence not specifically prepared in the context of the investigation of a competition authority but which concerns information that preexisted irrespective of the investigation, merely submitted in the context thereof, whether spontaneously or at the request of the competition authority, can be ordered at any time by a national court seized of a damages claim.[334]

1349. Finally, Article 8 of the EU Damages Directive provides for the application of penalties in certain circumstances: if a party fails or refuses to comply with a disclosure order, if the relevant evidence is destroyed, if the protection of confidential information is not adequately respected or, finally, if the evidence is used beyond the limit set forth by the national court when ordering the disclosure.

3. Substantive Issues

1350. In private actions for damages, the claimant must, out of principle, prove that it has suffered harm because of a competition law infringement. To trigger the liability of the defendant, this requires establishing a fault on the part of the latter, a damage and a causal link between the two. It is only when these three cumulative conditions are met that the national courts can proceed with the quantification of the damage.

1351. In order to foster the development of private enforcement in Europe, the EU Damages Directive establishes several presumptions that aim at reducing the burden of proof for claimants and facilitating their ability to obtain compensation for the harm suffered as a result of competition law infringements. However, given the rules governing the applicability in time of the substantial provisions of the EU Damages Directive, of which most of (if not all) the presumptions form part, these presumptions are in the vast majority of cases still not applicable, more than 5 years after the expiry date for the transposition of the EU Damages Directive. Against this background, this section will discuss both the rules derived from the EU Damages Directive and the current state of the law in the various Member States, based on recent precedents of the national courts.

A. *Establishing Liability of the Defendant(s)*

a. *The Wrongdoing (Fault)*

(1) General Considerations

1352. Pursuant to the principle of primacy of EU law, a national court cannot make a finding that would be contrary to a decision of the European Commission. Consequently, the decisions of the European Commission establishing a violation

---

333 Council Directive 2014/104 (EU Damages Directive), *supra* n. 287, Chapter VI, art. 6, ¶9.

334 Case C-57/21, *RegioJet AS*, ECLI:EU:C2023:6, (Jan. 12, 2023).

of Articles 101 and/or 102 TFEU should be regarded as proof of a wrongdoing by national courts in the context of follow-on damages claims.

1353. In addition, under Article 9 of the EU Damages Directive, a finding of infringement by a final decision of a NCA is deemed to irrefutably establish a wrongdoing for the purposes of follow-on damages claims brought before the courts of the same Member State. Final decisions issued by the competition authorities or courts of another Member State shall at least constitute *prima facie* evidence of a wrongdoing.

1354. In several Member States, although in most cases Article 9 is not yet applicable, national courts already tend to confer a probative value to the decisions of their competition authority, thereby facilitating the establishment by the claimant of a wrongdoing on the part of the defendant.

1355. For example, in France, the Paris Court of Appeal systematically considers that a finding of infringement by the FCA characterizes, in itself, a fault within the meaning of French tort law.[335] This solution in fact derives from the principle that any violation of the law constitutes a fault for the purpose of establishing civil liability. French courts have also given probative value to a commitment decision of the FCA, considering that, despite the absence of a finding of infringement, the content of the decision already constituted *prima facie* evidence of an infringement, on which the claimant could rely to establish a wrongdoing.[336]

1356. Similarly, in Spain, the Madrid Commercial Court considered that, in the context of a follow-on damage claim based on a decision of the CNMC fining five reinsurance companies for a cartel, it was bound by the facts established in the CNMC decision, which constituted irrebuttable evidence of wrongdoing.[337]

1357. In Italy, the Tribunal of Palermo considered that the decision issued by the AGCM against pharmaceutical companies Novartis and Roche constituted a presumption of proof of the anticompetitive practice and of the existence of harm to all consumers.[338]

---

335 For example, Paris Court of Appeal, Case No. 19/19969, *Sanofi*, comm., (Feb. 9, 2022); Case No. 19/22293, *Vania*, (Nov. 4, 2019); Case No. 20/04265, *Cora*, comm., (Nov. 24, 2021); Paris Court of Appeal, Case No. 17/23041, *Digicel*, comm., (June 17, 2020); Paris Court of Appeal, Case No. 17/21261, *Arkeos*, comm., (Mar. 6, 2019); Case No. 17/04101, *Doux Aliments*, (June 23, 2021); and Paris Commercial Court, Case No. 2017-021571, *Cora*, (Feb. 20, 2020); Paris Commercial Court, Case No. 2017-013952, *Carrefour v. Vania*, (Nov. 4, 2019); and Paris Commercial Court, Case No. 2017-013944, *JJSBF*, (Sept. 23, 2019).

336 Paris Court of Appeal, Case No. 18/04914, *PMU*, comm., (Sept. 12, 2018).

337 Madrid Commercial Court, Case No. 210/2020, *Realia*, (June 9, 2020). In Nov. 2009, the CNMC fined five reinsurance companies for fixing minimum prices of ten-year insurance contracts to cover construction damages (inherent defects) in buildings. In May 2017, property developer Realia lodged a complaint before the Commercial Court of Madrid, claiming compensation for the harm suffered as a result of the anticompetitive conducts fined in the decision. In its judgment, the Commercial Court ultimately granted damages to Realia amounting to €2.6 million.

338 Tribunal of Palermo, Case No. 2652/15, *Roche SpA v. Terrasi*, (May 17, 2017). In 2014, the AGCM fined Roche and Novartis for having allegedly colluded to promote the sales of *Lucentis* in the treatment of wet AMD (an ophthalmic disease), at the expense of *Avastin*, authorized for the treatment of several cancers but used off-label in the ophthalmic field. This case had also been investigated by the Rome Public Prosecutor's Office for fraud and manipulation of the medicines market and by the Court of Auditors, which looked into the consequences of such fraud in terms of additional costs for the public health service. In addition, without waiting for the AGCM's decision to become final, some Italian patients who had been treated with either *Avastin* or *Lucentis* decided to

1358. In Germany, the court is bound by the definitive decisions of the Federal Cartel Office, the European Commission, or the Competition Authority or court acting as such in another EU Member State.[339] This binding effect pertains to the factual and legal determination of the alleged competition law infringement but excludes questions on the causal link or the quantification of damages, which are subject to the court's free assessment of evidence.[340] Additionally, the binding effect does not encompass the question of fault, which must therefore be demonstrated by the claimant.

(2) The Specific Situation of Parent Companies or Legal Successors and the Concept of "Undertaking" in the Private Litigation Sphere

1359. Articles 101 and 102 TFEU apply to "undertakings" rather than individual legal entities. According to established caselaw of the ECJ, the notion of "undertaking" refers to "every entity engaged in an economic activity, regardless of the legal status of the entity and the way in which it is financed."[341]

1360. Using this concept, the European Commission and the ECJ, followed by NCAs and courts, have progressively extended liability for breaches of Articles 101 and 102 TFEU to existing or former parent companies of the legal entity that is the perpetrator of the infringement. Similarly, when the legal entity that has originally participated in the infringement has ceased to exist, its legal successor can be held liable under Article 101 or 102 TFEU.

1361. In the context of private enforcement proceedings, the question arose as to whether parent companies or legal successors that did not personally take part in the infringement could nonetheless be held liable for the payment of damages.

1362. In this respect, Article 1 of the EU Damages Directive provides a clear answer: anyone who has suffered harm as a result of an infringement of competition law by an undertaking can seek compensation from that undertaking.

1363. The ECJ provided further guidance on this matter in two recent judgments, in the context of follow-on damages claims not based on the provisions of the EU

---

claim compensation for the harm suffered as a result of this agreement before the judicial courts. One of such former patients won its case against Roche before the Giudice di Pace in a judgment on Dec. 27, 2014. Roche then lodged an appeal before the Tribunal of Palermo, which overturned the judgment of the Giudice di Pace on May 17, 2017, by ordering the restitution of what had already been paid by Roche and the accrued interest. The Tribunal of Palermo considered that the fact that the private action is based on a decision of the competition authority which is not yet final has no bearing on the value to be attributed to such a decision, since that decision constitutes, for the establishment of the facts, a "presumption of proof" capable of demonstrating, "in a privileged manner," the anticompetitive practice. It therefore lies on the defendant to prove to the contrary that the sanctioned agreement was in fact lawful. However, in this case no evidence had been adduced by Roche to rebut the presumption of the existence of an anticompetitive practice aimed at artificially obtaining a differentiation between the two medicines in order to favor Lucentis, which was more expensive. But in this case, the Tribunal was not satisfied that the alleged victim had actually suffered harm from the behavior sanctioned by the AGCM. It found that the claim for damages was vitiated by a lack of evidence since it was based solely on the decision of the competition authority, which did not include any finding regarding the situation of that specific patient. Therefore, the causal link between the unlawful conduct and the alleged injury could not be established.

339 *See* German Act against Restraints on Competition § 33b.

340 Federal Court of Justice, Case No. NZ Kart 2021, *Truck Cartel*, 117 ¶24 (Sept. 23, 2020).

341 Case C-41/90, *Höfner and Elser v. Macrotron*, ECLI:EU:C:1991:161, ¶21 (Apr. 23, 1991).

Damages Directive, which was inapplicable. In *Skanska* and subsequently *Sumal*, the Court held that the determination of the entity which is liable for damages caused by an infringement of EU competition law is directly governed by EU law and found that the notion of "undertaking" cannot have a different meaning in the context of the imposition of fines by competition authorities and in the context of actions for damages based on an infringement of competition law.[342] Therefore, according to the Court, "when an economic unit [i.e., an undertaking] infringes Article 101(1) TFEU, it is for that unit, in accordance with the principle of personal responsibility, to answer for that infringement."[343]

1364. In *Skanska*,[344] the Court deduced from this principle that, pursuant to the principle of economic continuity, the legal entity that has inherited the business of the perpetrator of an infringement of competition law shall be liable to pay damages to a victim of such infringement. In this case, the solution was justified by the fact that the perpetrator of the infringement had ceased to exist. Therefore, any other solution would have resulted in depriving the victim from the possibility to claim damages for the harm suffered, in violation of the fundamental right to compensation.

1365. In *Sumal*,[345] the ECJ reiterated that the concept of "undertaking" has the same meaning in the public and private enforcement of competition law. Therefore, a victim can directly sue a subsidiary of the perpetrator of the infringement, even if it was not an addressee of the European Commission's decision, subject to an important limit: the claimant must prove that the legal entity against which the action is directed is part of the undertaking responsible for the infringement of competition law. This means that such legal entity and the one(s) targeted by the European Commission's decision, having regard to the economic, organizational and legal links between them, belong to the same economic unit, within the meaning of competition law. In addition, to avoid situations where any company of a group, irrespective of its activities, could be sued in private enforcement proceedings, the claimant must also prove the existence of a specific link between the economic activity of the defendant and the subject matter of the infringement for which another company of the group was held liable.

1366. In the Netherlands, where many actions for damages have been brought, the District Court of Rotterdam applied the same approach, considering that a legal entity that is part of the undertaking responsible for a violation of Article 101 TFEU should also be considered liable for the payment of any damages suffered by a victim of that infringement.[346]

1367. Conversely, in France, under the traditional approach of the courts, pursuant to the principle of "personal liability," only the legal entity that participated in the infringement could be held liable in the context of a claim for damages, unless it could be

---

342 Case C-724/17, *Kaupunki v. Skanska Industrial Solutions Oy*, ECLI:EU:C:2019:204, ¶11 (Mar. 14, 2019); Case C-882/19, *Sumal, S.L. v. Mercedes Benz Trucks Espana, S.L.*, ECLI:EU:C:2021:800, (Oct. 6, 2021).

343 *Id.* ¶42.

344 Case C-724/17, *Skanska*, ECLI:EU:C:2019:204, (Mar. 14, 2019).

345 Case C-882/19, *Sumal*, ECLI:EU:C:2021:800, (Oct. 6, 2021).

346 Rotterdam District Court, Case No. C/10/547149, *Stichting Elevator Cartel Claim v. Kone B.V.*, (June 23, 2021).

established that such legal entity lacked autonomy in the conduct of its business, e.g., because it applied the directives of its parent company.[347] More recently, however, in line with the ECJ's interpretation, the Paris Court of Appeal considered that a parent company whose indirect liability for the infringement was recognized by the FCA could not subsequently escape civil liability in a follow-on damages claim, regardless of the fact that it did not take a personal part in the infringement.[348]

b. *The Existence of Harm*

1368. As a general principle, a distinction must be made between the existence of harm, which under the provisions of the EU Damages Directive can be presumed in certain circumstances (Article 17.2), and the quantification of the damage, which is a subsequent but mandatory step after the existence of harm has been established. This distinction has been confirmed by the ECJ which held that actions for damages aim to compensate as precisely as possible the victim for the harm suffered, "once the existence of and responsibility for that damage are established."[349] This approach was followed in several judgments by the French courts, which in a first step assessed the existence of harm, based in particular on the findings of the competition authority's decision, the additional evidence produced by the claimant and, as the case may be, economic analyses, and in a second step proceeded with the quantification of such harm.[350]

1369. Therefore, once the existence and responsibility of a damage has been established, a victim cannot be denied compensation, even in cases where it is very difficult or practically impossible to quantify such damage. In this respect, Article 17 of the EU Damages Directive indeed provides that:

> Member States shall ensure that the national courts are empowered, in accordance with national procedures, to estimate the amount of harm if it is established that a claimant suffered harm but it is practically impossible or excessively difficult precisely to quantify the harm suffered on the basis of the evidence available.

1370. However, in practice, this article must be understood as placing an obligation on national courts to proceed to a judicial estimation of the harm suffered when the claimant has demonstrated that it is not able to proceed to the quantification, on the basis of the elements available to it, including those to which it has been granted access on the basis of Article 5 of the EU Damages Directive.[351] Therefore, the ECJ clearly stated that, when the difficulty or practical impossibility of assessing the harm results from the inaction of the claimant, it is not for the national court to substitute itself to the claimant.[352]

---

347 For example, Paris Commercial Court, Case No. 2014-058853, *Orange Réunion*, (June 20, 2016); French Supreme Court, Case No. 13-24.854, *JCB Sale*, (Oct. 6, 2015).

348 Paris Court of Appeal, Case No. 20/04265, *Cora*, comm., (Nov. 24, 2021).

349 Case C-312/21, *Tráficos Manuel Ferrer SL*, ECLI:EU:C:2023:99, ¶52 (Feb. 16, 2023).

350 *See*, Paris Court of Appeal, Case No. 14PA02419, *SNCF Mobilités*, (June 13, 2019); Case No. 20/04265, *Cora*, comm., (Nov. 24, 2021); Case No. 17/04101, *Doux Aliments*, (June 23, 2021).

351 Case C-312/21, *Tráficos Manuel Ferrer SL*, ECLI:EU:C:2023:99, ¶57 (Feb. 16, 2023).

352 *Id.*

c. *A Damage in Relation with the Wrongdoing (Causal Link)*

1371. The causal link between the infringement and the damage suffered by the claimant is the third condition that must be met in order to trigger the liability of the defendant. In this respect, several presumptions facilitating the victim's burden of proof have been introduced by the EU Damages Directive. With respect more particularly to causation, the EU Damages Directive establishes a legal presumption that cartel infringements cause harm.[353] However, owing to rules governing the applicability of law over time, this provision currently does not apply in most damage claims brought before the national courts of the Member States. The ECJ has indeed recently confirmed that this presumption, insofar as it is directly linked to the attribution of civil liability to the author of the infringement and, consequently, directly affects his or her legal situation, is of a substantive nature rather than of a probative value, and therefore cannot apply retroactively.[354]

1372. In Belgium for example, the Ghent Court of Appeal found in 2022 that the presumption of harm only applies to cartels that persisted beyond the entry into force of the Belgian law transposing the EU Damages Directive, i.e., after June 22, 2017, or when a decision establishing the infringement was taken after that date. The court came to this decision because it considered that the relevant legal fact creating the presumption of harm is the existence of a cartel or a cartel decision.[355]

1373. Under the old regime, which still governs most of the follow-on actions being brought by alleged victims of competition law infringements, claimants must prove the causal link between the anticompetitive practices that form the basis of their claim and the harm they consider having suffered as a result. However, the standard of proof is inconsistent between the Member States and even sometimes within one Member State, where the case law fluctuates.

1374. For example, in Italy, national courts require the claimant to prove the causal link, i.e., that, absent the infringement, there would have been no harm.[356] In France, where the causal link is said to constitute an "autonomous condition" of civil liability, as a general rule the claimant is required to demonstrate the causal link between the infringement and the harm allegedly suffered.[357] However, in certain cases, the Paris Court of Appeal relied, among other elements, on the fact that cartels are presumed to cause harm.[358] Similarly, in Belgium, courts can rely

---

353 Council Directive 2014/104 (EU Damages Directive), *supra* n. 287, Chapter VI, art. 17(2).

354 Case C-267/20, *AB Volvo & DAF Trucks NV*, ECLI:EU:C:2022:494, (June 22, 2022).

355 Ghent Court of Appeal, Case Nos. 2019/AR/1255 and 2019/AR/1393, *Man S.E. and AB Volvo v. Bevatrans N.V.*, (Mar. 1, 2021).

356 Tribunal of Palermo, *Roche SpA v. Terrasi*, (May 17, 2017); the same is true in the UK, *see* Court of Appeal of England & Wales, Case Nos. A3/2018/2801, A3/2018/2802, *BritNed Development Ltd. v. ABB AB*, [2019] EWCA Civ 1840, (2019). (*See* Silvia Pietrini, *Causal link: The Palermo Tribunal rejects a claim for damages following the conviction for an anticompetitive agreement in the absence of proof of the causal link between the anticompetitive practice and the alleged harm (Roche SPA c/ Terrasi)*, CONCURRENCES May 2017, N° 4-2017, art. N° 85163, pp. 197–199)

357 Paris Court of Appeal, Case No. 15/05918, *Orange v. Outremer Telecom*, comm., (May 10, 2017); Case No. 17/04101, *Doux Aliments*, (June 23, 2021); *See also*, *Vania*, 2017-013952.

358 Paris Court of Appeal, Case No. 17/04101, *Doux Aliments*, (June 23, 2021); Case No. 07/10478, *Doux aliments v. Ceva Santé Animale*, comm., (June 10, 2009); Paris Court of Appeal, Case No. 14/15779, *SAS Cowes*, (Oct. 2, 2015); French Supreme Court, Case No. 13-24.854, *JCB Sale*, (Oct. 6, 2015); Paris Court of Appeal,

on a body of evidence to conclude that the victim necessarily suffered harm as a result of a cartel; using this technique, the Ghent Commercial Court recently considered, with respect to the Trucks cartel, that it was highly improbable that the claimant did not suffer damages following the cartel; and considered it evident that the impact of the cartel practices on gross prices (as established in the European Commission Decision) negatively influenced the price-setting downstream affecting end-customers such as the claimant.[359] In Germany, although out of principle it is for the claimant, in a follow-on damage claim, to establish that the cartel was capable of causing it harm, the German Supreme Court (*Bundesgerichtshof*, or BGH) recognized the existence of a factual presumption that long-lasting cartels lead to inflated prices and thus damage to those purchasing the cartelized products.[360] However, in practice, the case law is inconsistent. There is notably a lack of consensus on whether it can be presumed that a cartel has an impact on the prices of non-cartel participants ("umbrella effect").[361]

1375. In other Member States, the courts are less stringent in their approach to the causal link. For example, in Spain, the Audiencia Provincial of Barcelona established a rebuttable presumption in a follow-on damage claim that harm necessarily results from the illicit conduct sanctioned by the CNMC.[362] Similarly, the Audiencia Provincial of Alicante held that it is not necessary to invoke Article 17 of the EU Damages Directive to conclude that there is a presumption of harm; the examination of the circumstances of the case may justify applying a presumption that a damage has necessarily occurred.[363]

1376. In practice, the causal link can be established by reference to the infringement decision,[364] in particular when the latter directly cites the claimant as being the addressee of price increases decided between cartelists or as being the victim of exclusionary conduct. It can also be demonstrated based on economic analysis establishing the impact of the anticompetitive conduct.

B. *Quantification of the Harm*

1377. Quantifying the harm suffered by a victim of a competition law infringement, i.e., determining the amount of damages that should be awarded to the victim, is a complex exercise that often requires the use of economic experts, either appointed by the parties directly or by the court. However, even though expert opinions constitute a useful resource, they cannot replace the assessment of the courts, which are solely

---

Case No. 12/04441, *JCB Sales*, comm., (June 26, 2013).

359 Ghent Commercial Court, *Veurink v. DAF Trucks*, (Apr. 29, 2022).

360 BGH, Case No. KZR 24/17, *Rail Cartel II*, (Jan. 28, 2020).

361 *See, e.g.*, BGH Cartel Senate, Case No. KZR 8/18, *Rails Cartel – (Schienenkartell IV)*, (May 19, 2020),; Higher Regional Court of Karlsruhe (6th Senate), Case No. 6 U 204/15 Kart (2), *Grey cement cartel* (Nov. 9, 2016).

362 Audiencia Provincial of Barcelona, Case No. 1311/19, *Planeta*, (Jan. 10, 2020); Case No. 1965/18, *Misiones Salesianas*, (Jan. 10, 2020); Case No. 236/19, *Bankoa*, (Jan. 13, 2020); Case No. 1964/18, *Cortefiel*, (Jan. 10, 2020); Case No. 1197/19, *Manos Unidas*, (Jan. 13, 2020); Case No. 1128/19, *Mutua Madrileña*, (Jan. 13, 2020); Case No. 1127/19, *Caixa Ontinyent*, (Jan. 13, 2020); Case No. 1963/18, *CIFDSA*, (Jan. 13, 2020).

363 Audiencia Provincial of Alicante, Case No. 1083/2020, *Volvo AB*, (Oct. 15, 2020); *see also* Audiencia Provincial of Asturias, Case No. 690/2020, *Iveco*, (Dec. 18, 2020).

364 *See, e.g.*, Case No. 17/04101, *Doux Aliments*, (June 23, 2021), confirmed by the French Supreme Court, Mar. 2021; *see also*, Paris Court of Appeal, Case No. 20/04265, *Cora*, comm., (Nov. 24, 2021).

responsible for the quantification of the damage, having regard to the principle of full compensation laid down in the EU Damages Directive.[365] The principle of full compensation implies that damages should reflect the harm suffered, no more, no less. Thus, unlike the US, treble damages are not available in the EU.

1378. In addition, it should be noted that the right to full compensation does not concern the rules on allocation of costs between the parties in the context of judicial proceedings insofar as such rules, which vary from one Member State to another, do not aim at compensating the harm but at determining which party should bear the costs of the proceedings. In this context, the ECJ considered that it is not contrary to the principle of effectiveness of EU law that the claimant be obliged to bear its own costs in relation to the proceedings it brought as well as part of the common costs in case his claim is partially rejected, provided that the origin of the common costs can be attributed to the claimant.[366]

a. *General Considerations*

1379. Compensation means replacing the injured party in the position it would have been in had there been no infringement. Therefore, compensation not only includes the actual loss suffered (*damnum emergens*), but also the loss of profit (*lucrum cessans*) and the payment of interest. Actual loss means a reduction in a person's assets; loss of profit means that an increase in those assets, which would have occurred without the infringement, did not happen.

1380. In practice, the harm suffered by a victim of anticompetitive conduct can take many different forms, from the overcharge paid on cartelized products (direct damage) or even on non-cartelized products (umbrella effect) to the loss of certain sales (volume effect) or the loss of opportunity to enter a market or generate additional profits.

1381. The essential question in assessing antitrust damages is determining what would have happened if the infringement had not taken place. In practice, this requires hypothesizing a counterfactual scenario that reflects the situation as it should have been absent the effects of the infringement. For example, in a cartel that results in an overcharge for the direct customers of the cartelists, the counterfactual scenario should reflect the evolution of the supply prices absent the cartel. Damages can then be estimated by comparing the counterfactual price to the price actually paid by these customers. In an abuse of dominance case, the profits lost by rivals that have been excluded from the market or that have lost market shares as a result of the abusive conduct can be calculated by comparing their actual turnover and profit margins to the turnover and profit margins they would have produced if the infringement had not occurred.

1382. In practice, it is difficult to tell with certainty how a market would have evolved if Article 101 or 102 TFEU had not been breached. Prices, sales volumes, and

---

365 *See, e.g.*, in Germany, BGH, Case No. KZR 23/17, *Train Track Cartel*, (Dec. 3, 2019); in Spain, Provincial Court of Barcelona, Case No. 1964/2018, (Jan. 10, 2020); in France, Paris Court of Appeal, Case No. 20/04265, *Cora*, comm., (Nov. 24, 2021).

366 Case C-312/21, *Tráficos Manuel Ferrer SL*, ECLI:EU:C:2023:99, ¶47–49 (Feb. 16, 2023).

profit margins are all influenced by a variety of factors, as well as by complicated, often purposeful interactions between market participants that are difficult to predict. Therefore, by definition, building a counterfactual reflecting the hypothetical situation without the infringement requires reliance on a number of assumptions. There cannot be one single true value of the harm suffered, only best estimates. Furthermore, in cases where the infringement occurred many years before the claim, the unavailability or inaccessibility of certain data can add to this intrinsic limitation and make quantification more difficult and less precise. Despite these inherent limits to the quantification of the harm suffered as a result of a breach of Article 101 or Article 102 TFEU, national courts must determine the amount of damages to be awarded in any given case.

1383. In practice, when courts are unable to quantify the harm precisely, they can either decide on an amount themselves, based on the evidence adduced by the parties and, as the case may be, equity or fairness principles, or they can appoint an expert or rely on expert opinions produced as part of the administrative proceedings before competition authorities. For example, in France, experts are regularly appointed to help the courts decide on the quantification of harm.[367] In Germany, in the judgment of the Higher Regional Court Frankfurt am Main regarding the grey cement cartel, the court determined the quantification of harm based on an expert opinion obtained during the cartel administrative offense proceedings.[368] By contrast, the Regional Court Dortmund estimated a 15% price markup in a ruling on the rail cartel without a court-appointed expert opinion, despite gaps or ambiguities in the plaintiff's submission.[369] In Belgium, courts have sometimes chosen to award damages on an *ex aequo et bono* basis. Belgian courts used this option in *Honda*,[370] where the damage occurred more than 20 years before the judgment and was therefore extremely difficult to quantify precisely. The Ghent Commercial Court also chose this option more recently in the *Trucks* cartel case and quantified the damages using a fairness approach by applying a flat-rate percentage to the purchase price of the trucks.[371]

b. *Quantification in Practice: An Overview of the Various Methodologies Available to Claimants*

1384. Several methodologies can be used to construct a suitable and robust reference scenario which then serves for quantifying the harm. These various methodologies are based on different approaches and vary in terms of the underlying assumptions and the variety and detail of data needed. In this respect, it should be noted that the choice of one methodology over another shall be guided by the principle of proportionality, taking into account the amount of damages sought by the victim versus the cost of implementing a given methodology. Moreover, national courts can appoint experts to quantify damages when the victim has not provided its own

367 *See e.g.*, Paris Court of Appeal, Case No. 19/19969, *Sanofi*, comm., (Feb. 9, 2022).

368 Higher Regional Court of Frankfurt am Main, Case No. I ZR 43/14, *Grey cement cartel*, (Apr. 21, 2016).

369 Regional Court of Dortmund, Case No. 8 O 115/14, *Schienenkartell*, (Sept. 30, 2020).

370 Ghent Commercial Court, *TBM*, 179 (Mar. 23, 2017).

371 Ghent Commercial Court, *Veurink*, (Apr. 29, 2022).

expert analysis or when the courts believe they lack the necessary information to determine the amount of damages.

1385. The Practical Guide[372] outlines three principal economic methods that can be used to quantify harm. These methods are not exhaustive but are the most recognized in legal and academic circles. The Practical Guide explains that each of the three methods has its own strengths and weaknesses that make them more or less suitable to estimate the damage suffered in a given set of circumstances.

- *Comparator-based Methods*: Comparator-based methods are widely used in practice. Depending on the data available, comparison can be done over time (for example by comparing the evolution of the prices in the relevant product market during and before or after the infringement period),[373] or between geographic markets (for example by comparing the evolution of the prices in the market affected by the infringement with the evolution of prices in the same product market but in another Member State not covered by the infringement),[374] or between product markets, which requires identifying a market with similar characteristics.[375] When sufficient data is available, these comparator-based methods can be combined, enabling comparisons over time and across markets (so called difference-in-differences methodology).[376] The difference-in-differences methodology is particularly useful at isolating exogenous factors, but it requires a large set of data to be effectively implemented. When possible, it results in a very robust analysis on which national courts can rely to establish the causal link between thc infringement and the harm suffered by the claimant.
- *Economic Simulation Models*: The Practical Guide also presents the use of economic models that mirror actual market behavior to simulate the likely market outcome that would have occurred in the absence of the infringement. These models draw on economic theory to explain the likely functioning of a market in view of its main features. As such, an economic simulation model is a simplified vision of reality and relies heavily on assumptions about market characteristics and the behavior of suppliers and customers. However, when actual data is not available, a simple simulation still provides useful insights and should not be dismissed; more complex ones can be more comprehensive and produce a more reasonable estimate of the counterfactual scenario but are more technically demanding and require significant amounts of data and economic expertise.[377]
- *Cost-based and Finance-Based Methods*: The third approach described in the Practical Guide is the use of cost-based methods or methods based on the financial performance of the claimant or of the defendants. In the cost-based method,

---

372 European Commission, Practical Guide, *supra* n. 304, Chapter VI.

373 *Id.* ¶¶38–48. In practice, the comparison over time is widely used as a methodology to quantify damages (*see* Jean-François Laborde, *Cartel Damages Actions in Europe: How Courts Have Assessed Cartel Overcharges*, CONCURRENCES Sept. 2021, No. 3-2021 art. No. 102086, 232–242.

374 *Id.* ¶¶49–53.

375 *Id.* ¶¶54–55.

376 *Id.* ¶¶56–58.

377 *Id.* ¶¶104–105.

the production cost per unit is estimated and then a mark-up for the profit that would have been reasonable in the non-infringement scenario is added. The result is then compared with the price actually charged to the victim.[378] In practice, the cost-based method can be implemented using the actual production costs of the claimant or the defendant or by reference to more theoretical data, such as estimations in the sector. Methods based on the financial performance of the claimant or the defendant measure the profitability of an undertaking and may also provide some insight as to the amount of damages suffered. This method is similar to the comparator-based method as it requires establishing a counterfactual scenario using data from a comparator market or company. These methodologies notably present an advantage when the claimant lacks data, as information on the profitability of the defendant can be publicly available, for example in the case of publicly traded companies.

c. *The Passing-On Defense*

1386. The passing-on of overcharges is a defense traditionally raised in cartel cases by the defendants, when the alleged victim claims to have paid a higher price than it would have absent the infringement (referred to as the overcharge). When a defendant raises a passing-on defense, it argues that the overcharge allegedly paid by the direct customer has been passed down onto the distribution chain so that the direct customer in fact suffered no harm and cannot therefore obtain any compensation. In the case of indirect purchasers, the defense consists in saying that the overcharge was fully supported at an upper level in the distribution chain and therefore not passed on to the indirect purchaser.

1387. This defense is intrinsically linked to the principle of full compensation in EU law and aims at avoiding that victims be overcompensated for the harm suffered as a result of a violation of competition law.

1388. The EU Damages Directive establishes a double presumption in relation to passing-on:

- First, with respect to direct purchasers, Article 13 of the EU Damages Directive provides that "the burden of proving that the overcharge was passed on shall be on the defendant."
- Second, with respect to indirect purchasers, Article 14 provides that the latter shall be deemed to have paid an overcharge if the three following conditions are met: (i) the defendant has violated antitrust rules, (ii) this infringement has resulted in an overcharge for the direct purchaser of the defendant, and (iii) the indirect purchaser has obtained goods or services that were subject to the infringement from the direct purchaser. When these conditions are fulfilled, the burden of proof lies on the defendant to rebut the presumption of passing-on of the overcharge to the indirect purchaser.

1389. So far, the ECJ has not yet had to rule on the substantive or procedural nature of these presumptions and it has not yet been decided whether they should apply to all actions brought after December 26, 2014 or whether, as the other presumptions contained in the EU Damages Directive, they cannot apply retroactively.

---

378 *Id.* ¶106.

1390. Under the old regime, the approach varied between Member States. For example, in Germany, in line with the presumption set forth in the EU Damages Directive, the BGH held that the burden is on the defendant to show that its direct customers passed on the overcharge they paid as a result of a cartel by raising their resale prices to their own customers.[379] Similarly, in the Netherlands, the Supreme Court, referring inter alia to the EU Damages Directive, has ruled that the passing-on defense was valid under Dutch law but that the burden of proof that the overcharge has been passed-on by the claimant lies with the defendant invoking such defense.[380] Conversely, in France, according to settled case law, when the defendant to a damage claim raises the passing-on defense, it is for the claimant to prove that it has not or could not have passed-on the overcharge to its own customers.[381] Thus far, this case law has resulted in courts denying compensation to the victim in several cases.[382] However, the Paris Court of Appeal has finally recognized that the passing-on of the overcharge can be limited and, if the evidence adduced by the victim is sufficient and the economic analysis robust enough, compensation can be obtained.[383]

1391. In practice, estimating the amount of overcharge passed on requires complex and costly economic analysis that claimants cannot necessarily afford. Hence, in many cases, the courts must measure the passing-on based on theoretical or macro-economic evidence, such as the market characteristics, the share of the market affected by the practices, etc. Detailed guidance on how to quantify the passing-on of overcharges is provided in the European Commission's 2019 communication dedicated to this subject.[384]

1392. Finally, it should be noted that, from an economic perspective, the corollary of the passing-on of overcharges is a volume effect, which is another component of the damage that, in theory, must also be compensated. In other words, when a victim of a cartel increases its resale prices to pass on part or all of the overcharge paid to its suppliers, there is a high probability, except in markets with no price-elasticity, that such increase in price will result in smaller volumes being sold by the victim to its own customers. In such a case, the decrease in volumes sold results in a loss of profits for the direct purchaser that should be compensated. However, in some NCE cases, national courts have simply ignored this phenomenon and denied compensation to the victim.[385]

---

379 BGH, Case No. KZR 35/19, *Truck cartel*, (Sept. 23, 2020).

380 Supreme Court of the Netherlands, Case No. 15/00167, *TenneT v. ABB*, (July 8, 2016). This case concerns a follow-on damage claim brought by the Dutch national grid operator TenneT against the gas insulated switchgear producer ABB, following the decision of the European Commission of Jan. 24, 2007 sanctioning ABB for its participation in relation the Gas Insulated Switchgear cartel.

381 French Supreme Court, Case No. 11-18495, *Le Gouessant*, comm., (May 15, 2012).

382 Paris Commercial Court, Case No. 2017-013944, *JJSBF*, (Sept. 23, 2019); Case No. 2017013952, *Carrefour v. Vania*, (Nov. 4, 2019); *see also* Paris Court of Appeal, Case No. 19/19448, *JJSBF v. Carrefour*, comm., (Apr. 14, 2021) (confirmed by French Supreme Court, Case No. 21-19.197, comm., (Oct. 19, 2022); Paris Court of Appeal, Case No. 19/22293, *Vania*, (Nov. 4, 2019).

383 Paris Court of Appeal, Case No. 20/04265, *Cora*, comm., (Nov. 24, 2021).

384 European Commission Communication, Guidelines for national courts, *supra* n. 305, Chapter VI.

385 For example, Paris Commercial Court, Case No. 2017-021571, *Cora*, (Feb. 20, 2020) and on appeal, Paris Court of Appeal, Case No. 20/04265, *Cora*, comm., (Nov. 24, 2021).

C. *Joint and Several Liability*

1393. Article 11 of the EU Damages Directive provides that, in the case of an infringement of Article 101 TFEU, which by definition involves several undertakings, these undertakings shall be held jointly and severally liable for the harm caused by the infringement to which they are a party. Therefore, the claimant has the right to seek full compensation from any of the infringers, and it is then for the company held liable to go after its co-infringers to recoup their share of the damage. In this respect, the EU Damages Directive provides that the contribution of each co-infringer should be determined in light of their "relative responsibility" for the harm caused to the victim. This is a rather vague notion which, in practice, leaves room for interpretation by national courts in the assessment of the responsibility of each co-infringer.

1394. By way of example, in France, the Paris Court of Appeal has recently apportioned the amount of damages awarded to the victim of a cartel between the defendants based on the amount of their respective fine in the context of the public enforcement proceedings.[386] In two rulings dated 2019,[387] the Supreme Court of Finland also dealt with the allocation of damages between cartelists. The court considered that the allocation must be made according to two criteria: first, the share of the advantage generated by the infringement that has directly benefited the liable party and, second, the degree of fault that was attributable to each liable party. Applying these criteria, the court found that, in the first case, one cartel member was liable for a third of the damages and, in the second case, one cartel member alone was required to pay the entire damage.

1395. There are two exceptions to these principles. The first one applies to leniency applicants with immunity from fines. The EU Damages Directive provides that leniency applicants with immunity should only be held jointly and severally liable towards their own direct and indirect purchasers and, with respect to other injured parties, they are jointly and severally liable only when full compensation cannot be obtained from the other infringers. Immunity applicants are also protected in the context of contributory claims from a co-infringer required to pay full compensation to the victim. In such a case, an immunity applicant can only be required to contribute an amount up to the harm caused to its own direct and indirect purchasers.

1396. The second exception concerns small and medium-sized businesses (SMEs). Similarly to undertakings that benefited from an immunity from fine, SMEs whose market share was below 5% at any time during the infringement period and whose economic viability would be irremediably jeopardized if the normal rules on joint and several liability applied, can only be held jointly and severally liable towards their own direct and indirect purchasers. However, this exception does not apply when the SME concerned was a leading party in the infringement, pressured other parties to engage in the infringement, or was previously found to have violated competition law.[388]

---

386 *Id.*

387 Finnish Supreme Court, Case Nos. KKO:2019:57 and KKO:2019:58, (June 18, 2019).

388 These companies are solely accountable to their own direct and indirect purchasers, provided that their market shares are less than 5% at the time of the infringement and applying standard joint and several liability rules would put their economic sustainability in jeopardy.

1397. In practice, this concept of joint and several liability allows victims to devise a strategy and decide to either go after only one participant to the anticompetitive agreement or several of them at the same time for the whole damage. In the first case, it is likely that the defendant would then launch a recourse claim against the others, with a risk, from the claimant's perspective, that the courts subsequently join the two claims, thereby multiplying the number of defendants for the claimant. However, in France for example, even in case of a junction of cases, the victim continues to have one defendant and the others are only defendants to the recourse claim, which technically prevents them from responding to the claimant's brief, unless the claimant has direct claims against them.[389] In the second case, the claimant will face several defendants, making its case more burdensome (as several briefs and economic reports will be produced at the same time). However, such a strategy may also prove to be effective if at least one defendant settles: indeed, in such a case, this may encourage the other defendants to settle or, if they don't, it may influence the court's findings. Finally, another procedural strategy is to go after each participant to the anticompetitive agreement for their own share of the damage: such strategy appears to be the simplest one from a procedural perspective, as it avoids having to deal with several defendants at the same time but it may also create less incentives for defendants to settle.

4. The Future of Private Enforcement within the EU

1398. Since the adoption of the EU Damages Directive, private enforcement has clearly been on the rise in Europe. The Trucks cartel in particular has led to hundreds of damages claims being introduced throughout the EU, often by very small businesses that had bought one or two trucks from the cartelists. Between 2018 and 2020, more than 150 first instance judgments for damages in cartel cases were issued, with Germany being the most active Member State, followed by France and Spain.[390] It should also be noted that, in the aftermath of the EU Damages Directive, the overall success rate of private actions has significantly increased in the recent years.[391]

1399. Despite this positive trend, many challenges still lie ahead for national courts. The first one is the applicability of the substantive provisions of the EU Damages Directive, and in particular the presumptions it establishes: while it is clear that they cannot apply retroactively, national courts are often invited by claimants to interpret their national laws in light of the principle of effectiveness of EU law, and thus to give full effect to certain presumptions. According to the ECJ, this should be possible as long as it does not entail an interpretation *contra legem*.[392] However, in practice, courts rarely do so.

---

389 Paris Commercial Court, Case No. J2021000030, (May 10, 2021).

390 *See Cartel Damages Actions in Europe*, *supra* n. 373, Chapter VI, 232–242. This study is limited to damages claims in cartel cases and thus excludes the numerous claims that are brought on the basis of Article 102 TFEU. In reality, this figure is even higher than 150 because of the number of individual claims brought in Spain in the Trucks cartel, which have been counted as one claim for the purpose of the statistics presented in the study.

391 *Id.*

392 Case C-267/20, *AB Volvo & DAF Trucks NV*, ECLI:EU:C:2022:494, ¶77 (June 22, 2022).

1400. The second hurdle remains access to evidence. Although progress has been made, in practice, claimants are often faced with the fact that, in order to prove their case, they must adduce a lot of (often old) data, which are sometimes unavailable or at least incomplete. In addition, this work is often time-consuming and costly, which can constitute a significant obstacle in certain cases.

1401. To help overcome these barriers, financing solutions in the form of third-party litigation funding have developed in the market. Two models co-exist: the first one consists of accumulating claims by buying them from potential victims and leading the cases on the victims' behalf (this is notably the model of Cartel Damage Claims); the second one consists of providing funding to a claimant in exchange for a share of the proceeds if the action is successful, but the victim retains the control of their claim. In both cases, the litigation funder bears the financial risk in the proceedings. While these models are already quite popular in certain European countries (e.g., in the UK), in others they are far less developed (e.g., in France).

1402. Finally, the third issue lies with the fact that the EU does not currently have a harmonized collective redress mechanism similar to the US class actions. Only certain Member States provide for collective action mechanisms. Their efficacy depends on individual national frameworks. For example, in Portugal, where an opt-out mechanism applies, a follow-on collective claim was filed at the end of 2020 by a Portuguese Consumer Association against MasterCard; the association, which claims over €400 million in damages, argues that the cartel on interchange fees prevented Portuguese merchants from benefitting from lower rates and Portuguese consumers would be the indirect victims as the merchants would have passed the overcharge onto them. In Germany, where the law provides for an opt-in mechanism, a follow-on collective action including several hotels has recently been launched against Booking.com, arguing that the parity clauses imposed by the latter, which were found to be anticompetitive in public enforcement proceedings in Germany, would have resulted in a loss of opportunity for the hotels to offer better prices, thereby losing potential sales of hotel nights.

1403. It should also be noted that the European Parliament has recently passed the EU's Representative Actions Directive.[393] While the purpose of this directive is not the adoption of a single, pan-European collective regime and, for the time being, it does not cover damages caused by a competition law infringement, it is a first step towards effective collective actions for damages in Europe, which may subsequently foster their development, including in the field of competition law. More particularly, this directive requires Member States to adopt at least one collective redress mechanism whereby so-called "qualified entities" can bring representative actions before the national courts on behalf of consumers for compensation and/or injunctive relief. This directive applies to various types of damages, including those resulting from breaches of EU provisions on data protection, environment, travel, health, etc. but not competition law.

---

393 Council Directive 2020/1828 of the European Parliament and of the Council of Nov. 25, 2020 on representative actions for the protection of the collective interests of consumers and repealing Directive 2009/22, 2020 OJ (L 409) 1–27.

TABLE OF CONTENTS

Concurrences
Competition Laws Review

Concurrences Review

Concurrences is a print and online quarterly peer reviewed journal dedicated to EU and national competitions laws. It has been launched in 2004 as the flagship of the Institute of Competition Law in order to provide a forum for academics, practitioners and enforcers. Concurrences' influence and expertise has garnered contributions or interviews with such figures as Christine Lagarde, Bill Kovacic, Emmanuel Macron, Antonin Scalia and Magrethe Vestager.

Contents

More than 15,000 articles, print and/or online. Quarterly issues provide current coverage with contributions from the EU or national or foreign countries thanks to more than 2,500 authors in Europe and abroad.

Format

In order to balance academic contributions with opinions or legal practice notes, Concurrences provides its insight and analysis in a number of formats:

- Forewords: Opinions by leading academics or enforcers
- Interviews: Interviews of antitrust experts
- On-Topics: 4 to 6 short papers on hot issues
- Law & Economics: Short papers written by economists for a legal audience
- Articles: Long academic papers
- Case Summaries: Case commentary on EU and French case law
- Legal Practice: Short papers for in-house counsels
- International: Medium size papers on international policies
- Books Review: Summaries of recent antitrust books
- Articles Review: Summaries of leading articles published in 45 antitrust journals

Boards

The Scientific Committee is headed by Laurence Idot, Professor at Panthéon Assas University. The International Committee is headed by Frederic Jenny, OECD Competition Comitteee Chairman. Boards members include Douglas Ginsburg, Benoît Cœuré, Howard Shelanski, Richard Whish, Wouter Wils, Joshua Wright, etc.

Online version

Concurrences website provides all articles published since its inception, in addition to selected articles published online only in the electronic supplement.

Write for Concurrences

Concurrences welcome spontaneous contributions. Except in rare circumstances, the journal accepts only unpublished articles, whatever the form and nature of the contribution. The Editorial Board checks the form of the proposals, and then submits these to the Scientific Committee. Selection of the papers is conditional to a peer review by at least two members of the Committee. Within a month, the Committee assesses whether the draft article can be published and notifies the author.